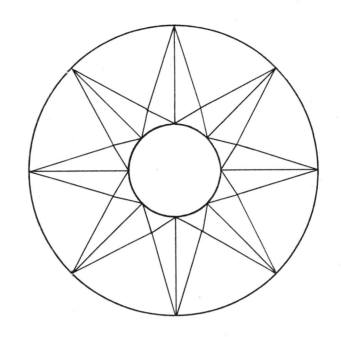

THE
WORLD
OF
MANKIND

THE AUTHORS

Peter Abrahams

John Houghton Allen

Hamilton Basso

James Warner Bellah

Paul Bowles

Eugene Burdick

Robert Carson

Hodding Carter

Joyce Cary

Bruce Catton

Bernard De Voto

David Dodge

Neil M. Gunn

A. B. Guthrie, Jr.

Hammond Innes

Nikos Kazantzakis

Richard Llewellyn

Hugh MacLennan

John P. Marquand

Aubrey Menen

Alan Moorehead

Frederic Morton

Sean O'Faolain

Alan Paton

Laurens van der Post

V. S. Pritchett

Santha Rama Rau

Harrison Salisbury

William Sansom

Jack Schaefer

Irwin Shaw

John Steinbeck

James Street

Han Suyin

E. B. White

THE
WORLD
OF
MANKIND

*by the
Writers,
Photographers and
Editors of*
HOLIDAY
Magazine

GOLDEN PRESS · NEW YORK

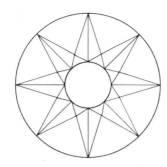

Staff of HOLIDAY

Editor:
TED PATRICK

Art Director:
FRANK ZACHARY

Editorial Director:
HARRY SIONS

Assistant to the Editor:
ALBERT H. FARNSWORTH

Production Director:
RICHARD L. FIELD

Senior Editors:
JAMES CERRUTI
LORING DOWST
HARRY G. NICKLES

Picture Editor:
LOUIS F. V. MERCIER

Associate Editors:
ARNOLD W. EHRLICH

Art Editors:
LOUIS R. GLESSMANN
GERTRUDE GORDON

Food Editor:
SILAS SPITZER

What to Wear Where Editor:
RUTH MASSEY

Assistant Editors:
JEROME K. ANDERSEN
DALE M. BROWN
RUTH GRAVES
JORN R. ROBERSON
WILLIAM C. WRIGHT

Editorial Assistants:
ELIZABETH COPELAND
MARY FRANCES S. MILLER
DIANA H. STAMBUL

ACKNOWLEDGMENTS

THANKS ARE DUE TO THE FOLLOWING AUTHORS, PUBLISHERS, AND AGENTS FOR PERMISSION TO USE THE MATERIAL INDICATED.

Peter Abrahams: *The Blacks.*

Hamilton Basso: *San Francisco.*

James Warner Bellah: *Alaska.*

Brandt & Brandt: *Hawaii* and *West Coast Journey* by Robert Carson; *The Mississippi* by Hodding Carter; *New England* by Bernard De Voto; *Scotland* by Neil M. Gunn; *Oregon Trail—Adventure With History* by A. B. Guthrie, Jr.; *Boston* by John P. Marquand.

Curtis Brown, Ltd.: *Mexico* by John Houghton Allen; *The Pacific* by Eugene Burdick; *The Meaning of England* and *Switzerland* by Joyce Cary; *The Caribbean* and *The Charmed Country* by David Dodge; *Wales* by Richard Llewellyn; *Ireland, Italy: Her Wonderful People* and *The World of Los Angeles* by Sean O'Faolain.

Bruce Catton: *Pilgrimage to Washington.*

William A. Collins Sons & Company, Ltd., (London): *Holland* and *Norway* by Hammond Innes.

Harper & Brothers: *Leningrad* from MY RUSSIAN JOURNEY by Santha Rama Rau. Copyright © 1958 by Curtis Publishing Co. Reprinted by permission of Harper & Brothers; *Bali* and *Burma* from VIEW TO THE SOUTHEAST by Santha Rama Rau. Copyright © 1955, 1956 by Curtis Publishing Co. Reprinted by permission of Harper & Brothers: *India* from THIS IS INDIA by Santha Rama Rau. Copyright 1953 by Curtis Publishing Co. Reprinted by permission of Harper & Brothers. *Here Is New York* by E. B. White. Copyright 1949 by Curtis Publishing Co. Reprinted by permission of Harper & Brothers.

The Hogarth Press Ltd. (London): *Denmark* and *Sweden* from William Sansom's THE ICICLE AND THE SUN.

Alfred A. Knopf, Inc.: *Holland* and *Norway* by Hammond Innes.

MCA Artists, Ltd.: *Paris! Paris!* by Irwin Shaw.

Hugh MacLennan: *Canada.*

Harold Matson Company: *Austria* by Frederic Morton; *South America, The Island World, London, Germany, Spain,* by V. S. Pritchett; *My Southwest* by Jack Schaefer; *The South* by James Street.

McGraw-Hill Book Company, Inc.: *Rome* from Aubrey Menen's ROME FOR OURSELVES (McGraw-Hill).

McIntosh and Otis, Inc.: *Always Something To Do In Salinas* by John Steinbeck.

William Morris Agency: *The Moslems* by Paul Bowles, copyright © 1959 by The Curtis Publishing Company; *The Remarkable French* by Aubrey Menen, © 1957 by The Curtis Publishing Company; *Tokyo* by Santha Rama Rau, Copyright © 1955 by The Curtis Publishing Company.

Alan Paton: *South Africa.*

Laurens van der Post: *Africa—Portrait Of A Continent.*

Reynal & Company: *Denmark* and *Sweden* from William Sansom's THE ICICLE AND THE SUN.

Russell & Volkening, Inc.: *French Canada* by Hugh MacLennan.

Harrison Salisbury: *Moscow.*

Han Suyin: *Peking.*

Dr. Max Tau (Oslo): *Greece* by Nikos Kazantzakis.

A. Watkins, Inc.: *The U.S.A.* © 1957 by Alan Moorehead; *Italy: Her Golden Hour* © 1955 by Alan Moorehead.

PHOTO CREDITS

Slim Aarons: p 11 tr; 15 c, br; 19; 66; 272.

Norman Ashe: p 53; 78.

Ray Atkeson: p 249 tl; 303; 326-7.

J. D. Barnell: p 62, 197.

Carl Biemiller: p 58 t.

Brian Brake (Magnum): p 99.

Brandt, Rapho-Guillumette: p 20 mr, bl; 21 tl, ml, bl.

Brazilian Government Trade Bureau: p 233.

Horace Bristol (East-West): p 200; 201.

British Travel Association: p 18; 26-7.

Brooks Studio: p 238-9.

Canadian Government Travel Bureau: p 351.

Cornell Capa (Magnum): p 13; 14; 97; 102; 103; 223.

Robert Capa (Magnum): p 54-5; 111.

CONTENTS

INTRODUCTION

It was not necessary to solemnly develop a theme for this book. Because of the nature of the magazine from which the material was taken the theme emerged naturally, and it is a simple one: men and women alive in the world, in all their brave variety, with all their quirks and greatness and folly, surrounded by beauty and harshness, moved by wonder and selfishness and love, aware of splendid ghosts in all their yesterdays, fearful or confident about tomorrow even while they dare, themselves, to shape it.

This has been the theme of HOLIDAY during the past decade, developed by some of the world's most distinguished writers and photographers. They have told not only of people. They have seen the world whole, exploring cities and seas and continents, bringing back the awful hush of deserts, the din of the brash metropolis, forest shadow, mountain peace, the long murmur of the ocean's fringe—a diversified background against which the patterns of man's life shift and mingle and reach tragedy or joy.

The World of Mankind presents a portrait of our time: always entertaining, but at the same time always informed, always candid. It is also, the editors believe, very necessary. Three centuries ago John Donne offered the sentiment that no man is an island, entire of itself. We lag behind our poets and our mystics; it has taken us all these years to realize the piercing truth behind his words: that no nation can be an island either, entire of itself. It should not be beyond us to see that now, more than ever since we first began to toy with civilization, we are interdependent or we are nothing; that no group among us, however well equipped with gold or bombs, can afford to claim superiority over any of the rest—or, worse still, to ignore them.

It is not enough—or even accurate—to say that men are equal. What is needed is an understanding of ways that are remote, rather than fear or an urge to alter them; laughter between nations, without malice and without sentimentality; the crossing of frontiers in family cars, and not in delegations; an end of intrigue, but not of curiosity; competition without greed; dispute without annihilation.

It has always been the intention and hope of HOLIDAY to take a part in extending the boundaries of men's thoughts and aspirations; it is therefore inevitable that this book should aim at the whole man, at his continuing delight and glory in the world, and at his desire to intensify those feelings and to share them.

TED PATRICK, *Editor*

EUROPE

*Bourton-on-the-Water reflects a
beauty that is warm, kindly and profound,
the unique serenity of the Cotswolds.*

England

THE MEANING OF ENGLAND

*This tribute to England was written by
Joyce Cary during the
final days of the illness which took his life in 1957.
Born in Ireland to an Anglo-Irish family,
he had a special feeling for England,
for to him she was the mother country,
not merely the homeland.*

A man's country is the home of his imagination, and men live by their imagination. A friend of mine from Somerset, touring in the next county, Devonshire, had a motor accident. He was taken up unconscious and sent at once to a cottage hospital, where he finally came to. He looked out of the window and was greatly distressed, saying over and over again, "Take me home." It was explained to him that he was in a hospital near Chard.

"Chard," he muttered; "that's Somerset."

"Yes."

He took another look at the fields and settled down peacefully to sleep. The scene, which he had taken, very reasonably, for Devonshire, had become Somerset—in Somerset he felt at home.

Not a twig or leaf was changed in the fields, but they were different, and this all-important difference was in the name and the associations attached to the name: not only my friend's childhood memories but the history of Somerset towns, battles, loyalties and disasters.

So, for good or evil, the name of a country becomes one of the most powerful symbols in the world; men will die for its glory who do not care in the least for their own. They will also commit the worst of crimes if some dictator can persuade them that the name has been insulted.

Many people have come to hate patriotism as the seedbed of hatred and war. But you can't abolish so fundamental and primitive an attachment as the love of home. You can only pervert it. Neither is patriotism necessarily an evil or a weakness. Its quality depends on the values embodied in the symbolic name.

My feeling about England is especially deep and conscious because I was born in Ireland to an Anglo-Irish family, long settled there. My earliest memories are of Donegal, its wild hills and the great sea loughs of Foyle and Swilly. I loved the country and the people, spoilers of children. But my heroes were the great men of English history, many of them Anglo-Irishmen like myself; and English history is world history. My imagination played on a world stage. I was engaged for England; I triumphed in her glories and suffered in her defeats and shames.

I was, like my family, sharply critical of the English and often of English policy, but my anger was that of a lover. I could not bear that England should be betrayed by her own children or by party politicians with narrow views and mean aims. I had, that is, a far more definite and romantic idea of England than the average born Englishman.

Of course, the early 1900's, when I was at school, was everywhere a time of romantic patriotism. If there is ever again a great war I don't suppose any nation will enter upon it in our

mood of 1914. Men will still fight and die for freedom but only as a bitter necessity. The soldier's duty, so far as fighting is concerned, has lost its glamour. There is nothing romantic about a bomb.

I had a special feeling about England, because, for my family, she was the mother country and not merely the homeland. She was for me not only all the riches of English literature and art but the long history of its free institutions. As the U.S.A. for an American does not suggest conquest or domination, but responsibility, especially to the ideal of freedom, so the British Empire for me was the liberating power which had begotten the free states of Canada, Australia, New Zealand, South

At Little Rissington, another Cotswold village, a trainer and his hounds—
still pups—set off for their daily sixteen-mile walk.

Africa, and was preparing many more to govern themselves.

This was not mere fancy on my part. I knew from friends in the Indian Service that the British governing staff were being replaced by Indians—those trained and devoted servants of State who now alone make Indian self-government possible. And when I myself joined the West African Service and found myself responsible for law and general welfare among primitive tribes, I was given the fundamental rule, "Act always so that the local native government, however primitive, can carry on without you."

I was to develop the beginnings of representative government if only by persuading chiefs to have consultative councils,

but I was not to break their authority. Native government at every stage of development must remain native so that when the time came for local independence the British staff could go without causing a breakdown in the machine.

The results of this policy are now being tested in Africa, where the first free African states of the Commonwealth are now being formed. And this development is keenly interesting to me, as a test and proof of the English Colonial policy that I helped to administer.

People think of me as a writer, but my years in the African Service, given to that England of my youthful imagination, are richer to my memories than any of my books.

THE ISLAND WORLD

England is small...a crowded country of
millions of neatly painted houses and
thousands of little green fields and woods where
a man living a mile from a village considers himself
in solitude. It is in this very smallness that
British author V. S. Pritchett
finds the source of English character and history.

Time out:
A Cornish farmer.

"*...this little world*": in that phrase, from the famous passage in *Richard II*, Shakespeare defined England simply and forever. The smallness of England is absurd, frightening and exquisite. It is a little sea garden. It is the toy country of millions of small, neatly painted houses with millions of small polished windows shining after rain, thousands of little green fields, of little green woods. The gardens are small, the famous rivers are small, the distances between villages and towns are small; no hill rises to much more than three thousand feet and most are less than eight hundred. Small motorcars travel down narrow, winding roads, small locomotives draw small railway wagons. A man living a mile from a village or a few miles from a town considers himself to be in solitude.

At Torquay: *"Bowls" clubs take*
their game seriously,
even to wearing uniforms.

How has it come about that an island so trivial and so private, a mere six hundred miles long, and, at its widest, not much more than three hundred, should have become, until fifty years ago, the wealthiest and most powerful in the world? And if that is not true now, the most densely populated country in the world after Belgium? The traveller who looks at the English landscape and considers the English character ought never to forget this. The moment he flies into the mist that on most days is streaked across this island, the moment he faces the long array of chalk at Dover or picks out the statue of Drake on the Hoe at Plymouth, or passes the Needles off Southampton, he is about to enter a country where people are shoulder to shoulder. The desire for privacy, the gambits for avoiding acquaintance are understandable.

Henley Royal Regatta: *Bright boaters, ties, and expectations.*

When Columbus discovered America he can be said to have created Britain also, for he moved the island to the centre or crossroads of the world. Since then, all sea traffic across the Atlantic has had to come this way for its shortest routes; the situation has been little changed by air travel. Set free by Columbus, the British discovered their Atlantic, non-European countenance.

As a result, the Englishman stands between two worlds, living by both. He is a European with a difference. You can prove to him that he is a European who has got his civil institutions from the Anglo-Saxon north and his Christianity and culture from the ancient Mediterranean; but he will insist that he is a fortress afloat off the European coast, unconquered since the 11th Century, and looking across the Atlantic to the countries his race has founded, or his ancestors have explored and exploited. He is a man facing two ways. In this, where he is

Etonians: *In tailcoats and white*
ties, they head for chapel.

Greenwich: *Personal Guards*
of the Queen pose
before the old Cutty Sark.

England/V.S. Pritchett **15**

chauvinistic, he has a national pride; he knows by long experience what it is to be admired, envied and hated, to make profits, commit crimes, to forgive those he has injured, to take punishment and laugh at himself. The songs of the Gilbert and Sullivan operas are full of national self-mockery. For behind the figure of the British as a figure of power, there is another: the kind, good-humoured man of the small island.

Islanders who live close to the great land masses develop an intense, defensive, local individuality; they live in continual fear of conquest. The British are nationally united because, in the last four hundred years, they have been in terror of Continental despots like Philip II of Spain, Louis XIV and Napoleon in France and, in our time, Hitler. Fear of this kind creates resolution and the spirit of aggression. In the late Middle Ages, the British were continually invading France, and when the long effort failed, their energies turned towards the New World. In milder times this aggressive spirit has become no more than a fruitful outburst against the claustrophobia which affects people on small islands, and especially one where the grey and relatively sunless climate turns the mind in upon itself.

We are liable to burst out. The man who delivers my whisky dresses up like a gentleman once a year, to let himself go in Monte Carlo.

Another important basic fact is that no place in Britain is more than seventy-five miles from tidal water; the frontier is the sea. One can see how much of British life has looked outward by the names of many of the little suburban villas: Durban, Poona, Kimberley, Nairobi, Waterloo. Or by the names of the streets in the seaports.

The main overriding difference in England is between North and South. The River Trent cuts English character in two. It passes through Nottingham—the region called "The Dukeries" because so many dukes have estates there—and turning northeast, runs into the Humber near Hull, the port for the Baltic. The North makes; heavy industry is there. The South rules; the Queen and the government are in the South. The Queen speaks in the standard southern English accent of the upper classes. Oxford and Cambridge are in the South.

The Southerner is gentler, more leisurely in manner, wittier, more self-concealing, more formal, politic and reserved than the Northerner. He is a bit of a snob, in all classes. If he is well off he conceals the fact. He is inclined to disparage himself. The Northerner calls him "soft." But if this north-south division is true of the people in a very general way, the landscape division of the country is really made by a line drawn from the mouth of the River Tweed on the northeast to Lands End in the southwest. The hills and mountains are mainly west of that line. East of it lie smaller hills, green plains and marshes.

Yet east or west, pastureland or sea marsh, moor or mountain, the delight of England is in the intimate and continual changes of a man-made landscape. It is the most gardened country on earth. The roads are rarely straight for more than

a mile or so; there is always surprise at the next corner. One moment the land is arable, the next it is water meadow or heath. We are in an island of oak woods. The beeches have their tall aisles in Buckinghamshire close to the Thames; the willow hangs over the small rivers and millraces of East Anglia, the counties of Norfolk, Suffolk and Essex that bulge out into the North Sea or "German Ocean." The poplar whitens against the slaty sky, the ash hangs in all the lanes, and the elm, the chestnut, the sycamore and hornbeam are in every hedgerow. The South is a country of hawthorn hedges. We live in a place of hanging woods, coppices, brakes and dells. Only in the flat country of the Fens southeast of Lincoln—a very Dutch part of England on the east coast protected by dykes—does one see

trees scattered singly, like separate people in long vistas, with the east wind and the dyke water between them.

The English counties are countries in themselves. Begin at Canterbury in Kent, in the extreme southeast, in the fruit garden of England, and work your way through the widest stretch of Southern England to Cornwall in the extreme west. The River Medway still traditionally divides the legendary Kentish man from the equally legendary Man of Kent—the man of the cherry orchards, netting his trees to keep off the birds, in agony about the late frosts—the "frosties," as country people call them—that are the curse of English agriculture. The russet towns and flint oast houses, or hop kilns, of Kent change to the birch woods of Surrey, adjoining Kent on the west, a county

given to stockbrokers and those golden, hearty, tennis-playing girls whose forearm drives John Betjeman has celebrated in his poem, *A Subaltern's Love Song:*

> *"Oh! full Surrey twilight! importunate band!*
> *Oh! strongly adorable tennis girl's hand!"*

Vast Hampshire, just west of Surrey, has its sandy heaths and those lovely houses on the Sussex border that some think as remarkable as the châteaux of the Loire; it has also its large nondescript population of squatters, eking out a hard independent living on a few ugly acres. In Hampshire are the chalk downs and the hangars on wooded cliffs where Gilbert White

Seaside: *Blue bay and sunshine at Torquay on the South Devon coast.*

wrote the most English of small English classics: *Natural History and Antiquities of Selborne*. White is a model for the eccentricity of the English country clergy—the oddest race in the country. All through Kent and Hampshire, and adjoining Sussex, Wilshire and Dorset run the bold chalk downs, rising like smooth green whales from the beech woods. Pause at Jane Austen's Winchester, in Hampshire. It is vivid to me, not only because of the cathedral but because there, the only time in my life, I saw a judge put on the black cap and condemn a man to death. It was a scene of horror from Thomas Hardy, but brought up to date in macabre fashion by press photographers who walked backward, like a court, before the mother of the murderer and the mother of his victim as they left the courtroom. I can still smell the brilliantine on the hair of the police. Soldiers were singing in the barracks nearby and the afternoon traffic of the cathedral town spanked on its way to Southampton.

Those chalk downs run north to Salisbury Plain, to Avebury and Stonehenge (they are pimpled by scores of burial mounds left by the people of the Stone Age and the Bronze); and southward into Hardy's Dorset, where the Gothic-looking stone cottages remind one that part of the variety of the English villages depends on the fact that they were built in styles, changing from century to century, by local men using local brick and stone. All these counties have their vestiges of dialect and their own accents. The radio is levelling this out; but the traveller who buys a post card in a village shop or

listens in the village pub will notice that the people talk two languages. They fall back into the dialect of their childhood (English people fall very easily into the talk of childhood) when they drop into craftiness or are telling comic stories against each other. Rustic phrases like "Be 'e talking to we?" are the language of succulent local comedy. It keeps the stranger at arm's length too. I once saw a la-di-da fellow go into a seaside taproom and call out cheerfully to the players, "I see you like playing shove ha'penny heah." The fishermen went on playing and, after a very long and freezing time, the oldest of them took his pipe out of his mouth and replied: "Some of us buggers be bloody artists at it." It was the war of town and country, between local and stranger.

But we must turn now and face the important fact that England is an industrial nation and that we have been dodging it. Ninety per cent of its people live in towns; and of those, 40 per cent live in the huge industrial conurbations. It is all very well: the most intelligent, alive and interesting people belong to the industrial population. Oxford dispels an illusion: an industrial city has engulfed the university, and the student body is formed, not by the privileged classes but by poorer clever boys up on scholarships from the red-brick suburbs and the industrial towns.

At Stratford, on Shakespeare's birthday, the long American cars of the diplomatic corps pack the streets for schoolboys to admire. A town councillor told me, as we watched the swans of Avon turning on the river, that he had never read Shakespeare until he came to Stratford. But now he had discovered, as a businessman, that "Shakespeare had the answer to every question." That's the spirit of the Midlands: practical.

Its capital is Birmingham, that huge concentration of engineering works, where town runs into town under the smoke, where the ground subsides over the coal fields, until we reach Arnold Bennett's Black Country. That is a region to see at night, when the kilns and the furnaces glow; it is inhabited by a race apart. Yet once these industrial wildernesses are passed, we realize that they have emptied the countryside and left enormous empty panoramas of moor and mountain. The North is the one part of this unspectacular island which is dramatic.

Suppose you drive up from Derby, where they make the Rolls-Royce engines, towards Manchester: you are travelling through ravines of the Peak District.

"What's life like in Derby?" you ask the man at the garage.

He gives you the set industrial look. "Dead," he says. "You coom here for the money and the work."

The North, you realize, means work, the love of work, the cult of work, the scorn for those who don't work. When you drive through the Peak to Buxton, looking down at the green curling River Wye, watching the water go over the weirs like glass, and passing through the spacious parklands where medieval Haddon Hall with its battlements looks across the centuries to Chatsworth, you see the busloads of industrial workers out on holiday. They have come out to see the spa waters blessed at Buxton, to hear the town band, drink pints of beer and eat potato crisps. Sheffield, with its steel and mines, is not far off over the hills.

A hard climate here. There is less sun than in the South. Snow blocks the roads in the winter. Hedges have gone, grass is poor on the hills. It is a country bony with rock. The bare fields are chained by loose, blackened stone walls; and from now on in the North, the stone wall will have taken the place of the hedge and there will be few flowers and grasses close to them. From the top of the high country you see Manchester lying twenty-odd miles away under a white chemical fume that makes you cough the moment you drive down into it. You have re-entered the poisoned-climate 20th Century.

The beauty of England lies in all its small towns. The cities have drawn away the growing population and have left the towns in their perfection. There is the market square, the parish church—almost always interesting: a Norman crypt perhaps, some superb murals of the 15th Century as at Pickering near Scarborough in the northeast, or angels and bosses in the vaulting—there are the red-brick or cream houses which so often turn out to be the patchwork of the centuries if you go down an alley and look at the backs of them.

I think of neat, stone Kirby Lonsdale on the way to Westmoreland and the Lakes, with its warm little square. It was one of Ruskin's favorite places. There's a lively blacksmith at Kirby Lonsdale whose family has worked for generations in wrought iron and who made the lovely gates of the churchyard. He is a TV "character" now, but he is a real craftsman and wanderer: he has ridden all over the sheep drives of the North into Scotland, and they have hardly changed since Sir Walter Scott wrote *The Two Drovers*.

I think of perfect Helmsley in the Pickering valley on the eastern side of Yorkshire. It is six o'clock in the summer, but it is cool enough for a big fire. People are sitting round it in the inn having tea. Two silent men are playing darts in the bar, and out of the window I can see the elegant grey square, empty,

Picnic: *The Eton-Harrow cricket match at Lord's.*

Coal miner: *A digger
attacks his victuals
at East Durham.*

Sculptor: *Famed Henry Moore
at work in his studio.*

Bell maker:
*His firm made the
bells of St. Paul's.*

Cricketer: *Saturday afternoons call
amateur batsmen to the pitch.*

Businessman:
*James Russell wears cap,
tweed jacket and sports car.*

Minstrels: *Musicians
at a medieval church fair.*

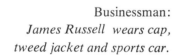

without a building to distress the eye, unchanged in gravity for centuries. Do not misunderstand me: the age of a place means nothing. Helmsley retains a perfect moment of domestic civilisation in silvering stone.

We used to climb the Fells and look across to the higher mountains of Westmoreland and to Solway Firth under their changing cloud. We were looking at what the Lake Poets have made into official romantic scenery. The traveller who leaves Lancashire or West Yorkshire for these little lakes has to prepare for those days when, as the people say, the weather is "dampening on"—as good a piece of English understatement as I have ever met. The caprice of the sky, the changes from wet to clear enhance the grace and variety of the scene as one drives, say, over the Kirstone Pass into Patterdale and Ullswater. Into that lake, red deer from the oldest herd in England will sometimes come down to swim. The Lakes are the country for walkers and climbers. The inhabitants are hardy, good, plain folk and taciturn; they have the Celt and the Viking in them.

The observant and thirsty traveller will have noticed by now how many inns are called *The Lamb, The Fleece, The Woolpack,* and so on; he will have read that the Lord Chancellor is said to "sit on the Woolsack." When you turn from Yorkshire and away from the machines and begin your journey down the eastern side of England from Durham to York, and then on to Lincoln and finally to that bulge into the North Sea which is called East Anglia, you will be travelling back in time to when the wealth of England was based on wool.

When we learned to weave our own cloth in the 14th Century, the beautiful wool towns of East Anglia were built and, in them, some of the finest churches in the country. I think of the churches at Lavenham and Stoke-by-Nayland, of lonely Blythburgh on its sea marsh and of the great church of Long Melford. I think of Norwich and the water-colour painters who learned from their almost-neighbors, the Dutch, and who were moved by the immense light of this flattish country which has been cleaned by the prevailing east wind. It was always a place for churches. Suffolk is called *selig* Suffolk, which is nowadays pronounced "silly"; but the word means holy and describes a land of monasteries and abbeys. The Anglo-Saxon is almost pure here. I went to school in Ipswich when I was a boy and we always called each other "boa"—the German *Bauer*—instead of boy; and in the singsong speech of the county we said, "Farewell, boa," instead of good-by.

Of all the East Anglian towns Bury St. Edmunds, I think, is the most beautiful. It is little known to travellers. The majestic Abbey churches and the vast ruin of the old Abbey in the middle of town have given the place the grand style. It has fine squares and streets, whose 18th Century façades very often conceal back ways and buildings of earlier times. It has the serenity of something fixed forever. It is a place of steep hills.

As the cars and motor bicycles roar through the town on a summer evening, the people walk into the Abbey grounds and there is the complete English summer scene. Couples go in for that expert examination of the rose garden which few Englishmen can resist, for they know the names of roses as they know the names of cricketers. Boys are swimming in the river, girls are playing tennis, youths are playing rough-and-ready cricket and quarrelling about whose turn it is next; and on the bowling green, that lovely close-cut lawn which is an English specialty and a sacred object of contemplation, sly men are rolling the big black balls.

The decorum of the people, the quiet, the evening scents, the silence of the courting couples—for English courtships are sedate in public—the rich shadows of the elms take your mind off the white scribble of the soundless jets in the blue sky. It is a thing we have got used to: the island is a fortress and you cannot drive many miles without coming to a runway.

I have written only about England and Englishmen, not about the Welsh or the Scots. It is all nonsense really; there are only the British. The English are a cultural fiction, the descendants of an early melting pot of Celts, Norsemen, Saxons, Teutons, Danes and Norman French, with an allowance of later Huguenots and the European immigrations of the last thirty years and the continuous inflow of the Irish. We now have West Indians too.

Hippolyte Taine, the French critic who came here in the middle of the last century, did not agree that we were a silent and reserved race. He found us quick, affable, talkative, easily unbosoming. Our leisurely manner was a necessary pose. God help everybody if we abandoned our self-control.

Taine found us unexampled in our individual relation to society but poor in personal relationships; our unrelaxed nature was deeply private, he said, and this privacy found its supreme expression in English lyrical poetry. For the rest, we were too closely packed, shoulder to shoulder.

I don't know. A few months ago I was standing on the walls of York looking over the rose gardens to the towers of the Minster and listening to the sound of the great bells. There were two bells, deep-sounding bells that hummed powerfully, covering all other sounds in the city. One was profound, grave and masculine, its note pronounced, impervious to argument. The other, though strong, was pitched a little higher, like an echo, still grave but feminine. I was listening to a colloquy of towers, a dialogue between those two aspects of the English nature, the outer and the inner, the governing and the private or poetic. They spoke for a long time and seemed to me to speak of the division that lies in the sober English nature.

In the end, if we ask what an Englishman is like, we have to say that he changes more from county to county than he does from class to class. The confident aggressor of the 19th Century has become the peculiar, considerate and self-disciplined being of today who so often sacrifices his obligations to his emotions and whose teen-age children show regular signs of wanting to burst out again. His fortune was once made out of wool; then out of coal, steel and ships; his skill—and skill he fosters and values far more than happiness—now has turned to the air and atomic power. If he accepts now a great deal of the standardisation imposed by a mass society he protects himself by a great tolerance of eccentricity and of what passes for madness. (All the English, Hamlet said, were mad.) He is a man who has always thought his own past was alive in him. It has been his fate to live in the crankish intimacy of that "little world" Shakespeare spoke of and yet to act compulsively on a far larger world outside in every century. It is the fate of islands.

Chimney sweep: *Tools in hand he goes forth to battle soot.*

Professor: *En route to Honours Day at Cambridge.*

Constable: *P. C. Pinchin's name decided his occupation.*

Dog lovers: *The Hyde Park sheep-dog trials.*

Civil servant: *His dress and bearing are immutable.*

Gatekeeper: *Welcome— and an umbrella when necessary.*

LONDON

No one, says V. S. Pritchett,
can be exact about London,
the monstrous and unreasonable agglomeration
of villages gummed together in the
course of centuries.
But those who have known that vast Victorian splodge
can never forget the mild, massive,
incontrovertible manner that is London.

No Londoner can be exact or reasonable about London. This place with the heavy sounding name, like coal being delivered or an engine shunting, is the world's greatest unreasonable city, a monstrous agglomeration of well-painted property. The main part of the city, 120 square miles of low-lying and congested Portland stone, yellow brick and stucco, slate, glass and several million chimneys, lies a few minutes' flight from the North Sea. There are immense acreages of railway track, and the subsoil is a tangle of tunnels running into scores of miles. Such is the mere core of London; another 700 square miles of what was once pasture and woodland is now continuous red-faced suburb. People talk loosely about the number of London's inhabitants: there are certainly nine million. To the police it seems much more.

It is impossible to be exact about London because no one really has ever seen it. Once in, we are engulfed. It is a city without profile, without symmetry; it is amorphous, like life, and no one thing about it is definitive. A natural guess, for example, is that it is as grey and yellow as it looks; yet, from any small height it looks entirely green, like a forest, with occasional stone towers sticking out. The explanation is paradoxical: by preserving trees the Londoner, by far the most urban living creature, convinces himself he is living in the countryside.

Of the world's capitals London has been the most powerful and important for a good two hundred years, the capital of the largest empire since the Roman. It is now the capital of a Commonwealth. But to be a Londoner is still to be immediately, ineluctably, a citizen of the world. Half of the mind of every Londoner is overseas. If the French government falls, if there is dock trouble in New York, a riot in the Gold Coast, even the charwoman cleaning the office will mention the lugubrious fact. There is an old story that someone was once mad enough to ask a Cockney whether the London he came from was London, Ontario; the Cockney groaned, "Nah! London the whole bloomin' world." Truculent, proud, even sentimental, yet the old hypocrite was piously complaining of the weight of the world upon the London mind.

Perhaps because of the weight and the worry, London is the least ostentatious of the world's capitals. It has little of the rhetorical architecture and the ambitious spacing of monuments and temples to be found in the capitals of the new democracies; none of the marble splash endowed by patriotic planners. Napoleon would turn in his grave in the Invalides if he

London's jumble of buildings is topped by a forest of landmarks, dominated by the great dome of St. Paul's.

could see Nelson's urn crowded among painters and bishops in the crypt of St. Paul's. The Houses of Parliament and Buckingham Palace are among the few great edifices to compose a view, and so—thanks to German bombers—was St. Paul's cathedral for a few years during and after the war; but, for the rest, though London has its fine quarters, its monuments, palaces and even a triumphal arch or two, these have been eased into the city and are not ornately imposed upon it.

London excels in the things that segregate and preserve an air of privilege: the lovely terraces of the Regency, the sedate faces of the squares and of the moneyed or modest Georgian and Early Victorian streets. These are not collectors' pieces; they are the routine of central London. The Londoner is purse proud and shows it in his domestic property rather than in imperial splash; and if he builds a Foreign Office that looks like a cross between a Renaissance palace and a Turkish bath, he redresses the balance by putting the Prime Minister in a small private house called No. 10 down a side street and with only an iron railing—and a couple of policemen—to prevent us from putting our noses against the window.

But I am writing as if I had *seen* London, when the confusing fact is that I have only lived in it most of my life. I have just looked at the smear of grey sky through the window of my top-floor flat. It is in one of those blocks of pink structures which went up like so many vending machines in London between the wars, when architecture broke with the Victorian rotundity and the cheese-coloured stucco of 150 years before. I closed the window to shut out the noise of the buses. Look at my hands. Already filthy.

I find myself siding with Henry James, who noticed the filth of London as soon as he arrived here, went on to say that it was not cheerful or agreeable, added that London was dull, stupid

Britain's peers gather here before the monarch's throne in the richly elaborate House of Lords.

and brutally large and had a "horrible numerosity of society." Was anything left after that? Yes, he said; there was magnificence.

London is a prime grumbler. The weather, the traffic, the smoke, the dirty colour get us down and we feel our life is being eaten up in those interminable bus and tube journeys through the marsh of brick—eaten up before we have even started to live. But gradually we begin to feel the magnificence that rises out of the grey, moody, Victorian splodge. We felt it in the sound of Big Ben growling like an old lion over the wet roofs in the silent, apprehensive nights of the war. Where Paris suggests pleasure, Rome the human passions of two thousand years, with assassination in every doorway, where New York suggests a ruthless alacrity, London suggests experience.

London is an agglomeration of villages which have been gummed together in the course of centuries. It is a small nation rather than a city, and its regions have never quite lost their original identity or even their dialects. The City of London, the administrative heart of the city, which begins at Aldgate suddenly, like a row of cliffs, is a province in itself. Yet a large part of central London is not muddle at all, for here it was planned in the late 18th and early 19th centuries, when the squares were laid out between Bloomsbury and Bayswater. The habit of making tree-shaded oases, in squares and private terraces, gave a respite from the vulgar uproar and ugly building of the general commercial scramble. The railed-in lawns and the green enclosures of the Inns of Court betray our love of privacy and privilege, and for delectable cliques, clubs and coteries, just as those acres and acres of little two-storey houses show how much we like a little property to ourselves. This has been the despair of urban planners.

There are immense cheese-coloured areas in Bayswater and elsewhere where Bernard Shaw's tall Heartbreak Houses have pillars like footmen's legs. Chelsea is one kind of place. Westminster another. Inner London is grey or yellow, outer London is red; that is about as much as can be said of the Victorian jungle, unless we name the slates shining like mirrors in the wet.

In that tired air, always heavy and often damp and lethargic, the grass grows green in the black soil of the gardens, the shrubs grow dusty and the dappled plane trees grow black. In the summer evenings we listen to their leaves turning over like the pages of endless office ledgers. We hear the ducks fly over from some pool of filthy water left on a bomb site to the wooded lakes in the parks. We hear the starlings at St. Martin's crying down the traffic. We hear owls. We even hear sheep in Regent's Park in summer. A city so countrified cannot be a megapolis.

We are tree lovers. In the winter the London trees are as black as processions of mourners and, like the weeds of some sooty gathering of widows, their higher branches are laced against the mist or the long, sad sunsets. The thing that reconciled us to those ruined miles in Holborn, Cheapside and round St. Paul's were the trees that grew rapidly out of burned-out basements where the safes had been kept; and the willow herb that grew in purple acres out of commercial brick.

The London tree grows out of poisoned soil, its roots are enclosed by stone and asphalt, and it breathes smoke. There is

one heroic creature, raising its arms between two overtowering blocks of office buildings and the church of St. Magnus the Martyr in Billingsgate. Typewriters clatter among its branches instead of birds; and a boy who climbed it would come down black. Its survival shows how firmly Londoners cling to nature and, in life, to some corner of what has been.

Except in the curve of the river between Westminster and St. Paul's, there are no large vistas in London, and our small ones have come to us by luck and accident. I have a typical view of the London muddle from my flat. There is one of those Victorian streets of carefully painted small houses, with their classical doorways and their iron railings. (The Victorians did not know what to do with all the iron they produced and simply caged up everything in it.)

London is prolific in its casualties, human waste and its eccentrics. We see that blowsy red-haired woman with the grey beard who skips about the pavement in the Haymarket.

A well-known trial to bus conductors, the woman always carries a spare hat concealed in a brown-paper bag for travelling by bus. She changes her hat and then sings out:

> He called me his Popsy Wopsy
> But I don't care.

And drops into a few unprintable words. We are very fond of her. There is the pavement artist who conducts a war with other street entertainers, especially those who use an animal to beg from the thousands of dog lovers, cat strokers, pigeon and duck feeders, the chronic animal lovers who swarm in London. "Worship God not animals," he scrawls in angry chalk on the pavement. There is the Negro bird warbler, ecstatic in his compulsion, and the King of Poland in his long golden hair and his long crimson robe. There are those solitaries with imaginary military careers and the frightening dry monotonous gramophone record of their battles and wounds. They are compelled, they utter, they click their heels, salute and depart. A pretty addled neighbour of mine used to mix up the washing of the tenants in her house when it hung on the line in her garden. She was getting her own back on the Pope, who had broken up her marriage to the Duke of Windsor. One has to distinguish between the divine mad and the people pursuing a stern, individual course. The elderly lady who arrives in white shorts on a racing bicycle at the British Museum every morning, winter and summer, is simply a student whom we shall see working under the gilded dome of the Reading Room. The taxi driver who answers you in the Latin he has picked up from the bishops he has been taking to and fro from the Athenaeum Club all his life is not consciously doing a comic turn. He is simply living his private life in public. As Jung says, we are dreaming all the time; consciousness merely interrupts. It was what Dickens noticed in Londoners years before.

We live in localities where we sharpen our particular foibles. The "local" public house is one gathering point, although television is emptying the pubs in the working-class districts. The London pubs are all different and live by character. For the stage, I think of the *Salisbury*, where a stage-door keeper the other day suggested to me that gin and eels made the ideal nightcap; *El Vino's* for the journalists, the *York Minster* for

Beefeaters, Yeoman Warders at the Tower, dress now as they did in Shakespeare's time.

the French. We live on strong beer and gin and drink them standing in moody or explanatory groups. At a pub we like to reveal ourselves suddenly and at length to a few new friends; but we respect privacy too. I have seen a man sitting in the midst of a packed and roaring pub reading *The Economist* from cover to cover, unaware of the quarrel between the sailor and the tart, the racing talk, the slow description of a hospital operation or the whispers to the girl having her neck stroked. He was simply insulated.

People began to say before the war that London was becoming continentalised. So it was, in a superficial way. You can buy *pizza* in the mass restaurants without going to Soho and *espresso* coffee in the bars. Popular London lives by its mass diversions. For generations the city has been the world's capital of ballroom dancing, and its "pallys" are packed most of the week to see the exhibitions. Africans and Indians colour the popular crowd and the great dancers are watched with a critical devotion that I have seen equalled only by Spaniards at the

Old pageantry and renewed excitement mark the Trooping the Colour which honors the Queen's birthday.

bullfight. The thousands who go to the ballet at Sadler's Wells or Covent Garden are a race in themselves.

And there is gambling; London is almost silenced in some quarters on Thursday nights, when people are doing their football pools, and again at six on Saturday when they hear the worst. There are the greyhound tracks—London's night betting machine; under the white floodlight that chemically green oval suggests the roulette tables of Monte Carlo. The mob goes to these places, the toughs, the spivs, the workers from the factories; but in the hot, carpeted bars of the people who are in the money you see the full heat of gambling, its secretiveness and its fantasies, as the floor is littered with betting slips. Living in London all my life, I had not met these Londoners before: the swarthy, brash, gold-ringed men, the Oriental-looking women in their furs or these startling blondes on the bar stools. Once more I had found another race, as I did when I followed the crowd who go to hear *Tosca* at Sadler's Wells or Shakespeare at the Old Vic, who have heard all the plays and all the operas you can name a dozen times over and call out for their favourite actors and actresses by name in an orgy of local religion.

Another London race is the race of arguers. We can never resist an argument. There are the human cockerels at lunchtime in squares like Lincoln's Inn Fields, crowing about every conceivable kind of political new dawn. But Sunday is the day for this essentially Puritan pleasure. We revel vulgarly in free speech. There are not only the dozen main meetings under the trees in Hyde Park, but there are those earliest known manifestations of dialectical life on earth: the conjunction of two men standing nose to nose, with two or three idle friends attending, each proving the other wrong, not in rage but in quiet and disparaging parliamentary calm and pith. ("You say the Buddha is living—how do you know the Buddha is living? Have you seen the Buddha?") From a distance the shouting of Marble Arch sounds like a dog show. The red buses go round the Arch and add the uproarious, band-playing suggestion of merry-go-rounds and racers, but nothing can drown the argument. "My friends," the speakers shout, "believe!" Half a dozen voices call back, "Get on with it. You said that before." And some wit yells out, "Where was Moses born?"

"Believe! Believe!" What are we asked to believe? Some well-informed man is telling us that there are millions of gallons of water up in the sky—"What? Up there, Dad?" comes a voice—and that there will be a repetition of the Great Flood. We are asked to believe that Ireland will be free, that Russia wants war, that America wants war—or that they don't—a hymn strikes up next door, all the Truth societies are at it like mongrels, a lonely figure disputes the Virgin Birth relentlessly, an elderly man, gnawing at a bone, tells us the Pyramids hold the key to human destiny. And then, five yards away, we hear the melting Oxford voice of a coloured man from the Gold Coast: "If I become Minister of Commerce in the Gold Coast——" What is he going to do? Something unpleasant to London, just as the

Irish are, the Egyptians, the Russians, the South Americans, the men of God.

Insult, doom, destruction are offered to us. The crowds stand round grinning. The Guardsmen stand pink with pleasure. Sailors are delighted. The police stand by like hospital nurses. For nurse is never far off, gossipy at the moment, but always with an eye open. There is a nurse in every Londoner and nurse says things have got to be fair. One would be relieved if, as in wicked countries like France or Italy, things could be unfair—just for once. It is our weakness that we cannot manage that. "No," someone shouts out to an interrupter. "Let him say what he thinks. Go on, mate, say what you was going to say."

The Park is Babel. But in Trafalgar Square, at the foot of Nelson's column and under that patriotic bas-relief of the Death of Nelson—for the British god is a sea god—you hear the Voice of the people. (They have put amplifiers on the noses of the lions there, which gives these soapy figures a new professorial look.)

The Irish poet W. B. Yeats, who used to wander, tall, remote and lonely, about the London streets when he had woken up from the detective story he had been reading in the Savile Club, despised Trafalgar Square meetings and once told me that in Dublin he had led a procession up Sackville Street and had smashed thirty thousand pounds' worth of plate glass. Such exaltations haven't been heard of in London—not since the days of the Duke of Wellington.

In any case London is traditionally free of hysteria, stoical and disciplined, but not beyond the resources of nature. Publicly powerful and often hated for that, London has always valued private life most. It is a place where whims have their rights, where nerves are not exacerbated, where one is at ease, where standardisation of behaviour is disliked and where the tone of casual conversation is affectionate. There is regard for what can last; this can be called vegetative, sentimental, unrealistic, muddled. A Londoner himself would call this feeling: passion.

Scotland

The romantic Highlanders of Sir Walter Scott, kilts, tartans, Bobbie Burns and the Ghost that went West are as far from the truth as the other picture of the canny, dour Scot who can only say "Ay" and look at a penny twice. Actually, says Neil M. Gunn, the Scots have been gamblers against long odds and supporters of lost causes, so reckless and headlong that the history of Scotland is often incredible.

Most people think of Scotland in terms of kilts, Robbie Burns, bagpipes, tartans, whisky and Scotch penuriousness. This fantastic picture shakes the ordinary Scot with laughter and drives the Scots comedian to carry it into the region of pure myth; so presumably it is used to hide something, to conceal the reality. Anyway, it is impossible to hide a country's history, and the sober fact is that the Scot's history shows him to have been a gambler against long odds, a supporter of "lost causes," reckless and headlong so often that much of that history has an incredible air. Not that he could not calculate the odds. He could—and did. But that did not stop him. When a wild gamble is over, a man may laugh at himself and his foibles and even strive to be thoughtful over his loose change.

Calculating odds is what an engineer does, so when the national battles stopped, the Scot became a notable engineer and built on a small river the biggest ships afloat. In Clyde shipyards the kilt and balmoral bonnet gave way to the foreman's dark suit and bowler hat. Quiet-mannered, thorough, the Scot got on with a job that seemed as remote from tartan romanticism as a Highland Calvinist minister from an orgy of jazz. And his Scots tongue may be heard in the engine rooms of ships in most parts of the world. But far in the sparsely popu-

lated areas of the Highlands a lobster fisherman, for whom time and blueprints have little meaning, talks slowly in a clear school English, patterned on the idioms of his native Gaelic. A stranger could be forgiven for thinking them different kinds of men—until he found still other kinds on the good farming lands of the east coast, on the trawlers and herring drifters that rake the seas, in the educational circles which derive from four ancient universities, or in the legal and administrative seats of the capital city, Edinburgh. In its scenery as in the ways of its people, Scotland is a land of great diversity.

Yet there is something in the tartan. A comedian doesn't make a myth out of nothing. And even in the case of Burns it is the simple truth that a nation which fought fabulous battles for its independence and produced warrior heroes like Wallace and Bruce has chosen a poet as its national figure. We may be getting near the heart of the matter if we say that the tartan stands for history, for the something which made the Scots cohere and quite literally fight to the death. His past is in the Scot as his blood is; and it is a long past. A bit of tartan, the swing of the kilt as the pipers march away, and the blood beats time to the old tune in the Clyde engineer as in the lonely Hebridean fisherman.

And it is really a very old tune. For example, it is doubtful if any war speech of our times more bitterly condemned totalitarian empire than the address delivered to his troops by the commander in chief of the Caledonians—as the inhabitants of Scotland were then called—before he ordered them to fall upon the invading Roman legions. "To ravage, to slaughter, to usurp under false titles they call empire; and where they make a desert, they call it peace." The words sound as familiar as a quotation from the Bible, but it was Tacitus the Roman who reported them. Caledonia, stern and wild, was being invaded, the fiery cross had gone round, the tribes and clans were out, and the year was about 85 A.D. Defeat and slavery—or liberty. "March then to battle," concluded the Caledonian, "and think of your

ancestors and your posterity." And some nineteen hundred years later, Scotsmen are accused of still being able to think of both.

So it is a long story. In truth, the first thing we learn about Scotland is that she is one of the oldest nations in Western Christendom; and the second, that her whole history is pervaded by this passion for liberty. The Romans fell back and dug themselves in behind a system of solid fortifications that ran along a line not far from what is to this day the border between England and Scotland.

The "romantic" Highlanders of Sir Walter Scott, the Bonnie Prince Charlies of glamour, the Ghost that went West, all the high-colored romances of the kind are about as far removed from reality as that other picture of the canny Scot: the dour careful fellow who can only say "Ay" and look at a penny twice. Scots comedians like Harry Lauder fastened on to this picture of the close-fisted, canny Scot, for they found that the English music hall loved it, and they guyed the invention to

the top of their bent. Most Aberdeen stories are manufactured by the wits in Aberdeen—for example, the photograph of Aberdeen on a flag day (money-collecting for charities), where all the streets are seen absolutely deserted. When the "Scotch comic" toddled onto the London stage, dressed outrageously in kilt and sporran, carrying a great twisted walking stick, he brought the house down. And that he appeared to joke "wi' difficulty" added the finishing touch. Perhaps there is something psychologically perverse here, and not least on the part of the audience. Perhaps we all feel good when we can unload our secret obsessions, our meannesses, onto some such solitary figure. The English music hall also had a similar sort of comic stage Irishman. But he vanished when a few gunmen shot him to bits over the Irish bogs. An American has asked me why the Scots never went in for direct action. The answer is that, unlike Ireland, Scotland was never conquered by arms; there is no "historic grievance" in the Irish sense. This is what makes clear-cut action in the "nationalist" manner so difficult in Scot-

A band of pipers winds across an Edinburgh crag known as Arthur's Seat.

land today. Anyway, it isn't that the Scots are more canny than the Irish or even as canny as the English make them out to be. Consider, for example, the Bonnie Prince Charlie episode.

Prince Charles Edward Stuart had his supporters in England as well as in Scotland, wealthy and influential Jacobites who passed their wineglass over the water decanter in secret toast to their king "over the water." But when he made his bid for the throne of his ancestors, he chose to land in the Highlands. The Highlanders whom he called to his standard knew that his chance of success was about that of the snowflake on the river, and knew also that failure meant all things between loss of possessions and the scaffold. Yet they answered the call and set forth and scattered an army in one wild charge and danced in Holyrood Palace in Edinburgh. Then they entered England and got as far as Derby. But the English Jacobites, who had schemed and passed their wine over the waterjug, did not answer the call. They were a canny, careful crowd who looked at the penny twice and decided not even to toss it. On Culloden Moor above Inverness, the weary, hungry remnants of the Jacobite army were defeated and the clans were finally broken. The senseless butchery that followed is something that no Highlander likes to remember, whether he was for the Prince or against him— and there were good reasons for being against him. Many simple clansmen who hadn't thirty pieces of copper with which to bless themselves guided the hunted Prince from place to place until he escaped abroad, though the London government had set £30,000 on his head. However that tragic episode in Scotland's story be assessed, it can hardly be held to prove that the Scot possesses, when he is moved, the excellent virtue of canniness.

But it is natural to attribute romance to the Highlands because in itself it is so varied and beautiful a country. There are bare, gaunt regions with outcrops of the oldest rock in the world, the earth's original crust. Glens with birches and tumbling streams and blue lochs. Mountain chains range most ways, yet the highest peaks are not much over 4000 feet, so that they never lose a certain intimacy. They can be encompassed, and many of them, like the Cuillin in the island of Skye, set problems for roped climbers that have given them a wide fame. The hills and moors for the greater part are heather-clad and divided into great sporting estates, where grouse are shot over trained dogs and, in the higher reaches, red deer are stalked. The rivers abound in trout and salmon.

Slantwise across this country stretches the Caledonian Canal, from Fort William in the southwest to Inverness in the northeast: an attractive excursion for any visitor, that can be savored the better from the deck of a boat, sailing through many lochs with wooded hillsides, and being stepped up or down at the various nests of locks. One of the lochs, twenty-four miles long, is called Loch Ness—where the Monster lives. I have never seen the Monster myself, but several of my friends have, including (to mention my last contact) my old companion, Ian McKillop, whose name recently appeared in the Royal Honours List in recognition of his public service to his native county of Invernessshire. He described to me, as he did to members of the County Council, how he watched the commotion on the loch's surface and the rapid speed of the mostly submerged "beast" as

it plowed the water. We know, of course, that the enlightened world generally regards the Loch Ness Monster as a fabulous creation designed by thrifty Scots to attract tourists with more money than sense. Alas, the Scots can't collect even that bouquet! So let it be said simply that a strange unclassified huge creature of some kind does exist. The loch rests on an old geological "fault" and is very deep. The bodies of drowned humans are rarely recovered from it.

Possibly this may seem the appropriate moment for introducing Highland whisky, but priority must be given to agriculture, which is still, as it always has been, the principal industry. And what a contrast is here between the few stony acres of many a croft among the hills or in the Hebrides and the highly mechanized farms on the flat eastern fringe, which broadens out between Inverness and Aberdeen and continues right down to those red lands on the way to Berwick. The Scots have long had a reputation for thoroughness in agriculture and it remains a simple fact that the average yield per acre of grain and potatoes surpasses that of most European countries. But their special pride is in their cattle herds, bred for the finest qualities, and sold whenever possible for export. At the moment, the percentage of attested herds in Scotland is much higher than in England. All this is not achieved without hard work and scientific husbandry, but at least it may help to dispel the notion of a poverty-stricken soil. Where the soil can be cultivated, the best is got from it—when the weather gives half a chance.

After agriculture comes sea fishing, all the way round the coast from the port of Aberdeen, along the fishing creeks of the Moray Firth, northward to Lerwick in Shetland, west to Stornoway in Lewis and down the west coast with its deep inlets.

The modern herring industry started nearly a hundred and fifty years ago on the Moray Firth, under favourable price conditions, and went ahead like a gold rush, the same old fury, carrying its thousands of barrels of cured herring eastward to the Baltic ports and westward to Jamaica; a trade sustained over a long period because of the care given to quality, but defeated towards the end by world politics, and particularly those following the first World War, when foreign governments started subsidizing their new fishing fleets but Westminster left the old fleet at home to sink as well as it could. Which is perhaps the appropriate moment for a dram of the real Scotch.

And the real Scotch whisky is still made in the Highlands, and made in the same old way as when history first found it and recorded its name. If most great discoveries are accidents, one can at least imagine some ancient bard murmuring *uisgebeatha* (the water of life) as the crystal distillate from a chance condensation of spirit vapor began to work miraculously upon him for the first time. The Scots have an expression: "He was miraculous," meaning wonderfully drunk; and in some such condition the long word was no doubt shortened to *uisge* (pronounced ooshke) or, as we now say, whisky. Yet drunkenness was a rare thing in the Highlands in those distant days when a man could have his own still.

But Scotland has had her lesson: the old industries are not enough, and today efforts are being made to bring light industries into production, while really large schemes for afforestation and the generation of hydroelectric power from the lochs

and rivers of the Highlands are under way. The economic decay of the Highlands may yet be arrested, and the bitter years of apathy following the 1745 Rising under Prince Charlie and the subsequent tragic evictions of the clansmen from their immemorial homesteads by a greedy landlordism that saw it could make more money out of sheep may yet be looked back upon as historic incidents in the long but undying story.

And prompting this thought from beneath is the stirring of the new life in Scotland or of the old life brought to a rebirth, to a Scottish Renaissance. Excellent poetry in Scots and Gaelic is now being published, but whether this literary revival can be carried over into the main prose stream, which is English, remains to be proved.

As for the English prose of the creative writer in Scotland, it has at its best that kind of uniqueness which distinguishes the prose of the American or Irishman. And when writing it, the Scot tends more and more to stay at home. For generations back, when he wanted to get on in his profession, he set out for London. James Barrie left his native Kirriemuir for London and fame and created Peter Pan. James Bridie, his successor as Scotland's premier dramatist, lives in the country outside Glasgow, goes to London only for a first production of one of his plays, and deals with themes ranging from Calvinism and the Devil to human anatomy and inheritance with a wit and thought and dramatic contrivance missing from the British stage since Bernard Shaw's heyday.

But whatever the aspect of Scottish life, there the resurgence will be found. Societies to promote or encourage this economic plan or that cultural aim seem to come to a self-supporting life by a sort of spontaneous generation, with the women sometimes more active than the men. The Saltire Society, large and flourishing, concerns itself with arts and crafts; Community Drama sweeps the country each spring with its one-act-play competitions in a sort of fever; the Scottish Council (Development and Industry) has had a strikingly successful Industrial Exhibition in Glasgow and is busy with new schemes of research and construction. Edinburgh is, as usual, thinking of its next International Festival. But in recent times the most arresting of all Scottish portents has been the quite astonishing success of the Covenant movement. The Covenant is a simple document whose important sentence reads: "We solemnly enter into this Covenant whereby we pledge ourselves, in all loyalty to the Crown and within the framework of the United Kingdom, to do everything in our power to secure for Scotland a Parliament with adequate legislative authority in Scottish affairs." Without propaganda or ballyhoo of any kind this Covenant has already been signed by over 1,600,000, or practically half of the Scottish electorate, and signatures still mount up. The bosses of the major political parties in Britain, Labour and Tory, are trying at the moment not to believe it, though the leaders of the Covenant movement include distinguished Scots from all parties, professions, and the arts, with John M. MacCormick, who has worked for Home Rule for twenty years, as

its versatile and able chairman. Much more will be heard of this, both at home and abroad, in the near future.

Such are the stirrings and heavings, the efforts, as it were, to break through all bonds into a free, healthy native air. Yet it is not altogether a matter of societies and groups and movements. For though the group, the clan, is a native expression of the feeling for community, it has always been based on the responsible actions of the free individual.

So the deeper meaning in the story becomes clear. It was as if the "fury" had always needed, was always searching for, a central point of cohesion, a natural or governing nucleus that would direct the energy the right way. That achieved, the Scot might then even have something valuable to give to the world; though he may not see it in that way but rather, with Carlyle, the old Scots prophet, believe that when a man has a zeal for reform he should reform himself first and so leave one rascal the less in the world. This kind of nationalism means not a theory in the head but an impulse from the living heart. It is the light in the eyes of the tired housewife who found grace again in the country dance; it is the long thought of the man sitting on the heather; it is the poem that is quoted, the song that is sung, the good heritage that is lost. When the ancient tap root dries up, the tree will blossom no more. When the flower of the spirit dies in one country, it dies for all.

Scotland/Neil M. Gunn **33**

Wales

The Land of Strangers, it was called.
Settled by invaders from Asia before recorded history,
occupied by Roman Legions 2,000 years ago, it became
the Kingdom of Arthur and the land of knights
and bards. It has produced billions of tons of coal,
thousands of poets and singers.
In this rich lore and tragic history the novelist
Richard Llewelleyn finds the heart of his native Wales.

From a point outside the United Kingdom of Great Britain, Wales is a place you must go somewhere else to get to. You can go to Finland direct, or Nicaragua direct, and a lot of other fine places, and some say you can go to hell direct; but you cannot go direct to Wales, unless, of course, you want a slow trip by tramp steamer. England, Northern Ireland and Scotland can all be got direct for the asking, but to get to Wales, the other quarter of the United Kingdom, you must first go to one of the other three and then on from there.

All this, however, is not to say that Wales is an unimportant country, or that Welsh people are averse to visitors, jealous of the national language, diffident about the beauty of some parts of their country, or ashamed of the scarring poverty in others. It is simply that Wales—"Gallant Little Wales" to some, "Dear Little Wales" to others, and "That Bloody Awful Hole Down

There" to the rest—has been protected territory since 1284, pampered by the attentions of noblemen holding it in the crooks—a good word, too—of strong arms to be dandled however daintily on Britannia's creamy thew.

When a mother feeds a child, that is natural, and purists call it mother love; but when the mother eats the child, anybody may be pardoned for calling it something less: and many a good meal has been made out of Wales by now, though some believe that a tidy bit of belching is on its way, and rude though belching undoubtedly is, sweet music it will be to many.

In 1284, Eleanor, queen of Edward I of the black stare and drooping eyelid, bore him another male child at Carnarvon Castle, in the Eryri country, home of the eagles. In the early dawn, so they tell us, the king escorted the child and his nurse into the assembly of Welsh princes and chieftains in the great hall, and raising the little bundle, declared him to be their countryman and gave him a motto for his coat of arms, part adjuration, part prophecy—"*Ich Dien*"—which means "I Serve."

With one Prince and many a pauper, Wales has been serving ever since.

Wales, the word itself, means Land of Strangers, and Welsh means stranger, from the Saxon Waelisc.

Of the two and a half million Strangers now living, almost a million speak their own strange language, Cymraeg. Their strange land they call Cymru, Land of Brothers; themselves Cymri, and each other, Cymro.

Caerphilly Castle dates from the 13th century.

Cymru, then, is bounded on the north and west by the Irish Sea, on the south by the Bristol Channel, and on the land side facing England by two rivers, the Severn reaching north, and the holy Dee bending south. A map of the country is roughly the shape of a pig's head looking perhaps hopefully across at Ireland which has, at last, come to adulthood with its own government, a happy state long desired by all good Cymri.

In the northwest corner, a group of hills—Snowdon is the highest at 3560 feet—reaches out along the Lleyn Peninsula, overlooking an island called Anglesey, now; but the Strangers call it Môn, Mother of Cymru, because of its green fruitfulness, and also, perhaps, because at one time it was the seat of all learning.

The hills of Wales are truly nothing more, but a dramatic quality in their form gives further stature, and most people call them mountains. They sweep down along the coast and then in a ridge across the south, dividing the country almost perfectly into four parts; and in olden times, Gwynedd, Ceredigion, Powys and Gwent were the four kingdoms ruled over by King Arthur, the Pendragon, guardian of the Holy Grail. Today, four cathedrals mark their royal passing—Bangor (it means "The White Choir") in Gwynedd; St. Asaph in Powys; Llandaff (Llan, in Cymraeg, means church; daff, a mutation of Taff, a river) in Gwent; and St. David's Cathedral in Dyfed. But no stone is marked for Arthur.

A bard, it is told, searched all the new-made graves throughout the land, beneath the trees of the forests, down in the valleys, and along by the grey sea; but then his muse awoke and told him "what folly it would be to think that Arthur had a grave," that kingly one, who always had a gentle word for the oppressed, and a sharp edge for the ruffian, and a spirit that put a blessing over all the world. He died in battle and the black queens took him in a barge across the torch-lit water and he was never seen again.

The most travelled route to Wales is through a city founded by the Celts, by them called Troynovant, or New Troy, by the Romans Londinium, and in a later Saxon day, London.

Welshmen still call it Llundain, and gather for worship in their own tongue at the great chapels in Castle Street and King's Cross, built by subscription among thousands of immigrants from the mountains and valleys; almost every shopgirl and certainly nearly all milkmen in London were Welsh in the late 80's. But the opening of new lands took the greater number of them to America, Australia and New Zealand in the years before the first World War. Not even Italy can show a higher percentage of migrants; and happy people do not migrate.

Starting from London's Paddington Station, under a glass arcade that has echoed from 4000 voices "up" to sing for Queen Victoria at the Crystal Palace, express trains go to Newport, Cardiff, Swansea, Pembroke Dock, Milford Haven and Fishguard; and north to Aberystwyth, Carnarvon, Bangor and

Holyhead. But only a Welsh eye feels the sting of those names lettered black on cream boards along the sides of the trains.

There is little of King Arthur's Wales, or his Welshmen, in the larger towns, though Swansea is Welshest of the harbours. Cardiff and Newport are Anglicized almost to the level of any English town, and so are the smaller market towns along the border.

To find the real Wales today, the best thing is to strike into the country, never mind where you start, along any of the first-class roads, and then turn off down any lane with a signpost—and watch for the signpost or you may find yourself headed into a bog—and keep going until you come to a village.

It seems strange that a people and a language, and indeed a whole philosophy or way of life, should survive tragedy after tragedy; and yet, walking through any Welsh village today there is nothing to tell of it beyond a certain subdued note in the primness of little houses and old stone cottages, the few modest shops, a public house or two, and The Chapel.

About the first thing to attract you will be the singular beauty of the village children, more particularly the girls, all of them distinct types easily defined. A lustrous redhead with the blue eyes of a Boadicea is common enough, and so is the brunette with a sprinkle of copper and the brown eye of a dreaming Athena; and Cerridwen is there, of the hooked nose,

that graceful crag, and eyes grey or blue in and out of mood as the smiling Atlantic, and sun-silver plaits to her waist; and always a sibyl with black curls in a cloud about her and a profile cut in Troy, but she will be off too quick for you to see whether her eyes are green or amber, or something wonderful between the two.

The village woman is often a natural beauty, reserved with a stranger though courteously so, and kindliest hostess when the ice is thawed and the kettle bubbles for tea.

You may be fortunate and find a village that has an untouched Old Part that will give you sight, sound, and smell of the true Wales. On a weekday, older women wear homespuns and clogs, and a man's cap. Younger women, of course, wear dresses copied from a fashion book and sewn in the evenings at home, or bought in the nearby market town; but they speak together in a strange language. Listen well, for this is Cymraeg and you will understand nothing; and fortunately, for they are probably talking about you.

If the water mill is working, it either grinds corn, or runs the looms for tweed; and down at the riverside you will see hanks of wool newly soaked in river water after steeping in the dye vat.

A fragrance is on the air from chimneys giving blue breath from log fires; and in a back yard you may see a woman mixing coal dust and clay to make pebbles of culm, a slow-burning heat-giver that saves money.

And money is important, for to many it is only another word for freedom; and for that reason the Welsh peasant's frugality may at times come within a touch of miserliness.

But there are times when money can be taken from them with unbelievable ease, for at heart they are simple as children and guileless as the hen; and the secret lies in one word—superstition. Sesame to a steady living by tramp necromancers is this rooted belief in powers going back to days when men allowed the oracle to guide their lives by auguries got from study of new-pulled chicken entrails.

About eight hundred years ago, an old Welshman of Pencader looked above the bridle plumage of a charger, into a face framed in gold armor surmounted by a jewelled crown.

"This nation, O king, may be troubled now as in olden time," he told Henry Plantagenet the Second, "and greatly weakened and destroyed by your, and other power; and it will often prevail by its praiseworthy exertion; but it can never be wholly subdued by wrath of man unless the wrath of God shall concur. Nor do I think that any other nation than this of Wales, or any other tongue—whatever may come to pass hereafter—shall in the day of severe searching before the Supreme Judge, answer for this corner of the earth."

The village at Seal Harbour, County Cork, is spread out on a barren, stony height overlooking Bantry Bay and the Atlantic. Its houses number ten, its total population, thirteen.

Ireland

"Perhaps," writes Sean O'Faolain of the Irish, "perhaps we are a race perpetually old and perpetually young, caught up in the conflict between aged wisdom and childish sensibility." But the real secret of the Irish nature is simply this: Every Irishman is a four-decker...

Ireland is one of the smallest of the nation-islands of the world. Cuba is bigger. Even Iceland is bigger. It is also a solitary island in the sense that it is not, like the Aegean Isles, part of an archipelago, or like Japan one of a chain of islands. It is the big toe of Europe dibbled out into the cold Atlantic. Before Columbus there was nothing at all west of us except the sunset and our awe-struck imaginings.

No Irishman can long forget this watery circumambience detaching us from the world. Even in the center of Ireland sea gulls follow the plow. Whenever we hear a plane humming above the frozen canopy of the clouds we know that it is going out over the sea or coming in from over the sea, a homing seabird. The longest straight line inside the map of Ireland measures only 302 miles, but our coast is so jagged that we are surrounded by about 2000 miles of waves. All our main cities are ports. On foggy days, when no planes take off, we feel very rim-of-the-worldish, thank God for Irish whisky and take a mean comfort in the hope that no planes are taking off from England either. It was on one such day that an English tourist asked me, outside my own gateway: "Tell me, please—when does the post leave for the mainland?" As if we were Nantucket or one of the Solomon Islands.

In wilder weather we are still more conscious of the seas around us. As a boy in Cork city, which is a good ten or fifteen miles inland from its great harbor at Cobh (pronounced Cove), I used to look forward with excitement to the equinoctial gales and the high tides that coincided with them. In those storms the old slated fronts of the houses shed their slates like feathers, the gutters spilled over, the lower-lying streets flooded, and the river, brown and foamy, bore out to sea the debris of its upper course—branches, a hencoop, perhaps a drowned sheep. An imaginative soul once declared that he saw floating by him a grand piano!

Not that the summer visitor will see any of these dramatic effects of our climate. He will enjoy watching the sea-borne clouds mounting the blue sky, rejoice in the bracing air by the sea, or inland feel pleasantly relaxed, not eager to indulge in vigorous athletics. But I doubt if it is the climate which produces this idle frame of mind and body. I suspect it is just the influence of the general easygoing *feel* of the Irish way of life. This, anyway, is as good an explanation of the restful nature of Ireland as the one produced by a visiting American contractor. He had been so delighted with his Irish-descended workmen in the States that he decided to inspect the wonderful island that had nurtured all this bounding energy and tireless vigor. Having wandered around the country for a week, and found the general tempo anything but bounding, he said: "I guess the reason my Irish workers are so full of pep is that their ancestors have been storing up their energy in Ireland for countless generations before letting it loose on America."

Islanded, then, and solitary. We are also remote. Our connection with Europe is more than ambiguous. The fact that we are at the end of the geographical queue makes Ireland not so much belong to the Continent as barely adhere to it, water-divided. The things that have always hitherto linked us to

Where the River Shannon flows: *Beyond a field of Irish potatoes lies Lough Allen in Leitrim County, third largest of the lakes formed by the river.*

Europe have been intangible. Religion, for instance, has always made Dublin far closer to Rome or Lourdes than to London or Paris. On the other hand, emigration to Britain has become heavy and constant over the last twenty years, and today Ireland is far more closely linked to England by brawn and blood than it was before we were separated politically.

I tuned in the radio recently to a rattling program of Irish songs and traditional Irish dance music. I presumed it was coming from Dublin. It turned out to be coming from Birmingham. A week later I picked up a similar program—this time from Sheffield. It evoked smoke-filled halls, pounding feet, flushed cheeks and hearty Irish voices. No wonder the steamers during the holidays have to make eight crossings a day until we begin to wonder whether the Irish are taking over parcels of Britain or Britain is taking old (or rather young) Ireland to her imperial bosom all over again.

A French friend of mine has well described us as *une île cachée derrière une autre île*—an island tucked away behind another island. To find us our continental friends must first discover us. Our American friends tend to overfly us. We are not disturbed. It means we are a serene and select pleasure, almost an exotic pleasure. We are one of the last of the small open spaces of the world. We shelter the lost silence of Europe. To break this silence we have to talk a lot. We shelter another refugee—Time. Because of our slow tempo, Irish hours are twice as long, as if the westering sun kept on forgetting to take them with her to America, where they arrive five hours late and twice as short. Sometimes, when we are very busy, talking, our hours kindly go anticlockwise until today becomes yesterday, and the future threatens to hold off forever. And this re-evokes an old, bitter and witty joke at our expense, coined by that inveterate hater of Irish nationalism, the old London *Morning Post*. It said that Ireland has always had a great future —and always will. I am glad to say that the *Morning Post* soon afterward learned all about the Future. It died.

A German could write a large volume on *The Economic Origins of the Irish Character*, composed entirely of statistics about rainfall, soil formation, grass, cows and horses. Just as a Frenchman might write a charming book about *The Moisture Content of Irish Leprechauns*—all about clouds trailing beards the color of dusk, and dark, high grass under old thorn trees, and the soft sound of cows munching at nightfall, up to their dewlaps in buttercups; and again, his book could contain many statistics about the rainfall, and the limestone soil, and the configuration of the mountains, and the prevailing winds, and the effects of the Gulf Stream which flows around our southwest coast and produces in places like Glengariff and Killarney a semi-tropical vegetation and a relaxing atmosphere which is ideal for the cultivation of all sorts of leprechauns, mostly rather damp and smelling of Irish Coffee. But whatever else these savants said, both of them would have to agree on one essential: that the slow, pastoral pattern of life in Ireland has changed very little since centuries before Christ.

After all, the oldest and greatest of our epic sagas—*An Tain Bo Cuailnge*, "The Cattle Raid of Cooley"—centers on the rivalry between a king and a queen for the possession of the country's biggest and best bull. At the close of that turbulent saga the two outsize bulls fight one another from end to end of Ireland, horning up valleys, leveling great plains, bulldozing mountains, manufacturing the face of Ireland. It is symbolic. That wild pre-Christian epic grew naturally out of a bucolic life that had been sanctified by so many generations that one begins to wonder why the tutelary deity of the ancient Irish was not the bull god, adored as the symbol of fertility, the guarantee of a grass-fed life that need never languish. As, in fact, it might never have languished if our island had been sited by the Almighty a thousand miles farther west, safe from John Bull.

The Irish have always loved the pastures, the moors and the woods. They never built towns. The Danes, the Normans and the Tudors founded every town we have. Long after the days of the Pilgrim Fathers these alien towns were still small and scattered; pastures brightened and forests darkened large areas of the island; the vast boglands were impassable; the mountains were impenetrable. A small but intensely virile population lived in secluded, disconnected groups, raiding one another bloodily. Nobody cared to venture far at night. The unknown was at every man's elbow. It is the background of the great battles, scandalous loves and tremendous exploits of the Rolands, Beowulfs, Siegfrieds and Brunhildes of the Celtic epic.

In my youth I often saw farmers in the poorer parts of Ireland flail the wheat with the same sort of wooden flails we find pictured on Etruscan tombs. By the fireside that night they might tell stories as old as Homer. The next day they would winnow the chaff in the golden wind. The basic fact is that the Irish have never taken tillage seriously. You may see it for yourself from every road you travel—great stretches of green broken by a few brown fields. Even in Texas there are more men than cows. In Ireland there are more cows than men. This has always been the Emerald Isle.

In a word, we are an antique people, our racial character formed and fixed by long-lasting life-modes. By the time we were finally conquered, late in the 17th Century, we were too old to change, old and obstinate, and we have paid for it and been rewarded for it. The history is there for all to read. We have, in the name of nationalism and religion, tradition and conservatism, been saying "No!" to the world for nine tenths of our life story, magnificently or foolishly, stubbornly or mulishly, heroically or suicidally, according to the way you look at it. And to this day we go on saying a great many "No's!"

Not that our Nay-men have it all their own way. Ever since the founding of the Irish Free State a war has been brewing between the Future and the Past. For example, the young farmers of Ireland have now banded into the *Macra na Feirme*, "the Sons of the Soil," whose sole aim is to increase agricultural production by scientific methods—words that ring as crazily in the ears of most of their elders as if, fifty years ago, it had been prophesied that one day the land would be ploughed by

A farmer accompanied by his dog drives his cart through the rolling countryside of County Cork.

The Rock of Cashel with its Round Tower and castle stands at a confluence of roads in South Tipperary.

motor power. These young Irishmen have not a trace of sentimentality in them, and, indeed, some of their achievements show this uncomfortably. Look at the tidy, concrete-built houses of the Eastern counties. They are as far as can be from the thatched, lime-washed cottages of the crofters of Connemara or West Kerry which have matured slowly, generation after generation, acquiring in time a beauty and a dignity that have made them part of the tradition of "picturesque" Ireland.

But all this modernization is raising new problems. It is reducing the labor needed on the farm. And the young folk get increasingly restless. Time was when on any Irish farm you could see the girls making butter, or baking bread on the hearth, maybe even spinning thread, or the sons making baskets. Today you have to search for these crafts. The factory product has replaced them all.

Here I propose to reveal to the world, for the first time, the secret of the Irish nature. Every Irishman is a four-decker. He lives, that is to say, on four levels of awareness. The first is his practical level. This is the realistic Irishman, keen as a needle, tough as nails, his eye on the main chance. He succeeds in whatever he sets his mind to. He is the sort of Irishman who, as the efficient colonial or military servant of the British Empire, used to win every nation's battles but his own.

Underneath this top-floor level lies the level of the historical memory, about which America, certainly, must know all it can possibly need to know. Poor Ould Ireland. The Famine. Saint Patrick's Day. The Boston Irish and Bunker Hill. This memory is generally about as inactive as Stromboli. It starts to rumble in us after about the third whisky.

Much deeper lies the third deck: a religious emotion as unconscious and as inescapable as childhood memories. The happiest visual marks of this inheritance are those old Romanesque oratories whose carved portals you will see everywhere, scattered throughout the country in remote, hermit places. You see a pleasant modern sign of it in the many grottoes to the Virgin by our roadsides. You will see a simple sign of it in a tiny altar to the Virgin, tended by the taxi drivers, in the center of O'Connell Street in Dublin.

And then, deepest of all, comes the old, old pagan folk mind, so deeply buried that when Irishmen act in response to its impulses they do not themselves recognize what impels them. It is this deep, dark folk mind that makes us a people of great stoicism, boundless fortitude, much indifference and small ambition, always eager for a laugh, cheerfully resigned, easily living along the waves of life, kindly, endless talkers, always inclined to exaggerate as if life were one long comedy or tragedy being endlessly recomposed, and loathing—this my conscience as an honest reporter obliges me to say and to italicize —simply *loathing* anything appertaining to the cold brain. I have sometimes thought that these are the qualities, or foibles, of old age the world over and that they come from and suggest our great age as a race. But when I reflect that the same folk mind accounts for our inclination to break out into sudden bouts of passion, crazy laughter, brief recklessness, the total combination as often strikes me as being characteristic not of age but of extreme youth, even of a sort of prolonged childishness. Perhaps we are a race perpetually old and perpetually young, caught up in conflict between aged wisdom and childish sensibility.

If, therefore (prospective guest), you should ever detect a certain shifty look in the eye of an Irishman of whom you have asked some general question, you may at once presume that his mental fingers are shifting and fumbling with the four press-buttons of his mental elevator. When his eye clears and he smiles at you with the frank and simple intensity of the utterly honest man, you may know that he has stabilized himself on his chosen deck. Temporarily! For by the time you have adjusted yourself to his chosen position you may suddenly discover that he is no longer before you—he has quietly gone up, or down, to another deck.

Is it because I happen to be an Irishman that I think that these are experiences that belong only to ancient lands like Ireland, or Greece, or India? Though many other countries are just as lovely as these, they have lost touch with the old traditional earth memories that can alone invest air and water and land with wonder and awe. God made the grass, the air and the rain; and the grass, the air and the rain made the Irish; and the Irish turned the grass, the air and the rain back into God. These people have always lived by the instinctive life of the soul and the passionate life of the body, and deep down in themselves they still do. Long may it be so! Nature is, in any case, not likely to be so utterly upheaved that it will ever be otherwise here. And if that upheaval ever, incredibly, did take place, there would be no need to say that we may as well draw a blue pencil through the map of Ireland. The Almighty would have already drawn a blue pencil through the map of the world.

The ruins of ancient St. Kevin's Church watch over the quiet graves in Glendalough.

France

THE REMARKABLE FRENCH

*The deeply civilized French still retain a
streak of the fervor which stormed the Bastille.
Aubrey Menen, long-time friend of France,
cuts through the glittering surface to reveal
the key to French logic.
Here is a wise and witty insight into the people who
love to be themselves, which is normal,
and love to let others be themselves—which is unique.*

A Frenchman of our own days, Saint-Exupéry, an aviator who became world-famous as a writer, once tried to sum up what the French people meant to him. He recalled that living among them was a sweet and gentle thing; he remembered the café waiter "who knows one half of Paris, and all of its secrets; who, when the first buds come on the trees will make a special trip to your table to assure you, 'This time it's really spring,' so that you, his old friend and client, can be as happy as he is. Yes," concluded Saint-Exupéry, "France is a happy land. Once over its frontiers, and alas, one has scarcely any more interest in spring. But one has, of course, a much deeper interest in such things as the destiny of the human race."

It is well put. The French people, like the rest of us, are dedicated to the pursuit of happiness: in addition, they have mastered the art of occasionally catching up with it. That is why it is the mark of a wise man to seek their company.

I would like you to meet some of them—those, that is, that I know. Not long ago, for example, I went to a party in Paris, at the home of my publisher. We were celebrating the publication of one of my books.

I went to a tall, gray house in a street filled with other tall, gray houses. The street was very quiet. I rang the bell. I heard it sound far away in the house. I waited in the silence. The door opened. I was greeted by a maid, my hat was taken and I was shown into a tall room lined with books and filled with men and women talking with great animation.

Now, should you go to a gathering like this anywhere else in the world, you will have to obey the odd rule that when a number of virtual strangers are gathered in one room, they must all search strenuously to find topics on which they agree. The only place, of course, where strangers can meet and be sure that there are topics on which they agree is a church. The Parisian, however, more sensibly sets out to find a topic on which everybody will disagree. By the time I arrived at this particular party, several such topics had already been found, and I and my book provided another.

I was introduced to various people by my hostess. I was not introduced with a cheerful mutter and left to guess the person's surname and his profession as though both were not to be mentioned openly in polite society. It was made quite clear to me that I was talking to M. Such-and-Such, who had written a book, or an article, or who was an expert or a diplomat or the man who put up the money for my publishers. I was instantly involved in conversation, and then, inevitably, in arguments. Each guest allowed me to feel important for three minutes and then had me fighting for dear life in order not to appear a fool and a clown. I began to enjoy myself.

Soon, it is true, there appeared a cloud no bigger than a man's hand to shadow my enjoyment. In spite of the general brilliance of the observations being made around me, it became clear to me that nobody had read my book. I mentioned this to my publisher. "No," he said, "they haven't, because it hasn't come from the printers yet. It won't be ready till tomorrow, if

Market Day: *At Chateau-Renault gossip and goods are traded weekly.*

Manpower: *A porter in the old Paris market, Les Halles.*

Bed and board: *Beaming owner and well-fed guest in a hotel at Gennes.*

then. But it doesn't matter. Even if they had, they wouldn't change their opinions. I've told everybody what's in it."

It appeared that he had, because the party had now divided into two factions, one which maintained that what he said I had said was excellent, while the other maintained that if I had said what he said I said, it was monstrous. A celebrated novelist came up to me in the middle of the storm, beamed and said, "Wonderful! You have created a scandal with your *first* French book. Now my first book, which sold thirty thousand——" The conversation of authors being largely arithmetical, I need not repeat it here. A little later I left the tall, gray house in the quiet street, feeling, as one should in France, deeply pleased with myself.

Should you wish to know more about these remarkable people, who have the secret of making you feel cleverer and more ignorant than you are, both at the same time, and with such enviable good manners, I would like you to meet Joël. He lives near Chartres, in a house in which I am sometimes invited to stay when I go to France. One evening, before dinner, I was lying on the vast, soft bed with its long, hard pillow which is the mark of a French bedroom, and dozing in the warmth of the central heating, which, in France—I do not know why— always seems to smell of cooking, when Joël knocked politely on the door and came in.

Joël is thirteen. He goes to school but I would hesitate to call him anything so frivolous as a schoolboy. He is handsome, studious and both charming and grave at once. He reminds me of those serious stucco cherubs that one sees in some French churches poring over plaster copies of the Gospels. He was dressed, as always, in one of those light fawn suits that French boys wear and which never seem to get dirty, with fawn shorts showing bare knees that never seem to have cuts on them. He wanted me to help him with some translation from a Latin text. Fortunately it was one which I had done at school. We made a rough translation, and he went away. An hour later I went down and on the way I returned his visit.

He was working in his room. His room was furnished with a bed, much frilled, with very white sheets, bookshelves, two or three pictures of landscapes and buildings, and a square, sensible table at which Joël worked under the light of a large, sensible lamp. There was none of the boyish paraphernalia one would find in other countries, because the whole room had been designed not by Joël but by his *maman*, to form his taste. Joël greeted me, and I looked over his shoulder to see his work. It was still our joint translation of Caesar, but disfigured by crossing out, by balloons with emendations and scribblings round the margins, themselves emended all in a careful hand. I blushed.

"Was my Latin as bad as that, Joël?"

"Why no," said Joël. "You made it all quite clear and correct, thank you."

"Then why are you altering it so much?"

"*That?*" he said, pointing to his crossings out. "Oh, that's different. I'm working on the *style*."

"Of course," I humbly agreed, and silently left him.

When I was at my English school, we, masters and boys alike, prided ourselves on the barbarity of our construing. We got the sense right, and then we went out to play football—to dirty our clothes and cut our knees, and not even the cleverest boys among us would bother about the *mot juste*. But Joël's work would be judged by the elegance of his prose, so he would sit another hour at the table, polishing the language he had inherited from Descartes, Pascal and Voltaire.

For a young Frenchman, that is a very proper thing to do. It is the glory of France that again and again in the history of civilization, while other races have been dimly feeling things in their bones (like the English) or in their bowels (like the Germans), the French have felt the same things and *said* them in crystalline phrases. They speak a language most marvelously adapted for describing and naming and defining. It is probably the one language which can give a man the certainty that, when he has said something in it, he has said what he means.

It is for that reason that the Frenchman delights to talk, but detests garrulity. He finds no need to say things over and over again in different ways to make his meaning clear. He learns, at school, or alone in his room like Joël, or in society, to say what he means at one blow and to say it with the utmost economy of words. The foreigner in France who fails to savor the exquisite art of the French language, fails to understand the Frenchman. "I have been brief," wrote Pascal, at the end of a dissertation. "I would have been briefer, but I did not have the time"; and Voltaire, perhaps an even greater master of the language, searching for a sentence to end a story of an Indian fakir who found the world took no notice of him when he gave up his bed of nails, finally hit upon eight perfect words: "*Il réprit ses clous pour avoir de la considération.*" ("He resumed his nails to [re]gain some respect.")

The words should be said aloud, because the ultimate beauties of style can be discovered only when French is spoken. If the Frenchman's pleasure in the written word is vast, his pleasure in the sound of his language when it is spoken with fire and artifice is unlimited, and I know of no better illustration of this enthusiasm than one which a friend provided me. He is a marquis, and when he was young he had money and position. He had gone one evening to the Comédie Française and there he had heard a young woman acting in a play by Molière. She was pretty, but it was the way she spoke her lines that ravished him. He went to see her performance again and again, and when the season came to an end he knew he could not live without hearing her beautiful elocution. So he married her.

After that he had many misfortunes, and when I met him he was an exile from France and earning his living, with his wife, in New Delhi. We met frequently. In the summer, when the wind blew from the desert, and there were locusts, and the temperature stood at 100° all day and all night, when, in a word, we were all ready to weep for sheer misery, M. le Marquis would say to his wife, "My dear, give us the speech from such-and-such a play." She would oblige, ringingly. She did not mind where she was—in a restaurant, a hotel bedroom at midnight, or the middle of the street. In minutes the sound of her voice would restore her husband's spirits as no alcohol could ever do. M. le Marquis loved her very dearly. He might—he would freely admit—have made a different marriage: he could have married an heiress, or a beauty, or a woman of intelli-

Hands across the counter: *A lady greengrocer of Perthus.*

The good life: *A farmer, a friend, and a joke at Chateau-Renault.*

Film festival: *Lovely ladies on both sides of the cordon.*

47

gence. Madame le Marquise was none of these, and he knew it. But never for a moment had he regretted his bargain. He called her, fondly, his audible bit of France.

The books in Joël's room do not deal only with literature He must study history, the mathematical sciences, the appreciation of art, geography, philosophy and a handful of other subjects that, in another country, would be thought more suitable for a student reading for a university degree than for a schoolboy. The French educational standard is the highest in the world, and there are those in France who maintain it is too high even for the French. This may or may not be so: the foreigner in France is wise to avoid the subject. Once I heard an American friend of mine criticize the French educational system in the presence of an official of the Ministry. The American—with some justice, I thought—said that the French system took no account of the great progress in educational theory that had taken place in the rest of the world.

"We believe," he said, "that children should not only study; they should be *happy*. School days can be, and should be, the happiest years of their lives."

The official was small and neat, with a small, neat rosette in his buttonhole to show that he was a member of the Legion of Honor, and he was a man of few words.

"In America, then, you teach children to be happy?"

"Yes."

"*Can* you?"

"Well—we try to, m'sieu."

"I see." The official paused, looked down at his neat shoes, and then looked up to ask: "And who teaches this happiness?"

"The teachers."

"Ah. Just so. And these schoolteachers are handsomely paid?"

"Certainly not."

"They are honored by the government and flattered by society and——"

"By no means, m'sieu."

"Then I take it they are not particularly happy people themselves? No? Well, then, we have a most interesting situation. Teachers who are underpaid and neglected, and unhappy, must teach little children how to enjoy life. I think that must be a very difficult objective. Here, in France, we have a simpler aim. Our teachers are supposed to teach their pupils how to be educated Frenchmen. Nothing more."

And, one might add, nothing less.

It is easy to see then why the guests at my publisher's party spoke so well, ranged so widely in their conversation, and were so quick-witted. They had not only been educated; they had survived their education—not all Frenchmen do—and they were among the French system's most brilliant products.

But we are still left with the question of their manners. We noted that they carried their brilliance with ease and courtesy. Where did they learn these accomplishments? At school? No: their curriculum scarcely left them time. Where then? I shall try to answer that question, and to do that we must go in to dinner with Joël—who has come down from his room—and with his mother and father.

The dining room is small—as dining rooms should be—and the table is long. Since we are foreigners we shall, at first, be a little confused by the seating arrangements. Joël's father, whom we shall call Monsieur D., does not sit at one end and Madame D. at the other. He sits in the middle of the long side, with his wife opposite him. It is Joël who sits at the end of the table, and since there are other guests, it falls out that he sits between two women, one a girl of twenty years and the other a matron. They are friends of Monsieur and Madame D., but not particularly close friends. Yet Joël is perfectly at his ease with them. He does not clown; he is not winsome; he does not talk too loudly and he does not fall into long silences. He is, I think, greatly to be envied, for this ease of manner with women will remain with him throughout his life.

I was brought up as an Englishman. Joël's ease will never be mine, so long as I live, because an Englishman is painfully trained, from his youth, to remain in a state of mental confusion about the other sex. For an Englishman a woman is always, to some extent, what a sister is to an English schoolboy. He likes her privately, but she embarrasses him in public.

Women no longer embarrass the average American, but in his rapid ascent to unheard-of prosperity, he finds, unless I am mistaken, that his womenfolk present much the same difficulty as his foreign relations: neither good will nor money ever seems really to fix them.

Now Joël has been taught that a knowledge of women is one of the marks of a gentleman. A Frenchman approaches women with immense confidence, simply because he is French, and he is therefore sure that he knows, historically, more about them than any other race on earth. This is not one of the national illusions of the French. It is the plain truth.

I would like now to tell you about Father X. I have known him since I was a youth, when I was spending my time and such money as I had on the Left Bank, trying to civilize myself.

He did not have the manner of a priest—if there is such a thing—nor even of the Order of which he was a member. He came from the Midi, the sun-drenched and lovely tract of France that lies back from the Mediterranean. He had the dark complexion and short stature of the men from those parts, and that towering sense of their personal honor and dignity that Daudet has portrayed so excellently; you could contradict him, but you could not treat him lightly.

He took me, one Christmas midnight, to Notre Dame and he showed me how, from a certain place in the ambulatory, you could stand within a few feet of the Cardinal-Archbishop's throne and watch him being publicly vested with the tremendous symbols of his office. Father X's eyes shone as he spoke; his pride in his Church was very plain. When the vast, glittering and hieratic dance that is Solemn High Mass was over—"dance" was his own word: "David," he said, "danced before the Ark of the Lord,"—and we were outside in the square by the statue of St. Joan, I said something to the effect that it was strange to hear a Frenchman talk as he had done. To me, France was Revolutionary France; it was anticlericalism and so forth. I repeat that I was young. It was only many years later that I learned most of France is fervently and unshakably Catholic.

He looked up, I remember, at the dark façade of the cathedral, where stood the statues that the revolutionaries had mutilated, and said: "Yes, I know what you mean. The Revolutionary Convention, you know, once brought an actress here and enthroned her on the high altar as the Goddess of Reason."

I said I thought that was excessive, but he shook his head.

"It was an insult to the Church, of course, but I don't think it was a blasphemy. Ours," he said, unexpectedly, "is the religion of reason."

I did not understand him at the time, not until I understood how these two things, Reason and Faith, have sometimes fought and sometimes combined in the thought of France.

The guiding principle of the French is that no man can be really trusted with the power to govern his fellow men. Most of us who are not French nourish in our hearts the belief that there do exist men who, given the chance to be our rulers, will be kindly, benevolent and just, even if it costs them effort and discomfort, rather like good King Wenceslaus. The French, however, do not have this mystical belief. They have observed that when a benevolent ruler looks out nowadays, unlike King Wenceslaus, he is usually looking out for himself.

To overcome this difficulty, the French middle classes have based themselves on a political idea called the General Will. This was a notion of Jean-Jacques Rousseau, a Swiss-born Frenchman and a most remarkable man, who wrote an essay, instantly famous, that said that the only natural and just government of mankind was one in which everybody expressed his opinion fully and thus revealed, in a way which Rousseau never made clear, the general will of the community—something which summed up all the individual opinions and in which everybody happily agreed, because he felt it was just what he had been saying himself all along.

The Frenchman thus forms his own opinion and then looks for some way in which it can be expressed in the councils of the nation—his opinion, with no compromise. Ideally, every Frenchman of voting age ought to elect himself to the Chamber of Deputies. Since this cannot be done (and that is the mistake in Rousseau's theories) the Frenchman tries to devise a constitution whereby the deputies he elects are so divided among themselves that lasting combinations are next to impossible. That is why he greatly prefers to elect a great number of small parties rather than two or three massive parties. Massive parties can never, in his view, reflect the General Will. They will have a will of their own. That, say the French, is not democracy at all.

They agree—they are not the fools that Anglo-Saxon commentators like to pretend—that their own system does not lead to a stable or a strong government. But France is governed, and not much worse than any other country. A foreigner, reading foreign comments on the French, might well expect France to be a country where one has to live in a state of constant alarm and uncertainty. When he goes to France, he will be surprised to find that the trains run on time, people sit down to three meals a day, hotels and restaurants cater for his needs as smoothly as anywhere else, and that he pays his bill not in eggs, chickens and gold watches but in French currency, which can be kept conveniently in a wallet and does not have to be carried around in suitcases. In spite of the fact that nobody knows who will be premier next week, he will find that fathers plan their sons' education for the next ten years and businessmen invest capital in long-term projects.

How does this come about? The answer is deep in the French character. All Frenchmen like to feel that they have a little something tucked away in a stocking under the mattress, which they do not talk about, but which they feel sure will see them through a crisis. The French have got something as reassuring as gold tucked in their political stocking and that is their civil service.

This civil service is hardly affected by the political changes and disasters of the Assembly. It obeys the orders of the government whenever there is a government and whenever the government can think of any orders to give. It will also supply ready-made orders for busy ministers to sign, and it will respectfully carry them out. Many a French statesman has discovered to his astonishment and delight that he has been governing France without knowing it.

But a strong civil service has its dangers. A civil servant likes things to be orderly. He does not like change. He deals with human beings, but he prefers them to be named, labeled, numbered, each in his own compartment and guaranteed to stay there. It is a good way to run a mortician's parlor, but intelligent Frenchmen are beginning to doubt if it is a good way to run a country in a boisterously changing world.

The French, say the French, are becoming an immobile nation. They, who changed Europe, cannot change themselves. For the first time in their history, they feel that it is no longer enough to point out that most of the things that distinguish Westerners from barbarians were taught them by the French. It is not enough to say that they showed the world that there could be joy in living. Such things once brought them the respect of all the world that counted. It does so no longer.

A long time ago, when the world that counted was a European world, it was said that France was every man's second country. I have tried to show why this was true. But France is not the second country of the Chinese, the Japanese, the Indians, the African Negro, the Arab—it is not the second country, that is, of the once-forgotten majority of the human race. They have had other teachers. We can only hope that they will turn out to be as good.

But, here we are, talking of the destiny of the human race, and that, as Saint-Exupéry warned us, is a sign that we are leaving France. Before we cross the frontier, let us recall Joël at his desk, the Marquis in exile listening to his wife, Father X and his lucid question. Is there any one thing about them that they would agree marks them as French? I doubt it. I doubt if they would agree upon any subject under the sun.

All Gaul, said Caesar, was divided into three parts. That was a long time ago. Now it is divided into some forty-three million, each of them a member of the French people, each of them insisting on his right to be himself, but insisting with grace, wit, intelligence and no rancor at all. Shall we, I wonder, find out one day that this is what being civilized really means?

PARIS! PARIS!

In Paris, city of dreamers and lovers,
novelist Irwin Shaw lets fancy take him on a
glorious ramble through the City of Light.
He wanders along the Seine, he climbs the
Eiffel Tower, he sips pernod at a side street cafe—
and to accompany him on this idyll,
he evokes a beautiful, laughing girl...

You start at a café table because everything in Paris starts at a café table. You are waiting for the girl you love.

She is young and American and perfect. She has straight legs and an enormous appetite and solid low-heeled shoes and she likes to walk and she has just arrived in the city for the first time in her life and she likes to listen to you talk and she is imaginary. She is late, of course, because you have been so conditioned by the women you have known that even the ones you invent can't meet you on time. You have invented her because you have been daydreaming; you have been playing

with the idea of pleasure and it has occurred to you that there could be few things more pleasurable in this sad world than to roam Paris for a day hand-in-hand with such a girl.

You sit there, glowing with the prospect of unfolding Paris for the first time to this superb, unreal and uninitiated creature.

It is summer or autumn or winter or spring and it is sunny and raining and there is snow on the statues and bits of ice in the Seine and the trees are all in full blossom and the swimmers are diving into the purified water in the wooden pools along the riverbanks and it is early in the morning and late at night and the President is giving a ball and the Garde Républicaine is out in breastplates and horsehair tails and the North Africans are rioting for autonomy at the Place de la République and all the policemen have dents in their shining steel helmets.

Mass is being celebrated at St.-Sulpice and they are burying an actor in Père Lachaise. There are long lines outside the mail windows at the American Express. Young lieutenants are leaving for stations abroad. There is a fair on the Esplanade des Invalides and the phrenologists are doing well next to the shooting galleries. They are selling perfume on the Rue de la Paix and the wine merchants are worried about this year's Burgundy and a thousand deep baskets of water cress are being stacked at Les Halles. The buses are coming in from the Orly airfield to the Gare des Invalides with the passengers from New York and South Africa and Warsaw, and the trains going south have whole cars filled with bicycles for the vacationers en route to the Côte d'Azur. It is August and half the shops are closed, with their iron shutters down, and it is February and the porters wait with wheel chairs at the Gare de l'Est for the skiers with broken legs.

It is Sunday and the couples are sprawled all over the Bois and the lions are roaring for the crowds across the deep moats in the Vincennes zoo. It is the fourteenth of July, and there are parades and the placing of wreaths in the memory of the dead and the memory of the Bastille and the memory of the unfortunate Foullon, whose head was carried on a pike up the Rue St.-Martin in 1789, his mouth stuffed with grass because he had said of the people of Paris, *"Eh bien.* If this riffraff has no bread, they'll eat hay." There is also the sound of jets flying in formation over the city, and there is dancing in the streets and in the gardens of the great houses, and there are fireworks in the sky behind the cathedral, and marshals of France standing at attention while the bands play the anthem, whose words include, "To arms, citizens!"

It is a workday and the open platforms of the buses are crowded with people who breathe deeply of the gasoline fumes on their way to their offices. It is market day and the housewives push through the stalls under the trees at the Place de l'Alma, next to the Salon Nautique, looking at the prices of the chickens and the cheeses and the celery root and complaining that life is too expensive.

There is the smell of freshly baked bread in the air and the streets are full of people hurrying home with long, unwrapped loaves under their arms. In the crowded *charcuteries* there are a dozen different kinds of *pâté* on the counters and Alsatian *choucroute* and *gnocchi* and snails and *coquilles* St. Jacques, ready to be put into the oven, and the salesgirls sound like a

Montmartre: *Apéritifs in the Place du Tertre.*

Sunny day: *Luncheon rendezvous in the gardens at the Ritz.*

cageful of flutes as they call out the prices to the customers. In the Métro, there is an experimental train that runs on rubber tires, to alleviate the nervous agony of being alive in the 20th Century. In the Berlitz classrooms the activities of the family Dupont are carefully followed as they say good morning to each other, open and close doors and lay various objects on a table. On the Ile St.-Louis, the owner of a convertible finds its top slashed for the seventh time and decides he will have to buy a closed car.

In the lobbies of the big hotels, sharp-eyed men are whispering to each other, making deals to import and export vital materials, and an American at the bar of the George Cinq says to his business associates, "I don't like to boast, but I am very close to the Virginia tobacco industry."

The all-girl orchestras are tuning up for their afternoon programs of waltzes in the big, bare cafés on the Boulevard Clichy, and in the *bals musettes* shopgirls dance with clerks under the paintings of thugs and apaches. There are thousands of people lined up at the Porte Saint-Cloud to watch a bicycle race and everybody is going to Deauville for the week end.

The fountains are playing at the Rond-Point, casting a fine spray over the flower borders and Notre-Dame is illuminated and looks as light as a dream on its stone island and the streets are empty and the traffic heavy and you sit there planning this limitless, all-seasoned, perfect day with your perfect girl in the city which is the Jerusalem of many strange pilgrimages and the capital of nostalgia and which you can never leave without tasting a faint, bitter flavor of exile.

You sip soberly at your drink and peer out among the passers-by for the bright American head which is bound to look a little artless and unpremeditated among the clever, artificially streaked, short hair of the Parisian women on the boulevard. The girl you love has not yet arrived, and you half-close your eyes and plan the first step.

First, there should be a general, bird's-eye view of the city, and the best place for that is the top of the Eiffel Tower. From there, the city lies embraced by its winding river and flows in a silvery haze over its moderate hills and its central plain. You can look out over the homes and the shops and the cemeteries and places of worship of three million people and you can see the hill in Montmartre where the Temple of Mercury used to stand and where St. Denis was beheaded. You can trace the course of the river and see where the canals join it and the Marne, and you can tell the girl about the Norsemen who sailed up the river in their oared galleys in the 9th Century, jovially axing the farmers and the city dwellers along the banks, as was the custom of travelers in that time.

There is one drawback about the Tower, though: the elevator makes you nervous. You know that you are unreasonable. You know that since it opened for business in 1889, it has carried millions of people safely up to the top. But you suffer a little from vertigo, and every time you get into the creaking, slightly tilted car you regret, with unreasonable chauvinism, being that high in the air and dependent for your life on French machinery. You would depend unhesitatingly upon French courage to get you out of danger, on French medicine to cure a stomach ache, upon French wit to make you laugh or a French wife to make you happy—but all that cable, all those girders, all those grinding gears....You decide to settle for a more moderate eminence; the top of the Arch of Triumph is quite high enough for a young girl's first view of Paris and its elevator is comfortably enclosed in a stone shaft.

Anyway, you will tell her, Paris is not a city of heights. Its architects, out of a respect for man, have made certain that man is not dwarfed by his works here. It is a city built to human scale, so that no man should feel pygmied here. Parisians are devoted to their sky and have passed a set of complicated laws designed to keep the height of buildings at a modest level, so that the sky—soft, streaked, gentle, beloved by painters—can be a constant, intimate presence above the roofs and the treetops. In defense of their sky, Parisians can be outlandishly fierce. Recently, a builder in Neuilly put up an apartment house taller than the legal limit and was ordered by the court to tear down the top two stories, although they had been leased in advance and there is a crucial housing shortage. In addition the builder was forced to pay a whopping fine for every day that the offending twenty feet of construction loomed above the skyline. And then, as an aesthetic afterthought, the judge sentenced him to jail. Oh, you think, remembering the caged and distant sky above your native city, if only there were more builders in Sing Sing.

From the top of the monument, staring out at the city, your girl doesn't say anything because she is perfect. The great avenues, which Baron Haussmann, Napoleon III's prefect of police, created to get the mob of Paris out into the open where he could use cavalry on them when they wanted a raise in salary or wished to murder a minister, sweep out to all points of the compass.

The boulevards are named after victories and soldiers, and on the Arch itself are the names of one hundred and seventy-two battles chiseled into the stone. Many of the streets of Paris are labeled for battlefields on which Frenchmen have conquered and you wonder what it must do to the spirit of the citizens of a city to have the sound of triumph on their lips every time they give an address to a taxi driver, and if they would be different today if, along with the Avenue de Wagram and the Avenue de Friedland, there were a Boulevard Sedan, a Rue Waterloo and a Place of the Surrender.

There are so many trees that when they are in foliage and seen from above, much of the city seems to be built in a giant park. Close by, the city leans against the green escarpments of Saint-Cloud and Saint-Germain, across the bending river, reminding you that Paris is more intimate with and more accessible to the countryside than any other great city in the world. The slate, jumbled world of the rooftops is pewter and lavender, Paris' own colors, and there is the gleam of innumerable studio windows, facing to the north. The pinkish Carrousel past the other end of the Champs-Elysées is like a distant and frivolous reflection of the Arch, on whose peak you are standing, and the wind up here carries a frail leaf-and-mold smell of the river with it. The white dome of Sacré-Coeur speaks of 19th Century religion on the heights of Montmartre and you can see the gray, medieval stone tower of Saint-Germain-des-Prés rising on the opposite bank from its nest of cafés.

Standing there, with the whole city spread around you, its palaces and spires and statues glistening in the damp sunlight, you reflect aloud to the girl on how wise Parisians are to have had ancestors who were ruled over by tyrants, because tyrants are egotists with an itch to build monuments to themselves. Then after a while you get rid of the tyrants and are left with the Louvre and the Tuileries and the obelisk and the Place Vendôme and the brave, sculptured horses and the great boulevards that were built because someone was ruthless enough and powerful enough to tear down acre after acre of people's homes and pave what used to be somebody's kitchen and plant chestnut trees in somebody else's bedroom. You reflect on the selfishness of being alive in your own time. You are delighted with what Louis XIV did to the city with the taxes he squeezed from the poor, and with what Napoleon built on the blood of a generation of young Frenchmen, though you would struggle to the death against a new Louis or a later Napoleon, no matter how many arches and palaces he guaranteed for your descendants to enjoy on their visit from America a hundred years from now.

At lunch you can remember that Victor Hugo said, "Paris is the ceiling of the human race," after which he was forced to flee to the islands of Jersey and Guernsey where he remained for the eighteen years of Napoleon III's reign. When he returned they began naming streets and squares after him and they have scarcely stopped since. Parisians seem to have a habit of exiling their heroes, or guillotining them, and making up for it later with street markers. Voltaire spent a good deal of

Place de L'Étoile *The whole city spreads around you.*

his life in Germany and Switzerland and when in due course they came to bury him in the Panthéon they discovered that his heart was missing and the rumor is that it was mislaid in a desk drawer which was sold by a junkman. Danton paid with his head for his activities in the city, but the city replaced it for the bronze statue of him on the Place de l'Odéon. Poor Courbet, too, who painted women's breasts so well, took down the statue of Napoleon from its pedestal on the Vendôme Column during the Commune, on the grounds that it was a warlike and inartistic creation. Then, when the tide of government changed, he was put in jail and had to turn into a painter of fruits and vegetables because they wouldn't allow his models into the jail. And, much later, the government demanded that he pay the costs of restoring the monument, which came to 323,000 francs. His paintings were seized as partial payment and with the balance staring him in the face, he fled to Switzerland, where he died, and now, of course, there is a Passage Courbet in Passy.

Replete with lunch and praising the wine, and happy that you will be hungry again in six hours, you and your girl leave the restaurant and find the Rue de Seine, where the little art galleries, the antique shops and the butcher shops stand side by side. There are larks in boxes on the butchers' marble tables, and partridge and wild doves flutter dead and head down, their wings outspread, in long strings across the open fronts of the stores, and the butchers in their sweaters and aprons look ruddy and frozen and keep blowing on their hands all winter. You buy a snuffbox and price some silver and haggle over a candlestick and notice the influence of Picasso on everybody and go into a tiny gallery which is having a *vernissage* of the works of a young painter who makes a specialty of lonely, moonlit cold walls around abandoned, dreamlike ports. The little room is crowded with people who are not looking at the pictures. There is a great deal of conversation and the young painter is standing alone in a corner, looking lonely and moonlit and abandoned.

Now you have to go to a cocktail party. It is a kind of house-warming, being given by a friend who waited for fifteen years to get this apartment. His old apartment, which was one floor above, had only three rooms, and this one has four. He really needs five rooms. On the floor below there is a five-room apartment. He inquires politely about the health of the tenant and looks forward patiently to the next fifteen years.

At the cocktail party there is gin, expensively imported from England, which shows that the host is serious about this collection of guests. People are standing in groups, smoking French cigarettes, which make your mouth smell like a small industrial town after you have gone through half a pack. Three or four of the guests have rosettes of the Legion of Honor and a plump, intelligent-looking lawyer is defending the ancient practice of dueling.

"There are arguments," he says, "which cannot be taken to law and which can only be settled by the duel. Otherwise they go on and on forever, with people cutting each other at dinners and in offices and making everybody uncomfortable and bored. A duel has the quality of a period at the end of a paragraph and civilized life has need of such periods."

In a corner, a group of Frenchmen are talking: "Americans," one of them says, "Americans may think they come to Paris for a number of reasons: To be artists, to be restless, to be young, to be free…but, essentially, they are all here in the same capacity. As archaeologists. To study antiquity. Nobody comes to the Paris of today, because Paris is a city of the past. Everybody visits a Paris which no longer exists except in ruins and memory."

"Paris is the only real city," adds another. "New York is four villages, London an industry, Rio de Janeiro a place where you have the feeling you must behave as though you are a schoolboy in a religious institution. Everything is possible in Paris, everything can be said, everybody can be met, often on the same day. It is the one city in the world which is not provincial."

And a sixty-year-old painter, looking back on his career and all the invitations he had accepted, says, "In Paris, fame is a telephone call."

"Let me explain about our government," a little round man with enormous glasses is saying to an American lady. "It is always falling and it is always Radical Socialist."

"There is only one country in the world," a journalist is saying, "which is rich enough to permit capitalism to work—and that is America. In France, capitalism cannot work." He pauses for a moment, reflecting on what he has said, then smiles happily. "In fact," he adds, "in France socialism cannot work. In fact, in France, nothing can work."

You leave because you want to go to the theater and there is just time for dinner before the curtain.

You go to the restaurant opposite the Odéon, where you can sit on the glassed-in terrace and look across the little square to the Greek-styled theater, now taken over by the Comédie-

Française, and whose columns are illuminated each night by marvelously theatrical blue floodlights. Just after the Liberation you could meet Jean Cocteau at that restaurant, and Christian Bérard, bearded and carrying a tawny, long-furred cat. You could also get a fluffy chocolate mousse there, made in American Army chocolate whose availability was no doubt connected with the nightly presence of the smiling, well-fed American soldier at the bar who must have been a mess sergeant.

Now it is crowded and fashionable and there is a rich smell of bouillabaisse in the air and you can eat your favorite oysters there, the enormous, deep-sea tasting *fines de claires*, which are scorned by the epicures, who favor the subtler Belons and Marennes, and who call the *claire*, or Portugaise, the working-man's oyster. The *sommelier*, who has an almost incomprehensible Midi accent, carries a corkscrew with an obscene device on it, but the wines are good and it is pleasant to sit there looking across at the floodlit columns and watching the polite people arriving for *Cyrano*.

You can see *Antigone* tonight or a dozen plays whose central theme is that of the cuckolded husband, including one in which the cuckolded husband is the magistrate who condemns to death for murder the man who was cozily tucked away in a hotel with the magistrate's wife on the afternoon on which the crime was committed. This last play, not unnaturally, drew some pained letters from the company of magistrates, who are overworked and underpaid and who feel sorry enough for themselves as it is.

You can even see a play which was put on at a little art theater and became a great success largely because it was a comedy which was not about cuckolded husbands.

You can see Molière or Racine or Bernstein or Sartre or Anouilh, a kind of one-man trust who pours out a seemingly inexhaustible stream of bitter, witty, elegant, slightly constructed popular plays, which follow so quickly on the heels of one another that there is a jealous legend about him that he writes all day every day and whenever he reaches twenty thousand words, sends them down to the nearest theater to be produced immediately.

The Parisian attitude toward food is one of loving care.

It is midnight by the time you get out of the theater. In St.-Germain, the ugliest bars in the world are jammed with the young unwashed of half a dozen countries and a lanky, recent graduate of Yale is announcing to the crowded sidewalk tables that his girl is deceiving him inside with the second son of an Indian prince. Nobody sympathizes with him and he laughs, showing the good old Yale spirit, and sits down and has a glass of beer.

On the Champs-Elysées the girls are prowling like jaguars, twitching their fur neckpieces under the cold, controlled stares of the police. The movies are letting out and everybody has been to see *Un Américain à Paris* and the couples are kissing frankly in the side streets. A young man, slightly drunk, comes up to an American group and bows and says, "You are Americans. Naturally, you are not communists. You do not have to work at the lathe. I, however, have to work at the lathe, so you must forgive me if I would do everything in my power to force you to the lathe." He says, "Thank you," and wanders politically and incoherently off in the direction of Passy.

In the night clubs, sad girls are singing that they hate Sunday, and there is a dancing horse and young men who sing that the Seine flows and flows and flows and sings and sings and sings and is a mistress in whose bed Paris sleeps. Off the Place Pigalle dark figures whisper out of the shadows, asking if you want to see a show, and in the big cafés, devoted to the almost-nude female body, parade all shapes of girls, bare from the waist up, but conforming to police regulations below that. After their turn, the girls line up, demure in ball gowns, on the staircase, and you can dance with them, if you will, by buying a ticket. Like most French women, they dance so tightly clasped to you that you feel like an infant strangling in his crib under blankets that have been tucked in too well.

Needing air, you and your girl walk to the river and step onto a tiny, crowded floating bar which is attached to a launch, and with a glass in your hand, and feeling, No, this is too romantic, chug off down the black river toward the cathedral. The city is quiet on both sides of you, the river wind is cool, the trees on the banks are fitfully illuminated by the headlights of occasional automobiles crossing the bridges. The bums are sleeping on the quais, waiting to be photographed at dawn by the people who keep turning out the glossy picture books on Paris; a train passes somewhere nearby, blowing its whistle, which sounds like a maiden lady who has been pinched, surprisingly, by a deacon; the buildings of the politicians and the diplomats are dark; the monuments doze; the starlit centuries surround you on the dark water. . . .

You turn, hesitantly, toward the girl at your side. . . .

You blink. It is daylight and you are still at the same café table. Your girl has never arrived, of course. At the table next to you a woman is saying, "I have a friend on *Figaro*. He says the war will start in September. What do you think will happen in Paris?"

"Paris," says the man who is sitting with her, "Paris will be spared."

"Why?"

"Because Paris is always spared," the man says, and orders a coffee.

The variety of France:
*ancient or modern,
simple or elegant.*

Apollo Fountains at Versailles.

THE CHARMED COUNTRY

*This motor tour reveals concretely what everything
else implies: that France is variety.
Outside the special focus of Paris
the countryside unrolls in a
mingled procession of
centuries, landscapes, architecture — a piling up
of civilizations from prehistoric caves through
cathedrals to the Riviera pleasure domes of today.
David Dodge culls many of the rarest sights during
a family trip through the charmed countryside of France.*

Paris, according to the poets, is a woman's town. The poets
aren't just versifying, either. Last July I spent several days in
the City of Light acting as chauffeur, delivery boy and disburs-
ing agent for three women. They were my wife, Elva; a sixteen-
year-old named Kendal, our daughter; her seventeen-year-old
cute but spendthrift friend, Charlotte. They were putting together a summer travel wardrobe, and they had unanimously
elected me payer of the bills for the party. I offer this apparently
irrelevant introduction to the account of our motor tour of
France only to explain why and how it is possible for a confessed Francophile to depart willingly from a city as lovely as
Paris, eager for the open road.

Mountain hamlet, St.-Cirq-Lapopie.

We had gone there to pick up a car, a Hillman Minx I had
bought on a repurchase arrangement made in New York. Because I had had experience with French red tape, I took a grain
of salt along with the New York man's promise that the car
would be ready at Paris when we arrived. I figured that an old
débrouillard like myself ought to be able to cut through the
formalities in a week, and allowed that much time for the
operation. The car really was ready when I asked for it, complete with plates, documents, insurance, luggage rack and the
rest. Thereafter the problem was to get the show on the road
before the time and funds we had set aside for the trip were
dissipated in the shops of the Rue du Faubourg St. Honoré.

Le Puy in the Haute-Loire region.

The schedule allowed us six long, lovely, unhurried summer
weeks for the tour, the budget enough money to enjoy ourselves without undue extravagances. Our itinerary was selec-
tive. Elva and I had explored the back roads of France several
times before, but while Kendal had been with us on a couple
of the trips, her age had been such that a re-enactment of the
Napoleonic Wars by the original cast wouldn't have pulled her
nose out of the comic books she traveled with. (*Small* children
are about as much fun as so many leg irons on a European tour,
take it from an authority.) As a result, she knew almost nothing
about France from personal observation, and Charlotte had
never been there before. My wife and I had a couple of fresh,
unspoiled and—we hoped—receptive young minds on which
to impress our ideas of the most attractive aspects of an attractive country.

Chapel by Le Corbusier at Ronchamp.

We began with Chartres, as a kind of test of adolescent re-
actions. The town, roughly sixty miles southwest of Paris, was

*Bike races, like the
Tour de l'Ouest, are
a French passion.*

Sunday afternoon: *the village square at Beaune.*

a little off our course, which I had plotted toward the northwest for a beginning, but there is only one Chartres cathedral. We went that way early one morning in July.

France has scores of cathedrals, literally, and each one has some distinctive feature not common to the others. The individuality of Notre Dame de Chartres lies, in part, in its location. This section of France is flat farming country, a huge wheat field. It might be Kansas in miniature, or Iowa. Tractors plow long regular furrows in its level soil, heavy traffic moves quickly along its straight roads. To come upon a hill here is an event. To come upon a hill crowned by a miracle of medieval artistry is startling, even before you are close enough to see the faultlessness of the miracle.

The direct approach to Chartres from Paris ordinarily gives you a sight of the cathedral towers rising against the sky from quite a distance off. This time squally weather hid the view until we were almost there, whereupon the clouds suddenly broke, the sun shone forth, and the most spectacular Gothic structure in Europe sprang unexpectedly into view on its hilltop, a rainbow arched like a band of glory over the soaring spires. It was a wholly satisfactory curtain raiser. The two voices from the back seat, which had been clacking teen-age *patatí-patatá* uninterruptedly, shut up for two whole minutes. The girls were tongue-tied with awe.

Superlatives flow easily at Chartres. It has been said that the triple west door, the Portail Royal, is the finest existing architectural production of the 12th Century, as the statuary of the north and south porches is the most wonderful of the 13th, the wheel-shaped flying buttresses the most original of the entire Gothic period, the 13th Century stained-glass windows the most perfect ensemble ever put together. You begin to understand why so many scholars have made a lifetime work of cataloguing all this, or aspects of it or even aspects of aspects. Later, if you carry the right guidebooks, you bone up on details, but to begin, at Chartres, you walk small, and do not feel either knowledgeable or important.

France has about 2000 miles of shore line, with dozens of fancifully named coasts. Besides the Flowered Coast of Normandy, there are the Azure Coast of Provence, the Vermilion Coast, the Silver Coast, the Coast of Granite Rose, the Coast of Love, the Coast of Legends, many more. Among the most attractive is the Atlantic shore near Biarritz, immediately north of the Spanish border. It doesn't have a proper name, or not much of a proper name. It's just the coast of the Basque country, and when you say it that way it doesn't sound like much. But it's one of the great playgrounds of Europe, where you can enjoy any kind of sport you like, from real bullfights and Basque pelota to roulette. Even *repassage particulier.*

The last-named game is a contest between hotel guests and hotel managements all over France, not exclusively in Biarritz.

The Cité at Carcassone, built in medieval times, is one of France's architectural wonders.

It means personal pants-pressing, an activity frowned upon by hotel valets everywhere. Unfortunately, French laundry, cleaning and valet services, generally first class, are also fantastically high priced and far too slow when you are on the road. The alternative is to carry certain basic equipment with you. Ours, besides soap and cleaning fluid, consisted of a light Italian iron that worked on any of three currents, plus a wide assortment of plugs, adapters, socket screw-ins and extension cords to tap a source of electric current through the barriers of intricate devices French hotel operators set up to defeat the attempt, such as papering over wall outlets and using lamp bulbs with non-standard bases. Against this kind of trickery nothing much can be planned in advance. You meet each challenge as it arises, by calling at the nearest electrical-supply shop for an appropriate gimmick after you have examined the situation. When you have built a fair collection of gimmicks, you are in a position to set up a home-valet operation for your womenfolk at the drop of a petticoat.

Another popular recreation in Biarritz is bikini watching, a healthful outdoor activity comparable to bird watching. The French, or minimal, bikini would probably not get by on an American beach but is very attractive on the young, slim female figure. I had two young, slim female figures to buy bikinis for in Biarritz, after which the responsibility for their entertainment, protection and petty expenses was taken over by a crowd of friendly young Basque lads they met on the beach. A better investment than those two sketchy bathing suits could not have been made.

The so-called French Riviera includes, vaguely, the Mediterranean coast from Italy to Marseille. The Côte d'Azur is usually thought of as extending only from the Italian border to Cannes, taking in Menton, Monaco, Nice, the Cap Ferrat area, Antibes, Juan-les-Pins and Cannes itself. Until a very few years ago that was it. Now the fashion carries summering crowds farther westward every year; to St.-Raphael, to Ste.-

The castle of Richard the Lion Hearted, at Les Andelys.

Maxime, to St.-Tropez and beyond. The chic crowd, the international-playboy-yacht-and-diamond set, still stick to their old stamping grounds east of Cannes' Quai St.-Pierre. It is to this fair and flowery coast that the heirs to fading European titles retire, if they can afford it, and famous figures of the international stage and screen come to enjoy their holidays.

In this glittering expanse of sun, sand and spending money, the center of social life is the terrace of Cannes' Hotel Carlton, a posh and well-run water-front lodging where you can easily

France/David Dodge 59

find your toes being trodden on in the elevator by a maharani, an ex-emperor, a Chinese philosopher, the eccentric wife of a Central American multimillionaire, an Oriental demigod and movie stars *ad lib*. The terrace itself is not quite so democratic; you have to spend a minimum of 200 francs, plus service, if you sit down there, but just breathing the same air as the Continental dreamboats at the neighboring table is worth the price of admission.

We left the lovely Côte d'Azur by way of the Route Napoleon, so called because Bonaparte used it for his comeback trail from Elba. This road, although it follows the general configurations of a bowl of spaghetti, is in this traveler's opinion the most beautiful mountain drive in France. It leads from the Mediterranean shore at Cannes northward to Grenoble, old capital of the Dauphiné and a university town of international repute, splendidly situated among Alpine surroundings about a hundred miles south of Geneva. Here, also, is one of the great French collections of modern painting.

Art galleries, like cathedrals, are ubiquitous in France. Every city has its museums, and even small towns contain respectable and interesting collections. Traveling French families visit them all conscientiously, papa, *maman* and the children together, because art museums are part of their national heritage and way of life, and you can get into a lot of them free, although not every day of the week. Traveling American families, unless they are prepared to spend the better part of their lives at it, must pick and choose. In this they are helped by the better guidebooks, which rate museums according to their relative merits, give the visitor a general idea of what he may expect to see, and tell him—not always too reliably—when the doors will be open.

What the guidebooks *don't* explain are the technical differences among Expressionist, Impressionist, Post-Expressionist, Neo-Impressionist, Cubist, Realistic, Surrealistic, Abstract, Primitive and other schools of contemporary painting, and when you come to a museum which, like Grenoble's, contains a rich and varied selection, you are weaving a tangled web indeed if you use these terms carelessly within earshot of your young. The inquiring adolescent mind always wants to know what you are talking about, and it is then necessary for you to put up or shut up. (A museum is not, of course, the only place where this can happen to you.) The safest and most rewarding plan is to study, briefly, any of several good books on the subject before you set forth. It is a delight simply to have eyes in a country so packed, crammed and loaded with fine art as is France. It is a far greater delight to see and understand what the artist is trying to get over, even when you don't have to explain to the youngsters.

Aix-les-Bains is near a mountain lake north of Grenoble, Annecy stands on the shore of another, and neither is hard to reach. This part of France, the Alpine country, has been a popular resort since the days of Imperial Rome. Aix-les-Bains, the famed spa, is perhaps a little stuffy for American taste; too much emphasis on gout and gallstones, too little on recreation. The British call it Aches les Pains. But Lake Annecy is as attractive a mountain vacation spot as anyone could ask, whether for a rest or to flex muscles. Swimming, boating, fishing, moun-

tain climbing, tennis, golf are the outdoor sports, the usual casino provides its own kind of attractions, and Annecy itself, the town, has charm, dignity and color as well as impressive surroundings, the soaring, snow-clad peaks of the Alps. Last, but far from least, Annecy is a good starting point from which to visit the unique and wondrous Chapel of Assy.

The Chapel of Assy should not be confused with the better-known Matisse chapel in Vence on the Côte d'Azur. Vence is pure Matisse, while Assy is Matisse, Rouault, Léger, Braque, Lurçat, Bonnard and other French artists who have there expressed themselves in stained glass, ceramic, mosaic, tapestry and paint. The Assy chapel does not submit to easy description. It has been photographed, but even color film does not do it justice. There is only one way to know it, and that is to go there. We did, taking the obscure side road that runs from Passy to Assy in the French Alps, not far from Mont Blanc, and when we arrived we entered the chapel reverently. No Frenchman cares what your religion may be, or if you have one. He does expect you to stand quiet in the presence of beauty.

Strasbourg has a cathedral that can best be described as stunning in its effect the first time you see it. How anything the size of a cathedral, a big one, can manage to lurk behind smaller buildings is difficult to explain, but lurk it does until you turn a street corner and find yourself unexpectedly face to face with one of the most impressive Gothic façades in the world.

The dramatic impact of that fine facade almost compensated for unseasonable Alsatian weather. Strasbourg faded behind us in a howling rainstorm which failed to dampen our holiday spirit. Rainy summers are not necessarily a tragedy in France. Although bad weather precludes *pique-niques*, it practically forces you to look at art galleries, can-can dancers and other indoor cultural attractions which you might pass up otherwise.

West of Alsace, Lorraine and the broad expanse of the Champagne country spread practically to Paris. You bear a little toward the north, leaving Strasbourg, to visit Metz and the battlefields of the first World War. Around Verdun, where the terrible years of trench warfare were fought to a stalemate, the ground is still so impregnated with explosives, the soil so thickly sown with death, that one-time farmland has been allowed to revert to *maquis*, worthless scrub. Here you find the graveyards of another generation of men who died for France. Here are their monuments; rusty war matériel, battered blockhouses, the grim trench where a line of bayonet tips protruding from bare earth marks the tomb of infantrymen engulfed by mud when the rain-soaked lip of their trench collapsed and buried them as they stood ready to go over the top. The scars of war are far more apparent here than in Normandy, even though Verdun's wounds have had more time to heal. You are glad to leave the *maquis* for the wide pleasant plains that have given their name to the king of wines.

Champagne, the region, holds out two main attractions to visitors: its wines, and the famous cathedral at Reims. The cathedral, badly battered by shellfire in the 1914-18 war, is even in restoration a mecca for admirers of medieval architecture, and the city is the beginning of one of the famed Wine Roads. These, of which there are three in Champagne, lead you gently and pleasantly from famous vineyard to famous vineyard. Later, when you make a tour of the caves and cellars of Reims or nearby Epernay, you stand a good chance of getting looped on free samples.

From Reims the roads led northward again, toward Picardy and Flanders. This triangular upper corner of France is generally left out of most itineraries, a mistake unless you are cramped for time.

The North is the home of some of France's finest historical monuments and several good resort areas, as well as the pit heads, slag heaps and smokestacks of industrial activity. There are hundreds of square miles of flat, fertile farmland as well, rolling meadows, small pretty villages, ancient cities and some of the best museums in the country.

The museum at Lille, far up near the Belgian border, is one of these. Our way there went via Laon and the small town of La Fère, where there is an inn which, I was told, is pretty good. We didn't get in. The season was then nearing the middle of August, the most competitive time of year for roadside sleeping accommodations, and we should have made a point of reaching La Fère earlier in the day.

This was the one occasion on which I really had to scratch to find rooms. Had we been a party of three, or five, rather than four, we might well have had to bed down in the streets. Four, for motorists in France as elsewhere in Europe, is the magic number. It fits two double rooms and one dinner table.

Beyond Lille a short road connects two towns of famous connotation for infantrymen: Armentières and Dunkerque. When young ladies are with you, do not make the mistake of remembering any of the verses of *Mademoiselle From Armentières* while driving through the town. Maidenly curiosity demands to know what comes next, and how do you explain to growing girls why you stopped singing so abruptly? I wrenched the conversation, with difficulty, around to the history of the region, inviting a rundown from the guidebook. That carried us safely away from hinky-dinky parlay-voo to Dunkerque, northernmost of French seaports and picturesque harbor of heroic memory.

The last lap took us southward down the coast again, to Calais and Boulogne. This region of France, a flat and unprotected plain, has been the battleground of Europe for centuries. Considering all the shot, shell and bombs that have been flung here, it is a miracle that so many fine ancient churches still stand, so many cities still preserve their distinctive Flemish Renaissance air. Residents of this war-torn area might reasonably be expected to regard life as a dour business, but Artois and Picardy, the coastal provinces, are quite gay. Grim reminders of the past are close at hand, of course. Nearer Belgium, red poppies still blow between the crosses, row on row, in Flanders fields. But the Channel shore from Calais south is lined with resorts for the lighthearted living: Le Touquet, Berck-Plage and others, annually overrun by a different kind of invasion, a horde of British, Belgian and French summer holidaymakers who do not know, or do not care, that the north of France is considered less chic than the south. We joined the invaders for two leisurely days on the beach at Le Touquet before our six-week holiday was over. Another afternoon, a last *pique-nique*, would see us again in Paris.

As the trip had begun with the most beautiful cathedral of France, so it neared end at the largest, in Amiens, and the most daringly vaulted, in Beauvais. At Grenoble I had learned how important it was to stay a clear jump ahead of Kendal and Charlotte in cultural and artistic matters (the tour, although it hadn't been planned that way, was more educational for the tour conductor than for anyone else), so I had again done a little surreptitious cramming. As a result, I was able to give an authoritative offhand lecture on the two giants of French Gothic architecture.

Strictly speaking, Amiens is the giant, Beauvais a might-have-been. Notre Dame d'Amiens, begun in the early 13th Century, is a wholly satisfying artistic entity. In size and grandeur it has no peer in France. Its external sculpture is harmoniously designed, superbly cut and well preserved, its interior impressively vast. The carved choir stalls, most beautiful in the country, reflect the wit and sophistication of their time as well as the designer's artistry, and although much of the stained glass has vanished from the windows, enough remains to tell of the blaze of beauty that must have shone down on the bowed heads of the people of Amiens.

St.-Pierre-de-Beauvais, less than forty miles away, never reached completion. Designed like its neighbor but meant to be even more huge, begun a generation later by builders with more faith than engineering skill, it collapsed in construction, was redesigned, completed in part—the central vaultings are the highest Gothic arches in existence—capped by a tower which also collapsed, and left, in the end, without the nave that was too mighty to be built. To visit Amiens and Beauvais on the same day is to see at once the glory of a unique art form in triumph, its dignity in failure.

All this I explained in a golden flow of eloquence. I was, I confess, carried away, as much by the sound of my own voice as by the cathedrals themselves. I did not notice until some time after I had finished that Kendal and Charlotte were unnaturally quiet. Driving the last few miles that still lay ahead of us, I began to wonder uneasily if the lack of *patatí-patatá* from the back seat meant that I had talked too much. You can prejudice most minds, at least at certain ages, against your own enthusiasms by being too enthusiastic.

I knew that Elva and I could never change in our feeling for the country we had just re-explored. The cathedrals, the museums, the gay resorts, the lovely tree-lined roads, the coasts, mountains, meadows, lakes, even the good crusty bread spread with cheese and washed down with cool wine while we sat under a tree by the roadside, all had too strong a hold on us.

But what about this penultimate moment, with Kendal and Charlotte sitting mutely in the back seat? Did their silence mean that my lecture on cathedral art had—awful thought—bored them? And did it not follow that the whole trip might have held more of boredom for them than of interest?

Had we, in trying to stuff them with too much of France in too short a time, provoked a reaction against the country we thought of as our second homeland?

I forget which of the girls spoke up just then, but as it turned out she was speaking for both. She said meditatively, "Gosh, think of all the wonderful things we *missed!*"

Italy

HER WONDERFUL PEOPLE

*Sean O'Faolain of Ireland marvels at the
ebullience of the Italian people:
they burst into song at the slightest encouragement;
rock with laughter when others would only smile;
become embroiled, for no perceptible reason,
in violent arguments that end in renewed friendship.
The Italians, O'Faolain finds, are paradoxical:
they are mature and childish, hardheaded and
impractical—a people to whom inconsistency is
one of the cardinal virtues...*

A distinguished English traveler once remarked that we cannot really begin to enjoy Italy until its monuments are off our conscience. Every visitor to Italy knows what he meant: the joy of total relaxation—the sunshine and the balm, the brilliant colors, the constant, pleasantly distracting to-and-fro of Italy's idlest hours. But, surely, he was thinking also that the greatest of its attractions are the Italian people themselves. And although nobody can hope to describe or define the character of a whole people—least of all a people so fascinatingly complex —here are a few fragments of personal impressions, and happy memories, which I have gained over many and many a day spent among my beloved Italian people.

One preliminary observation—and reservation. Here and there, throughout the peninsula, even the most casual visitor must recall a street called Via Venti Settembre. This street is a symbol; it reminds Italians that it was not until September 20,

1870, that their troops entered Rome and thereby finally unified *all* Italy. The name will remind American travelers of something even more striking: that United Italy, achieved by Garibaldi and Cavour, is politically younger than the United States.

So—if we are talking about the people of Italy we have to pause and ask ourselves: "But of which Italy?" For the Italy we visit today is a quite modern and still incomplete amalgam of many periods, many states and many influences. There is more than one Italy. Each region still retains—we must never forget—a great deal of the individuality of its origins.

We need only think what the map of Italy was like in the days of the medieval communes—to take only one period. It was like a jigsaw, whose pieces might suggest, at first, the parts of a curiously shaped plate that somebody had thrown on the ground. But those fragments were not parts of a plate with a unified design. Each bit was an independent state that had gone its own willful way—Milan, Como, Mantua, Parma, Pavia, Cremona, Bologna, Modena, Florence, Siena, Lucca and so on. Glue all these bits together and you may get your oddly shaped plate; but do you, even today, get your unified design? To glue is not to blend.

Blending takes time, centuries even. One of the most striking illustrations of this is an exquisite little chapel in Palermo, the Cappella Palatina. Its loveliness is unsurpassed by any building in the world, not even by Sainte-Chapelle. It is the creation of half a dozen successive cultures. It was built by a Norman ruler; its arches, resting on columns of peach-flower marble, are the broken Saracenic arch applied to the Roman curve; the pictorial mosaics that cover the walls with shimmering gold are part-Greek, part-Byzantine; the carved wooden roof drooping with stalactites of starred rosettes is a Moslem tribute to a Christian faith; into the pulpit pillars are carved the shadows

of the desert palms; there are Arabic motifs and inscriptions; Italian pupils have completed the designs.

Indeed, one may well ask on every occasion: "Which Italy?"

I once heard a story in Florence, told with true Florentine mordancy, which was supposed to bite off the Italian character in one neat mouthful. An Englishman, a Frenchman and an Italian went into a café and ordered a glass of beer apiece. In each glass there was a fly. The Englishman haughtily demanded another glass. The Frenchman politely asked for another glass. The Italian removed the fly, drank half the beer, restored the fly and then furiously shouted for another full glass.

When I retailed this story to a Sicilian he boiled with rage. "Just the kind of story a beastly Florentine would invent. We southerners"—how often one hears the phrase: *noi altri meridionati!*—"would never play so mean a trick as that."

And it is quite true that once we are across the Strait of Messina we become forcibly aware of a different character among the people; they are far more reserved, haughty, serious-minded, more idealistically romantic than any Italians of the mainland. It is a contrast that will strike us still more forcibly if we take the steamer from Naples to Palermo.

In both cities we will observe great poverty, some solid bourgeois comfort, and all the marks of bygone traditions of aristocratic wealth and grace. Yet how they differ in the techniques of living! The Neapolitan fights hardship with an insuppressible gaiety, the Palerman fends off discouragement with pride; but Florentine cynicism appeals to neither.

So one passes from region to region, and each offers its own view of the other, which is as often revealing of the teller as of the people discussed. A Roman will grant you that all southerners are as sharp as razors but are hopelessly lazy. The southerners will declare furiously that no Roman ever works, that he is merely the national middleman, the typical bloated bureaucrat exploiting the rest of the country. A Milanese will say that the only people in the country who work to produce (forgetting that farming is as productive as industry) are the Milanese. And if you counter this with mention of the Genoese he will scoff and say: "Work? The Genoese? They are merely cunning. If you ever see a Genoese falling out of a window, don't stop him; it would be unkind; he will fall on his feet, and get paid for it too!" The longer we listen the more bewildering it becomes until, remembering once again the many partitionings of Italy, we accept, perhaps a little wearily now, that every observation we make in one region has to be checked by what we observe in another; and then, gradually, with a pleasure that grows in rewards the more we travel, we begin to see that there are after all some basic truths about the Italian nature which harmonize all these internecine clashes of opinion.

Let us take some single subject—one of the most interesting of all subjects: the position of Woman in Italy. I suppose the popular idea is that Italy is the most romantic country in the world, where passion is unrestrained and love as free as air.

It must be admitted that the Italians themselves have unwittingly done much to spread this romantic legend. One thinks of all their throbbing songs about moonlight, and love and roses . . .

Specialmente fra le rose nell' primavera
Come bella fa l'amore nella sera . . .
(And especially among the roses in the springtime
How sweet to love when twilight falls . . .)

These are not songs for tourists; the Italians sing them all the time; roll them out on the radio until the twilight falls. Whether they believe this sirupy stuff is an entirely different matter to which I will come in due course. For the moment how does it fit in with the following cold little incident?

One summer evening in Marsala, that pleasant little port on the western tip of Sicily, a youngish Sicilian bachelor whom I have known for several years invited my wife and myself to dine at a restaurant.

When he came to collect us at our hotel he was accompanied by a young woman whom he cheerfully began to press to make a fourth at table. They both started to laugh gaily at the hugeness and absurdity of this joke, the point of which was that it would have been—as he well knew—contrary to all convention that she should do such a shocking thing.

"Shocking?" my wife said. "But you have two chaperones tonight!"

With sad-merry shruggings the young woman explained that if she were seen dining in public with a man it would mean either that they were formally affianced or were having an improper love affair. And yet, this young woman was twenty-three and had taken her degree at the University of Catania, while my bachelor friend is over thirty and a respected citizen.

"Do you think these conventions are strictly necessary?" we asked him, after his companion had regretfully departed for her parents' home and we sat dining *à trois*.

"Sicilian blood is warm," Beppo said humorously. "We are very near to Africa down here," and he pointed to the bottle of wine. For, as it happened, we were sipping a Moscato from the Italian island of Pantelleria, not forty miles from the African coast. He went on smilingly to quote an old proverb:

"*Non si mette la paglia vicino al fuoco.* 'There is no point in putting the straw too near the fire.' I mean, love in Italy is considered an undying fire, likely to burst into flame at any moment, at any breath, and of all places the straw is most combustible in the south."

"All right!" I laughed. "But come back to the conventions. When you, dear Beppo, go to dances are you not permitted to take girls with you?"

"Alone? Never! I may only invite them in threes and fours. There is only one woman in this town whom I may invite to accompany me alone. *La levatrice!* [The local midwife.] Midwives are supposed to be professionally immune to sex, like priests and nuns."

About a week later I found myself dining with another young man in Naples. The thermometer of love being here presumably three hundred miles cooler than in Marsala, I thought he would have somewhat different views on these conventions. Luigi is twenty-eight, married, eager, highly intelligent and rather idealistic. When he heard about Beppo and his young woman he nodded indulgently and said:

"I think we would be a little less strict in Naples, but I do see the point of these conventions. And, in principle, I agree with them. To understand the Italian attitude in these matters you must realize that we love our women utterly. We want them to be ours and ours alone. We want to marry a girl who has never been in love with anyone but ourselves. We impose ourselves on the woman we love." Here his ten urgent fingers pointed downward like Svengali mesmerizing Trilby. "We want them to share everything with us, we want to share everything with them. If my wife and I go to a picture gallery and enjoy a picture there, that experience becomes *our* experience. Listen! Last week my wife went to Florence. There she visited an exhibition in the Palazzo Strozzi. She saw a picture by Piero della Francesca which I have never seen. She has thereby had an experience which I have not had. Someday she will talk about this picture to a boy who has also seen it. That means that she will share an experience with another that I have not shared with her. For this I feel so jealous that I could almost hate her. You can see now why we do not like our young women to go about with other young men? They are *our* women!"

A week later still, having now moved this pulsing thermometer of love some three hundred miles farther from Africa, I found myself at a dinner party in Florence and tried out the effect of this new viewpoint on the company. I got an immediate illustration both of the skeptical nature of the Florentine temperament and of those variations within the general Italian character of which I have spoken. The whole company—there were about ten at table, all married, sound bourgeois types—exploded in scorn.

"Absurd!" cried one. "Impossible!" said another. "Besides," added a third, "no Neapolitan could feel like that!" A fourth, with true Florentine realism, demanded: "What is this picture anyway? Imagine falling out with your wife over a picture! Where can I see this picture?"—and he noted down the particulars. It still makes me chuckle to think of that staid, stolid, skeptical Florentine gazing and gazing at the *Madonna with Two Patrons* in the Strozzi, wondering what secret meaning it could have thus to come between husband and wife.

I then decided that this was just another example of the unbridgeable gap between north and south. But after dinner, four of us drove up to the Piazzale Michelangelo, to see again that view of Florence by night which is equaled only by the corresponding view from the opposite heights of Fiésole. There, seated at scores of little tables lit by Chinese lanterns, on the recessed terrace beside the restaurant, we found about two hundred people playing canasta. It was a charming scene. Then I noticed that it was chiefly the men who were playing and that the women were mostly onlookers; and I asked the lady of our little party why this was so. (She had lived in America for twenty years before returning to marry in Florence and has remained in outlook at least half American.) She smiled impishly: "Italian women like to keep an eye on their husbands. And husbands on their wives. They go everywhere together. I don't do this myself," glancing fondly at her handsome husband, who interrupted her to pat her hand. "I recognize that Carlo sometimes likes to be with his men friends. But my sisters-in-law are always warning me and upbraiding me and saying I am most unwise."

So, then, I thought to myself, this possessiveness is not confined to men, or to the south? All it does is to alter its quality a little from place to place, and person to person.

I ventured to mention "the heat of Africa" to Carlo. He was enchanted. He made *such* a pair of manly eyes at his wife as he chortled: "*Noi altri Italiani! Andiamo al fondo!*"

In Italy love leads to marriage. But here we seem at first to run into a contradiction. The Italian is as attracted toward love as a pursuit as the Frenchman is attracted toward love as a destination. This is an attitude which every woman who visits Italy finds delightful in the beginning and tedious in the long run. For the "run" in Italy is certain to be a long one, as protracted and sinuous and delicate as it is brief and pointed in France. One may well wonder whether at the conclusion of so extended a love game, after so much art and energy has been expended in maneuvering around the desired citadel, there can ever be enough energy and art left for the routine of everyday life. An Italian wife once said bitterly to me: "Before we marry we are treated like Madonnas. We are courted as if we were sopranos in an operatic love duet. After marriage we suddenly find ourselves transformed into tame German *Hausfraus*. And then the only songs we sing are lullabies."

The most damning word that an Italian can apply to a woman is that she is a *cerebrale*: a woman, that is, who is self-conscious in love, and therefore does not really love at all, because it is all happening in her mind. But where a force is elemental and unself-conscious one may expect to find that the flaw will show itself in a lack of formality. So that we come on the curious anomaly that courtships hedged by convention end too often in a married life that could do with more convention, in the sense of more art, more grace, more ceremony. Foreigners married to Italians have, therefore, to be very adaptable, and to accept above all that the pattern—immutable as destiny—is the family pattern. Divorce is forbidden by law. Contraception is rare outside the big cities and towns. Childlessness is a tragedy. The marriage ring encircles a life of devotion to children and home.

Before leaving the conventions of love and marriage I will risk one sweeping generalization: The traveler in Italy will make a grave mistake if he does not realize that, contrary to most first impressions, the Italians are among the most conventional people in Europe in all their behavior. Their apparently free-and-easy ways are not to be taken superficially. Take the illustration of bargaining. A Frenchman, if he bargains at all, will be more quiet about it, will use all the correct phrases of gentlemen, but he can be very biting and even quite disagreeable. An Italian will shout, wave his hands, appeal to God and the saints to witness his honesty, his generosity and your utter heartlessness, but he is rarely, if ever, rude or insulting; for this is in large part a game that you and he are playing and it must never, whatever the outcome, approach the sordid. We must always remember the great Italian desire to *fare bella figura*, to cut a fine figure. The poorest of the poor perhaps insist on this most of all. If we want to refuse a cameo seller proffering third-rate coral we may refuse him but we must not rebuff him. We must never belittle his wares. To rebuff or belittle him is *fare brutta figura*, to do things gracelessly, and he will walk away coldly, his natural human dignity wounded, and we will suddenly feel rather cheap.

Now, the Italians are hardheaded people and they live hard, tough, exacting lives. They are nobody's fools. The toughness of life in Italy does not let them fool themselves. But the catch is that the harder life is, the greater the temptation to imagine away its hardness—for the while. And who could blame them if they do, then, play the daring game of "Let's pretend"? This powerful, apparently irresistible, Italian capacity of dreaming enormously and articulately is their recompense, escape, analgesic. Where ambition has small scope time has small value; where time has small value one may as well play with it since one cannot sell it; a man may just as well dream that it is a night of romance and that Lollobrigida or Rita Hayworth has fallen in love with him, or that the girl by his side is a millionairess, or that he has a lot of money and will presently take her racing away in his Alfa-Romeo to Lake Como.

It is all a matter of the meaning or the meaninglessness of Time. Sometimes their days are too short, and then one will see them slaving in the fields, or sweating (for small pay) on some rush jobs, as near to dawn and dark as makes no matter. Sometimes the days are too long, and then the passing traveler looks at them and says that they are lazy or idle.

Where there are more opportunities and incentives—in Milan, Torino, Genoa, Rome—there will be more self-reliance and more steady ambition. In such cities a man can, with some assurance, foresee the shape of his life and of his sons' lives— elementary school, secondary school, technical institute or university, entry into business. In this assurance he will be content, by hard work, steadily to lay lire upon lire and gradually amass a modest competence. But in those parts of Italy where life is chancy and constricted—which means in three-quarters of the land—it is not a question of patiently laying one lire upon another but of holding on long enough to the first crumpled lire to let another lire press its dear if dirty cheek against it. In such regions time does not function, apart from the rising and setting of the sun, the movement of the seasons,

Seaside holiday: *The beach at Riccione, part of the resort's wide stretch of sun-soaked sands. Less tan-happy than Americans, Italians make good use of rented* tende *and umbrellas.*

the clock of the belly. You might just as well forget to wind your watch in the lofty hinterlands of Sicily; deep in the tawny uplands behind its crumbling southern coastline; down through the drowsy heel of Apulia where only the most persistent commercial traveler will penetrate, or some dejected Chinese selling baubles to the women, as Greek and Phoenician coasters must have done two thousand years ago. In such places we are in a land of toil, talk and reverie. What traveler has not seen these tireless talkers in every little piazza south and west of Naples— talking, talking, from morning to midnight—and wondered what they had to talk about?

And yet, some of the most vital minds in Europe have come out of these rudderless and rude Arcadias—brilliant thinkers like Verga, Crispi, Pirandello, Vico, De Sanctis, Gentile or Croce.

Ignazio Silone, who has himself lived in the south, once explained this to me—half seriously, half jocosely: it is, he said, the long, empty days that do it, those days whose vacancy faces every youth returning to his village from the seminary (the only sort of schooling available there) after years spent on logic and philosophy, metaphysics and the classics; days that will now be spent, from morning to dark, arguing, discussing, defining, hair-splitting, philosophizing, taking all the toys of life to pieces over the Campari, or the Cinzano, or the coffee at the little round tables under the dusty oleanders while the mules go by and the girls pass with slanting eyes. One should be able to guess from his plays that Pirandello, fretting away all reality into a huge, tragic joke, was a southerner. He came from outside Agrigento, in Sicily, a lost town where nobody would now dream of pausing were it not for the golden, Greek temples or the modern *Jolly Hotel*. Croce is typical: educated at a Catholic boarding school in Naples; finding all physical matter mere lumber, and all visible reality a despicable illusion. Naturally, the mass of these piazza gasbags never come to anything; they become petty clerks, utilizing one-hundredth part of their energies or intelligence on undemanding and underpaid jobs.

Life in Italy for such men can be completely aimless and irrelevant from one year to the next. I said this once to my friend from Marsala. He lifted his shoulders good-humoredly. "From year to year? We live from day to day." But when I repeated this to one of my Florentine friends he cried, not to be outdone: "From day to day? We live from minute to minute." They were both telling lies, of course, exaggerating, bragging of the Italian gift for improvisation.

We can see how all this fits in with what people sometimes call the histrionic quality of the Italians. Indeed, it is because they are, at once, so sensuous and imaginative that they can snatch from the most unpromising occasions so many brilliant moments, create so much brilliant color, get so much fun and excitement out of apparently nothing at all. At the slightest encouragement they will break into a snatch of song, turn any trivial occasion into a gale of laughter, seize the least excuse for a tremendous wordy quarrel—has anybody ever seen an honest blow struck in Italy in any of those high-blood-pressure street rows?—and then follow it up with the emotional pleasure (probably foreseen) of a joyful and passionate reconcilia-

Freshly scrubbed wine bottles are set out to dry in the sunshine at Certaldo, where Boccaccio lived.

tion. I often think they mustn't have a nerve in their bodies or they couldn't stand it. If they grieve their grief is bottomless— while it lasts.

If they enjoy an hour's sentimental dalliance it will seem to them a glorious and immortal romance, and it will be—while it lasts. It is a technique of dramatic improvisation amounting to genius. In their better days it went into their painting, their sculpture, their music, controlled and disciplined for the purposes of lasting art.

There is in the Borghese Gardens in Rome, in the children's corner under the great ilexes, in the vespertine summer shade, a charming fountain of a naked Pan, or satyr, and a nymph. The two naked figures laughingly uphold on the bridge of their clasped hands a laughing child. Water drips softly from their bare arms into the shallow bowl beneath their feet. Around the rim of the bowl is this inscription:—VITAE LAUDEM MURMURE SUO FONS CANIT. ("The fountain murmurs the praises of Life.") The place, the fountain, the figures and the inscription are an epitome of the Italian art of living at its best. One afternoon I was sitting in the open-air café a few steps away. The waiter brought me a beer and then, suddenly, uttered a little cry of apology: a petal from the ilexes overhead had drifted down into the beer. As he removed the tiny golden petal he looked up and said gently: "*Sempre qui una pioggia di fiori.*" ("It is always raining flowers here.") The waiter's choice of phrase, the murmur of the fountain of Pan nearby, the cries of the playing children became one. But it was he who had made the exquisite moment out of next to nothing.

This gift for sensitive improvisation colors all their lives. We know how neat and fresh and colorful even the poorest Roman girl looks as she emerges for her evening promenade, her frock as crisp as if it had just come out of a shop window.

Italy/Sean O'Faolain **67**

It is so because it is the only one she possesses in the whole world. To keep it new she took it off immediately when she got home last evening and she has been shuffling about in rope slippers and a peignoir all day. The shirt of the young man who meets her is snowy, his trousers creased, his hair brushed and oiled. You are looking at his total wardrobe. All his pocket may contain will be his bus fare. That boy and girl will have to invent a happy life between them out of as little as that.

Dinner with a view: *Venice's historic Piazetta and the church of Santa Maria della Salute.*

In the same way they manage to extract color out of the dullest-seeming work. It may amount to no more than the red rose in the paper cap of a sweating quarry worker, naked except for his ragged shorts. In Rome, this summer, a friend pointed in delight to the rusty barbed wire surrounding the military barracks in her quarter: climbing roses had been trained around the ugly entanglements. How often has one not noticed that the railway trackman between his screaming rails has smothered his hut in morning-glories? The traffic cop will turn his gestures into a movement from a ballet. You do not need to draw a blueprint for your carpenter or your dressmaker: they get the idea before you utter it, and possibly a better one born of it. It was Chris Serpell, the B.B.C. correspondent in Italy, who told us how one evening in Naples he took a bus and presently noticed that they were going off the route, around by the docks. When he protested the driver said: "True, signor, but the sunset is so beautiful over the bay this evening!" It all adds up to their burning instinct for Life expressing itself as colorfully as possible, with whatever humble material comes to hand.

All Italians (except their artists) are artists *manqués*. They live by feeling and instinct, not by reason. The persistent French Cartesianism ("I think, *therefore* I am") is alien to their natures, as it is to the nature of every artist. For art deals primarily with *felt* experience. If one rationalizes it the experience remains but it alters its nature: it becomes a thought. The experience is still valid; it was and remains true, but once we have rationalized it we have reassembled the parts of a machine in a new way, and though it may still work it is different. If Italians were to become ratiocinative they would become Frenchmen. They can only live the way they know.

Evidently there are some things in which it is not enough to have a genius for living from day to day, however dramatically, resourcefully or imaginatively. One can improvise for too long. Sooner or later the crash comes. Icarus, whose wings of wax melted when he flew too close to the sun, was an Italian.

The pattern of the Italian nature is one which has been woven over the centuries out of a series of inspired responses in terms of national temperament to a series of life-challenges in terms of historical vicissitudes and the economic pressures resulting from them. The economic tragedy of Italy has two main factors: persistent overpopulation and a tradition of privilege—native and foreign—without a corresponding sense of responsibility. There are too many Italians in Italy and since we have taken away her colonies this density will grow. All migration is internal (apart from a trickle to America), its chief line being from the underdeveloped south to the more highly developed north; which is why boys approach you so often in the street with fake American fountain pens and cheap watches supposedly smuggled from Switzerland. Poverty must do something. The south is thus endlessly swelling the population of the north, diluting its culture, and creating that sort of *lumpen* proletariat which is the natural fodder of communism everywhere. It was to adjust this state of affairs that, under Marshall aid, billions of lire have been spent since 1950 on the reclamation of the underdeveloped land in the south—one of the most generous plans ever initiated by a conquering country to reestablish the fortunes, and secure the future, of a former foe.

Italy has co-operated gallantly. The landowners of Italy include many admirable employers, but for the most part, especially in the south, they have been selfish to the point of savagery. In the north, likewise, too many industrialists have been exploiting the poor without pity for their present miseries or foresight for their future revenge. But changes are to be observed, and one could cite many examples of landowners and industrialists who have awakened alike to their natural human duties and to the long-term dangers of irresponsibility.

It is against this background that we have to see the modern Italian; and if we have the experience, the imagination and the historical knowledge to fill in the human picture we must be struck chiefly by the gallantry of these people who have, literally, come up smiling at the end of it all. That, with their hard lives, their chaotic history, their top-heavy economy, they should still manage to be resilient, high-spirited, undefeated, must fill us with admiration for their courage.

It is often said that Italians make bad soldiers, though many who have fought beside or against them would not agree—and the record of individual Italian courage would fill an encyclopedia. But it is probably true that they make bad armies, and that the barbarous art of dying *en masse* makes no appeal to their art of living felicitously, and bravely. It is this splendid courage in their lives that justifies them. To stand on a quay wall in Venice, or Naples, or Palermo, having lunched well, warm with good wine, one's pockets lined and to watch three or four fellows bare to the waist, cutting off slices of dry polenta, their main and probably sole meal for the whole hard working day, which began when the sun rose and will not end until the stars have come, and to hear them then, lying back in the sun, singing gaily, is a sight to twist one's heart, to make one feel that here are a people who have never known defeat in their souls and never will.

In some such gush of admiration, and surely also of love, one may well feel at last that one has come close to the Italian nature. And so, indeed, one might, were it not—the final discovery—that the tapestry of their natures is never quite still, and many of its threads are very old and the colors seem to run into one another as the light of circumstance changes. The Italian is not only split-minded, he has also the bewildering trick of oscillating between his own oppositions, some of which I have tried to intimate: his passion and his conventions; his sentimentality and his cynicism; that dreamy imagination and that sudden grasp of the dramatic opportunity; now warm, kindly and friendly, now swinging over into reserve, hauteur, ruthlessness, even plain rascality. If we do not realize that these are not so much contradictions in their natures as oscillations, we will feel, in despair, that at the very moment when we think we "have" them they have eluded us once more.

Yet of one thing we may always be sure: their one, clear, firm and indestructible certainty that, in spite of everything, it is well to be alive. I know no other race that, in equal circumstances, has this power to convey to us their joyous sense of the splendor of life.

starts out of the Middle Ages and declined in the same mysterious and indefinite way. Usually, however, scholars assign the year 1453, when the Turks seized Constantinople and Christendom collapsed in the East, as the beginning of the true Renaissance period, and 1492, when Charles VIII led the French across the Alps to the invasion of Italy—the same year that Columbus sailed to America—as the culmination; and the place where this extraordinary outburst of human genius was most apparent was Florence. From Florence the movement spread outward through the other city-states of Italy until it engulfed England and the whole of Europe. So in a certain sense the Renaissance created the modern world, the ideas we live by and the culture we follow, and you might even argue that the new cycle of history which began then is ending now, five centuries later.

HER GOLDEN HOUR

Fifteenth Century Florence under Lorenzo de Medici
was an island of intellect and learning
where the Italian Renaissance came to full flower.
Alan Moorehead evokes that glorious city on the Arno
when it was the artistic and cultural center
of all Europe...

In the past several years a vogue for everything Italian has sprung up in the outside world; for Italian movies and fashions, food and textiles and manufactured articles, even for the Italian way of life. Upon tourists in particular, who stream into the country in unbelievable numbers from early spring until late September, the country seems to have exerted a curious fascination, a kind of hunger for escape—not so much a geographic escape as an escape into time, into the past. And the particular moment of the past that appears to captivate visitors more than any other is the 15th Century.

No one has succeeded in explaining why the Italian Renaissance should have happened. It was not a conspiracy nor a religion nor the result of military conquest or of the genius of one man. Behind it lies a thousand years of darkness in Europe, when, with the exception of a few brief enlightened moments, human beings foundered in their own helplessness and ignorance. The marble palaces of the Roman Empire collapsed, and their civilization was buried under the debris. Greek and Latin, the two languages that contained the inspiration and the knowledge of the Classic age, were almost forgotten. Then following upon the Renaissance there was another chaotic period ending with World War II. Just this one bright island stands out in time: an island of intellect and discovery when the human brain flowered more wonderfully than it has ever done before or since, even perhaps in the Fifth Century B.C. in Greece, in the golden age of Pericles.

You cannot draw the exact coastline of this island, for there was no precise beginning or ending of the Renaissance; it emerged very tentatively with many backslidings and false

Florence in 1453 must have been a wonderful place to live in, at any rate for some of the inhabitants, the sort who believed that one crowded hour of glorious life was worth an age without a name. It was a city of roughly a hundred thousand people spread across both banks of the river Arno and enclosed within a circular turreted wall. Brunelleschi had completed his great dome on the cathedral and many of the noblest churches and palaces had already been built. We see them now only through a haze of traffic and crisscrossed wires, but they must have looked remarkably fine when there were no other high rooftops to block the view and in the streets below there were only horsemen and pedestrians. Already the gold doors were up on the baptistery outside the cathedral, Fra Angelico's frescoes had been painted on the walls of San Marco, Donatello's statues were in the Villa Medici, Luca della Robbia's blue-and-white

cherubs cavorted round a dozen fonts and doorways, and the church of San Miniato with its marvelous facade perched on its hill above the city. Across the Arno there were already four or five stone bridges, including the Santa Trinità, possibly the most beautiful bridge that was ever built; and while people trudged through mud in most of the other cities of Europe the Florentine streets were paved. Except that it was much more countrified, the surrounding view was very much as you see it today—a circle of low hills covered with cypress, olives and vineyards.

In all the narrow streets running down to the river tremendous activity was going on. Every other house was the workshop of some craftsman—a goldsmith or a weaver, a furniture maker or a stonemason, an armorer or a potter—and they were producing things of such beauty and originality that later the whole of Europe would copy them.

In their private lives the Florentines were far ahead of their own times and even of the times that succeeded them. They took baths regularly (a habit that was much neglected later on even at such splendid courts as that of Louis XIV in France), and although some of their fashions were capricious—the fabulous three-decker hats of the men, the striped stockings and the puffed-up sleeves—they were often made of the finest silks and velvets; and their everyday dress was either a comfortable loose-fitting gown or a jerkin and breeches.

Among women blond was the admired color, and girls would dye their hair or wear wigs on special occasions. They used cosmetics for their complexions, and although their practice of plucking the hair line above the forehead seems rather ugly now there was a great delicacy and poise about the Florentine women. Artists like Botticelli and Lippo Lippi saw them as slim romantic figures with very clear profiles and a gentle madonna-like sadness in their eyes.

It is true that Florence was swarming with prostitutes at this time, but the family tradition was very strong and no man would lightly have given up his wife and children for a mistress. Prostitution in any case was not yet surrounded by the half-secret squalor and misery of later centuries.

Politically the circumstances were exactly right to bring the Renaissance to its height. The banking family of the Medicis had established a subtle hold on the city, and while they were not yet dictators they were strong enough to keep a stable government going. Outside Florence there was always a latent menace from the two merchant republics of Venice and Genoa in the north, and from the Papacy and the feudal kingdom of Naples in the south, but none of these was powerful enough to attack alone. Although they were constantly maneuvering against themselves and against Florence in a series of petty wars there was a sufficient balance of power to maintain at least a rickety semblance of peace.

The Medicis at this early stage were far more interested in commerce than in conquest, far too involved in the spirit of the new age to sink their talents in corruption. Cosimo, who was the real founder of the family's greatness, was an avid

Florentine drummers, in plumes and pantaloons of 1530, parade in the Piazza della Signoria.

collector of classical manuscripts and of beautiful objects for his houses. He had a passion for the study of Greek philosophy and is said to have died listening to a Platonic discourse. Lorenzo de' Medici was born in 1449, and this perhaps more than any other event made possible the great age of the city that lay ahead.

Lorenzo grew up in his father's palaces and villas under a regime which would horrify a modern schoolboy: a remorseless round of Greek and Latin followed by logic, philosophy, rhetoric, mathematics and history. All this was imbibed at an age when the 20th Century child is still floundering on Caesar's invasion of Gaul. In the Renaissance life burned itself out very quickly. At fifteen or sixteen a boy was a man, and if he happened to be a man like Lorenzo his accomplishments were bewildering. He not only composed verses in the vernacular (and it was some of the first absolutely modern work in poetry), but he wrote and conversed fluently in Latin and was an amateur in half a dozen subjects—in agriculture, in Platonic philosophy, in the study of old coins and inscriptions, in music, painting and architecture. He was a fine horseman and fenced regularly.

This was an age of brilliant all-rounders, and it was not sufficient for a man to excel in any one subject. One of Lorenzo's tutors and companions was Leon Battista Alberti, who wrote comedy in Latin verse at the age of twenty and was considered one of the finest organists of the city. For a time Alberti's passion was philosophy, but then turning to sculpture and architecture he was employed on such works as the Trevi fountain in Rome. His books on these subjects are still regarded as classics. Naturally, too, he painted, and like Leonardo da Vinci he was interested in mechanics, and invented a device for raising sunken ships. In the end the list of Alberti's talents becomes tedious, for he was also a champion swordsman and horseman and was renowned for two special feats: he could jump standing over an upright man and he could fling a coin up to the roof of the cathedral in Florence.

Lorenzo may not have produced such virtuosity as this, but he was perfectly at home in the society of such a man, and when finally, at the age of twenty-one, he took control of the state he not only had the Medici millions behind him, he was also equipped with a brain that enabled him to become the greatest patron of the age.

Probably his chief claim to greatness was his power of bringing out the talents of the people who worked for him. He rejected nothing. He analyzed, encouraged and directed. When the leading scholars of the day came to him, full of ideas for the revival of learning in Greek and Latin, he founded a university for them and established a library. Agents were sent over Italy and the East in search of classical manuscripts. For the artists and sculptors he set up an atelier close to his own palace in Florence. From the architects he commissioned new villas and public buildings. He spent a fortune on jewels, ornaments, rare coins and antiques of every kind. The leading poets and musicians were given benefices and encouraged to perform at his banquets. At his dinner table you could find a geographer like Toscanelli, who held the astonishing theory that it might be

possible to sail around the world, scholars like Ficino, wits like Pulci, painters like Ghirlandajo and Botticelli, sculptors like Donatello, architects like Michelozzo and Bramante (who planned the building of St. Peter's in Rome). Even Michelangelo, the supreme genius of them all, first learned his art under the patronage of Lorenzo in Florence.

The list of the men who were supported by Lorenzo or directly influenced by his reign is fabulous. Very few people in the world today could compete with any in that gathering. With all the wealth and the resources of the modern mind no architect could now be found who could design a building as beautiful as a score of palaces and churches that were built about that time, nor would there be the craftsmen—the mosaicists and the carvers of wood and stone—to embellish it. Equally there exists now no sculptor of the stature of Donatello, no artist like Piero della Francesco (let alone Michelangelo), no poet like Poliziano, no scholar like Pico, no statesman like Lorenzo himself, no political thinker like Machiavelli, no scientist with the inventive genius of Leonardo da Vinci, no explorer like Columbus. Then as the Renaissance spread through Italy there arose a succession of extraordinary talent: Raphael in Rome, Titian, Tintoretto and Giorgioné in Venice, writers like Ariosto, historians like Guicciardini, scientists like Galileo, goldsmiths and sculptors like the rumbustious Cellini.

Even now in the 20th Century, an age of startling discoveries and inventions, it is difficult to comprehend completely the enormous vitality of the Renaissance mind. It was not only that these men had a passion for experiment and an imperative sense that to live they must create—they felt they were on the verge of vast discoveries, as indeed they were. Not only the forgotten past but the unknown future was opening up before them. Dug out of the ruins of Roman cities neglected for a thousand years came marvelous statues and marble carvings. One after another the manuscripts of the classical writers were rediscovered—the lost books of Livy, the lost songs of Sappho —and they revealed a world of which no living man had dreamed before. And remember, too, that the Roman Empire was twice as far away in time from the Renaissance as the Renaissance is from us.

The legend of the girl Julia which spread through Italy in the late 15th Century very well expresses the mood of the city. Julia was said to be a daughter of the emperor Claudius, and she was buried outside Rome on the Appian Way in an airtight tomb which remained unknown and untouched since Roman times. Then one day in April, 1485, the grave was discovered, and when the searchers lifted the lid of the coffin they beheld with awe the figure of the young girl marvelously preserved, with color in her cheeks, her hair still blond—perfectly expressing her ancient beauty.

To the men of Renaissance Florence this seemed a special revelation that their own age was chosen as the great moment for the rebirth of the world. Having gathered the resources of

The bust of Pope Paul III, one of the great figures
of the Renaissance, adorns a hall in the
Palazzo Farnese, which he began building in 1514.

*Alinari Brothers, on the elegant Via Tornabuoni
in Florence, caters to art students and art lovers.*

the past, they penetrated into mysteries which men had hardly dared to approach since the heroic age in Greece.

And for a time the possibilities did in fact seem limitless. When Copernicus and Galileo elucidated the solar system it was possible for explorers to embark on adventures that were impossible before. Columbus and Vasco da Gama, the forerunners of this era of exploration, opened up a world which was as strange then as the moon is to us now. In many other ways, either through the examination of old manuscripts or through new minds at work, science bounded forward in the study of anatomy, in hydraulics, in mathematics, even in the study of aerodynamics. One has only to look at Leonardo's drawings of flying machines, of the structure of plants and the muscles of the human body, to understand something of the universality of the Renaissance mind; at its best it was a combination of logic and poetry, the analysis and the vision, the artist and the scientist and sometimes even the philosopher all combined within a single brain.

Up to this time knowledge was imparted chiefly by word of mouth or through manuscripts laboriously written out on parchment by professional secretaries. But now printing was invented, and this was an even more important event than the development of radio and television in the present century. For the first time in history it became possible to broadcast knowledge over the world, and education was no longer confined to a tiny fraction of people, those in the monasteries and universities.

At the same time great experiment was going on in the arts. Between them Brunelleschi and Michelangelo solved the architectural problem of the unsupported dome. In painting the principles of perspective were realized at last, and artists became absorbed in the study of nature and the nude. In literature three of the greatest of the Italians, Dante, Petrarch and Boccaccio, had already shown the way to a new age in writing—the age that led to Cervantes in Spain, Rabelais in France, Shakespeare in England, Erasmus in Holland and Goethe in Germany.

It seemed indeed that the idea behind the legend of the girl Julia was true: this was the rebirth of the world.

But the most dramatic event—the event that perhaps brings the Renaissance closest to the present century—was the discovery of gunpowder. It was at the time as cataclysmic a thing as the splitting of the atom has been to us. The whole business of war was transformed into something far more terrible and far-reaching than it had ever been before. In addition to being the creator man had now become the destroyer.

Lorenzo plunged into these perilous seas at first with gaiety and then with the disenchanted persistence of middle age. The gay years lasted from 1469 to 1478, from the time he began to reign to the moment, nine years later, when an attempt was made on his life in Florence Cathedral and he was embroiled in war with the Pope and the King of Naples. Within this period he seemed not only to be living out his own youth but making Florence youthful as well. Morally no doubt it was deplorable. He squandered hundreds of thousands of florins (those handsome Florentine coins which his grandfather had made the most solid currency in Europe) on jousts and carnivals, employing the finest artists of the day on the most frivolous decorations. As these carousals succeeded one another through the summer nights it was Lorenzo himself who composed the bawdiest of songs and sang them to the public in the streets.

A thousand people would be invited to a banquet and the festivities would go on for perhaps three days and nights. It was not a period of outright debauchery—people were much too excited by their own lives for that—but the emphasis was always upon the idea that there was not much time. Life had to be enjoyed and burned up quickly before it was too late.

This was made painfully clear on the morning of April 26, 1478, when Lorenzo and his younger brother Giuliano went to attend Mass in Florence Cathedral. Lorenzo was well aware that he had made enemies. He had pursued the ancient policy of destroying his most powerful rivals in the city government, notably the Pazzi family, and promoting lesser people in their places. But he did not know that the Pazzis, encouraged by Pope Sixtus IV in Rome, had arranged on this particular morning to fall on him just at the moment of the ceremony when the Host was raised. The Pazzis, however, were not quite quick enough. They killed Giuliano but only managed to wound Lorenzo slightly in the neck before he escaped to the sacristy. The events that followed—the hanging of the conspirators, the excommunication of Lorenzo and the war with the Pope, even the final signing of the peace after Lorenzo had gone alone into the enemy's camp to make terms—are not much more than a repetition of the usual pattern of the teacup wars that bedeviled Italy at this time. Their real importance is in their effect on Lorenzo and Florence. The fecklessness and a good deal of the gaiety goes out of life: the adolescence is over and the middle age of the city begins, the period that throws out its steady light all over Italy.

In the last fourteen years of Lorenzo's career the university and the library became world-famous, and scholars journeyed to them from all over Europe. The churches and the palaces became filled with such a galaxy of paintings, sculptures and ornaments that not even the lootings, the decay, and the occasional indifference of five centuries have been able to disturb Florence's position as one of the great treasure houses of the modern world.

More important still, the tradition of humanism was established: the idea that the proper study of mankind is man himself. Life, to the humanist, was not a delusion, nor a short and wretched business to be got through as quickly as possible; life was an aim in itself, and they believed that it could be made a work of art.

Lorenzo suffered from inherited gout, and through these fourteen years he was often in pain. Early in 1492 it was evident that he was dying; and there is a predestined and symbolic quality about his death. He was only forty-three, and now that it was clear that all his years of passionate inquiry and experiment had never revealed the final answer to the mystery, he sent for a priest (according to Poliziano it was Savonarola himself), confessed his sins and received the benediction.

For Florence it was more than the death of another ruler; it was the end of an era and there was an immense foreboding in people's minds. The questions now were of a different kind. Had they not in fact gone too far and too fast under Lorenzo? Was man alone really able to command these mysteries? These journeyings of Columbus into outer space, for example: were they not flying in the face of nature, leading men on to places where they had no right to go? Was the invention of printing such a marvelous boon after all? Or did it mean that any sort of rubbish could now be disseminated wholesale through the world?

Worse still, gunpowder. Where would that lead? Would it create power for the building of new roads and cities? Or would it end in blowing the whole world to bits?

We have as yet no notion as to what the end of our own moment of history will be, but it is interesting to note what happened in Florence in 1492. In a sharp spasm of guilt and fear the people crept back to the Cathedral to listen to the blood-and-thunder sermons of Savonarola. They made a public bonfire of their exotic clothes and vanities, and huddled in dismay waiting for the deluge to descend and engulf them.

The deluge in the end turned out to be nothing worse than Charles VIII crossing the Alps into Italy, and presently in a more chastened spirit the Renaissance went on its way again. Other voyagers like Vasco da Gama appeared, other scientists like Harvey and Newton, other artists and architects, and a whole new world of music in Germany. And although never again has there been such an inspired combination of the artist and the scientist as there was in 15th Century Florence, the same spirit of inquiry has continued right down to the invention of the last hydrogen bomb.

One wonders, of course, if underneath all that brilliance the majority of the people in 15th Century Italy lived really satisfactory lives. Certainly the average Renaissance man (if there could have been such a creature) does not compare very favorably with the modern mass-produced man, with his mass habits and his mass ideas. The modern man is healthier and taller than his ancestor and he lives longer. He is probably more widely (if not more deeply) educated, freer of superstitions and less chained to the drudgery of living. Yet there was an element of creation in the everyday life of Florence which is sometimes lacking now—and it is possible that in the end this sense of creation, of being a thinking individual and not just one of the crowd, is the main craving of the human spirit. The crowd offers security but it makes a prison, too.

So perhaps there is a certain reassurance now in turning back to this time in Florence when all things were new and the emphasis lay not on machines but on the individual genius in man and his courage in venturing out into the unknown. This then may be the thing that is drawing so many people back to Italy and back to the Renaissance: this need they have to rediscover their own roots, the beginnings of their own emotions and ambitions. After five hundred years they have come home again.

Thunder clouds loom above the Ponte Vecchio in Florence.

ROME

Rome is still the treasure house of the past—
the ancient city of the Caesars, of the Forum,
the Coliseum and the Holy See. But here
Aubrey Menen writes of the new young Rome,
the modern metropolis where the present lives within
and beside the past, and where a vigorous young nation
is building literally on the foundation of
two thousand years ago.

Rome is young. It was not built in a day, but most of it was built in the last ten years. The Caesars lived here, the Sovereign Pontiffs still do. But the figure in history who has done most to shape this city today is Henry Ford.

This is the truth. You may escape it if you want to, as I did, for a while. To do that you should move about in a square mile or so of palaces, classical ruins and narrow streets. It is called Old Rome. I live in it. I came here three years ago because I wanted to study the past. But after a while I found that most of what we call history cannot be believed, and what is true cannot really be liked. So I let the dead past bury its dead and looked about me at the world today. Instead of the past I studied the present. I am very glad I did.

At first I did not look for the present in Rome. I visited a dozen other cities, some in Europe, some in America, two in Africa. I admired skyscrapers in Cairo, roads in New York and machinery in Milan. But whenever I came back to Rome, I was shut in the past again. It could not be avoided. I lived in a road lined with ancient palaces. Dead Caesars were carried past my door on the way to their funeral pyres, and each morning I was awakened by the bells of the oldest churches in the Christian world.

Then, one morning, I was wakened a little earlier. It was still dark. The bells had not yet begun to ring. But an errand boy was walking down the street, whistling. The tune was catching, but it did not sound very Italian. Besides, the boy had not yet learned it properly. The next morning he was better at it. The next, better still. On the fourth morning, he walked down my antique street whistling the tune without a mistake from beginning to end and so could I. It was a bouncing, fresh little tune that raised my spirits.

He whistled it every morning for the next week, and I would lie in bed looking at the dark shapes of the palaces through my window and whistling with him. I grew very fond of the melody. It reminded me of the bright, fresh things I had seen on my travels in the world of today. Then, one morning, he did not come, nor the next, nor the next. I waited for him, hoping

The beams of a Roman moon shed haunting light
on the Temple of Saturn and on the other relics of
the Forum which dazzled the ancient
world. In the distance looms the Colosseum.

St. Peter's, Vatican City: *The world's largest Christian church in the world's smallest state.*

to hear him with an intensity that surprised me. He never came again. It was left to bells once more to wake me, and they rang, for me, very drearily. I would get up, open the window, and glower at the palaces on either side of the street. Living in the past, I was seized by a profound nostalgia for the present.

I dislike all nostalgias. They are the subtlest form of self-pity. So I took myself in hand. I was living in an ancient city and I determined to do something to fit the fact. A card had come inviting me to the celebration of the anniversary of the founding of the city. I accepted and went.

The audience was made up of civilized, cultured Romans, all with a deep sense of history, since they were members of learned societies. The celebration was held in a place sacred with memories, the Capitoline Hill. Ambassadors, prelates, scholars and men with ancient names were there, surrounded by gorgeously uniformed retainers. We sat in a great painted hall in the Palace of the Conservators, once the rulers of Rome. We had been ushered up purple-carpeted steps by footmen in historic livery. We were the élite. Everything led me to expect a most impressive morning. In fact the ceremony turned out to be a flop. I am told that it always does.

The mayor of Rome was in the chair, the latest representative of the Caesars. Perhaps he was, after all, not so bad a representative. Some of the Caesars ran to fat; some of them made chaffing speeches; many, I imagine, scratched their rumps when listening to orators. Some, too, I'm sure, made a glorious muddle of a great occasion. This one made the worst I have ever seen.

Rome gives prizes to scholars each year for essays on history, for bibliographical studies, and for essays in classical Latin. As he gave away the awards, the mayor dropped the illuminated scrolls, grabbed silver wolves by their hindquarters, got names backward. Then he awarded the prize for Latin. "It has been won," he said, "by Father ——" He stopped. He squinted at the list in his hands. A Jesuit priest, smiling nervously, got up from my row and went forward. "By Father ——" said the representative of the Caesars. He looked up at us. "On the list it just says Father—and then blank," he complained. Father Blank hesitated in the aisle, blushed, and swallowed heavily. The rest of us tittered.

"Well," said the mayor, a man of action down to his last straining waistcoat button, "let's say it was awarded to a Father. Come forward, Father whoever-you-are. My congratulations." Father whoever-he-was tripped over his soutane, accepted a document, and enjoyed what the mayor had left him of a moment of glory for which he may have studied and composed for twenty years. Father whoever-he-was returned to his seat, red in the face, with our chuckles in his ears.

We were not cruel. We were bored. We had listened to a scholar telling us at length that Rome had been the tutor to the world. Another had described how proud he was to be a Roman and the mayor had described how proud he was to be a mayor. We were grateful for a touch of life in a dead morning.

I left before the ceremony ended. I walked down the empurpled stairs, past the liveried footmen, out into the fresh air. I sat on the steps of the church of the Ara Coeli and looked out over the ruins of the Forum. I remembered that the historian Edward Gibbon had sat on these same steps, looked at the same panorama and made up his mind to write the history of Rome's decline and fall. I reflected that he must have been in the same mood as I was, for in his view history was little but the record of the crimes and follies of mankind. I thought he might have added that the crimes and follies are monotonously alike.

That evening I was a guest at an entertainment. I use that word because I do not know a better one to describe the gathering of like souls that are the basis of upper-class social life in Rome. Since one goes in the evening, leaves before dinner, and one drinks, I suppose they are cocktail parties. No cocktails are served and there is no party spirit. The Romans call them *ricevimenti*, which means receptions, and that is altogether too grand a word. It suggests women in long white gloves and jewels, and shaking hands at the top of the stairs. Perhaps they were like this once. But long white gloves are now made only for the export market, and jewels went in the war. In all but the great families, Roman social life is very modest.

In Rome, too, as you enter the room, you see a circle of people and some empty seats, a circle of welcoming smiles and inviting looks. If you are lucky, there is someone who wouldn't mind if you sat beside them. The rest are wondering if you are going to wreck their evening. For once in a seat you may not, you cannot move. To get to your feet, except for an introduction, is a social crime, however long the entertainment lasts.

To be at your ease in polite Roman society, you must have, like diplomats, an iron seat and, like royalty, an infinite capacity for not wanting to go to the bathroom. As I was being introduced, I noticed a man whom I had seen at the morning's celebrations on the Capitoline Hill—and there was a vacant chair beside him. When my hostess released me I made for the chair. There were no hisses, though I thought I detected some sighs of relief, and I at once began: "Professor, I saw you this morning ——"

"At the ceremony, yes," he said. "You were looking bored."

He was, I suppose, about forty, slender-faced, with beautiful hands. His Italian was Roman, and that is to say he spoke the most musical language in the world, for the Roman prides himself on the lilt of his dialect and to keep it he will cheerfully murder the grammar of the language. I was aware that, to his ear, my Italian would sound like the grinding of a cement mixer. In as musical a tone as I could muster, I said:

"I was trying to concentrate on the grandeur of your eternal city. I didn't succeed very well."

"For three hours?" he said. "What a lesson you foreigners are to us flighty Italians. I can manage about five minutes. The mayor couldn't manage three."

"I noticed you looked very absorbed. I envied you."

"I was thinking of girls," he said. "I always do at functions."

I had no reason to doubt him. Every morning I read the best Roman daily newspapers. Each, on page three, has an array of scholarly essays on history, art, archaeology and similar topics. They are very erudite. But the page, without fail, is illustrated by pictures of bathing beauties and juvenile film actresses.

"I find," I said "I am growing a little tired of the past myself. Perhaps it's because in Rome there's so much of it."

He smiled. "It's my job to see that there's a great deal more. When anything is dug up I am one of the people who have to go and see it. I'm supposed to stop it being destroyed."

"Have they discovered anything recently?"

"They discover something about once a week," he said, sipping sweet liqueur from a tiny glass. "More often than that, for all I know."

"Do you mean that they dig things up and don't tell you?"

"Certainly. The things that are dug up nowadays are nearly all tombs. If the building contractors told me, I'd have to preserve them. If the contractors had any sense of history, Rome would be one big graveyard. Fortunately, they haven't. Two years ago they unearthed a Christian catacomb. It was too big to hide, so we stopped the building operations. It was discovered in the foundation of what was to be an apartment block for rehousing the poor. Two hundred men were thrown out of work and fifty people waited one year more to see the sun and air and sleep less than four in a room."

"What happened in the end?"

"That is an official secret." He changed the subject. "What do you do in Rome?"

"I—I write."

"Books?"

I nodded. My heart sank. The evening was ruined, I knew, for as any Roman will tell you, Romans do not read books.

The river god, Nile, reclines beside a colonnaded pool, one of three still left on the splendid 2nd century villa of the Emperor Hadrian.

They are the despair of publishers and they glory in it. He talked for a while of books in the manner of a man who has no intention of opening one, and very soon we were reduced to the trivialities that people talk when they have nothing in common. Soon a woman on my left was gossiping with the professor across my breast. Later, when at last we rose to go, he said: "Where do you live?"

"In Old Rome, professor."

"I see. And you're bored with it?"

"At the moment, yes, very."

"I quite understand," he said. "It often bores me too. When it does, do you know what I do?"

"You think of girls."

"No. I get in my car and go for a drive round new Rome—the one they're building outside the walls. I think you will find it beautiful. I do. Don't tell anyone I said so or they'll think I'm a Philistine and I shall lose my job. But take my advice. Go and see it."

Some time later, very much by chance, I did.

The wind, I remember, had failed. It is called the *ponente,* and it determines the mood of Romans more than anything else—more than love, more than money, more than the news of the day, which few Romans think about unless it is scandalous. The *ponente* blows in the evening. It is a light wind and it comes trickling into the narrow streets of Old Rome like a refreshing drink. The sun sets, the lights go on, and everybody, save the bedridden and the people in jail, goes out for a walk. You walk along the streets, you walk in the piazzas, you walk under the trees in the Pincian Gardens. You do not sit in cafés, unless you are imitating foreigners or you are with elderly women. Coffee costs money, and sitting still is a tremendous effort for a Roman when out of his house. He prefers to be on the move: to go from place to place, usually without any purpose at all.

His mind, like the professor's, will be on girls, whom he will eye from head to foot. I do not know for sure what Roman women think about when they are strolling because I am too shy to ask, but I should imagine that, if they are girls, they reciprocate, and if they are married women I suppose they worry about the girls their husbands are looking at. I would, I know. In the early evening in Rome, unfaithfulness is in the air. There is a play of eyes, of glances, of slight turning of pretty heads that must be very disturbing to a mother of a family. For others, it is a delight.

A delight, that is, to be enjoyed only when the wind blows. When it doesn't, the game is off. The air grows heavy, one's step is less jaunty, the streets seem narrower than ever. The men still eye the girls—I have seen them do it from doorways even in a cloudburst—but the girls look fierce and gaze straight ahead.

At such times I usually take my evening walk by the Tiber. On the evening I am describing, I walked farther along the

banks than I had ever done before. I walked, as I thought, right out of Rome. The road ended abruptly at the gates of a gas works. I turned off left and immediately I was lost. The neighborhood was shabby, ill-lit and profoundly depressing, even, I fancied, when the *ponente* blew. I walked more quickly. I got more lost. But ahead of me I saw brilliant lights, surprisingly high in the sky. I made for them. In a few moments I came out of the slums into the Piazza of the Navigators. It is named after the Italian seamen who discovered much of the New World. When I looked around me, I was almost as astonished as they.

The Piazza of the Navigators is a vast hemicycle of new buildings, perhaps a third of a mile across. The buildings are massive and run up to fifteen stories. The center building is crowned with a gigantic electric sign, the light that I saw in the sky. At the foot of these buildings runs an arcade, dazzling with more electric signs and brilliantly lit shop windows. From the open side of the hemicycle runs a wide road that leads, after several miles, straight to the sea. On this evening, one side of it seemed a river of rubies, because it was filled with swiftly moving automobiles, while the other side ran with gold from their headlamps.

I had never seen it before. I told myself it could not be Rome. But I looked about me and there were Romans in the arcade, walking to and fro, doing nothing, eying the girls. And there was a breeze. It was not the *ponente*. It came, I suppose, up the wide road from the sea.

As the professor had foreseen, I found it beautiful. It was brash, but I was enchanted with the lights, the size, the spaciousness. I felt alive. I wondered if I had felt so alive in Rome since I came there. In the middle of the piazza that honored the great discoverers, I made a discovery myself. I found that I was, at heart, vulgar. I thought this called for a drink in celebration, and I made for one of the bars. As I approached its chrome, glass and neon front my joy was completed. From out of the doorway came the thump and bounce of music from a loud-speaker, and it was playing the song that the errand boy used to whistle under my window every morning.

I went in. The bar was shiningly clean. A tall pillar in the center ran up to its high ceiling. On the sides of the pillar were ceramic reliefs, brightly colored, making fun of the more portentous episodes of Roman history.

I examined the ceramics and decided that the Roman dignitaries in togas were perfect portraits of the Romans that Juvenal and Martial describe. I went to the bar and ordered my drink. The bartender was polite enough to serve it, although I should have bought a ticket at the cash desk first.

The music was coming from a jukebox. I downed my drink to give me courage, and for the first time in my life I put a coin in one of these much-criticized machines.

I found that it was all very pretty. It is much better than having a violin played in your eye and slipping money into the violinist's trouser pocket, which is the chic thing to do in the part of Rome where I live. There are knobs, dials and twinkling lights, like some inaccessibly expensive toy that one saw as a child going Christmas shopping.

Colleagues: *Souvenir vendors in St. Peter's Square.*

But I am letting my memory run away with me. I did not, in fact, put my first coin in a jukebox with my own hands. I was much too stupid to follow all the instructions. A young boy next to me very kindly did the thing for me. He then asked me, with an apprehensive look, what tune I would like.

"That one that's just finished playing."

He beamed. I was delighted that my taste had been approved. Machinery turned, arms wove complicated patterns, and from a gold-and-silver grid worthy to be a screen in a Roman emperor's palace came my errand boy's song.

The record, to my surprise, was in English. The voice was innocent, the sentiments most worldly. "Bernardine," said the gold-and-silver grill, "Bernardine! *All your separate parts are not unknown, but the way you assemble 'em's all your own.*"*

I laughed. Some ten Romans—men, boys, girls, standing round about me—laughed too. When the record was finished, it occurred to me that it was most unlikely that any one of them would have understood a single line of the song. The tune elated them, as it had elated me each morning when it woke me in Old Rome.

I looked round the group. "Do any of you speak English?" I asked. All of them shook their heads, except one man.

"Yes. I speak it," he said. At once I knew I had made a mistake. In any casual group of Romans, in the piazzas, on the streets, in a trolleycar or in a bar like this, there is always one man who understands foreigners. Most Romans do not care for foreigners. They are not to be blamed. The majority of strangers in Rome are pilgrims, and people saying their prayers are interesting to Heaven and themselves alone. The rest come to look at the ruins. The Roman regards this as a worthy thing, but looking at the monuments of the dead gives the eyes a certain glaze that persists even when looking at the living.

The Roman finds this offensive. But there are some, like the natty little man who now elbowed his way to my side, to whom foreigners are a blessing. Foreigners can, with ease, be bamboozled, lectured, reprimanded or seduced. These things cannot be done to Romans without considerable effort.

He began with a reprimand. "You shouldn't be playing tunes like that trash," he said. "Italy is the land of music. We have the most beautiful songs in the world." He whistled, flat, a bar or two of *O Sole Mio*. "Now that," he said, "is real melody."

He fiddled with the knob of the jukebox, felt for a coin in his pockets, accepted the one I offered him with nimble fingers, and found a selection of old Neapolitan songs. They were largely about broken hearts, poverty and faithless women. A profound gloom settled on the bar. The group round the jukebox drifted away.

I made polite remarks in Italian. He answered in the same language. After three records of melancholy laced with treacle, he said, "What brings a gentleman like you to a low, vulgar place like this?"

"I got lost."

"Lost?" he said, with a flash of his teeth. "Suppose now I put you on the right path for . . . for an evening's entertainment, eh? I know one or two places in the center of town which are more fit for foreigners than a place like this."

*Music and lyrics by Johnny Mercer. Reprinted by permission, © Palm Springs Music Co.

"Which ones?"

The jukebox stopped playing. The happy friends of Bernardine were drifting out of the bar. Something had to be done.

He named some night clubs that I, in common with most Romans, had never been to.

"I've heard," I said, with a knowing look, "of a place at 42 Fontanella Borghese."

"Ah-ha!" said my persecutor. "That's the very spot to have a high old time. I've often been there with my friends," he winked.

"I'm interested to hear it," I said. "It happens to be my house. You and your gay friends must drop in some time. But I must warn you I usually go to bed at ten o'clock." I handed him my visiting card.

Since the butchering of Christians was put down, the only cruel sport that is left in Rome is the public and abject humiliating of one Roman by another. It is a sport with a great following, and every Roman from the age of eleven is an *aficionado*. A thrust such as mine—and it was, though I say it myself, quintessentially Roman—is greeted with long, loud, jeering laughter. I was rewarded with repeated salvos of this sort of applause.

"You look like a Roman. Are you?", I asked a boy.

"Roman of Romans. My father is, too, and so's my grandfather."

He spoke proudly, as he should. Three generations of Romans is nowadays a span to boast of.

"Do you go to school?"

"No. I work in a filling station."

"What are you going to be when you grow up?"

"A Teddy boy."

He used the English phrase to the delight of his listeners.

"What are you going to do when you're a Teddy boy?"

He brushed back the hair from his forehead. His black eyes grew intense with anticipated joys. "Run around in gangs."

"Doing what?"

"Wearing blujins. My father won't let me wear blujins yet."

Blue jeans (the word is pronounced with neat Italian vowels) are slowly making their way in Rome. Boys wearing them are frowned upon by their elders.

The boy at the knobs looked up at me, his dark eyes dancing. He had the round face and flopping curls that marked the Roman boy even in the times of the Renaissance. "Enjoying yourself?" he said.

"Very much. What's your name?"

"Nino."

"How old are you?"

"Thirteen."

"What crimes are you going to commit?"

His eyes sparkled. "Play flippers."

Every Roman is unshakably convinced that Americans call pinball machines flippers. Playing pinballs is considered by the older generation a vice so terrible that they have succeeded in having them prohibited by the police. Clandestine clubs in cellars have sprung up where adolescents furtively tread the primrose path, for joy, not money, since the boys do not bet.

"You like American things?"

He frowned. "American?"

"Yes. Blue jeans are American. So are pin—I mean flippers. That rock-and-roll record you have just put on is an American tune."

He looked away. He gave a quick little yawn, a sign among Roman boys that one is talking nonsense to them. I realized then that, to him, since he had never known Rome without them, such things were Roman.

It was eleven o'clock. The barman told us it was time to go.

Outside, the Piazza of the Navigators was still bustling with life. The great red sign still blazed. The cars were even thicker upon the road.

"I'm glad I lost my way," I said to Nino.

"Would you like to come again? I can show you the new houses. They're *bello—bello—bello*."

"All right. When?"

"Sometime. When you're this way again. Good night."

I found a taxi. I drove into Old Rome. I stopped the taxi near my house, for I felt I wanted to stretch my legs before I went to bed. I walked a little, then turned into the vast courtyard of the Borghese Palace. Fountains were playing. Great statues of Roman goddesses stood on plinths, broad-beamed and serene.

I stood in front of one of them, as I had done a hundred times before, admiring them. But the tune of *Bernardine* was running in my head. I hummed it. I thought of the words. Suddenly the goddess seemed very funny. I sang to her: "All your separate parts are not unknown, but the way you assemble 'em's all your own."

The policeman on guard recognized me. "Have you had a happy evening, sir?"

"Very, very happy, officer."

"A reception?"

"No. I've been seeing Rome."

"They say, sir," he remarked sagely, "that there's always something you haven't seen in Rome, even if you live here a hundred years."

"There certainly is, officer," I said. "There certainly is."

I suppose a housing settlement of great concrete buildings does not come within the province of beautiful things. But to me, standing there and remembering Garbatella, it seemed more beautiful than the palaces that line my street. I thought so then. I have just got up from my desk and looked out of the window at Prince Ruspoli's palace and Prince Borghese's palace, and I think so still.

But on the day that I first saw new Rome—or a single part of it, for there are a dozen of these new Romes ringing the old city—there was one thing wrong with it. There were hardly any residents. There were a few people on the balconies and terraces. They were mostly elderly. It was plain that all the apartments were inhabited, but nobody came in or out of the marble entrances, and the brand-new streets were deserted.

I asked Nino's father about it.

"Well," he said, "today's a national holiday, you see."

"I know," I said, "but wouldn't that mean that more people than usual would be at home?"

"Twenty years ago," said Nino's father, "you *had* to stay at home on a holiday, otherwise Mama or Grandmama would be offended. Now nobody does unless they're ill."

Nino looked down a road wistfully. He pointed to the west. "They've all gone to Ostia," he said. "I was going, too, but we hadn't any money in the house, so we went to church."

"They're due back about now," said Nino's uncle, once more embarrassed. "Let's stroll about for a while and watch."

We strolled. We went into a bar. I returned the hospitality that had been offered to me, and we watched. Ostia is the nearest seaside to the city, and about seven o'clock the return from the beaches began. It is an astonishing sight.

The roads slowly fill with hundreds upon hundreds of small family cars, mostly all alike. Packed into each are families of six or seven, bronzed, in beach dress, and inebriated with hours under the Mediterranean sun. They wave, they shout, they sing the latest songs. The cars stop at their houses and they tumble out, clatter up the marble staircases, pour into their apartments, fling open the balcony doors and come out onto the terraces to snatch the last pleasures of the day.

"And over there," said Nino's father, "is the Cristoforo Colombo."

The Cristoforo Colombo is a wide arterial road, with six lanes of traffic, that runs from the Piazza of the Navigators straight to the sea. It is the Tiber of modern Rome. The Tiber has lost its romance for the contemporary Roman. He barely mentions it, and then only in connection with traffic jams and suicides by drowning. But the six concrete ribbons of the Cristoforo Colombo have won his affection and engaged his pride.

The lanes on the far side of the dividing strip were filled with returning cars. The side that led to the sea was empty. A fast car making an evening trip to Ostia shot past us.

"Wow-aah!" said Nino, imitating its noise. He gazed after it, his eyes gleaming. "If only I could go in a car like that."

The very next week he did, because I took him. In the months that followed I hired every sort of car. I took Nino to Ostia, I took his father, his uncle, his mother, Nino's friends and my own. I no longer walked along the Tiber when the *ponente* failed. I rang the garage. Within fifteen minutes I was at the gates of Rome. In eighteen minutes more I saw the sea. Two more minutes and I was at Ostia. Rome has become a city by the sea.

Old Ostia is a stretch of ruins that nobody I know goes to see and to which I have so far never been myself. I pass it, usually at ninety miles an hour. New Ostia is a rabble of concrete buildings. Architecturally, it is a disaster. No Roman cares. Old Rome has the finest architecture in the world, and it is precisely that from which he wants to get away. New Ostia is ugly, vulgar and alive.

In any case, you do not stay there. You bathe, you eat sea food, clamber back into the car and spin farther along the coast. There are great pine woods that once belonged to kings. I have been shown their delights by Nino and his friends. I have hunted wild asparagus and taken it to a restaurant, had it cooked and eaten it with melted butter. I have picked the prickly red fruit they call a sea cherry and tasted its strange blend of the sweetness of fruit and the bitterness of the sea. I have hunted rabbits and watched the sky flat on my back under a pine tree. I have startled lovers. For young Romans, the pine woods are more part of the city than the Forum, in which most of them have never set foot.

I have even been to the rocky promontory called San Felice Circeo: it is known as the Capri of Rome, but it is not, thank heaven, like Capri except for the shape of its mountain. Everybody runs away from Rome, but some refined and expensive people find Ostia too coarse. They go to a hotel by the sea in San Felice, where they sun-bathe, water-ski, and in the evenings dance, secure that nobody will be in the hotel but their own sort. I explored this hotel a little. It is well appointed, and I was charmed to find that the refined Roman dances to the music of a jukebox. It was just an ordinary jukebox. Nobody had thought of adapting the mechanism to make it four times as expensive. Rich and poor alike pay fifty lire—about eight cents—to hear a tune.

The Cristoforo Colombo and the regular exodus have changed the whole Roman way of life. The road, and others like it, were completed just at the time when Italian engineers had applied their resourcefulness to the methods invented by Henry Ford, and produced vehicles which even the ordinary Italian could afford to buy. They produced the tiny automobile called the *Topolino*—the Mouse, a family car that costs little to run—and above all the motor scooter, which almost everybody in regular employment can afford.

Motoring immediately became a passion. The Roman, as I have said, does not like to sit still. Here was an ideal means of keeping on the go. He has even found a way of looking at the girls while he drives. He drives slowly beside her (the only time he will drive slowly), makes a Roman remark, and speeds off before she can slap his face. As an example, for those whom it may interest, I may quote a friend of mine who selects women who are plentifully endowed and remarks, in the politest of voices: "Young lady, tell me, does all that belong to you?"

The modern Romans enjoy their city, but periodically they empty it. The result is that Rome is the one capital city in Europe or America with only the vestiges of a theater. There are very few of them. They are open intermittently and they have been left to the intellectuals, who have succeeded in driving out ever the customers who, not yet having bought a motorcar, still kept up the habit of theater-going. The cinemas are so badly hit that in the summer most of them close down, while on a fine day in winter (and Rome has many) they are barely a third full. The opera, which used to depend on the well-heeled middle class, is now resigned to living off the foreigner. On one night, usually a Saturday opera tickets are cheaper, and on that night the modest Roman music lover used to attend in throngs. It is now the modest tourist. The native music lovers are all by the sea, or driving in the country, loving music by means of transistor radios.

Perhaps the greatest change that Henry Ford and modern road-making machinery have brought about is in the social life of Rome. The capital has been for centuries the seat of the greatest families of Italy. They had their own way of living, which largely consisted in impressing the rest of the Romans that they had an aristocratic disdain for money. But the great families were great landowners, and land, especially near the old limits of the city, has grown to be immensely valuable. The princes and princesses have dropped their well-bred disdain for cash (since there is so much to be made) and are rapidly turning themselves into landlords and landladies. I do not know what the Roman nobility talked about before the change. But I am told that it was the latest fashion from Paris, the latest shows in London, horses, hunting, marriage and adultery. They also had a continuous flow of private witticisms which were quite unamusing except to themselves. From my experience among them in Rome today, their conversation consists of the rental values of seaside villas, how to add a story to accommodate more people and what so-and-so said to such-a-one about where the new arterial road was really going to be built.

The change has its good side. Roman nobility has developed a pragmatical way of talking that I find pleasing. I once drove with a princess, the head of one of the most celebrated families of Rome, across her large estate on the other side of the Tiber. She is the Princess Doria-Pamphily and her name is Orietta. She is in the prime of life and beautiful.

Another person in the car was bent on making an impression. "Orietta," he said as we drove along. "What a lovely house! What do you do with it?"

"Let it. Are you looking for somewhere to live?"

He was not. We drove on in silence. Then he tried again. "Orietta," he said. "All this superb grassland. And the Roman sun. It must make wonderful hay. What do you do with it all?"

"Sell it," said the Princess. "Do you, by any chance, keep horses?"

It is as well that the head of so distinguished a family is a practical woman. I have just seen the large-scale maps of Rome's new system of encircling roads. A wide bypass will be driven right through the heart of her ancestral estates.

I think the upper stratum of Roman society will adapt itself to the new middle-class Rome of outings to the sea, small cars and suburbs. Indeed, I know they will. There is a restaurant to which I sometimes take visitors. It is a place where the gilded youth of Rome gathers in the evening. A short while ago an Italian who had returned home after many years in South America asked the guitarist to play some of the old Italian songs. The guitarist obliged with a heart-breaking song about somebody's mamma. The returned Italian sang it, in a sweet tenor. In the Piazza of the Navigators, the younger generation had merely moved toward the door for air. Here the young men all took out their handkerchiefs, buried their faces in them and heaved their shoulders as though they were moved to uncontrollable tears. The Roman is an excellent clown when he chooses: he is proud of the fact. The song died away. The returned Italian fell silent. The guitarist struck up another song which the young men greeted by cheering. It was not *Bernardine*, but it was an excellent Italian imitation of it.

But there is one group in Rome who will never, I feel, adapt themselves. These are the diplomats and their wives. A diplomat is, by profession, a man who is surrounded by every possible obstacle to getting to know the people in whose country he is living. Some do manage it, but not in the new Rome.

I went to a diplomatic party and listened for most of the evening to a woman who complained about her domestic staff. In the past, she said, it had been her custom to chat with them in their free time; she felt it helped her husband, the minister. Now they were never in the house except when compelled to be there for the sake of their jobs. They were out and away "on those dreadful scooters. It makes me feel very lonely. I don't seem to know the Italians any more."

I suggested a visit to Ostia on a Sunday afternoon. She had done it. She was a woman with a sense of duty, and she had gone. It had not taught her much. She had felt, if anything, more remote from the Italians than ever. Later, talking to her son (who ran a scooter), I learned that she had gone in the minister's car with its *Corps diplomatique* license plates.

A camera and a guidebook can be as much a barrier to knowing the New Roman as a diplomatic license plate. All that side of Roman life has no interest for the new Romans. Thousands of them do not come to the center of the city for months on end. New Rome is building its own suburban life, a more vigorous, more happy, more healthy way of living than Rome has known for centuries. New Rome is the thing which concerns, as I have shown, the Pope, princesses, scholars, priests, and everyone else down to bricklayers and filling-station hands. Put aside your guidebook and go see it. Perhaps it will dismay you. But you will return to the tourist sights with a better comprehension of what they meant to the men who built them. The romantically beautiful Spanish Steps were a piece of development. They were built to replace a patch of wasteland surrounded by hovels. A rabble of houses and a decaying palace were destroyed to make the wide and fashionable Via Veneto. The Piazza del Popolo was deliberately designed to make a grand finale to one of the roads that lead into Rome, precisely as the architects of today have designed the Piazza of the Navigators. The Imperial Forums, whose vast ruins are still noble, replaced the slums of a place called, in classical times, the Subura. The sweeping colonnades of Bernini before St. Peter's were intended to liberate the basilica from a warren of nondescript buildings, two of which remained down to the days of my boyhood. In the very heart of the city, under the Capitoline Hill, are the ruins of a Roman apartment house, a relic of another time when the population of Rome was bounding upward. The Via Giulia, the street in Rome most evocative of the past, was, in fact, a piece of planned urban development initiated by a Pope who detested the crooked streets and airless buildings of the city. Some of Rome has always been new.

As for Old Rome, there is some talk of banning traffic from it and making it a sort of historical reservation. If they do, my apartment will be very quiet, which is a good thing for a writer. As for me, I shall move: probably to Ostia.

Street scene: *Rome, by the Theater of Marcellus.*

Greece

"To the Greeks life seems a fine and inexhaustible thing," remarked the late Nikos Kazantzakis, greatest of modern Greek writers. "To love life, despite poverty, hunger and misfortune—this is one of the great traits of the Greek people..."

Before I take you with me, to travel through and get acquainted with Greece, let me tell you an incident that shows what hospitality means in Greece. This is not a story I heard from others; it happened to me.

A few years ago I was wandering through the mountains of Crete, alone, with a staff in my hand and a knapsack over my shoulder. At twilight I came near a village. Here I would have to spend the night. I entered the village as darkness fell; dogs began to bark, doors opened as I passed, women came out to see what stranger could be coming at such an hour. Where should I go? Whose door should I knock on to ask hospitality? Naturally, I turned where every stranger finds refuge—to the home of the priest.

As a rule, village priests in Greece are not highly educated; their learning is small, but they do have basic Christian virtues, and in every stranger who knocks on their door they see Christ and they open it for Him gladly.

So I knocked on the priest's door. The door opened and I saw an old man with a snow-white beard and long hair hanging down to his shoulders. He gave me his hand. "Welcome," he said. "Please come in."

I entered. I heard voices, doors opening and shutting. A couple of women darted into the next room and disappeared. The priest bade me sit on the sofa.

"You must excuse my wife," he said. "She isn't feeling well. I will cook your dinner and make your bed." His voice was heavy and sad. He was very pale, and his eyes were swollen and red.

I ate and slept, and in the morning the priest brought me a tray with bread, cheese and milk. Then I gave him my hand, thanked him and said good-by.

"Go to God's blessing, my child," he said. "Christ be with you."

At the edge of the village I saw an old man. He greeted me, palm on chest. "And where did you spend the night, my son?" he asked.

"At the priest's, old one," I answered.

The old man sighed. "Eh, the poor man," he said. "Or didn't they tell you?"

"Tell me what?"

"His son, his only son died yesterday morning. Didn't you hear the women keening?"

"I heard nothing, old one, nothing."

"They had him in the inner room, and I suppose they mourned him softly to spare you."

My eyes were brimming.

"Why are you crying?" the old man asked. "You are young, you aren't used to death. Go now, and good luck."

Now let us set out to get acquainted with Greece. Where do we start? Naturally with the city that is Greece within Greece, as the ancients called it—with Athens, the renowned city that has lived for thousands of years between Mount Hymettus and the sea. Many peoples have overrun her, and the traces of their passing may still be seen: the Parthenon, Byzantine churches, Frankish monasteries, mosques.

Athens today is a wasp's nest of lawyers, politicians, office seekers, merchants, poets—and chairs. Every Athenian takes up three chairs in the coffee house: one to sit on, another to lay his hat on, and a third to lean against. Go some evening to any of three big plazas—Concord, Constitution or Zappeion—

where Athenians gather to sip a coffee, drink ten glasses of cold water, and discuss the great political problems of Korea, Germany, Russia, the world. They talk and argue, swallow water, lean on chairs—and overhead the sky is violet, the sunset golden, and the evening breeze springs up to cool their sweating brows. The ladies come out, too, chic, wearing their finery like bunting, their large eyes filled with Levantine warmth. If it is summertime, the nightingales are warbling in the Royal Garden alongside the Zappeion, and the evzones—simple, unsophisticated soldiers from Rumelia in short and snow white fustanellas—twist their mustaches and stroll back and forth under the bright green pepper trees on Herodes Atticus Boulevard.

Athens is turbulent, teeming, alive. There are gathered here, from all over Greece, men who are greedy to reach their goals —to get rich, to enter politics, to land a government job, to rule Greece. They argue, they gesture, they shout. The old-time sophists live again; miniatures of Pericles, Socrates and Demosthenes walk about the streets, though no longer in mantles.

The two great rival plazas of Athens are Constitution and Concord. The first is aristocratic, genteely muted; only at noon, and from twilight to midnight, does it fill with people and chairs. On one side it looks down Churchill Street with its rich shops and big bookstores; on the other it faces Hermes Street, where the costly fabrics and sparkling diamonds spell hell and heaven for women. A little beyond lies the aristocratic Kolonaki section, where the newly rich, the big businessmen and the playboys have their mansions. The people say Kolonaki and their lips twist with hate and envy.

Concord Square is noisy and crowded. Its popular coffee houses are jammed. Its shoeshine boys line up in the middle of the square—alongside the stalls that sell the bright and fragrant flowers of Athens—and rattle big shoebrushes against their little boxes, eying the shoes of every passer-by, whether he stops to buy a bouquet or rushes past to disappear underground in the Phaleron-Piraeus subway. Here, in Concord Square, you rub elbows with a different sort of people; their faces seem lined, their clothes faded, their voices rough.

The two most popular shopping streets of Athens run into Concord Square—Athena and Aeolus Streets. What a welter of merchandise! Cheap ready-made clothes, thick-soled shoes and slippers and peasant sandals with pompons, and along the sidewalks, piles of vegetables and fruits. Greengrocers argue with their customers, scream their wares, and the air is filled with smells—rotting cantaloupes and oranges, fish being fried, cinnamon, fresh-roasted coffee and human sweat. Surely the goddess Athena would raise her tunic and pinch her nostrils if she had to cross the street that bears her name today.

Now you follow Athena Street to its end at the foot of the Acropolis. You climb the slope and stand before the famous temple of Athena, the Parthenon, the most beautiful work of architecture produced by Western man, and its harmony and grace leave you openmouthed with wonder. Then you look down on the white city spread out below and reaching toward the sea. In the distance, a blue pyramid rises from the glimmering water—Aegina, the splendid island that Pindar loved so well, and where, they say, Plato was born.

You enter the temple. The sun-weathered columns are pink, and on the walls you make out faded religious paintings of the Holy Virgin; in Christian times the temple of the Virgin Athena became a church of the Virgin Mary. You begin to understand the intrinsic harmony in the Greek makeup; on the ruins of their ancient, idol-worshiping temples, the Christian Greeks built churches to the corresponding saints. If the temple belonged to the sea god Poseidon, they built a church of St. Nicholas, protector of sailors; if it belonged to Apollo, god of light, they built a church to the Prophet Elias, whose name suggested *helios*, the sun. In the same way, here on the Acropolis, Athena's temple yielded to the church of the Virgin Mary, but deep down nothing was changed; one Virgin protectress of Greece was succeeded by another. (Actually the true deity in Athens today is not Athena, but Hermes—the two-faced, the god who is merchant and thief, the god of learning, the eloquent one. For Athens attracts not only politicians and merchants and big-time thieves but most of Greece's men of letters as well.)

If you are in Athens around Easter, on the night of Good Friday, you will see the *Epitaphios*, the bier of Christ. A little before midnight, every church congregation comes out in the streets in a bright candlelight procession, carrying the *Epitaphios*, a cubicle abloom with flowers, with lemon blossoms, lilacs, laurel and violets—and among them His image, painted on wood or heavy silk, lies at rest. The image has just been taken down from the cross inside the church, and now the faithful carry it about for all Athens to see and worship. The people of each parish follow the *Epitaphios* with lighted candles, and the priests, psalters and children's choirs chant a tender, sorrowful, poetic threnody for the God who died on the cross.

Across from the Acropolis, at the edge of Athens, stands the hill of Lycabettus with the church of St. George on its peak. If you climb Lycabettus that night and look down, you will see luminous rivers, many streams of burning candles moving slowly through the city until at last they flow together in one great incandescent sea.

I remember, one Good Friday, passing a small country church outside Athens and seeing, through the open door, a handful of peasant women bent over a table. They were singing dirges— for a dead relative, I thought. I entered and saw the figure of Christ stretched on the table, on a bed of lemon branches and lilacs. The plain little women, their kerchiefs awry, were mourning Him like a son of their own; and suddenly I understood, more deeply and plainly than ever before, how God took human form and descended to this earth.

Not one Greece but many.

To see Greece in its three chief aspects—modern, medieval and classical—you can take quick side trips from Athens—to Piraeus, Daphni and Sounion.

Piraeus is the largest port in Greece, a busy water-front city. Merchants, passengers, stevedores hurry aboard the big ships and hurry ashore again. Cargoes pile up on the docks, a tumult of sacks and barrels. Painted women prowl along the breakwater. In the taverns, meats are roasting, fish are frying, and the tavern keepers hustle about with pitchers of wine. The *fistikas* goes by once, twice, a dozen times, hawking his pistachio nuts, and on his heels comes the *pasatempos* with his roasted pumpkin seeds.

The market place down by the water is crammed with the good things of earth and sea. Here you will sit at a little tavern table, outdoors, perhaps near a sailor in a pointed woolen cap. His face is weathered by the sun, and his short curly beard smells of sea water and broiled crab and *retsina* wine. (In Greece today, the wine god Dionysus is embodied in the pine tree; its trunk is slashed, the flowing resin gathered and added to the wine in the barrel, and the result is the famous resinated wine of Greece—bitterish, aromatic, like a liquid pine tree.) With your *retsina* comes a variety of *meze*—olives, cheese, small fry cooked with garlic—and you sit and sip and nibble, take in the indigo sea, the black ships, the bare-chested sailors, the painted women, and for the moment you forget your native land.

Athens is the aristocrat, the *grande dame* of glorious descent, though somewhat humbled now. Piraeus is her thick-boned servant who lumbers all over the world to bring her cinnamon and pepper, Paris originals, books, Coca-Cola, radios and limousines. And dollars.

Your second side trip, a few kilometers out of Athens, will bring you to the medieval Frankish monastery at Daphni. You stroll through a thick olive grove and pause a moment to salute one hoary, hollow trunk—Plato's olive; here, they say, the philosopher used to sit and write. You pass pretty stands of pine and the air is flavored with resin and the sea smell blowing in from the Bay of Eleusis.

In the middle of a pine grove you come upon the monastery. A Byzantine dome, a green and quiet courtyard, cypress trees. Strewn about the court, open and empty, are the graves of bygone Frankish dukes who ruled Athens. The coats of arms carved in the stones are worn to a blur, the great proud names are erased and only the stones endure. Here in this lonely courtyard you give a moment's thought to the wealth and splendor of the Franks who conquered Athens. Then you step over the graves, cross the yard, and walk into the monastery.

You cross the threshold and gasp; the walls are covered from floor to dome with superb, precious, many-colored mosaics. Up in the crown you see the Almighty Jesus as the Byzantine artist liked to represent Him, stern of mien, with heavy eyebrows knit in anger, enveloped in a rainbow and holding the Bible as if poised to fling it down on the heads of the faithful. On every wall you follow the life and sufferings of Christ, each scene a mosaic of fantastic power and grace. And suddenly you see this little church as a walled-in heaven and yourself safely within it, untroubled by the cries and the concerns of the world.

Now for the third side trip. Again you travel a few kilometers, past pine forests and hamlets. The same sun shines, and the rocks reflect the scent of savory and thyme. You come to Sounion, high on a cliff above the sea, and the gracious marble temple of Poseidon. You enter now another immortal sphere, ancient Greece. You see the slim, lovely columns, and between them the endless, blue blue sea. You have come to one of the most beautiful ruins of antiquity. Ships sailed by here long ago, and their crews gave thanks to the mighty sea god when their homesick eyes picked out, on the far-off Athenian Acropolis, the gigantic bronze statue of the goddess Athena.

There is another sight in Athens you should not miss—the shadow play named Karaghiozi, after its principal character. At the foot of Lycabettus, the hill opposite the Acropolis, lies the reservoir section, the Athenian Latin Quarter. There you will find the Karaghiozi theater, a large court furnished with benches and chairs. At the far end is the "stage"—four posts stuck in the ground and wrapped in burlap, with a large white sheet stretched across the front two. Behind this stands the solitary performer who manipulates the puppets and speaks their voices.

The show begins. Always the same characters, from the same Levantine repertoire. The plots are full of cunning, of wit, of breezy and slapstick antics that draw explosions of laughter from the audience:

The pasha is beating Karaghiozi, and Karaghiozi says to him angrily, "Look here. Are you beating me for a joke or are you serious?"

"I'm serious."

"Well, it's a good thing I know it, because I don't stand for trifling."

Or Karaghiozi is dying of hunger but is ashamed to confess it. It is deep night, and he stands under his sweetheart's balcony.

"O my soul," he says to her passionately, "if only I had some small token to remember you by."

"What would you like, my Karaghiozi?"

"Oh, some little nothing. A pin. Throw me a pin."

"But it's dark. How will you see it, my Karaghiozi?"

"Stick it in a big loaf of bread, my love."

Athens has three faces, one ancient (the Parthenon, the museums), one old (Byzantine and Turkish), and one modern. Before the visitor says good-by to the city, he should take a stroll through the narrow, charming streets of old Athens, around the foot of the Acropolis. Here are humble little houses with potted basil and marigolds in their windows, tiny Byzantine churches that reflect nobility and grace in their small double columns, their freshly whitewashed domes and the old icons within. In this district lived the medieval rulers of Athens, the Turkish agas surrounded by the enslaved populace. For one who knows the bloodstained history of this spot, every little street brings tragic scenes to mind, scenes of martyrdom and love of freedom.

Now you leave Athens and begin your tour of the nation. You drive through Attica and enter Boeotia, you pass the famous mountains of Cithaeron and Helicon, where the Muses dwelt, you come to Parnassus—and you are in the storied land of Rumelia. Gradually, from Attica to Boeotia and from Boeotia to here, the light has been changing. The light of Attica is weightless and transparent, bringing to your eye the distant mountain, island, tree in sharpest outline. Somehow, I feel, this soft filtered light must have helped the ancient Greeks to see clearly within themselves, to impose order on conjectures, to

At Rhodes a temple to Athena stands serene on a hill above the dark Aegean.

separate concept from concept and create the holy trinity of the mind—the perfect syllogism of premise, argument and conclusion. The light of Attica is all spirit. Here man saw clearly for the first time, made order out of chaos, created a cosmos. And cosmos, the word, means harmony.

In the mountains of Rumelia there are many flocks of sheep. Now and then, as you round a big rock, you are hailed by a shepherd carrying a long hooked staff. "Stay, brother," he calls. "Have a glass of milk and a piece of cheese." And he whistles and his ewes come close to be milked.

Rumelia mothered the bravest of the valiant men who fought, 130 years ago, to free Greece from the Turk. Its people are simple mountain folk. They look down from the heights and wonder why anyone lives in the heat and dust of the plains.

Once I met a shepherd high up on Parnassus and he asked me, "Those people in the plains—do you suppose they have souls?"

Here in Rumelia was the fabulous Delphic Oracle. You tarry by the Phaedriad Rocks, source of the Spring of Castalia. You stoop and drink the water and it refreshes you in body and soul; this is the immortal water of poetry.

Then you look around you, from the tall mountains down to the plain where the river flows and glitters among enormous olive trees. It glitters like a gigantic snake; and snake it was, says the old myth, until the archer god Apollo fought with it and slew it.

Another combat took place at this oracle, the one which created the civilization of Greece. The fighters were Apollo and Dionysus; the god of light, logic and harmony against the god of darkness and frenzy, the god of water against the god of wine. Apollo won, and thus set the pattern of ancient Greek civilization.

The modern town of Delphoi is small and poor. Its houses are low, with whitewashed walls. Inside them you will see a hearth, dishes on display above it, an earthen jug of water, bright-colored woolen blankets. A shrine on the wall, with sacred icons and a small wick burning perpetually before them in its glass container. And in a corner, the loom.

The housewife bids you welcome, fetches a stool, offers you a tumbler of cold water and a tiny glass of fiery *raki*. The man of the house is often out, either in the fields or at the coffee house playing cards. If your hostess is young, her words to a stranger are few. If she is old, her mouth starts going and never stops. She rambles from old yarns to new ones, each a tale of disaster and death. The whole of Greece is leavened with blood and tears; and the last great war left hardly a house without its dead. So the old crone spins her yarns by the hour, forgetting nothing. Were she to write the history of contemporary Greece, it would be a tale of dragons, blood and starvation. It would also be, above and beyond the horrors, a tale of a love of freedom that is stronger even than death.

Hermes, the thief and the intellectual, may be the god of Athens; but the highest deity of Greece, the goddess who survives unchanged through the ages even with her feet dipped in blood and her eyes filled with tears, has always been Freedom. For centuries now the Greek has been fighting and dying for her sake. The mountains and shores of Greece are her birthplace; the Greek is her father, and the most illiterate peasant, the rudest shepherd, knows it. Surely Freedom was born here, in this holy air of Greece.

Now you return to Piraeus, where you board a caïque and sail into the Gulf of Corinth to explore the Peloponnesus. Again you come to an entirely different landscape, tame, peaceful, with grape vines growing in the plains. Try to be there in August or September, in the harvest season, the time of Dionysus' joy. The women sing a sorrowful refrain as they gather the vintage, as if they truly grieved to see Dionysus dismembered. Then they carry the precious seedless grapes to the drying ground and spread them under the sun, which turns them into the world-famous raisins of Greece.

You look in on the once illustrious city of Corinth, now a minor provincial town, dusty all summer and muddy all winter. Earthquakes have wrecked it again and again, and the Greeks have stubbornly rebuilt it every time. On a hill outside the town you will see the ruins of Acrocorinth, the ancient citadel. Here stood the temple of Aphrodite, famous in antiquity for its thousand priestesses. They were gorgeous, greedy, sinister women, and they so badly fleeced the men who came from all over Greece to worship the goddess of love that you needed tremendous wealth to enjoy the pleasures of Corinth. The Greeks summed it up in a proverb: "Not every man can sail to Corinth" —which means roughly you can't have everything.

Motoring southward from Corinth, you come to the patrician city of Nauplion, the first capital of Greece after her liberation from the Turks. It is a quiet city, and over its shoulder looms the fearsome Palamidi, a cliff with a thousand steps and a dreadful jail on its crest, where criminals, bandits, revolutionaries live out their natural lives or else mark time until the executioner beheads them.

You leave Nauplion a little hurriedly, the highway takes you to the edge of the peaceful plain, and suddenly beetling cliffs thrust up dead ahead. Anyone who knows what happened here, once upon a time is seized with fear. The cliffs are wild, naked, menacing, a setting for appalling deeds. You have come at last to storied, golden, bloodstained Mycenae, where the great chief Agamemnon ruled. You walk through the gigantic stone gates, between two rampant lionesses, and come upon the gaping graves of Mycenaean kings.

Next to Agamemnon, the hero of this place is Heinrich Schliemann, the self-taught German archaeologist. He had read Homer in his youth, and he believed naïvely every word he read —that the Trojan war had actually taken place, that Troy had been a real city, that the wondrous city of Mycenae, of which Homer sings with such love and awe, had existed; and he swore that he would be the first to bring to light these treasures covered over by the ages. Schliemann learned foreign languages, studied the ancient texts, and when he had learned all he wanted to know he went to Troy, where he dug and found the palaces, the graves, the gold; then to Mycenae, where his excavations unburied the royal graves and their contents of gold leaf, swords, goblets, and gold masks molded on the faces of ancient corpses.

Schliemann was convinced that he had found the tomb of Agamemnon himself, and the very mask that was pressed on his dead face just after he came back in triumph from the Trojan war to be murdered in his bath by Clytemnestra, his wife. Standing over the open tomb, you think back on this slaying and you shudder. All these centuries have gone by, and still the blood is not washed off these rugged stones. Why? Because in his tragedies the great poet Aeschylus immortalized the unholy deed with such poetic power and integrity that time is helpless to blot out its traces. Only the great poet can conquer time.

Cover your ears as you turn away from the bloodstained site of Mycenae, to shut out Agamemnon's hideous scream as his wife brings down the ax. You did not come to Greece to resurrect old evils, but to feast your soul on light and beauty, to see Greece in contemporary times and know it for the heaving, tortured, ragged, lovable—yes, and wondrous—land it is. So you strike out again, this time toward a smiling, gentle place— sacred Olympia. First you backtrack to Nauplion and Corinth, then you move westward along the lovely beaches of the Corinthian Gulf until you come to Patras, a good-sized city opposite the Ionian Islands.

The earth hereabouts is well-tilled, lavish. You no longer see just rocks and mountains with no growth and no inhabitants. Here you look out on delightful greenness and serenity. You walk through a village and the women run to their doorsteps to look at you, all curiosity and smiles. Many ask if you are thirsty, ready to bring out the ritual treat of water and *raki*. Some bring you bunches of ripe sweet grapes in a bed of vine leaves; others offer you fresh figs. It is summertime, and the porches and windows of their homes are strung with ears of corn, red peppers, tobacco leaves drying in the sun. The old men are sitting in the village square, under a poplar or a plane tree, and around them are the church, the school, the coffee house—the three main centers of Greek village life. The *kafetzis* goes back and forth with his tray, serving coffee, tiny glasses of *ouzo*, sweet *loukoumi* (Turkish delight) cold water. An old man calls for his narghile, sucks smoke from the mouthpiece with lowered eyelids, content. The world teeters on a brink, atomic bombs grow constantly more murderous, the heads of nations lie sleepless at night; but here in the village square, under the plane and the poplar, all is calm and secure.

You break away, finally, and reach Olympia. Your eye sweeps over the ancient palaestra, the ruined buildings, the half-toppled columns. When the ancients chose this gentle region as a place where all Greeks could compete at peaceful games, they chose unerringly. I have never seen another setting that filters thoughts of peace and harmony so subtly, so miraculously, into the mind. The ancient city-states warred ceaselessly among themselves—Sparta against Athens, Thebes against Sparta, Corinth against Corcyra. Here at Olympia they dropped their enmities, acknowledge that they were all one people, brothers, and contended only for a bloodless victory at racing, at wrestling, at throwing the discus.

Back on the road again, you drive southward. You leave the plains behind, you cross mountains. The peak of Taygetus thrusts up sharply, abruptly before you, and you are in Sparta. Here lived the ancient, dreadful enemy of Athens, the symbol of the brave, the rugged, the austere.

Athens, whose people knew how to laugh and how to contemplate, left many masterworks in words and marble. Sparta, whose harsh inhabitants despised abstract thought and beauty, left only a couple of piles of stones, and Sparta today is a mere town, sizable and insignificant, with wide streets and malarial fevers.

But we are not yet finished with Greece, even after the distances we have traveled. To the north stretches yet another Greece—Macedonia—with individual landscapes of its own, a distinct psychology, and different adventures in its history. From Athens, the simplest and quickest way to run up to Salonika, the chief city of northern Greece, is by plane. In a matter of hours you fly from a classical city to a city of Byzantine walls and towers, of splendid churches such at St. Demetrius and St. Sophia, and of people endowed with energy and practical minds.

Before the last World War, Salonika had a marked Jewish character. Sephardic Jews, driven out of Spain centuries ago under Isabella, found refuge in Turkish-held Salonika and rose to high positions in its finance and commerce. Before the war, they numbered 70,000; barely 7000 are left. The rest were murdered by the Nazis.

Salonika takes pride in its Byzantine history, its beautifully built churches and their brilliant mosaics, and in the busy trade its harbor handled in bygone years. Today her civic joy is the university, where the youth of Macedonia come to study for professional careers. Around the city spread fruitful plains, and farther to the east lie the great tobacco-growing centers of Drama, Xanthe and Kavalla. Tobacco, along with raisins and olive oil, constitutes the chief export wealth of Greece.

To the north of Salonika are the cities of Phlorina, Edessa and Naousa, set amid unstinting streams and lush vegetation. This is romantic Greece, amply watered and forested, a striking contrast to the classically dry and frugal plain of Attica.

Here in Macedonia you will also find a place that is unique on earth—Mount Athos, the Holy Mount. You board a little steamer in Salonika and overnight you reach the Holy Mount harbor and the tiny monastic town of Daphne.

If you are a man, you may go ashore and tread the sacred soil; if you are a woman—impossible. In all this holy area, which embraces twenty-one monasteries—eighteen of them Greek, one Serbian, one Bulgarian and one Russian—no woman has ever set her foot or tainted the air with her breath. And not only no woman but no female animal. You will see no ewes here, no nanny goats, no hens, no she-rabbits or cats; only rams, billy goats, roosters, he-rabbits, tomcats—and monks.

Once I spent six months on the Holy Mount. After looking around all the monasteries, I found one that appealed to me for its great strictness. The abbot assigned me to a cloister built high on a crag overlooking the sea, an hour's hike from the monastery. I had a small garden with two lemon trees and a laurel bush, two cells and a tiny chapel dedicated to St. John the Forerunner. There I lived completely alone; huge logs were piled beside the hearth, the fire blazed day and night, and I sat before it on a low stool reading my three favorite books, the Bible, Homer and Dante.

Each morning one of the monks, Father Lukas, climbed the crag to bring me my day's food and bread and a bottle of dark wine. He was always out of breath when he arrived at my cell, and he would sit down on the threshold and drink the wine bottle empty. Then he would rise, come in and greet me, and set my food down on the stool.

"How can you live here all alone in the wilderness?" he asked me once. "If I didn't have other monks around me, to talk to and argue with every day, I couldn't live."

"But you are a monk, Father Lukas," I said, "and the word means 'alone.' Isn't that why you came here to the Holy Mount, to lead a life of solitude?"

"Don't be foolish," he replied. "I came to the Holy Mount because I killed a Turk in Thrace. They were hunting for me, and I ducked into a monastery here and escaped. And that's the whole mystery."

He rubbed his hands together. "There is security here, my friend, and tranquillity—an easy life. And you get away from women and children and taxes, praise God. I tell you for your own good, don't budge from here. Become a monk and you will find your salvation."

"And don't you ever remember woman, Father Lukas?"

"I'll tell you, my friend, between us two. I do remember her once in a while, curse her, but in my sleep. And what do I do then? I wake up, dash a pail of water on my head, forget her and go back to bed."

I shall never forget the time I spent in that solitude. The

Holy Mount is one of the most beautiful places in the world, with wild cliffs and gentle beaches, forests of fir and pine, orchards of lemon and orange trees, all surrounded by blue and endless sea and dominated by lofty Athos, a calm, majestic, jagged peak capped with snow. And the life of the monasteries brims with mystery and fascination, its Byzantine rhythm beating on unchanged. In the morning a monk sounds the *semantron,* a long piece of wood which rings most musically as he strikes it with a little mallet on his rounds among the cells, waking the monks in the half-light of dawn. No bell ever rings so sweetly, or inspires in you such divine rapture, as this wooden *semantron* from Byzantine times.

The monks move out into the courtyard like black shadows. In the center stands the church and they file in. It is half dark inside; only two or three candles are lit, and by their glow you make out here and there the wan faces of the monks as they chant or stand unmoving in their pews, cross in hand.

The Matins over, the monks come out again, in single file with the abbot leading, and move to the refectory, an oblong chamber decorated with old, half-faded murals. Silently they take their seats at the long, narrow table, and the waiter brings their humble breakfast—lentils, olives, salt cod or, on high holidays, meat. From the rostrum above them, another monk reads from the Bible or the Lives of the Saints. They listen attentively. No one speaks.

Suddenly the abbot rings the little bell at his side, and all at once the monks gulp down the bite of food in their mouths and rise. Again the abbot takes the lead, the monks fall in behind him one by one. The procession moves toward the monastery cells, where the monks hole up for the day; or, if the weather is clear, they may stand on the threshold and sun themselves.

When I was leaving the Holy Mount I went to say good-by to an aged ascetic. He had been the monastery artist; his hands had created a multitude of Christs and Marys in the past. But now he was old, his fingers had grown wooden.

"Father Arsenios," I said to him, "I am leaving. You are a holy man, and I have come to ask for your advice."

"Achieve what you can," he replied. "Go to God's blessing."

"Give me one more piece of advice, I beg you, Father Arsenios."

"Achieve what you cannot," he replied, and spoke no more.

One final pleasure is in store for you—Crete. Here you will discover that there is more to Greece than the Classical, the Byzantine and the modern. There is a fourth Greece, a mysterious nation that lay buried in the Cretan earth and was only recently brought to light.

No one knew what went on in Greece, two and three thousand years before Christ, until an English archaeologist, Sir Arthur Evans, began to excavate at Cnossus, five kilometers south of Heraklion. What a marvel rose up from the earth! A vast palace with many stories, with a theater, baths, men's quarters and women's quarters, a throne chamber, storage cells containing huge sculptured vats. And walls covered with breathtakingly vivid murals—with fishes, birds, flowers, scenes showing bullfights, popular assemblies, noblewomen with their hair hanging in soft curls, their breasts naked, their lips painted, and white gloves tucked into their belts. And a young prince, slim waisted, in a gaudy feather headdress, with lilies, the symbol of royalty, beside him. And stacks of small earthen tablets inscribed with strange writing that the wise men of the world are only now beginning to read, to help us after all these centuries to hear the voice of this mysterious civilization.

Crete is, I believe, one of the world's holiest places. The island is like a ship plying about the three great mother continents, Europe, Asia and Africa. The civilization of Asia and Africa came here to make its first leap over to Europe; Crete was the first bit of Europe to know enlightenment of spirit.

Crete's ancient role is not its only attraction, however; the Crete of today is fascinating in its own right. Her people have struggled and suffered more than any other Greeks, and yet the joy and love of living is alive within them.

In a Cretan village one day I met a man who was a hundred years old. One morning a few years earlier, one of his grandchildren told me, while he was still able to get about, he had left home without a word and disappeared. It turned out he went wandering through the mountains where he had spent his youth herding sheep.

Once in a while a passing stranger would say to him, "Where are you going, grandfather? What are you doing here?" And the old man would always answer, "I am saying good-by, my son, saying good-by," and then go back to his wandering.

Three months later he came home. He had bade his mountains farewell, he was ready to die.

Now the old man was nearly blind, and he liked to sit by the village fountain at sundown, waiting for the girls to come and fill their jugs.

I was with him one day when the sound of wooden sandals came clattering over the stone pavement. His head snapped up.

"You, who are you?"

The girl told him.

"Bless you, child. Come close and let me see you."

He saw the girl not with his eyes but with his hands. His palms stroked her face repeatedly, hungrily, on the nose, the mouth, the chin. Then he let her go and sighed like a bull.

"What is the matter, grandfather?" I said. "Why are you sighing?"

"Why do you suppose?" he answered, annoyed. "Haven't you got eyes to see? I am going under the earth and leaving so many beautiful girls behind. Eh, if I were a king, I'd kill them all and take them with me, to keep me company in Hades."

Another day I said to him, "Tell me, grandfather, what is it like to live a century?"

He turned his red, lashless eyes toward me.

"Like a drink of cold water, my son," he said.

"And you are still thirsty?"

His hand jerked up in a malevolent gesture. "A curse on any man whose thirst is quenched."

To love life despite poverty, hunger and misfortune—that is one of the greatest traits of the Greek people. No matter how long they have been suffering, life seems to them a fine and inexhaustible thing. A drink of cold water, and devil take the man whose thirst is quenched.

Greece/Nikos Kazantzakis **95**

Russia

MOSCOW

Though it is the very heart of the surging new Soviet Union, Moscow in many ways remains grimly unchanged and unchanging. With the perspective of a journalist who lived and traveled for many years in Russia, Harrison Salisbury sees it still as "the city of peasants, of surging peasant crowds flowing like a slow muddy river over the streets, the sidewalks, the boulevards..."

If I talk of Moscow in terms of winter and snow, of gloom and aftermidnight, of footfalls and tentacles of fear, it is because, after many years of life in the Russian capital, these are the impressions most strongly in me. In the post-Stalin era many things are changing. But the mark of years of fear remains.

I lived in Russia many years before I began to feel that I knew Moscow. Not until I had gone away and come back several times, and lived there through times of peril and crisis, did the character of the city begin to be more clear.

My first sight of Moscow was from an airplane window. It was wartime and winter. The city sprawled over the half-forested Russian plain for miles in all directions. The only comparison which came to my mind was Chicago. But except that each is sprawling and that through each winds a namesake river, there is no similarity.

Far better to approach Moscow by train. Or best of all, were it possible, to come by jolting truck or bus. That would give you a chance to fix Moscow in space and era. Much depends, too, on the direction from which you come. Most travelers now approach Moscow through fastidious Stockholm, industrious Helsinki or bustling Berlin. Since there is much in Russia to offend not only the eye but the nose, invidious comparison is inevitable. The approach from the Middle East, which was common during the war, provided an opposite impression.

Wartime Moscow was surely the grimmest capital on earth. A city of few vehicles, no shops, no public restaurants, an early curfew, cold, hardship, much hunger and not a little bravery. I can still hear the soft shuffle of the felt *valenki* in the blacked-out Moscow streets of a winter evening. The low murmur of voices as the crowds passed unseen. And, suddenly, the gay sound of a man whistling in the profound darkness and the chuckle of my Russian companion: "There goes an American." Why? Because only an American would whistle on the street. Russians regard whistling as vulgar.

Moscow at war was a gray city—gray buildings, gray, lowering skies, the gray faces of the people and their colorless clothing. The windows of the closed shops were blank and more gray than the rationed bread. But in the monochrome of Moscow life there was one blaze of color, as incredible as a fairy tale by Pushkin. This was the victory salute.

When the Red Army achieved a great victory over the Germans, the loud-speakers which were hung up in the streets would rumble forth a *prikaz*—a triumphal communiqué in the name of Stalin, announcing that a salute would be fired in honor of the event. At the appointed hour of the evening, from bat-

teries located in the courtyards of the Kremlin, on the roofs of nearby buildings and in parks and squares close to the center of the city, the guns would roar and showers of skyrockets— red and green and golden—would explode high over the city. In the streets would be heard the exulting "ohs" and "ahs" of the crowds.

On such a night, standing in the white snow of the Red Square, with St. Basil's Cathedral glowing like a strange jewel in the fire of the rockets and the massed bulbs and turrets of the Kremlin silhouetted against the merlons, corbels and bartizans of its walls; and all about the people, silent and invisible as gray ghosts except when the red fire in the sky suddenly tinted their pale, upturned faces—on such a night, in such a moment, I now know that I was close to the essential mystery of Moscow.

Although I did not understand it then, the true agony of Moscow, of Russia itself, lies in the leaden burden of life which weights down the shoulders of the millions, year by year, in order that, fleetingly, the heavens may be lighted with sparks of heavenly beauty.

Russia's revolution was born in a slogan, "From the spark shall come the flame." Few of the idealists whose spirit was stirred by those words could have imagined that it would be a life-consuming, not a life-giving flame.

A city at war may be no nearer than a second cousin to the same city at peace, as anyone can testify who knew the moon- and fire-touched ecstasy of London under the blitz. But war or peace, czar or commissar, Moscow does not change.

When Vertinsky, the famous café singer, returned to Mos- cow after years of exile in Paris, he emerged from the station, set down his bags and exclaimed in awe, "The city is trans- formed! The wide streets! The new buildings! I should never have known I was in Moscow."

When he turned back to pick up his bags, they had vanished.

"Ah," he said, "the city has changed less than it seems."

The thieves in the railroad stations are not the only feature of Moscow which would seem familiar to Romanov expatriates.

It is some 800 years since Moscow was founded on a little pine-covered hill at the conflux of the Moscow and the Neglin- naia rivers. Of that Moscow hardly a reminiscence remains.

Moscow is filled with racial types from all over the vast U.S.S.R.

The name of one of the Kremlin gates—the Borovitzky or Gate of the Woods (the one Stalin used)—commemorates the little forest village on the hill. And, imbedded within the Great Kremlin Palace, like a fly in amber, is the tiny chapel of Spas Na Boru, the Saviour in the Forest, whose name also recalls the woods-on-the-hill where the city was born. But even this dates from the 14th Century, two hundred years after Moscow was founded.

The reason nothing of earliest Moscow remains is simple. It was called the City of Oak, and like all wooden cities it burned down, not once but repeatedly. Even after successive Princes of Muscovy began to transform the Kremlin into what travelers called a White City of Stone, it continued to burn down at frequent intervals. (The last time was in 1812, and the argument still rages as to whether Napoleon or the Russians set the fire. In the later years of his life Stalin laid down an official party dictum blaming the French, but the best guess still is that the whole thing was an accident.)

But fire was no more successful at changing Moscow's character than war. Moscow is set in the center of the great Russian forest plain like an island in the sea. This is the heartland of the Slavs, and Moscow is as surely the Slavic capital as St. Petersburg (now Leningrad) was not, despite the fact that for two centuries Peter's "window on the West" was the capital of the Russian Empire.

Lenin moved the capital back to Moscow as a military necessity in 1918. Thus, without realizing it, he sealed the doom of the intellectuals who had made the revolution and insured that the Soviet would become, essentially, a peasant state. Perhaps it would have come about anyway. But Moscow, being an urban island in a rural sea, inevitably is a peasant capital. This was so long before the revolution. It has become more and more true as post-revolutionary Moscow has doubled and trebled in size with the growth of industry and the bureaucracy. The men at the machines and the desks are peasants—direct from the village or one step removed.

The influx has been so great that a native Muscovite is almost as rare as a native New Yorker. The born Muscovite has a good deal of contempt for the people "from the village," and something of an inferiority complex toward the more sophisticated Leningrader. Over the centuries he has never learned to be friendly with foreigners, but his attitude may well warm up now that his masters are beaming smiles toward the outside world.

The man from Moscow, like most Russians, has a high (we might even consider it exaggerated) respect for what he calls "culture"—literature, classical music and science. His taste in art is not much higher than the peasant's. But he respects learning. Long ago he lost any real interest in government propaganda drives. His ambition is to acquire a small house in the suburbs with a garden where he can raise potatoes and cabbage. He wants to live quietly, obscurely, and keep out of trouble, which can be so serious in Moscow. In many ways he is a rather bitter man. But he has pride and loyalty for his city and loves it despite its hardships.

The native of Moscow is a fairly sophisticated person, yet you only need stroll down Gorky Street to see what a peasant world he lives in. Here are the faces, simple, broad hewn, high-cheekboned. Eyes wrinkled and squinting from long hours in sun and wind. Backs and shoulders bent from burdens and plowing. Sturdy, plodding, silent. The dark people, as they still call themselves. There are 6,000,000 of them there now, compared with a little more than 2,000,000 in 1917.

The incredible loveliness of the Kremlin, with its walls of old rose, its cream-and-yellow palaces, the gold and blue of its onion-domed churches—this is not what gives Moscow its character.

Nor is it the cobbled back streets, the *pereulki* of the Arbat, where diplomats dwell in the faded elegance of neo-Grecian and Empire houses built by Moscow merchants in the decades after 1812.

It is not even the churches, no longer forty times forty but startlingly numerous. There were something over 500 in 1917, exclusive of chapels in private mansions; today there are fifty-five.

No. Moscow's character is in the people, and the people are peasants. Nowhere in the world are there more peasants gathered together, and in some ways it is more significant that Moscow is peasant than that Moscow is communist. Moscow was peasant long before Lenin appeared on the scene. Even Moscow's merchants, who disappeared in the revolution (except from the stage, where, in Ostrovsky's old plays, they are more popular than ever), were peasants before they were

merchants—flint-fisted men who, nonetheless, flung their rubles like confetti at the feet of the gypsy dancers of the Yar. Moscow's workers, too, were peasants long before the revolution, country folk released by their village *mir*, or commune, to work awhile in the city. There is not much change today.

Moscow is a series of concentric circles bisected by great boulevards which radiate like the points of a compass. But no architect from Paris laid out Moscow. It grew out from the Kremlin, the first of the circles—actually a crude rhomboid set between the Moscow and now completely enclosed Neglinnaia rivers. Originally the Kremlin walls were the city walls. But gradually the city expanded and in time the new settlement was given the protection of battlements and was called the White City. Later another city sprang up beyond the second walls and this, too, was in turn enclosed.

The Kremlin is still the city's heart, still walled. On one side the Kremlin faces the Moscow River, but the barges and houseboats which once clustered between the Great Stone Bridge and the Moskvoretsky Bridge have long since been evicted and replaced by ramparts of granite, a decorative embarcadero and a broad boulevard. On the other facets of the Kremlin, where once were drawbridges and moats, it is set off by the Red Square and other central squares, some of which were opened up by the Bolsheviks to give the Kremlin garrison a better field of fire in event of a rising.

The walls which once surrounded the White City and the City Beyond the Walls long ago were leveled and transformed into broad thoroughfares, which Moscow calls the Boulevard Circle and the Garden Circle. The Boulevard Circle is little changed from the old days, but the outer circle is so useful for transferring troops, tanks or armored cars quickly from one quarter of Moscow to another, or from the outskirts to the inner city through the transverse boulevards, that today the

The Kremlin: Center, *Archangel Cathedral*; left, *the Cathedral of the Annunciation*.

"Garden" is a 200-foot-wide through way of asphalt, devoid of trees, grass or shrubs, sweltering in summer and freezing in winter.

Except for such scarification, and the blight of Stalinesque, the Revolution has probably done as much good as harm to Moscow's appearance. It was never a beautiful city despite the dreams of its poets. True, Stalin razed the great Church of the Saviour in anticipation of building a 100-story Palace of the Soviets, but the outbreak of World War II saved Moscow from this abomination.

In his final years Stalin went back to his early passion for bad imitations of American skyscrapers. He approved plans for eight tall buildings after seeing that they were appropriately bedecked with gingerbread, mostly in the form of small towers patterned after those of the Kremlin. Seven now embellish the capital, many of them in preposterous places. The thirty-one-story Moscow University building is the first thing seen by visitors approaching Moscow from the airport—a huge skyscraper, apparently located amid miles of open prairie. Yet there is enough implausibility about Kremlin-topped skyscrapers to allow them to blend with the Moscow scene, particularly at dusk or on misty nights when the towers are softly floodlighted.

But Stalin's passion didn't stop here. He proposed to put up a forty-seven-story skyscraper in lower Red Square. This called for wrecking some of the oldest structures in Moscow, and would have permanently altered the architectural *ambiance* of Red Square and the Kremlin. It would have transformed St. Basil's and the Spasky towers from living parts of an organic whole to sight-seers' curiosities at the foot of a bad imitation of the Metropolitan Life building. It was Russia's good fortune that Stalin died before this plan was very far advanced, and his successors abandoned the scheme.

The peasant soul of Moscow is unmistakable in its farmers' markets, around which so much of the city's trading life still centers. Here you see Georgians from Tsinindali with grapes and apricots; Tartars from the Crimea (some of them must have escaped deportation to Asia) with their watermelons; women from Vladimir with peonies or chrysanthemums; wood carvers from Zagorsk with *matushki*—those painted wooden dolls which are actually three in one, a doll within a doll within a doll. Watching these people you begin to realize that, if you are a Soviet subject and you grow something—lemons in Dagestan, walnuts in Armenia, peppers in Moldavia—or make something with your hands—say, *chorti*, little devils of blown glass, fitted with rubber tubes for squirting perfume in a rude fashion—sooner or later you will make your way to Moscow and offer it for sale. You will do your selling in or around one of the city's twenty-eight farmers' markets. Or in the streets and back alleys near the vast GUM department store. Or even in the store itself, around the plashing fountain where weary peasant women sit on the marble floor to rest their feet, eat their black bread and nurse their babies.

But Moscow is more than a mecca for peasants and for trade. It is a mecca for almost everyone in all the provinces of Russia. It is the city of hotels, restaurants and theaters, of the opera and ballet.

Communism has not improved the never-too-high standards of Moscow's restaurants. Still, it is a surprise to find decent caviar at reasonable prices in poor Moscow cafés—and tieless Russian workingmen shoving it down with large wedges of buttered black bread. Black bread, as always, is the Russian staple of diet—good, coarse and healthful. And recently the State Baking Trust has started to turn out excellent white bread in long, crusty loaves as crisp as those of France or Italy.

The big difference between the Moscow theater and Broadway is that you can leave Moscow and come back twenty years later to find hardly any change in the basic repertoire—and many actors at the Art Theater and the Maly Theater still playing the same roles. Russians like this. Regardless of politics they are great traditionalists. Even the revolutions in technique introduced by Stanislavsky and Nemirovich-Danchenko at the Art Theater have undergone a kind of petrification—what appears to be something alive is found, upon touching it, to have turned to stone.

And yet it is very fine to see *The Lower Depths*, just as Gorky envisaged it. Or Tolstoy's *Resurrection* or *The Fruits of Enlightenment*. Or Alexis Tolstoy's *Ivan the Dread* at the Maly. Or *The Cherry Orchard*. Or *The Seagull*. All are bits of Russian history and Russian life crystallized on the stage. The same may be said for the great Russian operas, *Ivan Susanin, Prince Igor, The Queen of Spades, Boris Godunoff* or the fairy tale of *Sadko*.

But most of all Moscow is the city of the Russian ballet, possibly the most wonderful anachronism of our time. For here in communist Moscow the Russian Imperial Ballet survives practically without change. The schools are the same. So are the stages and techniques, and many of the ballets—the eternal loveliness of *Swan Lake*, or a *Giselle* danced by Ulanova with feet so light you cannot believe she is mortal. And there are new ballets—*The Red Poppy*, poor propaganda but with classic ballet in the dream sequences; *The Bronze Horseman*, a Pushkin legend set to choreography (it may or may not have been the most subtle of criticisms of Stalin). And a dream come true—Prokofiev's final work, *The Stone Flower*, a Urals fantasy with a stern Princess of the Copper Mountain, and Ulanova, the incomparable, dancing her way into the heart of the Mountain—and into the hearts of all who watch her.

To anyone who has known Paris, Moscow would never seem like the City of Light. But to Russians it is just that. I hadn't been long in Russia when I first saw Chekhov's *Three Sisters* at the Art Theater, and I know I smiled a little at the way they talked about Moscow. About their aspirations and their hopes, eternally and desperately frustrated, to get to Moscow. I did not understand the pain and anguish in the cry: "*V Moskvu. V Moskvu*"—To Moscow. To Moscow."

Even after I had tramped Moscow's crowded streets, seen the Red Square and strolled through the run-down Coney Island attractions of the Central Park of Rest and Culture Named for Gorky (its name in the prerevolutionary era was the Not Boring Park), I still could not understand the attitude of the three Prozorov sisters.

But I did not wonder after I had seen the Russian provinces, the mud of the streets in provincial towns, the blank faces of the residents, the melancholy of the landscape. The Russians have a special word, *poshlost*, meaning utter boredom and banality, and it is used to describe life in the hinterland, the endless vastness which is Russia.

Once you understand *poshlost* and the provinces, you begin to appreciate what Moscow means to Russians. Returning from the depths of the "dark" country, I felt some of the emotion which comes into the voices of Irina, Olga and Masha as they talk about their beloved metropolis. I understood the mournful melodies with which the Russians are forever celebrating their *lubrimaya*—their beloved Moscow. Sentimental songs, sad and longing, filled with the nostalgia of the Russian heartland.

It was only after I had traveled deep into Russia and returned to Moscow that I could understand the feeling that is in the youths and girls of Moscow's university and institutes when mid-June comes and the sun mounts so high that night practically vanishes.

This is the time which Leningrad knows as the "white nights." But Moscow's nights are almost equally white. Dark falls at midnight but there is still light in the western sky, and by half past one streaks begin to show again in the east.

When examinations are over the girls put on their best long, white dresses and the boys their dark-blue serge suits—if they have them. They scrub their faces red and slick back their hair. In late evening, by classes and cliques, they go to the cafés where (frugally, for they haven't much money) they eat cake and ice cream and, perhaps, drink a bottle of wine. They dance a bit and they talk—especially, they talk—until closing at 3 A.M.

When they emerge on the street it is full daylight, a pale, colorless daylight with the sun still under the horizon. Linking arms, the youngsters move out into the broad streets and stroll slowly through the center of Moscow, singing song after song. For hours you hear their voices swelling and fading, swelling and fading, as they move about, meeting their comrades, forming larger crowds, dissolving into groups of eight or ten, reconverging. And always singing. Toward four or five o'clock the groups gather in the Red Square, and there the voices form a chorus that rolls and echoes from the pink walls of the Kremlin and the gray walls of GUM. Some of the songs are songs of love. Others are the sad songs of the Slav. Some are the new songs of Soviet patriotism, somehow muted by their fresh sopranos, altos and basses. And many are about their beloved Moscow.

It is only with the death of Stalin that the youngsters have brought their songs into the Red Square. Before that they stayed away, following one of those invisible but immutable rules which are the law of Moscow.

I have listened to the young wine of these voices and seen the clear blue eyes and the blossoming cheeks of these youngsters. And, listening to young Moscow singing its soul out for a beloved city, sadness has crept into my heart.

Here they were, the youth of Russia. The faces fresh in the cool morning light. Innocent. Still unmarked by the chains of the machine, by the whips of the dialectic. Youngsters who did not yet know that soon the Soviet night would begin to fall about them, and with it the clutch of fear.

Friendship of Peoples Fountain: *15 figures represent the 15 Soviet republics.*

LENINGRAD

Leningrad is haunted both by the elegance of the Tsars and by memories of the bitter intellects that launched the revolution. It lives among relics of other times, but in the lovingly preserved past Santha Rama Rau finds a key to the courage and vitality that still animate Russia's most beautiful city.

From the moment you arrive in Leningrad you are haunted by the city's past. It is all around you—in the innumerable monuments, palaces, churches that provide strange continuations and contrasts with life today. On any street, whether severe in its modern atmosphere or lavish in its old design, flanked by buildings both run-down and grandiose, you are haunted by the famous, the brilliant, the unhappy people who once lived here, by the scenes they must have known so well, by two of the most dramatic centuries of Russia's history. Leningrad's past has a curious vitality—more than in any other city I have known—surviving even in the unaccommodating climate of the new Soviet society.

The Soviets have a pleasing system of preserving the house or apartment of a very distinguished person as a sort of informal museum. As far as possible it is restored to its original condition, the furniture and pictures are reassembled, the décor copied from contemporary records. To me, these museums

formed an oddly moving aspect of Russia, they brought life and intimate detail to the vanished world of old Russia, and gave a sudden reality to those infinitely foreign people who lived in it. The seven elegantly formal rooms where Pushkin spent the last years of his life, and where he died after a romantic duel, still seem to enclose the air and the manners of the city at its grandest period. Here was the whole atmosphere of St. Petersburg, the city of the Tsars, more than a century away, but still a recurring echo in modern Leningrad.

If you stand in the dining room or in one of the salons of Pushkin's apartment and look out the long windows with their looped lace curtains, you see one of Leningrad's many canals. In summer, boats filled with young couples and sightseers cruise along the city's waterways, passing around the one hundred islands, to reach, at last, the magnificent sweep of the Neva River. You suddenly grasp the plan of the city—the river curling around islands and headlands, crossed by the graceful arches of bridges, and on each bank the disciplined lines of the palaces and churches (now museums and ministries). In the distance is the slender spire of the Peter and Paul Fortress (the grim prison of the old days), the distinctive rostral column on Vasilievsky Island, the pillared façade of the Winter Palace, and dominating them all, the celebrated statue of Peter the Great, who founded the city in 1703—the Bronze Horseman for whom Pushkin named his long patriotic poem, poised forever on his rearing horse atop a massive rock, the emperor with arm outstretched, the inspiration of St. Petersburg, the heart of Leningrad.

Pushkin's apartment doesn't face the Neva (it's on one of the lesser canals that lace the city), but from its windows, the sight of those pleasure boats, against the background of Leningrad's imposing baroque buildings, that still are painted in the light-hearted colors of past fancies—yellow and apple-green, dove-gray and rose—takes you almost effortlessly into the flamboyant days of the dead Tsars, when St. Petersburg was the new capital of "all the Russias," the center of intellectual life, the "Paris of East Europe," deliberately designed for kings and their courtiers.

Then, when you turn from the window to the cool stylishness of the early 18th Century furniture in the room, to the satins and brocades, it is easy to fill the apartment with imagined gatherings of Pushkin and his friends. Clustered at the dining table, perhaps, discussing contributions to Pushkin's literary magazine, *Contemporary*. Possibly deciding to publish a story by an unknown named Gogol, or the memoirs of that amazing woman Durova, who disguised herself as a soldier and fought, undiscovered, in the war of 1812. Or a group of artists and nobles at the round table under the huge portrait of Pushkin in the inner salon which he reserved for his special friends, deciding on the spur of the moment that each would write a couplet for a song, and that Glinka, Pushkin's lifelong friend, would write the music—the finished product is propped on the piano in the corner. The names, themselves, are evocative of an age: Prince Valkonsky, who had the chic literary and musical salon of St. Petersburg; Prince Baryatinski, versatile in the arts; Kiprenski, who, lacking paints while in exile for his part in the abortive insurrection of 1845, made a portrait of Pushkin in butter; Krylov, who wrote the wonderful Russian fairy tales; Linyev the painter, Zhukovski the aristocratic poet.

Even today Leningrad maintains its reputation for intellectual activity, and its artists and writers feel so strongly about their city that, according to a much quoted story, the eminent musician Shostakovich had to be forced to leave Leningrad on a stretcher during the German siege; he could not bear to desert his beloved city in a time of peril. Leningraders compare their ballet companies favorably with the world-famous Bolshoi of Moscow—and remind you that Galina Ulanova began her dancing career and made her reputation in Leningrad before Moscow took her over. They tell you with pride that Khachaturian's controversial ballet *Spartak* was first performed in Leningrad a year and a half before it was given to Moscow. They are loyal to their best drama company (called, predictably enough, the Pushkin Theater Company), and claim that it is both more original and more polished than the better-known Moscow Art Theater. They are justifiably proud of their university, their intellectuals and their writers who, though little known outside Russia, seem, to the Leningrad mind, to follow in the tradition of Pushkin, Lermontov, Gogol, Turgenev, Dostoyevsky, to mention only the greatest.

If the memorabilia in Pushkin's apartment of the intellectual life of the times—the first editions of his books, the holographs from musicians, writers, painters—remind you of a vital aspect of old St. Petersburg, the pervasive presence of Pushkin's wife, her photographs, bills and household notes, bring back with a new immediacy the other essential side of St. Petersburg— the social life of a major capital. You can see, in the charming femininity of her rooms, that she was giddy and extravagant and beautiful. She could spend in a month, without a thought, 471 rubles on hats from the exclusive French milliner Mme. Zoe Malpart—there is the bill addressed in French, as was proper for the nobility of the time, to *Son Excellence Mme. Pouschkine*. She saved invitations, loved the palace parties which were the pivot of the city's society. Pushkin, as an officer in the Tsar's government, was compelled to attend them though he had no interest in the fashionable life, and his disputes with the Tsar were a scandal in court circles.

Even in the old days of its splendor, of course, there was another life in St. Petersburg, far removed from the palaces and parties, from the doings of grand dukes and duchesses, from the salons of the intellectuals. Its most famous chronicler was Fyodor Dostoyevsky. Writing more than a generation after the almost legendary Pushkin, he was not so absorbed with the "Magnificent City of Peter." As the titles of his books— *Poor Folk, The Landlady, The Insulted and the Injured, The Idiot, Crime and Punishment*—indicate, he wrote about the other life of the city.

Not that Dostoyevsky was unaware of its beauties: ("I love the March sun in Petersburg.... The whole street glitters, bathed in brilliant light. All the houses seem to sparkle of a sudden...it is as though everything seems brighter, as though you were startled, or someone had nudged you with his elbow"); but he was equally conscious of its moments of intense gloom: ("Twilight was deepening and I felt more and more melancholy....I kept thinking that in the end I should die

in Petersburg...if only I could get out of this shell into the light of day, breathe the freshness of the fields and woods...").

One day, my husband and I decided to find Dostoyevsky's apartment to see if it held, as Pushkin's had, the air and feeling of his times, of his life in the city. Perhaps in this way we might see a little of that "other life" of St. Petersburg.

After considerable difficulty we found the apartment. It was not a museum. And it was not Dostoyevsky's life that it contained. As it turned out we had taken an unintentional excursion into modern Leningrad life.

The day we set out on our search was moist and cold. Leningraders said that the summer was really over now—no more long mild evenings. Now autumn would spread its penetrating chill through the city. I had been reading *The Insulted and the Injured*, that early, inept and curiously moving mixture of autobiography and fiction that Dostoyevsky had written nearly a century ago. When I came to passages like..."he pointed to the foggy vista of the street, lighted by street lamps dimly twinkling in the damp mist, to the dirty houses, to the wet and shining flagstones, to the cross, sullen, drenched figures that passed by, to all this picture, hemmed in by the dome of the Petersburg sky"...I had only to look out of my hotel window to find an almost theatrical re-enactment of the scene. Although it wasn't actually raining, the Leningrad sky was soft with clouds and St. Isaac's golden dome was a somber metallic gray.

After tea, my husband and I, following the directions we finally had obtained, walked to Dostoyevsky's apartment. It wasn't far, but it was in a poor part of town, where tourists seldom go. We had seen many beautiful and impressive things in Leningrad, but somehow this cold, undistinguished street corner was more memorable—or rather, memorable in a different way—than all the palaces, museums and gardens. It had the solid feeling of reality.

Resurrection Cathedral reflected in Griboyedov Canal.

It was already deep twilight, the premature evening of misty weather. The first trickle of people returning from work had begun, and there were customers at the cigarette stall on the corner and, surprisingly, at the cold-drink kiosk across the street. The entrance to the building was on an alleyway half blocked by a pile of lumber and building materials.

We walked through the archway to a dank and messy courtyard. Stacked firewood was partly covered with a torn tarpaulin. Next to it was a small shed or outhouse with a rotten door sagging on its hinges. There were shallow puddles between the flagstones. Four or five children with the pinched, thin-legged look of slum children anywhere played in the courtyard, taking turns climbing the outhouse roof, jumping to the firewood, and then to the ground. They stopped their game to stare at us, until we turned away uncertainly to examine the wooden board hung on a nail just inside the archway. It gave, in white painted letters, the names of the tenants and the numbers of their apartments, but, of course, there was nothing to indicate which had been Dostoyevsky's.

We were trying to collect the courage to knock on the door of one of the apartments—any apartment—and ask, when the biggest of the children, a shaven-headed blond boy, came over to us.

"Foreigners?" he asked without smiling.

"Yes."

"Poles?"

"No," my husband said, "I'm——"

"Hungarian?"

"No, American."

"Chewing gum?" the boy said hopefully.

"No chewing gum," my husband said, sorry to disappoint the child.

But the boy was busy fishing in the pocket of his shorts with a chapped hand. He pulled out a small, rather tarnished gilt-and-enamel badge, like a lapel pin. In Russian characters, it was inscribed: "1957 Youth Festival U.S.S.R." "Foreign money?" he asked.

"I'm sorry. But we will buy it for rubles if you want."

"Rubles?" He turned down the corners of his mouth and put the badge back in his pocket. He looked resigned more than disappointed.

"We are searching," my husband said, "for the apartment of Dostoyevsky."

The boy looked at us thoughtfully for a moment before he said, "Second entrance, third floor on your left," and ran back to his companions.

Inside the doorway marked "2," we found ourselves in a stone-floored hallway, colder than the evening outside. The stairs were uncarpeted stone, too, with iron railings and a small fogged window with iron bars on each landing. On one landing a metal bathtub was propped against the wall; its four little claw feet stuck out toward the stairs. On the third floor two doors faced each other across the narrow hallway. Both were heavily padded and strips of felt were tacked around them to cover the cracks. We rang the bell at the door on our left.

All the way up my husband had been composing sentences in his politest Russian: "Please forgive us for disturbing you,

but is this the apartment that was at one time occupied by Fyodor Mikhailovich Dostoyevsky, the writer?" But when the door was opened by a gray-haired woman in a dark dress with a sweater over it, he could only stare at her inquiring face and blurt out, "Good evening—did Dostoyevsky live here?"

Understandably, she looked astonished. "*What* did you say?" she asked, and added as an afterthought, "Good evening."

The second time it came out sounding better and she smiled. "Ah, Dostoyevsky. You are foreigners?"

"Yes. Tourists. And we are so sorry to trouble you."

"Ah, *tourists*. It is no trouble. Please come in. You are interested in Dostoyevsky?"

"We think him a great writer."

"Come in, please come in. Yes, this used to be his apartment."

She beckoned us through the outer and the inner door, equally padded against drafts. I was suddenly aware of how freezing the Leningrad winter must be. She locked both doors behind us, and remarked pleasantly, "You would like to see this apartment where he lived? It is nothing very special."

A woman's voice from another room called out something to which our hostess replied, "Come here, come here," and smiling at us, explained, "My sister—my younger sister."

The door on our left opened and a small round woman in black joined us in the cluttered hall. "Foreigners," our hostess said, as though that one word explained our presence. The four of us stood uncomfortably close, packed between a black leather bench on one side of the foyer, and a tall, white-painted cupboard on the other. There was an old-fashioned wooden coat rack in one corner, and simply no room for any other furniture.

The older woman said, "I have often wondered what kind of furniture Dostoyevsky had. This hall must have been empty —you can see that would be better. Really, there is only space for the bench and the coat rack. Probably he didn't have enough furniture to put here anyhow—he was always selling things to pay doctors' bills, debts." She smiled at us rather apologetically. "I know all this because I have lived here so long— thirty years, even before I was married. When we first moved here there were still old people in the building who remembered Dostoyevsky. They are dead now, of course. But they used to tell me how movers would come up the stairs and another piece of furniture would be taken away, another bill paid. He was very sick, you know. I was young when I heard these things, and it all seemed to me so sad." She shrugged her shoulders. "Now . . ."

I wondered how she would finish the sentence: Now worse things have happened to all of us? Or, now I have other things to think about?

But my husband said politely, "Now he would have free medical care?"

She laughed as if we had a secret together. "Yes. That is true."

The younger sister opened the door behind her. "This was his room," she said in a soft, deprecating voice. "The coldest and darkest room in the building. This is where he lived." *The Insulted and the Injured* had opened with the hero looking for a place to live: "All that day I had been walking about the town trying to find a lodging. My old one was very damp and I was beginning to cough rather ominously." We followed the sisters into his room. Smallish, with two narrow windows set close together in the wall opposite the door, it also looked crowded although there actually was little furniture. Two iron beds, one under each window, a cupboard, a round table covered with a plush tablecloth, a couple of straight chairs. I walked over to the windows, squeezing past the table, and stared out at Dostoyevsky's view. The dingy courtyard, the dark thin little figures of the children playing, the Leningrad evening closing in. Behind me one of the sisters switched on the light and said, "He worked here too. He was in bed much of the time and had to do his writing here."

I could think of no questions to ask, could not even imagine the sick tormented figure under that tidy white counterpane, writing away in the coldest, dampest room.

We crossed the tiny foyer to the door immediately opposite. This room was a bit bigger with French windows opening onto a narrow iron balcony. Here, too, there was a bed, but the room had been used as a parlor in Dostoyevsky's day—and there were three armchairs covered in white cotton, and another round table. "The sun comes in here in the afternoons," the gentle voice of the younger sister said, "—when we have some sun." We all smiled. Leningrad weather, like London weather, is always good for a mild joke.

While we were in this room, the doorbell rang. The older sister hurried out to open the door, and we could hear fragments of a muttered conversation in the hall. Almost immediately our hostess returned with a woman of stocky build and rather severe expression. She was still in her outdoor coat and scarf, and was carrying a string bag of onions, a large cabbage, a loaf of black bread and some packages wrapped in newspaper. She was introduced as "My older sister. This is her room."

In the awkward silence that followed, I said, "How nice that your family is all together."

When my husband translated this, our hostess replied without much interest. "Yes. We all lived here together when we were young. Now we all live here together again. Three old women."

"And in between?" my husband asked.

"In between we married. And the war. All three husbands killed. Again we live together—like girls." She laughed to emphasize the absurdity of her description.

Back to the foyer, and then into a thin sliver of a pantry obviously made by partitioning off part of the passageway. The oldest sister was there unpacking her purchases. Eggs in a plastic bowl on the table, cookies on a blue china plate. A small electric hot plate on the table transformed the narrow pantry into a makeshift kitchen.

With a touch of eagerness, the youngest sister led us through the pantry to curtained glass doors which opened into yet another bedroom. "My daughter's room," she said, almost whispering, and motioned to us to follow her. When we all stood around a baby's crib in the center of the room, staring down at the small pink child asleep in his closely wrapped shawls, she said, after an admiring moment, "My grandson."

I looked around at the rest of the room. Two large wardrobes were placed side by side, jutting into the room to form a kind of screen for the double bed in the corner. A desk and a bookcase. Two or three chairs. And the baby in his crib. "My daughter is a schoolteacher. Her husband too. They are not yet home." Rather timidly she asked, "Perhaps you will stay and meet them?"

"Oh, no," my husband and I said together, suddenly noticing how long we had been in the apartment. He added, "We have already disturbed you far too much."

"But at least you will stay and have some tea with us?"

"No, really. We must go." We stepped back into the pantry.

"But something," the middle sister said, looking worried. She passed the plate of cookies. We each took one, and since there wasn't room for more than one of us to sit at the pantry table, we all stood up nibbling cookies and smiling.

"Have we shown you what you came to see?" she asked.

"Yes, exactly," I answered firmly, lying shamelessly, for nothing could have held less of Dostoyevsky's atmosphere than this neat, cramped life, the quiet, the three old widows and the sleeping infant.

"I have been wanting to ask you something." The first touch of diffidence came into her voice. "What is it that you find in Dostoyevsky's writing?"

Before I could answer she went on hastily, "I do not ask out of ignorance. I used to be a doctor, I am retired now. I get a pension of a thousand rubles a month. My husband, before he was killed, was an engineer. So you understand that we are not uncultured. I have read Dostoyevsky—with particular care since we live in his apartment—but still, I must ask, what do you see in him? Why is he great?"

I couldn't think what to say, how to describe Dostoyevsky's calamitous power with words. At last I said, rather feebly, "He wrote of such extraordinary things—such strange unhappy people——"

She listened closely to my husband's translation with growing bewilderment. "Extraordinary?" she said. "Strange? But Dostoyevsky wrote of everyday, *ordinary* things and people. When I finish a Dostoyevsky novel, I forget it before I put the book down. What is there to remember? Now *Tolstoy*—a truly great writer. Who can ever forget Anna Karenina?" Anna Karenina, the rich, the aristocratic, the eternally romantic woman.

"To *us*," my husband explained, "Dostoyevsky's world is extraordinary. And powerful. And remembered forever."

For the first time the oldest sister joined in the conversation. "You are foreigners," she said.

Walking back that evening we came slowly to the good part of town near the Astoria, the wide streets and the fine buildings. I thought of the brightly lit lobby that awaited us, filled with music from the restaurant, the smiling greeting of the elevator operator, the lovely view from our windows. Now it was the hurrying pedestrians we passed who held the reality of the city, dark figures carrying packages and shopping bags. Now I had an idea of the life they returned to when they ducked into a dim entrance or through an archway, the world behind the beautiful facades.

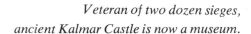

Sweden

Usually grave, pensive and even formal, the Swedes
are still capable of bursting suddenly
into gay and reckless activity.
They are, says William Sansom,
a nation of perfectionists whose character is as elegant,
as polished and as functional as the glittering
ball bearings their industry supplies to the world.

The master key to the Swede is the sun. There are several lesser locks to be negotiated; for with his Baltic soul and his era of 17th Century power and his exclusion from the last two world wars—and his comparative wealth—he is one of the most complicated of Europeans. But it is still the sun that turns him deepest, both with its absence during the long dark winter months, when resignation can sink to melancholy, and with its sudden marvelous blaze of strength in spring and golden summer.

On the first warm day of spring the citizens of Stockholm, a busy enough city, sit in hundreds on the steps of the Dramatic Theater or the Concert Hall, their faces toward the sun, their eyes closed, motionless, rapt. The first buds, a pleasure anywhere, become an obsessional joy with the Swede. Normally a quiet, grave people who tend to smile rather than laugh, their annual awakening from the condemned chrysalis is truly passionate and not easy for our more temperate hearts fully to understand—there is a certain splendor in such excitement; but one is reminded that all passion must be paid for. One suspects, too, that this split personality of the weather is reflected in the character of the Swede—somewhere beneath that kindly, pensive, ordered gravity, beneath his well-pressed cloth of sober gray, there burns a ball of fire yearning to explode. At times it does, and the cliché of the big crazy Swede comes

alive—sunshine, art, jazz, or a pair of skis can kindle this smoldering spark. And of course, in a people largely concerned with ice and long darkness, it flares prettily on alcohol.

However, that is the eruption. Ordinarily, the Swedish character is nearer the ball bearing than the ball of fire—it is as elegant, as polished, as functional as those fine steel spheres their industry has perfected. Elegance is noticeable in this country—elegance in craftsmanship such as the making of glass and pewterware; elegance in a formality of manners largely uninfluenced by modern laxity. But here again, though this might be a legacy of the great days of Gustavus Adolphus and Charles XII, we may be back with the sun motif—for love of the sun has given the Swede a consuming love of nature; he is unhappy without a tree and a plant and a mossy stone within reach, and it may well be that a sensitive colloquy with the natural beauties engenders a wider elegance. The Swedish flag is blue and yellow, the colors of the sun and the sunlit sky.

The countryside is more important to a Swede than his modern and functional city, and there are many facets to this countryside. For Sweden is a long country running north and south through several climates. Down in the south near Denmark the land is flat and flowering, and there is corn and thatch. Nearly a thousand miles north, harsh mountains of iron rise, icebound for most of the year, magic and desolate in the ephemeral midnight sun. Between, with its vast fir forests and its ninety-six thousand lakes, the country extends a gradual compromise between these different poles. So where to begin? Perhaps about the center, which is often called the heart of Sweden, the province of Dalarna, that is known abroad as Dalecarlia.

Here, in the villages of the long and lovely Lake Siljan, old-fashioned peasant costumes and handicrafts survive more than elsewhere in the country. The usual picture of the broad-hatted knee-breeched farmer, and of his wife in her striped apron and bodice, will more than likely come from here, and here the

fiddlers still gather and the long church boats strike out on the lake. These unusual craft, carrying from fifty to a hundred villagers, garlanded with green birch leaves and rowed by many white-shirted menfolk, were once the means of visiting the several white churches by the water. But with the advent of roads, they are now used only on ceremonial occasions. However, many of the people still wear the old costumes on Sundays, and though it may sound tourist-inspired to speak of a Dalecarlian walking through the white birch alley in yellow breeches with scarlet pompons, and his lady in one of her dozen formal costumes (different patterns for funerals, weddings, Christmas and so on), it is not so. They will be at ease, smoking a cigarette, chatting of crop or forest, and in a few seconds the costume is forgotten.

A sight always more startling than a pair of daffodil breeches is the number of white birch trees. This lovely eccentric, with

its slender branches that form so exquisite a filigree of silver in the hoarfrost, of misted green in spring, makes one feel as if someone had gone mad with a whitewash brush, splashing the dark forest with brilliant streaks of white. Sometimes the birches lead to a white church, or line the avenues of a small town. But the forests stretch far beyond, for mile upon monotonous mile, a vast melancholy of trees that the Swedes feel for intensely, as for a great and tender music.

Every great city has its different aspects; and one may first be impressed by the entrance into Göteborg harbor with its gray-black granite cliffs piling up like a dead school of whales, reminder that after the long reaches of Atlantic and North Sea hard land has been reached. Or one may be struck by the older town, with its 18th Century quays and its Dutch canals (most now filled in, though ghosts of them persist in the reflection of those remaining), and the open-air market of flowers. Or by the lovely park along the old moat where the town walls once stood; or—and this may be strongest—the feeling of well-planned space about the broad avenues and the tall, balconied apartments; or by Götaplatsen—a spacious square on elevated ground where theater, concert hall, art museum and the most modern Scandinavian hotel, the Park Avenue, converge round Milles' Poseidon fountain.

The Göteborgers are said to be different from other Swedes, more easygoing, like the southern people of Skåne. But do they laugh? Seldom in a restaurant do you hear a burst of laughter; seldom in the street is there more than a smile. What, one wonders, do the visiting sailors, tuned to the diversions of Antwerp or Copenhagen, find to do? There is a fine summer amusement park, and one big dance hall—apart from these a landfall here must reflect something of the granite tone of Göteborg's cool cliffs.

Boating about Bohuslän is another Göteborger joy. You can reach the sea in twenty minutes from the center of town. And this barren seacoast with its humpbacked rocks and small yachting towns like Marstrand attracts the summering Swede from all over—that is, if he is not adoring the sun in Lapland, or enjoying the sandier beaches to the south toward Lund, or painting a thousand miles off in the Balearic island of Iviza where a bearded, sun-glazed Swede with easel may be found round every corner.

But we are not in Iviza, nor Marstrand—we're still pumping up the green Göta canal on those leisurely three days to Stockholm; and by now threading between meadowed cows to the sleepy old spa of Söderköping (South Market). The town has that curiously attractive quiescent atmosphere of all those places which were once great ports and have now retreated inland. In the Middle Ages it was a commercial junction as thriving as Stockholm. But the river slowly silted up, the Hanseatic merchants from Lübeck or Visby directed their commerce elsewhere and one more great city of spires and monasteries faded to a village—but the atmosphere is thick.

Three miles farther on comes the bay of Slätbaken, and now the ship approaches the salt Baltic spray. A country has been crossed; these Baltic waters saw ancient Viking ships set off from Roslagen, farther north, to give the name *rus* to Russia, while Vikings on the west were beaching their longboats on the shores of America. But the present sea trip is less astounding; soon Södertälje embraces us with its harbor and the last stretch of canal into Stockholm's Lake Mälaren. This is Sweden's third-biggest lake, but it is more land than water, so profuse are its spruce-dark islands, and through these the boat approaches the first scattering of summer huts, the first suburban villas, and finally the first outcrop of big apartment blocks. Then, quite suddenly, you're in the city. Spires have risen around you, traffic swirls and the steamer is tying up opposite a broad quay on which stands a column like that of St. Mark in Venice, and beyond it a red-towered palace reminiscent of the Venetian campanile. This is Ostberg's famous City Hall of Stockholm, a sly comment on the loose old soubriquet "Venice of the North," but beautiful in its own right.

The City Hall is a fitting symbol, in some ways, of Stockholm itself, deep red brick with green copper turreting and golden crown work. Let us not so much marvel that here is a building of the 1900's that has achieved an integrated beauty, but that so many different styles have converged successfully. Stockholm is full of such exoticisms. "Lion gold" is a traditional color that blazes across large stretches of 18th Century plaster; Falu red may cover a tall gabled house in the Old Town or a great apartment block; there are domes of violent green copper, there are oriental motifs in some of the new carved granite buildings, and high above the white ships of the harbor hangs a suspended restaurant called *The Gondola*. But these, of course, are the eccentric spangles in a city that must mostly be remembered for its lucent stretches of water, its white ships, its clear glassy air, its green furring of landscape garden, its clusters of rectangular buildings and its involved traffic.

Stockholm is a deepwater port for big ships of the Baltic; it is the administrative center of a long land predominantly living off timber and iron. It has a million inhabitants, a seventh of the entire Swedish population, and they have the reputation among provincials of being busy, hardhearted and impersonal —the reputation of every capital city. Unlike most other capitals, it is not gay. It is beautiful, it offers exquisite food and fine theater and other metropolitan pleasures, and at night it is brightly lighted. Restaurants are luxurious and hushed; you may even be refused entry on suspicion of being drunk if you approach with too much gaiety. There are big dance halls, like the National, where youth has its more animated fling; and in some restaurants there is conservative dancing. The summer provides an amusement park on the Djurgarden island at Skansen—and then, with the sun and the open-air cafés, there is more liveliness. But generally the Swedes take it courteously, quietly.

For years, until it was moderated in October, 1955, Sweden has lived under the Bratt system of liquor rationing. Hard liquor could be bought only from State shops on a ration card (3 liters a month for adults). In restaurants, liquor was served only with food, and even then consumption was limited, with half measures for ladies. The plate of hash obligatory with a drink was seldom consumed, being brought out again and again for new customers. Light wines were fairly free, but expensive in a land without vines, and beer was only about two per cent alcohol. It is probably this, rather than the Swedish temperament, which has kept the city so quiet. But one cannot be certain, for the Swede is difficult to predict—with his stiff traditional manners yet his delight in modern design, his puritan air yet his sexual casualness (about 10 per cent of all Swedish children are illegitimate). Where this sexual freedom, which is a general Scandinavian tendency, derives from is difficult to say. It may be part of the climate of social progress—part of the throwing off of restriction, of planning for comfort and equality (including sexual equality). Paradoxically again, in a country given to benign bureaucratic restriction, there is a straightforward lack of prudery. Unmarried mothers are well looked after, at least without official opprobrium. Nor is there any fuss, in a country otherwise inclined toward formality in dress and manners, about near-nakedness on the beaches. The love of fine physique and sun worship, sees to this. Magazines of nude photographs decorate every tobacconist's window.

But despite her equality in most matters, the Swedish woman still faces one old drawback—a superiority in numbers. The male tends to pick and choose, giving him an attitude of superiority. "The Orient begins at Malmö," it has been said, with reference to these sultanly tendencies.

It may be suggested that life in Stockholm, with its fine music, theater and art, and its accessible sports, is enough. Yet one wonders; and one feels an air not of simple enjoyment but of light tension, of some kind of spiritual dissatisfaction. The perfectionist Swede works hard and pays high taxes and enjoys a high standard of living. Poverty is nil. It is a welfare state that has progressed far. But perhaps the achievement of such a physically sound position, with its emphasis on the reasonable middle way and its implicit condemnation of excess and eccentricity, leaves the bewildering question: What for? But in any case, no one could wish the situation retracted and the cruelty of the old stews returned. Perhaps, after all, and in terms of temperament, we are back with the sun again—and with a discontent more divine.

The sun returns us to the right life of Stockholm, and one grave omission. For Stockholm does offer a unique summer diversion—the flight to the midnight sun. The plane leaves in the morning between ten and eleven; by one o'clock the well-dined Stockholmer is circling above the great lakes and wild valleys of northern Lapland, a moth in the light of the low lantern sun; sometime after four he is back home again in the capital. In that time, he will have passed up and down his entire long country, far above the spires of Upsala of the white-capped students, up and up over log-bearing rivers and forests and charcoal burners' huts, past Skelleftea whose iron deposits contain so much arsenic it has to be hidden away in concrete vats, past Boliden where gold is mined, over bears and wolves and elks and deer and eagles and the great long-skirted owls of the north, up to the land where Lapps live in hide-and-birch wigwams with their reindeer herds, up to the mining town of Kiruna which boasts the largest city area in the world (about 5000 square miles), up to the long glass roofs where tomatoes and cucumbers and strawberries are forced in the few months of strong sunlight, and finally to Lake Torneträsk, near the Norwegian border, a magic of flowering desolation in the light of the low-lying, lambent, night-loving sun.

The shadow of your airplane might remind the Lapp of his gray reindeer herd as it moves in winter like a shadow across the distant mountain snows, or cause him to wonder whether a friend's catch of fish was aboard, or a sick person for the hospital, for this most modern form of transport is the most reasonable one in emergency for this least mechanized of Sweden's people.

As a pork packer uses up all of the pig, so a Lapp rationalizes his reindeer. Its strength is used for transport (pack or sleigh), its flesh for meat, its hide for clothing and for building, its fur for warmth, its horn for knives. Of an estimated 10,000 Swedish Lapps, about three or four thousand are nomadic.

Following their reindeer down from the wolves in winter and up from the mosquitoes in summer is an arduous, though profitable, life. It is no longer right to talk of the Lapps generally as a nomadic people; for they are beginning to prefer huts to tents, to form settled communities, to cultivate the land and to fish. They still wear a decorated traditional costume, the woman in her apron and big skirt and lace cap, the man in a loose-fitting blue-and-red coat and a cap topped with a huge red pompon. The nomadic Lapp child attends nomadic school in the summer, and although at heart his worship is still very close to nature—there are strange tales of telepathic powers over great distances and of an ability to hear "music" from stones—he is properly a Christian, though he may be able to visit the church only twice a year, when accumulations of marriages and christenings are celebrated en masse.

The land these strange, slit-eyed little people live in is surprisingly luxuriant in summer, and malicious. Flowers grow to twice their normal size, the sun remains out all night—and the mosquito breeds in millions. Over the flowered wilderness one may see at midnight a nearly naked hiker glistening with mosquito oil, his pale sun-cast shadow stalking behind; one may see also the luxurious electric carriages of the Land Cruise train from Stockholm humming along in comfort over the reindeer moss and heather, past snow-capped mountains and immensely calm lakes, over country softened by Atlantic warmths, though on a parallel with the center of Greenland. Like all lonely, unpopulated places, Lapland beggars description. Its essence is the sense of time and space that permeates the air, of age and of permanence.

But in winter? Then life must seem frustrated, extended unendurably through dark hours endlessly long. *Lappsjuk*, Lapp sickness, the Swedes call the languor of the northern mind in winter. The country is snowbound throughout its length—the Bothnian ports are frozen fast, you can drive a car over lakes frozen with ice a yard and more thick, the petrol-blue rivers of summer turn to bottle-green torrents snaking through bull icicles big as organ pipes, locomotives arrive hoary and ice-hung like those heavy black monsters met in 19th Century Russian novels; and indeed the whole of the mystique of ice and fur and snow and fire invigorates the cold white land

Because the Swede and the visitor to his land like to think in terms of summer, this account has emphasized the golden months—but that is only a third of the story. The rest is snow and frost and the bravura of torchlit sleigh rides under a blue velvet sky studded with icy stars. Or, if you like, sitting by a rubber plant in double-windowed steam heat—for the Swedes are not like the camp English, they make themselves comfortable. Even the reindeer's horns are covered with a warm, mossy fur.

And it seems finally that it must indeed be this long winter, with its long introspective hours—plus a comparative wealth for so northerly a nation—that has made the Swede a perfectionist. He flavors his envelope glue to taste sweet, winds up the end of his tooth-paste tube with a key, places a litter box outside a country school; and in larger matters is fair and socially progressive for the good of all, and has become peaceable after having been, like the Swiss, one of the ablest militarists of Europe.

But other people have long winters, little sun? So they do. We are back with a question mark where we started.

Norway

To the tourist, Norway may be a fairyland of snow and ice, a country slashed by spectacular fiords and lit by the Midnight Sun.
But to the rugged Norsemen, Hammond Innes points out, the real Norway is still the wild, glacial, windswept land of the Vikings.

Viking means the dweller in a *vik*—a bay or inlet. The translation is too soft. *Viks* are sudden gashes in precipitous mountains; the homesteads little patches of emerald green, crevice-tucked at fiord head among towering crags capped with snow. Glimpsed from the air, the men of the *viks* are dwellers in a moonscape half submerged in sea; barren, glacial land with ragged fingers deep-thrust in arctic waters, scattering from their tips rock islands like drops of molten lead congealed. And yet, somehow, a fairyland country.

The clouds were breaking up below us as we crossed the Svartisen, that black ice glacier whose dirty, frozen skirts have only recently been drawn back from the sea. We were barely two thirds the way up Norway, yet already inside the Arctic Circle. North from Bodo the sun shone in a clear blue sky and the coast of Norway smiled up at us. Beyond the flapping, corrugated wing of the old JU 52 seaplane the Lofoten Islands emerged from the horizon's haze, a serrated, Alpine outline of incredible brutality. Below us the mountains of the mainland hefted the sea aside into narrow strips with rippling, ice-worn shoulders that rose 2000 feet, their snow patches gleaming white in the sunlight only a little below the bumbling course of our aircraft. Away to port the sea was littered with skerries, islands of rock, white and bald from a million years of glacial polishing.

Three quarters of Norway is barren, uninhabitable. Surely this included the land below us? Yet here and there the gleam of a white-painted wooden house proved the contrary. Man was here, clinging precariously to the scree skirts of the mountains, building on barren rock and harvesting the sea in default of land that bore a trace of life-giving soil. Occasionally, glacial deposits provided root purchase for crops and here the fresh-cut hay showed a tiny carpet of green marked by the sun-shadowed bars of the hay hung to dry on wire fences.

Directly below us the islands seemed to float in patches of livid green as though rimmed by mineral discoloration; the sun coloring the water in the shallows. Elsewhere the water had the flat, black look of great depth. Flat, with no corrugation, for we were over the Inner Lead, that maritime highway that runs a thousand miles almost uninterrupted from North Cape to The Naze, a salt-water river protected by island banks. Boats like toys arrowed the mirror stillness, plowing the water thoroughfare that has cradled the sea's toughest sons.

The men of the *viks*, originally Teutons from Asia, were in Norway almost before the glacial ice had receded. Long before Christ was born the Land of the Midnight Sun was a legend; Homer had heard of it and Herodotus wrote of a people who slept like bears six months of the year. In the search for whale

and walrus (the hide was used for ships' ropes) and in the crossing of the Folda, that forty-mile break in the Lead where the gale-torn might of the North Ocean has been as effective as an Iron Curtain separating North Norway from the South, the fishing "coracles" underwent a sea change and emerged as ships.

The Viking as we know him—the trader, the marauder, the explorer, the settler—was born.

One, Ottar, a trader to England with furs, walrus tusks and rope, and the down of the *ærfugl*—the eider duck—reported to Alfred the Great of a voyage he had made eastward to Russia's White Sea. This was in 875. But already the longships were further afield, thrusting out into the ocean to establish colonies in Iceland and Greenland. They were in America, called Vinland because of the grapes, more than five centuries before Columbus.

But for all their reputation as raiders and seamen they were, and still are, fishermen. The warmth of the Gulf Stream brings them a silver harvest and fish dominate all my memories of the Inner Lead. Oksfjord, typical of a thousand tiny *vaags*, or wharfs, seen at two o'clock in the morning with the sun already high and blazing bright in the translucent air; a trailer of blue smoke hangs over the sheds and oil tanks of the fish factory, drifting vertically against the shadowed bulk of a mountain whose scree slopes support a dozen wooden houses. Nothing else but the silence of the mountains, bare, ice-scarred, devoid of living thing. The stillness of the fiord, the harshness of the unnatural sunlight, has a frozen quality. And as we touched the *vaag* and our warps were looped over the hooks of mooring chains run through hawse holes in the wooden quay, we could smell the fish oil.

The reek of fish oil hangs like a cloying mist over almost every *vaag* the length of Norway. "It is a good smell," I was told once, and the Norwegian rubbed his hands and his salt-wrinkled face cracked in a grin. "It smells of money."

When first I came to Norway just after the war, I came by

Sogne Fjord is the longest in Norway. Against the granite vastness midget farms climb upward from mirrorlike water to tree-covered cliff sides.

sea. The Bergenske Dampskipsselskab, the steamship company whose black funnels ringed in white dominate Bergen's much-photographed fish market and the old Hanseatic houses of the Bryggen, runs a fast luxury service from England. To wake up and find your 9000-tonner gliding into the heart of Stavanger, into what would be the market place in any other country, and mooring at the very doorsteps of the gaily painted wooden houses of this old town, is to be put into the mood of the adventure from the start.

The English language comes easily to the Norwegian, for there has been a two-way trade in words between the two countries since very early days. On the bridge of any Norwegian steamer you can hear the officer of the watch ordering *starboard, midships, steady.* Some speak it with an American accent, some with an English, depending on where their ships have taken them or what nation has hired them as crew. The people of Oslo speak it with the singsong of the Welsh. But apart from school-taught English—youngsters mostly have a good command of the language—the biggest single influence has been World War II and the trek westward across the sea to fight for the king they love.

This was on the scale of a migration. A few went overland via Sweden and Finland, some to Russia to fight with the Red Army—there is a statue at Kirkenes near the Russian frontier to commemorate twelve Norwegians killed by the Germans after being captured in Russian uniform. But the majority moved across the sea, to Iceland, the Faeroes, the Shetlands and Scotland, mainly by fishing boat, but some by smaller boats under sail and even rowing boats with nothing but oars and the strength of their arms with which to fight the westerly winds. Many were lost. But many got through.

Others, like Petersen, a diver's helper, stayed to fight in the Resistance. He told me stories of train wrecking and gun duels high in glacial wastes as he fed air to his partner from a boat moored off Bovaagen's inlet. These two were disentangling a big diesel marine engine from a Dutch barge blasted by a bomb and sunk between two rocky islands. A local man had bought the wreck for a few kroner just for the engine.

Norwegians have an innate business sense. What other country with almost half its length inside the Arctic Circle has turned barren mountain and icy glacier to capital account and exported it as scenic beauty? The towns they build are business towns, centering round the ports—quiet, almost self-effacing, yet bursting with civic pride. Most of them date back about a thousand years—to the days, in fact, when the Norsemen were spreading out into Europe.

The mountains are the Norwegians' playground. In summer their sturdy legs carry them and their piled rucksacks far into the wild hinterlands of rock and snow, following the course of mountain torrents from one tourist hut to another, some to fish the trout- and salmon-full rivers, the majority just to breathe God's good air and feast their eyes on the beauty of Nature.

Nature is their God. And if it is a simple, uncomplicated God, those of us who take advantage of the hospitality provided by the many tourist hostels established through all the finest mountain country will admit that it is a God that harms nobody and makes for a clean-living, friendly people. To eat trout as I have done, fresh-caught in a mountain lake high up in the great solitudes and cooked in a sour-cream sauce, and to listen to the youth songs of boys and girls uninhibitedly tramping the mountains together, is to be as near to the Elysian Fields as one may get in an Atomic Age.

And in winter they don their skis, again to face the mountains for the exhilaration of the clean swoop down through

virgin snow, the feel of freedom and the cold oneness with Nature. At the age of two a boy gets his first pair of skis. At four he tries his first small jump. Grown up, he'll ride the air with whirling, balancing arms as he swoops from the springboard of one of the tall ski- ump platforms that stand at the back of every town. Trekking on ski and on foot, his tough body quarters the mountain ranges winter and summer and he is as astonished as any ardent fly-fisher at the sedentary "salmon-looking" visitors to Sogne Ford who sit all day on a scaffold platform of pine poles under a black umbrella staring down through the waters of the ficrd, waiting for a salmon to enter the net.

As for the sea: this is to Norway what the Corn Belt is to America, and only a playground for the townsmen and the people of the rich forest lands of the South. Indeed, on the coast, from the great whaling ports of Tonsberg and Sandefjord in the south to Alesund and Lofoten where the toc-a-tocs gather to harvest the herring and the cod, there is little talk of playing, summer or winter; nor along the steamship highway in the shelter of the islands, nor on the high seas carrying the world's goods. This is the real Norway. These are the real Norwegians. The ships may have changed down the ages, but the sea hasn't, nor have the men. They are still the men of the *viks*—still sailors, tracers, fishermen, whalers—still Vikings.

Sailors, artists and writers frequent
the cafés of Copenhagen's Nyhavn, a canal street
whose 18th century houses belie its name,
"New Port." The anchor commemorates
seamen who died in World War II.

Denmark

*Denmark is that remarkably individualistic country
where women smoke cigars, the King does
his own shopping, and hard-working citizens refuse
to take themselves seriously.
William Sansom explores the paradoxes of
a land where industrialists donate their profits to
scholarship funds, the government places
no restrictions on the pleasures of a tenaciously gay
people, and the visitor gets
a royal welcome.*

Five hundred islands, giant pink horses, cigar-smoking spinsters, ships in the streets, blood-red cottages with green plush roofs, a sky line of bottles and a capital with a twenty-four-hour-a-day night life—these are some of the ingredients of a country which is too often loosely thought of as a flat green conveyor belt endlessly emitting eggs and bacon and butter; or too vaguely embraced as "part of Scandinavia." But royal Denmark is part of nothing but itself; it is a national entity jealous of its character and customs, properly peculiar.

Denmark is in many ways a middle land. It lies on a latitude with Labrador and a longitude almost as far east as Berlin. It is thus not truly northern, no iceland of winter-long snow and fir forest like its Scandinavian neighbors; nor is it properly separated from the Teutonic influences of the south Baltic coast. Yet you will see snowplows waiting in the railway sid-

ings, and any attempt to use a German dictionary will be confounded by a language wild with ø's and ae's and aa's. Our parcel-loving minds like to align national character, but if one tries to make the Dane into a Swede or Norwegian, one finds he is as far apart from the formal graces of the first as from the athletic *brio* of the latter. The Dane is an easygoing, broad-living fellow, but if one searches south, and tries to relate him with that relatively easygoing German, the Rhinelander—there again the trip rope rises, for the Rhinelander's ease is largely Catholic and wine-growing, and the Dane is nationally Lutheran and a beer drinker.

The Dane, with his large sense of humor, his imagination, his independence, yet his ideal of co-operation, remains distinct. The key to him most probably lies in another direction, in the word "skipper," which is Danish for master of a ship. For Denmark, scattered over hundreds of islands, at the head of the Baltic and abreast the North Sea, is essentially a seafaring nation; the salt sea is in the winds and in the bone. Traveling about the inland sea roads on the ferry, among witchlike buoys mounted with brooms and past churches in which always hang model ships, the green sea suddenly seems rather greener than usual, the green waves hump up a little too solidly for water, and in fact are not water but green turf suckled by the sea, grassland of a low-lying island, one more evidence of this wide integrity of little pieces, purple earth and green grass and blue sea that still goes by the old name of its southern mainland border, the march of the Danes, Denmark. It is neither rugged and keen like Norway, nor low and drenched like Holland, nor built on the ice-age rock of Sweden; this is bright, fresh and lively sea country, soft and sand-born country, freshened by winds from the sea.

A bewildering map shows Denmark, very roughly, as three pieces of land divided by two vertical sea belts. To the left Jutland, springing from the mainland of Europe; in the middle, the rich cluster called Fünen and to the right Zealand and its islands, with the capital Copenhagen. Of four million Danes, one million live in Copenhagen; so whether you arrive by sea from England to Jutland, or from Germany to Zealand, or via the North Pole to Kastrup airport, the capital must finally be the place of destination.

Copenhagen—or as the Danes with a northerly bite have it, København—is a salt-sea city whose deep-draught steamships berth hard up against the main streets. Through the delicate rococo quarterings of the royal Amalienborg Palace, you can see the giant red-and-black funnel of an ocean-going liner, modern steel bright against the weathered gray pediments; the King, sailor himself and monarch of a democracy, often waves from his balcony as these great ships sail off into the Baltic night. It seems, as you wander among the gracious old

dinner in one of the large music halls, such as the Atlantic Palace or Lorry, or in the world-famous Tivoli gardens. You will sit in a restaurant of grand dimension, serving perhaps a thousand diners, and see a creditable variety performance (Copenhagen has a particular reputation for this, a good billing in Copenhagen ensures interest in an artiste throughout the big music halls of Central and Northern Europe); you can stay and dance, or go to one of a dozen more intimate restaurants; at one or two o'clock, you carry on to a night club such as the Adlon (entrance via your passport and a few *kroner*); when this closes at five or so in the morning, other restaurants with music, such as *Hanegalet* (The Cock's Crow) or *Jomfruburet* (The Maiden's Bower) conveniently open their doors; around eleven in the morning there will be dance bands playing at, say, one of the small bars in Nyhavn; fit in thereafter a tea dance somewhere, followed by an apéritif dance at some such place as Wonder Bar, and you are ready for the Atlantic Palace again.

Tivoli demands special mention. Elsewhere the more graceful tradition of the pleasure garden has fallen away; but here still, in the center of a capital city, is a large enclosed garden, planted with trees and harboring its own idyllic lake, where one may enjoy a variety of pleasures—a fine orchestra, a performance of the *commedia dell'arte*, a military band, a number of excellent restaurants, and thereafter all the fun of the usual fair. It is a place that is far from the raucous pleasuredrome of modern conception; and although it boasts a switchback and bright-lighted booths, it still remains a tree-shaded pleasaunce where the best may be enjoyed for little money among a pleasure-strolling crowd not much removed in spirit from those earlier Copenhageners who opened their beloved gardens to the enlivening measure, the "madly racing strains" of the celebrated *Champagne Galop*.

One can only pick at random: the Glyptotek, rich with sculpture and a momentous iron-pillared palm garden, and a fine collection of French impressionists that includes Manet's terrifying *Absinthe Drinker* . . . or the crown jewels in rosy Rosenborg Palace that disappear from view if a pilfering hand extends across an invisible beam . . . or a performance of the Royal Ballet at the gold-and-cream Royal Theater with its richly mirrored promenades and that formidable gilded message above the proscenium EI BLOT TIL LYST (Not only for pleasure). Or the hundred philological surprises that erupt on all sides: STOP FOR BLINK says the traffic light (*stop when the light blinks*); HJAELP yells the security button in the lift (*help*); GOD MAD announces a restaurant (*good food*). Such terrors as FYSISK can be reduced phonetically to a simple "physical," and TOBAKKER makes nice baby talk for "tobaccos." But half the Copenhageners speak English, no need to worry—the language can be left simply to delight the eye.

The coast road to Elsinor takes you north past the startling skyscape of empty bottles piled outside the Tuborg brewery,

houses by the quays, past great Christiansborg Castle that houses the government, and through much of the center of this city, that there is a ship at the end of every street. Against a graceful copper spire the rigging of sailboats describes a sharp calligraphy that in other cities would be made by the winter branches of a tree; and on the green lawns of the Rosenborg park, white seagulls strut the part of pigeons. There is a seaman's roll about the place, streets quickly turn into bollarded quays, and into the main square of Kongens Nytorv, where among old mansions the Royal Theater stands, there debouches the dockful of tarted sailors' dives called Nyhavn—as if Hoboken led off Times Square or Limehouse lay by Piccadilly.

Ships. And spires. The copper spires of Copenhagen are the city's other fable. Castles, churches, and most other buildings of eminence vie to strike with bright verdigris the gray winter sky, the summer's high blue. These green writhings are as dreamlike as the ships—the spire of the copper-roofed Bourse is made up of dragons' tails entwined upward to end in a point of unique delicacy, that of Christianshavn's church is wreathed with a gilded copper staircase spiraling to the sky, the spire of the Russian Church spangles its three great onion bulbs over the high roofs of Bredgade, Christiansborg and the Nicolai church topple giant crowns and high gilded balls dizzily to the heavens. Stand at a high window and see these green-and-gold towers and spires appearing and disappearing in the weaving of a morning mist, one moment gilded by the sun, the next suddenly vanished, and you may feel properly diminutive among these immense decorous chessmen striding —formally, gravely—the streets of a dream town.

But beneath the spires lies the real city, the one so well called the Paris of the North. For Copenhagen is a most lighthearted city; Parisian frivolity laces the rococo of the older buildings; the air is bright, an enlivening clarity glasses the northern sunlight and—an unequivocal fact—you can dance and drink throughout the twenty-four hours. To test this, first take your

*Old tradesmen's signs, traditional symbols of retail shops,
decorate a lane in Tivoli Gardens, Copenhagen's beloved, fantastic pleasure park.*

by villas and small estates set among gardens and birches and the nearest of Copenhagen's bathing beaches at Klampenborg, which offers such diverse distractions as a race course and tuna fishing. A Copenhagener can be out of his office and in the sea within half an hour. Beaches and a residue of small fishing villages line the waters of a tideless Sound, and across the way lies the coast of Sweden. Perhaps now for the first time one realizes the wideness of life on these flatlands, how much more immense the sky becomes, with life a pinprick beneath a consciously curved dome of blue and endless air. Here you can breathe. In the immediate distance rise the fairy-tale towers of Kronborg, Hamlet's castle. Despite a levity of romantic turrets and Dutch gabling, this is a monster fortress and one can well see how its cannon for so many years weighed an iron stopper

Deep-driven oak piles support Egeskov Mansion, the home of nobles since the 16th century and among the loveliest of Fünen's fairytale castles.

into this bottleneck of the Baltic. Ferries land here from Sweden, and they are popular, for by Elsinore lies Marienlyst, a large beach hotel that runs the only gaming tables permitted in the whole of Scandinavia—the Swede who wants to drink freely and ruin himself at the limit of ten *kroner* is a hungry week-end visitor. Even the Swedish elk, a beast of intractable size and truly of the North, has been known to swim across.

Inland lies peaceful green wooded country, the royal deer forests round Lake Esrom and the lovely palace of Fredensborg, a white and classic edifice with roofs of a brilliant dark-blue tile, and the autumn residence of the royal family. It was here that King Christian IX, known as the Father-in-Law of Europe for the number of daughters he provided for her scattered thrones, used to entertain on his lawns the Tsar of Russia and the Empress Dagmar, the Prince of Wales and Princess Alexandra and others of the related royal families and courts of Europe. And it is here that one might realize the curious insistence of blue in the Danish colorscape. On an autumn day, against green lawns and the tawny and gold of great beaches, those royal dark-blue tiles, glazed and richly brilliant, stand insistent against a sky of paler blue; and in the park two guards approach, black bearskins and pale-blue trousers. Blue hits sharply against the greens of nature; it is this insistent wink of blue—on uniforms, in the Royal porcelain, in the bright clothes of children, in the sky, in the sea, in blond eyes, and always in that subtle blue of the roof tiles—that in its very unorthodoxy seems more to mark the country than its natural colors of purple earth and green field and even the ubiquitous red flag. Colors are important. The pleasures of travel lie not only in the enjoyment of strange excellencies but also in the feeling of strange detail; and here colors, and small daily habits—the way the doorknobs move and how the sugar is wrapped—can be in total more impressive than isolated instances of fine architecture and distinguished landscape. What more Italian than the papery flutter of those giant lire notes—what more Danish than the big brass coins, with their feeling of plain *money*, felt in the pocket nowhere else? The windows of every house in Denmark are jungled with green plants, such as mother-in-law tongues, that thrive in steam heat; house builders, like sky-blown angels, wear white caps and white overalls and decorate the skeleton rafters with flags and wreaths; the six-seater taxis are shaped like charabancs and called "half-a-loaf-of-rye-bread"; coffee is drunk with cream, not milk; a white eider-down serves for blankets; and there's always a bicycle behind you and the postboxes are yellow and the King is called a *Konge*.

Denmark is old. But new too. Industry has compelled such cities as Aalborg with its great *akvavit* distilleries, and Aarhus whose fine new university and well-wooded town planning present a spacious outlook for the modern industrial city.

The old and the new, the scientifically packed and frozen butter deriving from a venerable thatched farmhouse—again we find that easy, sensible admixture, that middle way which, like its middle status between the true North and the European main, makes Denmark so difficult to define, so amiable to encounter. A land of sun-charmed castles and tall silver oil tanks, a royal democracy whose king sits one moment on the ritual throne and the next conducts the orchestra publicly in the pit of his Royal Theater. A country where every time you drink a glass of beer you know you are doing somebody somewhere some good, for lager and learning go hand in hand—all the Carlsberg profits are devoted to educational or artistic foundations, or to general scientific research. A land where criminal alcoholics are ordered a most fitting, but elsewhere unusual, corrective: the antialcoholic drug, Antabus. A country whose main railway station in Copenhagen is rich with stained glass and chandeliers but has no trains—they run underneath it—and where a day's run might land you up against an eel farm, an archipelago, a stork's nest. Or in a sudden village of green weatherboarding built by Dutch pirates, or near the abrupt rise or Møn's white cliffs, ghosts of the flat seas, or on a wild shore where crofters still collect the sea-drift amber, or at a large inn (*Kro*) by a trout stream, or in an extremely comfortable hotel in a modern town of progressive excellence. Or anywhere else in a diverse land of hard-working people who refuse to take themselves too seriously, whose government has for years subsidized perhaps the most remarkably successful system of adult education in the world—the Folk-High Schools, where a month's stay, with all accommodations, costs only 185 *Kroner*, or perhaps nothing to a student subsidized by his local council —yet a government that puts no restriction on the pleasures of a gay and tenaciously pleasure-loving people, one of whose endearing small charms is to welcome, sincerely, with real and unrapacious interest, the foreigner.

Changing guard at Amalienborg Palace: *Four fine rococo buildings surround a square in Copenhagen. The palace is the winter home of Denmark's king.*

Some towns in Holland still cherish the costumes of earlier times. On the island of Marken even the children dress in the old style.

Holland

Holland, land of windmills and tulips, dikes and diamonds, is a country that was literally created by its people.
And today, says Hammond Innes, the Dutch, who retain both their monarchy and their enterprise, are among the most democratic and progressive people of Europe.

Holland as a country is unique, and to anybody who knows the sea and its destructive power, utterly fascinating, for geologically it has no right to exist. Half the population is living in what should be water or swamp. As one Frenchman put it: "God created all the world except Holland, which the Dutch created themselves."

I remember the first time I saw it, sailing into the Hook of Holland on a yacht. It was high tide and the breakwaters of the Maas entrance were awash, and my impression was of a vast expanse of sea and sky with only the spire of a church or the sails of a windmill to show that we were coming in to land. We sailed up to Rotterdam, past oil refineries and cranes and miles of warehouses; it was hard to realize that this, the second-greatest port in the world, was all built on piles in a quaking land of bog. And then down through the rivers and canals to Flushing—locks and bridges and barges everywhere, and from the deck no land visible except the dikes on either side, their green tops in silhouette against the cloud-spattered sky. But when I climbed the mast, then I could see all the rich land of Holland laid out below the level of the water on which we sailed—way, way below it, as much as twenty feet.

Holland is, of course, the delta of the Rhine. Combined with the Maas and the Scheldt from the south, it fans out into a great delta area of sand and silt and peat bog with tide-built dunes along the coast. And far inland are heights of sand—old sand banks left by the eroding Rhine waters. In a few cases they reach up to three hundred feet above sea level, a truly mountainous height in a land where a standing field of corn looks high as a hill in the surrounding flatness.

A man who looked at this tidal delta in the 9th Century—a Moorish merchant—described it as a *sebcha*, a plain of salt water and mud. How different it is today, with its two thousand eight hundred polders or reclaimed areas, each protected by its dike; and beyond the polders lie the main sea defenses—first the Watcher or main dike, then the Sleeper and after that the Dreamer. A hard land to create, with the enemy of sea and river water ever at the gate. A hard land to hold. But the enemy at the gate provides nearly five thousand miles of waterways and floats the products of Germany's industrial Ruhr to every quarter of the globe. Go to Rotterdam and in the dust of rebuilding you can feel the thrusting industrial might of resurgent Germany.

The Dutch are afraid of that resurgence. They admit this quite frankly, particularly the Dutch of Rotterdam. They have reason. On May 14, 1940, German bombers tore the heart out of old Rotterdam, and the center of the city was laid flat in a holocaust of high explosives and incendiaries. I can still remember, after all this time, with what a sense of shock we in England heard the news of this attack. It was brutal, cold-blooded obliteration of a city. Later the defeated Germans destroyed half the port of Rotterdam, but it is that first murderous *Blitzkrieg* that the Dutch remember—and so that future generations shall not forget, Zadkine's statue stands in the middle of the rebuilt city, a tortured, impressionistic figure with arms upraised to ward off the blow, and the heart torn out of the contorted body.

But the Dutch are a practical people, and the waters of the Rhine flow through Rotterdam to the sea. Go up to the top of one of their new buildings and look over the half-built city to

A spot of solid Dutch contentment, Middelburg sits on land created by pushing back the North Sea.

the cranes and the silver thread of the Maas. The tideway is black with barges, black with trade flowing down the Rhine. "Already the port is too small," Anton Schutter told me. We were high up in the blitzed cathedral, looking at the city from the top of the partly reconstructed Laurens Tower, and he pointed to an expanse of green meadowland on the outskirts of the city. "We are going to dredge all those fields and make a new harbor. Then Rotterdam will be the greatest port in the world." Jacob Hardingsveld, whose life's work is the painstaking reconstruction of the cathedral, took my arm and drew me to the other side of the scaffolding, not to show me his own great work but to point to a big modern building erected before the war. "Next year we will demolish that," he said, "and drive a great new motorway through to the Maas. Then," he added, with the intensity of a man looking into the future—"then we are in contact with our existence."

Walk through the Lijn Baan, the new shopping center which is largely completed. Everything is very modern—the design of the buildings, the manner of display. The Dutch have a special feel for the straight-line patterns of concrete and brick and glass. For generations they have landscaped their country with trees and public buildings to overcome the monotony of its flatness. By now they have an inherited sense of the look of things, particularly the look of their sky line, and this artistic sense is apparent in the new Rotterdam that is rising like a phoenix from the ashes of the old.

The sea is Holland's Enemy No. 1, but it is also their friend. You have only to visit Amsterdam to see how much they owe to it. Here is a city of a million people with a great history. Its broad concentric canals or *grachten* make it more fantastic than Venice, a giant spider's web of water with fifty canals and four hundred bridges that have remained intact for centuries.

It is difficult to believe, as you stroll in the quiet of evening along the brick-paved streets bordering the canals, that you are seeing it much as the rich Amsterdam merchant saw it three hundred years ago. The buildings, largely of brick, look quite new as they stand shoulder to shoulder in solid ranks, their big windows looking out onto the canals. Then you notice, in the apex of each stone gable, a sturdy wooden gallows with a hook on it, and you realize that these were built as merchants' houses, the upper floors their warehouses and the gallows for tackle to hoist the wares. Here and there you find a date inscribed in the stone. It always seems to be around 1670.

But there are some older buildings too. The Oude Kerke, for instance, which dates from 1300 and is one of the few examples I have seen of a church that stands as it was built, with the houses crowding so close that they are an integral part of the whole. And nearby, at the bottom of the old Zeedijk, is a little tower called the "Tower of Tears" because it marked the end of Amsterdam and so many women stood there and wept as their men warped their vessels out into the harbor at the beginning of a voyage to distant parts. One such voyage is commemorated in a bronze plaque erected by the Greenwich His-

torical Society of New York in 1927. It reads: "*From this ancient 'Tower of Tears' erected 1482 A.D. Henry Hudson set sail April 4th, 1609 A.D. on the vessel 'Half Moon' on that voyage of discovery destined to bring him to the Harbor of New York and the Hudson River.*" Did anyone weep, I wonder, for this Englishman who was obsessed with the idea of a Northwest Passage and died a tragic death in search of it? He was in Dutch employ when he sailed from here, and twenty years later

Dutch settlers followed the trail he had blazed to the Hudson River and built New Amsterdam, later to be renamed New York.

Wealth poured into the merchant houses you see along the *grachten*, until trade developed into banking, and the precious stones from the Indies and from Africa made Amsterdam the diamond center of the world. Since the last war, the marketing side of the business has moved to Antwerp in Belgium, but the Dutch are still the world's cutters. At the Moppes & Zoon factory you can see how it is done—and also look at crystal replicas of the world's most famous jewels. The exhibition has been open only two years, but Robert Streep, who handles the buying and selling, told me he had already had a hundred thousand visitors. He also told me that the loss in cutting a rough stone was 50 per cent and that one third of what you pay for a finished brilliant represents the work put into it. Wives please note—mine did!

Holland/Hammond Innes **123**

There are fifty-eight facets to be cut in a brilliant, a lot of work. Going round the factory, handling diamonds like beads of glass, Peter van Rosendaal tried to explain to me how he was able to keep track of each individual stone, however small—and they have cut one brilliant as small as a pin's head. I never did discover how it was done, for in this one factory they have two hundred and thirty people all busily cutting and polishing. There are many other factories in Amsterdam, and in the south of Holland, particularly in Brabant, hundreds of farmers spend the long winter evenings cutting stones that they have bought and will sell again when they have worked them into brilliants and baguettes and eight-cuts.

The Dutch alone seem to have this art developed to the highest pitch, probably because their national characteristics include co-operation, patience and industry—characteristics essential to convert a tidal estuary of mud flats into the market garden of Europe. Since the sunken lands first grew crops, the Dutch have always made sacrifices for the good of their country. This is a basic factor in their social and political life and is even carried into their labor relations, which is why the word "strike" is virtually unknown here.

Of all peoples the Dutch are perhaps the most fundamentally democratic. Class distinctions are concealed. Yet, paradoxically, their country remains a monarchy, though the visitor is seldom conscious of this. The monarchy—particularly under Queen Juliana—has fitted itself to the mood of the people. In her reign, the curtsey was dropped and the royal children

bicycled like the rest of Holland's children. The result may not be as colorful as in other monarchies, but it suits the Dutch. They refer to her as Juliana, as though she were a personal friend.

It is a pity, but modern clothes are now swamping the traditional village costumes. However, if you go to Arnhem's Open-Air Museum you can still see them all. Here, among the pine woods of the Hooge Veluwe, the Dutch are gathering their past together. Old farmhouses have been transported bodily, each representative of its particular region, and each furnished with original pieces. There are windmills, too, of every type; and in a big new building, beautifully presented in wax-figure groups, are exhibited all the costumes of Holland—some that you can still see in daily wear, but most of them the products of a bygone age that you could otherwise see only by prying into the trunks of farmhouses up and down the land.

Becoming these costumes may be, but look at all that needle-work, all that elaborate embroidery, that fine lace! Such finery has to be made, and in a modern world the girls no longer have time on their hands. Like the windmills that had a sign language of their own, telling of birth and death and disaster—a language used by the Resistance in the last war—the costumes of the women, by color, knot or headdress, proclaimed the age and condition of the wearer, her district, even her village. All this proud love of place has already vanished in the inland districts, lost among the neat little houses with their picture windows that line the modern motor highways. Soon it will

The porters at Alkmaar's market carry Edam cheese on shoulder-slung cradles.

vanish from the doomed coast of the Zuider Zee as farmers from the outside move into the new polders. And in the south —in Zeeland and Beveland—it will vanish, too, when the Delta Plan is completed and the estuaries sealed by dams.

At the far end of the great Zuider Zee dike is Friesland. I remember once arriving in Dokkum, where they killed St. Boniface, and asking the way in English.

"Sorry—speak no English," was the reply. "I Friesland." So might a Welshman reply west of the border in Britain.

Here great farms, house and barn all one and elaborately tiled in dark blue, shoulder their huge bulks against the sky, and the place names all seem to end in "um"—Dokkum, Hallum, Irnsum, Arum, Winsum, Tzum. Go north along the coast to Holwerd, out along the shell-encrusted causeway that stretches a dead-end arm into the sea to meet the Ameland ferry, and all along the horizon you can see the apparently uninterrupted stretch of the dun islands, low and flat like Pacific atolls strangely transported to northern waters. All this will be land one day.

From this view of the Friesche Wad, its waters chopped by the wind the way Dutch artists paint their shallow seas, I drove south and west through the canal-encircled capital, Leeuwarden, and the great barn country beyond, to the shores of the old Zuider Zee. Here, close under the age-old dike, is one of the loveliest roads in Holland, one car wide, with the green dike on the right and still water mirroring grass and reeds on the left, and every ten miles an ancient port: Makkum, where a master potter paints colors bluer than Delft; Workum, making its own individual pottery, with a great brick tower and a beautiful crest; Hindeloopen, a tight-packed huddle of ancient houses, with miniature cobbled streets and a tiny humpbacked bridge lit with carriage lamps. And then eastward from Stavoren, on a little road running a causeway thread through a great mere, the road surface seemingly no higher than the surrounding water.

All this is old country, but go south from here and cross the dike at Lemmer, and suddenly it is different. You are in a flat pan then, the barns all new, the roads straight and the farms neat little rectangular holdings. This is the Nordoostpolder, Holland's dream come true. They drained it during the war with young men working, safe from the Germans in a sea of mud. You would expect to sleep in a rough bed here, for it is a raw, agricultural land. Instead, Emmeloord has a hotel that is one of the best in Holland, 't Voorhuys, or as they like to call it, *"Het hotel op de bodem van de zee"*—the hotel at the bottom of the sea. Only fifteen years ago the table at which you dine would have been sixteen feet below the wind-swept surface of the Zuider Zee.

Visitors pour into Emmeloord from all parts of the world, and it is nothing for Henk Wierenga, who manages 't Voorhuys, to serve lunch for 500 guests. They come to see the work of Engineer Elizabeth van den Ban, who planned the town before the war, and they come to see the polder, for it is pure socialism, and socialism at its best. Everything is owned by the state—the fields, the farms, the workmen's cottages, the villages, even Emmeloord and its $300,000 hotel. And, strangely,

the Dutch like it that way. They are co-operative by nature. There were more than 400 applicants for each holding, and a seventy-five-acre farm costs the state about $100,000. On present rentals it will take one hundred years to pay off the initial cost. But what is a century when your are reclaiming land for all time?.

There is a museum at Schokland in the Nordoostpolder that is as fascinating as any in the world. No less than 156 wrecks were located in the reclamation of this one polder, and the remnants of some of them can still be seen, together with examples of rigging and cargoes going back several centuries. And in the church, that is all that remains of a once-thriving island community, you can see everything of interest brought up by the dredgers from the wrecks and the drowned hamlets and the prehistoric sands of the Zuider Zee—pipes and silver buttons, pottery of every period back to Roman, Bronze Age tools and Stone Age axes and flint sickles and daggers.

If you go south through Kampen, down along the coast to Harderwijk, you can see the land in course of reclamation. I went to Lelystad, an artificial island built in the very middle of the Zuider Zee. Here there will be a big town, but when I saw it the few houses were lost amid a litter of stone heaps and floating machinery. To the east were fishing boats under full sail, brown canvas dipping gently to the lift and fall of the waves. Soon, I was told, all this would be a sea of mud, the water pumped out and the first reeds growing. Those ships with their brown sails would be things of the past.

Fancy striped shirts add color to the
otherwise somber costumes of Volendam fishermen.

Nowhere in Germany is the past better preserved than in Rothenburg ob der Tauber, a 9th century town in western Bavaria, famed for its crooked, half-timbered houses.

Germany

*Nobody has explained what sparked the
unbelievable rebirth of Germany;
nobody has discovered the source of its formidable gifts
for good and evil. It remains an unsolved and,
perhaps, unsolvable riddle.
"The enigma of Germany,"
writes V. S. Pritchett, "is permanent.
It is something the Germans themselves feel:
so modern, yet so medieval; so prosaic,
yet so disturbed by emotions or visions that
are never stabilized for long..."*

To begin a portrait of Germany at its unreal former capital may seem to overweight the untypical. I do not think so. Berlin is a symbol of divided Germany. I had a similar sensation of unreality outside the city, despite the "miracle" of Western Germany's economic prosperity. The hollowness we are aware of in Berlin can also be detected in the boom of the Ruhr and the luxury of Düsseldorf. That hollowness contains all the unanswered questions which haunt the foreigner and the Germans themselves. The only exceptional thing about Berlin is the claustrophobia felt in the West Zone. The West Berliners are, as one of my German friends puts it, like bumblebees bumping in vain against a window. They make that four-hour drive, without stop or contact, to Lübeck, Nürnberg—anywhere in the West—and for a short time they can breathe.

Noise and dust all day long: Berlin is bulldozing, drilling, rebuilding. It is building a new city. It is building the fine new motor roads. Technical recovery is fast in the modern world. But the nightmare gapes in nearly every street. Ornate and

pompous architecture looks more obscene in its ruin than the prosaic, and Berlin's old pomp looks hideous. The concrete of Hitler's bunker heaves up in a wilderness of nettles. The embassies are smashed up. The Nazis' own self-made and prophetic monument—the gutted and gaping Reichstag—is grotesque. The wind drives over the leveled trees of the immense Tiergarten, which has grown up in brushwood or in newly planted young trees. What bombardment did not level, the inhabitants cut down for firewood in the first terrible winter of the defeat.

We are looking back not only on war but on the robbery and murder that followed it. Even in Cologne one does not see so many miles of ruined masonry. But the Berliners are clever and a little cynical, like the dwellers in all capitals; they are now adapted to their absurd and dreadful city. The underground railway runs through both the West and East zones but it is administered by the East. The Zoo station, the Times Square or Piccadilly of West Berlin, is an Eastern property; it was left half ruined until last year, but the West has nagged the East into repairing it. You go through to East Berlin without change or inspection on the underground, just as you drive through untroubled in a bus and not much troubled if you go by car; if you take the tram you have to change at the check point. The political farce of Berlin transport amuses the Berliners.

To drive out of the thriving and thronged streets of West Berlin, and to cross to the East at the Brandenburger Tor, is to enter an emptier region, with far fewer people in the streets. At night it is poorly lit. The advertisement signs and neon lights of the West give place to the immense red banners and public boredom of state propaganda: calls for production, for unity against nuclear war, and so on. There are few cars. No Westerner buys in the shops full of poor goods; at four West marks to one East mark the exchange is absurd. For the Easterner himself life is expensive and political control unending.

The official Soviet architecture—reminiscent of Fascist architecture in Italy or in Hitler's Germany—is cold and commonplace. The famous Stalin Allee is dreary, pretentious and is said to be shoddily built. The imagination—for better or worse—is in the new architecture of the West; but the theater and opera—a test in Germany—is a little more alive in the East; at the Theater Schiffambauerdam, the productions are by general consent brilliant, though there is a glut of Brecht plays.

In West Berlin, architects like Niemeyer, Gropius and Le Corbusier have let themselves go in the high buildings of the ruined official quarter of the city; and if the future catches up with them, these exercises in altitude and box-building may be assimilated. You have to get used to the violent contrast in all German cities between the new gray, flat-roofed standard town and the old. The Germans have been mad about the future for forty years now. Size and the "modernistic" have always had a dramatic attraction to Germans; and on the whole, it has been aesthetically disastrous; they really excel in their smaller buildings—there are delightful small houses in Berlin; and there is one church that does not look like something out of an amusement park.

The beauty that is left in Berlin, as in all German cities, is in the profusion of trees, lawns, flowers and gardens. The suburbs around Dahlem, seat of the new Free University—a delightful modern building with no arrogance, reminding us that modern architecture excels in its interiors—recall Princeton or the greenness and amenity of the pleasant suburbs of London.

Ever since Bismarck and the rise of German nationalism, a very large number of Germans—even liberals—have been nonplused by the enmity they have aroused abroad. The Spaniards, the French, the British have in turn dominated the world; the Russians, the Americans, the Chinese are striving for domination—why not themselves? They are no less equipped or gifted. The British could have helped them achieve domination, yet they behaved as "bad cousins," betraying the unity of the Anglo-Saxon cause and behaving hypocritically. German political writing up to and through the Nazi period is imbued with such opinions. And these views are still held by ex-Nazis settled in North and South America, Africa and Spain.

You do not hear them in Germany, though the unimportant neo-Nazi group holds them. Occasionally, however, a word let slip made me wonder. My friend X, a staff officer during the war, tells me, for example, that the Germans might have escaped their disasters in war and politics, if only "like the British, they had been gifted with tact." One of the difficulties of talking about the war in Germany today is that the Germans alternate between a tacit, guarded toughness and intense self-criticism. Like any adolescent they have two faces. ("Two faces!" says my exasperated Jewish friend in Hamburg. "They have a dozen.") They deny nationalism. They hated the Nazis, but—"What could one do? You don't understand a totalitarian state"; they "weren't there," they "didn't know," and in their craving for sympathy they become sentimentalists to whom forgetting is automatic. "We want to forget all those horrors."

It is said that these orderly people, in their hearts, are a pagan race of tree worshipers. They get out of the bus at the inn and rush emotionally for the woods. *"Wunderbar!"* they exclaim—"Wonderful." It is shouted, with a full heart. The old man in the dockside roughhouse, in Hamburg, who wanders among the drunken sailors offering to cut out a paper silhouette, will get out his nail scissors and in a couple of minutes will deftly make you a picture of wild deer standing under fir trees. It is a common German scene. There is a Christmas card in every German mind. Yet the oldest and traditional trees of Germany are not firs but the oak, the lime and the beech. In the German beer halls and taverns, they sit on oaken benches and at tables of scrubbed oak.

So much of German country life is woodland life. You catch the smell of cut wood at once as you go into a town in Bavaria or Württemberg. You hear the sound of the sawmill there, and in the evening, in the villages, the sound of the ax. The winter's logs are built up as neat as houses in the gardens; and outside, in the street, the women of the family are splitting firewood. Some old woman is always there sweeping up the sawdust in the street. I have never seen anywhere else so many women with brooms. Untidiness, uncleanliness and waste they abominate.

Just as we are always near forest and forest flowers in Germany, where the wild lupines grow tall in the summer, so are we also near water. The Germans worship water as they worship trees. The motorists, the hikers, stop to look at the Elbe, the Danube, the Oder, the Iser, the Rhine and innumerable other rivers with something more than common curiosity. The rivers are living beings to them. "I live near such and such a river," they will say. Or, "Over there is the source of the So-and-So river." They will make pilgrimages to the local spring. A waterfall must not be missed. They have a childish love of echoes. On the Königssee, the great lake below Berchtesgaden, a man stands up in the trippers' boat to blow his bugle or to yodel so that the magic echo jumps from precipice to precipice over the water. The lakelands close to Berlin, the lagoons that come into the middle of Hamburg and are so gracefully gardened, the Rhine marked by its castles and its terraces, the deep oil-green Alpine lakes of Bavaria, with their wooded islands and castles—all these enchant the Germans.

The reason is not, I think, that they are immersed in Romantic literature, although the travel agencies have worked the Romantic theme to death. The wanderings of water appeal to the deeply felt wandering instinct in the Germans. They are simply people who love nature and who work off a lot of their strong but formless emotional life upon it. Sitting behind me on the bus going to Oberammergau was a bright Berlin lady who chattered for hours about shops, flats, prices, clothes, cousins, sons and daughters in Berlin. The only thing that made her pause and change the subject was the sight of snow high up in a cleft in the blinding rock. "Snow," she cried. "Look." And then rapturously, and I'm afraid repeatedly: "White snow." We grinned at the German weakness for using two words when one will do and theorized about the literalness of German thought. After all, snow is white anyway. We were wrong. Snow is snow, but white snow is *new* snow. At the beginning of summer she had spotted a new fall. Here was intense delight in a detail of nature.

The German is also a flower lover. He is more given to his plants and flowers than even the English or the Dutch. It is rare in villages or in cities to see a window sill without flowers. The flower shops of Germany are the most remarkable I have ever seen, for they are filled not only with carnations, roses, lilies, irises, and so on, in their season, but with tropical flowers, waxy flowers from the hothouse, with water flowers and all strange ferns, giant stems and creepers. A shop in a back street will display its water lilies. That fond, famous old 19th Century picture by Spitzweg, called *Herr Pfarrer als Kakteenliebhaber* and found in every post-card shop, commemorates a German passion. The old German with his spectacles on the end of his nose, the long pipe drooping from his mouth, is peering at the startling bloom that has appeared on his precious cactus. Flowers, not ribbons, decorate the bride's car at weddings.

One aspect of German material success (on which everyone agrees) is the silence of the artists. Regional pride has seen to it that there are fine state-subsidized theaters in every city, and the people pour into them. The public habit of "culture" is unabated. The German theater, German music, and especially the orchestras, have never recovered from the massacre of the Jews and the exodus of the survivors to other countries. "If we want German violinists," a critic said, "we have to send to Pittsburgh for them and they won't come anyway." The loss to the arts is irreparable. There are few German plays; people go to see Giraudoux, Sartre, Arthur Miller, John Osborne, Priestley, Tennessee Williams. The cinema is pretty dead. The great days of UFA are gone; and although one or two companies are turning out a good many films, the quality is undistinguished. The war-hero films are alarming—but then what war-hero films are not?

The radio thrives but there are no important novelists. Only through the grotesque satire in Berlin cabarets does one get that clownish, mad, macabre circus gift of the German wits. The inner life of the Germans has been stunned. Those old morbid themes of this emotional race—the German death wish, the dream orgy, the Gothic nightmare, the love affair consumed by introspection, the wanderings of the insatiable seeker— have all gone. German writing in this century was interesting only because it was part of the great blaze of Europe's literary genius which started about 1890 and went on to 1930. Now the writers are numb. What I have read has not interested me and critics tell me there is nothing in it. The modern painting has violence without taste or skill—to judge by the big show at Munich last year. The German writers are handicapped by having poor newspapers and few reviews. They earn their living—very well—on radio and television and especially by foreign works. West Germany has become a vacuum filled by foreign things.

I went to the Bonn Parliament House—the Germans are staggered and quaintly puzzled because it has become an enormous attraction for tourists of all nations—and then over to the little Rhine resort of Königswinter to drink a bottle of wine in a cool, quiet court of flowers. Back in Bonn it was funny to see a few students marching round, each with a bar stool and a mandolin. They sat on the bar stools under the chestnuts, even on the pavements, drank their beer, and once more set off on their comic, decorous, harmless follow-my-leader round the streets. They looked stern, perfect gentlemen in the evening when they turned up in velvet caps and colored sashes in a private room at the restaurant. They stood in rows facing each other, bolt upright, and sang long songs while each held a stack of pierced caps on his drawn rapier with solemn ceremony. It looked like, and perhaps was, part of their childish love of traditional gestures. It only alarms that they look so stiff, correct and serious.

My mind goes from them to the young people of Hamburg —with Munich it is for me the most attractive place in West Germany—sailing their dinghies and sculling in eights and fours across the beautiful lagoons that come into the middle of the city. Despite their fanatical work, Hamburgers have the energy left for pleasure late into the night. They love night clubs. They arrange life so that they can eat and drink what they like at any hour.

Hamburg has a very English air, but a more thoroughgoing eye for pleasure than any hard-working British city. Society in Hamburg is said to be starchy and strictly mercantile, but it is a cheerful place, and the Sankt Pauli night town is fantastic. It was here I remember seeing an enormous, tipsy, middle-aged man trying to cuddle and kiss his girl friend of the same age while she ate a pound or two of cold pork and red beef. Such pinches, such squeezes; how he tipped her best hat over her eyes and disarranged her blouse while she prodded him with her fork and shook—the whole 170 pounds of her— with coy giggles. The waiters loved it. The grotesque that so often appears in German art and literature has its counterpart in life.

But behind these pretty and jolly things, there is something austere and of the North. The enigma of Germany is permanent, for it is something the Germans themselves feel: so modern, yet so medieval; so prosaic yet so disturbed by emotions or visions that are never stabilized for long.

My last look at the country left me with most of my questions unanswered. I was torn between admiration and alarm. I had traveled up through the final ruin of the Rhine where the destruction becomes worse and worse as you approach Cologne. Across the Rhine, over the railway wilderness and the water, was the mass of the great cathedral, powerful and gray on its wasted slope, where hundreds of buses are parked. Injured but surviving, coarse and unpleasing in its stone, the structure conveys more than any other cathedral I know an idea of the armored and feudal power of the Middle Ages. Above all it is a symbol of the massive Northern will. It is Will *in excelsis*. Of all cathedrals it is the least tranquil, the most soldierly, the most overmastering; Charlemagne might not have died. Yet medieval though it is, it does not seem remote from the factories and railways nearby. The profound boom of its bell is like the voice of all the metal in the Ruhr, the hard masculine voice of German permanence and inexhaustible German energy.

Austria

*To many a casual visitor Austria is merely quaint...
a Franz Josef museum called Vienna and a charming
Tirolian hinterland liberally sprinkled with
wine gardens where the melodies of
Johann Strauss go on forever.
In a way, says Frederic Morton, all this is true,
or half true. But the important thing to remember,
he points out, is that today Austria is
far more than a mere relic of the past.*

I will begin, of course, with a coffeehouse. This particular one, in the Styrian city of Graz, was visited daily by a certain young man—a somewhat seedy-looking gentleman, I'm afraid. He seldom showed up before eleven and hadn't yawned the sleep out of his system before noon. Somehow he was very charming, though. He ran up a huge debit account, but he tipped generously. His waiter loved him. "Good morning, *Herr Direktor* Huber," he would say each day to the young man. "How does the *Herr Direktor* feel this morning?" And he would bring his patron coffee and whipped cream and brioche. And the young man would eat and drink and loll on the soft upholstery, glancing at the newspapers the waiter brought him, then tossing them aside with a mild, smiling melancholy. "Illustrated magazines for the *Herr Direktor?*" the waiter would promptly inquire. And the young man would nod and spend the rest of the day looking at pictures of pretty girls and humming Mozart.

One day, however, he appeared very early. He wasn't so seedy, but he looked very pale. "Oh, *Herr Direktor* Huber," the waiter cried. "At this hour! How does the *Herr Direktor* feel? An extra-strong mocha for the *Herr Direktor?*"

The young man shook his head as he assumed his accustomed seat. "You can cut the *Herr Direktor* stuff," he said. And added with worried pride, "I have a job now."

Like Herr Huber, Austria's staple has always been sheer personality. In the 15th and 16th Centuries, for example, the Habsburgs took over huge parts of Europe, not with powerful armies but with personable bridegrooms. Austria did not have to conquer Spain, Bohemia or Hungary. It married them. Its invincibility on the dance floor won the Congress of Vienna and choreographed an empire that was to perform continuously until 1914. It was very photogenic and civilized, that empire, and magnificently sideburned, but not entirely real. Austria-Hungary was less a state than a costume ball aswirl with Ukrainian astrakhan hats, the silvery scabbards of Budapest dragoons and the swish of Bierdermeier-era bustles. But the bullet at Sarajevo set off the first World War and broke up the long, long waltz.

What remained in 1918 was a little rump state, politically viable but an economic cretin. It was a very photogenic and civilized and square-mustached little country, but the Austrians lounged in their coffeehouses and chose not to wake up to the fact that they were small fry. In point of culture, in the arts and in social progress, they continued to live as a great Western power. They poured out Nobel Prize winners, pastry

An artist's conception of a pair of horses on a wall in Salzburg contrasts with the team which passes by in the street.

masterpieces, Ph.D.'s and housing projects like a nation of 70,000,000 instead of 7,000,000. Their relationship to reality was like that of the bullfighter to the bull: no one else could avoid the truth with such grace. They worshiped the late emperor's memory—and voted republican. They outlawed the nobility with all its titles—and called every successful greengrocer *Herr Hofrat*—court councilor. In an act of collective moral myopia, in 1938, they confused Adolf Hitler with Franz Josef and applauded the *Anschluss* with an overwhelming *ja*—

yet today they have forgotten this almost unanimously, as if anti-Nazi attitudes could be made retroactive.

After the second World War, Austria resumed its career characteristically. It was, by Allied decree, free—and yet occupied by the four powers. It was democratic, yet Red Army boots thumped down the corridors of all trains entering the Soviet Zone. It was partitioned, yet Austria had a single government that dealt capably with bomb damage and with litigation concerning the name of a cake; it seems that the present owners of the Café Sacher, historic birthplace of a chocolate miracle known as the *Sacher Torte*, claimed the sole right to call it by that name, and their dispute with other patisseries became a national issue.

Austria was also the only country to make an operetta out of the cold war. The Four-Power jeep—in which an American, a British, a French and a Russian MP patrolled Vienna together —looked like a car pool shared by extras from *Die Fledermaus*. At Russian headquarters in the Hofburg, the guard could have understudied a Sigmund Romberg baritone. The fantastic green scarves sported by American MP's in Salzburg were, so help me, regulation. In 1955 the United States, Britain, France and Russia signed the Austrian peace treaty, which emptied the country's soil of foreign troops and fully restored its independence. It was an act regarded by many Austrians as one of a series of preliminary celebrations that led up to the opening of the Vienna State Opera. History took liberties with Austria. Austria took liberties with history.

It would be unfair not to note that lately some of this has changed. An oddly solid element has been creeping down the Danube. Agriculture and industries are making a strong recovery, and the country has begun to enjoy a practically unprecedented prosperity, with added income from its mushrooming tourist trade. But most remarkable is the Austrian's recent willingness to accept Austria seriously. For hundreds of years he has had unlimited confidence in his sophistication and *savoir-faire*, but entertained a poetic doubt as to his existence. Now he knows that a resuscitation of the Austro-Hungarian grand monarchy is impossible, and he is coming to believe in his national self, however small, however unhyphenated. He is plain *Herr* Huber in the coffeehouse—for the first time really conscious that he is on his own.

Since the Austrian has only tardily come to terms with himself, it is understandable that others have formed a rather pixilated image of his country. Much of the world still sees Austria as a great big Franz Josef mausoleum called Vienna, with Salzburg for a suburb and the Tirol as the hinterland; sprinkled all over, presumably, are wine gardens where Sigmund Freud yodels with Johann Strauss. It's not an entirely accurate picture, but not a very wrong one either. For one thing Vienna *is* the pre-eminent fact in Austria. It has 1,800,000 inhabitants—more than a fourth of the Austrian population. Its huge intellectual energies dominate the arts and the professions of the country. And many of its civic peculiarities have become nationwide habits. The famous Tirolean suit, for instance, caught the fancy of the Viennese aristocracy in the 19th Century, and much of Austria has been perpetrating the fad ever since.

In Linz, the capital of Upper Austria, a young Italian lady of my acquaintance had a startling but not altogether untypical experience with this sartorial idiom. As she told it to me, "I arrive in the station. I don't know anyone. I am lost. Then I see a guide. He has on leather shorts and the jacket with the green lapels and big red suspenders, just as the guides in Italy are dressed in ancient folk costumes. So I ask him if he can take me to a good hotel. He is very nice and he takes me to a very good place. I want to pay him, but he says no, no, he wants to take me to dinner too. So I think why not, he wants to make more money and I don't know a good restaurant. I say *si*. So he guides me to an excellent place to eat. Afterwards he still refuses money, and offers to guide me to dancing. I think that is a little strange, but he has been so nice, I say *si*. But by the time we go dancing, I have finished looking at the sights, I am looking at the people. And I find out there are a lot of guides in Austria. There is a man in leather shorts sitting at every table! I ask my Austrian, 'Are you a guide, yes or no?' And he says, 'No, I am not a guide. I am a man. I love you.' A lover of me! In leather shorts!"

Equally confusing to the outsider is a certain Viennese speech habit that has been nationalized. In Austria, you must understand, pronunciation is a mark of social standing. Most people speak the local dialect of one of the provinces or of Vienna itself. High German, equivalent to the King's English, is the language of rich squares. Intellectuals and social nobility, however, converse in a highly esoteric tongue known as *Kaiserdeutsch*, or imperial German. It is in essence the common, but softened, Viennese brogue pronounced in a deliberately weary way.

The closest American counterpart would be the speech of an overworked Brooklyn grandmother taking a break at teatime. You may not believe it, but to my native Viennese ears it sounds very graceful and beautiful.

Hand kissing constitutes another Viennese rite that has become part of the Middle European mystique. It can imply courtesy, coldness or adultery, depending on how it is performed. All Austrian hand kissing (the French and Italian varieties are pitiable imitations) begins with the smiled murmur, "*Küss d'Hand*," which is *Kaiserdeutsch* for *Ich küsse die Hand*." The kisser then brings his heels together with a non-Prussian click. Simultaneously he bends—not too fast, not too slow, and only from the waist—to the lady's hand. If he wishes to convey a frigid formal greeting, his nose will stop a withering two inches short of her knuckles. If he is confiding a discreet passion, he can brush his half-closed lips across her fingers, making them a sort of secret boudoir. If he wants to lend his devotion a tender and public note, he will rest his mouth for two whole seconds against the back of her hand and then touch it gently to his cheek.

But if Vienna exports its mannerisms to the rest of the nation, in the food department it is a confirmed importer from the provinces. Many of the best national dishes are drawn from the hinterland—dishes with a certain rustic heartiness. In fact, in or out of the capital, the Austrian hates the so-called international cuisine; he disdains sauces and garnishings and culinary chicanery. If you insist, he'll make you pay dearly for his reluctant imitations. But it's far better to choose the indigenous and above all the unpronounceable: *Krenfleisch* (meat with horse-radish), *Backhendl* (fried chicken), *Zwetschgenknoedel* (plum dumplings), *Palatschinken* (sweet omelette). They're all deliciously prepared and very cheap. Many good restaurants—excepting, of course, obvious tourist traps—charge about twenty schillings (eighty cents) for a meal.

In hotels and entertainment, too, the bucolic represents the best. I suspect any Austrian hotel, save those in Vienna and Bad Gastein, with an urban exterior. I give a wide berth to neon signs that yell "night club"; Austria's best boast artists who wouldn't quite make the grade in Labrador. What the country does have, besides the world's leading opera and most intellectual cabarets (for which you need a perfect command of German), are the "merry cellars" (for which you need nothing except vocal chords and wine). You are in the right place if, ten minutes after your arrival, you find yourself arm-linked and swaying with people you don't know, singing a song whose words you don't understand, and having a good time for no perceptible reason.

You've picked the right hotel if it meets three requirements: it must look like a chalet, preferably just the slightest bit weather-worn; it must have, instead of one dining room, several cozy little *Stuben*; and its waiter, the moment you order coffee, must ask the crucial question, "*Mit oder ohne Schlag, bitte?*"—"with or without whipped cream, please?"

Every Austrian puts whipped cream on practically everything—on coffee, hot chocolate, cake, pie, on compotes and fruits, and symbolically, healingly on his sorrows. *Schlag* represents all the good things in the world. *Schlag* proves that even today life can be noble, and corpulent.

Hard work as well as beauty is part of Tirolean farm life.

Switzerland

The late Joyce Cary loved Switzerland, for there, as nowhere else, he found the peace he sought. In the mountains and in the people themselves he felt a mood and quality which he described simply as "the feeling that Switzerland is a country at peace with the world and within itself..."

My first Swiss holiday, thirty years ago, was to Lenzerheide for the skiing. Lenzerheide was then peaceful and remote. From the station at Chur we were taken up the high winding mountain roads by a post wagon, set upon a sledge for the winter and drawn by two horses. Lenzerheide was still as primitive as its transport. There was no ski lift—I believe such things existed, but not on our mountains. We did not miss it because most of us had never seen a ski lift, and we had plenty of snow, plenty of open slopes, a good skating rink, the marvelous winter climate of the Alps, the sunshine so hot in January that we climbed in the thinnest of vests or no body garment at all, and in the evening wonderful food, music and dancing, bridge and billiards, whatever you chose. And, after all, that deep sleep which comes from long days in the air and a great deal of hard work, for we had climbed every foot of the slopes on which we made our runs.

And what a pleasure it was after an hour's climbing to rest in some high pass, to look at the new view on the far side, to hang up one's skis to dry and take the lunch sandwiches out of one's rucksack. Down below we could see the village like a toy, and skaters performing their elaborate antics on a rink about the size of a postage stamp, like animalculae circling and dodging under the microscope in a drop of water. We did not despise them but we wondered how anyone could spend the day revolving about half an acre of ice.

Most people go to Switzerland, as I went first, for winter sports or summer climbing. They are attracted by the rich variety of its pleasures as a holiday ground—no other in Europe gives at once the same facilities for climbers, skiers, skaters, walkers, bathers, not to speak of botanists and ornithologists. And these pleasures are suited to every strength and capacity. There are high mountains to be climbed in perfect safety by a novice who has never before worn climbing boots or carried an ice ax, and peaks which still defeat the most skillful. One can stroll through pine woods for an afternoon or trek for days through the wildest country, carrying a pack and sleeping in the huts provided. And Switzerland's greatest virtue as a holiday center is that there are pleasures for the whole year in an area half the size of Maine.

The last skiers are not off the northern slopes before spring is coming to the valleys immediately beneath, and the whole lower country is full of fruit blossoms, especially in the great cherry orchards that produce the jam, black and white, which no visitor to Switzerland can ever forget.

And as the blossoms fall, covering the ground with a new

snow just as the last of the old is melting off the ski slopes, the cows begin to go back from their winter quarters to summer pastures. For several weeks the air of all Switzerland seems to be full of bells. Now, too, the first botanists are hunting for alpines, and walkers begin to travel the lower mountain passes.

In June, while the lakes are covered with sailboats and the bathing beaches with sun-loungers, the climbers gather in Zermatt, Grindelwald and Pontresina, or, for rock climbers especially, Chamonix. It is in Chamonix that one finds the best guides for the special art of rock climbing. Zermatt is still a small village, standing at more than 5000 feet, very conveniently placed among a group of high peaks and great glaciers. Zermatt is not only for mountain climbers; it is a center also for winter sports, and especially for walkers and sight-seers. Nowadays it also has summer railways running to the Riffelalphorn and the Gornergrat, famous for views. These sight-seeing railways, incidentally, are now very common among the high Alps and enable anyone to see sights formerly open only to climbers.

Guide books urge you to see the painted house fronts of North Switzerland, but they are not peculiar to the country. They belong to all the North Germanic lands as the farms of Lake Leman, among the vineyards, are like those of all Southern France. But what is native, always interesting, often beautiful and little mentioned in guide books is the magnificent timber-work to be seen everywhere, not only in farmhouses and villas but in the underpinning of a mountain tunnel or the trestles of a country bridge.

The ancient wooden bridges of Lucerne are famous; the oldest dates actually from 1333. It is all of timber, and it is roofed from end to end to keep off the snow. It carries within it, fitted into the rafters, a picture gallery as unusual and attractive as itself, over a hundred small triangular paintings of Swiss history, painted about 1600.

Lucerne must be visited, in any case, to see the lake. I recommend the steamer, not so much because a motorist cannot see typical aspects of the view, the sudden opening of new distances, of new gulfs, and mountaintops, through some narrow gateway in a precipice, as because lakes should be seen from boats.

On Lucerne the landscapes are dramatic and extraordinary; they remind one of stage scenery in some Wagnerian opera, with precipices and headlands for side scenes—the blue distances, range upon range of peaks, are suddenly revealed as by the lifting of a curtain, so that the placid movement of the steamer working to its timetable, carrying its commuters, its market women and bales of merchandise, from one little port to another, the regular thump of the engine like a pulse that could not be hurried by the most exciting tragedy, is in contrast rather than concord with the backcloth. But it is a contrast which gives the strongest value to the grandeur and the color of the scenery.

In every corner of Switzerland there is water—the milky streams, full of stone dust, running down from glaciers; clear mountain brooks with their pools; lakes of every shape and size; fiords like those of Lucerne; inland seas like Zurich, Constance and Leman; and everywhere waterfalls, waterfalls unnumbered and often unnamed. You come upon them tumbling over unexpected cliffs into the tops of the pines, as you walk in the woods; you hear them all the time; you hear of them sometimes even too much. In all my Swiss visits I never went to see the Falls of the Rhine until last year. They had been described to me as overpraised, a tourist commodity. And though one can be on guard against the talk of vulgarization, the tourist commodity—the sight, the view, vamped up and publicized to catch tourists—is a trap, like the cheap souvenirs from tourist shops. But the Falls of the Rhine are not a fraud. In spite of all the praise, in spite of Ruskin's enthusiasm a hundred years ago, they can still surprise. For one thing, they are not a mere sheet of water folded over a shelf. There are three main falls, divided by rocks, and as the great weight of water pours over it is broken and molded by other rocks below, so that the surface offers new angles and new colors to the eye at the slightest movement of the head. Also, if one stands at the best viewpoint—a jutting balcony on the right bank below the castle of Laufen and within a few feet of the water—one can hear in the midst of the general roar a whole orchestra of other noises, ringing, knocking, sighing, murmuring, on quite high notes as well as in the bass, so that one gets in nature something of the effect of those water gardens of the Moguls in Kashmir, so artificially contrived to give in unison all the different notes of which water is capable. I do not mean that there is the same refinement of sound. You do not get the tinkling of small fountains on a pool which the Moguls used as treble—so to speak—as the first violins. But what the Rhine Falls lose in refinement of sound they gain in majesty and volume. No connoisseur of waterfalls should miss this one, even if he has seen Niagara, Victoria on the Zambesi and, in

Switzerland, such other beauties as the unkindly named Pissevasche near St. Maurice (in the Valais) or the Alpien-Bach in the famous gorge of the Gondo where we can also follow Napoleon's military road over the Simplon Pass.

The Swiss constitution is carefully designed, like the American—from which it took many hints—at once to establish a necessary degree of lawful authority, and control it. It not only allots different powers to different departments of state but puts them in different places. Berne is the parliamentary capital, but the Supreme Court is at Lausanne, and its real diplomatic center might be found in Geneva. Here is the International Labor Office and the International Red Cross founded by a Swiss in 1864—he had been horrified by the sufferings of the wounded after the battle of Solferino in 1859.

In Geneva, too, there is the Palace of Nations, once headquarters of the old League, now used by the U.N. for some of its European branches, and recently by the Great Powers for an Asiatic conference. Geneva is also a sacred city to Protestants who come from afar to visit its monument of the Reformation, carved with the text of the Mayflower Pact.

Lausanne and Geneva are both on Lake Leman, the biggest lake of Central Europe. This great lake may seem tame after the romantic gorges of Lucerne, but it has special charms in the variety of its scenery and its wide expanse. It is usually compared with the Italian lakes for its deep blue color, its tranquil air of a beauty long domesticated among a reasonable, a Latin people. And it is truly part of Latin Switzerland; more than a third of its shores are in France, and when you travel from Geneva or Lausanne to Evian-les-Bains you go through the customs. Leman is an international sea, and although it is famous for its Riviera climate, a favorite place for winter quarters and girls' schools, yet I am not sure I don't prefer it as I saw it last, in a storm.

I was on my way to Chillon, a place like the Falls of the Rhine that I had hitherto avoided for the same reason—too much fame, too much glorification by travel agencies.

I went by steamer from Ouchy, the port of Lausanne, a charming place in itself, and already waves were breaking on the quay, the yachts at anchor were tossing their masts at the most surprising angles. The wind was strong and the sky was full of clouds, but there was plenty of space between them, so that the broad rays of the sun were passing all the time like searchlights over the mountains, the vineyards on the foothills, and the white farmhouses with their red roofs. The yachts sparkled as they rolled, and the trees on the terrace, shaking their leaves, sent down a shower of bright salt drops. Beyond the shelter of the bay there were true white horses, or at least white ponies, cantering in the stately manner of white horses, all before the wind. One could see their names thrown forward at each gust, and white horses on Lake Leman are all the whiter for the blue of the water which, on a day like this, takes on the tint of indigo.

At Montreaux, where I landed, the spray was blowing across the little public garden on the lake front as far as the shop windows, and as I came to Chillon I saw the waves breaking against the castle walls and remembered Byron's verses to

Bonivard. I won't quote them; they are in all the anthologies; they were in the pamphlet handed to me at the castle gates before I went in. In short, they are hackneyed like most good things.

Chillon castle stands actually in the lake and is a perfect specimen of the military art of its time, the 13th Century, before gunpowder came in. Its site was so well chosen that modern experts could not find a better; their fortifications are just behind. It is still a strategic position, after six hundred years.

Swiss archaeologists have lately restored Chillon and the work has been well done. Of course some romance, some interest has been lost by patching up the walls and cleaning away weeds. It is a nice question here, as elsewhere, whether taking an ancient monument out of the stream of history and preserving it as a museum piece adds more pleasure to the historian than it loses for the sight-seer. Restoration of an old building is as critical a job as patching up an old hero for a public appearance. If you paint out the scars and fill up the wrinkles you may improve his looks, but you don't add to his attraction or his significance, you only make him seem cheap and false. Chillon is in some danger, but it is not yet spoilt; at least the repainting and refurnishing of some of the chief rooms give one an idea of what the place was like when it was lived in. And the prisons remain exactly as they were in the 16th Century when Bonivard was shut up by the Duke of Savoy for asserting the liberties of Geneva.

True, he was chiefly out for himself; the Bonivard of fact was not quite the noble character of Byron's poem. But when he fought and suffered for his own rights he served the rights and liberty of others. One can respect him as a man of principle and courage. The dungeons at Chillon, as Byron described them, are actually below lake level, and the prisoners chained to the pillars could see only a patch of sky out of the windows.

And on this day the effect of the waves, beating against the walls outside with that peculiar hollow noise of waves heard within a building, had a melancholy which owed nothing to archaeologists. It was the same noise that those prisoners had heard during their years in this same stone vault.

The effect was not so much to take one back into history as to make history contemporary, to bring it to life; it gave me a strong unexpected impression of a past that is never out of date because it is repeated forever in the present.

Byron has made Chillon famous, and now one cannot separate the castle from the poem. They enter into feeling together. Our lives, in fact, are so mixed up with what we have learned and heard—the arts and literature of thousands of years, working upon us even when we don't notice it—that we exist almost entirely by and in the imagination. The mountains that two hundred years ago were found simply dangerous nuisances to travelers are now symbols of beauty and majesty. Chillon, which was built only for a fort and a prison, is now part of a great poem to liberty.

A holiday is chiefly an act of the imagination. Wherever we go in the world, even if it is only into the next room, we carry with us an idea and a feeling based on that idea. Every

Charming Zermatt lies near the base of the Matterhorn.

member of a nation has an idea of the character of his people and country, and therefore of himself, and that idea is present with him everywhere. It is probably the most constant single political force in the world, though so well hidden, so little noticed.

In Switzerland we carry always in our imagination the idea of a state which has been at peace for a hundred and fifty years, and which has fought for it. We feel that here is a people which has solved the problem that faces the world—unity of different races and religions under one government.

One may not think of history in one's travels abroad, but history is at work all the time in our minds and nerves. I daresay one reason for the special peacefulness of a holiday in Switzerland is simply in the feeling that Switzerland is a country at peace with the world and within itself.

An old, grilled courtyard in Córdoba sparkles with
color as bright Spanish sunlight falls on
roses and geraniums and a warmly tiled floor.

Spain

*Of all the countries of Europe,
Spain is perhaps the most baffling...
an almost impossible blend of arrogant elegance
and unspeakable poverty,
of melancholy and gaiety, of Don Quixote and Carmen.
In the interplay of these extraordinary contrasts
V. S. Pritchett finds the secret of this
"other Europe" beyond the Pyrénées.*

It was in the middle of Madrid at four in the morning. The
scene: a thieves' kitchen, a shabby cellar lit by one weak and
naked electric light, where a couple of dozen seedy, sad men
were watching a gypsy. A poker-faced guitar player was cynically, monotonously twanging. The gypsy was dancing. In the
Spanish fashion, one or two people began to taunt him. An-
gered by the sneers, the gypsy cleared a wider space in the
middle of the room and prepared to give a wild dance that
would silence his tormentors, but he lost his head and made a
terrible mistake: he started to take his jacket off. There is a
right way and a wrong way of doing the smallest thing in Spain
and Spaniards are pitiless to error. Every man in the room rose
to his feet and in one voice shouted, "None of that!" The
drunken proprietor rushed forward: "No jackets off here."
Spain is the country where "No" means "No and No." It is the

country of male pride where no one, unless he is a laborer
working in the sun, would lower himself to taking his jacket
off. The correct thing would have been for the gypsy to raise his
jacket above his hips and tie the two front ends into a knot. The
country of "No and No" is also the place where there is always
a formula or way out.

To the foreigner arriving at the frontier or the airport, Spain
immediately presents itself as the silent, unchangeable, challenging country. The first sight is of the heavy, blind walls of
crumbly yellow churches. Their domes dominate. In their belfries the bells sound like buckets beaten with a spade. For centuries, Spain has rejected the West. With the air of a dilapidated
grandee, the ill-paid customs officer puts on his white cotton
gloves and slowly examines your luggage. The white gloves
are *de rigueur*. You can insist that he wear them. And as he dis-
dainfully rummages, you remember that this is, in theory, the
last obstinate Fascist state in Europe, the onetime ally of Hitler
and Mussolini. You cannot help remembering what you have
read of the Inquisition, the pride of the Spanish Armada, the
cruelties of the conquest of South America. You also remember
that Spain founded the first great modern empire, and that,
with English, its language divides the New World. Though you
may travel to Madrid in the *Talgo*, the fast luxury train like a
silver pencil, with its load of silent rich people who sit staring
into nothing for ten hours, or sometimes reading a Western,
you will see a withered and aged country, empty and marked

Castle in Spain: *The mighty Alcazar of Segovia.*

by neglect, and you will think of an empire lost by pride, intolerance and indolence.

That is to say, you will think of all this if you have been brought up on "the black legend" of Spanish history. You may have been brought up on the gayer legend of Carmen and romantic Spain, where the guitar mutters all night and the castanets are like birds in the hands, of the girl with the rose in her hair and the black mantilla, and the lover in velvet cloak and Córdoba hat, pinned to the iron-grilled window like a moth at night. Which legend is true? Both are true and untrue. Nearly everything one says about Spain can be countered by the opposite; only one thing is indisputable: though Spain has been ruled through most of its history by absolute kings and military dictators, its people are the most various, the most individual, in Europe. The formality is a disguise; the Spaniards are human beings to the limit.

The Spaniards put in long hours of work, take long afternoon rests in the heat, and sit up half the night. Luncheon is at two-thirty and goes on till nearly five, dinner is never before ten. The theater opens at 11:30 and the play doesn't start until the audience stamps and whistles. The country places shut up earlier, for the peasant starts at dawn, riding on his donkey to his work, but there is always someone hammering or shouting at the top of his voice all night. At six in the evening Spanish towns are suddenly reborn: the women are out for the day's *paseo.* Rich and poor put on their best clothes, the hair of the women has been brushed for an hour to the point of agony and, buttressed by Victorian underclothes, they go to the main street or to the cool colonnades of the Plaza Mayor, to walk round and round in formal procession for the next two or three hours. The women's hair has to be superbly dressed, for none of them wears hats; only on Sundays will they wear a black mantilla and on fiestas a high comb. The idea of a "fine appearance" for the street is imperative. The street is their drawing room. Their house or flat or room is the secret living place, visited only by relations. Except in the smart, Europeanized set, there is so little social life in the home that it can be said not to exist. The cocktail party is uncommon and awkward; the women do not drink and still drift into the old custom of segregating themselves in one part of the double room. In the hours of the *paseo* the women rarely walk alone, but almost never with a man unless he is a son, a brother or a husband. They walk with a maid or a woman friend. They walk to be admired, to be stared at—and the Spanish stare fixes itself for minutes on end upon its object—they do not move a muscle when a man calls out at them. The habit of shouting at women in the street is an old custom and delights the women. They do not reply or respond by a look. Their brilliant eyes never meet the eyes of any man as they walk, but stare straight through until the moment of passing when, by a quick movement, they glance away. Eyes are never modestly lowered. The Spaniards understand reserve, but are untouched by shyness, and the women carry themselves with boldness and decision. They seem to be more militant and dominating than the men and,

in fact, they do dominate. The males alone have the run of the city and all the freedoms. Later at night the streets will be crowded with men alone; it is a country made for men. But it is also made for the family; the families are very large and the mother rules them. The apparently free and privileged Spanish male is like putty in the hands of his mother. His wife is a mother above all; indeed Don Juan is the most mothered man in Europe.

Spain/V.S. Pritchett

This *paseo* at six o'clock is the hour of the challenge of the eyes, a kind of ritual bird dance of the sexes. It is the hour of secret messages, concealed signals, and of maids running with notes. The whole of life in its beauty, comedy or horror is displayed publicly in the streets. Everything is exposed without self-consciousness—except love. Love might not exist. There is marriage after a long engagement going on for years during which passion is kept alive by a hundred tiffs, doubts, head tossings, attentions and reconciliations; there is the public brothel which is more like a club, a place for conversation, than for sex. But romantic love or the light love affair makes little public appearance. No embraces, no kisses, no holding of hands in the street. The public love-making of the French or the naïve explosions of the Italians horrify the Spaniards. There are cat-calls in the cinema if the film shows people kissing. A kiss on the mouth in a film is thought obscene. Bishops denounce it, and the people agree. In the last twenty years and especially since the great changes of the civil war, the duenna or chaperone is disappearing; one now hears of girls being allowed out until eight in the evening with a group of friends; but if the duenna has gone, her ghost remains. On Sundays in the lovers' lanes of the beautiful Spanish parks one sees the lovers sitting on two chairs opposite each other with a third, empty chair close by. There, to placate public opinion, an imaginary duenna sits. Spanish men and women freely use sexual oaths and speak with untroubled candor about their physical feelings. They are free and natural in speech, are never shocked and do not talk to shock. But though they talk a lot of rhetoric about sexual passion, the tone of their love affairs is Victorian, sentimental, domestic. They like custom; every Sunday afternoon the housemaids of Madrid have the habit of meeting their young men outside the main gates of the Retiro park. It has been the custom for generations.

One sits at the café table drinking a glass of beer and eating olives or prawns or some nutty little piece of fried octopus. There are no Spanish *apéritifs*. The Spaniards used to drink coffee half the day, before the war, or thick chocolate flavored with cinnamon. Now those who can afford it drink Italian vermouth, or a soft drink of nut milk called *horchata*. Except in the Basque provinces and in Andalusia, little alcohol is drunk and wine sparingly. One can go for months without seeing a drunken man in Castile or the eastern provinces; in Granada and Seville, on the other hand, the sherry drinkers are apt to totter home.

In no country in Europe is there so little class distinction; there are no class accents, and despite the violent differences in wealth, ranging from luxury to starvation, all Spaniards act and speak on a general assumption of human equality. "We are as noble as the king, only not as rich," the poor peasants of the Aragonese mountains used to say. I have seen a prime minister embrace his gardener in the traditional male embrace, the men standing chest to chest and resting an arm on the other's shoulder. I have seen a waiter who had come back from a holiday embrace a customer. It is an equality of the heart based on the idea fundamental in all Spanish relationships: the dignity of manliness. "*Hombre!*" they exclaim. Even the women address each other in this way.

The Spanish genius has expressed itself in building—they have been the greatest builders since the Romans—in mystical poetry, in great religious figures like Santa Teresa and Loyola, in inspired acts of discovery—Cortes and Pizarro—in the carving of tombs and altar pieces and in a small but superb group of painters and sculptors. The Spaniards have surpassed all Europe in the popular arts. They have a genius for the popular: dancing above all.

There are two kinds of dancing: the regional dances like the discreet, monotonous folk dance of the *sardana* which goes on every Sunday in the squares of Barcelona to the sound of pipe and tabor; or the gay dance of Huelva, near Cadiz. Every region has its dance. There is the Aragonese *jota*, gracious, fiery, full of verve as the body leaps and sways and seems to quiver and burn under the snapping thumbs of the dancer or the crackle of his castanets that circle the body like a Catherine wheel.

There is the lightness and speed of the *sevillanas*. Spanish dancing is the dramatic language of the body: fear, challenge, voluptuousness, languor, hatred and irresistible sensual life come out in it. The heels stamp with animal, sexual defiance and enticement, yet at the crisis of abandon or fury the dancer is not disordered, but still controlled by the dramatic pattern of the dance.

The other Spanish dancing, chiefly seen in Granada and Seville, comes from the gypsies and, like the gypsy songs, it is violent, sexual, an allegory of physical love and death. Here fury or passion whirls into disorder. In the black nights or under the moon, one can go up to the smart, electrically lit caves in the hills above Granada and see the gypsies dancing in the packed rooms. Hands clap in rhythm, guttural cries of *olé!* and *anda!* come from the troupe, as the dancer turns his body into a serpent or into flame. Since the civil war the puritan archbishop of Seville has checked a good deal of the dancing, but nothing can stop the gypsies. Mothers make babies roll their hips, as they lie in their arms. The long-nosed Spanish gypsies are not all vagrants; some have made fortunes in the bull ring. In Granada many have entered the liberal professions; the brief case has replaced the guitar.

After the dancing, there is the strange art of singing—*cante hondo* (deep song) or *cante flamenco* (popular song)—as it is called. The radio blares it everywhere, that high Hindu or Arab falsetto, splitting its semitones, and coming out like a sustained, wavering desert whine. The driver of the last empty tram at night will sing it to himself as he goes by, or the peasant jogging on his donkey across the plain will sing it, in a long, lonely, drawling voice.

You sit in one of those tiled back rooms in a bar off the Puerta del Sol in Madrid—a bar with bulls' heads on the walls, full of roaring men standing on a floor littered with sugar papers and prawn shells—and you hear the guitarist cunningly working upon his audience and the singer like a hypnotist. Suddenly the singer breaks out in a high guttural voice with a long sighing "*aye*" or "*lele*" prolonged for several bars; he stops, the guitar begins to gallop and threaten and then, suddenly—and drama is everything to the Spanish—on an even higher and more piercing note the singer cries out his dramatic opening line: the guitar breaks in again, the singer springs into the remaining lines, pausing on notes, hesitating and rising to the crisis of the song which falls away into a rapid, melancholy cadence as the guitar gathers it up again. The poems are simple: "The trouble with women is that they are like cherries; fail to pick them in time and you have lost them." Or, "I warn you, now that love has come to us, that I will punish your pride."

The audience may chatter loudly at the beginning of these songs and behave with the familiar indifference which the Spaniards regard as their right; but they are waiting for one or two difficult split notes and subtle variations of the vowels at the crisis of the song which will put the singer's strange art to the test. When this crisis comes the audience is dead silent, expectant, quick to detect error and passionate in applause—or its opposite.

Close to a *cante hondo* are the blood-freezing *saetas* which are sung in Holy Week. The procession of hooded familiars of

The past is always close at hand in Spain. Outside Avila, this landscape of stone-colored, stone-walled city, with its cross and shepherds, might be a scene painted by Goya or Velázquez.

the brotherhoods walk up the white streets of Seville which are polished by the grease of the twinkling candles they are holding. The penitents walk barefoot. One man is bowed under an enormous cross. The image of the Virgin, or some painted sculpture of the Christ, is borne by on a platform by men concealed beneath. Suddenly the silent procession stops. The whole street is silent and then a solitary figure breaks out into this short, half-savage song. The atmosphere of Seville is heady and voluptuous in that springtime week and the short cry of the singer seems to express the remorse and the agony of the sinner, tearing his heart in physical longing for God. The Spaniards are inclined to lay this on with a knife and the composer de Falla once complained in a loud voice about the way one of these religious songs was sung. He was in the street and he had to be hurried out of sight, for the crowd would have lynched him.

The Holy Week processions in all Spanish cities, and the fiestas that follow, bring out the popular love of ritual and spectacle. Military parades are shabby in Spain—though Franco's official Moorish guard is picturesque—but the religious processions combine the tragic with the sumptuous and pagan. The jeweled Virgins are very pretty and the carved Christs are done with that carnal and realistic unction which is present in so much of Spanish art. Seville, in the Feria, which follows Holy Week, is intoxicating. The short-waistcoated riders in their tall Córdoba hats, the dark Sevillanas with their high combs and the roses in their hair, riding behind them on lively horses, are—as the Spaniards say—tremendous. "Spain!" the novelist Galdós cried. "With one side of your face fiesta and the other misery!" The fiesta expresses the Spanish genius for the good life; at the other extreme, in the misery, is the deep obsession with the death of the body. One moment

the Spanish spirit is vital, fantastic, luxurious, excellent; the next it is plain, monotonous, consumed by boredom, torpor and the thought of death. There is no middle way.

But, above all, the bullfight shows the love the Spaniards have for excellence in the popular occasion, for display, elegance and ritual, combined with strong emotion and the sight of skill and fearlessness. Many Spaniards dislike bullfighting: Europe is pulling at them. They have turned to football. But bullfighting has not become less popular. It has perhaps become safer because bulls are now bred small and are fought younger and because the public has come to like virtuosity and speed. Stoical and indifferent to suffering in themselves, the Spaniards are astonished when the foreigner suggests that bullfighting is cruel. There is nothing sadistic in the crowd; they are strong-stomached and unimaginative; because the emotions roused are strong and tragic; they are not turned by

Arrogance and elegance, love of ritual and of spectacle,
preoccupation with death and emotion and courage—
all these make up the most Spanish of dramas, the
bullfight; all these are visible on the face of a torero.

the sight of the bull coughing up his blood or by the sight of the wretched padded cab horse of the picador rolled over by the enormous force of the bull's charge. The crowd goes to the ring for the spectacle and after that for drama and for the style, the beauty and precision of the matador's passes with the cape. The virile grace of the male body is seen to perfection. The art of inciting and dominating danger is what the crowd has come to see: it is quick to spot cowardice, dishonorable behavior or incompetence. Incompetence, alas, is common. The matador often misses the famous "moment of truth"—when the sword goes in—and the result is a bloody fiasco. The audience at the bull ring is as extraordinary as the fight itself, for it breaks up into protesting and counterprotesting factions at any moment. The bullfight is not a sport—except in Pamplona —but something between a rite and a spectacle. The bull is bred to be dangerous. He dies in hot blood, at the top of his rage. He will die anyway, and the Spaniards consider he dies more heroically than under the mallet of the stockyard.

"Bread, bulls and tomorrow is another day," says the proverb. Spanish hunger, Spanish passion and Spanish fatalism are summed up in it. The children play bullfighting, not cowboys and Indians, in the streets. They make the famous "passes," using their jackets for capes. They "play" dogs and donkeys. At a fair outside Seville you will hear the cry, "The bulls!" and off will go the lads to worry the long-horned herds in their pastures. Belmonte, one of the greatest bullfighters of all time, a rich man now, who has large estates, started as an urchin in the Triana, the gypsy quarter of Seville, and used to "poach" bulls by moonlight. Like the other lads he stripped off his clothes and played the bulls naked. Bullfighters are scarred from childhood. In the "great fiestas" of the year, after the corn has been threshed on the village threshing floors, the villages are flagged, the Plaza Mayor is barricaded, the mayor and corporation come out on the balcony and the bulls come into the ring. The fights are amateur and brutal. One hears now and again of the bull getting upstairs into the Town Hall and bumping the authorities off the balcony.

Spain is a poor country, at once naturally hostile to industrialism and yet seeking it. It is the seeping in of industrialism which is, at bottom, responsible for the three civil wars, the innumerable parliaments, the two republics, the *coups d'état* of the army, the bitter quarrel between the Catholics and the anticlerical Catholics. There is a mere handful of Protestants whose few chapels periodically get their windows broken. One moment in Spain Don Quixote speaks; the next moment Sancho Panza replies.

"We live under a tyranny," says the malicious Madrid cynic, "and are in consequence the freest country in Europe. We have no free press, but we can do exactly what we like." Then he raises his glass and slyly gives a toast: "To the Pope's intentions," he says.

"Here," says the taxi driver charging at the crossroads, "we are all anarchists. And"—he winks—"there are some secret ones with contacts over the frontier."

The well-behaved foreigner finds a people hostile to government, socially un-co-operative, and who seem to find life endurable without these virtues. Beautiful laws are drawn up, Spain is nominally a "state of vertical syndicates" on Mussolini's model; but Sancho Panza has turned it into something different.

"Who," I asked, after crossing the Ebro, "who blew up that bridge?"

"The others," said the café proprietor.

"But which side? Franco or the Reds?"

"The others," said the café proprietor.

Then he lifted a finger and rubbed it slyly along the tip of his long nose. "After a civil war it is always the others. Whoever wins is right."

General Franco began as a Moroccan general, out for a traditional *coup d'état*. He was obliged to get foreign Fascist allies who were anxious to practice bombing civilians in preparation for World War II. Instead of a *coup*, Franco got a war and a Fascist party. He won the war, he wriggled out of his alliance with Hitler and Mussolini when he saw they were losing. A practical man, he wanted grain, not glory; the Allies fed him with just enough to keep him out of Hitler's hands. The Church, the Fascist (or Falangist) party and the army tried to capture him. He clipped back the Falange, which is not much more than a noisy but discredited youth movement. He was for long vindictive to his enemies. Now he is a little more tolerant and is trying, with a good deal of success, to get the less important exiles back to Spain. He still has far too many political prisoners; but people have got bored with him and used to him. They are bewildered and anxious for the future, but no one inside Spain or outside seems able to agree on his successor.

The fact is that Spain depends on personal government, just as life in Spain depends on influence. ("My cousin will see you win your lawsuit," or even "My uncle will see you get a seat on the bus.") There is not necessarily bribery in it—except to get something through the customs, or a large contract, or a long-distance call on the once efficient and now ruined American telephone system. In one sense Franco has been obliged to watch the success of the revolution he defeated in battle. He wanted to preserve the traditional Spain, but by his own act that Spain has gone. The night watchman who called the hours through the night in the villages has vanished; the lorry is driving out the mule. Women have far more liberty. The peasants are leaving the land. The despised foreigner, suspected for his Western ideas, is now welcomed as a tourist to excellent hotels. And to him Spain is one of the few cheap countries left. It is also one of notable honesty and cleanliness. The Spaniards may be dilatory, but they are to be trusted absolutely. Their patience is a great virtue; their dignity and self-respect unforgettable.

"How much do you earn?" I asked a car-park attendant in Barcelona, an elderly man.

"Seventeen pesetas," he said with quiet irony. "A wage not large enough to live on but on which one can die with dignity."

AFRICA

Laurens van der Post
Paul Bowles
Peter Abrahams
Alan Paton

PORTRAIT OF A CONTINENT

*Alone, aloof and resistant, the immense continent of
darkness seems to have been armed by nature to
discourage foreign contacts. Yet it is immensely rich,
teeming with vivid, uninhibited life.*
*In this genius for life and growth Laurens van der Post
finds hope that Africa will be able to
resolve the bitter tensions and the conflict between
what is oldest in man and what is newest.*

Always, it seems to me, whichever way and at whatever time
one approaches Africa, one faces a mystery. Even as a child,
in the shimmering interior of Africa, when I asked, "Why is
it called the Dark Continent?" the answer came pat: because
for so long Africa had been a great unknown quantity, a dark
place in the mind of man. One understood readily enough why
the New World and Australia remained undiscovered for so
many centuries. No one in Europe had known of their existence. Not so Africa. It had lain for many thousands of years
in full view of the thrustful civilizations that came and went
along the Mediterranean seaboard. It was a known unknown,
a dark secret in the full sun. Yet it stayed unraveled right into
our own restless era. Why?

The answer is not just indifference on the part of the Mediterranean world, nor its tendency to double back toward the
fabulous East. It is true that the discovery of both the New
World and the Cape of Good Hope, at the beginning of the
modern epoch, were mere by-products of European determination to break back into Asia. Nonetheless, there are indications

enough that Africa at all sorts of odd moments strangely excited the early world. Almost everything the ancients said
about it implied a sense of wonder, from the trite Roman saying, "Out of Africa always something new," up to Shakespeare's "I speak of Africa and golden joys" and Sir Thomas
Browne's observation in another dimension: "There is all
Africa and her prodigies in us." Homer, who launched the real
adventure of the European spirit in the 7th Century B.C.—and
possibly much earlier—refers to Africa as a place fit for the
vacation of gods, and Herodotus, who lived some generations
later and collected all possible information about Africa, describes the Sacred Nile as descending from the heavy clouds
poised over the high mountains of Ethiopia.

I feel keenly that these and many other fragments of the
past suggest more coming and going between the emerging
world and Africa than is recorded in our history. But why did
it stop where it did? Consider that the Carthaginian general
Hanno nearly 3000 years ago sailed by the Pillars of Hercules
as far south as Kakoulima on the west coast of Africa and
brought home strange tales of his adventures. Other Phoeni-
cians appear to have steered the opposite way from Suez, right
around Africa, in the 6th Century B.C. The Israelites, too, are
said to have traded with ports along the east coast of Africa,
and I myself have seen strange cities of stone crumbling in the
suffocating jungle and mangrove fringes of the same coast.
There are also some ruined fortresses standing by a few strategic footpaths in the interior, suggesting an even deeper pene-
tration. But that is all. Africa remained merely a vast coastline
in the mind of the world until the middle of the 19th Century.

The conventional reaction is to blame it on the nature of
Africa. To use the animistic terms evoked by the spectacle of
this immense continent, striding alone and intact with the pace
of a sleepwalker into our crowded time, it was as if the land
itself abhorred foreign contact and was organized to resist
accordingly. Nearly everywhere, hard by the coast, the land
rose steeply to form a great plateau that stretched for thousands of miles east, west, north and south. The waste of the
Sahara sealed the widest and most likely invasion route from
the north. The sterile Red Sea hills and the gleaming, turreted
redoubt of Ethiopia guarded the eastern flank, and the single
gap made by the valley of the Nile was blocked with one of
the world's most formidable marshes. In the south, where a
temperate climate might have suggested another Mediterranean venture, more desert stood in the way, and a foreshore
so bleak that it is still known as the Skeleton Coast. In between
north and south and subtropic and tropic, bush and jungle
descended in dense masses sullenly to stand sentinel in their
own reflections by creek, lagoon and mangrove swamp within
the sound of the sea.

All these defenses were manned in depth by a vast force of
parasites dealing out contagion and death. Thus the tsetse fly
closed the vulnerable low-lying bush-veld against man and
his chattels by injecting them with the fatal sleeping sickness.
Despite DDT and other determined stratagems of the scientist,

White mist and a torrent of thunder: *Victoria Falls.*

In Tanganyika a safari is almost lost against the vastness of African sky and land.

more than half of Tanganyika remains fly-ridden. Even in areas far longer in European hands, like my own native South Africa, total possession of the land is denied to man through the same cause. Indeed many of us are grateful to the tsetse fly for protecting some portion of Africa against exploitation, and preserving its innate loveliness for a future wherein we may become more caring of our mother earth.

As ardent a defender of Africa's ancient natural rights was the mosquito, an airborne force that attacked the invader with diseases like yellow fever and several varieties of malaria, to name only a few of the many malignities in its armory. There were hosts of other parasites as well, but these examples should be enough to show how discouraging and ugly the scene must have appeared to men reared on the better-mannered European earth. I myself certainly understand how they turned from Africa to look elsewhere for treasure, and how D. H. Lawrence could dismiss it as "the continent of dark negation."

Yet I cannot accept this as the whole answer. Instructed as I was from birth in the idiom of Africa, I am tempted to counter indignantly that the world without was a world of "bright rejection," one that denied the spontaneous, vivid, uninhibited and unending abundance of life that was the true glory of Africa. The Mediterranean was a man's world, more and more obedient and bent to man. Africa was a stronghold of life that was obedient only to life; a great and splendid barbaric woman longing for an equal mate.

These considerations traveled with us as we flew south. But, flying through the blue air, the horizon traveling evenly and effortlessly before us like a blue ripple over a still blue sea, watching a plume of thundercloud 3000 feet long curling over the peaked cap of a far range of purple mountains, and seeing the earth take over from the towns and carry on as if they had never existed, these considerations seemed more and more secondary.

The right words for the change were found for me by a young inspector in the international locust-control organization, who was on his way from Ethiopia to the northern frontier of Kenya. After three years in Ethiopia, he said with a smile oddly fresh and tender, he could not yet get used to the scale of the land. All his spare time had gone into seeing "as much as I can of the world down there," where everything was conceived in the grand manner, even its pests and plagues. At this very moment he was on his way to intercept a swarm of locusts a quarter of a mile broad and some hundreds of miles long.

I, too, had watched similar swarms down south descend on our broad acres of young corn and move on, as hungry as ever, an hour later with not a blade left standing above the ground. I had seen storks, hawks and a score of other birds that specialize in this kind of diet turn away from the swarm before the sun was hot, disgusted with their feed. Once an overland express, every gleaming cog a symbol of 20th Century achieve-

Behind them, touching the clouds, rises Mawenzi, the east peak of Mount Kilimanjaro.

ment, was held up from dawn to sunset, its wheels spinning helplessly in locust corpses knee-deep on the track. I remembered a tattered black son of Africa laughing at the sight with an uninhibited delight which nowadays I understand better.

Yet there were less destructive examples of the land's abundance and genius for sheer life. I thought of Vergil's "Africa, breeding ground of the great," and wished we could descend to where the waters of the great marsh of the White Nile were spreading. From the air the marsh looks impersonal and empty, burning with a bronze flame among islands covered with palm and thorn, and with reeds, papyrus and quivering elephant grasses crowding its lagoons and creeks. But I knew that, within, it bubbled with life, a vast porridge churned by pike, perch and tiger fish, by hippopotamus and crocodile.

As the sun broke through the vapors drawn by the night over the sleeping waters, wherever I looked the smooth water face was speckled, like an antique mirror, by the black nose tips and dark ears of the hippopotamuses leaning their long chins on the slow current, patiently waiting for the sun to air their dank beds among the reeds. They would emerge from the water like creatures coming out of a prehistoric dream of life and with a slow somnambulistic step vanish in their tens of thousands into the land beside the marshes. I would not believe it possible that so many could be absorbed without a sign of protest or strain by the land. Yet they would vanish effortlessly, leaving not a trace behind. They would be followed by croco-

diles appearing in tight formations on the banks to sleep, eyes shut with ecstasy or mouths wide open for some oddly privileged little birds to pick clean their teeth.

These birds of Africa: they moved in swarms more dazzling than the locust. There in the marshes, in unimagined numbers, were all the classical waterfowl: giant mauve herons and their cousins in peacock blue with a crest of gold on their helmets; storks with white bathing shorts, black tops and yellow beaks; cranes in lilac velvet strutting on mannequin legs; duck in Joseph's-dream colors and bustling geese officious in pinstriped suits and small black bowlers. Scarlet bee-eaters, blue African rollers and yellow finches would make gay overhead, and long lily-trotters race from one massive leaf to another for insect prizes translucent in the light, silver spurs of water flashing at their heels, and all around them royal-blue lilies and white water daisies opening wide tender hearts to their own chosen ray of sun.

In the migration season I have seen their numbers swollen to such an extent that even so great a water had acute mooring crises. For an hour before sunset the sky overhead would be filled with fowl pleading with their crowded kinsfolk for room on the waters below. When the noise and confusion was at its greatest they would never leave their own formation or get entangled with another. The temptation to lose their neat little heads and to despair must have been almost irresistible in that world of whirring wings over the strange, packed and problematic water. Yet even in the last flight to make the water in the red of evening, they would come down in perfect formation. Then they would stop their cries and quickly croon their beating hearts to sleep, until there would be only a whisper of wind and water among the reeds.

Nor was this abundance of bird and animal life limited to the water. I had turned my back on them one yellow dawn not long before and walked toward that far escarpment of mountains in the east. All day long somewhere ahead of me some feathered swarm made dense smoke in the blue of the day. Whenever I rested, the silence was loud with their song, and curiously intimate and unafraid birds pecked at the seeds of grass in the shade beside me or rested within reach of my hand, some so still and tiny and well clothed in spectroscopic red, orange, yellow, green, blue and violet colors that they might have been Oriental jewelry scattered as largesse to the impoverished earth. There were fever birds singing of sunstroke and hallucination in the noon of day overhead. There were natural lanes beside the game tracks where trees leafless and smooth like ivory would be topped mile after mile with vultures, their raw unfeathered necks tucked well into their drooping shoulders, their undertaker spirits full of longing for murder and sudden death. Wherever there was a glimpse of blue, at its center was some hawk, kite, buzzard or eagle hanging like a spider on a shining thread of air.

And after the abundance of birds, the abundance of animals. Where the hippo tracks and crocodile slithers fell away behind one, the massive buffalo took over, grazing in dark sullen crescents far out into the plains. All day long, even when not visible, they charged the electroplated air with their deep, silent power. Between and beyond them ranged the elephant; it was useless to guess at their numbers. The bush contained them as the sea the fish. But if one knew how to look for them there, they were close at hand, moving silently from tree to tree in their long resilient stride, Saracen tusks gleaming and trunks delicately curling, or else perhaps standing with eyes shut like a child's, innocent with fatigue at night, and ears working like a fish's fin, to sleep in some broad stream of mottled shadow flowing deep underneath the forest leaves sizzling in the sun.

The same went for rhino, lion, leopard, the lynx and many another lesser breed without the law. Even at night, in one's rest, their many varied sounds—the leopard's startled cough, the cheetah's birdlike whimper, the lynx's snarl, the lion's roar, solemn and full of fate as a roll of drums in a Beethoven symphony, all added to the anguished cry of the werewolf hyenas, the jackal's mournful wail, the wild dog's urgent yap, the bush buck's challenging bark, the owl's screech, the night plover's bosun's pipe and the far sea sound of the stars—never let one forget how crowded with natural pilgrims was this ancient African way.

Beyond the escarpment on the great plains the view was more open but hardly less full. Vast herds of purple eland, dazzle upon dazzle of heraldic zebra, troops of hartebeest in cyclamen satins, battalions of chocolate wildebeest or gnu and leaping herds of more than a hundred kinds of buck and gazelle moved with a restless gypsy brilliance before one's eyes. At dawn and sunset they stood hip to hip, drinking lip to lip of their own fiery reflections on the burning waters around their feet, while the dust rose like swarms of golden bees from the impatient hoofs of the colorful crowds stamping the earth behind them.

So it continued, each element and level of the land equipped and fully stocked with its particular achievement of life. The great primeval forests would present their anthropoids beating themselves on the chest in the leafy darkness like drums summoning cannibals to a ritual. Monkeys with pink baby faces and black apes with silver collars swung over an abyss between one giant treetop and another, while far below them copper pygmies, mauve okapi and the wide-eyed dik-dik, with ears like canna petals, moved as silent as the dappled and remote sunlight over ground covered with moss and ferns. And after the forests, the bush, where high-strung baboons in auburn coats stared out of wise and alert amber eyes.

The earth, too, had its own particular children, the snakes and serpents with a glory all their own, adorned and nourished with the impartiality of a mother dedicated without fear or favor to all she has brought forth: cobras in ebony black, with a ring of startling white around slim throats, lying in the sun beside their holes, and adders, round and compact like Maya bracelets, their triangular heads poised on jeweled tails, or passively stitched, point by gleaming point, into the background tapestry of olive-green grass. Indeed there was one breed dedicated not to the sun but to the moon, emerging when it was full (so a black child of Africa told me), to sit on its tail swaying rhythmically and hissing at the pallid light as if in pain. There were Spartan mambas, black and green, long and athletic, speeding through the bush seemingly airborne on coils of fire, or gleefully dangling in the trees after a surfeit of birds' eggs. There were the wise old pythons, out of love with effort, coiled ponderously in the colors of fabulous orchids on a tree branch commanding the coming and going of game along the bush-veld tracks.

Then last of all came my own native South Africa. The way to it by air was narrow and long and wound through deep valleys of cloud. The sky was shuddering with thunder, torn asunder with lightning, and the air was dynamic with foreboding of change and eventfulness—so much so that a party of a dozen white sisters seated near me took out their rosaries and with closed eyes chanted prayers. But when we came out of the cloud at last I thought I had never seen the land more beautiful or poignant.

Physically, humanly and spiritually the whole of Africa comes to a dramatic point in my native land. From desert, plain, mountain and river, from mosquito and tsetse fly to lion and elephant, from the first man of Africa, the Bushman, to the Hottentot and Bantu who succeeded and oppressed him, right up to the European, all are held together in a striking microcosm of the gigantic whole. From the air my country looked as if made to the measure of immeasurable creation.

Yet down below, negative obsessions, wounding and embittering tensions of mind and spirit were most powerfully at work. Even my oldest friends, seeing me after a long absence, seemed compelled not to ask after my health but to dive, with their first breath, deep into a discussion of the problem between white and black. Thus at Cape Town, in the hotel I have used since boyhood, I found a revered senator sitting in the lounge. He had been in Parliament for thirty-five years and was now a gray-haired elder statesman. But the expression in his eyes and the thought in his mind had not changed in that time. "Come," he said at once, drawing me into a seat beside him. "Come and talk to me about the native question." And a famous judge whom I deeply respect took me by the arm at tea to confess rather ruefully: "I don't understand myself. When I come out of chambers at the end of my day and walk along the streets, I try to relax by playing a game of guessing what the passers-by do for a living. I did not realize until this afternoon that I have never included a black person in the game. It's odd, isn't it?" Again I took a black friend to Pretoria with me, and agreed on a place at which to meet him an hour later. I found him at the place, sitting on the pavement; in Pretoria, the capital of a country with nine million black inhabitants, there is not a public seat on which they are allowed to sit.

I could go on indefinitely giving similar examples but I wish only to illustrate how quickly one can be seized in South Africa by the basic obsession. Indeed if one took the surface values in command here at their face value, one would despair. Yet the paradox is salutary: where the conflict is greatest, I find most cause for hope.

No individual and no people have been able to achieve full maturity without terrible inner conflict. We are all condemned to *act* the new meaning that is seeking expression in our lives before we can *know* it. And new awareness presupposes suffering. One thought that has always depressed me about the new emerging nationalisms in Africa is that they are getting their power too easily. But no one could say that of South Africa. The conflict there is truly joined. The new meaning has everyone by the throat and will not let go until all men surrender to it. Although, for the moment, its denial seems greater than ever, I have no doubt that the meaning itself will prevail. When I was a boy, only one clear South African voice was raised on behalf of the wholeness of life in Africa: the voice of Olive Schreiner. By the time I was eighteen there were three of us apprenticed to the cause. Today there are thousands, of all races and colors, who refuse to be silent on behalf of an Africa wherein these crippling obsessions with color and race must no longer exist.

And yet, if it depended on humanity alone, I might succumb to fear. Happily, the outcome depends, too, on Africa—not the Africa of the towns which sit on the land incongruously, like a top hat on a Hottentot, but on the old Africa which surrounds them and which is still so deeply at one within itself and life and time. That Africa I am certain is slowly gathering together all that is old and new, and shaping it in the image of the oneness of itself. It is a process of immense significance for the whole world.

Seen in this light, the mystery encountered on the northern shores of the Mediterranean is mysterious no longer. I myself no longer wonder why Africa was left undiscovered for so long. I believe it was miraculously preserved for precisely this hard-

pressed moment in time. The world is dominated by men and cultures that have lost contact with the natural spirit in themselves. Life is denied its true increase and daily more imperiled because what is oldest in man and what is newest are separated; and not only separated but thrown one against the other in deadly conflict. That is why the scene being enacted in Africa is watched so breathlessly from the wings of the world. Two halves must joint and, however painful the process, out of it a greater reintegration of the spirit of man will come. Paul could come to revelation on the road to Damascus only through persecution of what he was about to love. Great hatred is often only fear of a greater love.

All this was very alive in me as I watched at sunset from the deck of my ship. The Cape of Good Hope, "the fairest" (as Francis Drake described it) "in the whole circumference of the earth," was falling astern into the sea and the night. More than four hundred years ago, the Portuguese poet Camoëns sailed round the Cape on his way to China. Afterward in his *Lusiad*, one of the great epic poems of the world, he described a vision which Vasco da Gama, who rounded the Cape first of all in 1497, had had in those waters. Suddenly the sky went dark, Camoëns says, the wind dropped, the sea moaned and a great Negroid giant loomed over da Gama's ship. The brave admiral, trembling, could hardly ask who was the giant. "I am that great, that occult, that much tormented Cape," came the booming answer, and the giant went on to warn the admiral that great trouble and suffering would come as a result of his breakthrough into these distant waters. He himself, the giant said, was the last of the Titans, turned to stone because he had dared to love a white nymph of the sea who rejected him. To me this poem has always read like a prophetic allegory. Africa has been turned to stone for the Europeans simply because Africa has been denied white love. But once loved for its own sake, it could live again for the white man, a Promethean Titan bringing the light of a greater fire of life into the dark hour of the European.

Lions stare serenely across the great Serengeti Plains.

THE MOSLEMS

*North Africa is changing, but the traveler
who still expects to find an aura of mystery
will not be disappointed. Paul Bowles finds it in
the faces of the people, in patterns of
sunlight and shadow in the bazaars, in a way of life
that is strictly ordered according to an
ancient pattern of concord between God and man.*

It had taken the truck fourteen hours to get from Kerzaz to Adrar, and except for the lunch stop in the oasis of El Aougherout, the old man had sat the whole time on the floor without moving, his legs tucked up beneath him, the hood of his burnoose pulled up over his turban to protect his face from the fine dust that sifted up through the floor. First-class passage on the vehicles of the Compagnie Générale Transsaharienne entitled the voyager to travel in the glassed-in compartment with the driver, and that was where I sat, occasionally turning to look through the smeared panes at the solitary figure sitting sedately in the midst of the tornado of dust behind. At lunchtime, when I had seen his face with its burning brown eyes and magnificent white beard, it had occurred to me that he looked like a handsome and very serious Santa Claus.

The dust grew worse during the afternoon, so that by sunset, when we finally pulled into Adrar, even the driver and I were covered. I got out and shook myself, and the little old man clambered out of the back, cascades of dust spilling from his garments. Then he came around to the front of the truck to speak to the driver, who, being a good Moslem, wanted to get to a shower and wash himself. Unfortunately he was a city Moslem as well, so that he was impatient with the measured cadence of his countryman's speech, and slammed the door in the middle of it, unaware that the old man's hand was in the way.

Calmly the old man opened the door with his other hand. The tip of his middle finger dangled by a bit of skin. He looked at it an instant, then quietly scooped up a handful of that ubiquitous dust, put the two parts of the finger together and poured the dust over it, saying softly: "Thanks be to Allah." With that, the expression on his face never having changed, he picked up his bundle and staff and walked away. I stood looking after him, full of wonder, and reflecting upon the differences between his behavior and what mine would have been under the same circumstances. To show no outward sign of pain is unusual enough, but to express no resentment against the person who has hurt you seems very strange, and to give thanks to God at such a moment is the strangest touch of all.

My experience since then has shown me that this was not untypical, and it has remained in my memory and become a symbol of that which is admirable in the people of North Africa. "This world we see is unimportant and ephemeral as a dream," they say. "To take it seriously would be an absurdity. Let us think rather of the heavens that surround us." And the landscape is conducive to reflections upon the nature of the infinite. In other parts of Africa you are aware of the earth beneath your feet, of the vegetation and the animals; all power seems concentrated in the earth. In North Africa the earth becomes the less important part of the landscape because you find yourself constantly raising your eyes to look at the sky. In the arid landscape the sky is the final arbiter. When you have understood that, not intellectually but emotionally, you have also understood why it is that the great trinity of monotheistic religions, Judaism, Christianity and Islam, which removed the source of power from the earth itself to the spaces outside the earth, were evolved in desert regions. And of the three, Islam, perhaps because it is the most recently born, operates the most directly and with the greatest strength upon the daily actions of those who embrace it.

For a person born into a culture where religion has long ago become a thing quite separate from daily life, it is a startling experience to find himself suddenly in the midst of a culture where there is a minimum of discrepancy between dogma and natural behavior, and this is one of the great fascinations of being in North Africa. I am not speaking of Egypt, where the old harmony is gone, decayed from within. My own impressions of Egypt before Nasser are those of a great panorama of sun-dried disintegration. In any case, she has had a different history from the rest of Mediterranean Africa, she is ethnically and linguistically distinct, and is more a part of the Levant than of the region we ordinarily mean when we speak of North Africa. But in Tunisia, Algeria and Morocco there are still people whose lives proceed according to the ancient pattern of concord between God and man, agreement between theory and practice, identity of word and flesh (or however one prefers to conceive and define that pristine state of existence we intuitively feel we once enjoyed and now have lost).

I don't claim that the Moslems of North Africa are a group of mystics, heedless of bodily comfort, interested only in the welfare of the spirit. If you have ever bought so much as an egg from one of them, you learned that they are quite able to fend for themselves when it comes to money matters. The spoiled strawberries are at the bottom of the basket, the pebbles inextricably mixed with the lentils and the water with the milk, the same as in many other parts of the world, with the difference that if you ask the price of an object in a rural market, they will reply, all in one breath: "Fifty, how much will you give?" I should say that in the realm of *béah o shri* (selling and buying; note that in their minds selling comes first), which is what they call business, they are surpassed only by the Hindus, who are less emotional about it and therefore more successful, and by the Chinese, acknowledged masters of the Oriental branch of the science of commerce.

When I meet fellow Americans traveling about here in North Africa, I ask them: "What did you expect to find here?" Almost without exception, regardless of the way they express it, the answer, reduced to its simplest terms, is a sense of mystery.

*The faces of Moslem women are still veiled in public.
This unveiled girl dances at
a family festival in a courtyard enclosed on all sides.*

They expect mystery, and they find it, since fortunately it is a quality difficult to extinguish all in a moment. They find it in the patterns of sunlight filtering through the latticework that covers the *souks*, in the unexpected turnings and tunnels of the narrow streets, in the women whose features still go hidden beneath the *litham*, in the secretiveness of the architecture, which is such that even if the front door of a house is open, it is impossible to see inside. If they listen as well as look, they find it too in the song the lone camel driver sings by his fire before dawn, in the calling of the muezzins at night, when their voices are like bright beams of sound piercing the silence, and, most often, in the dry beat of the darabukka, the hand drum played by the women everywhere, in the great city houses and in the remotest tents of the wilderness.

It is a strange sensation, when you are walking alone in a still, dark street late at night, to come upon a pile of cardboard boxes soaked with rain, and, as you pass by it, to find yourself staring into the eyes of a man sitting upright behind it. A thief? A beggar? The night watchman of the quarter? A spy for the Secret Police?

You just keep walking, looking at the ground, hearing your footsteps echo between the walls of the deserted street. Into your head comes the idea that you may suddenly hear the sound of a conspiratorial whistle, and that something unpleasant may be about to happen. A little farther along you see, deep in the recess of an arcade of shops, another man reclining in a deck chair, asleep. Then you realize that all along the street there are men both sleeping and sitting quietly awake, and that even in the hours of its most intense silence the place is never empty of people.

At the moment, writing about any part of Africa is a little like trying to draw a picture of a roller coaster in motion. You can say: It *was* thus and so, or, it is *becoming* this or that, but you risk making a misstatement if you say categorically that anything *is*, because likely as not you will open tomorrow's newspaper to discover that it has changed. On the whole the new governments of Tunisia and Morocco are desirous of furthering tourism in their respective countries; they are learning that the average tourist is more interested in native dancing than in the new bus terminal; that he is more willing to spend money in the Casbah than to inspect new housing projects. For a while, after the demise of the violently unpopular Pasha of Marrakesh, Thami el Glaoui (one of whose sources of income was a percentage of the earnings of the twelve thousand prostitutes of his city), the great public square of Marrakesh, the Djemâa el Fna, was used solely as a parking lot. Now, anyone who has visited the region will tell you that the biggest single attraction for tourists in all North Africa was the Djemâa el Fna in Marrakesh. It was hard to find a moment of the day or night when tourists could not be found prowling around among its acrobats, singers, storytellers, snake charmers, dancers and medicine men. Without it Marrakesh became just another Moroccan city. And so the Djemâa el Fna was reinstated, and now goes on more or less as before.

Both Tunisia's Bourghiba and Morocco's King Mohammed V are interested in retaining close ties with the West, but in order to ingratiate themselves with their constituents they find themselves obliged to make increasing numbers of concessions to its enemies within their own governments. The fate of both countries hangs upon the outcome of the war in Algeria. The longer France continues hostilities, the less likelihood there will be that any part of North Africa can remain within the orbit of the Western world. And doubtless France will continue to insist upon her "rights" in Algeria as long as we support her side in the struggle.

The political prospect for Barbary does not look bright—except to those who would like to see the neutralist bloc extended to the Atlantic coast. These latter people are likely to present the argument that such a development would be a natural one since the countries are Moslem and adhere to the Arab League. The point is that North Africa is inhabited, like Malaya and Pakistan, by Moslems who are not Arabs.

Encyclopaedia Britannica's estimate of the percentage of Arab stock in the population of Morocco dates from two decades ago, but there has been no influx of Arabs since. It gives 10 per cent of an approximate figure. The remaining 90 per cent are Berbers, who anthropologically have nothing to do with the Arabs. They are not of Semitic origin, and have been living where they are since long before the Arab conquerors came.

Even after thirteen hundred years, the Berbers' conception of how to observe the Moslem religion is by no means identical with that of the descendants of the men who brought it to them. And, the city Moslems complain, they do not observe the fast of Ramadan properly; they neither veil or segregate their women and, most objectionable of all, they have a passion for forming cults dedicated to the worship of local saints. In this their religious practices show a serious deviation from orthodoxy, inasmuch as during the *moussems*, those gigantic pilgrimages which are held periodically under the auspices of each particular brotherhood, men and women *together* dance themselves into a prolonged frenzy which can last for thirty-six hours at a stretch. Self-torture, the inducing of trances, ordeal

by fire and the sword, and the eating of such delicacies as broken glass and scorpions are also usual on these occasions.

The traveler who has been present at one of these indescribable gatherings will never forget it, although if he dislikes the sight of blood and suffering, he will probably try hard to put it out of his mind. To me these spectacles are filled with great beauty, because their obvious purpose is to prove the superiority of the spirit over the flesh. The sight of ten or twenty thousand people actively declaring their faith, demonstrating en masse the power of that faith, can scarcely be anything but inspiring. You lie in the fire, I gash my legs and arms with a knife, he pounds a sharpened bone into his thigh with a rock— then, together, covered with ashes and blood, we sing and dance in joyous praise of the saint and the god who make it possible for us to triumph over pain and, by extension, over death itself. For the participants, of course, exhaustion and ecstasy are inseparable.

This cult-worship, based on vestiges of an earlier religion, has long been frowned upon by the devout urban Moslems of North Africa, and as early as the mid-thirties various restric-

*A professor at ancient Al Azhar
University sits in meditation.*

*The Gezireh Sporting Club on Gezireh Island has
a race track and facilities for many other sports.*

*"Get your ice-cold drink!" A hawker
sells fruit juice from a fancy container.*

tions were placed on its practice. Now at last, all public manifestations of it have been effectively suppressed. There were several reasons why the educated Moslems objected to the brotherhoods. During the periods of the protectorates in Tunisia and Morocco, the colonial administrations did not hesitate to use them for their own political ends, to ensure more complete domination. Also, it has always been felt that visitors who happened to witness the members of a cult in action were given an unfortunate impression of cultural backwardness. Most important was the fact that the rituals were unorthodox and thus unacceptable to true Moslems. If you mentioned such cults as the Hamatcha, the Derqaoua, the Aissaoua, the Haddaoua, the Jilala or the Gnaoua to a city man, he invariably cried: "They're all criminals! They should be put in jail!" without stopping to reflect that it would be difficult to incarcerate more than half the population of any country. I think one reason why the city folk are so violent about the cults is that most of them are only one generation removed from connection with them themselves and, knowing the official attitude toward them, feel a certain guilt at being even that much involved with them. Having been born into a family of adepts is not a thing anyone can quickly forget. Each brotherhood has its own songs and drum rhythms, immediately recognizable as such by persons both within and outside the group. In early childhood rhythmical patterns and sequences of tones become a part of an adept's subconscious, and in later life it is not difficult to attain the trance state when one hears them again.

One of my acquaintances, who has always been vociferous in his denunciation of the brotherhoods, eventually admitted to me that all the older members of his family were adherents to the Jilala cult, citing immediately afterward as an example of their perniciousness an experience of his grandmother some three years before. Like the rest of the family, she was brought up as a Jilalía, but was too old to take part in the observances, which nowadays are held secretly. One evening she was alone in the house, her children and grandchildren having all gone to the movies, and since she had nothing else to do, she went to bed. Somewhere nearby, there was a meeting of Jilala; the drums penetrated her dreams, and in her sleep she rose and, in her night clothing, made her way toward the sounds. She was found next morning unconscious in a vegetable garden near the house where the meeting had taken place, having been badly bitten by ants. The reason she fell, the family assured me, was that at a certain moment the drumming had stopped; if it had gone on, she would have arrived. The drummers always continue until everyone has been brought out of his trance.

"But they did not know she was coming," they said, "and so the next morning, after we had carried her home, we had to send for the drummers to bring her to her senses."

This is the sort of story that infuriates the younger generation of French-educated Moslems if they hear it being told to foreigners. And for the latter to be interested in such things upsets them even more. "Are all the people in your country Holy Rollers?" they demand. "Why don't you write about the civilized people here, instead of the most backward?"

I understand them. They would like to see themselves presented to the outside world in the most "advanced" light possible. They find it perverse of a Westerner to be interested only in the dissimilarities between their culture and his. However, that's the way some of us Westerners are.

Hospitality in North Africa knows no limits. You are taken in and treated as a member of the family. If you don't enjoy yourself, it is not your host's fault, but rather the result of your own inadaptability, for every attempt is made to see that you are happy and comfortable. Some time ago I was the guest of two brothers who had an enormous house in the medina of Fez. So that I should feel truly at home, I was given an entire wing of the establishment, a tiled patio with a room on either side and a fountain in the center. There were great numbers of servants to bring me food and drink, and also to inquire, before my hosts came to call, whether I was disposed to receive them. When they came they often brought singers and musicians to entertain me. The only hitch was that they went to such lengths to treat me as one of them that they also assumed I was not interested in going out into the city. During the entire fortnight I spent with them I never once found my way out of the house, or even out of my own section of it, since all doors were kept locked and bolted, and only the guard, an old Senegalese slave, had the keys. For long hours I sat in the patio listening to the sounds of the city outside, sometimes hearing faint strains of music that I would have given anything really to hear, watching the square of deep-blue sky above my head slowly become a softer and lighter blue as twilight approached, waiting for the swallows that wheeled above the patio when the day was finally over and the muezzins began their calls to evening prayer, and merely existing in the hope that someone would come, something would happen before too many more hours had gone past. But as I say, if I was bored, that was my own fault and not theirs. They were doing everything that they could to please me.

Just as in that 12th Century fortress in Fez I had been provided with a small hand-wound phonograph and one record (Josephine Baker singing *J'ai Deux Amours*, a song hit of that year), so all over North Africa you are confronted with a mélange of the very old and the most recent, with no hint of anything left over from the intervening centuries. It is one of the great charms of the place, the fact that your today carries with it no memories of yesterday or the day before; everything that is not medieval is completely new. The younger generation of French and Jews, born and raised in the cities of North Africa, for the most part have no contact at all with that which is ancient in their countries. A Moroccan girl whose family moved from Rabat to New York, upon being asked what she thought of her new home, replied: "Well, of course, coming from a new country as I do, it's very hard to get used to all these old houses here in New York. I had no idea New York was so *old*." It is hard to remember that the French began to settle in Morocco only at the time of World War I, and that the mushroom cities of Casablanca, Agadir and Tangier grew up in the thirties. Xauen, whose mountains are visible from the terrace of my apartment in Tangier, was entered by European troops in 1920. Even in southern Algeria, where one is inclined

to think of the French as having been stationed for a much longer time, there are war monuments bearing battle dates as recent as 1912. Throughout the whole first quarter of the century the North African frontier was continuously being pushed southward by means of warfare, and south of the Grand Atlas it was 1936 before "pacification" came to an end and European civilians were allowed, albeit on the strict terms laid down by the military, to look for the first time into the magic valleys of the Drâa, the Dadès and the Todra.

Appearing unexpectedly in out-of-the-way regions of North Africa has never been without its difficulties. I remember making an impossible journey before the last war in a produce truck over the Grand Atlas to Ouarzazat, full of excitement at the prospect of seeing the Casbah with its strange painted towers, only to be forced to remain three days inside the shack that passed for a hotel, and then sent on another truck straight back to Marrakesh, having seen nothing but Foreign Legionnaires, and having heard no music other than the bugle calls that issued every so often from the nearby camp. Another time I entered Tunisia on camel back from across the Great Eastern Erg. I had two camels and one hard-working camel driver, whose job it was to run all day long from one beast to the other and try, by whacking their hind legs, to keep them walking in something resembling a straight line. This was a much more difficult task than it sounds; although our course was generally due east, one of the animals had an inexplicable desire to walk southward, while the other was possessed by an equally mysterious urge to go north. The poor man passed his time screaming: "*Hut! Aïda!*" and trying to run both ways at once. His turban was continually coming unwound, and he had no time to attend to the scarf he was knitting, in spite of the fact that he kept the yarn and needles dangling around his neck, ready to work on at any moment.

We did finally cross the border and amble into Tunisia, where we were immediately apprehended by the police. The camel driver was sent back to Algeria where he belonged, and I started on my painful way up through Tunisia, where the French authorities evidently had decided to make my stay in the country as wretched as possible. In the oasis at Nefta, in the hotel at Tozeur, even in the Mosque of Sidi Oqba at Kairouan, I was arrested and lugged off to the commissariat, carefully questioned, and told that I need not imagine I could make a move of which they would not be fully aware.

The explanation was that in spite of my American passport they were convinced I was a German; in those days anybody wandering around North Africa who was not an obvious tourist was suspect. Even the Moslems looked at me closely and said: "*Toi pas Français. Toi Allemand,*" to which I never replied, for fear of having to pay the price that would have been demanded if my true status had been revealed to them.

Algeria is a country where it is better to keep moving around than to stay long in one place. Its towns are not very interesting, but its landscapes are impressive. In the winter, traveling by train across the western steppes, you can go all day and see nothing but flat stretches of snow on all sides, unrelieved by trees in the foreground or by mountains in the distance. In the summer these same desolate lands are cruelly hot, and the wind

Working in the town bazaar, a silversmith of Yezd, in Iran, turns out fine pieces of art with the same crude tools his ancestors used for centuries.

hara," came into being. Here, sheltered from Algerian guerrilla bands, the French have conducted their own nuclear tests.

From the point of view of the onlookers here, the crucial Algerian struggle is to the 'fifties rather what the Spanish Civil War was to the 'thirties. Friendships break up as a result of bitter arguments, and the same old epithets of "Fascist" and "Communist" are tossed back and forth. But regardless of how the tragic episode terminates, no part of North Africa will again be the same sort of paradise for Europeans that it was during the past fifty years. The place has been thrown open to the 20th Century. With Europeanization and nationalism have come a consciousness of identity and the awareness of that identity's commercial possibilities. From now on the North Africans, like the Mexicans, will control and exploit their own charms, rather than being placed on exhibit for us by their managers, and the result will be a very different thing. Tourist land it is still, and doubtless will continue to be for a while, and it is on that basis only that we as residents or intending visitors are now obliged to consider it. We now come here as paying guests of the inhabitants themselves rather than of their exploiters. Travel here is certain not to be so easy or so comfortable as before, and prices are ten times higher than they were, but at least we meet the people on terms of equality, which, we must admit, is a healthier situation.

If you live long enough in a place where the question of colonialism versus self-government is constantly being discussed, you are bound to find yourself having a very definite opinion on the subject. The difficulty is that some of your co-residents feel one way and some the other, but all feel strongly. Those in favor of colonialism argue that you can't "give" (quotes mine) an almost totally illiterate people political power and expect them to create a democracy, and that is doubtless true; but the point is that since they are inevitably going to take the power sooner or later, it is only reasonable to help them take it while they still have at least some measure of good will toward their erstwhile masters. The die-hard French attitude is summed up in a remark made to me by a friendly immigration officer at the Algiers airport. "Our great mistake," he said sadly, "was ever to allow these savages to learn to read and write." I said I supposed that was logical, if one expected to rule forever, which I knew, given the intelligence of the French, they did not intend to do, since it was impossible. The official ceased looking sad and became much less friendly.

At a dinner in Marrakesh during the French occupation, the Frenchman sitting beside me became engaged in an amicable discussion with a Moroccan across the table. "But look at the facts, *mon cher ami.* Before our arrival there was constant warfare between the tribes. Since we came the population of Morocco has doubled. Is that true or not?"

The Moroccan leaned forward. "We can take care of our own births and deaths," he said, smiling. "If we must be killed, just let other Moroccans attend to it. We really prefer that."

swirls the dust into tall yellow pillars that move deliberately from one side of the empty horizon to the other. When you come upon a town in such regions, lying like the remains of a picnic lunch in the middle of an endless parking lot, you know it was the French who put it there. The Algerians prefer to live along the wild and beautiful seacoast, in the palm gardens of the south, atop the cliffs bordering the dry rivers, or on the crests of the high mountains in the center of the country. Up there above the slopes dotted with almond trees, the Berber villages sit astride the long spines of the lesser ranges. The men and women file down the zigzagging paths to cultivate the rich valleys below, here and there in full view of the snowfields where the French have built their skiing resorts. Far to the south lie the parallel chains of red sawtooth mountains which run northeast to southwest across the entire country and divide the plains from the desert. It is at this natural frontier that Algeria proper ends. For administrative reasons the French originally decided that Algeria was to include the desert itself, straight down to French West Africa, but recently a border was created and a new political entity called simply "Le Sa-

In the shade of orange trees, Moslem women patiently wait their turn in the courtyard of a small-claims court in Tangier.

THE BLACKS

*Dominated by harsh ancestral spirits and
ordered by the insistent throb of drums,
the tribal man of Africa has not been changed
by the remote touch of Westernism.
But this is the man, says Peter Abrahams, who will
have the crucial voice in determining the future of Africa.*

It was a hot, humid, oppressive August day in Accra, capital of the Gold Coast that was to become Ghana. The air had the stillness of death. I walked down toward the sea front. Perhaps there would be the hint of a breeze there. As I neared the sea front I was assailed by a potent stench of the sea with strong overtones of rotting fish.

The houses were drab, run-down wooden structures or made of corrugated iron, put together any way you please. The streets were wide and tarred, and each street had an open-drainage system into which young boys and old men piddled when they needed to relieve themselves. I have seen women empty chamber pots into these drains in the early morning. The fierce sun takes care of the germs, but God help you if smells made you sick.

In about eight minutes of walking, some fifteen "taxis" pulled up beside me: "Hi, massa! Taxi, massa! Me go anywhere you go cheap!" They are all private taxis with no meters and driven by strapping young men with flashing teeth. The place is full of taxi drivers willing to go anywhere and do anything cheap.

The street traders here are women. "Mammy traders," they are called. They trade in everything. They sell cigarettes, one at a time; round loaves of bread and hunks of cooked meat on which the big West African flies make sport. They love bargaining and haggling. They are a powerful economic factor in the life of the country. The more prosperous ones own their own trucks, some own fleets of trucks. These "mammy trucks" are the principal carriers of the country. They carry passengers as well as produce and go hurtling across the countryside with little regard for life or limb. Each truck has its own distinctive slogan, such as: REPENT FOR DEATH IS ROUND THE CORNER, or ENTER WITHOUT HOPE, or THE LAST RIDE or IF IT MUST IT WILL. My own favorite, and I traveled in this particular truck, pleaded, NOT TODAY O LORD NOT TODAY.

I passed many mammy traders, many mammy trucks, before I reached the sea front. I crossed a street, jumped over an open drain, and there was the sea. But there was no breeze, and no shade from the terrible sun. In the end I gave in to the idea of "taxi, massa, taxi" and looked about for one. But now there was no taxi in sight. Instead, I saw, suddenly, a long procession of many women and a few men. The procession swung around a corner and came into full view, twenty or thirty yards long. The women wore white flowing robes and white kerchiefs on their heads. Their faces were painted into grotesque masks made with thick streaks of black, red, white and yellow paints. The heavy thud of bare feet rose above the hum of the sea.

Then, all at once, the drums burst forth and there was no other sound about me. The marching women began to jig, then dance. As the tail of the procession passed me the drums reach a frenzy. A thin, pure note from a reed rose above the drums. The whole procession became a shivering, shaking mass. The reed note held longer than seemed human. And then, dramatically, there was silence.

I thought of Richard Wright, with whom I had had breakfast that morning. This was his first visit to any part of Africa and he seemed to find it bewildering. Countee Cullen, the late American Negro poet, had speculated:

*One three centuries removed
From the scenes his fathers loved,
Spicy grove, cinnamon tree
What is Africa to me?**

Wright was finding the answers and finding them disconcerting. He had been astounded by the casual attitude to sex. There was, he had said, too much sex, too casually given and taken; so that it worked out as no sex, with none of the emotional involvement associated with sex in the Western mind. He shook his head with a slight disgust. The open drains into which young boys and old men piddled had led him to conclude that Africans piddled rather more than other people. The sight of young men dancing together, holding hands, disturbed the puritan in him. He expressed to me that morning what he later summed up in his book on the Gold Coast: "I was black and they were black but it did not help me."

What Wright did not understand, what his whole background and training had made difficult for him to understand, was that being black did not of itself qualify one for acceptance in tribal Africa. But how could he, when there are thousands of urban-bred Africans up and down the vast continent who do not themselves understand this? The more perceptive of the urban Africans are only now beginning to comprehend, but slowly.

Being black is a small matter in tribal Africa because the attitude toward color is healthy and normal. Color does not matter. Color is an act of God that neither confers privileges nor imposes handicaps on a man. A man's skin is like the day: the day is either clear or dark. There is nothing more to it until external agencies come in and invest it with special meaning and importance.

What does matter to the tribal African, what is important, is the complex pattern of his position within his own group and his relations with the other members of the group. He is no Pan-African dreaming of a greater African glory when the white man is driven into the sea. The acute race consciousness of the American Negro, or of the black South African at the receiving end of *apartheid*, is alien to him. The important things in his life are anything but race and color—until they are forced on him. And "mother Africa" is much too vast to inspire big continental dreams in him. She is a land of huge

*In a time of transition, tribal customs are still
remembered. Women of the Venda tribe (Transvaal)
in silver girdles and bracelets perform a Python Dance.*

*From *Heritage*, copyright 1925 by Harper and Bros., reprinted by permission.

mountains, dark jungles and vast deserts. In her rivers and in her jungles and in her grasslands lurk creatures that are the enemies of man: the leopard and the lion, the snake and crocodile. All this makes travel, by the old African methods, extremely difficult and makes for isolation between one group of people and another. The African who is in Britain is likely to be a deal better informed on what is happening all over the continent than would be his fellow African in any of the main centers of both tribal and nontribal Africa. In terms of communications the man in the tribe lives in the Dark Ages.

Richard Wright was surprised that even educated Africans, racially conscious literate people, had not heard of him and were skeptical of a grown man earning his living by writing. They could not understand what kind of writing brought a man enough money to support a family. Wright really wanted to understand the African, but—"I found the African an oblique, a hard-to-know man."

My sympathies were all with Wright.

The heat and salty rancid fish smell had made me desperately thirsty. Across the way a mammy trader squatted beside her pile of merchandise: cooked meat, sweet potatoes—a whole host of edibles—and some bottles of opaque white liquid that could be either coconut milk or palm juice, as well as the inevitable little pile of cigarettes priced at a penny apiece. I had been warned of the risks involved in eating anything sold by the street traders. But to hell with it, I was thirsty and not exactly a stranger to African germs. I crossed the street, felt the bottles and chose the one that seemed coolest and looked the least opaque.

"How much?"

"One shilling." The carved ebony face looked at me with dead eyes.

I pulled the screwed-up newspaper stopper from the bottle, wiped its mouth and took a swig. I could not decide whether it was coconut milk or palm juice. It had been heavily watered down and sweetened. But it was wet and thirst-quenching. I drank half the bottle, firmly ignoring the little foreign bodies that floated in the liquid. Then I paid her and drank the rest. I put down the empty and began to move away.

"You African?" She asked in her harsh, cold, masculine voice.

I stopped, turned and looked at her face. It was as deadly cold and impersonal as before: not a flicker of feeling in her eyes. Like an African mask, I thought. But unlike Wright, I did not try to penetrate it. I knew the futility of trying. She would show feeling if and when she decided. Not before.

"Yes," I said, and added, "from the south. Far, far south." She paused for so long that I began to move again.

"You like here?" Nationalism had obviously touched her. I turned back to her. "No," I said.

"Why you don't like?"

"I don't say I don't like."

"But you don't like?"

I showed her my teeth, African-wise, which is neither smile nor grimace but a blending of the two. "*You* like Africa?" I asked.

Now it was her turn to show me her teeth. There was a flicker of feeling in her eyes, then they went dead again. She nodded. I had established my claim. Only outsiders—white people or the Richard Wrights—liked or disliked Africa.

I left the mammy trader and carried on up the smelly and hot street. Much and little had passed between us. Out to sea some fishing boats appeared on the sky line. About me were the citizens of Accra. Some wore the cloth of the country—the men looking like pint-sized citizens of ancient Rome painted black and the women looking extraordinarily masculine—and others wore Western dress.

My thoughts shifted to my forthcoming meeting with

Savage wrestling is the favorite sport of the Korongo Nuba village of Buran, in central Sudan. The men, all over six feet, crouch, glare, spar and circle warily before beginning their fierce grappling. As several pairs battle in the dust, the crowd shrieks and a club-bearing referee watches the action.

Kwame Nkrumah, Ghana's first Prime Minister. It was well over seven years since I had last seen him, in London. Then he was a poor struggling student; now he was the head of a state and the spokesman for the great Pan-African dream of freedom and independence.

This was the man who later made common cause with the people of French Guinea, when they voted for independence in 1958 and against membership in de Gaulle's Fifth Republic —a move by Nkrumah that can have great significance for the British Commonwealth. Prime Minister Macmillan has indicated that Whitehall is watching Nkrumah's "closer association" moves with Guinea with keen interest. Prediction would be idle, yet it is intriguing to speculate that an ex-colony of Britain might bring an ex-colony of France into the Commonwealth. This could be a dramatic underscoring of the changing nature of colonialism in Africa. And at the center of it is Kwame Nkrumah.

I remembered our past friendship and wondered what changes I would find in him. Anyway, it was now nine A.M. and my date with him was 9:30. I would soon know.

A few minutes later I flagged a taxi and simply said, "Kwame's office."

As we talked in Nkrumah's cool office that hot August day in Accra, my mind kept slipping back to our mutual friend Jomo or Johnstone Kenyatta, now imprisoned in his native Kenya for leading the Mau Mau movement. Significantly, though we mentioned many friends, both Nkrumah and I avoided mentioning Kenyatta. I had decided not to mention him first. I had hoped Nkrumah would. He did not.

A year earlier, I had flown up to Kenya from South Africa and visited Kenyatta. I felt terribly depressed as I got off the plane. Things had grown so much uglier in the Union. The barricades were up in the ugly war of color. When I had left South Africa in the dim-and-distant past, there were isolated islands where black and white could meet in neutral territory. When I went back in 1952, the islands were submerged under the rising tide of color hatreds, and I was glad to quit that dark, unhappy land which yet compelled my love.

It was in this mood that I got off the plane. I had not seen my friend Jomo for years. Now there he was, just outside the airport terminal building, leaning on a heavy cane, bigger than I remembered him in Europe, paunchy, his face looking puffy. And behind him was a huge crowd of Africans.

I began to move toward him when a lean-faced, lean-hipped white colonial-administrator type suddenly appeared beside me and said: "Mr. Abrahams."

I stopped and thought, "Oh, Lord."

Kenyatta also came forward. The two men ignored each other. Lean-face introduced himself and said the Colonial Office had alerted them that I was coming to do some writing for the London *Observer* and they had drawn up a provisional schedule for me. Had I done anything about accommodation?

Before I could answer, Kenyatta said, "You are staying with me, of course." The old detachment was back in his eyes. They seemed to say, "You've got to choose, pal."

Lean-face said, "We've got something set up for you for tomorrow and——"

"I live in the bush," Kenyatta added.

It dawned on me that I had become, for the moment, the battlefield of that horrible animal, the racial struggle. I made up my mind, resenting both sides and yet conscious of the crowd of Africans in the background. A question of face was involved.

"I've promised to spend this week end with Mr. Kenyatta."

Lean-face was graceful about it. I promised to call at the Secretariat first thing on Monday morning. He gave me a copy of the schedule that had been prepared for me and wondered, *sotto voce*, whether I knew what I was letting myself in for.

Arms raised in triumph, the victor is carried through the village. Other wrestlers resting in the shade look like some fantastic ballet troupe, their faces covered with ashes and their hair shaved to tiny tufts.

Kenyatta assured me that I would be perfectly safe, that nobody was going to cut my throat. I was aware that they were talking to each other through me. I was aware that they knew I was aware, and that made me bad-tempered.

"Then I'll say good night, Mr. Abrahams," Lean-face said pointedly.

As soon as he was out of hearing Kenyatta began to curse.

"It's good to see you again, Johnstone." I gripped his hand.

"Jomo," he replied. The hint of ironic speculation was back in his eyes. A slightly sardonic, slightly bitter smile played on his lips.

"Welcome to Kenya, Peter," he said. Then, abruptly: "Come meet the leaders of my people. They've been waiting long."

We moved forward and the crowd gathered about us. Jomo made a little speech in Kikuyu, then translated it for my benefit. A little old man, ancient as the hills, with huge holes in his ears, then welcomed me on behalf of the land and its people. Again Jomo translated.

After this we all bundled into the fleet of rattling old cars and set off for the Kikuyu reserve in the heart of the African bush. Kenyatta became silent and remote during the journey.

We stopped at the old chief's compound, where other members of the tribe waited to welcome me. By this time the reception committee had grown to a few hundred. About me, pervading the air, was the smell of burning flesh; a young cow was being roasted in my honor. Before I entered the house a drink was handed to me. Another was handed to the old chief and a third to Kenyatta. The old man muttered a brief incantation and spilled half his drink on the earth as a libation. Jomo and I followed suit. Then the three of us downed our drinks and entered the house.

A general feasting and drinking then commenced, both inside and outside the house. I was getting a full ceremonial tribal welcome. The important dignitaries of the tribe slipped into the room in twos and threes, spoke to me through Kenyatta for a few moments, and then went away.

"Africa doesn't seem to change," Kenyatta murmured between dignitaries. There was a terrible undercurrent of bitterness behind the softly murmured words. I was startled by it and looked at his face. For a fleeting moment he looked like a trapped, caged animal.

He saw me looking at him and quickly composed his face into a slightly sardonic, humorous mask. "Don't look too closely," he said.

And still the dignitaries filed in, had a drink, spoke their welcome and went out.

The ceremonial welcome reached its high point about midnight. Huge chunks of the roasted cow were brought in to us, and we gnawed at the almost raw meat between swigs of liquor. Outside, there was muted drumming. Voices were growing louder and louder.

Suddenly, in the midst of a long-winded speech by an immensely dignified Masai chief from a neighboring and friendly tribe, Kenyatta jumped up, grabbed his heavy cane and half staggered to the door.

"Come, Peter," he called.

Everybody was startled. I hesitated. He raised his cane and beckoned to me with it. I knew that this would be a dreadful breach of tribal etiquette.

"Come, man!" he snapped.

I got up, aware of the sudden silence that had descended on the huge gathering. By some strange magic everybody seemed to know that something had gone wrong.

"Jomo," I said.

"I can't stand any more," he snapped. "Come!"

I followed him to the door. I knew the discourtesy we were inflicting on the tribe. I also knew that my friend was at the breaking point. We walked through the crowd of people, got into Kenyatta's car and drove off into the night. The African moon was big and yellow, bathing the land in a soft light that almost achieved the clarity of daylight.

He took me to his home. It was a big, sprawling, empty place on the brow of a hill. Inside, it had nothing to make for comfort. There were hard wooden chairs, a few tables and only the bed in the bedroom. There were no books, none of the normal amenities of Western civilization. When we arrived two women emerged from somewhere in the back and hovered about in the shadows. They brought in liquor, but I never got a clear glimpse of either of them. My friend's anguish of spirit was such that I did not want to ask questions. We sat on the veranda and drank steadily and in silence until we were both miserably, depressingly drunk.

And then Kenyatta began to speak in a low, bitter voice of his frustration and of the isolated position in which he found himself. He had no friends. There was no one in the tribe who could give the intellectual companionship that had become so important to him in his years in Europe. The things that were important to him—consequential conversation, the drink that represented a social activity rather than the intention to get drunk, the concept of individualism, the inviolability of privacy—all these were alien to the tribesmen in whose midst he lived. So Kenyatta, the Western man, was driven in on himself and was forced to assert himself in tribal terms. Only thus would the tribesmen follow him and so give him his position of power and importance as a leader.

To live without roots is to live in hell, and no man chooses voluntarily to live in hell. The people who could answer his needs as a Western man had erected a barrier of color against him in spite of the fact that the taproots of their culture had become the taproots of his culture too. By denying him access to those things which complete the life of Western man, they had forced him back into the tribalism from which he had so painfully freed himself over the years.

None of this was stated explicitly by either Kenyatta or myself. But it was there in his brooding bitter commentary on both the tribes and the white settlers of the land. For me, Kenyatta became that night a man who in his own life personified the terrible tragedy of Africa and the terrible secret war that rages in it. He was the victim both of tribalism and of Westernism gone sick. His heart and mind and body were the battlefield of the ugly violence known as the Mau Mau revolt long before it broke out in that beautiful land. The tragedy is that he was so rarely gifted, that he could have made such a magnificent contribution in other circumstances.

What then is tribal man? Perhaps his most important single characteristic is that he is not an individual in the Western sense. Psychologically and emotionally he is the present living personification of a number of forces, among the most important of which are the ancestral dead. The dead have a powerful hold on the living. They control and regulate the lives and activities of the living from the grave. They hand out the rules and codes by which the living conduct their daily affairs. If there is a drought, if there is a famine, it is a sign that the ancestors are angry because someone has broken a rule of the tribe, a law laid down by the dead. There will be no peace, no order, no prosperity until the ancestors are appeased.

So the chief calls the whole tribe to a meeting in which the guilty ones will be "smelled out." The procedure begins with the drums—a key factor in African life. Their insistent throbs call the people to the gathering on a placid, almost momentous key at first, but working on the emotions.

Everyone in the village will be present; neither man, woman nor child would think of not obeying the summons. They form a circle, with the witch doctors or medicine man and the drummers to the fore. When all the people are assembled the throbbing of the drums increases. They beat in tune to the heartbeats of the circle.

The witch doctor is dressed in lion or leopard skin, sometimes in monkey skin. His face is painted in bold streaks of color: white, black, red. There are crisscrossing lines on his body too. He wanders about the center of the circle, almost idly at first. Every now and then he pauses and looks straight into someone's eyes and keeps on looking. For the person looked at, this is an encounter with fate. Few stare back. Their eyes slide past his face or go glazed. They fear but are not supposed to fear. They know the ancestors are just, that the innocent are never punished. To experience fear, therefore, is an acknowledgment of guilt. It is not necessary to know the nature of your guilt to be guilty. If you were not, there would be no fear in your mind.

The tempo of the drums increases. The witch doctor begins to dance, slowly at first. He begins to talk in a high-pitched nasal voice; spirits always talk through their noses. The drums and the incantations go on and on, getting faster and wilder, dominating the hearts and minds of all the circle. People begin to tremble and shiver. Some crop down in a trance and lie moaning on the ground. Everyone is possessed by the frenzy of the drums. The spirits of the ancestors are abroad.

Suddenly the drums stop. The witch doctor stands fixed for a dreadful moment that seems without end. Then he pounces. He grabs his victim and drags him or her into the center of the circle. The victim does not resist, does not protest. The ancestors are always just.

There may be one, there may be many victims. But once the victim or the victims are "smelled out," the hypnotic spell of the drums is broken. People relax. Their hearts beat normally once more. Now the ancestors will be propitiated and the living freed of the evil which beset them. Now the famine or the drought or the plague or whatever had beset the land will depart from it. And so, while the victim or victims are put to death, the rest of the tribe celebrates the passing of the evil.

A Nuba girl of Kordofan in Sudan wears the traditional cosmetics and jewelry of her tribe.

It may be that in this particular village—almost anywhere in tribal Africa—the spirits of the ancestors rest in a sacred tree. In that case the victim is taken to the tree and executed there so that the ancestors can taste his blood. Or his heart may be cut out and put at the foot of the tree. Or it may be that the spirits of the ancestors have entered the body of a snake, a very popular sacred symbol in certain areas of West Africa. In that case the living victim is taken to the snake and left there, bound, to be executed by the ancestors acting through the snake. Or it may be that the village is on the edge of a lake, especially one of the lakes of Central Africa, where the spirits of the ancestors enter the body of a crocodile. In that case the victim is fed to the crocodiles. Wherever the spirits of the ancestors may be—and they are always in some living animal or plant—it is there that the victim is taken to propitiate them and so deliver the rest of the tribe from the calamity.

The world of tribal man is so dominated by the spirits that some tribes will not eat birds because of the spirits that dwell in them; some will not eat fish; some are vegetarians; some eat meat only.

Tribal man is hemmed in, imprisoned by his ancestors. His horizons are only as wide as they permit. He is also protected by them. The rules are such that there are no orphans in the tribe, no misfits, no neurotics. And of course, the ancestral dead are hostile to change.

This, then, is the "oblique, the hard-to-know man" whom Richard Wright encountered on his first visit to Africa. He is the man who raised Nkrumah to power. He is the man whose pressures led Jomo Kenyatta to the Mau Mau and then to his lonely prison-exile in a barren and isolated spot and, probably, to banishment from Kenya in the end. He, tribal man, will have a crucial say in the future of Africa.

The ancestral dead notwithstanding, change is being imposed on him. How he reacts to the change will have a powerful bearing on tomorrow's Africa.

If the men inaugurating the new ways have the sense and the patience to preserve the finer qualities of the old ways and fuse these with the new, then we can expect something magnificently new out of Africa.

The Blacks/Peter Abrahams **167**

SOUTH AFRICA

Speaking of the country of his birth, Alan Paton says that despite racial and cultural antagonisms "there is one South Africa common to us all... the physical land." A great raised plateau that falls off sharply to the sea, it is a land that is at once exciting and depressing, attractive and repelling, majestic and fierce.

I was born in the town of Pietermaritzburg, the capital of Natal, in the year 1903. Natal was then a colony of the British Empire, and on the King's birthday red-coated soldiers would march down the street where we lived, filling the air with music. And with excitement, too, for the white people would pour out of the houses, and the black servants would pour out, too, and the Indian children would come up from the back streets to share the excitement.

It was a pioneer town. Between our street and the surrounding majestic hills there was nothing but the wide-open veld. We lived in both town and country. In the school holidays we slid on sheet-iron toboggans down the steep grassy hills, or swam in the Dorp Spruit (the Town Stream), and smoked cigarettes made of fallen leaves.

The town of Pietermaritzburg was named after two Afrikaner heroes, Piet Retief and Gerrit Maritz. In 1836 those Afrikaners of the Cape of Good Hope who could no longer abide the British Government trekked away into the unknown interior. Some of them founded the republics of the Orange Free State and the Transvaal, but others turned east till they reached the edge of the great escarpment of the Drakensberg, and looked down on a country the like of which they had never seen before. They were used to the Great Karroo, with its flat *koppies* and the thorn trees seeking sustenance in the rocks and stones, to dry river beds, and to a light that poured down harshly and ceaselessly on the endless plain. But here was a paradisiacal country, a prodigal endowment of hills and valleys and rivers and streams, a rich lush grass abounding in flowers and game, a warm air full of colored birds, a promise of reward and foretaste of happiness to come.

The Trekkers' wagons came down over the rampart of the Drakensberg, a feat pictured today on the walls of many an Afrikaner home. And Dingaan, king of the Zulus, watched them come. Piet Retief and sixty of his followers came to the king seeking a grant of land, and Dingaan slew them all. And the king then sent an army to the Trekkers' camp and slew their women and children also, at a place now called Weenen, which means weeping.

The Trekkers finally broke the power of Dingaan at Blood River and founded the town of Pietermaritzburg. Yet, because the British drove the Trekkers out of Natal, I never heard the Afrikaans language spoken when I was a child, and I can remember my astonishment on discovering that the names of the streets of my town were Afrikaans names. What an innocent preparation for life in South Africa today, where the Afrikaner, having tasted British rule and having not liked it, is now giving the British a chance to taste his rule and not like it either; where the Afrikaner remembers Blood River and the Zulu remembers it too.

But this fierce country is exciting too. Would I live somewhere else? Sometimes I would, but not now. For she evokes something deep and powerful, that satisfies even when it is painful, something exciting and depressing, attracting and repelling; she is the mistress that one hates and loves, a worshiped and a wanton thing. She is finally and inescapably the land where I was born; when I write about her, I draw on the memories of childhood, the boy silent, hardly moving, listening breathless to the sounds of the world into which he is so wondrously born, innocent, knowing nothing, yet understanding everything. And the land where he was born can break his heart but not his love.

South Africa appears differently to each of her lovers. The Afrikaner loves her as the land that is his own, fiercely and possessively; the Englishman loves her as part of the British Commonwealth; the black African as part of a continent in which he has the power of numbers if no other; the Cape Colored people endure her caprices with an outward show of gaiety. But the Indian people, if they by miracle can love her at all, do so with fear, and the pain of having been wanted, used and thrown away.

Yet all move together through the streets of Cape Town, Johannesburg and Durban, making them as colorful as any cities can be. We go about our own separate affairs, not pushing one another about, but showing impersonal courtesies. Yet we are separate enough: we live separately, see films separately, swim in the sea separately, send telegrams separately, worship God separately, and separately are committed to the fire or the ground. At times this separation lies lightly upon us, but at other times—suddenly and frighteningly—it seems a monstrous offense against God and men, and against the beautiful country we call our home.

Yet there is one South Africa that is common to us all: the physical land in which we live, the great interior plain, elevated and treeless, reaching to the edges of the escarpments, below whose walls are the countless streams and valleys of the coastal lands. That is what South Africa is, a great raised plateau that falls sharply to the sea, more sharply on the east than on the west, the whole country being set between the Atlantic and the Indian oceans. It enjoys a climate as wonderful as any in the world. The heat of summer in the interior is tempered by the altitude, and at the coasts by winds. The cold of winter in the interior is tempered by the sun that pours down month after month out of cloudless skies, and on the eastern coasts winter comes hardly at all.

Our forests—and there are only a few—run like fingers into the southeastward-facing *kloofs* that catch the wet ocean winds. South African scenery is wide and sweeping, set under

A woman of the Ndebele tribe, near Pretoria.

a wide and sweeping sky. Its beauty is vast, a matter of light and color and distance, not of field and stream and tree.

Cape Town is our Mother City. She lies under the wall of Table Mountain, that stands 3600 feet out of Table Bay. At the narrow base of the mountain is built the city. To live in this part of South Africa, called the Cape Peninsula, is to live always in the shadow of some mountain. The drive from the city to the tip of the Peninsula is one of the most spectacular in Africa; at Cape Point you leave the bus or automobile and walk to the lighthouse, looking out toward the South Pole, with the Atlantic on your right and the Indian Ocean on your left. These ships that you see are following Vasco da Gama's line of voyage up the east coast of Africa.

The architecture of Cape Town is stately and striking: the Dutch gables, the whitewashed walls, the spacious and lofty interiors, the massive furniture, the long stoeps, the oaks that surround the noble dwellings of Stellenberg, Alphen, Vergelegen, La Gratitude and Rhone, and the vineyards that run to the very feet of the mountains. Many of these houses may be visited by permission; one of the oldest of them, Groot Constantia, is a national monument. Here may be seen the original slave quarters, part of the house itself.

In the streets of Cape Town you will hear many languages: English, Afrikaans, Zulu, Xosa, and the tongues of sailors and travelers from many lands; for this is the Tavern of the Seas. All public notices are in English and Afrikaans, the two offical languages of the Union, but there is one in particular that will engage the attention of the visitor—"Europeans Only—Slegs Blankes" and "Non-Europeans Only—Slegs Nieblankes." These notices will be found at entrances to public offices, at public counters, on public seats.

Among the sights of Cape Town are the stands of the Cape Colored flower sellers. In September and October the color and variety of these flowers are wide-ranging; for this is the southern spring, and the mountains and valleys of the Cape of Good Hope, for hundreds of miles along the eastern coasts to Fort Elizabeth, are covered with a diversity of wildflowers unequaled in the world. These are disas, gladiolas, ixias and numerous heaths of unsurpassed beauty on the mountainsides; the vleis are white with arums. Most striking of all are the porteas of all kinds and sizes, appearing outwardly as a cup of green leaves changing to the most delicate of colors within, the whole enclosing a pin-cushion type of bloom. This is one of the national emblems of our country, and must be classed with the delicate antelope called the springbok.

To the north of Cape Town is the semidesert region of Namaqualand, and at this same spring season the whole country bursts into flame: the dimorphotheca, the ursinia, the aus daisy, the arctotis (poetically called the desert ephemeral), and mesembryanthemums of every size, habit and hue. Those plants seem to be always trembling on the brink of delivery;

the flower is locked in the womb, awaiting some word from the sky and earth that it is time to come forth. Clouds bank up into the months-long-empty heavens, the lightning flashes, the thunder rolls, the rain falls, the buds burst, and the traveler drives hour after hour through a rioting desert of orange and yellow miracle.

Yet the whole area around Cape Town is the holidaymaker's paradise. If we travel across the Cape Flats, the twenty miles of sandy land that separates the peninsula from the continent, we move into an entrancing country, the land of Stellenbosch and Paarl and the Drakenstein Valley, of the old Dutch houses and oaks and vines, and with streams rushing down the village streets. For every place here is under a mountain, and every mountain is full of streams, and every stream might as well run through the village streets as any other place. Small wonder that South Africans speak wistfully of the Cape. There is everything: mountains and rivers, flowers and trees, white-gabled houses and museums and galleries; cinemas and theaters and shops, and an absence of that fierceness that characterizes the rest of South Africa.

If we head northeast through the mountains and valleys of the Cape, we are soon in this fiercer world, and its first name is the Karroo—the plain that the Trekkers reached as they got further and further away from the shadow of Table Mountain and the easy, fat life. I can imagine them climbing onto the interior plateau with a sense of liberation. They were finished with white-walled houses and vineyards and the interfering officials of the Dutch East India Company. Here was a wide-open world where you didn't need to live near your neighbor, though, by God, if anyone threatened him, he threatened you too; where the supreme law was, as it is now, *stand together, all white people, if you would survive*. That is really what *apartheid* means.

The Karroo is a region of rock and stone and thorn, but the stunted vegetation of its arid hills nourishes some of the best sheep in the world. The only green patches are along the watercourses, and they are beautiful with tall Lombardy poplars, peach and apricot trees and fields of lucerne. But no one who understands the Karroo, or indeed any desert, looks for local and immediate beauty; it must be found in the sweep of earth and sky, in peace and soundlessness, in the alternation of dawn and sunset, and in a night that is black, with a million stars. If a day or two of harsh traveling is too much to pay for this, then we can do our steady seventy miles an hour along the thousand-mile highway to Johannesburg. Or we could take one of these trains that every now and then appear so astonishingly out of the veld. Or we could go back to Cape Town and take a plane. But our understanding of this complex country would be so much the less.

Bloemfontein lies on the great interior plain, now less rocky and stony, and more flat and featureless. This city of over 100,000 people is the capital of the Orange Free State, one of the first Afrikaner republics founded by the Trekkers. Some Trekkers stayed here, while others continued north to found the Transvaal Republic, and others trekked east until they reached the Drakensberg Mountains and the drop into Natal.

The scenery of the Orange Free State, except where it borders on Natal and Basutoland, is a subject of jest for other South Africans. The winter is as severe as that experienced in any part of the Union, because of the 5000-foot elevation of this naked plain. Yet it is mild compared with the winters of North America. The thermometer may fall to 15° on a winter night, but if the day dawns windless and cloudless the temperature rises into the sixties, and people, wrapped up a little more than usual, love to sit in the sun. Snow, except on the mountains, is a rare visitor; I lived in the neighboring Transvaal for thirteen years at an altitude of 5700 feet, and snow fell three times in that period. A snowfall in Johannesburg is enough to bring commercial activities almost to a stop, and the traffic of the city becomes lost, not in confusion but in wonder.

At Bloemfontein stands Anton van Wouw's austere reminder of that past which is the key to all our present—the Vrouemonument, the moving memorial in somber stone to the twenty thousand Afrikaner women and children who perished in the concentration camps in which the British had placed them so that their farms and farmhouses could be destroyed in the Anglo-Boer war. I myself visit this Vrouemonument with reverence, and with humble acknowledgment of past sins, not only because they are the sins of my forefathers but because I am involved in all mankind.

Before we leave the Orange Free State we will notice one thing more. Every thirty miles or so we come to a small town dominated by the spires of its Afrikaner churches; many of these churches are new, and have evolved a style of architecture that is striking and indigenous. On the whole these churches frown on dancing, drinking and all the less sedate pleasures. They are bringing greater pressure to bear on local authorities, who under English influences have allowed public places to be used for Sunday sports; the authorities are thus caught between two forces: what the public says it wants and what the public really wants. A swim suit of Victorian lines was once designed for Free State ladies on British Natal's beaches; the courage required in Bloemfontein to reject it was equaled only by the courage required in Durban to wear it.

When you approach the Vaal River, to cross, naturally, into the Transvaal, something is quite clearly going to happen. On the left, unseen, is Welkom, the new gold town; on the right, unseen, is Sasol, the new oil-from-coal town; and, on the left, partly seen, is Vanderbÿl, the new steel town. Ahead of us lies Vereeniging, with its great condensers, mines and factories, growing at a great pace. The traffic doubles, trebles, increases ten times, twenty times. This can only mean that we are nearing Johannesburg, City of Gold and Uranium, seat of the University of the Witwatersrand, home of extreme wealth and extreme poverty, See of Bishops and University of Crime, City of Pleasure and the place where women—white women and black women—don't walk alone in the streets at night, if they walk at all. This is the city that imperial money and brains made with republican gold, and the black man sold his labor at a price that made it all possible.

The black people streamed into Johannesburg, not only into the white mines but into the white kitchens and the white gardens and the white factories. They choked up the "locations," those outlying parts of the city set aside for them. They spilled over into the shanty-towns, preserving in all this squalor an incredible lustiness of life. Wives lost husbands, and husbands lost wives; parents lost children and children parents; neglected youths became dangerous ones, and sent white people to gunsmiths and locksmiths and psychiatrists. Rock was hauled out of the earth and, when the gold had been torn out of it, lay in great white dumps all over the city and veld. Buildings went up and, with each cycle of development, got pulled down to make way for taller ones.

Everyone hurried through the streets, at a pace faster than in any other part of Africa. Today Johannesburg has nearly a million inhabitants, and another million live in the satellite towns that stretch east and west along the surface of the fabulous Reef of Gold. Nearly half of the world's gold comes from here, and, made up into bars, goes back into the earth in far-off America. And now there is uranium as well. Johannesburg is often compared with American cities, and rightly; but it has so much of its own that it is like no other city.

It is Johannesburg that houses its thousands of black mine-workers in monastic compounds to preserve the tribal system, that sent the tribal system reeling. It is Johannesburg, with its rigid racial separation, which has loosed the new ideas that will bring racial separation to an end. It is Johannesburg which gives such stability to our economy, that will see revolution first, if any revolution comes.

The Cape Peninsula, the Kruger National Park and the Natal Coast from Durban to Port Edward are the three premier vacation areas of white South Africa. From Durban to Port Edward stretch holiday resorts, rejoicing in names like Isipingo, Amanzimtoti, Illovo, Umgababa, Umkomaas, Sezela, Umtwalumi, Umtentweni. As children we spent many a holiday here, burning ourselves black on the beaches.

We always traveled by night train from Pietermaritzburg, and my brother and I would spend the whole time on the open platforms between the coaches, watching the dark countryside go by. There was the excitement of reaching Durban, which in those days was a town of sixty thousand people, but a metropolis to us. Then the train would turn south, and soon would be running a few yards from the shore itself, crossing lagoon after lagoon, and giving us frequent glimpses of the early morning bathers.

In those days the resorts were small, and most of the holidaymakers would be, like ourselves, people from inland Natal. But the motor car has changed all that. Now during the school vacations at Christmas and in July, and the two shorter periods between, thousands of cars leave Johannesburg and Pretoria, and pour down to the sea.

Life at a South Coast resort is an idyll of simplicity; the supreme attraction is the sea itself. The beaches are as Nature made them of firm yellow sand, often rocky. The coastal bush comes down to the beach itself, and palms and wild bananas give a tropical air to the scene. A short distance from the shore, the trees become taller: the idomba, the umkuhla, and the giant fig, that grows often as a parasite, sprouting from a bird-dropped seed in a forked branch, growing up and down in pythonlike coils until its host is swallowed up. Often in June and July we cannot resist a cry of astonishment when

amid all this greenery we encounter the Kaffir boom, a true flame of the forest.

When I was a boy most of the cottages along the coast were built of wood and corrugated iron, with monastic furnishings, but today modern villas have taken their places. Everywhere is the hibiscus hedge, with its dense foliage and handsome red-starred flowers. Hibiscus is prodigious as well as beautiful. You plant it by pushing sticks of it into the sand; and if you neglect your hedge too long it is a major operation to bring it back under control.

The climate, too, makes this a holiday paradise. Midsummer can be warm and robust, midwinter is warm, sometimes cool, almost never cold. Only the old and infirm find the seashore too sharp for them in mid-July. The hottest time of the summer day is about ten in the morning, when the land breeze has died down and the sea breeze has not yet begun. It is surely one of the world's most favored places to live in. But not actively; the sea is too blue, the breeze too balmy, nature too generous. We lived there five years and ran away.

Here in June, occasionally July, happens one of Nature's strangest events. Up from the cold southern seas come the sardines, herringlike fish perhaps a foot in length, in stupendous shoals. They strike the coast of South Africa at Port St. John's, and continue northeast almost to Durban, where they again swing out into the ocean. They are accompanied by screaming flocks of sea birds, maddened game fish, barracuda, sharks, jumping, snapping, tearing, gorging; doctors leave patients on the operating tables, judges jump from the bench, teachers leave classes if the classes have not already left them. The beaches are a pandemonium; fishermen hook fish, birds and men with fine impartiality. The color bar is forgotten. As if this were not enough, sometimes the sardines erupt in tens of thousands onto the sand, where people fill baskets, boxes, hats, skirts and dresses.

The English-speaking people of Natal are full of concern about their future, and about the future of the Union which they joined in 1910. The two outstanding Afrikaner leaders of that time were the Boer War generals, Louis Botha and Jan Smuts, both of whom were trusted and loved by the English-speaking people. Botha and Smuts were apostles of conciliation, and had been deeply influenced by the decision of the British Government in 1906 to restore self-government within the British Commonwealth to the two defeated republics of the Transvaal and the Orange Free State.

Since that time, however, Afrikaner nationalism has grown in strength, until now it is able to rule the country. It is committed to the establishment of a republic, and whether we shall remain within or without the Commonwealth no one can foresee. It is also committed to the policy of *apartheid*, the policy of racial separation, which however justly men may attempt to apply it, is offensive to the emergent nations of Asia and Africa. The future is dangerous and obscure.

Yet how lovely is the land, how generous her space and sun, how fascinating her different peoples, how rich her endowment. If flowers could bring peace, and mountains justice, how beautiful South Africa would be. For she is a mistress most fair of face, and most unquiet in her heart.

ASIA
and the
PACIFIC

Santha Rama Rau

Han Suyin

Eugene Burdick

At rest outside the frescoed walls of the maharaja's palace at Udaipur, a girl looks out at the fast-changing Indian world with ancient eyes.

India

In a country that is unknown rather than inscrutable, the Westerner constantly meets the unexpected. Santha Rama Rau, here serving as a guide to her native country, demonstrates that it is next to impossible for a perceptive person to be unmoved by India where endless diversity creates an extraordinary richness of life.

Not long ago an Indian woman dressed in a sari was traveling in a train in England. Sitting across from her was the only other occupant of the compartment, an Englishwoman. As the train pulled away from London toward the countryside, the Englishwoman, who had been studying the appearance of her companion with considerable interest, was unable to contain her curiosity any longer. She swept her hand across the window, indicating the lovely scenery of the Thames valley. "Don't you find the Thames beautiful?" she asked.

"Yes, I do. Very beautiful."

"Do you have rivers as big as this in India?—if you don't mind my asking."

"We have rivers bigger than the Thames. In fact, in my home, Allahabad, where the Jumma and the great Ganges meet, the river becomes so wide you cannot see across it."

After a pause the Englishwoman nodded toward the woods and trees passing outside the train window. "Do you have trees to any extent? Like our oak, for instance?"

"Oh, yes, and what's more we have the great teak forests of the east, the pine forests of the mountains——"

"Mountains? Are they anything like the English mountains?"

"Surely you must have heard of the Himalayas," said the Indian, sounding, by now, rather defensive. "They are the highest in the world. Next to them the English mountains are scarcely even hills."

To this the Englishwoman said with admirable patience and sweetness and entire disbelief, "You *do* love your country very much, my dear, don't you?"

This is a true story and I tell it to illustrate two things that any traveler to India should remember—the widespread innocence abroad about India (even in her ex-ruler's homeland), and the deep pride that Indians have in their country.

Any girl who has worn a sari in a New York restaurant and been asked by a stranger to tell fortunes, or any Indian who has been asked by good-natured hostesses to give them the recipe for curry, or, inevitably, for information about the rope trick, beds of nails, caste marks or sacred cows, recognizes the familiar misconceptions and preconceptions that are common conversational currency about India. Set these experiences (that any Indian abroad can duplicate a dozen times) against the Indian's own feeling about his country and you can see that a degree of tact is needed when you want to ask even reasonable questions. One aspect of Indian feeling is shown in the much-quoted sarcasm of the Indian's reply to the American who asked, "Have you been to America?"

"America?" the Indian said. "Ah, that is the country Columbus found when he was looking for India."

A more naïve and equally arrogant story which has been attributed to the Nagas, an Indian hill tribe, tells of the creation of mankind: God put His first model of man into the oven to be baked. Being unpracticed, He took the model out while it was still white and doughy—that became the white man. The second model He left in so long it came out burned —that became the Negro. Finally He timed it exactly right and the model came out an even, perfect brown—that, of course, became the Indian.

These two things—the foreigner's misinformation and the Indian's touchy pride—combine to make traveling in India a complicated, sometimes confusing, often irritating and always unexpected experience. But whatever the complexities of the Indian character or country, one thing is certain—it is impossible to be disappointed in India. In the fantastic diversity of the country, from the frozen peaks and plateaus bordering Tibet to the tropical Malabar coast, in the inexhaustible variety of the Indian people—their faces, manners, costumes, jewelry, arts and way of life—there is something to everyone's taste.

The misconceptions about India take a number of different forms. One sort, which a friend of mine calls "the lean, bronzed horsemen" school of literature, reduces Indian life to the simple code of fighting men—honor, revenge and treachery; this appears mostly in the writings of people like Kipling or Yeats-Brown.

Another sort, the "Mother India" school, dwells on the primitive customs and miserable living conditions in India. Yet another prepares you for a land of mystics and holy men. One way and another, a formidable screen of fantasy and half-truths has grown up between India and the West.

Most people, for instance, think of India as a hot country. If you find yourself on the edge of the Rajasthan Desert in June, certainly the temperature will be around 115° in the shade and there will be a scalding wind as well. But because of such extremes of heat, people tend to overlook the fact that all of North India has a very cold winter, that a large part of the country is mountainous, and that you can ski in Kashmir. Even Bombay, which is sometimes considered part of South India and can't possibly be called cold, because the temperature rarely goes below 70°, is still very pleasant. Residents of the city consider 90° a heat wave, and try to avoid the sticky weather of the month before and the month after the summer monsoon.

Then again, you are bound to have heard that India is dirty. When you arrive here and see the city streets and the people in them, you will feel this is no exaggeration. They look filthy. But the interiors of the homes are not. And it is worth remembering that Indians in their turn are likely to consider foreigners dirty because they shake hands with strangers, wear their shoes indoors and eat with knives and forks. My grand-

Cities of India: *Udaipur* (top)—*a view from a palace balcony. Calcutta—fakirs, one on a bed of thorns. Banaras—bathing ghats by the Ganges. Madras—women in festive finery.*

mother used to say, "You know whether your own hands are clean. But who can be sure that the servants have washed the silver?"

Perhaps you have been told of India's extensive illiteracy. Only about 15 per cent of India's three hundred million people can read and write. But don't make the mistake of thinking that this means they are uneducated or primitive. There is a strong tradition of the oral transmission of learning in India, and in spite of scanty communications and the small range of newspapers and radios, you would have to travel to a very obscure village indeed to find Indians who haven't a good idea of their country's needs and problems, its leaders and what they stand for. In the first free elections in India's history, held in January, 1952, over 60 per cent of the electorate voted.

Whether the various sorts of misconceptions romanticize, patronize or disparage India, one thing is certain—they are a great barrier to the foreign traveler's understanding of the country. So perhaps the most important things he can bring with him are an open mind and a great deal of tact.

I would suggest that any visitor to India arrange to see at least one of the great festivals, for India is among the few remaining places where a sense of pageantry and extravagant display is still accepted as a necessary part of life. A festival will provide not only a very good show but a contact with a warm and expressive side of the Indians as well. Certain festivals have become famous because custom, tradition or history has made them more important than the others. In Bengal it is the Durga Puja (otherwise known as the Kali dances) that has become the most elaborate. This celebrates the day of fighting between Rama, the hero of the *Ramayana*, and Ravana, the king of evil. For this period the goddess Durga, in her aspect of Kali, the goddess of destruction, is worshiped with offerings of flowers, fruit and food in the usual way, as well as with frenzied dancing. In some places the Durga Puja is accompanied by the public sacrifice of animals to the goddess, and the severed heads are piled high in front of her shrine.

In the past, the festival of the Great Cart in Puri, the sacred place of pilgrimage in Orissa State, gained notoriety because the excesses of religious devotion caused some of the pilgrims to throw themselves under the huge wheels of the ceremonial cart of the Lord Jagannath (Juggernaut). It is still the best known of India's religious processions, although the hundred thousand or so pilgrims who flood into Puri in June or July seem less impulsive these days.

The cart itself is a wooden chariot approximately forty-five feet high in which is placed the image of the Lord Jagannath (literally, king of the earth and an aspect of Vishnu). On the day of the festival, pilgrims pull the cart from the temple and take it in a fantastic procession through the town.

Of all the hundreds of local festivals perhaps the grandest are the Dusserah celebrations of Mysore. For ten days in Sep-

Sights of India: *The whiskered guard* (top) *of a Rajput maharaja. A flower-decked leopard in a mock funeral. A snake charmer and friend, a cobra. A sacred cow enjoying the freedom of the city.*

tember or October all of Mysore rejoices in commemoration of the victory of Rama over the forces of evil. The festivities center in Mysore City, the site of the palace, where the maharaja holds a ten-day durbar with all the splendid panoply of his ancestors. All the nobles from every part of the state come to Mysore to pay their traditional homage. Each brings a sack of gold coins which he places at the maharaja's feet. In the old days this was their annual tribute to the throne, but now (because the nobles pay land and income taxes) only the gesture remains—the sacks of gold are small and are later returned to the nobles. The maharaja gives each noble a *paan* (chopped areca nut and spices wrapped in betel leaf) to signify his blessing. This ceremony takes place in the vast throne room of the palace. On one side of the hall the maharaja sits cross-legged on the gold brocade cushions of the throne. Over his head, as the chief decoration on the elaborate canopy, is a golden, jewel-encrusted peacock carrying an enormous emerald in its beak. The throne itself is carved figwood overlaid with gold and silver.

The maharaja wears different ceremonial dress each night, but all are of gold or silver brocade and his turban is usually made of "cloth of gold," with cockades of precious stones. Around his neck he wears some of the fabulous state diamonds that seem to glitter with a special light of their own. I remember watching the scene from the visitors' gallery and noticing that as the maharaja breathed the slight movement of his chest was enough to make the diamond necklaces give off a regular, dazzling flash, like a lighthouse beam.

Seated on the floor in front of him are the nobles, dressed in the formal long black jackets with jeweled buttons over tight, white trousers. Meanwhile, outside the palace the state troops are displaying feats of equestrian skill, and acrobats, clowns, sword swallowers, singers and dancers and performing. Since the whole side of the durbar hall opposite the throne opens directly onto the palace grounds, the maharaja can watch his nobles and, beyond them, the performance outside. The nobles can watch only the maharaja, but the crowds of Mysore's commoners can come into the palace grounds and see everything. Without question, that gathering is, for sheer magnificence, one of the most impressive in the world.

For those ten days the town of Mysore more than trebles its population. Villagers think nothing of walking a hundred miles to be in Mysore for Dusserah. Within the exhibition grounds a miniature city is set up with representative arts, shops, costumes or houses from all over Mysore, and there are also restaurants, coffee shops (Mysore is famous for its coffee), side shows, theaters, puppet shows, storytellers, and most of all, the thousands of people all in a holiday mood, wearing their gayest clothes, asking questions about each other's homes and listening enthralled to stories about parts of Mysore they will never visit even though they live only fifty miles away.

On the last day of Dusserah the biggest show of all is put on—the maharaja's ceremonial procession to the temple where he does his *puja*. The Mysore troops lead off carrying the state colors, and then come the palace guards carrying lances, the nobles with their retinues, the maharaja's personal bodyguard,

mounted on matched black horses with leopard-skin saddles, the royal camels, and then the maharaja himself riding on the largest of the state elephants, and behind him the lesser elephants, chariots, horsemen, outriders and foot soldiers.

The maharaja's elephant is elaborately decorated for the procession. He is painted with auspicious designs; red and white flowers curl up his legs, his eyes are elongated with paint, even his toenails are painted. Finally the elephant jewelry is brought out. He wears a massive gold necklace, huge gold earrings, a jeweled plaque on his forehead, anklets, gold tips on his tusks. Sitting in the howdah on top of this incredible animal, the maharaja rides in state through the city, and returns in a torchlight procession to his palace in the evening.

It is easier to face the relatively colorless days of the rest of the year after Dusserah.

The centuries have brought many shifts in population in India. From the important cities of the landlocked interior, people have drifted to the coastal towns. Or, as industrialism grew, people flooded in from the country to the cotton mills, the steel works, the new factories. As a result many of India's major cities have now an entirely alien character. Arriving in Bombay, for instance, you would have to recognize that fat and ugly arch, the Gateway of India (designed by an Englishman to commemorate the landing of King George V and Queen Mary), before you could say with any certainty what country you were in. If you happened to come in by air you wouldn't have even that landmark. The drive in from the airport would take you through the usual dingy industrial outskirts of any big town. You would catch a glimpse of the sea from time to time as the road curved around the many bays and inlets of Bombay Island, but the residential sections, the shops, the blocks of apartment houses along the sea front could belong in any town with a warm climate.

By Indian standards Bombay, like all the big present-day cities, is of recent origin. For years the island was rented by the East India Company for ten pounds a year, but it wasn't until the 18th Century that it began to grow into a town. Even Madras, the oldest of the modern cities, was only about fifty years ahead of Bombay. And New Delhi, the capital of the country, was inaugurated only twenty-two years ago. However, it is from these cities of India, modern, unrepresentative, and with practically no contact with the main body of India, that most visitors form their impressions of the country.

This is not to say that modern Indian cities are without compensations. It is in the cities that you will shop and see the full range of India's ancient handicrafts and modern manufactures. You will go to Indian movies (an average feature is three hours long), to the theater, to museums or shows. Each city has its special excellences. When an Indian goes to Delhi, for instance, he will make a point of buying some *halva sohn*, a delectable local sweet, to take home, as well as the beautifully hand-worked silver for which the city is famous. To the visitor there is the added interest of finding one's way to Chandni Chauk (the Silver Street) where on each side of the narrow alley, deep in the crowded bazaar section of the old city, the stalls displaying their silver jewelry and ornaments glitter like moonlight.

Although the seat of the government is in the brash new buildings of New Delhi, it is old Delhi, only a few miles away, that has the fascinating bazaars and such nationally famous places as the Jama Masjid—a huge and beautiful mosque—and the Red Fort and the Kashmir Gate. There, too, inside the walls of the old city, you will see the humming life of the Indian sidewalks. Early in the morning there may be the village women who have been walking since four or five o'clock to bring their fruit, flowers and vegetables into town, and they will transform the street into a market. Later in the morning those stalls will have vanished and perhaps basket makers, or men making children's toys out of colored paper or palm leaves will have taken over. In the early afternoon the street will be deserted except for a few coolies sleeping in the shade of the wall. By evening there may be sweet stalls, people selling betel nuts, a man with a traveling tea urn and little metal cups which he clinks to attract your attention, or a stall with the heavy, pervasive attars of musk or rose or jasmine for which Delhi is famous.

In Madras you will turn off the long gleaming sweep of the seashore into the narrow roads leading to the silk shops where you can buy heavy, luminous saris in colors that you will not find anywhere else in the world. If they seem stiff at first,

remember that the more you wash them (in soap and water, like a handkerchief) the softer and more beautiful they will become. In Hyderabad you will ask for the hand-woven silk brocades called *himru*, which are made in ancient and lovely designs and which can be found nowhere else in India. Agra, already famous for the Taj Mahal, is known to Indians as well for its precise and decorative mosaics—semiprecious stones like carnelian and jade set in dead-white marble. In Jaipur, artisans whose skill has been passed down from father to son for generations produce a more extraordinary kind of mosaic —precious stones set *in* precious stones. A necklace, for instance, made of large cabochon emeralds will have sprays of red and white flowers, made of rubies and diamonds, set in the emeralds themselves.

To go into any of these shops the visitor should learn the pace and technique of Indian shopping. To be in a hurry is fatal. Many shopkeepers won't bother to bring out their exquisite wares for someone who is in too great a rush to appreciate them. In the old-fashioned shops you will probably take off your shoes and settle down cross-legged on the white-cotton-covered mattress that takes up most of the floor. Almost certainly you will be offered very sweet milky tea or, if it is a very hot day, lemon soda. You will answer formal and polite

Worshippers await a ritual procession of elephants.

questions about where you come from, how long you have been in the country, whether you are married, whether you have children, and possibly how old you are. Then the silks and brocades will be unrolled or the antique jewelry displayed.

Perhaps the most celebrated and most extraordinary of Indian cities is Banaras, the holiest city in India. To Hindus, a chance to bathe in the river Ganges there equals the value a Muslim might place on a journey to Mecca. The sacred river Ganges flows, according to Hindu mythology, from the head of the God Shiva, in his aspect of the Creator. Prosaic geography shows it as rising in the Tibetan Himalayas and flowing south and east to empty into the Bay of Bengal at Calcutta. In either case, it is certainly a lifeline without which a vast area of India would become desert and the great cities of North India would vanish. At Banaras, the Ganges is supposed to acquire healing properties, and one of the sights most likely to repel the foreigner is the procession of the sick, maimed, leprous and emaciated going down to the river to bathe in its magical waters. On the banks you will see, besides, the fakirs who are almost as familiar in cartoons as the men doing the Indian rope trick. I have never actually seen one on a bed of nails, but I have often seen them at various other penances designed to achieve spiritual conquest over the feelings and pains of the body.

Many foreigners leave India still convinced that all Indian food falls into the comprehensive and meaningless category of "curry," by which they mean a sort of floury yellow sauce into which you can throw any sort of meat or fish and serve it with rice. One of the pleasures of finding your way into Indian homes will certainly be the variety and novelty of Indian food. North Indian cooks who specialize in cooking meat claim to be able to produce a different mutton dish for every day of the year, ranging from the simple kebabs grilled on a skewer over a charcoal burner to *roghan josh*, which is cooked for hours in clarified butter and curds, or *ran*, which must be soaked for twenty-four hours in buttermilk before it is roasted in a very slow oven. Each has its special spices, which must be ground fresh for the ocassion, and each has certain vegetables, pickles, varieties of bread, rice or pilau that are served with it.

Every part of India has distinctive food. The South, which is largely vegetarian, plays endless variations on the very simple theme of rice, lentils and a vegetable. There are at least five kinds of lentils in India and each can be cooked in a dozen ways. *Russum*, for example, which has lentils for a base, is a kind of hot consommé flavored predominantly with sour tamarind and chilies. And *patrel* is a lentil paste made to taste both sweet and salt, baked in a bland green leaf like spinach.

Bengal is famous for its sweets, Bombay and the coast on each side of it for ways to cook fish. North India, where people eat wheat as a staple rather than rice, has dozens of different

Monumental India: *A priest-guide* (top) *at Temple of Love, Banaras. Dancing Shiva at Elephanta Caves. Moslem architecture at Jaipur. Kailasa Temple, cut from a solid rock cliff.*

kinds of bread, and Kashmiri food is supposed to be the richest in India. You can tell from the food served in any Indian home what part of the country your hosts are from.

In an Indian home you will be served your food in a *thali*, a round, shallow tray, usually made of silver or brass, and you will eat with your fingers. In most Indian homes you will sit on the floor, or possibly on very low wooden stools, and the *thali* will be placed in front of you. In its middle will be a small hill of rice, and around the edge, in little matching bowls, will be meats or fish or vegetables, lentils, curds, pickles and chutneys and sweets. Everything is served at once and you decide in what order or combination you want to eat the various dishes.

If you are with an orthodox family, your hostess will not eat with you. She will serve you and watch your *thali* to refill the little bowls as you empty them. The Indian breads must be served hot, so your hostess will bring them to you one or two at a time and this will keep her moving in and out of the kitchen. Neither she nor her daughters will join in the conversation.

Eating with your fingers is not too difficult, as even the liquid food becomes manageable if you mix it with enough rice, but certain rules go with it. Never use your left hand in eating, even if you are left-handed, as the left hand is considered unclean. Never try to serve yourself; your hostess or a servant will do it. This is because your right hand, with which you are eating, will leave the serving spoon sticky and you mustn't touch food with your left. If you want to be perfect in your technique, don't let the food cover more than the first knuckle of your fingers—this is how people are judged for their grace in eating. Never offer anyone food from your *thali*—even if it is in one of the little bowls that you haven't touched. Any food that has been on your plate is *jhuta*, which means that it cannot be eaten by anyone but an untouchable; offering it will only embarrass or insult your Indian friends.

An Indian meal usually ends with a spoonful of plain boiled rice mixed with some plain curds. This is considered a digestive. Usually there is fruit as well, perhaps the most abundant and various in the world, and certainly you will be offered a *paan*, which may be an elaborate arrangement of strips of coconut, saffron, tobacco, cardamom, cloves, aniseed and many other spices wrapped in betel leaves and covered with silver leaf, or may be quite simple, with only lime, a sort of earthy paste called *katha* and *areca* nut as a filling. In any case, your hostess will probably bring out her *paan daan*, the metal box (often a work of art in itself) in which the ingredients are kept, and make a little ceremony of filling and wrapping the betel leaf. This is traditionally supposed to be the most beautiful activity in which a woman's hands can be engaged.

The food that you are given in Indian homes may be bewildering in its variety and richness, but in contrast, the home itself is apt to be simple to the point of austerity. Indians who do not fall into the "westernized" category seem to be entirely unaware of the barrenness of their surroundings. There is practically no furniture in their homes—beds are usually wooden frames webbed with criss-crossing wide tape, and a large chest or trunk in the bedroom will hold clothes and linen. Living-room furniture usually consists of a wide wooden platform covered with a sheet and some bolsters and cushions. There may be an odd table or two, or a book case, but these will have the look of being there by mistake. Floors will be bare or covered with reed mats or, in the North, with heavier carpets, and it is on the floor that most Indians eat and sleep, where the children study their lessons and the adults sit.

On the wall there may be a brightly colored religious picture of Lakshmi, the goddess of wealth, rising from her lotus, wearing a shiny sari, possibly with the border picked out in tinsel. Or it may be a picture of Krishna with his flute; his skin will be a murky blue, the result, according to legend, of a snakebite. There will almost certainly be a picture of Mahatma Gandhi somewhere in the house, and probably a large garish calendar of the sort that is given free by, say, Tata's soap manufacturers or Standard Oil. None of these is intended to have aesthetic value. They are on the wall for their usefulness or as reminders of spiritual values. The Indian doesn't, as a rule, think of his home as a place to beautify except to be sure that it is spotlessly clean.

If Indians have no sense of decoration for their homes, their sense of personal decoration is extraordinary. More than any other women in Asia—and perhaps in the world—Indians wear, collect and enjoy jewelry. It is worn at the wrist, neck and

Indian splendor: *An elephant clothed in gold and decked out in jewels. At Agra, the Taj Mahal. The lavish frescoes in the palace at Bundi.*

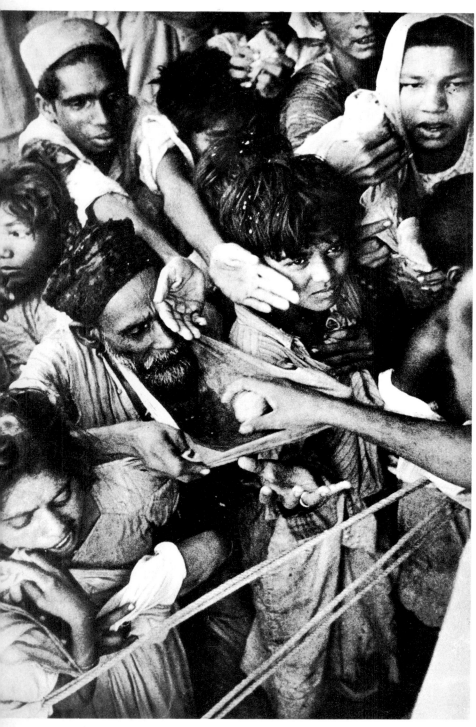

*The hands of young and old reach out eagerly
for the free food distributed
on the birthday of a Rajput prince.*

An economic factor partly explains this great concern with jewelry. Under Hindu law a woman's property consists only of her jewelry and the clothes, silver and other gifts she is given for her wedding. Her husband cannot take them away, sell them or use them in any way. From her they pass to her daughters, and this, in a large part of India, is the only economic security a woman can count on. Her jewelry, then, becomes an investment and insurance as well as adornment.

Clothes, too, are for the Indian woman a kind of investment. The metal threads that are woven into her saris and into the brocaded borders and accessories are silver. When the silk of her sari begins to wear out, she can burn it. The silver will remain to be sold or rewoven into a new sari. There are other advantages to her way of dressing. A sari is never out of style and can be handed down from mother to daughter until it falls apart. Because a sari is simply a length of cloth which is wrapped and draped individually each time it is worn, it can fit anyone, and requires no dressmakers.

In all its different ways, the Indian home and family can provide you with not only an important insight into the country and its people but with a warmth, a generosity and a friendliness with which Indians surround people they have accepted into their homes. It is this that gives them their reputation of emotionalism, and it can be their most endearing quality.

In every Indian city, however, the vast majority of the inhabitants—the mass of Indians—are out of reach for the foreigners. You will see them everywhere, sleeping on the sidewalks at night, crowding the bazaars, the industrial areas, the water front or the slums in the daytime, sitting and talking with their friends on street corners in the evenings, or bargaining cheerfully with the girls in the Bombay red-light district of Kamatipura. On holidays the women will put on their bright cotton saris and follow their husbands to Chowpatty, the city's beach. There, they will buy an anna's worth of roasted chickpeas from one of the little stalls for their children and will spend the day walking about and watching the other people.

They are the permanent backdrop to everything you do or see in India. Your only contact with them will be through the coolies who carry your luggage, the small boys who pester you for money or offer to run errands or fetch a taxi or watch your car, the servants in a hotel, the cook in a dak bungalow. You will probably never know anything much about them, never exchange an intimacy or a joke.

The Indians that you get to know will show you and tell you a lot about India, but even they will probably provide only the most tenuous of bridges to the great mass of Indians. Perhaps this is the only real meaning of the "mysterious" or "inscrutable" Orient. Your best clues to the Indians will be in what you see of their country. The threadbare, ingrained, desperate poverty of the villages you pass through or the shabby parts of cities—this is their life. The magnificence of the temples you see, the sculptures or the dances all contribute to their cultural heritage. The pageantry and processions or the excitement of a village fair or a city festival make up their glamour. For them India can offer only a poor living, but even for them, in its endless diversity, India can offer a rich life.

ears, of course, but pieces are designed as well for the forehead, nose and upper ear, and sometimes an entire gold ear studded with gems is made to fit over the natural one. There are rings for toes and thumbs, and there is a plaque for the back of the hand from which extend five short chains. On the end of each chain is a ring and the five rings fit over the fingers and the thumb. Also attached to the plaque is a much larger ring which fits around the wrist as a bracelet.

There are jeweled hair ornaments; there are anklets; there are sets of bracelets made in graded sizes to be worn in a solid mass from wrist to elbow and from elbow almost to the armpit. There is a limitless variety of brooches, pendants and clips.

BURMA

There are no flying fishes on the road to Mandalay,
and Santha Rama Rau says that the dawn comes up
quite prosaically from across a wide and dusty plain.
But the people of Burma
are so delightfully friendly that even during the
ravages of World War II the country was
called the Land of Laughter.

Of all the countries of Southeast Asia, Burma is probably the one with the most immediate appeal. This may seem like too extravagant a statement to those foreigners whose memories of Burma are concerned mostly with the bitter wartime years, who connect the place names of northern Burma with stops on "Vinegar Joe" Stilwell's famous retreat, or who remember the difficulties and the triumphs of the cutting of the Burma Road through almost impenetrable jungles and mountains to link the Chinese armies with their Western allies. Even now Rangoon (the capital and your most likely point of arrival) is not a startlingly beautiful city. The ride in from the airport shows only a somewhat scrubby landscape and the usual undistinguished suburbs. But almost at once you are aware of the special character of the people—a blend of charm, *laissez-faire* and a lively sense of the ridiculous.

A Burmese once remarked to me, "Burmans have really only three basic moods—good, better and bored." Another Burman explained, "I suppose you could call us arrogant, but we can't make ourselves believe there is a better place to live than Burma." (The Burmese quota for immigration to the United States is never filled.) This attitude makes Burma refreshingly full of fun, and her people a delight to know.

Under the Burman's good-humored tolerance of the world about him, however, there is an occasional quick anger and a sharp spirit of independence. The combination explodes from time to time in sudden bursts of violence. Burmese history hasn't been particularly calm. Sandwiched between Asia's two largest nations, India to the west and a 1200-mile frontier with China on the east, Burma, with only nineteen million people, has had its share of invasions, peaceful and military, from its neighbors. The fact that they invariably paid tribute to Burma's appeal by giving the country complimentary names was not much consolation. Burma has been known in its history as "Golden Peninsula," "Golden Earth," and "Golden Land"— descriptions which cover the typical Burmese landmarks of gilded pagoda spires, the wealth of the soil, and the sunny disposition of the people.

Four times in its history Burma's many small independent states and principalities have been welded together to form a free and united country: in the 11th Century (Burma's Golden Age); in the 16th Century when Bayin Naung unified Burma; in the 18th Century when the capital was named "Yangon" (Rangoon) or "The End of Strife"—a remarkably poor prophecy, because soon afterward Burma fought three wars with

The Shwedagon Pagoda dominates Rangoon.

England which resulted in the country's becoming a British colony in 1885; and, a few years ago, when Burma's prime minister, U Nu, quelled an insurrection and set up the present socialistic regime.

Throughout all this the Burmese sense of identity was never really shaken. You notice immediately, for instance, even on the streets of a city as Westernized as Rangoon that Burmese men, more than any other Asians, wear their national dress— the *longyi*, or sarong, a short loose jacket, and a most dashing headcloth in frivolous ice-cream colors. Asian women are more conservative about their clothes, so it is not particularly surprising that you almost never see a Burmese woman in Western dress, but always in a *longyi* and white jacket fastened with fanciful buttons that may be made of diamonds and jade or glass and bone. The passion for permanent waves or the Audrey Hepburn cut that has affected most major cities in Asia has not touched the Burmese women. Their special pride is long, heavy hair beautifully arranged and decorated with flowers. Even many children wear their hair in the old-fashioned style—long, on the top of the head and tied in a knot, around which the hair is clipped into a short, flopping fringe.

In their daily living, too, the Burmese stubbornly prefer their own ways—foods (including a source made of dried fish which foreigners find smelly, but which is necessary to any Burmese meal); entertainment (theater and dancing), and sports (boat racing). In their politicians they like a quality they call "being a Burmese Burman"—un-Westernized, that is. They tell you that their Foreign Service is an unpopular vocation because it involves living abroad. They remind you that Burma was one of the last British colonies and the first, since America showed the way in 1776, to gain independence.

Still, the Burmese can make fun of qualities they most admire. Prime Minister U Nu, for instance, famous for 'his devotion to Buddhism and his austerely simple life, was nicknamed "Not-so-Simple-Simon." The point was that his devotion and simplicity paid off by winning him the support of Burma's huge Buddhist population. Once, when I remarked to a Burmese friend on the pleasant attitude of his people, he said, "Oh, yes, we are very good at living in abject luxury." For by Asian standards, Burma is rich. Its biggest economic problem is a surplus of rice.

Because the Burmese are so hospitable and so ready to share and explain their country, the traveler feels an instant closeness with Burma and its life. He makes friends and shares Burmese interests with no sense of effort. Another factor that makes social life casual is that Burmese women are independent and very far from the conventional picture of the retiring Oriental woman. Burmese women keep their maiden names even after marriage. They share equal property and inheritance rights with men, and they can divorce their husbands simply by announcing their intentions to a few respected elders. They are good businesswomen; many of them run commercial concerns and if, at first, it seems strange to see a slender Burmese woman with elegantly knotted hair and a bright silk *longyi* smoking a cigar and shrewdly discussing business, you soon accept it as another example of Burmese individuality. About one thing, however, Burmese women are most careful. Despite her equality a Burmese wife never destroys her husband's *hpon*—his maleness, or rather, as a friend explained it, "the glory or holiness of man." She is always respectful, and she is careful to avoid putting her *longyi* on his bed or touching his possessions with her feet.

Next to the appeal of the Burmese people, your strongest impression of Burma is likely to be of a deeply felt, if casually observed, religion. It is probably the most intensely Buddhist country in the world. The two indispensable features of any Burmese scene are the tapering, gilt peaks of pagodas and the saffron robes of priests. Even in Rangoon, a busy, crowded modern port, architecturally an unfortunate mixture of public buildings in a "British colonial" style (onion domes, meaningless towers, weirdly ornate arcades and cornices) and the concrete cubes of offices and new apartment buildings, the whole city is given character by the dominating spire of the Shwedagon Pagoda, while the smaller Sule Pagoda marks the exact center of town.

Any morning on Rangoon's streets you will see the groups of shaven-headed priests, monks and acolytes standing before shops and houses, their begging bowls held before them, waiting for whatever food (vegetarian) the devout townspeople may give them. Every Burman in his youth enters a monastery as a novice. He may stay only a few weeks, or for years, or even dedicate his entire life to religion. He may go only to learn to read and write, or to study the fundamentals of Buddhism, or to acquire his full education. But he is sent there by his mother with the traditional request that he be beaten if he is bad. (Burmese mothers are too affectionate to beat their sons.) And he leaves the monastery with respect for his religion and a familiarity with its principles that last him all his life.

Even with this rigorous background, there is little that is forbidding to a Burman in his religion. He will take off his shoes before he enters a pagoda, but no further deference is expected of him. In the immense, circular Shwedagon, Burma's most famous place of worship and the world's largest Buddhist pagoda, the Burmese patter briskly up the four huge stairways. They stop to greet friends, pausing at one of the stalls to buy flowers for offerings. At another stall, they bargain for toys for their children—gay and imaginative wooden animals, comical puppets, painted umbrellas. Perhaps they buy a small lacquer figure of Buddha to send to some unfortunate provincial cousins who have no chance to visit the sacred Shwedagon. Almost certainly they stop for a cup of coffee, sweets for the children or a coconut to offer at a shrine. These long entrance passages have the air of a thriving bazaar.

Even on the high main terrace where all the many shrines are built and where Buddha statues tower in alcoves or huddle in tiny niches, the atmosphere remains casual and friendly. Children slide about on the tiles, kicking aside the withering flowers from past devotions; women wander by carrying their bundles, talking intimately as though they were going marketing; men who may be prostrating themselves will pause to stare at a stranger. But, also, there will be a mystic, so lost in meditation that no expression alters his face as he sits crosslegged in a corner, no muscle moves when people gaze at him, there is no hint of weariness or distraction to relieve his rigid pose.

From somewhere comes the chanting of scriptures punctuated by the sharp resonance of a bell; priests and devout laymen are saying prayers among the twinkling crystals, the mirrored shrines, the lacy, gilded decorations of the pavilions. Rising high into the pale Burmese sky above the worshipers is the golden spire of the Shwedagon.

The Burmese, with their natural sense of enjoyment, make their religious festivals among the most entertaining in the world. Except during the Buddhist Lent (usually July through September) there is a festival of some sort almost every fortnight. There are big festivals at both the beginning and end of Lent when all Burma is decorated with lights and for three days there are feasts and almsgiving.

New Year (which comes in mid-April) is celebrated with a water festival when the images of Buddha are ritually washed in perfume; the children have converted the solemn business of being blessed with holy water into a water fight.

Then there is the fire festival of mid-November, and festivals for the various important stages in the life of Buddha. And besides all these, every full moon deserves a celebration, and every pagoda has its own annual festival, and every family has its special ceremonies when a boy shaves his head to enter a monastery, or when a girl has the lobes of her ears pierced.

Next to Japan, Burma is more theatrical minded than any nation in Asia, and their *pwes* (a word which covers everything from historical drama to musical comedy) always seem to be packed with people who are happy to sit all night on reed mats watching a biographical play about an ancient Burmese king or a variety show with dozens of changes of scene and costume. You may be invited to go to the theater at midnight or at three in the morning—your host may have been watching the show since nine at night, but since foreigners don't have such stamina, he may, politely, have asked you only for the most interesting part or for the moment when the lead dancer appears. In any case, you will see a profoundly Burmese art and entertainment.

Unless it is one of the rare modern plays, music and the dance will undoubtedly be mixed in with straight theater. The Burmese orchestra—one of the most decorative I have seen—is set a little below the level of the stage.

The *saing-waing*, the most important instrument, looks like a fantastic mirrored and gilded circular cage. Inside it are a series of graded drums, each tuned with a blob of rice paste in the middle, and in the center the musician sits on a tiny stool, swinging from side to side, beating the drums, setting the mood and the pace for the orchestra.

Around this leader are ranged the flute and drum players, and on one side, slung from a fabulous golden frame, are the two huge gongs that maintain the basic beat of the music. The dancers appear, dressed in the most luxurious of *longyis*, jackets and jewelry, and face the audience with almost formidable assurance. They joke and flirt with men in the orchestra, and then, suddenly, they flare into short bursts of dancing, as brilliant and surprising as firecrackers.

Immediately after a famous dancer has been wildly applauded, a comedian may do an absurd take-off on the same dance, and his casual ridicule of a great art form draws equally enthusiastic appreciation.

Though Buddhism plays so large a part in the life, entertainment and character of the Burmese, at the same time they prudently keep on good terms with the *nats*—vaguely defined as spirits of inanimate (and sometimes animate) things. You may meet a Burman who seems in every way sophisticated, realistic, even cynical. As you get to know him better you may discover that he never takes a journey without first checking with an astrologer, or never sets the date for an important family event—a daughter's wedding, or a move to a new home —without first determining the most auspicious day and hour. In the case of a new house, he would first hang coconuts from its eaves to keep the evil *nats* out. Even the Prime Minister, they tell you, once returned a defective radio with the comment that his house *nats* didn't like it.

Outside a Buddhist pagoda there is often another shrine for the *nats* so they won't be jealous; and in the spring, when, for some reason the *nats* most need to be pacified, all over Rangoon there are *nat* dances and offerings.

When you see a *nat* dance, you realize it is a trance dance.

The woman dancer sits on the ground in front of a shelf piled with offerings. As the orchestra plays loudly, she gets up smiling quite ordinarily and begins her dance. Somewhere in the course of it the *nats* take over and give her a new personality. She may become, for instance, a little girl with a pettish expression, childish gestures and the inexpert, touching movements of a child learning to dance; she will seem to be bouncing a ball, tying ribbons in her hair, playing with her friends. Or she may become a drunkard, reeling clumsily about, belligerently pushing away friends who try to restrain her.

One *nat*-dancer I saw became the soul of generosity—she gave away everything she possessed to people in the audience or the orchestra. At the end I found myself, considerably embarrassed, holding a bunch of bananas, three eggs, an orange and a four-yard length of silk. The finish of the dance is marked by an uncontrollable shaking as the *nat* leaves the dancer's body.

To anyone who knows Mandalay only sentimentally from Kipling's poem, it comes as a dispiriting lesson in geography to learn that Mandalay is nowhere near the sea, there are no flying fish (even the Irrawaddy River, Burma's great waterway, is a couple of miles away and you can't even see it from the city unless you climb to the top of Mandalay Hill) and the dawn comes up quite prosaically from across a wide and dusty plain. However, Mandalay is, in every other sense, a magnificent place, and, as the Burmese are sure to tell you, "it is the indestructible heart of Burma."

From Mandalay eastward begins the great Shan plateau, sheltered to the north from Tibet by a gigantic horseshoe of mountains where dozens of different groups of hill people live —the Chins, Kachins, Nagas, Lolos, to mention only a few.

The best way to visit the northern Shan states from Mandalay is by car. You can hire a jeep to take you up the alarming (but quite safe) road that climbs eastward to the hill resort of Maymyo where even in February you will find delicious strawberries sold on the roadside by Gurkha tribesmen (eight big baskets for a dollar), roses in the gardens and, most precious of all, what the Burmese call "two-blanket weather." Beyond Maymyo, the road dips perilously down hillsides, spans ravines on slender bridges, climbs past the northern Shan capital of Lashio to the jade-green mountains and incredible vistas of the Chinese borderlands. On your way you spend your nights in government "Travelers' Bungalows," and your days exploring villages or tea plantations, and in the dry winter season there is nearly always a *pwe* somewhere in the vicinity.

From the lookout pavilion on the border you can stare into the rocky, improbably dramatic gorges of China itself, resembling the most stylized of Chinese paintings. To those whose knowledge of Burma is associated with wartime memories of the bitter jungle fighting in these hills, the winding track has a different significance—this was the western end of the vital Burma Road.

If you are a bit more adventurous, you can follow the China frontier to the town of Namkam (headquarters of Dr. Seagrave, author of *Burma Surgeon*) and from there continue to Bhamo, the country of the Chins and Kachins who still tattoo themselves from thigh to waist in fantastic designs. Their tattoos are a matter of great pride. In one dance I witnessed, a Chin boy was the only one who stubbornly insisted on dancing in long trousers. The others wore tight loin cloths. When the dance leader told him to roll up his trouser legs for the sake of symmetry, he shamefacedly explained, "I haven't yet been able to get my thighs tattooed."

From Bhamo you can take the magnificent three-day boat journey down the Irrawaddy to Mandalay. In the Shan states southeast of Mandalay is Taunggyi, capital of the whole Shan plateau, an untidy-looking town, casually scattered about the side of a hill. If its architecture is undistinctive, its gardens and flowering trees are theatrically lavish. The town and the surrounding hillsides are covered in exuberant succession all through the winter with pale clouds of cherry blossom, the unearthly blue of jacaranda, white bouhenia (its flowers are used in cooking a fragrant stew), poinsettia (both the color of parchment and the more familiar scarlet), flame of the forest, the sharp incredible pink of cassia, and a tree I never identified whose bark is said to be an antidote to drunkenness. Altogether they give Taunggyi a light-opera air, intensified by the friendliness of almost any Shan you meet.

If your visit coincides with one of the "Five-day markets" (held every five days, not lasting five days), Taunggyi will offer an exciting glimpse of the people and handicrafts of the Shan countryside. For on market day the people come down from their mountain villages, the members of each tribe in their distinctive costumes and jewelry, to exchange their finely woven cloth and their capacious, decorative shoulder bags for salt, staples and town goods. You will see beautifully carved and etched silver work as well as the wonderful lacquerware for which Burma is famous.

About an hour's drive from Taunggyi is the strangely lovely country around Lake Inle, home of the Inthas. To reach the lake, you hire a boat in the nearest village and follow a narrow channel cut through the marshes. Winding among the high reeds, you feel curiously adventurous, isolated and somehow

Spring and a season of ceremonial processions conveniently coincide to persuade the young ladies of Burma to show off their prettiest clothes.

ominous, like a scene from the *African Queen*. Here and there along the channel are gingerbread pergolas with lotuses carved on their eaves; beyond the reeds stretch the paddy fields with always a flight of white herons swinging down in sleek lines to settle on the young rice.

Suddenly from the narrow tunnel you come out into the open lake, a calm, pastel, misty expanse of water, like a painting on silk. All around are tiny green islands and between them the slender Intha boats flit to the fish traps, the duck-shooting marshes and the villages on the far shore. The boats are hollowed-out teak trees, which are propelled by the most extraordinary rowing technique I have seen. The Intha oarsman stands at the back of the shell, a leg wrapped around the oar, and with a backward kick he forces the oar through the water.

The lake people have a peculiarly gentle nature and so great an affection for their shallow, beautiful lake that they are said to grow thin from misery if they ever leave it. There is no robbery among them, so the story goes, and no bandits, even though parts of northern Burma are still plagued by that hangover of wartime guerrillas. The Inthas live entirely off their lake, even raising vegetables on floating gardens. In the middle of the lake there is a most surprising and pleasing resthouse, built on stilts, where you can spend the night or stop for a meal.

On the far side of Inle are weaving villages whose women produce intricate designs in clear primary colors that are typical of the Shan peoples. The largest of the lake villages, Ywama, has the enchantment that goes with places that make only a casual distinction between water and land. Most of the houses are built on stilts over the water. The twelve monasteries with their towers and domes throw crinkled reflections on the village's main thoroughfare, a wide, half-tamed strip of the lake.

With all these diversities of country, populations and cultures, post-war Burma was presented with some of the most formidable problems of any Southeast Asian country. Its towns and countryside had been ravaged by the war, it had been the battlefield for two huge armies. It then had to come to grips with a nation-wide communist-led insurrection. Three things, the Burmese feel, saved their country: the pacific and unifying power of Buddhism, the determination of their prime minister, U Nu, and the fact that a Burman refuses to be bullied. To which a foreigner is inclined to add a fourth: the Burmans' independent and down-to-earth character. The astonishing and admirable results have been that within a few years the many states and tribes have become a more or less unified country, internal communism is no longer a threat, and a free and democratic government is getting ahead with the work of building a Welfare State. But the endearing thing about the Burmese is that through all this they have retained their sobriquet of "the Land of Laughter."

On one occasion, when I went to a *pwe* with some Burmese friends, some of us got sleepy before the end of the performance (it was then four in the morning). On the way home I asked my host to tell me the end of the story. Did the tangled romance end in separation, death and tragedy? Or were the lovers reunited and the obstacles overcome?

"Don't you know?" he said laughing. "All Burmese stories have happy endings."

PEKING

*After an absence of twenty years Han Suyin
returns to her native city,
now the capital of Communist China.
Loud-speakers howl political exhortations but the
winds still sough in the
dragon-shaped pines of the temples.
And Peking, she finds, remains Peking in
spite of stupendous progress and
equally stupendous errors.*

In a soft-gray and lavender twilight, heavy with the dust and dusk smell of North China, I heard the loud-speaker of the train I had been riding north for four days intone its final, hundred-and-tenth announcement: "Beloved travelers, gather your luggage. Count the pieces, lest some stray from you in the haste of departure. Pray do not hurl yourselves violently off the carriage; help the children and the women, give a hand to the old. In ten minutes we shall see the walls of Peking, glorious capital of the People's Republic of China." Then followed, as usual, the lesson in health and good conduct which, like the morning and afternoon gymnastics (one-two, bend: one-two, rise—for ten minutes in every institution, bank, office, school, department, university, all over China), pour out of the omnipresent, frantically audible loud-speakers: "Once more, beloved travelers, respect the hygiene and cleanliness of your country. Eliminate the four pests: flies, mosquitoes, rats and sparrows. Do not spit on the platform; use the spittoons. Do not allow your esteemed children to relieve themselves elsewhere than in the W.C. . . ." and the conclusive outburst of marching music with which all Chinese trains arrive and depart.

Pom pom pom went the engine, with sudden meaning pounding its way forward, and now on the horizon rose the long line of gray walls, their battlements softly indenting the sky, with a sudden uprush here and there into a tower, wistful and gravely balanced and so well remembered. Soon the train was running along the outer face of the walls of Peking, their plain brick surface split by bulging roots and centuries of rain. Twenty years ago, in the space between railway track and wall, there had been dingy coal sheds and great pyramids of coal balls, shaped by hand out of coal dust and water and a little clay. And now they were there the same heaps, the same sheds, ensconced between bulges of the gray wall.

I was going home, home to Peking after twenty years. Sometime before, Premier Chou En-lai broadcast an announcement that all Chinese abroad could visit their families on the mainland, stay as long as they wished and leave when they pleased. Eight days later I applied for a visa from my home in Malaya. Seven weeks after that it arrived. In time, I made my way to Hong Kong and boarded a train to the frontier of China. I was going back to see my birthplace, to see my family, to see, for the first time, the new country that has aroused the

*Girls stroll in the grounds of Peking's summer-palace,
resplendent with gardens, artificial lakes and
pagodas built by the Empress Dowager Tzu Hsi in 1888.*

speculation, the hopes and the fears of all the world, the People's Republic of China.

Pom pompom pom went our singing train, and the wall drummed the music back. Suddenly there rose a mighty crescendo of double towers above the horizontal line of battlements, the loud-speakers crashed a triumphal last chord and we ground to rest. Peking. I was back after twenty years, and to confirm this fact the face of Third Brother (returned from the United States a year ago) flattened its nose at me against the windowpane.

"The railway station is the same, only cleaner," said Second Uncle, waving his cane at the medium-sized red-and-white cupolaed hall, built in the 1920s, which, at the moment, seemed crammed with the close ranks of The Welcoming Family. Astonishingly, we started shaking hands. We did not shake hands solemnly, like the Swiss; we did it with mirth and smiles, as if it were at the same time a joke. (In the modern Chinese plays which I saw later, in Peking, hand wringing is performed at all solemn, fraternal and inspirational moments, for instance when the counterrevolutionary spy is finally unmasked by the heroic girl friend who is a model worker in the factory, while the gullible engineer—obviously an intellectual with the shamefully low political awareness to which intellectuals are prone—stands by with bent head, realizing that if he'd only spent a few more hours a week studying Marxism-Leninism, he wouldn't have been outwitted by the spy. But his intentions were good, the girl friend forgives him with a long, forceful, repeated shaking of his hand, while the audience cheers and claps, knowing that they will be happy ever after.)

Beside the famous pink wall a worker exercises with shadow-boxing calisthenics.

China's youth is organized into Communist groups, each with emblems like the red flag carried by this small Pioneer.

Elaborately costumed, a youth burlesques a coquette at a Peking New Year's celebration.

But I digress. After shaking hands with cousins, sisters-in-law, uncles by affection, aunts by curiosity and a few school children with the red scarves of Pioneers (one of them turned out to be a seventeenth Brother), my luggage was seized by assorted relatives and we all walked out to catch the big red Skoda bus, mainstay of transport in Peking.

Before me, straight, massive, splendid, rose the tiered gate towers of *Cheng Yang Men,* the Gate Facing Straight the Sun, also known as The Front Gate. It stood against what could be nothing but a Peking sky, translucent as an old bronze mirror of the Han dynasty, with undertones of purple to its silver-gray, its polished surface skimmed by handfuls of swifts.

In front of the station a large banner was being taken down. On it was inscribed, in French and Chinese: *Welcome to the French Basketball Teams.* Below it two men held another banner, ready to hoist in its place. In Hindi, Nepali and Chinese, it proclaimed: *Welcome to the Nepali Fraternal Delegation to China.* A large billboard spread a Picasso dove, like a small elephant on the wing. Rows of taxis, American Cadillacs and Packards and Buicks, a few elegant Czech and Polish cars, were in front of the station. I turned to Third Brother: "Why so many American cars?" He laughed. "They left them behind; we use them now." Beyond the taxis were two lines of ramshackle pedicabs, their parts held together by string, dirt and good nature, and, wonder of wonders, a row of those extraordinary horse coaches, looking like French 19th Century landaus, with two lamps of copper on each side and a coachman on top, and pulled by small, crestfallen Mongolian ponies. "These are used by the farmers when they come on holiday," said Second Uncle.

The street was bright with shops, crowded with people buying things, going in and out of restaurants, or just laughing and talking. There was a flower garden around the large gate tower now, and girls walked hand-in-hand, many in trousers and blouses, but nearly all wearing long, thick pigtails, some down to their knees. This Gretchen hairdo is now the most popular in China, irrespective of age. Some women wore the Chinese dress with slits, which is returning in vast quantities in all the department stores, ready-made in all colors, in three sizes and vastly ill-fitting. Others were in skirts and blouses or western-style dresses. The men wore shirts and gray or blue suits with collars (a garment wrongly identified with communist doctrine, since it was first worn by Dr. Sun Yat-sen forty-five years ago). Some of the men pushed prams, some carried babies for their wives, and many married couples went arm in arm, obviously happy and unashamed—a strange sight for an Asian country even today.

But it was the prams which provoked another small explosion of reminiscence. They were made of wicker, had four small wheels, irregular, wobbly and squeaking, and were exactly the same as my own pram, later passed on to my sister and finally used for airing our dolls. "They still make them, near the Drum Tower," said Second Uncle, who sensed I was looking at my rediscovered childhood. "People talk as if all were new," he said, "but things don't change so much. There is birth and marriage and death. If man is happy, he is good. If he is hungry, he is bad. And now we are not hungry."

Peking lies as it has always done, massive yet full of grace in the ash-gray northern plains, itself full of color and glaze, green and gold, red and blue; flatly it lies on the flat earth, a horizontal city under the enormous petal of the turquoise sky. The imperial palaces are now a museum, but Peking willows, surely the most languid and with the longest droop, still sigh and rustle and seem to recite poems from the *Book of Songs*. The lotus in the man-made lakes and moats of the Forbidden City swing their heavy corollas, and couples row their boats and sing old folk airs with new brash words. With Chinese tact, the Western Hills lie just far enough away to remain swathed in light-blue mist by day, yet not too far for buses to carry large families and school children there for Sunday picnics at the Perfumed Mountain, the jade-green Cloud Temple. Under the slim, white Jade Pagoda the spring still pours into rice fields and on into Peking's lakes. The Ming tombs, repaired and repainted as are all Peking's monuments, are visited by tourists and youngsters sucking ice-cream sticks and climbing on the heads of the longevity turtles. Wind-blown with history and dust, Peking breeds peonies in summer, chrysanthemums in autumn, goldfish with fancy eyes and enormous tails the year round, just as it used to—even if there are nine new universities, three million people, and a whole new city. New Peking, growing swiftly just west of the old walls.

Peking is communist, and to many that means that it is no longer what it was. But history sometimes has a way of making a change, however abrupt, however incompatible with our vision of the past, however opposite and therefore to us strange and horrifying, the very link which may one day appear a logical and necessary continuation of long-prepared, long-drawn scenes in a never-ending play. How easy to say, "Things are not what they were."..."This is the end."..."China is no longer China." But it is not true for us Chinese.

Peking is Peking, intact and eternal, itself in spite of change, or rather because of it. China is Chinese, and is also now the Asian miracle, the country that has achieved sufficiency in food in the shortest time for the largest agglomeration of people on earth. From all the countries of Asia and from the rest of the world they come to see it—professors from Scandinavia and Ceylon; slim young men from Japan or from Jordan with cameras and GI caps; robed priests from Lebanon and Greece; businessmen from London; artists and doctors from Indonesia—a cavalcade taken in massive delegations or in solo importance to see the achievements of the New China, in a fanfare of steel mills, blast furnaces, cotton factories, tool plants, coal mines, oil wells, railway tracks, huge dams and colossal bridges. Euphoric, dazed, enthusiastic, hostile, prejudiced, conquered, they come and go. Propelled, conducted by the Chinese equivalent of Intourist, they are interested only in the difference with "old China," "old Peking." They see what they call "The future of Asia" unfold, and sometimes forget that every future has a past.

Here you see them both, past and future. Socialist Peking shows off its palaces and temples as well as its new universities, factories, nurseries, hospitals and sanatoria. At the Gate of Heavenly Peace, the first gate of the Great Within, Mao Tse-tung, chairman of the People's Republic, and his colleagues stand, on May first and October first, facing due south, toward the Gate Facing Straight the Sun, and review the mammoth parades, half a million strong, which tell the greatness of New China. Guests and delegates from nearly every country throng the tiered seats. To foreigners there may be great differences, a yawning gap between the past and the present, but to the people of Peking, at least, it looks strangely as if there were continuity.

Magnificent things are done, and also mean ones; stupendous progress and stupid errors; admirable enthusiasm and trivial vileness; a growing spirit of criticism and free discussion, and arguments against this dangerous freedom. Everybody works. There is no leisure class. Women all work too. Children all go to school. Illiteracy, I was told, is nearly abolished. Architecture is somewhat idiotic. There are no crimes. Peking is so puritan it seems nearly sexless, and there are no night clubs, no prostitutes, no singsongs, and an extramarital affair is a punishable offense. Everyone talks of productivity, most of all the writers, but there hasn't been a Chinese novel worth reading in the last few years.

Very few people from outside keep their balance while in Peking, especially if they stay longer than three weeks (but most "do" China in twenty days). The impact, if one is thoughtful, is a little like turning around in bed and finding a dinosaur in the room. To condemn a dinosaur for being a dinosaur is somewhat futile. Notions of "good" or "bad," "right" and "wrong," and of the meaning of freedom are re-evaluated. This produces something resembling a mental breakdown because few of us can remain unemotional before something so vast, so utterly beyond experience or even adequate description. The notion of the individual human being gets submerged, as much as one fights against it; one feels selfish to feel individual, apart, uncollected within the collective. It is a sensation of guilt which can only be terminated by giving up oneself to the collective, or by accepting a state of being perpetually alone and outcast. And yet, even spoken of in terms of standard of productivity, even reduced to a social function, the human being is still there. It was my function to find the human being, and I found him.

I, too, had my moments of transport and exaltation—and within the next half hour, I just wanted to go home and be sick. I alternated between admiration and indignation to the point of physical pain; yet the day came when all fell into place, and though I would not acquiesce, I could understand.

In the constant interaction of old and new, in rediscovering my Peking childhood and exploring a new domain as strange as the moon, I was much helped by my refusal to have an Aim and a Purpose: I kept the pretense of a leisure now immoral and useless, and in my pocket, a mooncake.

Leisure meant refusing to do what everyone else did, and that was easy, for there is no obligation. No one in Peking forced me to do anything; if I wished I could have gone and looked at ducks quacking in the moats rather than at the 156 new projects of Manchuria. I watched magnolias blossom and wither, as well as intellectuals squirm their way out of argument; I listened to the wind soughing among the dragon-

In a dueling dance, a tradition of Chinese New Year,
contestants fence to the rhythm of cymbals and drums.

shaped pines of the temples in the Western Hills, as well as
to polemics for and against Hu Feng, thought-rebel and counterrevolutionary. I looked at peonies blossoming as they have
done for the last 1200 years, and discussed the lotus with
workers who also stared, but hastily assured me that their
Purpose was Inhaling Healthful Air to become more Productive. The mooncake—which I had carried in my pocket and
nibbled after festivals and parties in my childhood—I obtained
at the Laughing Autumn Arise shop, in the Eastern Peace Market, which is where it always was, on Wang Fu Ching, once
known to foreign tourists as Morrison Street.

Wang Fu Ching Street is full of shops: curios, carpets,
furniture, clothes, books, photographers, bicycles, musical
instruments, toys. It has lost a Swiss jeweler and acquired
several always-filled bookshops. There is also Peking's new
pride, the Hundred Goods Store, as large as a modest department store in New York, shining, marbly, clean, five-storied,
and crowded seven days a week and until nine at night. Rows
of ready-made dresses, blouses, skirts and of course shapeless
slacks. All salaries have been raised recently, and there is an
enormous shopping spree for radios, sewing machines, bicycles, shoes, coats, rubbers, dresses, blankets, and especially

children's clothes and toys. On Wang Fu Ching Street alone
there are five shops for children, plus a whole new floor at the
Hundred Goods Store.

The loud-speaker here sounds very much like a cross between an English nannie and the Board of Rites: "Beloved
women comrades must dress cleanly and well, with modesty
but attractively. There is *no harm* in looking attractive in a
dignified manner. Beloved comrades, dress in keeping with
your new, your many-splendored life . . ."

Foreign visitors to Peking are classified, as everyone else.
V.I.P.'s and government guests live at the former Peking Hotel;
less important guests overflow into other hotels, including my
favorite, the Sinchiao, situated next to the decrepit Hatamen
gate. The Peking Hotel is twice its former size, has allergy-
making plush chairs, a green marble lobby with fake bronze
pillars, reception rooms like basilicas, and excellent elevators.
From its roof can be seen the entire extent of the Forbidden
City—an unforgettable sight. The Sinchiao is comfortable
though not so grand, the rooms are excellent, each has a bath
and telephone, and the staff is cheerful and most obliging.
There is no tipping anywhere in China, and at the end of your
stay the room boy will ask you for your "criticisms and valuable suggestions." This is done everywhere you go: factory,
hospital, university, theater, trains, airports. The Chinese
genuinely want to learn, even from "capitalist" visitors.

Sipping coffee in the morning on the sixth-floor European
restaurant of the Sinchiao Hotel is a way of keeping tabs on
who's in Peking today: One morning the French girls' basketball team wafts in on a wave of perfume, emitting soprano
bursts of laughter and followed by a unanimity of stars. They
have come to play the Chinese at the grim, monumental,
Soviet-inspired gymnasium outside the Heavenly Bridge. Next
day the newspapers print their smug, pleased regrets: "The
French teams, both male and female, showed the utmost in-
trepidity. The struggle was exceeding fierce. . . . Our teams
won 84 to 12, 87 to 14 . . ."

Another day it is the Rumanian song-and-dance delegation,
forty strong, marching into the restaurant. Or a visitation of
Soviet experts (all Soviets are experts). These are a sober,
hardworking lot, the women spontaneous, unaffected, easy
to talk to. One woman doctor hugged me to her ample bosom
shouting, "*Krasivaya, krasivaya!*" and that was the only time
I needed an interpreter in China; it means, roughly, "you
pretty creature." They carry commuter brief cases. Watching
a Soviet delegation eat breakfast is like seeing a mountain
avalanche engulfing a valley, only the valley here is a mon-
strously overloaded table: two cream cakes each, pots of yog-
hurt, French bread fried and speared upon knife points, three
boiled eggs per person, buns, jam, tea. . . . "All the comrades
So-lean get fatter in our country," says my comrade-waiter.
"So-lean" is the Chinese onomatopoeic for "Soviet."

Another morning, three demure English ladies are entertained by an Australian in shirt sleeves who keeps repeating
vengefully: "'E 'adn't kept up with the woiking class...'e
was tot'ly out of touch with the woikers...." (Who is "'e"?
I wonder. Stalin?) Then there appears a Polish expert on porcelain who speaks English and to whom I lend *The Unquiet*

Grave, by Palinurus—a talisman book which, like my mooncake, keeps me sane, selfish, desperately believing that truth and art are eternal values. He laughs as he reads: "The true function of a writer is to produce a masterpiece and no other task is of any consequence." "That's politically retrograde," he says. But he copies it out. "We have no such good books now in our country," he murmurs sadly.

Most stupefied of all the visitors are French and Belgian Marxists, grounded in the intellectual Marxism of Western Europe, astounded by the neo-Confucian Marxism they discover in China. "But this is not Marxism, this is not what Lenin meant . . . *mais pas du tout, pas du tout*." Meanwhile an Italian girl with Lollo curls and gold bangles comes in with a black-robed, black-bearded priest who looks exactly like Archbishop Makarios and who distributes orthodox signs of the cross upon us, the waiters, the lifts and all down Hatamen Street.

The Chinese restaurant downstairs is a wonderful section of Asia. Here are Overseas Chinese, who have come to visit "the ancestors' land." They are loaded with cameras and watches, which they will sell at 400 per cent profit. They buy jade, which they will take and sell at 300 per cent profit in Southeast Asia. There are fifty Japanese with 100 cameras; there are Mongols in orange and Mongols in blue suits, calling out "Ha-ha!" with gruff voices; Annamites who sidle quietly and Burmese who are nearly invisible in their quietness; Moslems from Arabia, Egyptians in close curls, Mexicans in berets, Buddhists in yellow robes. The most fascinating guests of all were the people's representatives to the National People's Congress, held in Peking while I was there.

From all over China they assembled, 4000 of them including staff and secretaries. There were slim little girls delivering speeches on factory productivity; old men in long silk gowns, spouting classics; ladies in white hair and bound feet, respectfully supported by Party commissars in blue suits; ladies in slacks, in *cheongsams*, barefoot farm women wearing aprons with silver chains. Cobblers and capitalists, cooks and bankers, chauffeurs and railwaymen, professors and ex-Kuomintang officials—they were all there.

Later I attended sessions of the Congress, held in the South Sea Park, in a large hall with painted friezes, Chinese lacquer columns and klieg lights. I don't know about previous assemblies, but this one was extraordinary for the vigor of the criticism, and the outspokenness of some speeches—all, of course, an outgrowth of the Hundred Flowers doctrine. The final speech by Chou En-lai was also a remarkable thing: "We have to keep in touch with reality. . . . If we don't know what really happens, if we are not criticized we cannot correct our mistakes, and we govern in a vacuum. . . ." But everyone was careful to emphasize that "free" discussion must never leap the boundaries of "socialist realism," which was a little confusing. My French journalist friend was amused. "Here you say to people: 'Please discuss and criticize.' In my country we say: 'When for the love of God are you going to shut up?' "

Comrade Kang, the taxi man, is my friend. He drives me when I go long distances. He is the new, the technical man of Peking. Like his colleagues, he has a tendency to drive in the

*In puritanical Peking
a young couple experiments
with dancing in the
Working People's Palace.*

*Applying the
traditional make-up, an
actor gets ready
for a performance of
a Chinese opera.*

*A child in the playground
of North Sea Park,
a juggler playing for a
street crowd: lighter
moments in sober China.*

middle of the street, and when a car approaches, they rush at each other and veer only when the fenders are about to touch. In a shaken voice, I tell Comrade Kang how well he drives. "I drove a truck in Korea," he says proudly.

Comrade Kang takes me one day to the theater, generously paying twenty-five cents for my seat. In a country where monthly salaries vary from twenty-five to one hundred U. S. dollars, he is well off with fifty dollars a month, a flat, two children, a radio, plenty to eat, and a machine, his taxi, to look after. He loves machines, reads about mechanics all the time, and through him I understand why plays about fairies are popular in Peking.

Let Comrade Kang see a sophisticated play where people torture themselves deciding whether they will sleep with this man or that, and he would be horrified, his puritanism insulted. Give him instead a good black-and-white theme: good technician versus crafty spy; virtue rewarded, justice triumphant, Evil vanquished by Good, if not through human (and fallible) agency, then through a supernatural one. Since there is no God for Comrade Kang, he goes back to his childhood and invoke fairies. Of course fairies are not "true," but they are agreeable. Hence the popularity of fairy plays. Sitting with him in the theater, I lose my cynical and weary layers of complex wisdom and the seesaw variety of moods and moments which go to make up a human being in a sophisticated society. Two-dimensional, the play unfolds. The last handshake. We clap and go away. "My loved one has seen it three times," says Comrade Kang, referring to his wife. His wife is on night

Members of the Peking municipal legislature attend a session in Sun Yat-sen Memorial Hall, a former palace of the Imperial City.

shift. One evening when she is off we three go together, and they hold hands all through the play.

It was while looking at the goldfish in the zoo that I found what I had been missing in Peking. I joined a fascinated crowd of children from a nursery bending over the huge vats, and stared and stared at the tiger-head fishes, the lion-head fishes, the fish with bubble eyes, the fish with eyes-that-look-to-heaven, the red, white and violet dragon, the fish that wears a hat—monsters by ordinary goldfish standards, but what monsters! Such tails, such heads, such eyes on bulbs, on stalks, such chrysanthemum excrescences, such flashes of mandarin red and gold and scarlet, such touches of silver, such glimmers of tulip pink with pale gray and black honey fish melting in the green, green water!

I looked at them and suddenly said, "Funerals."

Marriages in China are down to bare-rock simplicity. Two people register at the court, invite friends to dinner. Often there is no honeymoon, though officially a week off is given. It usually isn't taken because of moral pressure; people feel their neighbors would criticize them for "putting private affairs above public need." But there is always a way of having one's cake and eating it. Peking gives a three-day general holiday on the occasion of the old, lunar Chinese New Year (now back in style in the calendar), so most marriages are now celebrated on New Year's Eve.

But funerals—those mile-long processions winding their disorderly columns along the dusty streets with the bearers carrying paper men and women, paper chairs, tables, motorcars, houses to be burned at the grave; with the immense hearse, covered in red brocade and borne by thirty-two coolies (what a surprising word in China now, the word coolie!) —I missed the funerals, the fish-bright funerals.

"What happens when people die, Comrade Kang?"

For the first time he did not like a question of mine. "People don't die very much now, we are all so healthy," he murmured. No, I realized, people couldn't die, for to die would be nearly sabotage, depriving the State of some useful cog. Yet people do die, of course, and some have died of sheer exhaustion.

"A funeral isn't anything much. Some people dress the body in new clothes—such a waste of necessary cloth!" said Kang, man of the New Age. "Some families call the Buddhist priests to chant prayers." He told me that prayers are so much per hour (Is there *anything* that Peking has not regulated, fixed, organized, estimated, categorized?). The coffin is buried in the public cemetery. No flowers, no brocade, no fuss. Families just wear a dark band around the sleeve. "But many people are now practicing cremation," said Kang.

Suddenly Comrade Kang's face lost its jolliness and showed the haunted, cheekboned mask of the peasant, generations of starvation behind him. "All this land given to the dead," he said angrily. "All those mounds of graves everywhere, until the Northern Plains looked like one vast cemetery! We need all the land we can spare to grow food. We never want to starve again. We were wrong to treat the dead better than the living."

It is thus everywhere in Asia: the touchstone is freedom from want. If one is hungry, what is the use of talking of other freedoms?

TOKYO

*A city surrounded by Asian tensions, Tokyo still
remains one of the gayest and liveliest capitals on earth.
It has, says Santha Rama Rau,
a unique quality of its own—
"something brash, pushing, irrepressible."*

Styles of East and West meet at a geisha party.

There is a moment of the Japanese evening, about six o'clock, that seems to suit the city of Tokyo particularly well. It is a moment when the ordered movement of the day shifts suddenly to the excitement of evening. Standing on the Sukiyabashi, a bridge in the center of town, you watch thousands of people stream past in kimonos and wooden sandals or in Western clothes. You see their intent or smiling faces as they turn towards a subway entrance, a movie house, a Japanese restaurant, or as they pause at a shop window. You listen to the streetcars racketing toward the Imperial Palace. You watch the shoeshine girls and sidewalk vendors of toys, food, newspapers. You hear the music and advertising blaring from corner kiosks. You look up to the moving lights of the Asahi Building flashing the day's news in Japanese characters, or down at the scummy water of the canal and the slow Japanese barges moving under the bridge. You are standing at the heart of a city as noisily individual as any in the world, an extraordinary mixture of cultures, ages and continents—each contributing to the Tokyo atmosphere, all fused and modified by the special personality of the city.

By Japanese standards Tokyo is a new city. Until the end of the 16th Century it was little more than a seaside village backed by a huge, windswept plain, desolate and marshy. Unlike Kyoto, which is over a thousand years old, Tokyo—or Edo, as it was called in those days—grew to national importance only during the 17th Century when the strong military ruler of all Japan, the shogun, established his headquarters here, reclaimed the Edo swamps and built the roads, harbor and bridges of the city. It didn't become the capital until 1868, after the Emperor Meiji restored imperial supremacy and changed the city's name to Tokyo. Today it is not only the most important city in Japan but, with nearly eight million people, the third largest in the world, with an emperor who represents the oldest ruling dynasty anywhere, yet it still remains a gay, vigorous, gaudy town.

Flattened and mutilated three times in three generations by a succession of fires, earthquakes and the bombings of the last war, humiliated by the recent Occupation, Tokyo still has a special vitality of its own, something brash, pushing, irrepressible. Business is here, politics are here, the biggest fortunes are made and lost here, the biggest scandals break here. From all over Japan the young and the ambitious come to Tokyo. The citizens of Kyoto may say scornfully that Tokyo is only "a branch office of New York," but in all the scattered islands the Japanese know that Tokyo is where things are happening. Tokyo decides what is chic to wear, to think, to

say, to see. It is the Big City, and its air carries a special excitement, its crowds a denser anonymity, its people a special city-bred pride.

I went to a Tokyo bar with some friends for a late drink after the theater. It was a large, shabby room where the guests sit on benches at scrubbed wooden tables. As usual, the men at the next table stared at us inquisitively, and then one of them reached across with his bottle of sake, filled our cups, invited us to drink and asked the inevitable question—where were we from? When we made the same inquiry he replied, surprised, "Tokyo, of course Tokyo."

One of us apologized and explained the silly question by adding that there were so many country people in Tokyo these days one couldn't always be sure.

The man laughed. "You can always tell the Tokyo man," he said. "He will be the only one enjoying himself."

To enjoy yourself in Tokyo you can spend thousands of yen a day or practically nothing. But on the whole, Tokyo is a big-spending, amusement-loving city geared to pleasure. Thousands of restaurants, bars and night clubs cater to its people. Hundreds of theaters, movies, girly shows, puppet plays, dancers and street singers provide their entertainment. Art shows, concerts, big sports events, shops and the endless magic of the crowded Tokyo streets, the millions of people, the lovely parts of town—all go to form the changing backdrop of Tokyo life.

They say you haven't really lived in Tokyo until you have done these things: seen the double bridge to the Imperial Palace, admired the glamorous women of downtown Tokyo, attended a geisha party, eaten river eel late on a summer night, strolled of an evening along the Ginza avenue, and been to the Kabuki-za, the biggest legitimate theater in the world. Characteristically, half these activities cost you nothing, a couple need at least a little money, and a geisha party, if you are the host, can come to anything from twenty to a thousand

Looking like members of a fat-men's ballet, three of the highly honored sumo *wrestlers make their formal bows.*

Ceilings and doorways are apt to seem too low, the lower edge of a painting will be only six inches off the floor, the glass pane in a paper window is at eye level only if you are sitting on the floor, and it offers a view in which the sky is the least significant aspect of a landscape, in which branches and bushes in the garden seem to crowd closely about you but you seldom see the tops of trees. Suddenly, a number of peculiarly Japanese arts make sense—you can understand why they create gardens composed entirely of stones, gravel and sand, for viewed from the ground, rocks can become mountains, a patch of moss a forest, a small stretch of sand the endless expanse of a desert. The technique of stunting a tree so that after fifty years of growth it is only two feet high seemed to me at first a curious but slightly repellent trick, but in a Japanese house, or in that part of the garden that you see from a window, the *bonsai* is a complete tree, almost a necessary art.

It seems odd, however, that a people with so unfailing an eye for the appropriate and the beautiful should go so far astray in Western décor. It is very fashionable just now to furnish a room or two in the Western style, but I have hardly ever seen one which isn't both dowdy and graceless, usually with a weird mixture of antimacassars and "moderne."

But with all its Westernization, the traditional Tokyo character remains unchanged, marked by a sort of carefree toughness, quick and astute, hot-tempered, even quarrelsome, but widely generous. A Tokyo man, they say, can make a hundred thousand yen in the morning and spend it before nightfall. He can always rattle money in his pocket but he is never rich.

The Japanese find these traits enormously appealing. Even now, a Japanese will tell you with pride that he is an *Edokko*, a child of Tokyo, with the city's distinctive character. When Uzaemon, the most admired and handsome actor of prewar Tokyo, appropriated part of an old saying as his personal motto—*Azuma otoko*, the Tokyo man—even his enemies had to admit that it was suitable because he fitted that Japanese ideal in every way. His favorite role was Sukeroku, a gallant, touchy, magnanimous hero who at one point makes a romantic speech listing his faults and his qualities.

"Take my name," says Sukeroku, "then you will never be refused by a courtesan in all your life. My stature is small, but my deeds are great. News of my prowess has traveled far and wide—from the toothless charcoal seller of Hachioji to the pickled-plum-like attendant at Sanya, all gossip over their tea of my exploits. I am first to lose money and last to lose a fight ....The more numerous the enemies, the greater my strength —like a dragon in water. In all of Edo I am not unknown. My crest is leaves and peonies. My domicile is cherry-flower-scented Naka-no-cho."

To this day, when they hear these words, Tokyo audiences cheer.

dollars, depending on the fame of the geisha and the extravagance of the food. However, all these things are representative of Tokyo's special life and flavor. Follow them, and you will see the Tokyo that its own citizens value most highly, the life they remember with the greatest homesickness when they are away. The great poet Basho summed it up in one of his short poems, an attenuated suggestion of mood: "Autumn. Ten years have passed. Now it is of Edo that I think when I say home.'"

Of all the facets of Japanese living, perhaps the one that most foreigners find appealing and beautiful is the Japanese house. By now, I should think, most Americans have at least a vague idea of what a Japanese house is like. They know of the almost total absence of furniture, of the deliberately unobtrusive juxtapositions of wood, grass matting and paper doors and windows, of the infinitely studied use of even five square yards of garden to give every window a lovely and varied view and to bring a carefully tailored version of the outdoors indoors.

One point, however, to which you have to adjust your eye, is the perspective of a civilization that lives on the floor. Until you get used to it you may feel clumsy in a Japanese house.

Simplicity and fine taste mark Japanese homes. On his restful veranda, Keizo Yoshiiye and his family take afternoon tea. O-cha—honorable tea—is drunk all day long, even at bedtime. Flower arranging, as traditional as the service of tea, is an art in which every Japanese lady is accomplished.

Bali

In Bali there are no ulcers, no neurotics.
According to a Balinese proverb,
if you get angry, you soon grow old.
Those who are fortunate and rich are expected
to support friends who are in difficulties.
And—on this island where art and beauty are
the elements of daily life—there is no race for fame and
no fear of the future, for, as an artist friend
told author Santha Rama Rau,
"When I am dead there
will be many to paint good pictures."

When first I was in Bali, I remarked to a Balinese friend—an old and distinguished man in the village where I stayed—that he should travel and see the world beyond his island. With surprise he replied, "I have already traveled. I went to Java when I was young."

"But that's not very far," I insisted. "Java is your closest neighbor."

"It is far enough," he said with finality. "I could see from the faces of the people that they had unhappy hearts. Their rice fields were not as beautiful as ours, and their dancing did not belong to everybody. When I came home I knew that Bali was the best place in the world."

After a good deal of traveling on several continents, I find that I agree with him.

The tiny island of Bali, among the smallest in the Indonesian archipelago, has been admired for the beauty of its people and its countryside, for the vitality of its arts, for the gentleness and charm of the Balinese nature, even for its religious exu-

berance. Even the most casual tourist can hardly fail to be pleased by the Balinese countryside. From the wonderful sandy beaches of Kuta, and the strange, stark tableland of Bali's southern promontory, the island extends northward in graded planes of rice fields and coconut groves—the typical tropical landscape—to the windy mountains of Central Bali and the sharp cliffs jutting along the north shore.

They tell you in Bali that the island has just enough of everything—enough jungles in the west for tiger-shooting; one live volcano and the high improbable perfection of the extinct Gunung Agung; a couple of lakes between the volcanoes; pine forests on the slopes of the hills; and then, with a pleasing inevitability, the rice fields and the cocoanut groves again.

But the thing I came to like best of all when I lived in Bali was the extraordinary pleasure, diversity and excitement of Balinese village life. In the years since, I have often tried to analyze just what is so appealing about day-to-day living in Bali. The people are friendly and have a sense of humor combined with a kind of tough realism that I like. The pleasures of dancing, music, gambling and cockfighting can be endlessly absorbing. Life, even without electricity, radios, newspapers, running water and other trappings of civilization, can be extremely comfortable. In a Balinese village one seems to be busy all day without time or inclination even to read. I gossiped with friends, went for long walks with the village children through Bali's incredibly beautiful rice fields, and in the evenings there was nearly always a dance, a play or puppet show within walking distance of the village. And somehow all of this seemed to give Bali the most attractive life in the world.

Of course I went back to Ubud, the village where I had lived before, to spend a few days with my best friends there—Chokorda Agung and his two wives. (Chokorda is a Balinese

The djanger *is a dance popular with Balinese boys and girls.*

title meaning, roughly, "prince," and second only to raja.) I had sent no message, but simply arrived one afternoon.

Chokorda Agung was sitting in a small pavilion atop the wall of his outer courtyard, watching the village world go by and chatting with his cousin and a couple of friends who were on their way to Bali's chief town, Den Pasar. In the usual Balinese way, they had stopped by for a visit and an exchange of local news.

A stocky, jolly man, Chokorda Agung scrambled down from the wall, laughing and calling out explanations to his friends. "I was wondering when you would return to Ubud," he said

to me. "You are married, I hear, and you have a child. A son. Very good. Your old house has others living in it, but you will stay with us until we can find you another."

"This is only for a few days," I protested.

"That is what you said the last time. Come and see the wives."

We walked through the courtyards of his *puri*—palace, the literal translation, makes it sound pretentious. Still, it is a big compound in accordance with his rank, and represents the wealth of many rice fields. I remembered the time many years ago, when we sat in his wall pavilion looking out over the *puri*, which was extraordinarily lovely in the dark blue twilight of late evening, and he had asked me casually, "Do your Indian princes have such palaces?"

I had been at a loss to describe the obviously unimagined richness, size and grandeur of Indian palaces, and had answered at last, "Not so beautiful as this."

Chokorda Agung jumped up and announced that we should pay our respects to the other Chokordas. Agung's old uncle who lived in the adjoining *puri* was sitting in his living pavilion, listening to the story of someone's troubles. Most likely the man would come to live in the *puri* and be supported by the old Chokorda until he got back on his feet. In Bali, if you have money you expect to support a number of people— relatives and friends—who are in difficulties. One of the aspects of Western life that most upsets the Balinese is what they describe as the "loneliness of misfortune"—the unwillingness to receive or give help casually. I asked a Balinese friend what would happen if a man got into trouble through his own foolishness; if, for instance, he sold his fields and went off to Den Pasar and lost all his money gambling.

"He would walk back to his village. Nowhere in Bali is too far to walk within a few days."

"But when he reached his own village—suppose he was a bad man and had no friends?"

"Nobody in Bali is without friends," was the astonished answer. "They would help him."

Chokorda Agung's old uncle politely greeted us and almost at once announced his chief news to me. He was eighty years old, but last year he had married again and now he had a three-month-old baby. "It is a good sign that an old man should have a baby. It means that the era of Kali in which we have been living is near its end. Wars and fighting will diminish and a new period of peace and fresh life will begin."

We next called on Chokorda Rahi, who is about sixty and one of the handsomest men I ever saw. He was performing his daily devotions before a small shrine at the back of the courtyard. After a few minutes he came out formally dressed in an elegant *kain*—the straight, three-yard length of batik tightly tied at the waist; he was bare-chested and wore a smartly folded headcloth embellished with hibiscus.

He called to his wife to bring out the sweet, bland rice wine that she makes herself, and while we sipped it slowly Chokorda Rahi, who forty years ago had been one of Bali's best dancers, brought me up on the local dance news. I told him that what I most wanted to see in Ubud was the *gabor*, which I remembered as the most beautiful dance I had ever seen.

"But we no longer have a *gabor*. It finished three years ago."

"Oh, what a pity!" I said, thinking sadly of the eight young girls moving through the angular, exquisite turns and flourishes of the *gabor*, dancing for the temple or for village feasts and festivals. "Can't it be revived?"

Chokorda Rahi smiled at this example of foreign irrationality. "When Ubud people want the *gabor* again it will be revived. They became bored with the *gabor*, the girls grew up and got married, the boys began working on the Ubud *gamelan*. Now we have the best orchestra in the district."

"But no more dances?"

Chokorda Rahi looked as if he doubted my sanity. "Of course there are dances," he said, "but different ones. People in Bali get bored very easily. That is our greatest security. They constantly invent new dances and sometimes revive the old ones. But competition is fierce, so the standard must be kept high, and you can't keep high standards if people are bored." He began to name the nearby villages and their specialities. "Pliatan has an excellent *legong*, and that is the oldest Balinese dance—hundreds of years old. Blangsinga has the best *kebyar* and that is only about twenty-five years old. Sayan has a good *joget bum-bum* that was invented since you were last in Bali. But people come from everywhere to hear the Ubud *gamelan*."

The Balinese seem to have very little of what I think of as "the museum mentality," no compulsion to preserve old and beautiful things. They demand more immediate vitality from their arts. They are confident that every generation will produce beautiful new things, that it is silly to waste time keeping old ones. Temples are rebuilt every twenty or thirty years, old carvings and sculpture are casually tossed out and new ones installed. This keeps the artists and artisans busy and the people interested.

Once I asked a Balinese artist why he never signed his work. He replied seriously, "It is more difficult to write my name than to paint a picture."

"But don't you want people to know your name?"

"If a man likes my pictures I will know it. Why should he also like my name?"

"What I am trying to say is, if your pictures are good and if your name is on them, then even people who have never seen you will admire you."

"They will admire the pictures."

"Listen," I said desperately, "even after you are dead perhaps your pictures will be famous and your name will be respected. Otherwise people may forget who painted them."

He smiled with that odd Balinese assurance and, entirely missing the point, said, "Don't worry, people will not forget how to paint good pictures. After I am dead there will be many to paint good pictures."

As usual, the days in Ubud were full of small events and melted into the past with bewildering speed. I visited several friends and again got used to the curiously antiseptic yet very intimate "women's talk" of Bali; the immediate question, "Are you pregnant?" the clucking sympathy when I said, "No," the prompt advice to have a baby quickly before my son is three years old. I listened with fascination to the list of Ubud girls

An older man performs the baris, *a ritual war dance.*

who had reached puberty and were eligible for love-making and marriage; and the young women who were unhappy with their husbands and what should be done about it (everything from patience to divorce, which is quite simply obtained in Bali: "no man is happy unless his wife is happy too").

Sitting informally like that in their houses, Balinese women usually wear no covering over their breasts. Or, if they are working in the fields they wear no blouse because to cover your breasts in Bali is not a sign of modesty, only of wealth. If you have so many blouses that you don't mind getting them dirty in the household or field work that almost any Balinese woman does, whatever her rank, then you can extravagantly wear them all the time. Recently the government and the Balinese council of rajas, irritated by the publicity Bali's bare-breasted women had received, announced that the tourist photographs were "undignified," and that in the future Balinese women would wear blouses. Predictably enough, the Balinese didn't take much notice of this announcement and continued to dress and behave as they always had. There are two occasions when women must always cover their breasts: any visit to a temple, and any formal ceremony or social event. However, girls of marriageable age usually wear blouses. In this, as in almost everything else, the Balinese have their own rules and their own flexibility.

On those Ubud mornings, visiting the women and asking questions, the hours slipped away. We sat on the raised pavilion floors eating bananas, cubes of papaya speared on toothpicks and sweet, gelatinous rice cakes, and talking with solid realism about the common material of most people's lives.

Once I went to hear an orchestra rehearsal and was again impressed and tired from concentrating on Bali's astonishingly strong, disciplined and inventive music. One evening Chokorda Agung said that he was going to a village half an hour away to see a dance class, and would I like to go along? The teacher, he said, was famous for his skill. A couple of the boys from the Ubud orchestra decided to come with us to keep an eye on the competition and make scornful comparisons.

After dinner we set out carrying a couple of torches, palm fronds lashed together and soaked in coconut oil, walking at the brisk Balinese pace. Chokorda Agung explained that this village, until recently, had been too poor to afford an orchestra and dancers. In the last year, however, crops had been good and they had achieved a mild prosperity so, of course, the first thing they wanted was their own dance troupe. They had hired the teacher, an old man, who was fed and housed in the village and received a fee as well. He had picked four of the most talented village girls to learn a version of the *legong*. One of the girls gave promise of being really outstanding; the others merely seemed adequate. In Bali it doesn't seem to occur to people that anyone can't dance; everybody dances, some, of course, better than others.

Soon we turned into the paths through the rice fields, walking single file by the light of the uncertain torches. On summer nights the boys would catch fireflies and slip them inside the leader's shirt where their flickering would give him an oddly luminous figure, easy to follow but not too glaring to spoil the enjoyment of the starlight reflected in the water, or the silhouetted palms. Occasionally Chokorda Agung burst into song, adding nonsense syllables to the *legong* music. "I am happy," he explained in the offhand Balinese way that reminds you how rarely you hear such a comment in other societies. As we passed each village we would hear the shrill barking of the dogs, and someone would call across the fields to know who we were and where we were going, soft disembodied voices in the darkness.

It was easy to tell that the village of our destination was poor. It had no rehearsal pavilion, and the troupe was using the shed where fruit, vegetables and cloth were sold on market days. The earthen floor had been swept clean and the dance area was illuminated with oil lamps while the *gamelan* played in a shifting semi-darkness at the far end. The little girls danced in their everyday clothes, with set, serious faces, eyes darting to match the hand gestures, concentrating intensely on the music and on the old teacher as he corrected the position of an elbow, or the fluid weaving of the head and neck. All around the shed the villagers crowded three and four deep, each wearing a faded *kain*, a shabby piece of cloth thrown with unstudied elegance around the head to produce that magnificent top-heavy look that is peculiarly Balinese, each watching to see that their money was well spent and to take pleasure in the inevitable beauty of the dance even at a formative stage.

If I had to choose the quality that most impresses me about Bali, I suppose it would be that everyone is an artist. It is the only society I know of which accepts the creation and execution of art as a usual activity. Yet on the island there are practically no artists who are "professional." Extremely few people actually earn their livings from art. Mostly they are farmers, owners of fruit and coconut trees, of cows, pigs, chickens and always of rice fields—and the major part of their day is spent working the land. But if "amateur" implies a lower artistic level, they certainly are not amateurs, for their music, dancing, painting and sculpture can reach the highest international standards. A well-known Balinese musician once told me that anyone could learn to be an artist.

"But other countries have not found it so," I argued.

"I do not know other countries, but perhaps it is because other peoples are not free in their minds."

"Well, perhaps," I said, not entirely convinced.

"Any man can be trained to be a farmer," he told me confidently. "In the same way anyone can be trained to be an artist."

"But you need talent as well for art. Few people have that."

He kept a politely disbelieving silence, and from the Balinese evidence, I was talking nonsense.

I stayed in Ubud much longer than I had intended, but eventually I had to leave and for my last two days Chokorda Agung invited some of my favorite dancers to perform in the *puri*. One of the best *penchak* dancers lived in Ubud, and one evening he came to do the brief, dramatic dance that is accompanied only by drums and cymbals and is really a stylization of the art of self-defense. The Balinese have never fought a war and their idea of fighting has taken the form only of defense, and even then in such a remote way that it has become a dance with the flimsiest reminders of its origin. The first invasion of the island was a cultural one when Hinduism was brought to Bali by Madjapahit, the great Javanese emperor who fled with his court to Bali in the 14th Century to escape the waves of encroaching Islam. The Moslem conversion, for some reason, skipped Bali, and the island still remains the only Hindu country outside India.

Forty-nine years ago when the Dutch invaded Bali, the Balinese might have been called on to fight their first war, but what actually happened is Bali's most romantically tragic story. The Dutch ships were sighted off the Balinese coast and, as they came closer, the people in the seaside villages could see the soldiers. The local raja declared that Bali must defend

Graded plains of rice fields stair-step down a Balinese hillside.

itself. All the young men of south Bali went to their houses and carefully dressed as they would for a very grand dance or a formal temple ceremony. They wore their gold-and-scarlet *kains*, wrapped their headbands with a special flourish, decorated themselves with the bravest of red flowers, and each carried a ceremonial dagger called a kris. They took a traditional cup of wine before they left their houses, and in a fantastic, glittering procession, marched down to the beach. There they formed themselves in long lines and each man, with a flash of the kris, took up a *penchak* pose and faced the enemy.

Apparently the Balinese believed that this would show the soldiers that Bali did not wish to be invaded, and that the Dutch would go away. With astonishment rather than fear they saw the Dutch open fire. When the first group of young Balinese in their scarlet-and-gold finery fell, and died on the sand, the rest of them turned their krises on themselves rather than acknowledge such an inexplicable defeat. It was probably the most incredible mass suicide in history. Bali was conquered without more than one casualty to the Dutch.

After the *penchak* dance in Ubud, I said to Chokorda Agung, "I have been counting the hours and I have only thirty-two left in Bali. That makes me very sad."

"Well," he said briskly, "there's a good cremation over near Den Pasar tomorrow; that should cheer you up."

It proved to be a wonderful way to spend an afternoon. The bodies to be cremated had been put in a series of the most improbable effigies of cows. They were made of wood and painted in frivolous colors—pink, turquoise, yellow—and embellished with curlicues of gold. One cow was black, but even that didn't look funereal because it had gilt horns, and red and white ribbons streamed from its tail, and it was decorated with garlands of flowers. A long line of women in their finery carried offerings of flowers, food and trinkets to the cremation grounds, walking with that marvelously confident Balinese grace, backs erect, heads steady; occasionally an arm smoothly raised to adjust the palm tray of offerings on the head.

The young men of the village, in gangs of twenty and thirty, picked up the cow effigies and went whirling and galloping down the road. There was a wild, hilarious mud fight among the boys in one of the rice paddies. Three different orchestras provided music—a big, full-scale *gamelan*, a bamboo orchestra and a four-toned *angklung*. At last the effigies and their contents were burned, while the older men, dressed in checkered clothes, danced a *baris jaga* and got high on rice wine.

I returned to Ubud feeling much more cheerful. I remembered the time when one of the Ubud youngsters had offered to read my palm. He held my hand open and with a grubby finger traced the letter *M* formed by the lines (most people have it). "Do you know what the *M* stands for?" he asked. "It stands for *manusia musti mati* (mankind must die), and that's all the fortune anyone needs to know." He rushed away laughing.

The Pacific

*The Pacific is the biggest physical fact on earth.
It covers a third of the world's surface, more than all
the continents combined. Its islands are home to millions
of people whose lives, Eugene Burdick believes, are
shaped by the might and the moods of the sea around
them. He suggests here something of the scope and
power and meaning of a vastness that is almost
beyond comprehension.*

By a staggering amount the Pacific is the biggest ocean of the
world. Its waves have the longest fetch of open water in which
to travel. The two deepest "deeps," the Mindanao and the
Marianas, are in the Pacific, and so are the next four deepest
"deeps." There is no other body of water which seems so
empty, in which distances loom so depressingly great. In the
early days of exploration, sailors dreaded the Pacific because its
vast distances made it certain that many of the crew would die
of scurvy, heat, suicide and assorted afflictions which seem to
grow simply out of the immensity of the place. Today, when it
is possible to barrel cleanly across the whole expanse in fifteen
hours, in a jet at 35,000 feet, passengers arriving at Hong Kong
have the slight gnawing sensation that they have defied something by making the trip so swiftly. Everywhere, among everybody in the Pacific, there is this shared sense of awe at the
brutal cosmic size of the place.

When the Pacific does show its violent side the results are
terrifying. The thin skin, passive and flat for so long, can rear
itself into the most ghastly and fearful shapes. It is like a nightmare taking liquid shape, especially if one is aboard a ship.
Gentle swells work up into towering combers which lift and
drop a ship, casually at first, then in plunges of sixty and eighty
feet. The highest wave ever authenticated was 112 feet high
and no sailor was surprised that it occurred in the Pacific. From
the trough of such waves it is *technically* true that the wave
does not blot out the world; the wave only occupies a small
fraction of the bowl of sky. But *psychologically* the huge
Pacific waves are mesmerizing. Each one looms like destruction,
and then, as the wave relents and the ship lifts to the crest and
you can see nothing but a wind-whipped, foam-flecked army
of even bigger waves advancing, the waves do seem to blot out
the rest of the sky; to command all of one's attention. You have
the capacity for only one emotion: pure fear of the Pacific.

There is no ocean where more often the log entry is made:
"Beaufort Scale: 12," meaning a hurricane speed of over
seventy-five miles an hour. Such winds, combined with the
great fetches of the Pacific, produce not only staggeringly high
waves but also a sound one can never forget or describe. Every
protrusion on a ship, even the rivet heads, will sing or howl or

Costumed as ghosts, mudmen from the Goroka uplands assemble not for battle but for an agricultural show.

hum depending on its shape. Signal lanyards, which have been hanging loose for months, will draw tight as violin strings and then give off a dangerous fierce humming. When they break, one by one, they instantly snap out into the wind and become as stiff as rods. At some point the ocean itself starts to give off a sound: the great fundamental clash of wave trains colliding with one another, the soft unendurable suck of foam, the hiss of wave tops suddenly converted into liquid shrapnel. The sight of the Pacific lashed into a kind of Brobdingnagian madness, at war insanely with itself, is chilling. But at the height of the chaos there is a kind of visual relief: the face of the ocean disappears in a haze of water which looks precisely like smoke. The awful war of wind and water goes on, but one cannot see it.

When the face of the Pacific changes the consequences are just as awesome for land dwellers. Old-timers tell of watching typhoons pull coconuts off trees and send them shooting like cannon balls across the sky. As the ferocity increases whole rows of trees will be wrenched loose and disappear into the sky in orderly intervals. Rivers, under the force of wind and tide, will back up and pour water into the surrounding countryside at precisely the moment that mountainsides turn into liquid mud and start to flow toward the sea. Paddy fields, nipa huts, asphalt roads, sandalwood trees, the slimy outpouring of fish preserves are all stirred in a gigantic mass. The coral atolls themselves survive because their rocklike roots reach to the bottom of the sea, but waves wash completely over them and great chunks of coral, often weighing several tons, will be torn loose and flung about.

Most of the time, of course, the Pacific seems a calm and orderly place; the trades blow, the currents pour in their endless cycle, the sun is hot and even, the clouds are predictable. Its sheer size, however, conceals the fact that it has the most restless, mercurial and raw personality of any of the Seven Seas. Strange islands bubble and steam into existence and then subside. There are the awful cracks of doom like Krakatoa, the island that went up with its thousands of people in a great explosion. Large annual streams of fish will suddenly vanish and then reappear. One half of an island will receive a rainfall so intense that rowboats in the harbor sink beneath the feet of men who cannot bail out the downpour fast enough—and the other side of the island will have the stark lunar look of a desert. In the Solomons recently, a brand-new radar- and radio-equipped government ship disappeared without a trace, and although there was regret there was little surprise. Some thousands of sailors live today who watched a World War II destroyer try to maneuver in waves which, under the pressure of typhoon winds, increased their "length" (the distance from crest to crest), until finally there came a wave which lifted the destroyer high, poised her on a crest of salt water and broke her back as if the wave had been solid steel. There was a splinter of time when the sailors from other ships could see both halves of the destroyer falling through midair. Only a

Outriggers head home for Bora Bora, in French Oceania.

handful of her men survived. The pressures of wind and sea were such that had any of the accompanying destroyers altered course, even by a degree, they might have suffered the same fate.

The traveler in the Pacific will see very little of what goes on below the skin of the ocean. If he goes to Kona on Hawaii, or to any of the resorts behind the Great Barrier Reef of Australia, he can see into the upper layers either by skin-diving or by peering through a water glass into the life of the reef. But most travelers will see only what is above the surface of the ocean, perhaps not realizing that everything above water is determined by what lies below. In this great expanse of salt water the land is utterly determined by the sea. Everything, from the growth of pineapples in Hawaii to the fertility rate among Tongans and the dances of the Solomon Islanders, is determined by the sea. Were the temperature of the Pacific to rise or fall even slightly, were the currents to shift their directions by even a few degrees, cataclysmic changes would take place. This knowledge is bred into the bones and blood of everyone in the Pacific; it is part of the personality of the Pacific.

Take, for example, the two types of islands which exist in the Pacific. They could not be more different in appearance or in origin. One is the result of a cosmic patience; the other is always born in some sort of natural catastrophe.

An atoll is a misery to describe and stupendous to behold. It is simply a ring of coral which has been building up for thousands of years out of the dead bodies of tiny coral polyps. These dead husks calcify, and each foot of coral growth represents endless generations of polyp life. Because the coral polyp can live only in salt water, the atolls seldom rise high above sea level. Some of the newer ones are literally awash at every high tide. The older ones have developed sand by the constant motion of sea and wind, but the soil, if any, is usually poor. Occasionally a deep convulsion of the sea will jerk a coral atoll high out of the water, and this "uplifted coral" produces such

places as Tongatabu. Usually the atoll is circular and encloses a lagoon, which is a great shallow shoal of coral. Almost inevitably there is a seabeach, a great rugged shoulder of coral which the atoll pushes in the direction of the prevailing wind and sea to protect itself. Here the surf comes smashing in. On the lagoon-beach side the surf is almost nothing. There is a kind of monumental aspect to an atoll, but it lies almost entirely beneath the water. The slight ring of coral that rises above the surface represents eons of calcified life and death; it is the tip of an enormous structure of matter reaching down to a plateau in the ocean bed. The atoll itself seems almost trivial; a monstrous expenditure of life and energy to produce so small a thing.

But *seeing* an atoll is something else. Most Westerners when they see a place of beauty experience a "shock of recognition"; they have been prepared for it. We behold Chartres, the Grand Canyon, the skyline of Manhattan, Notre-Dame, the Valley of the Loire, the Rhine River, the Matterhorn—and we know what each is like before we see it. Post cards and motion pictures and parents have told us what to expect. We see each sight and it is beautiful, but beautiful as we expected it to be. We get out our cameras with a slight sense of duty, not with a surprised thrill.

But let the traveler see the atolls of the Tuamotus or the Societies or the Australs for the first time and he is stunned. The atoll is foreign to our eyes, to our notions of aesthetic balance, to our standards of color and balance and symmetry.

Say, for example, that you first see an atoll from the air. Swooping down on it from a great distance, you will note the sharp classic stems of the coco palms. This is a wonderfully simple tree, it rises in a curve and then breaks into a burst of fronds. By some prescience the coco palms arrange themselves nicely along an atoll. Abruptly the deep bottomless blue of the open sea ends and the reef begins. It is only when the sea-blue ends that you realize how deep, pure, almost black a hue it is; it absorbs the sun like a vast sponge, it sends back no softened colors. As the water shoals rapidly, new shades of the blue appear—unfamiliar, unnamed primitive colors. And then, in a flashing second, the entire expanse of the atoll is visible, the new colors claw their way into the sky, make a physical assault on the eyeball and brain and past training. The colors are astonishing. The mind fights to tone them down, to moderate the chromatic attack, to re-establish some sort of control.

The eye picks out the familiar and fastens on it with a kind of desperation—the tin roof of a trader's hut, the neat rectangular shape of a pier, the nipa huts of a village, an occasional path, a parade ground, the whitewashed school with children playing in the yard, dogs running in yapping circles. All of this is pedestrian, sometimes even dingy.

The colors, however, transform everything. The seabeach is generally made up of many blues, owing to the splintering and irregularities in the coral: azure, lapis lazuli, pure cobalt, occasionally a smoky-blue twist that runs like a river through

For a celebration, a Mt. Hagen maiden wears fantastic makeup, cowrie shell necklace and eagle plumage.

the deeper hues. Each color, however, seems to be primary, to have an integrity and intensity of its own. There is no admixture of the blues, no running together of colors. Each patch will have distinct limits as if aware of itself and proud.

The raised part of the atoll is tawny and green and lined with an edging of white sand. The lagoon is shallow, often with knobs of coral that rear themselves above the water. Here is a green and white world. But again the greens have an almost weird clarity; a fierce, pure intensity. The white is sand and it ranges from a dead-white when the sun is directly overhead to a dazzling crystal-like brightness when the sun is lower. During the day the whole lagoon is made up of these shimmering combinations of green and white, which intertwine with one another, take on different shapes, but are always distinct and pure. There are long slits of creamy green, banks of jade which tremble when the wind moves over the water, circles of bitter green, a tongue of striking emerald. The greens are liquid and they move, but they are all strange. There are no familiar greens, none of the weaker and more civilized colors. Everything shimmers and is deliquescent, but it is also primitive and raw.

As the sun goes down, the greens in the lagoon go out abruptly, one at a time, and the great flat stretch of water takes on an even, deep and flawless green that looks as solid as a vast thin sheet of crystal. When a fish jumps, you suck in your breath, expecting a high crackling noise as the brittle surface is shattered. But nothing happens, and soon the lagoon turns black and the white rim of sand comes up luminous as old bone. The coconut trees merge into a solid line and bend over the water in a short luscious curve.

I once flew over an atoll with a distinguished French painter who is also extremely articulate. We took off from Papeete, where he had arrived only two days before. Papeete and Moorea he found attractive, not wildly exciting but different. We flew for two hours and then the amphibian plane began to circle a group of atolls which happened to be deserted. We circled for five minutes before I noted that his eyes were closed and his face was pale. I asked what he thought of the view.

His words came back bleached, diminished, tiny. "No more. Let's go back. Something like this is bad for me. It burns out the fine artistic nerve endings which civilization develops." He wet his lips. "Some things are too primary, too violent, too raw."

"But it's gorgeous," I said energetically, reaching for the only word which came to mind.

"Exactly. Gorgeous, fantastic, spectacular," he replied, his eyes still squeezed shut. "Even wonderful and savage. But it is not art." Then he added wistfully, in a whisper, "I think."

He left two weeks later from Papeete without leaving the inside of Quinn's bar and his hotel. He was a man with courage, but he also wanted to preserve his training and his balance, and he was sure, with an iron certitude, that the Pacific would bleed him white.

SOUTH
and
LATIN
AMERICA

V. S. Pritchett
John Houghton Allen
David Dodge

V. S. Pritchett is, in the opinion of many of his colleagues, the most skillful observer and reporter of our time. He is also a remarkably sentient and perceptive writer, ideally equipped to make this journey of exploration into modern South America.

South America

ECUADOR

In Ecuador the ancient Inca highway begins at Quito. But the city is graced, not with relics of a proud empire, but with monuments to its conquerors. Here in the high thin air of the Andes is preserved the essence of Spanish baroque civilization.

Ecuador is a small country and, like the others of the Spanish corner, it is divided into three parts: the tropics, the tableland and the peaks. Between ten and fifteen per cent of its people are white of Spanish blood, with some Central European refugees; the remaining 2,000,000 odd (they guess) are Indian, mestizo, Negro or mulatto. There are also a few Asiatics. In Ecuador you stand in soundless and breathless leagues of acacia scrub, among the volcanoes and, for the first time, among Indians. From Quito to Cuzco and on to La Paz, in the Tibet of South America, you are always at 10,000 feet or more, breathing thin air, deafened by the hammers in the head, and a little mad. The skin cracks, the voice goes husky. You stare back at the expressionless stare of Mongolians who seem to have been cut out of mahogany by an imperceptible dry wind that is as fine as a knife. These men and women, sexually distinguishable only because the woman has a little mahogany baby sticking its head out of the blanket on her back, are the dispossessed heirs and slaves of the Inca empire, and now the bond servants of the feudal estates of Ecuador and Peru. (The Inca empire lasted four hundred years and stretched from Quito down to Chile, where the Araucanian Indians fought it off.)

The Indians squat, still as stone, against the walls under the arcades of Quito, motionless in their ponchos, oddly sophisticated in their brown trilby (fedora) hats. They seem to possess the city by force of peaceable but perhaps meaningful vigil. They camp in the markets, they cry "Oh, Father" or "Oh, Mother" as they kneel before the altars in the churches.

Quito is the most Spanish-looking city in South America and architecturally the richest. The fine things of all this Pacific coast are survivals. Earthquakes have destroyed city after city. Travelers complain of the lack of Gothic architecture but— who knows?—there may have been Gothic brought down in a cloud of rubble three or four hundred years ago. The wonderful churches of Quito are now drenched in the Inca gold of the baroque. The Spanish artists came out here at the beginning of the 16th Century and (it is evident) there must have been Moorish converts among the conquerors. You look up at magnificent ceilings of cedar conceived in the Moorish geometry and honeycomb. The noble doorway of the Compania is in the full flourish of Spanish baroque; San Francisco echoes the Escorial outside Madrid; the tiled domes of churches and cathedral recall Valencia and Saragossa and, as the day ends, you hear the rancorous Spanish bells.

In Quito there was gold for coloring the decorative orgy and there were hardwoods for carvers of pulpits and chapel rails, choirs and organ lofts; for the sculpturing of angels' wings and climbing flowers and peeping cherubs and saints that seem to waltz like people in a painted enchantment. Fancifully they carved the nipples of fertile women or the faces of demons upon the choir stalls; with naïve terror they cut the wing and eye and claw of the condor or of some mythical bird; under the severe thumb of the classical master, his Indian craftsmen copied the classical Spanish austerity. In Mexico, where the Spaniards were extirpating a bloody religion and felt themselves more violently challenged, they allowed the

Timeless Otavalo is a quiet country market town.

shake to dust in their earthquakes. You see the Indians at a country market like Otavalo, stirring their stewpans or eating some yellow mess, one or two eating, one or two against the wall brooding, one or two stretched out dead-drunk. They have been at the market since the hard cold dawn. They stand before their sacks of beans, their yellow and speckled corn, their heaps of newly sheared wool, the wool they have dyed and woven into ponchos, blankets and scarves, before their trays of golden-looking glass beads. These, coiled many times round the neck or dangling in great loads, indicate the wealth of the woman who wears them. The women, in their heavy, white, basinlike hats, sit and stare across their earthenware, their carven bulls, their heaps of purple pineapples and tropical fruits. These markets are crowded and silent—though you hear the loud-speaker in the modern market—and there will be no sound but the whisper of bare feet on the ground. Speak to the Indians and few can answer, for they do not speak Spanish, but they will utter an obsequious and bashful twittering.

By midday they will be drunk on *chicha*, the sugared alcohol made from maize, or on the alcohol that has been collected in a hole cut in the stems of the aloes which stand along the roads of the wilderness like swords. A pole with a white rag sticking out of a doorway is the sign of the *chicha* seller; a red flag denotes not the Communist Party but the butcher; a bunch of flowers, the seller of coca leaves. There are sacks of these dried leaves in the market. They are bitter-tasting and the Indians add lime leaves to sweeten them. The coca comforts, but the lime dries and draws the mouth. Out comes the flask of *aguardiente* and the market place is harmlessly drugged and drunk at once—harmlessly because the Indian, unlike the mulatto, does not get out his knife, but rolls stiffly about with the innocence of an un-co-ordinated marionette.

There is continual controversy about the evils of coca chewing and the wickedness of the landlords who grow it and the governments that allow it to be grown. The Incas knew the power of the coca leaf. The rulers controlled its use. They reserved it for soldiers; for the wonderful runners who carried news and royal commands along the mountain highway from Quito to Cuzco; and for their priests. To the soldiers and runners the coca leaf gave energy in the thin and exhausting air of the high mountains; in religion, the leaf was used only in those annual ceremonies which required religious ecstasy. The coca leaf was rare and valued. The Spaniards broke the monopoly and allowed it to everyone, and now it has become the general drug that takes the mind of the Indian off his continual hunger.

The Inca highway ran from Quito down to Cuzco. You can sometimes see it scratched and zigzagging up the flanks of the mountains—miles of it are still paved—and imagine the relays of royal runners who brought the news of the Spaniards' arrival over a thousand miles in a day or two to the Emperor Atahualpa, whom Pizarro captured and murdered.

In Ecuador umbrellas grow on trees—or jungle vines.

Indian craftsmen less freedom. In any case, Mexico felt the first passion of the Spanish impulse; South America felt the second, less exalted wave. Pizarro was not Cortes and the Indians were less bloody. The madonnas have sometimes an Indian look and are, at any rate, less fair than the Mediterranean goddesses; the Christs bleed at the knees for, no less than the Spaniards, these people delight in the sight of blood or at least do not show the usual northern aversion to it.

A great many of the Indians in Ecuador are the tied serfs on the great estates. They live in clay-colored adobe huts which

PERU

*In Lima and in Cuzco the courtliness of the
old Spanish tradition still lives on,
buttressed now by modern wealth.
But high above, in the solitude of savage mountains,
stands the lost city of Machu Picchu,
a silent reminder of an almost forgotten civilization.*

An ancient Incan funeral mask.

Under its pan of gray cloud Lima is Londonish. Its pavements are always wet and greasy in the small hours at which, inevitably, you set out on all South American journeys. Lima ought to be an oven, but the cloud from the Humboldt current has made it livable. You sweat in the sun, but there is a deadly cold and continual flutter of air in the ears; you shiver in the heat. It is really a pleasant climate made for civilization, like the climate of Chile or the Mediterranean, but you have to get used to it and use the Peruvian cunning. I was ill in Lima. The Peruvian doctor said, "Don't go to the mountains yet." The maid said: "Don't go out today. There is a cloud."

It is a city of flowers. In the cloisters of the University—the oldest in South America—you might be in one of the ecstatic patios of Seville; in the gardens and avenues that run down to the sea at Miraflores, along the smart *corniche* and in the gardens of the hotels, the tropical trees blossom heavily and all blooms are brilliant and large. You walk at a saunter, taking peaceful breaths. You are breathing something else. What is it? It ought to be the serenity of the Mediterranean, but here, in Peru, the serenity is what they call "the Pacific sadness," a loneliness in the midst of well-being that comes, perhaps, of looking across a sun-slashed ocean for thousands of miles, into nothing. The Andes lock out the wars and troubles of the world.

Earthquakes, sudden incursions of new wealth from oil at Talara, from mines, precious stones, wool, tea and cotton, have destroyed a great deal of the old Lima, with its single-story houses with the iron-grilled windows, the high doors, balconies, the painted porches and the inner courts. Round the pretty square of the Pueblo Libre with its remarkable National Museum of Anthropology and Archaeology—it has the richest archaeological collection in Peru, indeed in South America—and in the streets by the bull ring, you see the old city. Life here is simple and shuttered. It goes on in courtyards, roofed by matting against the sun, where the smoke of the charcoal fires rises and the flowers grow and the mulattoes and cholos sprawl with their hats over their eyes and the tarry-haired women call out.

The old Lima had its fantastics. There is a pagoda-like building near the bull ring, built (I was told) by a jealous rich man so that his wife could sit at the top of the painted-glass tower and, from this purdah, see the bullfight for nothing.

Of course, the fine, new white schools and popular suburbs, the streets of painted villas, the mixture of architectural styles copied from the Californian and Mexican and the half-timbered Tudor English, are dramatically modern. They indicate that (with Venezuela and Colombia) Peru is solid in the South American boom and by solid we mean it can deal abroad in foreign exchange and not be on the rocks like Bolivia, shaking like Chile, unbalanced like the Argentine and living breathlessly off its prospects like Brazil. Oil! There is a sigh of relief. And if not oil, there are mines hardly touched, in the mountains.

No South American state speaks well of another. To the rest, Peru is at once privately fantastic, outwardly formal in the Spanish manner, stuck fast in pride and the past. Peru has some of the Spanish pomp, the lazy official pride, the obstinate and moneyed addiction to custom. Pizarro founded Lima; he is buried in the cathedral. The city was the solid administrative capital of Spanish rule.

The struggle between the outlying regions and the center goes on in all South American states. Here, in Peru, where distances are great, local corruption and indifference is the inevitable result of overpowering central government. The Inquisition looked after religious heresy; but Lima had the administrators and the 17th Century courtiers, the vested interest in the distribution of trade that Spain imposed, and even the caste system that put the creole (or colonist) under the thumb of the Spaniard. Spain had even the fantastic notion that it could reconquer Peru as late as 1866, after Peru had known independence for a generation.

There is a somnolent weightiness in the Spanish inheritance, the habit of sitting impregnably on wealth, the strengthening of related families into nations within the nation. Brash, pushful, Italianized people from the Argentine come up to Lima and find society impenetrable. They play polo with the rich but never find friendship. As in Spain, casual encounters

Machu Picchu in the Peruvian Andes. Remote, mysterious, heaven-high, the last Inca citadel looks down upon the sacred Urubamba River storming through a corridor of granite.

everywhere; in the home never. The young girls are chaperoned. There is even a fixed day upon which sea bathing begins; it would be solecism, vagrancy, a sin, to bathe a day sooner. Custom, custom. Lima has its tea hour, as elegant as it used to be in Madrid in the '20's. The rich women and their beautiful daughters sit stiffly, speechlessly, dressed by Fath and Dior, manacled in gold, set off by diamonds and emeralds in that silent and most deadly of all warfares of women: the warfare of jewelry. Each diamond is an accurate shot at neighboring diamonds in the room; even more it is brilliant with contempt for the luxury of Buenos Aires, Rio or New York. The flash of a sugar estate answers the challenge of an oil well or a mine, the fortune of a hacienda weighs itself against the emeralds of a fortune cut out of the Andean rock.

Behind the glitter are the ruthless struggles of politics, the suppressed political parties. And as the tea party goes on, the German, American and English engineers and commercial men go boisterously past the tables—having already drunk too much—foreign capitalism that has built the railroads, the factories, drilled the wells and opened up the country—and with intelligence and disdain the clever and lethargic Peruvians watch them and then drive off in their Cadillacs to enjoy themselves, or sit playing poker dice and sending out messages by the page boys.

And, being Spanish, Lima has kept the bullfight, where the other countries, except Venezuela, are either bored by it or have forbidden it. The bull ring is across the bridge at the top of the city, under the mountain that looks like Vesuvius in the sun-shot haze, that gives a veil of blue heat when the cloud gives way to the sun and the skin begins to burn. I went twice to the bull ring, first when it was empty and they were sweeping the sand and cleaning it for the *corrida* on the next day, in the company of an excitable Argentine who, with the push and intensity of his race, wanted to know the points.

"Look now," said the shameless Argentine, a serious man and a polo player, a colonel in the army and an old enemy of Perón—which was why he had left his country—"look now," he said to the mulatto guide. "Explain to me. I know nothing. I am the bull now—" he crouched—"you are the picador. Now you try to get the lance—where? Here? On the shoulder. Right. Then why does the crowd whistle with disapproval? What have you done wrong?" "Gone in too deeply," said the mulatto in his hoarse kind voice. Up and down the alley, the mulatto in his shabby jeans and singlet was playing the sporting colonel, making veronicas and coming in for the moment of truth. "Good, now I understand," the Argentine said. The mulatto looked with dignity and grave irony at the excitable man and winked at his mistakes. "Come and have a bottle of beer," said the colonel.

We saw the bulls arrive in their packing cases. We sat sweating in a bar on a street noisy with grinding trams and a jukebox. It was the day for getting ready for the annual fiesta, the religious procession of the Señor de los Milagros, the image of the Christ that was strangely preserved in one of Lima's disastrous earthquakes. The mulatto, a huge, heavy man in his fifties was one of those who would bear the image for his parish, expiating—as he gently said—his sins.

That night the procession shuffled round the streets, the crowds blackened, the booths of the open-air fair were lit up; over the loud-speakers came the voice of a popular priest in the full, angry roar of Spanish imprecation, scarifying the sins of the multitude and making their skins tingle with the dread of eternal punishment. It was a blasting and relentless voice whipping up the lethargy of the passing crowds in the night.

Peruvians, like Spaniards, get the bull fever young. A boy of ten beside me was disputing the finer points of the *corrida* with his father, but both were seized, as the whole ring was seized, by that short, frightening and unanimous gasp of admiration which punctuates the intensely critical calm of the bullfight with short crises of masculine ecstasy. There was a Venezuelan who circled like a heavenly messenger with unfailing banderillas, but who was uncertain in all else and unnerved at the kill. Just before he thrust home the sword, some man bawled out to him, "Do better than last time!" Even the easygoing Peruvians have inherited the Spanish gift for total abuse.

There was a young, plump Portuguese in pale blue who looked as if he lived on sweet cakes and had been trained for the ballet, who swept us all by his courage and his art. He fought like a rocket breaking and blooming into star after star. There was a young Spaniard, new to Lima, wonderfully indifferent as he dominated the bull. When the bulls got bored and the fighting went all over the place, Lima shouted out satirically, as Seville does, "Music! Music!" asking the band to play in contempt. And scarves, coats, purses, handbags went down in showers in the moments of triumph. There is one tall gentleman of great dignity in Lima who sends his straw hat spinning into the ring when he is pleased, and it goes spinning faultlessly back to him, so that it is never off his head for more than twenty seconds. For twenty seconds that man lives.

The visitor to Cuzco flies there in two or three hours from Lima, spends a few days there, takes the light railway to Machu Picchu and then flies back from Cuzco to Lima. You can travel to Cuzco by train—they supply oxygen at the great altitudes—but it takes a long time. I flew there. It is the most exciting short flight in South America.

On this flight the Andes give us one more sensation. We have flown beside them and kept our distance; now it remains for us to fly over them, to exchange voluptuousness for a terror that, at the breaking point, suddenly becomes the sublime. We have looked down upon the patterns of desert or plain and have had the impression of seeing a mind in the earth itself and of reading its hieroglyph. But when we cross the Andes they rise up and assault the flier. When we cross those hundreds of miles of peaks and brown ranges, the rock wilderness that lies between viceregal Lima and Pizarro's Cuzco, it is like flying over the blades of knives. Shoulders and summits, ravines, whole systems of them by the thousand are spread about us and are not exhausted at the hard horizon.

The Plaza de Toros in Lima draws huge, enthusiastic crowds.

It is a sea of solid iron and almost without feature. There may be a blue-eyed lake, like single, hard sapphire dropped there; an enameled vein of green in a ravine so deep that it might be a mere snick in the bed of the sea; but these are glints, like malice rather than beauty, in a world that is obdurate, upheaving and unconquerable beyond our conception. The sight hurts the whole body and appalls the mind; we are so high above it that we fear we could be whisked off the curve of the world into outer space. Suddenly, rising out of the roof, the snow peaks jut up one by one in the higher courts of the sky like cruel kings. There is hierarchy even among rock. We approach them clumsily bumping; we pass slowly between their silence. They stand, withered and distraught, caparisoned with snow. We have been clambering over rock walls for hours, and now, hardly beyond the touch of our wing, we come into these white and royal presences. They look as mad as Lear and as lonely. Slowly they pass—for it is they who seem to move away, not ourselves—with, perhaps, a rag of cloud drawn after them like ermine whipped away with the fretfulness of old kings. And there behind us, they wait. The horrible thing is that they wait: we have got to return. It is not a place, you feel, as the pilot finds his way between them toward the bare and winding stairway into the valley of Cuzco, where you would choose to hear one of those motors stop. These ravines are solitudes and are—in a word whose meaning we had not realized till now—savage. Now we can say we have seen the savage with our eyes, the landscape of the condor.

We landed at Cuzco in the dust and sunlight and, taking the tip of those who know how cautiously one must make the change from sea level to the high altitudes of the Andes, I went straight to bed for a couple of hours. Cuzco looked as if it had been bombed. Five years before there had been an earthquake. Builders were still working on the colonial houses where the Spanish copy has been imposed on the great locked stones of the Incas. In the baroque churches the belfries had crumbled, the walls split and the ceilings brought down. In 1950 two thirds of the buildings in a city of 80,000 had been made uninhabitable. If the people had not gone in thousands to a football match—football at that altitude!—the casualties would have been far greater.

The Pacific coast is the region of earthquakes, from the tiny quakes that wake you up for a second or two in the small hours of the morning, the sudden rattle in the day that shakes the roofs, the windows and the floors and brings down stones and dust on the mountain roads, to the catastrophe that occurs once or twice in a generation.

The aspect of Cuzco is perfectly Castilian, in the austerity of its arid mountain setting and its bare brown tilled fields, which are marked by the poplars the Spaniards brought from the dusty roads of Castile. Pizarro entered Cuzco in 1533. He had marched his paltry army of 177 men up from the coast to conquer an empire and capture Atahualpa, its ruler. The Spanish genius is the gambler's. Pizarro, remembering the boldness of Cortes in Mexico, got his blow in first and took the Inca by bloody stratagem; and then, after a terrible march over the Andes, arrived in Cuzco, the capital of the kingdom. He had fought his way there, but he had murdered Atahualpa by then and arrived a conqueror.

Pizarro came to Cuzco in November, when all is brown and the air is clean and cold under a changeless sky and when a white cloud will stand still like a piece of sculpture; and the landscape must have reminded the conqueror of the land he had known in his youth. Spanish and yet not Spanish. For he saw the heavy, low-built Inca temples and houses, built of huge blocks of stone, the temples shining with walls of gold and silver inside.

Those implacable walls of the Incas, beautiful in their mortarless, ingenious interlocking, became foundations on which the Spanish manors and cloisters, the Spanish arcades and green and brown balconies, the rich Spanish churches, have been built. Here and there, the religious symbols of the Incas are embossed on a building; the cabalistic sign leaps like a serpent close to the Spanish coat of arms or the richly ornamented doorway.

The Inca stone blocks are a timeless and simple geometry, one of the fundamental inventions of the human race. What hands first moved them? We see their silvery bloom in the streets of Cuzco, in the fortress of Sacsahuaman, and in their unanswering mystery at Machu Picchu. Old explorers of the Andes regret that Hiram Bingham's almost impassable mule track from Machu Picchu has now been replaced by a light railway which wanders down the gorges and connects the Indian villages, and that vulgar tourists can get to a lost city that is lost no more. But is Pompeii the worse for being visited?

You journey to Machu Picchu—some fifty miles north of Cuzco—by rail, through high and flowering valleys of broom. Then the mountains close in, the corridors of the gorges begin. You shiver at 10,000 feet and stare at the sky for a sight of the condor that never comes; you drop down into the dripping tropical forest that clots the air. The mountains shut you in. The train whistle sends echoes bounding from wall to wall; outside their huts, the Indians stand, dirty, bedraggled, the last hopeless heirs of the race, or trot in panic on their donkeys along the track in front of the train. You follow the "river with three names," the Urubamba, that storms over its boulders for tens of miles. You see the rope bridges spanning it; and then, when the gorge divides and you are at the bottom of the mountain hole, a furry cone of rock shoots upward for a couple of thousand feet. On the wall opposite, out of sight from below, is the lost city, the condor's nest. There, terraced on the summit, with its altars open to the sky, its ruined windows turned for the rising and setting sun, its worshipers gone, is Machu Picchu.

This is one of the supreme sights of the Andes and one of the unsurpassed archaeological finds and mysteries of South America. Not even a swarm of tourists could take from the height and the surrounding mountain mass their overpowering communication of solitude. The silence belongs to the earth and the rock, and the human voice and person are trivial beside it. We know, in any case, that one step beyond the precincts and we could be lost, starved and infallibly dying. The most insensitive of us is forced to see here that he has come to an end, that a town not only can die but that all memory and knowledge of it can pass out of mind.

Machu Picchu was discovered in 1911 by Hiram Bingham, the American archaeologist. He climbed the precipice and found the ruins buried in undergrowth. At first they were thought to be purely Inca, but then pottery was found which suggested at least part of the town had been built in pre-Inca times. There is no tradition to say how the town came there or why it was abandoned, yet it can have been no more than four hundred years ago that one of the Inca princes fled there with his nobles from Pizzaro. A very large number of female skeletons have been found and some have thought the prince fled there with the Virgins of the Sun. The huge stones of the walls, the cells, the temples and the altars and places for observing the rising and setting of the Sun God stand smooth and silvered and perplexing. Did the Spaniards not know of the place? Did they never march up the gorge? And why did the town die? Did the inhabitants perish of some plague? Did they simply die out, from hunger or old age? One pictures, as one stands there, the last aging handful and then the last human being of all among the dead. Yet it may not have been like that. The people may have gone down to the jungle of Peru; they may have been wiped out in war.

Pre-Inca pottery has been found in Machu Picchu. Legend overlaps legend, as one master race with its new propaganda overlays another in Indian history. On the topmost stone of Machu Picchu we see with awe "the stone that measures the sun." First it is the moon who sends her child, the sun, in the form of a jaguar to beget a child with an Indian woman and create the race. Centuries pass and then it is Viracocha, the god who comes out of Lake Titicaca to create heaven, earth and men, but forgets to create light. In darkness men destroy each other and Viracocha turns them to stone. Then, trying again, he creates Manco and Oello, son and mother or brother and sister, to redeem the fallen world and to create a civilization of which perhaps the triumphant Incas before Pizarro were the descendants. The scholars dispute, the archaeologists dig, there is no written tradition. We can only know that the Indians of today, living on a little maize and sometimes a bit of dried guinea-pig meat, are worse off than the Indians of those times who discovered and grew the potato and made maize flour, bread, drink and honey. They used the seed, the leaves and the roots of the aloe. From the roots they made soap and, even now, you see the Indian women beating their washing with the aloe leaves so that the soapy pulp froths out. Even now you find the hole in the root where the sap gathers and ferments and from which comes the liquid they boil or used to boil for treating their black hair. Their dyes come from plants, their wool from the llamas. A constant sight on these roads is of women trotting along with their distaffs, frantically spinning their wool as they go.

Death is familiar to the Indian: the Incas—as you can see in the wonderful museum at Lima—mummified their dead and buried them in a sitting posture, binding the bodies in grave-clothes that are now spidery with age. From its cobweb of clothing the shrunken face, oddly Hindu in appearance, gazes back at us with cynical intensity. The dead person's spirit placated by being buried with his favorite things, he does no

How large is an Indian boy in the shadow of the Andes?

ill to his survivors. The Jivaro Indians of the Amazon shrink heads. In the fields you sometimes see a ring of men and women squatting in the evening outside some village. It is a wake. They are eating the dead person's favorite dishes and soon they will sing and, as the *chicha* works on them, they will dance and get drunk. In a year's time they will mark the anniversary of the dead person to fend off any ill intent of his spirit.

I saw the priest—a hearty Irish-American from Chicago—rapidly baptizing the newborn babies in the church on the plain outside Lake Titicaca. The mothers knelt on the floor afterward, took their babies that looked like little skinned rabbits, bound them in their shawls, slung them onto their backs with the swift skill of a lifetime, and trotted off to the market.

"Most of them die very soon," said the priest, "but if the babies are not baptized before they die the parents think their spirits will return in the form of hail and destroy the crops. And now," he said, "I've got to bless all those clothes, the clothes of the dead, so as to free them from evil spirits until the next anniversary."

"As far as I can figure it out," said the man from Chicago, "their life is a system of elaborate insurance policies."

CHILE

Isolated between an immense mountain wall
and the sea, Chile is safe from the rest of the world,
if not always secure from the cataclysms of nature.
It is alternately grim and graceful.
But among the countries of South America, it is the
one that almost became modern
before the 20th Century swept past.

You take off from La Paz for the thousand-mile flight south to Santiago, the capital of Chile. The moment you have flown off the tableland of Bolivia—over the Chilean nitrate desert, over the largest copper mine in the world, lost in its vast pitiless amphitheater of rock and sand—the plane turns toward the kinder sun of the subtropics and you are in a different world.

Once again you see how irreconcilably the South American states differ. Peru is courtly; Bolivia is barbaric. In Chile the Spanish spirit has been diluted: Central Chile has the classical grace of the Mediterranean; Southern Chile of the lakes, with its cool and rainy climate and its blossoms hung against the snow mountains, suggests a Japanese print, or again, because of its plantations of firs, some part of Germany or Scandinavia; in the extreme south the cold and harshness of the uninhabitable country are Antarctic.

I have heard the Chileans called the English of South America. There is a long tradition of English settlement there, and a strong link with the British navy. I have also heard the Chilean described as frank, uncouth, masterful, ill-mannered and efficient. He has no equal in South America as a soldier and is, in the sense that the Northern races understand this, a strong character. That is, a man of action, more honest, less sensitive than is general among Latins; less subtle, and with less of that "delicacy" which is one of the fundamental qualities of the South American, and that marks him off from the Northerner in the New World or the Old. In Peru and Bolivia, and even in Ecuador, the Spanish stock is being Indianized; but in Chile, the Araucaman Indian is being Europeanized. But if we left the primitive in Bolivia for something that is nearer the modern world in spirit, the modern world of Chile is, to be frank, circa 1900. The Chilean has the island temperament. He looks out from the pretty harbor restaurants of Valparaiso—the food in Chile is the best in South America—and sees the Japanese merchant vessels lying there. This long narrow country, shut off in a narrow strip 2600 miles long and, on the average, 110 miles wide between the Andes and the South Pacific, is far away from the rest of the world.

And there are economic reasons for Chile's isolation. The opening of the Panama Canal cut down the voyages round the Horn. This took away the trade of Valparaiso, where every sailor in the world once called. The manufacture of synthetic nitrates has eaten into the wealth of the nitrate deserts, the copper market has dropped. Less than a quarter of the land in Chile is arable. There are fine horses and cattle but the country cannot keep itself in beef.

In Santiago the Andes seem to come down into the top of the main avenue. A foreground of wild, yellow poppies, a bruise-colored haze that darkens in the sunlight, and then those sudden helmets of the peaks and the flashing snow. Aconcagua, the highest (22,835 feet) mountain in the Americas, lies in its glaciers beyond, in the pass that leads over to the Argentine. Here, in all Central Chile, the light swims and shimmers.

In the spring heat, the scent of carnations and roses blows along the roads, the long tresses of the white acacia are in bloom, the broom is in flower; in the pastures, there are the dark orange flowers of the espino tree and those large, broad, drooping willows that stand like green crinolines in the meadows and flow and float in the soft breezes. From the green-painted valleys the mountains rise gracefully. The cactus is cultivated and also the vine. Between Valparaiso and Santiago is the Pan-American highway, no longer a dream or a surface of grit, but a concrete road. Long avenues of poplars or eucalyptus go up straight to the *fondas*—the small manorlike farms—and brown streams lie under the womanish tresses of the willows. Oxen are plowing fields. Vines are trellised between the adobe cottages; there are fields of carnations in the market gardens, of snapdragons and white roses, beds of arum lilies and geraniums. The chestnuts are heavily in flower and the hydrangea in its electric colors. It is November—the Chilean spring—and the wheat is on the turn from green to gold.

The walls of the *fondas* are tiled in blue, in the Spanish fashion. There are oak beams, open fireplaces and fine polished iron such as you see in rich men's houses in Spain. The furniture and the pottery have the formal style of modern Spanish. The designs came from the famous patterns of Talavera in Spain. The young owner will seem like a gay, horse-riding Andalusian, grave but always with a candid smile and the impulsive gesture. He is, it is clear, a gentleman. He wants immigrants but from Northern Europe. He prays at night, you may be sure, for an oil refinery to be built, for Chilean aircraft, for something to raise the rather faded economy of this beautiful country. He is a parliamentary democrat who fears the miners' unions.

I will say this for the young landowner: his family is rich. He could have had a good time. Instead he is a practical farmer, getting down to work on the land and in his community. He rounds up the cattle with his brilliant cowboys—the rodeo is the great sport of Chile. For gaiety he has the rather solemn "boites" of Santiago, the packed cinemas. On Sundays he can go down to Viña del Mar, the Rapallo of the Southern Pacific. The tea dance starts, the couples sit on the terraces and listen to the sea roll in. The ladies are heavy, voluptuous, lively. Tea —it is the great Chilean extravagance and elegance. With the best food, the most enjoyable fruits, and the only drinkable wine, he has an agreeable life. He can forget how much his country depends on grim copper mines like El Teniente up in the Andes or on Anaconda in the desert.

Balsa boats, actually made of bulrushes, rest gently on the icy waters of Lake Titicaca, two miles above sea level.

ARGENTINA

*Though its culture is derived basically from
Spain and Italy, the Argentine has
borrowed freely from all of Europe and from America.
It displays its wealth and progress lavishly.
In Buenos Aires, with its glittering Parisian manner,
you will feel the unmistakable
shock of the 20th Century.*

In Buenos Aires you are very near to what you know in London, Paris or New York. Once more you are in contact with the great cities, the million windows built into severe walls; by day impersonal as print, by night a brilliant geometry of light standing still high in the sky or moving in endless traffic along the ground. Every light represents a human being like yourself, the electric man. By instruments the pilot lands you in a city of instruments and tensions. The nerves tighten. You are caught between the artificial screams of the modern world—fire engine, police and ambulance—and a hygienic quiet that is not exactly silence; simply a current that has been switched off.

You feel the tension sixty miles out of Buenos Aires when the lights of this continually spreading urban area begin to form in a countryside that one hundred years ago was a pampas of thistles and clover. The cattle have yielded to the wheat, the wheat has yielded to the market garden, the market garden to the factory and the extravagantly spaced suburbs and their electric railways.

Like the other cities of the east coast of South America—São Paulo and Rio de Janeiro—Buenos Aires is a Babylon shot up suddenly out of the prairie, plantation and jungle. It shouts money and progress from its skyscraper tops. It is almost impolite to mention that it was established toward the end of the 16th Century. The people like to regard themselves as no older than their sudden and tremendous wealth and expansion, no older than the furs and diamonds in the street called, with classical Spanish lettering and economy, Florida; they are the latest edition of Bond Street, Fifth Avenue, the Rue de la Paix or the Avenue Hoche. Latin conservatism and sensibility are their weapons against the Anglo-Saxon. If the sense of time is to be valued, for them it is the future. It belongs to them, they feel, yet they cling to the illusion that money can keep the old Faubourg St.-Germain alive. Upon the future they act aggressively and without apology; they have the aggression and arrogance of the Americas mitigated by sensations of loneliness and insecurity.

Argentine writers say that the Argentine is a lonely man not only because behind him is the loneliness of the pampas where he once made all his wealth, but because he has built a city that might be a lovely importation of Paris, Genoa, Madrid or Milan and yet is inconsolably far away from the great centers of power in the United States and Western Europe. The Grands Boulevards glitter with traffic uncontrolled, under the thick

The gaucho's home is a vastness of sky and pampas.

plane trees. The Argentine flatters Paris by imitating it, like the newly rich; but he hates it because, in making money out of Europe and America, shaping his life and economy to theirs, he feels he has made nothing that is his own. Or perhaps he has lost what he had in the cattle-raising days.

His blood is Spanish, scarcely touched by Indian. Italian stock has been grafted onto him to redouble the dramatic sense of the virile and masculine sensibility and the ethos of Southern Europe. His culture is French and profoundly so. In the 19th Century the British bankers were his servants; in the Twentieth he looks toward New York. A chauvinist and proud, he rails against foreign capital. Yet he will build himself an English Tudor house and racing stables, play polo like a Virginian, re-create Longchamps and throw up a skyscraper or two. Is not the Argentine the most powerful, the most advanced of the South American states, the one chosen to lead, unify and even to conquer? The dilemma has been how to allow the indigenous to grow amid so much assertion of the will and so much copying. Among Spanish Americans, it is he who has the publishing houses, the bookshops, the writers, the newspapers and reviews that have an international standing. He wishes for foreign cultures, as the Mexican and Brazilian seek strength in their own.

In the streets and the beautiful parks walked the brown-eyed women, with their strong Roman noses and that carriage of body and limb which is meant to display sexual attractiveness to the utmost for admiration only and for its own sake. The men gazed and were provoked by the sight of sexual arrogance and were left staring the Argentine stare, alone, to consider its fatality. You sense in the men and women a mingling of Italian virility and violence with that alternation of passivity and compulsion which is the Spanish inheritance. Buenos Aires is a city of lovely flowers. You may see a girl carrying a bouquet of fifty roses as she walks between two men; and when a private celebration takes place, say a cocktail party for the opening of a new dress shop, scores of superb bouquets of flowers, fit for opera singers, are sent by friends.

Six in the evening is the hour of the *paseo*, when the street called Florida is closed to traffic and the women, who have spent hours preparing for this moment, walk in groups. This *paseo* is less militant than the *paseos* of Spain; the sexes are not segregated, and the exhausting Spanish eye warfare has been softened by Italian gaiety. The Italians have improved rich, bourgeois Buenos Aires. Diamonds, emeralds, sapphires, pearls are in the shop windows. Inside, the jewelers sit formally at their velvet-topped tables, like croupiers waiting for the rich gambler. For the true inhabitants, Buenos Aires is the delightful city. They have the American gregariousness, the easy feeling for the surface of life. They live in sets and groups that are always in and out of each other's houses, always giving parties with energetic gaiety, always amusing themselves. They bubble along, hating to be alone. The elegance and liveliness of the rich in the smart bars is diverting; the gaiety is not noisy and it is free of the boring Anglo-American drunkenness. I have never liked the look of the rich so much, the young above all.

At evening he prepares his supper, inevitably barbecued beef.

In shops, they prefer long transactions. Four assistants will hang about a man buying a hat; it will not be a matter of a hat for hat's sake, as in London; or a sale for sale's sake, as in New York; it will be a hat for life's sake, an opportunity for the buyer to talk about his life, his friends, his family, and a pretense at bargaining which will interest everyone completely. They sigh to see a customer go; a life has gone, they gossip about him afterward.

The personal is everything for them. They inherit from Spain the wish to preserve the sense of personal favor, that one is buying a hat there through the influence of a friend of a friend of a friend. The dictator, in the personal politics of South America, is simply the dominating personality, the man himself with all his anecdotes, interests, deals, habits, passions, friends, whims. He is not the father of his country, but, perhaps, the uncle on the make. To the general American alacrity is added refinement; the cardinal thing in manners is not candor or directness but indirection and the importance of not wounding susceptibility.

There is often a damp haze or a dust haze over Buenos Aires. Its parks and open spaces are gracious, planted with the lovely flowering trees of the subtropics, and they sweep in little hills and drives to the reddened waters of the estuary which stains the sea for miles outside. The river is too wide for us to see the farther shore; its mouth is an ocean in itself, but only an hour's flight away is Montevideo, and on the far windy beaches of Uruguay the sea becomes fresh and blue again. Up the great river Plata, for tens of miles, Buenos Aires has spread its low white-walled houses with their heavy carrot-colored tiles, with all the space of the pampas to use up. Along the modern highways and the cobbled avenues, no police or traffic lights control the traffic, which has its own skin-of-the-teeth methods of cutting across. Occasionally, you see an empty pagoda where the white-helmeted policeman is supposed to stand. He is rarely there.

The light in the Argentine is strong; the sky seems higher and steeper, a vertical wall at the plain's edge. Trees and buildings stare like cutouts. Clouds are hard. If ever a landscape was made for horse racing, it is this one. The eucalyptus trees and the poplars are planted in platoons around the farms. These trees are immigrants. The characteristic tree of the pampas, where, in its fertility, nature has hardly troubled to make a tree, is the low and spongy ombú. It does not burn, it cannot be used for anything except its rich shade, and, under it, when the land was not wired off and the cattle were wild, the gaucho rested with his horse, his knife and his guitar.

Little trellised restaurants are outside Buenos Aires, dancing places where men take their girls. At the home of the rich landowner, whose family may have built an English country house, you are back in the society of the Edwardian rich. The English house has been copied almost too perfectly: the oak beams, the open fireplaces, the English prints and the grim manorial bedrooms. His English lawn has fine grass, not the coarse grass of Europe, and is religiously watered. In the meandering *jardin anglais*, you stand under the comical rain tree that spits water from its leaves. You see the slap-up flower beds, the swimming pool, the stallion and race horses

in the stables, the grooms and the gig to trot the visitor round the orchards and the fields where the sheep or the beef cattle graze. A butler of fifty years ago will bring an English tea and, by some touch of excess, a bottle of whisky too. Where is "the family"? In England? No; in Biarritz, Paris, Monte Carlo. The pony trots round, we hear for the first time since childhood the delicious flick of a whip, feel the rumble of hard wheels in our spines, the scented dust rises; some burned-up peasant from Spanish Galicia, lisping his "c's" or his "z's" with snobbish contempt for his Argentine masters, gossips away to the jaunty foreman and calls him señor. "Before Perón went," laughs the foreman, "he was the head of the local Peronista delegation and was going to shoot us all. We've done with all that nonsense now. He's an innocent." But no Galician is an innocent. It is country life, lazy-voiced drawling, merry, shrewd.

You have flown over this scene, over the green watery-looking billiard table of the pampas. This is far, far from being the whole of the Argentine. There is the scrub forest of the Chaco, from which (when I was young and worked in the leather trade in London) we used to get our quebracho wood —the "ax breaker"—there is the flood plain that lies between the Paraná and Paraguay rivers; there is wild Patagonia, where the English shepherds emigrated last century and the Welsh colonists still sing their hymns and speak to no strangers, as clannish as the Basques. Along the Paraguay River they grow the *yerba maté*, which the Jesuits were the first to cultivate in this meat-eating country. The maté supplies the ordinary man the vitamins he would get from green vegetables. And up on the frontier where the Argentine and Brazil and Paraguay meet, the water of the Iguassú Falls comes crashing in broad beards out of the tropical forest. It is an irony that this rich country disappointed the early travelers. They called it Argentina in despair, for there was no silver. The wealth came first from the clover and the grass, from the horses that sprang from the seventy-two which the Spaniards let go wild four hundred years ago; and from the cattle. Then when the Italians came, bringing the energy of Europe, crops were planted: grain and the *frigoríficos*, those vast freezing plants and slaughterhouses that stand by the waterside in Buenos Aires, created a nation. At the turn of the century began that industrialization which has enormously enlarged Buenos Aires, drained people into the towns. A new urban middle class appeared. Behind all South American cities lies the empty land where no new emigrant wants to settle.

The cities of that coast from south of Capricorn to the Equator—how violent is their difference! European in one respect, they are not standardized. Little in Rio recalls Buenos Aires, except a phalanx of tall buildings; and Montevideo has nothing in common with its neighbor over the estuary of the Rio de la Plata, except the *frigoríficos* and the meat ships waiting in the harbor. Across the continent in Chile the people have one official meatless day a week, apart from any religious fast; in Uruguay it is reckoned that everyone, rich and poor, eats one pound of meat daily; in Buenos Aires they eat more. Good meat on the east coast, poor on the west; so the gourmand might divide the continent.

URUGUAY

Uruguay has been described as "prudent, distrustful, sterling, efficient, realistic." Pritchett found it a country with many ways of contentment, a little Sweden, "...the one unmistakable democracy and the world's first pocket Welfare State."

From Buenos Aires to Montevideo is scarcely an hour's flight. You take the flying boat from the dock close to the center of the city and fly across the estuary whose opposite bank you cannot see. Some travelers prefer the night journey by the ferry steamer, to see the lights of Buenos Aires drop away and Montevideo come up. I took the plane. Like any week-end Argentine tripper or escaping politician, I arrived in South America's little Sweden. Sweden (they call Uruguay) for cultural and political reasons. It is, for a large part, a very flat country and bears no physical resemblance to Sweden at all. Uruguay acts as a buffer between the ambitious Argentines and the Imperial Brazilians. Montevideo is an ordinary city with the provincial air blowing in from its pines, its dunes, its flat plains and little hills. Uruguay is a mild place, so well-behaved that foreigners smile: all the school children in neat aprons and carrying their notebooks, hardly any illiteracy, higher education free and generally available; retirement on full pay at sixty; no income tax, no president, but rule by a sacred committee of nine—their nine Cadillacs stand outside the Presidential Palace. Uruguay is the one unmistakable, working democracy and the world's first pocket Welfare State. One could imagine Ibsen rewriting his plays there. "Prudent, distrustful, sterling, efficient, realistic," Count Keyserling wrote of the Uruguayans.

Montevideo is the least American of modern South American cities. It is very Germanic. It even goes in for small British and German motorcars. The Italians have brought it gaiety; from Central Europe has come something very serious, the latest books and the best music. And Uruguay *is* provincial; it is so democratic that even its handsome parks and streets are littered with wastepaper, its people wear standardized clothes, its night clubs are dim and decorous. They call them *boîtes* as in Chile, or—horrible word—*whiskerias*. But conversation is good here; learning is considerable; books are read. There is no dread of "dangerous thoughts." In José E. Rodo, Uruguay has produced the only great South American thinker. There is intellectual liberty, liberal civilization without the horrors of mass society. Life is like a long week-end with the like-minded. Montevideo is the one place in South America where you see people of all classes enjoying family week-ends on the beaches. Acres of bodies brown in the sun. Out they drive in thousands along the miles of Atlantic sands and bathe, sit in the little restaurants and bars, and indulge the national passion for picnicking in the thoughtfully planted pine woods or by the sea. It was once a treeless country, but the good Uruguayans saw *that* defect was put right. The wealthy can drive out beyond the miles of hotels and villas to the fashionable resort of Punta del Este and look out on that island where nature, with an eye for our education, has placed one of the world's largest colonies of sea lions. And do not say that the lovely harbor of Montevideo is dull: the Antarctic whaling fleets put in there for the winter. Mr. Onassis had an office there before he moved to Monte Carlo.

Montevideo is a capital bemused with the magic of the number nine. A Committee of Nine, representing the political groups, runs the country. So well regulated are the Uruguayans, so caught by the prosaic magic of fair shares, that even the jobs in the many state organizations are distributed proportionately to the numbers of their political groups. If nine stevedores are required on the docks, they must be in the correct party proportions. This making everything go by nines is a religion.

And how do the Uruguayans raise money for the government without an income tax? By direct taxation on property, pensions, sales, reserves, profits, banks, and so on, and a good deal by the manipulation of a sliding scale of exchange rates and price regulations in certain areas. This leads to little comedies; on the way to the airport you notice a group of new bungalows and huts. They are really butchers' shops. Anyone with a car can drive out here and buy meat at half price—on Sundays only. He is avoiding the city sales tax by buying in the country. A day on the beach and then a drive into the pines to buy meat; there are many ways of contentment in Uruguay. There is one alarming thought: why should so much happiness have led to inflation?

Montevideo: *Busy, democratic, prosperous and pleasantly provincial. Sleek modern buildings change its skyline, but the whaling fleet still winters in its harbor, its beaches are heavily populated and picknickers fill its woods.*

Uruguay/V.S. Pritchett **229**

BRAZIL

In Brazil jungles curtain the ends of the streets,
architecture is exuberant, the past
sometimes leaps toward the future and sometimes merely
glosses ancient poverty with the glitter of modernity.
Here, in the vast melting pot of South America,
the present is awakening tensely, almost ominously.

You leave Montevideo, fly up the Atlantic coast of Brazil to Rio de Janeiro. The arrival over Rio at night is a magnificent experience. Flying has not stolen the drama of the most fantastic harbor in the world. At night all capitals are the *ville lumière*, but Rio displays an unexampled intricacy in the hard and ingenious magic of light. You never knew that electricity could be so fantastic simply in the course of fringing hills and water. Those brooches high in the sky as we turn are golden ships; those long insectile shapes like centipedes, devils' coach horses and sacred beetles fixed in their jeweled battle pieces are the quays, the peninsulas, the promontories, the sugar loaves. There are the pearl strings that go from bay to bay, from mountain to mountain, with a recklessness that turns you into a child exclaiming with wonder. Nature has gone the limit of its possibilities in South America—in mountain, snow and glacier, in prairie, desert and jungle, in the huge red-river systems like the Rio de la Plata, the Amazon and the Orinoco. But in Rio, a sort of theatrical folly has been added to the natural fecundity. For here are harbors in colonies, mountains upended in collections of furry cones and shaggy pyramids. The jungle curtains the ends of streets, hangs over the roofs of the low, pink-walled colonial homes, or sets off modern buildings that shoot up in stacks of steel and shuttered glass. Even the sea is rich as it breaks along the splendid curve of Copacabana and sends up a soft smoke of hot foam over the high buildings. At night Midas changes Rio to gold.

By day, when the gold has gone, if we climb a few hundred yards from the sea's edge, we are looking into the pulpy green, underwater world of the tropical forest. It hangs heavily down upon us, entices from shade to shade. Flowers are as big as faces, leaves are like bodies, stems are like human legs. You half expect to hear the sap pumping and the strange plants speak. Those leaves like swords, like scissored cardboard, like fire, like feathers, like the lolling tongues of huge animals; those trunks so bulbous; those flowering creepers like bursts of colored smoke—all combine to give the tropical hothouse the look of an overpowering court. A court which suddenly becomes silent and motionless the moment your step is heard. We stand only a yard or two off the road, in one of these tropical gardens, and have the baffling sensation that someone or something has, in that very instant, slipped away to tell someone else. We are left with the impudent sexual stare of flowers (they have none of the innocence we imagine in the flowers of our milder climates)—the jacaranda, the flame drip, the yellow cassia and silver imbauba, the hibiscus, the banana and the little red flower called "the shameless Mary."

Cities that are crushed between mountains and sea commonly spread up the mountains, if only for air. Not so Rio. Its originality is that the rich keep to the flat and drive the slums into the hills of the city. So there is not only 20th Century Rio fitted between the hills, but the hill villages, the shack villages or *favelas* which crop up just above the roofs of the offices, the rich apartment houses and even the brilliant tunnel that takes the speedway out of Flamengo into Copacabana. It is as if slums of native huts, made of old timber, corrugated iron, flattened petrol cans, bamboo, palm leaves and sacking were built on the sky line of the Rue de la Paix or were dotted about Manhattan in the 50's at the twentieth-floor level. There is old 19th Century Rio, three stories high, a refuge from the blinding light, where the houses lie in the shade of large trees and the rooms have the relief of air and semidarkness. And there is Rio of the mid-20th Century, built at an astonishing speed, a place of tall steel and glass boxes where people fry in the summer, are blinded by light, catch chills from the air-conditioning or are driven quietly mad by its relentless buzz. It is not quite like that, of course; but the Brazilians inherit the Portuguese weakness for leaving nothing alone. They bulldoze the hills away, tunnel under them, fill in large areas of the central bays—so that some people fear the lovely colony of anchorages will one day be solid concrete. So the wretched are driven up to the *favelas*. There are dangerous *favelas*, perilous at night, hardly policed. At least one of them is better off and has television sets and night clubs. But most have no light except the candle or the oil lamp on the table; and the life of the women is the perpetual journey for water. You look out of the office windows and watch the women carrying their empty petrol cans down and their full ones up the steep red mud paths. When the tropical rains come the red soil dissolves, the hillside slips, the shacks are crushed.

Brazil, more than any other of the republics, is a country that absorbs the alien life. It is the one major melting pot of South America, the one place of positive ferment. Our only chance of judging it is by its cities and it would of course be true to say that only the cities are modern, that the rest is backward, often wretched and isolated; but we can make certain guesses from the cities and above all from their architecture. The sudden awakening from long colonial sleep came first with the late abolition of slavery in 1888, later than anywhere else, but (most important) without bloodshed or deadening race segregation; and then with the late arrival of industrialization. Lucio Costa (who with Niemeyer, Serrador, Baumgart, Rino Levi, Warchavchik, Burle-Marx and others, is a leading figure in Brazil's architectural revolution) puts these two facts first in explaining it.

The abolition of slavery had shown that the traditional style of building was no longer efficient. Brazil's first modern building to be mounted on pillars—*pilotis*—was designed in 1931, and since then Brazil has been exuberant in its bold modern designs. A final stimulus—as so often happens in art—was a fundamental difficulty, the lack of steel. The architects had to do what they could with reinforced concrete—on this coast there are no earthquakes. Sun, concrete, vegetation—"these," Costa said, "are the *données*." Sometimes originality has been

Rio de Janeiro and its landmark mountain, Sugar Loaf.

extravagant, as in Niemeyer's famous church of Saint Francis at Pampulha outside the astonishing new city of Belo Horizonte. The church, a series of parabolas of glass and concrete and tiles, decorated by the painter Portinari, looks like a fantastic phosphorescent snail on the march. (The bishops refused to consecrate it.) In the same town Niemeyer built the lake casino, a minor masterpiece which follows the shore line of the lake, and which combines a theater, cinema, restaurants, cafés and swimming pools. Some of the luxury hotels, like the hotel at Petrópolis, said to be the largest in the world, are built on a casino plan.

What must strike the connoisseur of Brazilian architecture is its *élan*, its variety and its freedom from those boring surfaces to which the cult of shape and function too commonly leads. In the new villas of Belo Horizonte the sharp, boxlike lines have been ingeniously broken, the impersonal stare has gone; graceful snakelike ramps, cagelike galleries all light and air, verandas shaded by grille and Venetian shutter, and outer walls in beautiful patterns of color as if they were textiles or even wallpapers—which is, incidentally, an extension of the old Portuguese tradition—relieve and divert the ennui of the eye. The *brise-soleil* (or outer shutter), which brings shade to these tall buildings in the tropics, is a Brazilian device though it was Le Corbusier who suggested the movable shades which project from the walls of the Ministry of Education. These interest the eye and, like the honeycomb grilles in the walls of schools, hospitals and apartment houses, make fascinating patterns of light and shade in the rooms.

Personal privacy is as strongly desired by the Brazilians as by the English, and modern architecture—so obviously designed for the collective life—hardly seems to offer this intimacy. There are, however, many examples of private building. Above all, gardens and trees have been drawn into the setting.

It is typical of the present generation of Brazilians to want the new, rich thing, whatever it is. São Paulo, as sudden as Chicago in its growth, was ambitious to possess famous French pictures and has bought a collection which, however, has not yet been housed in the city. In so far as they inherit from the Portuguese, the genius is decorative and exotic, even indiscriminate. "The Spanish-speaking republics," an old diplomat said to me, "are pyramids tottering on their apexes. Brazil is a pyramid standing on its base. It is as well founded as Mexico and is the one country that is really creating an indigenous and original culture."

That sense of the loss of loved, hated and continually imitated Europe is absent. There was no violent break with Europe. The relationship between Brazil and Portugal is close. The Spanish-speaking countries were separated from Spain by wars of independence. Brazil separated peacefully with a lawyer's sigh, and some writers have said that to the practical virtues of the Portuguese the Brazilians have added an aristocratic sense which the Portuguese have lacked. For until 1889, Brazil was a monarchy, the only monarchy on the American continent. The Emperor's palace—now the National Museum —may be seen in Rio, and up in the mountains at Petrópolis is a summer resort that recalls Cintra or Saint-Germain-en-Laye.

Just as, after visiting Spain, you are struck by the gentleness and sensibility of the Portuguese, so you are struck by these qualities in the Brazilians when you come here from other republics. They have added great wit and a taste for wild comedy. The dislike of violence, the apparent passivity of the Brazilians, has been despised by Northerners and has been laid to the tropical climate and to a disintegration and decadence of character which, it is argued, comes from the tolerance of mixed blood. The latter argument, however, finds no support from science, and sociology shows it to be nonsense. Climate has its influence, but it is only oppressively tropical along the Amazon, where the white race does indeed degenerate rapidly.

The most dramatic transition from new to old, from present to past, is the journey from the new city of Belo Horizonte— 250 miles north of Rio—to the old gold-mining town of Ouro Preto, not far off. It was from this town, the greatest producer of gold in the world in the 18th Century until the mines gave out, that the Portuguese kings and the Church gathered the enormous riches of the Portuguese abbeys and churches. The glory of Ouro Preto is in its lovely and fantastic baroque churches, each different in design, in its use of tower and scrolls of masonry and color, in its sixteen famous fountains, but most of all in the works of the greatest of all Brazilian masters, the crippled mulatto sculptor, Aleijadinho. He has been called the El Greco of Brazilian sculptors, because of the audacity of his religious carvings. Their distortions are imaginative; Brazilian art and literature have a strong feeling for exaggeration, distortion and satirical caricature and wit. The huge figures at the church in Congonhas do Campo are his.

Traditionally, mining is an industry that is violent in its human relationships, whereas the slave life on the adjacent plantations of old Portuguese Brazil was patriarchal and, within restrictions, self-indulgent and benevolent. I flew in a number of small hops through this region. First up the coast from Rio to Salvador in Baìa; then to Aracaju, Macao (Maceió); afterward to Recife in Pernambuco and on to Fortaleza and Belém. These were charming journeys. You are never far from the sea; you are going round the hot bulge of the sizzling South American leg of mutton. You find yourself in the Brazil of the 17th and 18th centuries, among lovely churches and monastic establishments, pretty streets and fine houses, and all the painted grace of the *ancien régime* where life is modern enough but retains the old idle things of more leisured times.

Salvador is a town of churches and old doorways, of gramophone shops that blare out sambas and tangos all day while the crowd hangs round the doorways listening. The population is chiefly Negro or mulatto. It is a place of cotton frocks, beauty parlors, barbershops. White trousers, white shirts, white frocks, everywhere, give these places a littered appearance. In the superb blue and steaming bay, the steep-prowed fishing boats in the Portuguese style come in with their lateen sails; and the purple pineapples, the bananas, the mangoes and the innumerable other fruits are heaped in the market and carried in baskets on yokes in the street. We never, in the North, eat pineapples like these, without acid or stringiness, as soft as scented water ices to the mouth. The Brazilian picks out his mango and smells it first, as if he were pausing to accept or reject the bouquet of a wine, making sure it has just the right, faint exhalation of the curious turpentinelike fragrance. In tropical countries, the scents and savors of the fruits are a refined pleasure of the senses. They are like wines in their vintages; indeed the fruit of South America is really the wine of the country, and the juices offered at the stalls belong to a world of natural soft drinks that is closed to palates hardened by alcohol. For myself, though I cannot drink the sweet Guaranà which is consumed all over Brazil, I find the dry Guaranà sold in the Amazon delicious. Most of the whisky in South America, by the way, is a swindle, the gin deserves only to be drowned, the lager beer is excellent and the various vodkalike fire waters are for desperation.

North of Salvador is a foaming coast of white china clay, scrub and coconut palms. The country scene is made delightful by the sight—made so well-known to us by painters—of Negro women washing their linen and spreading out the sheets on grass that is as green as parrots. I watched a team of expert, nearly naked men play football at midday and some sweatless Negro athletes running through the town in training! At noon, on some little plane, a "mixed" of goods and passengers, you bump over the estuaries of the copra trade, tip giddily over the palms and come grating down on a blazing strip in the low jungle oven.

The company in these planes is familylike: a nun meeting relations, a couple of sailors, a Swiss trader, mothers and children. A car picks them up at the airport and takes them off into the trees. You step out into flame, crawl to the shade of a shed, where some silent man with a wheelbarrow of large green coconuts hacks the top off with one frightening slash of his machete, sticks a straw in it and hands it to you without a word. He knows what you want: a drink of that cold, refreshing milk; the knowing scrape out the yoghurtlike pulp afterward.

This is copra- and cotton-growing country. The plane comes down at Recife, which is called Pernambuco by sailors. It is on the most easterly hump of the South American leg of mutton, halfway between Rio and the mouth of the Amazon on the coastal route. Recife is the direct Atlantic airport for Africa and Europe. You land among the mango trees and a car bumps you over the bad roads into that flat Venetian city. The families, the young men and girls sit, silently, on the low walls of the serene, lagoonlike rivers in the hot night that is unendurable indoors. In your hotel you lie listening to people talking all night long in the street below. When do they sleep in these places? Not in the morning. They are up at seven. Most journeys begin before dawn, when you pull yourself together with three or four cups of strong black coffee, before getting down to the real bouts of coffee drinking in the daylight hours. In this climate you are always drinking, sitting, mopping until—acclimatized at last—you watch without interest the flies sticking to your shirt. Recife has some of the oppression and desuetude of the tropics; a gray day there will be like lead. The trousers of the dock workers are dirty and torn, coconut shells litter the gutters, beggars are numerous. You see the mulatto women asleep over their babies against the walls, or whining for alms, and others crying lottery tickets. Quite a portion of the population seems to be peddling ties and belts on the streets. It is a packed and dusty, swarming little town. There are sores and scars on the mahogany and malarial faces. To the mixture of races you saw at Salvador there is the addition of the old Dutch stock at Recife. There are pictures of the Portuguese victory over the Dutch in one of the churches. There is a superb golden sacristy here which has the beautiful blue Portuguese tiles; and in all the churches the decorations, the little pillared and petticoated balconies, are made of hardwood painted chalk-white or in clever imitation of marble. There was wood here, but not much stone, except the gray soapstone; much of the granite and stone and tiles, even the cobbles and bricks, were originally brought from Portugal in ballast.

All these coastal towns, where scrub and jungle and palm grove are not far off and sometimes come in to engulf, are interesting chiefly for the people. At the barber's in Recife, the fat man cutting your hair is almost asleep as he leans against you; some of his customers are fast asleep at eleven in the morning. On the blue river at Recife, with its brown Venetian shadows from quays, bridges and buildings, the crabcatchers go out on their curious plank boats, poling what seems no more than a board across the water; later, they will carry dozens of these electric blue crabs on strings through the streets. The suburbs of Recife are enchanting. The pretty houses are under the deep shade of the trees: the mangoes holding their fruit like large solid green tears, the palm, and the banana, that joyous and giant vegetation which is itself a kind of light masonry. In the gardens grow the millions of empty, vivid flowers and among them the golden and silver birds fly. At a street corner I remember the bamboo cages of a bird market where the birds gave their piercing tropical whistles and the blue macaws screeched like temperamental opera singers who have lapsed into vulgarity.

Brasilia: *Tomorrow's buildings rise in a city hewn from yesterday's wilderness.*

Mexico

Mexico is neither Spanish nor Indian.
It is mestizo—and very much itself.
Old Spain lives on in colonial Guadalajara
and there are Indians in the mountains.
In the plains and in the sierras, along the tropical coasts
and in the metropolis of Mexico City
John Houghton Allen finds both quietness and violence.
And always there is the timelessness of mañana.

In Southern California we are week-end travelers. Los Angeles is a great city-state, and it has everything, but we also like to get away from our city. In a few hours' time we can be at the beach, or sailing to the Channel Isles, or climbing the High Sierras, or driving over the Mojave Desert to Palm Springs, or down into Baja California to a first-rate bullfight. Tijuana is Mexico to most of us, and a fine town, a friendly border town. It has cabarets and good restaurants, jai alai and horse racing. Thirty miles down the coast of this peninsula is the playground of Ensenada, with its white beach and luxury hotels and casinos, as much a Mexican Riviera town as Acapulco; so the confirmed Californian doesn't have to look very long for what he wants or go very far into the interior of Mexico. But I cannot forget that south of all this, and pleasant as it is, there is a land.

Another world at our doorstep, a land of great plains and sierras, a vast continuation of the terrain that makes our own Southwest colorful, a land that falls away to tropical coasts and climbs to the central temperate highlands and crawls down at last to the malignant enervating jungle of Quintana Roo. Here is a vast land, and a lotus land as well as the land of *mañana*. Men like myself, who love the north of Mexico almost nostalgically, or men who love the rich Aztec-Spanish culture in the central plateaus, the great city of Mexico and the timeless Indian villages, or men who are lost in the archaeology and the Noa Noa of the Mexican tropics, we all have been marked undefinably by this quiet and violent land, and always we feel a kind of nameless exile away from Mexico, a compulsion to return.

It is the damnedest country yet. The longer you live here, the less you know, but it's still your favorite country. There is never a happy medium in Mexico. It is peaceful and turbulent, it is *simpático* with earthquake in the air, fantastic with history, fluorescent with contrast, always unpredictable—and yet the peace is here, deep and satisfying, the individual's peace that we all thought was lost.

It is in the *mañana* perhaps, the timelessness, the changelessness. There is custom to believe, and in this way black is black and white is white in Mexico. It's fine to have something to believe, and to live in a country where the rules aren't changed every day. Juan Diego, the average Mexican, is all smiles, but he won't budge, if it's not the custom. The menus don't vary, and the programs never change, but that, also, is the custom.

Or perhaps the peace is in the commonplaces of the plaza where people come and go like actors in a play, with drama to their idleness. There is always a feeling about the plaza that the curtain has just gone up, and you are watching something on a stage. In the center stands the Victorian bandstand which Porfirio Díaz left in every plaza of Mexico. And people taking their ease, gentry getting their shoes shined, families sitting on the grass, the Latin lovers flirting portentously, and well-behaved children everywhere.

The peace may be in the picturesqueness that is never quite healthy but always heart-warming. Or the cure-all of the afternoon siesta, for even the Revolution must trim its sails to the sacred siesta. There can't be very much wrong with a people who can sleep away their cares. Or the peace may be in the fountains playing in the sun and the blessed church bells ring-

Taxco is a lovely survival from Spanish Colonial times.

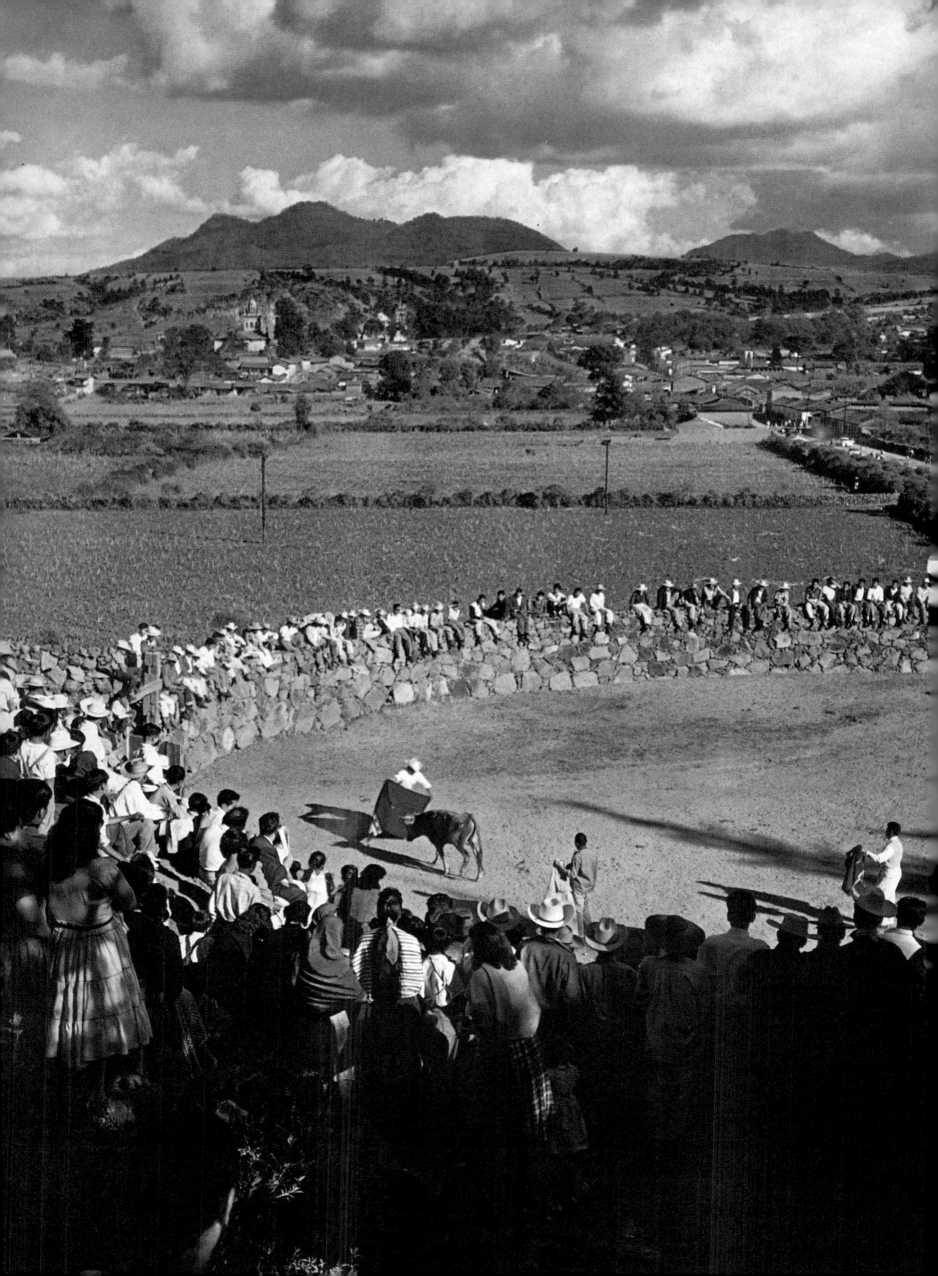

A country matador in Pátzcuaro shows off his skill. The show goes on until bulls, fighters and tequila are exhausted.

ing; we are less aware of such things in our land. Or perhaps the peace is general, in the very way the Mexicans *fit* in their environment, for they are not so foolish as to be in conflict with it. They *belong* in their times and therefore they are not strangers in their own land, and even their cities are built *in* the landscape and not away from the earth and humanity like modern cities.

Or perhaps the peace is spiritual, I don't know. I am not a religious person, but this seems as good an explanation as any in a land where explanations don't make sense, or are not needed. The real peace may be the Church. Every Mexican is born a Catholic and everybody is named after a saint. There is something abiding about the great democratic cathedrals in Mexico, something profound about the pilgrimages to Guadalupe Hidalgo, that Mexican Lourdes outside the capital, and the processions of the Virgin of Zapopan in Guadalajara, and the naïve symbolic Indian dances at feast days in the villages. And I don't believe any traveler who ever heard the church bells on the dry clear northern plains of Mexico, ringing out from a dim colonial town that looms softly ahead in the early morning hours, shattering man's ancient aloneness in all the alien lands of this world, will ever forget them.

More than half the area of Mexico is comprised of Baja California and the northern frontier states of Sonora, Chihuahua, Coahuila, Nuevo León and Tamaulipas. The last three states have been my second *patria*, for I was raised along the Rio Grande. It is grand country, still a frontier, even though the macadam roads have come and the men on horseback and the great haciendas are gone forever. You drive through on the Pan American Highway now, and between Nuevo Laredo and Ciudad Victoria you are in a raw ancient land, brilliant and cruel in the sunlight. There is a zest, a vitality in the desert air. There is no end to the horizon but the eroded mountains that stand in the distance in a purple haze, like lunar pieces in the Never-Never of everyman's memory. And off the main highway, hidden, waiting, lie the little white colonial towns that are like benedictions in the cruel landscape. You see them in the distance and they make the heart ache for their cool loveliness, you come upon them after a hard drive and they make the world right.

Monterrey, which is four hours down this Pan American Highway from Nuevo Laredo, is the most important industrial city of Mexico. This, a sleepy white colonial town in a pastoral country before the Revolution, is today a bang-up commercial city, very progressive, very rich, very American.

Mexico has the face of Spain, but the Mexican national is a mestizo. Juan Diego, the average citizen, used to be an Indian, but now he is a mixture in varied degrees of conflicting Spanish and Indian bloods. There is still ferment in the mixture, but Juan Diego is typical of Mexico. Seventy per cent of the population is mestizo, while the Spanish, the aristocratic, articulate, cultured minority who built Mexico, are today a class negligible and unrepresentative. The pure Indian is of no more consequence than the European. The last indigenes are being

translated rudely into the 20th Century of necessity, in spite of the fact that they belong to the ruins of a civilization that was flourishing when Spain was ruled by the Moors and the United States a wilderness. The Indians are a Mexican problem. They will be assimilated, and they are coming out of the hills as fast as they learn to read and write, but just now it is only the artist and the aesthete who can take them unadulterated. It must be very pleasant to sit in the cafés of towns like Taxco and have the natives go native for you, but I doubt if Mexico will let the artist hang on to its past for local color.

In appearance Juan Diego is not impressive, when you consider he has a complex personality with almost gorgeous ingredients. In him are Spanish and Indian traits—Oriental fatalism and African ruthlessness and Spanish individuality and Indian patience. He is not cast in the heroic mold, and there is serenity and humor and anarchy and travesty in Juan Diego. He is a paradox, in fact. He has small hands and feet and more grace than muscle, for even the *peónes* have quality. He believes in justice but he will settle for the customary. He is pantheistic and also Catholic. He is a handicraftsman at heart, communal by instinct—but in Mexico even the Communist is an individual.

Now, as Juan Diego begins to coalesce, to realize his own peculiar humanity, he faces swift industrialization, for better or for worse, and I cannot imagine my friend the potter, or the mechanic who works by intuition, or the lottery vendor who recites Calderón de la Barca, or the professor who is an amateur bullfighter, or my great, good and temperamental friends the woodcarvers and ironmongers and plasterers, working on an assembly line, although anything can happen in Mexico. It bores them to repeat, to make any two things alike.

And I doubt whether Juan Diego has any talent for dying on the installment plan. He has always revolted against his peonage, but usury is a dragon's trade in Mexico because Juan Diego will pay the interest cheerfully and forever but never gets around to the principal. Also, he is wantless most of the time; if he can't have it he doesn't want it, and his sales resistance makes me want to cheer. There is a lot of him that doesn't make sense to us, and you mix all the ingredients together and the mestizo should be a mess, but he isn't. Here is a man who doesn't even have complexes. He likes being Juan Diego, it is a career in itself, and with his Indian humility the chances are he will endure. He may be here after the rest of civilization makes its final mistake.

It was the enlightened viceroy and the Church and the native craftsman that made Mexico great. Mexico has a colonial history rich as anything in literature. The Spanish were the greatest builders since the Romans, and in the Spanish crown jewel of Mexico they excelled themselves and built for all time. The cathedrals in Pueblo and Mexico City rival anything by Herrera in Spain. The priests created the homely architecture of the mission on every frontier. In the towns the glazed faïence on the great cathedral domes and towers reminds one of Seville. The colonial houses and grand stairways and loggias, like those that remain in the Santiago Palace, and the old patios today make you think of a time when the heart of the world beat more serenely.

The Spanish built the aqueduct at Querétaro, and that masterpiece of a cloister a La Mercéd, and the mellow old buttressed cathedral in Cuernavaca, and the holy city of Cholula with its 365 churches, one for each day in the year. That was sheer fantasy, and yet the Spanish were practical. They loved their New Spain, and they gave every town its *portales* around the Spanish square. And it was during the Golden Age of Spain that its men built in Mexico the incomparable colonial towns of Morelia, Cuernavaca, San Luis Potosi—towns that have music for their names and stand with a baroque loveliness until this day in the luminous rains—and, above all, the city of Guadalajara.

Here is the most typical Old World city in Mexico. It has never lost its *hispanidad*, its character. It is still a great Spanish town in the hacienda country of Jalisco that once was the garden of the world to Mexico, a land of gentry, of proud peasants that were never hungry and craftsmen of high order in stone, ironmongery, woodcarving, pottery, silver, leather and textiles. The first time I saw Jalisco, I said this is where a man goes when he dies; and Guadalajara, like a *ville lumière* in the strange unearthly light of another world—this is the city I have been looking for all the days of my life. The colonial haciendas abandoned and dreaming in the golden valleys, in the golden day, the warm tawny plains with the poetic quality of what might have been. . . . *Ay*, Jalisco, and *ay*, Guadalajara! There is always about it the echo of the Spanish proverb: That was a long time ago, and this is another country.

The landscape is not vital and cruel, like the North of Mexico, but idyllic and pastoral, the meadows now and again seas of yellow flowers, the houses with thatched roofs and the villages fenced with organ cactus—a semitropical land and at the same time arid. In the *barrancas* between the mountains are palm trees and tropical fruit, while all the hillsides are covered like giant pincushions with great pronged joshuas or maguey. You can still see the large-wheeled cart and wooden plows behind oxen, the blindfolded burro at the rotary wheel. Fine horsemen ride the Spanish ponies at the *pase-trote*, sitting straight in the saddle like soldiers. You used to see women washing white linen on the flat stones, or bathing naked and unashamed by the village streams. They were always combing their long black hair. And you heard the *mariachi* music, that originated in Jalisco, heartbreaking and tender as balladry and yet light with allegro.

In Guadalajara is the last of what is left of the Spanish pride. The gentry there are the last sahibs in our dull world. They have beautiful manners, European educations. Castilian blood —a little too fine, perhaps. The sign of extinction is on their brow, they are awry in their own land and they have lived to the end of their time, but they are not going offstage out of character. All they want is Yesterday.

By highway from Guadalajara to Mexico City you drive past the misty lake of Chapala, and through the clean town of Morelia with its great bishop's palace that is now a hotel and its pink cathedral, and past Lake Patzcuaro with its Tarascan Indians fishing in boats with their butterfly nets and looking like Orientals. Then you come to what the Indians call the Mixteca, the Cloud Land of the central plateau. Here in the

Cloud Land you find such diverse cities as Querétaro, still haunted by Maximilian, and Puebla, a fair colonial town with the snow-covered volcanoes of Izataccihuatl and Popocatepetl for background, and the holy city of Cholula—and the always-foreign and fascinating capital of Mexico.

The most surprising thing about Mexico City is that it is not Spanish but French. It seems never to have really wanted to be Mexican, any more than New Orleans wanted to become a part of the United States. French influence was strong in Mexico during the time of Santa Ana and all through the dictatorship of Porfirio Díaz, both of whom fancied themselves in the pattern of Napoleon. Under the rule of Maximilian and Carlotta, Mexico City was for a little while a genuine European city.

An Austrian prince and a Belgian queen—it was a lost cause from the start. I can feel the phantom touch of Maximilian, who was shot by his subjects, and his Empress, who went mad, wherever I go in Mexico City. There is an *alas* to it. I half expect to see his spahis and the legionnaires and the White Austrian Cavalry in the streets, or ladies in costumes right out of the old daguerreotypes. It was a storybook time, and yet genuine—for a little while Mexico City was another Vienna, although there was always disaster like a twilight in the air.

The Mexicans killed Maximilian but they remember him with a strange redeeming pathos. Even today the classic song *La Paloma* is rarely sung in public out of respect for the memory of his tragic queen. When the Mexican people learned how she languished in a château in Belgium, mercifully imprisoned, singing over and over her favorite song *La Paloma* —and it was said she sang it like a little prayer, muttering every once in a while *Mejíco* and *Maximiliano, Maximiliano*— they never asked to hear it in a theater again.

Mexico City is high in the mountains, white with palaces, lush and green from the regular rains. It is a very great city, the oldest metropolis in America. There are things about it I shall remember: the cypresses, five hundred years old, that shatter the gravel paths in Chapultepec Park, and the mosaicked fountain of Don Quixote there, that gallant knight crowned with the golden helmet of Illusion. And the floating gardens of Xochimilco, the canals covered with *camolote*— lilies—and the drab gondolas poled through the soft sheets of rain. The flower markets and the Volador—the Thieves Market—and the Zócalo where the great cathedral stands. Dining at Préndes and drinking the golden manzanilla. . . .

Random things I remember: the pyramids of the Sun and the Moon at Teotihuacán, the grotesque idols of the Aztecs. The clowning of Cantínflas, pathetic, wistful, his tongue in his cheek like Sancho Panza, a master of travesty and pantomime. A symphony orchestra in *charro* costume with a hundred strings that made music like the harps of the wind. Ancient colonial houses in the slums of the town with worn façades and the scrubbed old flagstones stale with age. The sun that shines every day of the year, and the luminous rains.

I remember the Church of La Soledad where, it is said, thieves go to pray. And the public scribes in the arcades of the Plaza de Santo Domingo, not picturesque old gentlemen of much Latinity and the florid goose-quill style but cynical penurious young men banging away at typewriters. The stagnant crowds of the market and the street theaters with the Rabelaisian humor. And the fine proud women in the cabarets, who walk like the Aztec Virgins of the Sun.

The pensions terrifically over-furnished, decorated in this city of flowers with artificial roses, a Victrola with a horn in the parlor, daguerreotypes on marble-topped tables, kitchens with open fireplaces hazed with charcoal smoke, like greasy Flemish interiors, dark corridors with the cages of despondent birds that never sing; and the tenants bickering with all their hearts and hands, and how the servants always cry when you leave. It is very touching.

I remember the old hotels with their glassed observatories, the rubber plants and oleanders in the patios, the tall windows and the transoms over the palatial doors, and the stained glass in the bathroom with the fixtures from the days of the Second Empire, the elegant brass bed, the sitting room bare as a railway station but very proper if you were holding audiences—the whole *déclassé* but not in the least uncomfortable, with an exquisite service that verges on personal regard.

You used to feel at home in the old hotels. In the new and the modernized versions the manner is more impersonal and the bars are very swank. There is much modernity in Mexico City because it is a city that keeps abreast of the times, even if that makes some of its buildings look like grain elevators. You find as much novelty here as in Paris. It is a city distinguished and cosmopolitan, in the suburbs are fine examples of extreme modern architecture, and of course in modern painting the Mexicans are supposed to be in advance of the world. This is an opinion I don't share—I think their stuff is already dated—but I will admit the murals by Orozco, Rivera

and Montenegro have verve, vitality, a primitive Aztec impact, and I am impressed by them in the same way I am impressed by the strange stunning spectacle of the bullfight.

The one place in the tropics I want most to go to is La Paz, at the bottom of the peninsula of Baja California. I don't know why I want to go there, except that it has a lovely name, The Peace. I have always thought of it as an oasis in that Painted Desert of a land, something hidden and remote like the little white towns in northern Mexico. I have stopped over in Mazatlán several times, opposite it on the mainland, but I never got over the bay to La Paz. It takes longer than *mañana* to get to La Paz, and after a few days of the tropical heat in Mazatlán I get out of the mood and pass it up until the next time.

La Paz may be the last colonial town of them all, off the trail and unchanged; there may be rich remains there of an old Jesuit mission culture—I don't know. But I have a feeling I shan't come to La Paz, because it will always be there for tomorrow or another day. And perhaps it would be only a fishermen's village, after all, with buzzards in the street and malaria at one's elbow like a dark presence, and no baroque cathedral or fountains playing in the sun, only the deserted carrousel of the Porfirio Díaz bandstand in the solitary square, with no smiling people or dark Spanish eyes behind the iron-grilled windows, and at the hotel a handful of my countrymen down for the sports fishing and cursing their luck, stranded with the heat 120° in the shade, and the taxis standing hopefully with no place to go, like taxis in Purgatory.

I think of these things, and I think I will just keep La Paz, with the lovely name, in the heart, where it belongs, and that way I shall have it forever—the peace that is illusion, the peace in the heart, the extravagant peace of Mexico.

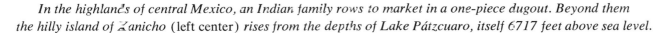

In the highlands of central Mexico, an Indian family rows to market in a one-piece dugout. Beyond them the hilly island of Janicho (left center) rises from the depths of Lake Pátzcuaro, itself 6717 feet above sea level.

The Caribbean

The islands of the West Indies are dappled with a stimulating melange of human ways and creeds and skin colors.
Place names are English, French or Dutch, but there are monkeys in the forest and mongooses in the fields.
Here, where the pace is too gentle ever to overtake the 20th Century, David Dodge finds foreign worlds that survive almost intact in remote reaches of the sea.

On a world globe, the islands of the Caribbean Sea lie equally distant from the capitals of Western Europe, the palm-plumed atolls of the South Pacific and the dark valley of the Congo. Pictorially and culturally they combine aspects of all these extremes. Early Spanish, French, Dutch and English settlers carried to the West Indies their languages, their tastes, their ways of life; slaves kidnaped from Africa brought manners and morals of their own. And because for centuries many of the islands were hard to reach and thus immune to outside influences, old ways have survived among their inhabitants. Here the crack of an English cricket bat sounds from beneath the soaring feather dusters of a grove of coco palms; a Gallic *sommelier* offers the proper wine to go with French food served on a hibiscus-hung terrace overlooking a coral reef; blue-eyed, flaxen-haired Dutch girls with the warm brown skins of Polynesian *vahines* bring tea in Delft cups to be drunk in the shade of a divi-divi tree blown lopsided by the trade winds. Here black-skinned, white-toothed islanders, whose forebears arrived in chains, speak archaic English on one island, Spanish on another, Creole French on a third, on yet another a patois containing elements of Spanish, French, English, Dutch, Portuguese and Ashanti, sometimes with a Scotch burr superim-

posed. Here Europe and Africa remain Old World transplants in the New World's tropic waters.

Travelers who know only the Bahamas and the Greater Antilles—Cuba, Jamaica, Hispaniola, Puerto Rico—may not recognize the picture. It is not a true portrait of the islands most easily accessible from the North American mainland, because Americans traveling *en masse* carry their own ways with them as inevitably as did the early colonists. An inescapable truth about us was well put by the Commissioner of Grand Cayman Island: "No magic carpet has yet been patented which can give you simultaneously the splendors of an endless, deserted, moon-drenched beach and the amenities of a handily located hot-dog stand.... Arcadia and the lush night club are brief and incompatible bedfellows." But even in the more sophisticated areas of the Caribbean there are islands which still retain their exotic flavor, odd corners still with uncorrupted charm. In the more remote reaches of the sea, entire small foreign worlds survive.

From the butt-stock of Puerto Rico, easternmost of the Greater Antilles, the Lesser Antilles swing in a great whipcrack east and south, missing the flank of South America to curl westward again along the Venezuelan coast. Deep-water sailing men saw in this looping string of coral-crowned submerged volcanic peaks a different metaphor, calling the northwestern islands the Leewards, those of the southeast the Windwards. As far as ocean breezes go, the names mean nothing. Prevailing trades, blowing from the northeast, strike the archipelago broadside on, treating all the islands to the same unfailing natural air-conditioning that makes them tropic paradises instead of sun-scorched miniature hells.

A good place to begin a Lesser Antillean expedition is Antigua, 250 miles east and a little south of Puerto Rico.

Westward out of Antigua a boat is within sight of one landfall or another almost all the way to Puerto Rico. A plane sees them as toy lands on a plate-glass sea. In these waters rise Nevis' cloudy peak, the rolling green of St. Kitts' cane-clad hills, tiny Saint Eustatius and the surf-lipped volcanic mouth

that is even tinier Saba; Sint Maarten—or, if you prefer, St. Martin—where Hollander and Frenchman celebrate each other's national holidays in insular fraternity, ignoring the cleavage line of empires that divides the island into two countries; strange, remote St. Barthélemy, whose Swedish inhabitants are French citizens; farther on, beyond the windy gap of Anegada Passage, a multiplicity of shoals, cays and islets that are the American and British Virgins. Among these islands are allures for every taste, from the incongruity of St. Thomas' neon-lighted movie-houses, Sears Roebuck displays and jukeboxes to the bleak loneliness of Dead Man's Chest, where legend left fifteen marooned pirates to die of thirst.

St. Kitts and Nevis are two peaks of the same submarine upthrust separated by a narrow sea strait. Nevis, smaller of the two, as yet has no landing field for planes. St. Kitts' airport serves for both islands, and though one is accessible from the other in less than an hour by regular boat service, little of the trickle of air-borne tourism that has begun to reach St. Kitts flows as far as its sister isle. Nevis' several small hostelries, fine palm-fringed beaches and pretty little capital city, Charlestown, remain unexploited and almost unknown to outsiders.

I journeyed to Nevis on the afternoon launch from St. Kitts. I meant to go back the same evening, by the same boat. There was little about Nevis, according to the St. Kittsians, to entertain a visitor for more than a few hours. The beaches were nice, Charlestown attractive enough for a small port, and that was the end of it except for the boat ride. I was warned not to miss the returning launch. Why would I miss it, I thought, if what they said about Nevis was true?

When the launch left that evening, I watched it go from the balcony of an island pension overhanging the small roadstead that was Charlestown's harbor. How I found the pension or how it found me I don't remember, but it seemed wholly natural to be sitting there on the balcony tranquilly watching the launch putter off. Minutes before, a squall had blown in quickly from the sea, hammered land and harbor with pounding drops, then disappeared in a mist downwind, leaving a rainbow hanging over the roadstead. Beneath the rainbow's arch a sloop was raising its clumsy sails to catch the evening breeze, slight at first but quickening as the sun went down. The rainbow faded. Lights began to blink on along the harbor front, a chain of bright jewels reflected in the water. Boats rocked in the gentle Caribbean swell. Somewhere, far off, music played.

I was sitting on the balcony again the next afternoon, looking at the sea with my hands folded and my mind peacefully blank, when the launch came across from St. Kitts. I didn't intend to catch that one either. At the pension rate of three dollars a day, with rum selling at a dollar a bottle, I had already calculated that I could cash what was left of my plane ticket for enough to last six months. After that, beachcombing, with a bed under the coco palms. It was hard even to look that far into the lazy future. I had found my island Eden at last, my Bali Ha'i, my private garden of opium poppies, and if it hadn't been for the captain of the launch, who had stern orders from the island governor to sell only round-trip tickets to Nevis and see that the return fares were used, St. Kitts and the rest of the outside world would have known me no more.

Except for St. Thomas, one of our own outposts in the cosmopolitan archipelago, the Leewards are host to few American visitors. Cruise ships make port in some of the more important harbors, but their passengers generally stay no longer than the ship. Island hotel accommodations are indifferent, running hot water a rarity. Food is usually an import, therefore expensive and too often canned, frozen or smoked. Other drawbacks exist; mosquitoes on some islands, sand flies on others, on all the problem of inland transportation.

But running hot water is not a necessity where the sea itself is a warm plunge, where mangoes, papaya, pineapple, custard apples, bananas, coconuts, avocados, citrus, lobster, crab, crayfish, conch and other natural bounties are available to supplement an otherwise spiritless diet, and it is no great inconvenience to sleep under a mosquito net. If road transport is slow it gives you more opportunity to enjoy the scenes that summoned you, more time to fall under the nostalgic influence of the islands' past. Here are the great houses of a vanished aristocracy who lived like medieval lords on a rich traffic of sugar and slaves. Fields of cane still break in rustling waves around the sailless stone corpses of old plantation mills standing like sentinel towers in the wind that no longer powers them. Here rise the still solid fortresses of men who fought off raiding pirates, the cities that were sacked and ravished by the raiders when defenses failed. Rum, blood and the bitter acridity of slave sweat have all dripped upon these soils. The colors and stains they left are still to be seen.

Since the trade winds themselves pay no attention to any of the authorities, it makes no practical difference that cartographers, encyclopedists and colonial historians disagree about the point at which the Leeward group ends and the Windwards begin. It lies somewhere within the waters surrounding three islands halfway down the Lesser Antillean chain: Guadeloupe, Dominica and Martinique. Dominica, no relation to the Dominican Republic, sits squarely between the other two and is a British colony classified by its government as a Windward. Map makers generally hold it to be a Leeward. Guadeloupe, to the north, is indisputably a Leeward, while Martinique, to the south, is a Windward by consensus although not by unanimous vote. It is easier to think of Guadeloupe and Martinique, the two most important islands of the French West Indies, as twin links which tie the island chains together rather than as boundaries which divide them.

The French islands have a social personality unlike any other in the West Indies except that of independent Haiti. Under Dutch or English rule the black man is a citizen but remains a "native." On the French islands there are no "natives." Black, brown, mulatto, quadroon, octoroon, *griffe* and *sang-mêlé*, all are *citoyens de la République*. Guadeloupe and Martinique might be called the Corsicas of the Caribbean. Shops with French names, standing in French market places, sell French goods for French francs, and the dark girl who makes

Carnival time in Trinidad brings out
this fantastic conception of an
American Indian. Saved and refurbished each
year, some heavy costumes need wheeled supports.

your change counts "*Cent, deux cents, twois cents*" in her soft liquid voice because her African ancestors did not have a purr in their throats. But she is, or thinks of herself as, French first, dark-skinned second. Not the other way around.

Guadeloupe has perhaps less appeal for travelers than rival Martinique, although there are those who would argue the point. Both islands are lush, fertile and flowered. Guadeloupe's principal port, Pointe-à-Pitre, is bustling and ugly; Basse-Terre, its capital, more attractive but less often seen. Gosier, a seacoast hamlet only a few miles out of Pointe-à-Pitre, is the home of a small hostelry as surprising to stumble upon as the foot of a rainbow. Here guests enjoy an unparalleled view of beach, reef, island and sea from a cliffside terrace-restaurant where pretty waitresses in *foulard et madras*, a French chef and an Italian *maître* combine their several talents to challenge the canard that true Continental cuisine cannot be exported. The *maître's* wine cellar alone would justify a stopover on Guadeloupe.

The same amenities are even more readily available in Fort-de-France, Martinique's capital, at first glance a neat, colorful French city which might, except for its tropical foliage, fit the coast of Provence. Closer inspection uncovers the same cluttered back streets that fringe most West Indian seaports, but these are not immediately visible. From the seafront a broad savanna of green grass, graveled walks and tall palms reaches into the city's heart. Around *La Savane* on three sides are banks, hotels, shops, clean modern constructions ranked with stately old colonial buildings. A white marble statue of Martinique's most famous daughter, the beautiful Creole who became Napoleon's ill-starred Empress Josephine, stands in the middle of the park, and behind Josephine and the city rise the verdant hills of the land that Paul Gauguin called paradise.

A wholly different land is Barbados, an hour's flight northeast of Grenada. Easternmost of all the West Indies, Barbados has been variously nicknamed Little England, a seabound Shangri-La and the Poor Man's Jamaica. It is free of disease, jungle overgrowth, dangerous animals, snakes, noxious insects, volcanic eruptions and earthquakes, rarely brushed by hurricanes. Its water is pure, its land productive, its manners civilized.

Barbados alone among the West Indies has never known Spanish, French or Dutch occupation. Its mood is undiluted British colonial. Bridgetown, the island capital, is Gilbert and Sullivan played on a tropic stage. Bridgetown's Broad Street runs into Bridgetown's own Trafalgar Square, where a statue of Lord Nelson frowns at the shrill wails of a woman hawking *maubee*, a spicy drink she dispenses from the spigot of a cooler balanced on her head. Bridgetown harbor police wear Jack Tar uniforms of Admiral Nelson's time: white middies, widely belted bell-bottom trousers, round flat hats. You look in vain for pigtails under the wide hat brims. Barbados place names are English—Hastings, Christ Church, Newcastle—but monkeys swing in the trees of its small, carefully nurtured forests, and mongooses run among its sugar-cane fields. You are always aware, on Barbados, of the firm, guiding hand of Empire.

Still another world among the Crown colonies is Trinidad. This pseudo-island is literally part of the Spanish Main, a piece of South America isolated from the rest of the continent by shallow sea straits. In other respects its roots extend under all the oceans. No other land in the Americas has a more diverse, motley and polyglot population. Hindu, Moslem, Chinese, Japanese, Syrian, Lebanese, Portuguese, Spanish, English, French, Dutch, African, Jew, Gentile—these and other faiths, breeds and colors have gone into its makeup. Temples, mosques, synagogues, cathedrals, shrines, churches and meeting houses of all the religions open their doors to Trinidad's faithful. Turbaned Sikhs, fezzed Moroccans, pith-helmeted colonial planters, Frenchmen in berets, Venezuelans wearing the snappiest of snap brims, bare-headed Americans and a jigging, posturing old crone of a flower vendor with an enormous basketful of blooms on her head jostle each other in the streets. Trinidadians wear saris, dhotis, slit Chinese skirts, mantillas, Indian embroideries, Japanese silks, madras, batik and African prints. You see caste marks, ceremonial ash-stainings, strange tattooings and a brown girl with a jewel in one delicate nostril. Like schools of bright tropic fish intermingling in the shallows of a coral reef, the cultures, bloods, faiths and colors of the world teem and intermingle in Trinidad's vital, virile capital city, Port of Spain.

Port of Spain reminds you of a prosperous Port-au-Prince, stimulating and creative. But where Haitian creativeness is intellectual, Trinidad's is earthy. Trinidad invented Calypso, a better vehicle for bawdry than for such uses as praise, satire, electioneering and the promotion of soft drinks. Trinidad invented the steel band, finding music in pieces of junk when wartime restrictions left it with no other outlet for its urge to bounce and rhyme. Trinidad's Carnival celebrations are unsurpassed for color, costume, originality of ideas and the time and energy that go into their presentation. The Trinidadian is an artist of the streets; a West Indian Villon; he calls himself Saga Boy, Smart Man, Robust Man. He is not above a con game now and then, if the mark looks easy. But he works hard to make the flimflam a good one, and no hard feelings if it doesn't come off. A Saga Boy saying is that a stranger who eats the *cascadura*, a Trinidadian fish, must inevitably return to the island to end his days. Port of Spain hopes that he will bring a fat, not too tightly pouched purse and arrive in time for Carnival.

Outside of the great city, Trinidad's life is oil, asphalt and agriculture. For a change of pace and scenery Trinidadians go to Tobago, twenty-five minutes away by air, a pleasant overnight cruise by boat. Tobagonians boast that Defoe had their island in mind when he wrote *Robinson Crusoe*, and if the facts don't justify the boast nobody cares: it *could* have been so even if it isn't. Coconut palms and shady cocoa plantations forest the little island, a reef defends it, its several small hostelries are comfortable, breezy and clean. Those who live on Tobago, as wards of Trinidad, have untaxed access to Trinidad's bountiful production of rum, limes, sugar, nutmeg and bitters, the essential ingredients of a planter's punch. Punch drinking is the most popular activity on Tobago mainly because there isn't much else to do. The sun shines, sea waves lap the shore, trade winds sway the palms. You lose track of the days easily, learn to enjoy the purposeless pleasure of a hammock, and neglect to shave as often as you might. The island has only one real drawback. Crusoe was exempt, but other residents can stay only six months without paying colonial income tax.

Far west of Trinidad and Tobago, snappers on the curling West Indian whip, are the Dutch Leewards—Curaçao, Aruba, Bonaire. Willemstad, Curaçao's most important port and chief city of the Netherlands Antilles, is pictorially unique among the Caribbean settlements. Gabled Dutch buildings of 18th and 19th Century design, their narrow high fronts a glowing palette of pink, buff, lavender, green, orange and yellow, stand primly along both sides of a narrow inlet that leads the sea through the city's heart into a sheltered harbor, the Schottegat. The stout walls of old fortifications loom on either side of the inlet's mouth, and a preposterous pontoon bridge with the happy name of Queen Emma swings back and forth across the inlet like a crossing gate, opening to admit ships through the channel, closing to let traffic move from one side of the city to the other.

Oranjestad, on Aruba, and Kralendijk, on Bonaire, are smaller, less colorful editions of Willemstad, minus Queen Emma, and the three cities together house a population almost as polyglot as Trinidad's. Dutch is the official speech, but other tongues have blended with it over the centuries into a weird linguistic goulash, papiamento, that is understood by most of the islanders and few other living people. Dutch, papiamento, English or Hindustani, it is all one to Curaçao's enterprising storekeepers. They can, and do, negotiate with customers in any of twenty-two different languages.

Curaçao is the bazaar of the West Indies. Several other island governments permit the operation of free-port shops, where duty-free or almost duty-free imports are sold to cruise-ship passengers and other transients at attractive prices. Curaçao was one of the first to see the advantages in the business, and still holds a good proportion of the trade. Stores in Willemstad's Punda, the commercial side of the inlet, bulge with bargains in French perfumes, Swiss watches, German cameras, Italian silks, Japanese binoculars, English china, Danish porcelain, Indian brassware, Swedish crystal, Irish tweeds, diamonds, pearls, gold, silver and other loot that would have made old Blackbeard wet his lips. Pirates no longer call at Willemstad, but the Schottegat's Queen Emma opens annually to thousands of other ships. Most of their passengers find at least the time to lunch ashore, snap a photograph or two, and spend more money than they had intended to spend.

Ships bring the shoppers, oil brings the ships. Two of the largest refineries in the world function on Curaçao and Aruba, converting crude petroleum from Venezuelan wells into gasoline, bunker fuel and profits. Some of the profits are being reinvested by the Dutch in an attempt to develop these islands as a vacation resort; new roads are being laid down, new beaches developed, new hotels constructed. Although the Dutch Leewards are arid—Willemstad distills most of its drinking water from the sea—they are also hurricane free, and their appealing Dutchness could well attract a holiday trade. Unhappily, oil money seems to blotch as badly here as it does on Trinidad. A new hotel on Aruba is a modernistic monstrosity, new buildings that glare across the harbor inlet at the Punda's attractive spectrum of gabled house fronts set the teeth on edge with garish "modern" façades, as out of place in their surroundings as gold teeth in a pretty girl's smile, and only the earnest opposition of a few far-sighted burghers and businessmen has so far kept functional architecture out of the Punda itself. Another hotel, opened recently within the walls of one of the fine old fortresses guarding the Schottegat's entrance, has wisely been designed to harmonize with its surroundings. Here, where muzzle-loading cannon once roared Dutch defiance at sea raiders, rises this most modern Caribbean hostelry south of Puerto Rico, complete with air conditioning, cocktail lounge, coffee shop, swimming pool, dance floor and a casino, the first to spin a roulette wheel in the Lesser Antilles. The oil refinery, far at the other end of the Schottegat, will not be visible from the new hotel's broad seaside terraces. But its unseen shadow looms over the whole island.

Curaçao was the end of my pilgrimage. The plane that was to carry me back from the warm southern sea to ice, snow and the chill clutch of March took off late at night. As it rose into the wind I saw below the Schottegat's giant refinery, pulsing as strongly with viscid black blood at night as it did during the day. The scene was lit with the harsh blue-brightness of thousands of electric lights glaring from distillery, cracking tower and tank, and yellowed over by smoking plumes of flame from the high torches of waste-gas flare-offs. Its symbolism depressed me even in the few moments before the glare disappeared under the plane's wing and we were flying at last over the featureless dark sea.

High-octane fuel, ever faster and more efficient planes, ever-multiplying airstrips would, I thought, inevitably bring the last West Indian island out of its isolation. I remembered the Cayman Island Commissioner's acid warning about magic carpets and hot-dog stands. Was progress to overwhelm the golden Caribbees, steal their individuality, standardize their charms? Brooding on it, I thought of flamboyant Port of Spain and dreamy, do-nothing Tobago; sailed again in my mind along the jungly coast of Dominica; listened to the mournful *adieu foulard, adieu madras* on Martinique; smelled the spicy odor of nutmeg and mace awaiting shipment on the wharves of St. George's. In the blank screen of the plane window I saw again the wonderful Buster Brown hats of Barbados' harbor police; a trading sloop careened for tarring in Castries' turquoise lagoon. St. Kitts was in the screen, hot and somnolent under its cloak of gray-green cane; Nevis' cool clouded peak rising from an encirclement of coco palms and white sand beach; bleak Dead Man's Chest and incredible, captivating Haiti.

Would the pictures I remembered fade, lose color and give way to drabber scenes as the magic carpets converted to jet power, the hot-dog stand came within easy reach?

In the end, I remembered Jamaica's Cockpit country, a scant fifteen miles from the fleshpots of Montego Bay, and felt better about it all. A few places will always be left. The gentle West Indian pace is too slow ever to catch up entirely with the whizzing 20th Century. For that, let visitors to these lovely lands be grateful.

The Caribbean/David Dodge **247**

NORTH AMERICA

Alan Moorehead

Bernard De Voto

John P. Marquand

E. B. White

Bruce Catton

James Street

Hodding Carter

Jack Schaefer

Robert Carson

Sean O'Faolain

Hamilton Basso

John Steinbeck

A. B. Guthrie, Jr.

James Warner Bellah

Hugh MacLennan

U.S.A.

No book can encompass the inexhaustible marvels of the United States and no individual can ever comprehend its sprawling complexities and contrasts. We see it only in part and in glimpses. But in this full-circuit journey, Alan Moorehead, the distinguished British writer, looks at our country with the fresh insight of an outsider, and with high originality sees significant aspects of our nation that most of us have overlooked or simply taken for granted.

I asked a number of Americans last summer where a man should go if he had a couple of months to spend in the United States, and never got the same answer from any of them. The South, they all said vaguely, out to the Coast, New England—but when it came down to details they were in total disagreement.

The truth is, of course, that no one man ever sees America, least of all the man who rushes around the forty-eight states. In my own brief journeys about the United States in the last ten years or so I have never altogether got around this difficulty. Friends listen to me and say, "But you don't seem to have seen anything. And you sound as though you were bored." I haven't been bored at all and as a rule I see quite a bit. What has happened is that, confronted by the enormity of the United States, the sheer impossibility of seeing everything, I have retreated into the minutiae of my own experiences. Mine is not the telescopic view. It is the microscopic one. Not Cyclorama and the Wide Screen, but the snapshot for the family album. And I find it fascinating.

In the end the trip I planned was the obvious one: down to the South, then across to the West Coast and back again east through the center: finally New England. But first I stopped at Washington.

I have, I must confess, a slightly bemused approach to this heart of the American nation, and that is because some years ago I went there as a member of an official government delegation to an international conference. There we were, my fellow negotiators and I, brief cases in hand, the green baize table before us, and although we were in and out of many of the great buildings and attended many banquets and receptions, I find I can remember nothing of them, neither the words that were spoken nor the decisions we made. All I can recall is an intense preoccupation with our business. It cast a spell over one's vision, so that one saw nothing of the outward scene; one was always hurrying to a meeting, changing one's clothes, turning to address some necessary remark to one's neighbor at the dinner table. Washington, one supposes, must be like this to quite a number of people who have business there, and that is the way it must be. Yet the outward scene can be enthralling, and to see it—to feel the historical pull of the place—one must be an idler there and without importance.

The National Gallery is usually the first place I make for. I don't happen to like the new acquisition, Salvador Dali's *Sacrament of the Last Supper*, but that is neither here nor there: this is one of the really great galleries of the world, and I know of nothing better on a hot Washington day than to stroll through these halls of cool marble and there survey some of the greatest masterpieces on earth.

Next I like to drive slowly past that lovely chain of white Georgian buildings from the White House to Georgetown. Not the Pentagon, not the latest massive National Archives Building, not even the passing traffic has yet succeeded in overwhelming these charming, airy houses where people were meant to sit and talk instead of rapidly going somewhere else. As for the modern part of the town, I would recommend a visitor to visit the Capitol, of course, and attend one of the congressional hearings if he could. I would urge him to prowl around the wonderful Library of Congress. But best of all, I think, he should drive through the trees and the lawns along the Potomac to the Lincoln Memorial, because it is a moving thing for anyone of any nationality to read the words of the Gettysburg Address carved on the walls of that special place.

After that, if he has a taste for history, he can move on slowly into the South, taking in the great landmarks of the Civil War on the way.

It was early June, and an Indian equatorial heat was beginning to blanket the Atlantic coast when I arrived at Charleston, South Carolina. Although it was nearly midnight when my train got in, there was still a woolliness in the air, a heaviness such as you have before a thunderstorm; and in the morning the view from my window disclosed a flat sea the color of gunmetal lapping up against the walls of the Battery. A harsh white glare was filtering down from the sky. I know this heat. I have felt it in India and Southeast Asia just before the monsoon breaks, and on the island of Ceylon. It can engender strong hatreds in the human mind—it tends with a kind of lazy violence to bring emotions to the surface—yet its basic quality is soporific. It gives a strange significance to the most trivial events. An improbable Navy blimp was drifting down the coast. In the hotel lobby the ladies' club had settled down to a morning's bridge. They were playing a tournament of some kind, and when their chairwoman handed out the cards the chatter died on a note; it was the kind of abrupt and apprehensive silence you have in a school examination when the pupils first see the questions.

Later I took a bus to a place called Folly Beach. This bus was a hot and rattling affair, and it was filled with teen-agers on their way home from school. They kept teasing the driver, a good-looking young man, with a rapid bantering conversation which, clearly, they had had with him the day before and were going to have again tomorrow. Every few blocks the bus stopped and Negro women, their arms full of parcels, got in and made their way silently and gracefully toward the back. If there was animosity in the atmosphere I did not notice it, but instead there was something else, a sort of wariness, a watchfulness.

At Folly Beach it was the immemorial American seaside scene—the hamburger and the ice-cream stands festooned with strip lighting, the colored beach umbrellas, the distant view of a fairground and a Ferris wheel, the children coursing among the prone figures on the sand, and somewhere in the background the voice of a jukebox gnome moaning of rock 'n' roll. It was the dead hour of the day, and Folly Beach is not a fashionable place. It looked a little run down, even a little squalid, and this comes as a slight shock to a foreigner, for he seldom thinks of this country as anything but rich. He knows about the Log Cabin to White House tradition, but he doesn't believe that there are poor log cabins left in America, let alone slums with leaking roofs and rubbish in the gutter.

I came back in the same hot bus to keep an appointment with some people who belong to the other side of the South— the South that has nothing to do with Tobacco Road and the early works of Mr. Faulkner. Their home was one of those lovely Charleston houses, pillared and balconied, which are surely among the most beautiful buildings in America. All around us, as we sat on the cool green lawn, the dogs at our feet, there were other such houses and other gardens, and trees with their hanging webs of Spanish moss.

This family had lived here for generations, and their

Negro servants had grown up with them. As courtly and distinguished an old gentleman as I shall ever see was saying gently: "I hate New York. I hope never to see the place again. You cannot conceive the lies that are told there about the South. They know nothing about it and they do not choose to know the truth. But if they force this issue, if they try to force our children to go to school with negras and to learn about our traditions and our culture from negra teachers, then they are asking for trouble."

It was not a threat, not even a declaration of defiance, but the old man's voice had a curiously convincing ring; it was as though he were stating some simple basic truth, some absolute axiom like Pascal's "Christians are right: pagans are wrong," which, for some frivolous reasons, pure cussedness perhaps, the rest of the world was incapable of understanding.

Back in the lobby of the hotel, the television was competing with an electric organ in the bar, the ladies' bridge club was replaced now by an eager group of men listening to the results of an election for a local sheriff. I turned up the air conditioning in my room and I read the hotel's pamphlet on what I was to do in case a hydrogen bomb fell on us in the night. I found the whole of this day slightly unreal.

Now I grant you that as a description of the South this is altogether inadequate. None of these small events makes a pattern and there are no neat answers anywhere. It was, indeed, a little like living in a Tennessee Williams play. Yet it represents the South to me more than the plantations do, more than the lovely countryside one sees riding down through the Appalachians, more even than the battlefields of the Civil War —and simply because it was a part of my own experience and not something recommended by a guidebook.

In Washington I had managed to get hold of a book which for a long time has been out of print—Charles Dickens' account of his journey through the United States in 1842. It is now no more than a collector's item, but I found it an excellent companion on the next stage of my journey—to New Orleans, Texas and the southern Rockies. "In going to the New World," Dickens wrote, "one must utterly forget and put out of sight the Old One and bring none of its customs and observations into comparison." Frankly I find this absurd, if not impossible. A traveler can no more stop himself from making comparisons with his own background and his own way of life than he can prevent himself from breathing; and in any case it is half the fun of any journey.

Certainly I found it absorbing to see how much this southwestern corner of the continent reminds one of other, older parts of the world, especially the Mediterranean and the Middle East. The big cities of the Eastern seaboard and the Great Lakes are entirely American and could never exist anywhere else. The Deep South is a phenomenon on its own. But here, paradoxically, in the most isolated part of the continent, the part that is supposed to be the least affected by influences from the outside world and the most directly committed to the future, some of the oldest themes in civilization are at work.

You notice this directly you cross the Mississippi. New Orleans clearly is the most Mediterranean of all American cities, another Marseilles with perhaps a flavoring of Genoa added. In Texas you don't have to look far to see the Middle East again, with its dry heat and deserts and stark mountains and warm, sluggish sea; and in New Mexico and Arizona you are back in Spain.

The Mississippi, and particularly that vast frightening Delta to the south of New Orleans, is to my mind one of the great spectacles of America. The region gives me horrendous visions of sinister green swamps, of quicksands that suck you down, of monsters splashing through the wet undergrowth; but one can also see its practical possibilities. The view from the air is best. Then you see the great veined net of waters spreading out like a chart showing the circulation of the human blood, and it is as strange as the Nile rushing down through Egypt in its summer flood.

As for the river upstream, I know of no more vivid description of it than the one I found in my century-old copy of Dickens: "An enormous ditch, sometimes two or three miles wide, running liquid mud, six miles an hour . . . the banks low, the trees dwarfish, the marshes swarming with frogs, the wretched cabins few and far apart, their inmates hollow-cheeked and pale, the weather very hot, mosquitos penetrating into every crack and crevice of the boat, mud and slime on everything: nothing pleasant in its aspect but the harmless lightning which flickers every night upon the dark horizon."

He added morosely, "We drank the muddy water of this river while we were upon it. It is considered wholesome by the natives, and is something more opaque than gruel."

Dickens was in an irascible and querulous state of mind when he visited America, and Old Man River didn't please him very much. It would be rather pleasant if he could return now and see how the wretched cabins of New Orleans and the hollow-cheeked denizens of Memphis and St. Louis have been transformed.

Better still, I would have liked him to accompany me on my own journey westward. He never got to Texas, and heaven knows what he would have made of such places as Dallas. I arrived there on a Sunday, and a Dallas Sunday is something to conjure with. "Dial a Prayer. TE 2146," says an advertisement in my morning paper. "A prayer there 24 hours a day." A blinking sign proclaims that "Jesus Saves." Behind my bathroom door there is a bottle opener. In the coffeeroom a very large man at the next table is speaking to a small man:
"I'm not broke, see? I'm rich. *You* know that."
"Yes," says the small man, "I know that, Harry."

A few blocks down the street from Nieman-Marcus, which must be one of the most elegant stores in the world, a burlesque show of an incomparable sordidness has opened its doors to a handful of sad young men carrying their jackets over their arms in the blistering heat. Sunday in Dallas has begun.

One can go on a good deal like this not only about Dallas but about most of the other big towns in Texas; and it is, one soon realizes, bunk. It is the sort of superficial truth that becomes more lying than a lie. I hold no particular brief for Dallas, but on that Sunday I discovered things about the Southwest, admirable things, which nobody ever thought worth mentioning to me before.

The city has, for example, a first-class repertory theater which apparently gets packed houses for the most abstruse and difficult plays, and the Metropolitan Opera can find an audience here any time it likes to come. I did not much care for the uninhibited blaze of modern painting in the art gallery, but at least it was a display that has come up spontaneously from the local talent, and their "art for rent" scheme is surely an excellent idea: if you cannot raise the price of a picture you like, you can rent it for three months for ten or fifteen dollars.

Then there is the Natural History Museum, which is as good as or better than anything of the kind I know abroad, and the fine little aquarium of subtropical fish, notably my friend the horse-eyed jack and a whiskey seal that was gazing out on the Sunday crowds with an air of odd self-mockery and complaisance. I mean no offense when I say he bore a remarkable resemblance to that splendid comic, Mr. Bert Lahr.

Sunday in Dallas, with the temperature at 97° in the shade. Just for these few hours after lunch there is a pause in the headlong rush. Is it eight or nine million people they have in Texas now? And how many oil millionaires, how many fine cattle out at the King Ranch, how many hundreds of square miles of new industrial development? The Texans don't have to boast any more; they do in fact live on a scale beyond anything the nabobs of the Victorian age dreamed of, and not even this pool of semisilence on a hot Sunday afternoon can diminish it. In my hotel, for instance—and it is like a hundred others in America—all goes by with a marvelous efficiency. One departs as one arrives, on a sort of assembly line. All is taken care of with the smoothness of a ceremonial in a temple. The bill, the luggage, the forwarding address for one's mail, the tickets for the plane— then you are shot out of the place like Puffed Wheat, and it leaves you with the disconcerting impression that you have never been there at all. There is a certain bloodlessness in all this, a lack of flavor, but it is very soothing.

Provided one is not in a hurry, it is a mistake, I think, to fly out to California from Texas. One should drive, not only because there is so much to see, at any rate at the start of the journey, but because here one can enjoy to the heart's content the sensation of sheer space and the feeling of freedom that goes with it.

Somerset Maugham in one of his early books had a word about such places. He claimed that in order to enjoy traveling, especially in wild country, you have to pay for it: pay in terms of hot long rides in the sun, of dust and mosquitoes, of being cold and hungry and even a little anxious about whether or not you will reach the journey's end. I cannot pretend that I ever found New Mexico and Arizona quite such hard going as this, but I did run into a sandstorm down there. It blew with such incredible fierceness that we had to stop the car, and we could actually see the paint being picked off the fenders. Then a tornado of hail and rain burst down on us, and for the next two days one misfortune followed another: we ran out of gas, we had punctures, we got lost, we felt ill and exhausted.

Finally our evil star departed, and the things we had come to see looked perfectly marvelous. Never can the Painted

The brilliance of buttes and wind-carved valleys dazes
the motorist who follows a ribbon
of highway—U.S. 66—as it winds across Arizona.

Desert have glowed with lovelier shades of rose and green and lavender, never can the Grand Canyon have been deeper or the Petrified Forest more absorbing. And as a fancier of deserts and open spaces, especially at night, I can remember nothing finer than the moonlight falling on the high peaks of the Sierra Nevada. Death Valley (and here again we are back on the southern shores of the Mediterranean, in the Libyan Desert perhaps) adds a final pleasant whiff of forlornness and despair; and then at last the Pacific breaks into view. It's a wonderful journey.

In California I went north along the route that winds along the Pacific coast to San Francisco; and this, too, can be a wonderful part of any journey round the United States. If you can find a seat in a quiet car away from the loudspeakers and the perambulating souvenir salesmen, I would recommend the train rather than the road. There you sit all day, detached and cool as in a theater, and the changing scene flows past, the Pacific at your left a yard or two away, and to your right the orchards and the green foothills of the coastal range. Of all the oceans the Pacific is the one I love the best, and here it is beside you stretching away into an infinite milky distance, the scene of the great sea battles of the last war, of dreams of coral reefs and idleness, the noblest and the greatest mass of water in the world.

The towns the train goes through have charming names: Santa Barbara, Point Conception, Guadalupe, San Luis Obispo, Santa Margarita, Paso Robles, San Jose. And finally San Francisco: San Francisco of the Golden Gate, of Alcatraz, trolley cars on dizzy slopes, the Top o' the Mark, Chinatown, a remembrance of earthquakes. It is an unusual mixture, and one can understand how it is that eight out of ten Americans will say that of all the great cities of the United States San Francisco is the one they most prefer. It is, of course, a remarkable town, a port to be compared with Rio de Janeiro and Sydney. In San Francisco, people say, tensions relax, one lives the good life and there is just the right mixture of leisure and work, of ambition and *laissez-faire*. Outside New York it is probably the most cosmopolitan of American cities, and it seems to have a special niche in the affections of writers from Mark Twain and Bret Harte onward. Rudyard Kipling, in a little book he wrote about America at the end of the last century, raved about the place, and another Englishman, C. S. Forester, one of the best of living storytellers, has made his home close by for many years. Quite a number of his Hornblower stories have been written looking down upon the Golden Gate.

There is an atmosphere of holiday, too, in some of the fishing villages along the neighboring coast. One such place I liked in particular was Martinez with its strange abandoned fleet of wartime ships. There must be ten thousand of them, all neatly anchored side by side in lines, and they are quite deserted. For some reason, a practical reason no doubt, these phantom vessels have been painted a dull red, and it gives them an operatic quality, a feeling that they might not be real but simply painted on a backcloth: Agamemnon's fleet waiting to set out again for Troy. And in fact this long arm of San Francisco Bay does very closely resemble the Dardanelles in Turkey with its Narrows, just about the same width, and

the same golden summer hills and deep-blue sky. San Francisco, like Troy, lies close to the fortieth parallel.

And now one turns back toward the east again, back to regions which are purely American. I have with me still the timetable of the City of San Francisco, the express that runs through to Chicago, and although I find most railway timetables about as difficult to decipher as the Dead Sea Scrolls, this one is different. It directs you forward on a steady course like a ship at sea. Nevada, Utah, Wyoming and Colorado, Nebraska, Iowa and Illinois. Some poet must have been at

U.S.A./Alan Moorehead **255**

Above the Owens River Valley the eastern front of the Sierras rises in wave after wave of peaks in the nation's highest, most impressive mountain block.

work when they named the American states. Had Melville written about the land as he wrote about the sea he would have rolled these words round his tongue with abandon, conjuring up marvelous allusions to mythical empires in the Red Indian past.

I love this journey. Late in the afternoon you climb directly to the heights of the Sierra Nevada, where snow lies beneath the trees even in summer, and all night long you can catch glimpses of distant mountain peaks in the starlight. The morning discloses the Great Salt Lake floating like a mirage under the wheels of the train, and from then on, through another day and another night, the great flat plain unfolds. Now finally the traveler has the illusion of complete remoteness, that he has got away from the influence of both the East and the West at last. It is like the Ukraine in Russia: one knows that great cities are building here, great dams and factories, mines and ranches and universities, but they remain as detached from New York as Rostov is from Moscow.

I know of no large city in the world which is quite so independent as Chicago. "I have struck a city," Kipling wrote in 1899, "a real city—and they call it Chicago. The other places do not count. San Francisco was a pleasure-resort as well as a city, and Salt Lake a phenomenon. This is the first real American city I have encountered."

Well, this is still the great point of rendezvous, the inland capital of an American world within an American world, and it is also the city where the traveler can most acutely feel a sense of utter antlike anonymity. In Chicago, as nowhere else in the United States, he is exposed to the weather in the streets, and by that I mean the weather of public places, of the hotel lobby and the airline terminal, of the traffic roaring by, of crowds upon crowds of strangers all hurrying off upon occupations with which he has no connection whatsoever. He realizes presently that this is not an unfriendly city, but for the moment he is trapped in a limbo. I know that this kind of loneliness can descend on any traveler in any foreign city, but Chicago is so big, so preoccupied with its own affairs, it never fails, just at first, to reduce me to the sort of bewilderment that overtakes a boy on his first day at school.

Then of course, the strangeness passes. On this trip I spent a few days with friends in a country club outside the town, and they gave me a glimpse of what it is like to be rich in America now. The girls and young men who gathered at the swimming pool in the morning had grown up together. They had been to the best schools in the East, they knew all about horse shows and country race meetings (how much now, in the jet-propelled age, the horse is becoming the symbol of wealth), and they had made their first educational trips to Europe. There was an excellent cold buffet in the clubhouse, the locker rooms were almost clinical in their spotlessness and whiteness, and at night there were a score of things to do. Once, for example, we drove over to an open-air theater to hear Marian Anderson sing (an odd experience, watching that carved tragic

*The towers of the colossus, Chicago,
the hub of midwestern America, stand
tall above the green expanse of Lake Michigan.*

face and hearing the words of the song, "None but the lonely heart may know my sadness"); but we might equally well have gone to some private dance, played bridge, taken a speedboat out on the lake. In town my friends had an apartment furnished in the kind of good taste that is familiar along the Avenue du Bois in Paris.

Now all this was a thousand miles away from the slaughter yards, the steel mills and the Negro districts of the city. It had nothing to do with Carl Sandburg's poem on Chicago, the one beginning "Hog Butcher for the World." But it was not an idle life, and it was not a pattern familiar in Europe. The men here were off to work first thing in the morning, very few of the women had servants, and no one I met was yet overtaken by the listlessness and boredom that seem so often to become the curse of wealth.

I came back into the city at the height of a heat wave on a Sunday morning, but still the streets throbbed with an immense intensity, the traffic poured along the roads, and huge buildings were going up on every other block. When, I thought, in any American city, does the last workman lay down the last pneumatic drill and declare the city is finally finished?

That night, on the train going east again, I made my way to the lounge car in search of a long cold drink.

"No liquor," the attendant said. "This is Indiana and this is Sunday."

The passenger alongside me heard the conversation and, delving into his brief case, produced an array of small significant bottles. "What will you have?" he said. He was from Chicago, and, having supplied me with drinks, would let nothing deter him from buying my dinner. He was the sort of man I always associate with Chicago: large, confident, rich and healthy. But this kindness was something added, a last gesture from the roaring city, a reminder of the ordinary human warmth within the huge machine.

Now finally New England and the northeast. I spent a few days on Long Island, drove north to Boston, and then, wandering westward, fetched up at Lake Champlain by the Adirondacks. It was the kind of journey one would prefer not to write about but to draw in a series of pictures on an illustrated map. Long Island for restaurants like The Hedges, for the slow roll of the Atlantic breakers on the beach, and for the old family houses that have stood against hurricanes and every other sort of disturbance for two centuries and more. Massachusetts and Vermont for the forests and the lakes. Even in England I have never seen such greenness, nor towns more lovely than Greenfield and Williamstown, nor universities so well designed to project an image of a better life. The Adirondacks for their odd combination of summer camps and landmarks that go back through every stage of American history. A speedboat with a water skier in tow goes racing across the same lake where the French came down from Canada to fight the British in 1758; and here the Americans won their first great victory in the Revolution. The European doesn't often think of

America as an old civilization, but after three centuries of wars and settlement these hills have probably changed less than many parts of Britain and the Continent.

In summertime it is hard to think of the change that overtakes this region in rough weather. Yet at Lake Champlain they say the water sometimes freezes over entirely, so that one can go skidding across the ice in a land yacht for a distance of a hundred miles or so, faster than the wind, at eighty miles an hour; and that fanatical fishermen, thinking nothing of the cold, will cut holes in the ice and crouch like Eskimos all day dangling their lines into the green depths below.

But now it was midsummer, the ice had melted, the wars were over, and for my part I could see no more of America. Not on this trip, anyway. I had come a long way. I was tired. I sat down beside the lake.

Often at the end of a crowded trip like this there emerges in the traveler's mind that fatal desire to generalize, to nod his head sagely in the club and say, "Well, you know the main thing about America is ——" The British have been doing this about the French for years. "France," they say, "is going to the dogs"; and what the French have to say about the British is perhaps not printable.

So now what to say about America? Well, first it seems to me to have changed enormously within the last ten years. There is a new seriousness everywhere. It emerges in a dozen different ways: in the clothes the men wear, the darker suits, the plainer neckties, the slower, more careful way in which conversations are carried on, in the discipline of the traffic and—most striking of all—in the much more sober tone of the advertisements. I have no statistics, but it is my guess that Americans drink less alcoholic liquor than they formerly did—or at any rate they don't drink in such a hurry. Clearly, too, the all-seeing omnipresent eye of television is fixed chiefly upon the family audience, and the programs are much more respectable than many of the stage shows and movies one used to see in the old days.

The cult of the pretty girl continues, of course, as relentlessly as ever, but now she is a nice girl, and although implausibly she may be selling such things as cement and electric generators in the advertisements, she belongs to the world of junior proms and healthy breakfast foods. Sex magazines may dominate the newsstands, but Marilyn Monroe is the girl men look at, and in her attitudes there is more than a hint that she is laughing at herself, that she is making a game of the whole physical feminine racket. In other words, the *femme fatale* has become a mild joke. That nice Philadelphia girl Princess Grace delivered the death blow.

Another thing about the United States was new to me— the preoccupation with ill health, even death itself. Never can there have been an age in America or anywhere else, in war or peace, when there was such an intense concentration upon the frailty of the human body. No magazine I bought was without its article on cancer, on infantile paralysis, on tuberculosis, on heart disease, on sleeplessness, on the evils of smoking. No newspaper was without its news from the laboratories and the research institutes. This to a stranger was very odd, considering that Americans are the healthiest and probably

the least inhibited people on earth. Is life so good, then, that they cannot bear to leave it?

Is this a part of the whole sobering process of taking up the responsibility of being the leading nation on earth? Is it some natural reaction against the breaking of the sound barrier and the discovery of the atomic bomb—a feeling that, in the midst of unimagined prosperity and progress, there must be these grisly reminders of the bitter end?

Most Americans to whom I talked could not see this new seriousness in themselves at all. They thought, in the main, that America was going the other way, that she was becoming oversold on pleasure. A million advertisements, they pointed out, keep urging people on toward the dream life, the new car, the delights of new foods and perfumes and gadgets, the possibility of traveling anywhere at any time ("See our booklet on our new scale of easy payments"), and even sleep itself is made a captive if you take the right pill or invest in some wonderful insomnia-proof mattress. Then there is the American genius for packaging, for wrapping up even so mundane a thing as an ironing board so that it looks like a birthday present. And music follows you everywhere.

All this, my American friends argued, is an attempt to squeeze a bogus excitement out of life, to give to each moment an unnatural quality of zest and pleasure—and they didn't think it was right. "What, I would like to know," one magazine writer asked, "is so all-fired wonderful about prosperity?" —and he went on to argue humorously, but still with serious intent, that Americans were in reality happier, healthier and nicer people during the years of the depression.

I don't agree with any of this. I think Americans work hard, harder than most people in Europe, and much more efficiently. I think, too, that they know, perhaps unconsciously, perhaps instinctively, that they are up against the old unanswerable enigma: can you really set up a new civilization which is not based upon slavery, nor upon religion, nor upon conquest, nor upon a territorial empire? It has never been done before on a major scale in all history. But the Americans whom I met all thought they could do it, provided they worked hard enough and invented enough machines, provided they stuck together.

This "togetherness" is in the end the most striking thing in America now. It is the most communistic—or, if you hate the word, the most communalistic—country I have ever visited, the only place where the old Jeffersonian and Marxian idea that all men are born equal has been given a proper chance. Now more than ever, every man seems to have the right to share in everything, to ride in a car, to smoke the same cigarette and send his child to the same school as the millionaire. By and large he eats the same food, looks at the same movies and goes to the same places for his vacation.

This distribution of cheap goods and services right across the United States is a staggering thing, and is certainly unknown in countries like China and Russia. And since one has to pay for everything, the American, it seems to me, pays

for this shared wealth by forfeiting a certain flavor in life. You cannot altogether get over this difficulty by packaging or even by the high standard of the goods inside. Anyone who has ever lived in a French or Italian village will never be entirely deceived by alluring descriptions of dishes on the American restaurant menu, nor by the attractive appearance of food. He goes for flavor—and that comes not from the freezer nor even from variety but from manure, from salts and from the untreated earth itself. Often, of course, the Italian and the Frenchman never got enough to eat. But that is another story

that we need not go into here. I simply say that there exists in everyone in every country, the U.S.A. included, and especially in a time of security, a simple zany urge for eccentricity, a longing of the individual to be different: not to drive at a regulated fifty miles an hour on the throughway but to walk alone.

Meanwhile, and let me hasten to say this, I have known nothing quite so good as this life in America, so friendly, so easy to enjoy, and, in the end, so sane. I hope I can often come back again.

U.S.A./Alan Moorehead **261**

NEW ENGLAND

New England is the quiet street of a town.
It is a wooded landscape. It is Yankee logic.
And, said the late Bernard De Voto,
wherever we come from, New England
is in our blood, New England is still our home.

"It is a small college," Daniel Webster is supposed to have said of Dartmouth, "but there are those of us who love it." The New England to which Dartmouth belongs is small, too, the smallest of our regions as well as the most continuously and diversely beautiful, and everybody has a lot of fixed ideas about it. Also about the people who live in it and who will be called here, with forthright originality, the Yankees.

The Yankees, we are told, are provincial. So a member of the Explorers' Club told me this: Out in Mongolia or Tibet or some such place his small expedition was nearing what was going to be its triumphant end: he was going to reach some high pass, back of beyond, that no one except the local natives had ever seen, with some province untrod by alien feet beyond and below it. The elation that far wanderers feel at such a time was on him when, a couple of days short of his goal, he met a party of nomadic herdsmen. It was startling and even heartbreaking that they knew quite a few words of English, but it was certainly interesting that they spoke them with a Boston accent. (That accent has been described by Mr. Charles Morton as part Boston, part Harvard, and part hick.) A couple of days later he breasted the last rampart of that high world and, sure enough, there, with his feet dangling over the edge of the abyss, was Hallowell Bigelow Cabot-Lowell, of the class of '27, reading President Pusey's annual report. "You know," said my informant, who comes from Dedham and is named Lowell-Cabot, "the last time I'd seen him was in Spitsbergen."

On the other hand, the Yankees are a cosmopolitan breed, with an itching heel and a genius for adapting to far frontiers. That is why so many New Bostons, New Salems, Portlands, Newports, and Portsmouths are scattered over the other forty-four states. So a friend of mine in San Francisco told me this: His daughter roomed at Smith College (Northampton, Massachusetts, providentially convenient to Amherst and Williams) with the daughter of a prominent member of the clan whom Mr. Cleveland Amory calls the Proper Bostonians. Last summer the roommate spent part of the vacation with my friend's daughter, and while in San Francisco had her nineteenth birthday. Her father telephoned his congratulations and affection. He had some difficulty hearing her pleased response and bade her speak up. She didn't speak up and he demanded, "What are you whispering for?" "But, Daddy," the girl said, "everybody is asleep. It's only five o'clock out here." Then Boston: "Nonsense. I've been in my office for an hour."

Endlessly misconceived, misrepresented, and even caricatured as New England has been, the most striking thing about it is this: no American ever comes here for the first time. Wherever he grew up, whoever his forebears were, he seems to bring with him something that could be called an ancestral memory

except that, most likely, his ancestors never saw New England, either.

Some elements of this feeling are easily accounted for. The history and literature which the visitor was taught in school were crowded with images and emblems of New England. Moreover, in this harried age there is an intense longing for our lost serenity, and nostalgia for what we may call Currier & Ives America has pretty well identified itself with the landscape of rural New England. That tranquility of heart is associated in the visitor's expectation—by paintings, post cards, and calendars if by nothing else—with hillside fields marked off by stone walls, and village greens where a spire rises from a white meetinghouse and is seen through the branches of great elms.

Another element is more mysterious. For there is a faint, evanescent feeling of personal recognition. Whether at first sight or after quite a while, it may be after initial dislike or resentment, the visitor frequently experiences a *déjà vu* of the heart. He seems to have been here before. He lived here a long time ago; some part of his boyhood was spent here. He had forgotten about it but now, in momentary glimpses of things gone before he can identify them, he seems to be beginning to remember. In some profound and subtle way he has come home.

We have touched on two of the accepted symbols that mean New England to the general consciousness. Though frequently employed for counterfeit effects, they are true to the region: the fields marked off by the stone walls that are so picturesque and signify so much labor through so many generations, and the elm-bordered village green with the meetinghouse topped by a spire that shows the influence of Christopher Wren—the Georgian or "Colonial" meetinghouse. But now we need several additional images and symbols of New England.

I take you first to a mill pond anywhere in the region except the industrial centers. It provides fine swimming and fishing for boys but the masonry dam from which they dive, though built for eternity, is now functionless; the water that flows through its penstock turns no wheels. Next a reminder of the migration that Mr. Stewart Holbrook calls the Yankee Exodus—and this, too, could be anywhere in the region. Make it a marker in the village of Whitingham, Vermont, up a long valley, deep in the forest that has recaptured most of the fields once hacked from it. A memorial in Vermont granite has been erected on the village green, but this is recent and the one I have in mind is older and on a hillside above town. It looks like a gravestone till you get close enough to read the text. "Brigham Young," it magnificently says, "born on this spot, 1801. A man of much courage and superb equipment."... who ended up in the Rocky Mountains, in what the hymn calls our lovely Deseret where the Saints of God are met.

Finally to another church building, this one at Gloucester, Mass. Whereas the meetinghouse with the Wren spire is Congregational, this is a Catholic church, the Church of Our Lady

This Congregational Church has had many lives. Built in
1829, it was hauled away in 1873, put to a number
of uses—even as a movie—until the Yankees
of Litchfield brought it home again to their green.

of Good Voyage. Two things about it. The Yankees who make up its congregation are, most of them, of Portuguese ancestry. And Our Lady, whose image stands between the two towers, holds a fishing schooner on one forearm and has raised her other hand to still the stormy sea.

She looks out across Gloucester Harbor to the Atlantic and, because in New England the sense of the past is always with you and the sense of the sea seldom absent for long, we may begin with both. The Yankees, who invented a fair half of the machines and institutions and ideas that produced the contemporary United States, also invented about ninety-five per cent of the American religions. Their sects have contended mightily without reaching agreement on what man's fate is. But there has never been any ambiguity about New England's fate: it is geographical. It begins here, at the coastline.

A long coast. Its western end is almost at the western end of Long Island Sound—Greenwich, Connecticut. It stretches to Eastport, Maine, and beyond it to where the St. Croix River comes out to meet the twenty-foot tides of Passamaquoddy Bay. It is multitudinously indented, an always changing succession of coves, inlets, bays, and estuaries. Most of them are short and narrow, but Narragansett Bay has room for the world's navies plus whatever multimillionaires' yachts may still survive; and Penobscot Bay, beautiful in all weathers and beloved by sailors of small boats, trends deeply into Maine. Creeks and rivers come down to many of these inlets. Most of the streams are short (though the Connecticut River bisects the region from north to south) but they were routes to the interior long before there were roads. They and the inlets they end in turned the Yankees to the sea.

So Mr. T. S. Eliot, who grew up in St. Louis and has spent his life in England but seems nevertheless to have lived some secret part of his boyhood in New England like the rest of us—Mr. Eliot hears the lost sea voices. Others heard these voices long before the Pilgrims got to Plymouth—Portuguese, Breton, Basque, and half a dozen other stocks who came to this coast for fish; and a gilded cod still watches over the proceedings of the General Court of Massachusetts. Fifty years after Plymouth, the Yankees were shipping lumber as far as Madagascar and long before that the King's men were ranging the forest to mark with a broad arrow the pines that would make masts for the royal navy. The Yankees have traded in timber, shingles, and the like ever since; if Paul Bunyan had a birthplace anywhere, it was Maine. After the great days of lumber it was the coastwise trade; then it was the trade in slaves and molasses with Africa and the West Indies.

The whalers were in the Antarctic, the slavers off the Guinea Coast, and the merchant captains and supercargoes everywhere. Wherever there was a profit to be taken there was a Yankee shipmaster to lay his craft on her beam ends if need be, to get over the bar first and snatch it from the British. The names of Boston, Salem, Portsmouth, New London, and a dozen other towns were known in Asiatic ports and South Sea

islands that had never heard of the United States. Yankee children worked into their counting-out rhymes such names as Surinam, Diamond Head, Pernambuco, Ilo-Ilo. The mansions that should be common beside the inland greens, but aren't, cluster at the ports. See them on Newburyport's High Street, at Wiscasset, wherever the ships came home. They are gracious with carved interior cornices, mantel pieces, and dadoes by artisans who had learned their Adam and McIntire. They were full of treasure-trove from everywhere, chinaware, silk prints, ivory, lacquer work, jeweled statuettes of heathen gods.

Collateral heirs quarrel over that loot nowadays, or it has passed to the institutions which its collectors so handsomely endowed. The great age lasted to produce the clipper ship, which may well have been the most beautiful object American craftsmen have ever made, and then it ended. Bowsprits no longer thrust over the cobbled streets of the water fronts. You must look for the tall masts and intricate rigging in the museums—at Salem, New Bedford, Mystic, Newport. The shipyards build only small boats now except at Bath, Fore River, and Groton, where the Navy keeps the ways busy. But the big stone wharves still traffic in aromatic stuffs, coffee, spices, sandalwood; and New England, so early shaped by the sea, still looks out to sea.

Along the coast a man is a captain if he owns or sails a boat, any boat at all. At Chilmark, Chatham, Yarmouth, and many similar places you can be ferried about the harbor by weather-beaten, salty, indestructible sea dogs in their seventies, spouting their inherited lingo and recounting personal adventures with lovely brown wenches, cannibals, mooncussers, and mutineers—sea dogs doing their stuff for five dollars an hour, who have never been beyond the breakwater.

A still more rigid protocol is that of amateur captains and crews, from the myriad Snipes to the racing yachts whose balloon spinnakers, with the sunlight on them and clouds for background, make them almost as beautiful as the clippers. A landsman may not venture to say much about their rituals of precedence, procedure, idiom, and costume. Enough that the coast is the summer-sailor's paradise. A Sunday at Edgartown, Marblehead, or Boothbay Harbor is a maritime traffic jam. The Gloucestermen have not raced the Bluenoses for some years now, but there is nothing gentle about the annual Bermuda Race that sails from Newport. And from some headland such as Highland Light watch a freighter making out to sea, to the sea wine-dark with evening or slate gray with the anvil-topped clouds that mean a blow is coming up. It remains New England's portal on the infinite.

The blow coming up still brings the sea foaming over Norman's Woe, the Dry Salvages, and a hundred other reefs, shoals, and races. Every equinox and every winter adds to the heroic chronicle. Gloucester still needs the intercession of Our Lady of Good Voyage. It has an annual ceremony for those lost at sea, and on Memorial Day many another coastal town scatters flowers on the ebb tide. The Yankee names on the new gravestones are Portuguese, Scandinavian, Greek, or Italian for the most part, and they are those of fishermen. Fishing is the principal maritime commerce remaining to New England, with diesel-powered draggers and seiners, much different from the schooners of yesterday. No poetry celebrates the little hookers on their innumerable errands, and the lobstermen remain unsung.

Years ago when William Allen White was working on his life of Calvin Coolidge, I drove with him to Vermont. Repeatedly he shook his head and asked, "Aren't there any fat men here?" And in the Coolidge barn, at Plymouth, looking at fragments of sadirons, old harness, and the usual clutter, he asked the question a Kansan must always ask, "Don't these people ever throw anything away?"

Why, Yankees come in all sizes and configurations but it is true that one marked type has always been common: lean and compact, thin-cheeked, bony, looking but little older at seventy than at thirty. It is true, too, that the immigrant stocks have tended to take on these same lineaments. As for throwing something away, not while a use for it can be conceived. Let dwellers in a more opulent geography waste their substance if the fools will; work has always been too hard here and solvency, which is heavenly grace, too hard to maintain. I twitted a friend of mine about a trivial display of parsimony. A member of a family that is rather more than wealthy and married into an equally rich one, she blushed. "You mustn't say such things to me," she said, "I was taught that when I couldn't squeeze any more toothpaste out of the tube with my fingers, I must use my heel." They say that when Erskine Caldwell quitted Maine after an unsatisfactory venture there, he announced that he was going back to his own country, where there wasn't no difference nohow between ten cents and eleven cents. An exact awareness of that one-cent difference is at the very basis of the New England mind. Ignorance of it in regard to the public funds has always been the accusation made by the Proper Bostonians against the Irish Bostonians who have succeeded them in the city government. I heard one such sum up his kind's condemnation of a man he liked and admired: "Jim Curley don't know the difference between principal and interest." You will remember the young Boston widow whose stanchness was widely approved; she took up prostitution, though she was tempted to dip into capital.

Hold this frugality to the light. One aspect of it has created ten thousand derisive anecdotes, and can indeed lead to meanness and miserliness that corrode the human spirit. And yet another aspect leads straight to the neatness, clarity, and precision that are true elegance. This elegance is the swept and garnished New England countryside, the houses and town halls and meetinghouses whose white paint is spiritual dignity, the fanlights of the mansions, the scrubbed stoops (with a pumpkin on them at harvest time) of the farmhouses, the farmhouses themselves, sited not only so that they are sheltered from the prevailing wind but so that they take in the vista of the creek curving toward the fold in the hills.

It is almost inconceivable now that the hill farms were once a wheat country and a sheep country. That period could not possibly last; the upland soil washed into the creeks long ago. The Yankee Exodus that Mr. Holbrook writes about began even before the Middle West was opened up, and there was no stopping it once the Yankee farmer heard about cropland that was flat, had deep soil, and was free of stones. Concern

The Common at Townsend, Massachusetts:
Once a public grazing ground, now a pleasant park.

The hill farms ceased to be agriculture but remained landscape. New England has been a summer resort for more than a century and has steadily increased in popularity as a winter-sports center. Moreover, the exhausted fields and sagging houses, which up to the last war could often be bought for less than the timber in the woodlots was worth, attracted people who wanted respite from city noise and strain. "Summer folks" turned from renting to buying and so went on the tax rolls. Rich outlanders bought up such showplaces as the hill towns had, chiefly in southwestern Vermont and Connecticut's Litchfield Hills. Where nothing sufficiently imposing existed they built their own; because they invaded the Berkshires at the nadir of the national taste, a beautiful area is freckled with monstrosities almost as appalling as those at Newport. (Change has overtaken them, too; many are schools, hospitals, and religious retreats now.) But most of the summer folks who became taxpayers were professional people, especially academics.

A more important immigration that had been going on for a long time was accelerated by the depression—people whose workrooms or studies could be anywhere: writers, painters, musicians, hand craftsmen. A New Hampshire town is typical; it has an orchestra, founded by such an immigrant, that plays

about the abandoned New England farm and the abandoned New England spinster became a fixture in American journalism. The forest began to take back the fields which that nightmare labor had cleared. Many miles of stone walls it was a weariness to build are deep in hardwoods now. Family burying grounds are thickets of weed trees. Lilacs, strayed garden perennials, and apple trees blossom among maples that have choked off what once were lanes.

The farmers who did not go west moved to the valleys and to whatever flatland New England has, mainly in Connecticut, Down East in Maine, and along the Connecticut River. Sometimes they moved their town halls and meetinghouses with them. Valley soil, truck gardening, and dairy farming saved the stricken agriculture. Aroostook County has made the potato famous; in summer the Connecticut Valley is wonderfully pleasing striations of green and white, the onion fields and the cheesecloth tents that shade the tobacco fields. But the truth is that not many of the original Yankees were talented farmers; their genius was of a different kind. So agriculture largely passed into the hands of those who had the talent: Poles, Italians, French-Canadians, Slavs, a few Russians and Greeks, and of course the Finns, who would work in a mill only long enough to raise the first payment on an abandoned farm. They knew how to make the glacial rubble yield the comforts that their predecessors could not get from it. They knew, too, what the quintessential Yankee Robert Frost (also an immigrant; he was born in San Francisco) meant by his commandment, Build soil! . . . And agriculture will profit even more than the small industries if the contentious and hood-winked states ever sanction some public power projects.

Small farm: *The backbone of New England sustenance
in the still-remembered past, it has often
in recent years been allowed
to revert to forest or been converted
to a retreat for summer vacationists.*

New England/Bernard De Voto 267

Sea trade brought the world's goods to Salem's homes.

on antique instruments the music written for them. That some instruments are hard to come by does not bother its members, for they make what they cannot find. "Vermont's actual farming farmers amount to less than a fourth of its population," says a treatise just published. The explanation is not only the small industries; it is also the writers, painters, etchers, illustrators, composers and dancers whom the state has attracted and the craftsmen who work in wood, metal, ceramics, glass, fabrics and plastics. In their small shops they practice an exquisite and fastidious workmanship, entirely true to the tradition of New England. What do you lack? Gunstocks, fiddles, cabinets, precision instruments of brass, ornamental ironwork, glass mosaics or stained-glass windows, carved semiprecious stones, models of the night sky or of molecules, laminated tables, chairs of inlay, miniatures, intaglio work? There are native or naturalized Vermonters to provide it.

Still another immigration has recently been making itself felt, even in upper New England. Big manufacturing firms are establishing branch plants where highly skilled labor is abundant, and where there is quiet, and clean air and the rural outdoors. Thus a cycle of change has come all the way round to the beginning again. It requires a final note on geography as fate.

Of the highlands, the most fateful were those farthest west, especially the Berkshires. For one fundamental feature of New England geography lies outside New England—the Hudson

River. It is a water route for freight to New York Harbor; and the Mohawk Valley which opens off it is a route, along which the Erie Canal was built, to the Great Lakes and the Mississippi. No canal could cross the granite spine of New England. New England lost the industrial lead that it had achieved over New York and Pennsylvania. It was forced back on the mechanical skills which have become its specialties and has flourished by means of them ever since.

For the Yankees who turned to the glacial waterfalls had found the genius of their breed. We may now return to those masonry dams that are the vestiges of another age. They are on all rivers and creeks and on some brooks so small that you can hardly believe the evidence. Beside them are brick walls it would take high explosives to demolish, though roofs and windows have been gone for two generations or more. The walls are those of little mills that were powered by the dams, the mills to which the Yankee genius brought precision, versatility, and unsurpassed craftsmanship. The Yankees were predestined smiths, mechanics, artificers, contrivers, innovators. The direct and orderly progression of machine processes was their intellectual idiom. Indeed it was their spiritual wellbeing, for what is the logic of machines if it is not the identical economy, exactness, propriety and neatness that I have already called elegance? At the village green, the exquisite steeple and the scrubbed stoop with a pumpkin on it; in the shipyards, the lines of the clippers; in the shop, a turret lathe or a drop forge growing ever more complex and automatic as Yankee logic works out its functions. Note that the sects held God Himself to the demands of logic and machined their dogmas to tolerances of a ten-thousandth of an inch.

The mills were everywhere. The town where I have spent the pleasantest of my summers is far to the north; it has five hundred inhabitants and a single woodworking mill. A century ago it had 1200 inhabitants and the two creeks powered a grist mill, a sawmill, a planing and turning mill, a fulling mill, a fanning mill, and one of those primordial "machine shops" that would do anything the surrounding market wanted done. What ended this happiest period of the industrial revolution was not only the spread of steam and later electric power that made industrial concentrations economical, but even more the development of the railroad network. Massachusetts and Connecticut, whose geographical relationship to the railroads was favorable, developed the mill town as we now know it—and learned the vulnerability of a one-industry economy when later shifts came. But in upper New England the loss of the mills was a greater disaster than the passing of the hill farms. At about the same time large-scale lumbering began to peter out; the forest was as exhausted as the hilltop fields.

The towns hung on. I point again to the tenacity and ingenuity of the breed who built them, but something else is to be stressed more: The New England town, which is a township and may contain several villages, has always been a community. We speak of it as the society that first gave self-government to America; in the farmer on his feet in town meeting to hold the *se*electment to account we see the primary mechanism of democracy. That is true enough but the Americans were traveling toward that goal by other roads as well; the greater point here is that from the beginning the town was a society where people were members one of another. That explains its vitality and is the reason why anyone who writes about New England must keep coming back to the towns. On the successive New England frontiers civilization did not have to develop slowly, step by step. It was taken there fully developed in units already organized and of established community habits. Nor does the community stop at some Tenth Street boundary, with the fringe and farms excluded. It extends all the way to the next town line and incloses the proprietors of the farthest fields, trap lines, and summer camps in the common consciousness. It is remarkably independent of that next town, though practiced also in co-operating with it. And if the towns are independent of one another they are even more remarkably independent of the states. Indepedence is the other face of elegance.

As the towns hung on, so did a surprising number of woodworking mills. They had made everything for a wide market; now they made shoe pegs, heels, toothpicks, hoe handles, bowls, end tables, or toilet paper. Sometimes a town's solvency depended on a single mill that provided a small payroll and a market for the woodlots. You see them in the most thinly populated valleys; every few years they are rebuilt after a flood has swept them downstream. The forest began to return a larger yield; pulp mills came to utilize the wood that would not make lumber; the veneer and plywood business came into being. The mechanical specialties proliferated; as far up the Connecticut Valley as Springfield, Vermont, there are famous machine-tool plants, and your maple sugar may have been processed farther north. Today the town is a complex equilibrium: truck farms, dairy farms, mills, summer residents and winter sports, the tourist trade, a preparatory school or a sanitarium. And now that the wheel has come full circle, the branch plants. The more the New England town has changed, the more it has remained the same thing.

Stereotypes about the Yankees are also much too beloved to be given up. Most of them go back to the Yankees of the Exodus. By the hundred thousand they went out to Oregon and Nebraska and Minnesota and Arizona, and to all wildernesses and way stations in between. They sowed the land with colleges and loan companies, with transcontinental railroads and inconceivably woozy utopian experiments, with revolutionary political ideas and Lydia E. Pinkham's Vegetable Compound. They furiously peddled the Yankee notions, both kinds: tinware and whittled bowls and brass clocks and, so the comic weeklies proclaimed, wooden nutmegs; the abolition of slavery and the prohibtion of strong drink (which they had conspicuously omitted to institute in New England), humane treatment of the insane, and the immediate Second Coming of Christ, tax-supported schools, celibate marriage, and polygamy.

The stereotypes are as various as the actuality. The Yankee as bumpkin with a hat all bound 'round with a woolen string, chewing a straw and talking about the caows—the earliest

figure of farce in our literature and still a fixture on the radio and in Eugene O'Neill's plays. The Yankee as Sam Slick, just too dum'd smairt for other bumpkins and for you city fellers, peddling lightning rods for cows and swamproot bitters and stock in the Portland city hall. The Yankee as busybody, reformer, agitator. The Yankee of our oral facetiae; Cap'n Simmons, "no kith or kin of mine, thank God," will do for a sample.

And down this corridor are so many images of the Yankee as Puritan that I can only shrug and check the bet. I tell you severely that the Puritan had little to do with Maine, less with Vermont, and nothing at all with Rhode Island—or half of New England—and that he was a divided soul. He was a beset artist, a lover of fine glass and fine silverware, of bright colors, of the art of rhetoric, of (outside the meetinghouse) music; he created our most beautiful architectural styles. God knows he feared the poisons that lurk in well water and could not graduate a class or ordain a minister without floods of alcohol in which the unrighteous man would have foundered. He reproached himself for yielding too eagerly and often to the seductiveness of women and the statistics show what he was talking about.

Boxing the compass, the stereotypes assert too much. As one who is without New England blood, breeding, or inheritance but has spent his mature life here, I demur. The Yankees are supposed to be a taciturn and laconic breed, speaking little and in unstressed, epigrammatic irony, hiding their private thoughts and private lives behind a cool impersonality of speech. They are the most indefatigable talkers on earth, of a more than Sicilian volubility. It takes an outlander years to learn how to break in even momentarily on their logorrhea. The stranger who comes among them never gets accustomed to the reckless and unbuttoned outpouring of their most intimate secrets. A repressed people? Orgiastic is the better word; I would be happy to take you to a dog track, to any town or county fair, or for that matter along any river bank or down any country road when evening has fallen. Graceless and bad-mannered? Well, yes, the Bostonians. They always have been; even the naturally courtly Irish have lapsed by attraction into a belligerent crankiness. But away from Boston they are warm and gracious. Prone to eccentricity? Yes, thank God, both the old stock and the immigrant or galvanized Yankees . . . It means that in the Yankee commonwealth the right for a man to be himself is exercised and respected.

Which brings us back, as always, to the New England countryside and the New England town. And to the question with which I began, why so many Americans from other regions, on coming here for the first time, feel at home.

By whatever distant rivers the Yankees sat down, they wept when they remembered Zion, and they still do. In the last desert between the last blue rocks, Mr. Eliot rejoices in the lost lilac and the lost sea voices, the bent goldenrod and the whirling plover. (Killdeer, he would have said if he were more recently from Zion.) On the far side of the continent Stewart Holbrook remembers great-aunt Sharon picking up a great pink-and-white conch shell to sound over the Vermont hillside the note which was a "warning that a Yankee God had brought noontime again."

It is the street of a town. It is quiet, almost as quiet as the woods, the hill crest, and the pond that can be reached in ten minutes from the center. The town has no vision of becoming a city. None of its inhabitants expects to become a millionaire. The basis of its vigor and its magnetism is quite simple and it is also quite real. One is freer here than elsewhere to be oneself. There are space, leisure, and freedom for personality to develop. One may follow his calling and raise his family in decent self-respect with less pressure to conform to the prepossessions or timidity of others, with more immunity from the dictation of fashion or belief or group passion or group orthodoxy. The feeling of being at home in the New England town is an augmentation: a fuller knowledge than one is likely to get elsewhere that there is reason to respect oneself and that one's independence and individuality are respected. Independence, orderly citizenship, self-respect, they are more easily come by here. Meaning more, they are more sought after and therefore more often achieved. They sum up as the life of elegance.

That is one part of the feeling I am trying to account for. The rest will be revealed by another immigration to New England. In my time at Harvard, the most beloved teacher was Dean Le Baron Russell Briggs. Shortly after he died, a friend of mine, trying to phrase our feeling about him, said, "To thousands of alumni he stood for the invisible Harvard." This other immigration is to the invisible New England. For the first instance, the Boston doctor.

Those who have intractable or little-understood ailments, or who need the most expert surgery, or who can't afford to pay for the needed treatment, come to Boston by the thousand every year. Now there has always been an honorable medical tradition among the Bostonians, and in some families medical talent seems to be hereditary. But the Boston doctor comes not only from New England but from everywhere else—London, Johannesburg, Vienna, Prairie du Chien, Podunk. He does not come to make a fortune. Having come here, he cannot be drawn away. He will refuse chairs and appointments that pay three times as much in money and power; he will relinquish to other hands the cosseting of Texas billionaires afflicted with the rheum.

Other cities have medical schools, foundations, hospitals and research laboratories quite as distinguished as those in Boston. There is no reason why medical men should come to Boston in such numbers. No reason except one: that, like the townsman along the village green, they will live more fully here because they will be at home. They hold citizenship in the invisible republic.

The Yankee Institutions were founded on the difference between ten cents and eleven cents. They grew out of the Yankee logic, the Yankee scorn for slovenliness, the Yankee passion for order and precision. They are magnificent. Take me, a man who practices his profession by means of libraries. Within reach of a fifteen-minute drive from my door there are two of the largest general libraries in the world, nearly a dozen specialized libraries that are unsurpassed in their fields, a good many lesser ones.

Think of the colleges. And take for granted and so pass over the famous universities, the "name" colleges. To understand more fully, consider the little-known ones plentifully scattered over six states: the experimental colleges that spring up and flourish, the junior colleges and technical institutes and normal schools. A YMCA night school becomes Northeastern University. Brandeis in Waltham was born of dream and exile less than fifteen years ago. Institutes on back roads or over garages are founded for farmers' or workingmen's children, for bright boys in the mills, for immigrants and displaced persons. Once founded, they grow.

Think of the schools and again pass over those that are known in all parts of the country. Get on to two other groups, the upstate academies with the microscopic endowments that teach the young of eight towns and some from Iran and Luxembourg, and the small specialized schools that teach everything, posture or lip reading or electronics or foreign exchange or oratory or design to the ambitious, the elderly, the handicapped, and even the dimwitted. Now to complete the map of the republic, bring in the museums, laboratories, herbariums, arboretums, conservatories, experimental farms and forests and fisheries and print shops, and the membrane that connects them with one another.

People have kept coming to study at the Institutes, to work or teach at them, to pursue inquiries or investigations or researches, or simply to live where they are near at hand. In regard to their staffs and satellites, the word "Yankee" has come to have the same meaning that the generations have given it in the cities and towns and on the farms. Some derive from the old stock. Some are Yankees in that they came to New England and stayed. They came as the maker and player of obsolete musical instruments came to Littleton, the craftsmen in glass or walnut to Burlington, the medical researcher to the Back Bay.

For a long time only a trickle, this immigration has been in full flood for two generations. It has been partly a conscription, for the Institutions can call almost anyone they may want. But they attract more than they summon. Between the two wars brilliant and courageous people kept coming here in loathing of the Italian, German, and Russian tyrannies. During and since World War II the émigrés have been joined by exiles and refugees. They are an important and seminal part of the invisible republic, these displaced scholars, thinkers, and artists—the gifted and talented, the rebellious, the unconquerable. They were drawn here by the same magnetic field that has attracted a corresponding society from all parts of the United States.

A heterogeneous, miscellaneous, astonishing society. They were sent for, they were drawn here, they came in curiosity or in hope or in a restless, sad conviction that There Must Be Some Place. They found a place; it had been prepared for them a long time ago. They found they were at home. They are Yankees.

BOSTON

*The face of Boston has changed many times
in 300 years, but its personality is as yet unaltered.
Its spirit is in every stick and stone, its
beauty in the accumulation of memories which
nothing can ever wholly replace.
In this biting and affectionate report,
the late John P. Marquand draws a Bostonian's
portrait of the city of the Last Puritans.*

Though a large city, Boston has many small-town attributes. Everyone seems to know a little about everyone else there, and all good Bostonians are partial to local gossip and anecdote. These tales may be apocryphal but unusually they rest somewhere on truth's foundation—like the timeworn one about the Beacon Street butler announcing some newspaper reporters—"A man from the *Post*, a man from the *Globe*, and a gentleman from the *Boston Evening Transcript*."

There is a commonly accepted legend that one of Boston's most famous nonagenarians still walks each morning several miles from his home to his office in Boston's downtown business district. Whether or not this is literally correct, the idea is reassuring to Boston citizens, who all pride themselves on being hardy individuals—like, as a random example, the Bostonian, who, while taking a Sunday stroll in the country, slipped from a stone wall and broke his arm, and simply said, "Oh, sugar."

Not very long ago, when a kettle of deep fat in the kitchen of the Somerset Club burst suddenly into flames, it was reported that the firemen answering the alarm were told to use the service and not the members' entrance. It seems that this was a true report but one which still hurts the feelings of loyal members, because it implied exclusiveness. It should be added that these directions were given the firemen because the service entrance was the shortest way to the kitchen. Almost daily there are new additions to this wealth of Boston lore, but ancient tales are also passed on by succeeding generations. Even today you can hear a story about old Mr. Thomas Handasyd Perkins, the great merchant in the China trade. It is said that a Boston jeweler, noticing that Mr. Perkins wore a leather thong attached to his gold watch, asked if Mr. Perkins would not like a gold watch chain, considering his position, and Mr. Perkins answered that his position was such that he could afford to wear a leather thong.

It is reported that Mr. Justice Holmes once made the observation that Bostonians, even in times of national crisis, when referring to The President, do not mean the President of the United States, but the President of Harvard. Then, of course, there is the story of the Boston lady, who, on returning from

*Bostonians and pigeons collect on the Common
across from Park Street Church, constructed in 1809.*

Beacon Street—still a good address in the best Boston tradition.

a trip to California, was asked what route she followed, and answered that she went by way of Dedham. There is also the one about another Boston lady, who corrected a stranger who spoke of the state of Iowa, saying gently, "In Boston we call it Ohio." All these anecdotes are known to almost every citizen, and one could add dozens more to the collection, but the one which I still like best concerns one of Boston's senior diplomats, who was absent for a long period of time on a tour of duty in the Orient. "If he does not come home soon," one of his relatives is reported to have said, "he will get completely out of touch with Milton"—not the poet, of course, but Boston's famous suburb.

This in a strict sense is truer than one might think, for Boston is a complex of intricately developed manners and of delicately balanced values which demand constant association if the city is to be fully comprehended. Otherwise one does indeed get out of touch with Boston. I am acutely aware of this, although an orthodox Bostonian would say that I am in no position whatsoever to make any authoritative remark on the subject, since I come from Newburyport, Massachusetts, and was born in Wilmington, Delaware. He might also add that I am not even what is sometimes called a professional Bostonian, like certain enthusiastic Westerners and Jerseyites who have settled in the city limits and have carried the torch until they have out-Bostoned Boston. Nevertheless I have developed a certain superficial awareness of the city, since most of my life has been spent shuttling in a schizophrenic manner between Boston and New York.

Nothing, I believe, is more spiritually difficult than an attempt to adjust oneself to the life of these two utterly divergent cities. A true Bostonian is fortunate in that he has never made such an effort. There is no necessity, because he is completely content with his environment. A genuine Bostonian is always anxious to get home. New York, he will tell you, if you meet him on the five o'clock as it leaves the Grand Central, is not a place to come to but it is a very good place to get away from. Bostonians, when in New York, used to frequent the Hotel Belmont, presumably to be as near to the New York, New Haven, and Hartford Railroad as possible, but now that this hostelry has disappeared, a Bostonian is a man without a country. It is very easy and, for one who has his roots there, dangerous to get out of touch with Boston. Nevertheless, it is surprising how quickly this city reclaims an erring son, once he has returned. The more things change, as the French say, the more they remain the same things, and here perhaps the French are right.

There is no city in this kaleidoscopic country that has not suffered its growing pains of change, but Boston, I imagine, has undergone more startling and soul-shaking upheavals than most, in spite of what untutored critics say about its static qualities. No one who delves even superficially into the record can ignore all the terrific things that have happened and are still happening there, always accompanied by the protests of an outraged citizenry. It would be possible, if one wished, to start with the making of the Back Bay from the mud flats of the Charles River, a stream which, in spite of its alterations, still separates Boston from the hazy and enigmatic reaches of Cambridge, but by now the Back Bay and all its brick and brownstone houses have become as permanent, almost, as Beacon Hill.

Since that time, however, other shattering changes have reared their ugly heads. As an example, there was the construction of the subway through Boston Common. To achieve this improvement it was necessary to excavate a graveyard at the edge of the Common and to re-establish many remains on top of the subway, a pious act which still stands in the minds of a few as an outstanding exhibition of civic gymnastics. Then there was the damming of the Charles River to make what is now the picturesque Basin, an encroachment on individual rights which aroused the wrath of dwellers along the water side of Beacon Street, who had enjoyed watching from their back windows the rise and fall of the tide and who were obliged to alter their household systems of drainage. Even a brief perusal of the public prints show that some group of Boston citizens has always been protesting against something. Around the latter twenties, there was the difficulty over the erection of a large electric sign overlooking Boston Common advertising a popular automobile. Many persons felt that the sight of an electric sign over the Parkman Bandstand and the Common's educationally labeled trees was a desecration of hallowed ground and that the electric advertisements bordering the Common on Tremont Street were quite enough. History may prove that this event was the source of a new rush of bad ideas which have yet to cease. Only a year or so ago housewives on Beacon Hill were compelled to move their Boston rockers outside their dwellings and to sit in embattled formations in order to prevent a city contractor from tearing up the bricks of their sidewalks and substituting a modern and unsightly concrete pavement, and worse was soon to follow.

The recent Governor of Massachusetts, the Honorable Paul A. Dever, is blamed in many quarters for the latest bouleversements, and with some justice—for not even James Michael Curley himself, Boston's perennial mayor as long as one can remember, and a name frequently used to frighten small Beacon Street children, has done as much to change the face of this splendid city. Under the generous and friendly Dever administration "A Great New Highway System"—as Mr. Dever has called it on hundreds of billboards, always asking passers-by to excuse the inconvenience—knifed its way through Boston. Skyway ramps arched over its ancient winding lanes, and intricate clover leaves, flanked by swimming pools and playgrounds, appeared at unexpected points. The Esplanade along the Charles, the generous gift of Mrs. Storrow, where it was once possible to wheel babies, walk dogs, and even to sail toy boats in comparative security, now—excuse the inconvenience—has a six-lane concrete highway running through it, with underpasses, overpasses, and bridges for pedestrians. The old North End—excuse the inconvenience—where the Old North Church and the rewarding residence of the late Paul Revere, not to mention the old Copp's Hill Burying Ground, still presumably remain intact, and where one once purchased Italian goat cheeses and spaghetti dinners, was vastly altered. Block after block, fragile shops and tenements, which frankly could not have stood up much longer anyway, were leveled down to rubble, so that our cradle of liberty, Faneuil Hall itself, now stands nakedly before the intricacies of the Great New Highway System.

These physical changes, imposing though they may be, are only symptoms of an era's social change. For more than a century, certain sections of Boston's population have been endeavoring, like defeated armies, to break contact with pursuing elements. Irish Bostonians have held the South End so long that they have lost their brogue and are today in many ways as aloof as the Boston Brahmins, but the Italians, who have staked their claim to the old North End, are constantly treading on their heels. Besides these larger quotas, orthodox

Jewish communities, a small Chinatown, and a growing Harlem, not to mention colonies of Syrians, Poles, and Greeks, have all taken root in Boston; but no other group has yet duplicated the migrations of Boston's most publicized minority, sometimes termed "the Proper Bostonians" or "the Last Puritans."

From the earliest history of Boston to the present these individuals have been assiduously engaged in escaping from strange neighbors and, more recently, from themselves. When Bonner drew his inviting map of Boston before the middle of the eighteenth century, the Brahmins, if there were Brahmins then, dwelt in gambrel-roofed houses in the vicinity of the North End, only to move south under the pressures of business and population growth. The days of Gilbert Stuart and the China trade saw them building on Beacon Hill, and also in the region where the shopping district now flourishes, on Franklin, Summer and Winter streets. Some of them tried Tremont Street for a while, ending by building the beautiful Colonnade Row, recalled now only in ancient prints, but their culture vanished from these districts years ago, leaving only an occasional square or church behind it. They also experimented with the South End for a while, evolving exclusive residential developments, still visible in the vicinity of Worcester Square. Eventually, however, they were attracted to the Back Bay and began living life anew on the right and wrong sides of Commonwealth Avenue, on Newbury and Marlborough streets and on the water and wrong sides of Beacon. It almost seemed, around the turn of the century, that polite Boston was permanently established in this area. Conservatives even began to venture from their Bulfinch fronts on Beacon Hill to settle behind the uglier but more fashionable façades of the new land beside the Public Garden. There they dwelt—and some do still—in a soberly intellectual affluence, accounts of which still linger like a happy echo in the pages of Doctor Holmes or the novels of William Dean Howells and Judge Grant and occasionally of Henry James.

Space prevents any full description of their remarkable and often endearing customs. There is only room to observe that though they have long been a minority surrounded by a population as much a part of Boston as themselves, their vigor and their impeccable instinct for order and tradition, combined with their capacity for making and conserving comfortable sums of money, have always given character and tone to the whole city. They have even contrived, in spite of their small numbers, to run financial State Street, and more often than not to govern the state and represent its people in the halls of Congress, and their genius has not yet evaporated. It has been assisted always by the infusion of new blood, as Mr. Howells has observed in his novel, *The Rise of Silas Lapham*, depicting the career of an astute and aggressive Yankee from the wrong side of the tracks. There are plenty of Silas Laphams still, revered figures in the Chamber of Commerce, if not in the Somerset and Union clubs, but most of these somehow prefer rural life in the Newtons.

It is disturbing to report that proper Boston, so well defined and so conspicuous, is now undergoing the greatest change of all. In the last two decades, and indeed even before, proper Bostonians have been leaving Boston, and the exodus has now become so great as to remind one of Philadelphia, that strange city now almost completely devoid of proper Philadelphians.

The vacant houses and the sales signs on Commonwealth Avenue and Marlborough Street chant in a mute chorus the lament of a vanishing way of life. Few persons can afford and fewer wish to live in their grandparents' mansions now, in drafty rooms with dated heating plants and plumbing. Boston servants, whose wages plus their food frequently exceed the salary of a Harvard instructor, are neither so spry nor so hardy as they used to be, granted that their services are obtainable. Neither do their loyalties and spirit of sacrifice meet the standards which any Beacon Street housewife once felt justified in expecting. They have somehow lost that fine old pride in work which once kept the shadowy dining rooms, drawing rooms and libraries spotless, and they show a marked distaste for cozy unheated quarters beneath the slates. For years the real value of these dwellings has dropped below what they are assessed for tax purposes. It is cheaper to leave them than remodel, and besides, Beacon Street and Commonwealth Avenue are shaken now by a roar of traffic, and parked cars are jammed all day along the curbs. It is better for the children to move to the country.

Thus many peculiar contradictions are appearing on Boston's proudest streets. First the dentists and the doctors and the osteopaths appeared, and then small apartments and larger apartment buildings and next a few restaurants. The Slater House with its great ballroom became an eating establishment known as the Fox and Hounds, and a casket company has its offices at the far end of Commonwealth Avenue. Several imposing dwellings now house secretarial schools and colleges and academies of song and dance. Outlanders by the hundreds, according to older standards, are now quite at home on Beacon Street. It is growing increasingly difficult to reconstruct old Boston now.

The protesters against the automobile sign and kindred desecrations are still calling for the moving vans, and not for any conventional trek to the now citified suburbia of Brookline and Chestnut Hill. They are moving to more distant, less disturbed perimeters—to Concord, Dedham, Beverly Farms and Hamilton, and even to points beyond. Incidentally it is interesting to note that the Boston Irish too are not unsusceptible to the travel virus. Their comfortably situated lawyers, brokers, contractors, and plenty of their politicians are now living the year around in Cohasset and Scituate and other South Shore points. It is true that the breadwinners of all these solid families still spend their days in Boston offices, own Boston real estate, park their cars in front of the No Parking signs, and with their wives and children patronize Boston stores, hotels and theaters, but they no longer live or vote there. Imperceptibly at first but with growing momentum the conservative balance and leadership of the town is disappearing to parts unknown, leaving vacuum in its place. Soon, if the trend continues, only a corporal's guard will be left behind the ancient and purpled windows of Beacon Hill and around the Public Garden. New baby carriages and new juveniles will gather in that Garden soon, in the vicinity of its little lake and the bronze statue of George Washington. Dogs of a different type will follow their masters on what is left of the Esplanade. New faces by the hundreds will appear in the congregations of the Arlington Street Church, of the Advent, the Emmanuel, and Trinity. It may even be that the Scruple Room of the Boston Athenaeum will someday be freely opened to proprietors.

It is all very well to remark that something has always been happening to Boston. In all probability, since the days of that well-disposed Indian, the chief Shawmut, whose name still adorns a local banking house, and who had real-estate interests on Boston Neck when the first Puritans arrived, there have been individuals who have said that Boston is not what it used to be. Furthermore, nothing anywhere is ever what it used to be. Nothing is easier to lament than the good old days, and most lamentations can be discounted in the name of progress. Nevertheless the fact remains that the physical face of Boston and its habits and institutions have undergone more alterations in the lifetime of its present generation than ever before in its history. Boston has been shaken by impacts that may well make strong men weep, and no one can foretell what the final results may be; but it is curious to discover that nothing of its personality has been basically altered yet. It still remains one of the few cities in America with an individuality and flavor entirely its own. It has never forgotten its past in terms of its present and to anyone who has lived in it long enough to know its way, Boston is still, from a prejudiced viewpoint, one of the most satisfactory cities anywhere, and one of the most beguilingly beautiful.

It may be that Boston has only beautiful elements and that the gold-domed State House—crippled by its more modern marble wings—the Old State House, Park Street Church, King's Chapel, Trinity, the Public Library, the Fenway, and Mrs. Jack Gardner's Palace are beads on a string that have no relationship or unity. Nevertheless I doubt this, because most of these critics have not lived there long enough to have the loyalty that makes all of Boston beautiful. They may have seen it after a fresh snowfall. They may have seen it at the end of a hard winter, in early spring, or in the dry heat of summer, but they have seldom lived through the full palette of its changing seasons. They have not seen an early spring sunrise there, or the glow of its bricks in summer or winter sunsets. It would be fantastic to compare the naïvely Victorian planting of the Public Garden with the beauties of Kensington or the Tuileries, but still there is nothing anywhere else that is just like the Public Garden, any more than there is anything else like the Common. It would be equally fantastic to compare the islands and the chill murky water and mud flats of Boston Harbor with the Bay of Naples, but then as one sails into that harbor and sees from a ship's deck what is left of the old water front and watches the buildings of the old town rise upward to its hills, there can be no doubt it is unique. It is a harbor that can speak in terms of both the future and the past. There is nowhere else where one can both think of the atomic

Swan boats sail on the lagoon in Boston's Public Gardens.

age and still hear the echo of the gunfire of the *Chesapeake* and *Shannon* in the War of 1812, when Lawrence, the Captain of the *Chesapeake*, said as he was dying in the surgeon's cockpit, "Don't give up the ship."

To a Bostonian, Boston's beauty lies in an accumulation of memories which nothing can ever wholly displace. Its charm lies in the varied memories of the great men and women who have lived there and have left their indelible imprint. Dr. Holmes' Autocrat of the Breakfast Table might have a hard time finding his way about right now, but he would still understand the town. He would understand it as anyone who has lived in Boston does the moment he returns, because its spirit is in the air he breathes and in every stick and stone.

Boston/John P. Marquand **275**

HERE IS NEW YORK

The island of Manhattan is the greatest human concentrate on earth, a majestic, perpendicular city. E. B. White calls it a poem whose magic is comprehensible to millions of permanent residents but whose full meaning will always remain elusive even to them.

On any person who desires such queer prizes, New York will bestow the gift of loneliness and the gift of privacy. It is this largess that accounts for the presence within the city's walls of a considerable section of the population; for the residents of Manhattan are to a large extent strangers who have pulled up stakes somewhere and come to town, seeking sanctuary or fulfillment or some greater or lesser grail. The capacity to make such dubious gifts is a mysterious quality of New York. It can destroy an individual, or it can fulfill him, depending a good deal on luck. No one should come to New York to live unless he is willing to be lucky.

New York is the concentrate of art and commerce and sport and religion and entertainment and finance, bringing to a single compact arena the gladiator, the evangelist, the promoter, the actor, the trader and the merchant. It carries on its lapel the unexpungeable odor of the long past, so that no matter where you sit in New York you feel the vibrations of great times and tall deeds, of queer people and events and undertakings. I am sitting at the moment in a stifling hotel room in 90-degree heat, halfway down an air shaft, in midtown. No air moves in or out of the room, yet I am curiously affected by emanations from the immediate surroundings. I am twenty-two blocks from where Rudolph Valentino lay in state, eight blocks from where Nathan Hale was executed, five blocks from the publisher's office where Ernest Hemingway hit Max Eastman on the nose, four miles from where Walt Whitman sat sweating out editorials for the *Brooklyn Eagle*, thirty-four blocks from the street Willa Cather lived in when she came to New York to write books about Nebraska, one block from where Marceline used to clown on the boards of the Hippodrome, thirty-six blocks from the spot where the historian Joe Gould kicked a radio to pieces in full view of the public, thirteen blocks from where Harry Thaw shot Stanford White, five blocks from where I used to usher at the Metropolitan Opera and only a hundred and twelve blocks from the spot where Clarence Day the Elder was washed of his sins in the Church of the Epiphany (I could continue this list indefinitely); and for that matter I am probably occupying the very room that any number of exalted and somewise memorable characters sat in, some of them on hot, breathless afternoons, lonely and private and full of their own sense of emanations from without.

When I went down to lunch a few minutes ago I noticed that the man sitting next to me (about eighteen inches away along the wall) was Fred Stone. The eighteen inches were both the connection and the separation that New York provides for

Manhattan dusk: *Tower lights glitter against the darkening blue night.*

its inhabitants. My only connection with Fred Stone was that I saw him in *The Wizard of Oz* around the beginning of the century. But our waiter felt the same stimulus from being close to a man from Oz, and after Mr. Stone left the room the waiter told me that when he (the waiter) was a young man just arrived in this country and before he could understand a word of English, he had taken his girl for their first theater date to *The Wizard of Oz*. It was a wonderful show, the waiter recalled—a man of straw, a man of tin. Wonderful! (And still only eighteen inches away.) "Mr. Stone is a very hearty eater," said the waiter thoughtfully, content with this fragile participation in destiny, this link with Oz.

New York blends the gift of privacy with the excitement of participation; and better than most dense communities it succeeds in insulating the individual (if he wants it, and almost everybody wants or needs it) against all enormous and violent and wonderful events that are taking place every minute. Since I have been sitting in this miasmic air shaft, a good many rather splashy events have occurred in town. A man shot and killed his wife in a fit of jealousy. It caused no stir outside his block and got only small mention in the papers. I did not attend. Since my arrival, the greatest air show ever staged in all the world took place in town. I didn't attend and neither did most of the eight million other inhabitants, although they say there was quite a crowd. I didn't even hear any planes except a couple of westbound commercial airliners that habitually use this air shaft to fly over. The biggest ocean-going ships on the North Atlantic arrived and departed. I didn't notice them and neither did most other New Yorkers. I am told this is the greatest seaport in the world, with six hundred and fifty miles of water front, and ships calling here from many exotic lands, but the only boat I've happened to notice since my arrival was a small sloop tacking out of the East River night before last on the ebb tide when I was walking across the Brooklyn Bridge. I heard the *Queen Mary* blow one midnight, though, and the sound carried the whole history of departure and longing and loss. The Lions have been in convention. I've seen not one Lion. A friend of mine saw one and told me about him. (He was lame, and was wearing a bolero.) At the ballgrounds and horse parks the greatest sporting spectacles have been enacted. I saw no ballplayer, no race horse. The governor came to town. I heard the siren scream, but that was all there was to that—an eighteen-inch margin again. A man was killed by a falling cornice. I was not a party to the tragedy, and again the inches counted heavily.

I mention these merely to show that New York is peculiarly constructed to absorb almost anything that comes along (whether a thousand-foot liner out of the East or a twenty-thousand-man convention out of the West) without inflicting the event on its inhabitants; so that every event is, in a sense, optional, and the inhabitant is in the happy position of being able to choose his spectacle and so conserve his soul. In most metropolises, small and large, the choice is often not with the individual at all. He is thrown to the Lions. The Lions are overwhelming; the event is unavoidable. A cornice falls, and it hits every citizen on the head, every last man in town. I sometimes think that the only event that hits every New Yorker on the head is the annual St. Patrick's Day parade, which is fairly penetrating—the Irish are a hard race to tune out, there are 500,000 of them in residence, and they have the police force right in the family.

The quality in New York that insulates its inhabitants from life may simply weaken them as individuals. Perhaps it is healthier to live in a community where, when a cornice falls, you feel the blow; where, when the governor passes, you see at any rate his hat.

I am not defending New York in this regard. Many of its settlers are probably here merely to escape, not face, reality. But whatever it means, it is a rather rare gift, and I believe it has a positive effect on the creative capacities of New Yorkers—for creation is in part merely the business of forgoing the great and small distractions.

Although New York often imparts a feeling of great forlornness or forsakenness, it seldom seems dead or unresourceful; and you always feel that either by shifting your location ten blocks or by reducing your fortune by five dollars you can experience rejuvenation. Many people who have no real independence of spirit depend on the city's tremendous variety and sources of excitement for spiritual sustenance and maintenance of morale. In the country there are a few chances of sudden rejuvenation—a shift in weather, perhaps, or something arriving in the mail. But in New York the chances are endless. I think that although many persons are here from some excess of spirit (which caused them to break away from their small town), some, too, are here from a deficiency of spirit, who find in New York a protection, or an easy substitution.

There are roughly three New Yorks. There is, first, the New York of the man or woman who was born here, who takes the city for granted and accepts its size and its turbulence as natural and inevitable. Second, there is the New York of the commuter—the city that is devoured by locusts each day and spat out each night. Third, there is the New York of the person who was born somewhere else and came to New York in quest of something. Of these three trembling cities the greatest is the last—the city of final destination, the city that is a goal. It is this third city that accounts for New York's high-strung disposition, its poetical deportment, its dedication to the arts, and its incomparable achievements. Commuters give the city its tidal restlessness; natives give it solidity and continuity; but the settlers give it passion. And whether it is a farmer arriving from Italy to set up a small grocery store in a slum, or a young girl arriving from a small town in Mississippi to escape the indignity of being observed by her neighbors, or a boy arriving from the Corn Belt with a manuscript in his suitcase and a pain in his heart, it makes no difference: each embraces New York with the intense excitement of first love, each absorbs New York with the fresh eyes of an adventurer, each generates heat and light to dwarf the Consolidated Edison Company.

A poem compresses much in a small space and adds music, thus heightening its meaning. The city is like poetry: it compresses all life, all races and breeds, into a small island and adds music and the accompaniment of internal engines. The

Manhattan fantasy: *Photographed through one window with the reflection of another cast in it.*

island of Manhattan is without any doubt the greatest human concentrate on earth, the poem whose magic is comprehensible to millions of permanent residents but whose full meaning will always remain illusive. At the feet of the tallest and plushiest offices lie the crummiest slums. The genteel mysteries housed in the Riverside Church are only a few blocks from the voodoo charms of Harlem. The merchant princes, riding to Wall Street in their limousines down the East River Drive, pass within a few hundred yards of the gypsy kings; but the princes do not know they are passing kings, and the kings are not up yet anyway—they live a more leisurely life than the princes and get drunk more consistently.

New York is nothing like Paris; it is nothing like London; and it is not Spokane multiplied by sixty, or Detroit multiplied by four. It is by all odds the loftiest of cities. It even managed to reach the highest point in the sky at the lowest moment of the depression. The Empire State Building shot 1250 feet into

the air when it was madness to put out as much as six inches of new growth. (The building has a mooring mast that no dirigible has ever tied to; it employs a man to flush toilets in slack times; it has been hit by an airplane in a fog, struck countless times by lightning, and been jumped off by so many unhappy people that pedestrians instinctively quicken step when passing Fifth Avenue and 34th Street.)

Manhattan has been compelled to expand skyward because of the absence of any other direction in which to grow. This, more than any other thing, is responsible for its physical majesty. It is to the nation what the white church spire is to the village—the visible symbol of aspiration and faith, the white plume saying that the way is up. The summer traveler swings in over Hell Gate Bridge and from the window of his sleeping car as it glides above the pigeon lofts and back yards of Queens looks southwest to where the morning light first strikes the steel peaks of midtown, and he sees its upward thrust unmistakable: the great walls and towers rising, the smoke rising, the heat not yet rising, the hopes and ferments of so many awakening millions rising—this vigorous spear that presses heaven hard.

It is a miracle that New York works at all. The whole thing is implausible. Every time the residents brush their teeth, millions of gallons of water must be drawn from the Catskills and the hills of Westchester. When a young man in Manhattan writes a letter to his girl in Brooklyn, the love message gets blown to her through a pneumatic tube—*pfft*—just like that. The subterranean system of telephone cables, power lines, steam pipes, gas mains and sewer pipes is reason enough to abandon the island to the gods and the weevils. Every time an incision is made in the pavement, the noisy surgeons expose ganglia that are tangled beyond belief. By rights New York should have destroyed itself long ago, from panic or fire or rioting or failure of some vital supply line in its circulatory system or from some deep labyrinthine short circuit. Long ago the city should have experienced an insoluble traffic snarl at some impossible bottleneck. It should have perished of hunger when food lines failed for a few days. It should have been wiped out by a plague starting in its slums or carried in by ships' rats. It should have been overwhelmed by the sea that licks at it on every side. The workers in its myriad cells should have succumbed to nerves, from the fearful pall of smoke-fog that drifts over every few days from Jersey, blotting out all light at noon and leaving the high offices suspended, men groping and depressed, and the sense of world's end. It should have been touched in the head by the August heat and gone off its rocker.

To a New Yorker the city is both changeless and changing. In many respects it neither looks nor feels the way it did twenty-five years ago. The elevated railways have all been pulled down. An old-timer walking up Sixth past the Jefferson Market jail misses the railroad, misses its sound, its spotted shade, its little aerial stations, and the tremor of the thing. Broadway has changed in aspect. It used to have a discernible bony structure beneath its loud bright surface; but the signs are so enormous now, the buildings and shops and hotels have largely disappeared under the neon lights and letters and the frozen-custard façade. Broadway is a custard street with no frame supporting it. In Greenwich Village the light is thinning: big apartments have come in, bordering the Square, and the bars are mirrored and chromed. But there are still in the Village the lingering traces of poesy, Mexican glass, hammered brass, batik, lamps made of whisky bottles, first novels made of fresh memories—the old Village with its alleys and ratty one-room rents catering to the erratic needs of those whose hearts are young and gay.

Grand Central has become honky-tonk, with its extra-dimensional advertising displays and its tendency to adopt the tactics of a travel broker. I practically lived in Grand Central Terminal at one period (it has all the conveniences and I had no other place to stay) and the great hall always seemed to me one of the more inspiring interiors in New York, until Lastex and Coca-Cola got into the temple.

The subtlest change in New York is something people don't speak much about but that is in everyone's mind. The city, for the first time in its long history, is destructible. A single flight of planes no bigger than a wedge of geese can quickly end this island fantasy, burn the towers, crumble the bridges, turn the underground passages into lethal chambers, cremate the millions. The intimation of mortality is part of New York now: in the sound of jets overhead, in the black headlines of the latest edition.

All dwellers in cities must live with the stubborn fact of annihilation; in New York the fact is somewhat more concentrated because of the concentration of the city itself, and because, of all targets, New York has a certain clear priority. In the mind of whatever perverted dreamer might loose the lightning, New York must hold a steady, irresistible charm.

It used to be that the Statue of Liberty was the signpost that proclaimed New York and translated it for all the world. Today Liberty shares the role with Death. Along the East River, from the razed slaughterhouses of Turtle Bay, as though in a race with the spectral flight of planes, men are carving out the permanent headquarters of the United Nations—the greatest housing project of them all. In its stride, New York takes on one more interior city, to shelter, this time, all governments, and to clear the slum called war. New York is not a capital city—it is not a national capital or a state capital. But it is by way of becoming the capital of the world. The buildings, as conceived by architects, will be cigar boxes set on end. Traffic will flow in a new tunnel under First Avenue. Forty-seventh Street will be widened (and if my guess is any good, trucks will appear late at night to plant tall trees surreptitiously, their roots to mingle with the intestines of the town). Once again the city will absorb, almost without showing any sign of it, a congress of visitors. It has already shown itself capable of stashing away the United Nations—a great many of the delegates have been around town during the past couple of years, and the citizenry has hardly caught a glimpse of their coattails or their black Homburgs.

This race—this race between the destroying planes and the struggling Parliament of Man—it sticks in all our heads. The city at last perfectly illustrates both the universal dilemma and the general solution, this riddle in steel and stone is at once the perfect target and the perfect demonstration of nonviolence, of racial brotherhood, this lofty target scraping the skies and meeting the destroying planes halfway, home of all people and all nations, capital of everything, housing the deliberations by which the planes are to be stayed and their errand forestalled.

A block or two west of the new City of Man in Turtle Bay there is an old willow tree that presides over an interior garden. It is a battered tree, long suffering and much climbed, held together by strands of wire but beloved of those who know it. In a way it symbolizes the city: life under difficulties, growth against odds, sap-rise in the midst of concrete, and the steady reaching for the sun. Whenever I look at it nowadays, and feel the cold shadow of the planes, I think: "This must be saved, this particular thing, this very tree." If it were to go, all would go—this city, this mischievous and marvelous monument which not to look upon would be like death.

PILGRIMAGE TO WASHINGTON

Washington today hastens to the tempo
of government at work.
New buildings rise and vistas change, but there are
things here which are changeless and in them
Bruce Catton finds the sense of
living history which still rests upon the city.

Washington is first and most obviously the seat of government. As far as the destiny of the American people can be said to be under conscious control, the control is exercised here, along with the immense housekeeping job connected with keeping the republic a going concern. If the people of the United States are to make war, tame a mountain river, increase the tax rate, tap a new source of energy, curb gangsterism, open a national park, overhaul their transportation system or introduce a new set of postage stamps, the decision is taken in Washington; after which, somebody in Washington will see to it that the job is carried out.

If, conversely, anyone in the country wants something from his Federal Government—and a great many people do want a great many things, in season and out—he comes to Washington to demand it. He comes, often enough, as an individual; he also comes as an organized association, planting elaborate headquarters here so that he can exert a continuing influence on the legislators and the housekeepers and, with Washington as a center, can keep a stream of information and exhortation

directed at his fellow citizens in the rest of the country. The relationship between the electorate and the elected can be extremely complicated, and most of the complications are visible in Washington.

Beyond all this Washington serves a separate purpose. It is where the people of the nation can see just what they are up to and how they are doing it; and while they are seeing this they can also, sometimes almost in spite of themselves, see how this compares with what they have been up to in the past. Here, as nowhere else in America, they meet their own history, and it has a curiously contemporary quality. History is real in Washington. Its overtones can be so pervasive that they subdue the present. Washington's magnificent distances have an extension in time as well as in space. Here the weight of the past can be felt.

Probably this, more than anything else, accounts for the fact that Washington is above all other things a center for tourists. Nobody has an accurate count of the Americans who come here each year just to have a look around, but the total is certainly well up in the millions. Some of the figures that do exist give an indication. One year 2,300,000 people visited the Lincoln Memorial, about half that many signed in at the Washington Monument, an equal number went down to Mount Vernon, and 5,400,000 visited the various buildings which go to make up the Smithsonian Institution. The number that simply strolled through the Capitol building itself is beyond estimation.

When we assume the guise of tourists we tend to be somewhat noisy. We chatter a good deal, and we are often accompanied by our young, who chatter even more. Yet many of these introspective moments in front of national shrines are strangely silent. Post yourself, some day, in the impressive Exhibition Hall in the National Archives Building, where the Constitution and the Declaration of Independence are on display behind plate glass, with a little elevated runway to lead visitors past them. Far underneath, out of sight, there is a ponderous bomb-and-fire-proof vault to safeguard them from any imaginable catastrophe, with machinery ready to lower them into this place of security at a moment's notice. The room itself is silent, getting its effect from its vaulted stillness, with state flags ranked against a wall giving a touch of color. The people who come here accept the silence when they enter, speaking in hushed whispers. The documents are eloquent. There they are, in faded script, bearing the signatures of men long dead, John Hancock's enormous scrawl still bespeaking its defiance of majesty, two huge pieces of paper which have carried an unimaginable burden of human affairs down through the generations—and you can almost feel the impact. The communication between the moment of the nation's birth and this moment of its full maturity is almost tangible. A surprising number of visitors pay twenty-five cents to buy a booklet which gives facsimile reproductions of these two documents.

In Statuary Hall, once the meeting-place of the
House of Representatives, stand honored Americans
whose statues were placed there by their states.

The same thing is true elsewhere. The desire to see Statuary Hall, for instance, is no ordinary wish to look at a collection of statues. As a display of sculpture this semicircular room with the tall pillars and the lofty ceiling leaves a good deal to be desired. Each state was originally allowed to put two statues here, celebrating the deeds of its worthiest citizens (the limit is one now), and some of the states responded too promptly, putting up monuments to men now known only to the guidebooks. In addition, many of the sculptors were chosen hastily: if Gutzon Borglum, Jo Davidson and Daniel Chester French are represented here, so are others whose artistic abilities were unhappily minor. If you had nothing here but this mixed collection of statues, most of us would pass it up and look for something more stimulating.

Yet this hall contains echoes from the great past, and no American can stand in it without hearing them. This room for a solid half century was the meeting place of the House of Representatives. It is a fragment of the original Capitol building; when the British captured Washington, in the War of 1812, jubilant redcoats swarmed into this room and held a mock session of the Congress which had fled the town, and ponderous Admiral Cockburn sat in the speaker's chair and shouted: "Gentlemen, the question is, shall this harbor of Yankee democracy be burned? All in favor of burning it will say aye."

The soldiers shouted in jeering affirmative, and when the admiral called for the nays no voice was raised. So a fire was lighted, with the books which then constituted the Library of Congress used for kindling, and the room was gutted, with all but the outer shell destroyed. After the war the Capitol was restored, and the harbor of Yankee democracy functioned again. Henry Clay sat here as Speaker of the House, helping to build that office into the place of power it has been ever since. In this room the Missouri Compromise, with Clay as the driving force behind it, was adopted.

Here John Randolph, the famous and bizarre Randolph of Roanoke, served his time as a representative, stalking into the chamber all booted and spurred, carrying a riding whip and attended, as often as not, by one or more of his favorite dogs, raising his thin derisive voice in opposition to Clay, with whom his argument became so bitter that at last, in 1826, the two men fought a duel. (No one was hurt; Randolph contemptuously fired in the air, Clay's bullet pierced the skirt of Randolph's coat.) Here, also, in 1824, the House voted that one of Randolph's most hated rivals, John Quincy Adams, was to be the next President of the United States. After he had been President, Adams sat here as a representative for seventeen years, engaging in heated debates which centered about his outspoken opposition to the extension of slavery; and in this chamber, on February 21, 1848, Adams fell unconscious with apoplexy, dying two days later without having emerged from his coma. A metal plate on the floor marks the spot where Adams fell. Oddly enough, it is just a few feet away from a statue to Jefferson Davis.

Go down the list: the names of the men who made the United States Senate great in the immense years before the Civil War. Here they sat and here they spoke, and among them

was Daniel Webster, the man who looked more like a statesman than any statesman should be permitted to look—Daniel Webster, who lived hard, shifted his position when expediency overpowered him, and looked out from under beetling brows with the practiced gesture of the actor-turned-orator, to be remembered ever since as one of the thundering spokesmen for the American dream. Webster made his famous "Reply to Hayne" in this room, and although few Americans today remember who Hayne was or what he had been talking about, Webster answered him in words which schoolboys still recite. These walls echoed to that voice, saw Webster and Calhoun struggle bloodlessly a decade before the guns took over.

There was also Stephen A. Douglas of Illinois, undersized and underaged—he was only forty-eight when he died, in 1861—who here jammed through the famous Kansas-Nebraska Act, and whose voice, echoing against these familiar walls, helped to shape the turbulent future of the country. Clay, Calhoun, Webster, Douglas—this little room held giants in its day, and their presence here is unmistakable.

The visitors who want to see these things want also to see today's Government at work, and legislators who direct constituents to Statuary Hall and the old Supreme Court Chamber must also provide passes to the House and Senate galleries. Almost uniformly, the people who get into these galleries and watch today's Congress going about its work come away disappointed. The business is much less impressive in actuality than in retrospect; statesmen seldom impress us as statesmen until after they have gone to their graves, and the actual mechanics of democratic government look shoddy, ill-fitted and distressingly lacking in dignity.

One trouble is that few sessions of either House or Senate are well attended. The big jobs are usually done off the floor. Men who make speeches—and speeches are constantly being made—are talking less for their colleagues than they are for the record, for the voters back home, or, as a phrase-coiner said long ago, for Buncombe County. And ordinarily, they do not look very impressive. (Did Webster and Calhoun, back in the 1840's, disappoint people who looked down on them from the galleries, expecting to see giants with no human frailties?) Much of the important business of the country is done by overworked men who detest the steamy heat of Washington's summer months as much as the lowliest Government secretary does, and who are looking ahead to the chance to get back home and catch up on some sleep.

Some of the things that have happened under the shadows of the Capitol dome are of recent memory, a reminder that we ourselves make history even while we read it. Go to the Senate Office Building—the *old* Senate Office Building, it is now, because they have built a new one to handle the overflow— and climb a flight of marble stairs to the big caucus room, an enormous chamber, its ceiling lifted two stories high, a dais running across one end. In this room many meetings have been held; among them, the meetings of what we now know as the McCarthy Committee, where senators looked down on men who, for one reason or another, had either defied the faith they were born into or had managed their lives so ineptly that they seemed to have defied it. Men were exposed and ruined, or ran into ill-luck and were broken through little fault of their own, in this echoing chamber. Among them, finally, was Senator McCarthy himself, who at last ran upon the sharp prongs of a New England lawyer, Joseph Welch, and who sat in this room, after the crowds had left, crying out to intimates: "What did I do wrong?"

The Capitol Building itself is changing. It is a noble building but it was built in the old monumental style—a magnificent façade, with its interior poorly arranged for human use. A few years ago Congress decreed that the east front of this building should be moved eastward by about thirty feet, to allow more room inside for working people. Lovers of tradition and of the past have objected bitterly, to no avail; whatever the architectural effect may be, the Capitol is expanding, and the day-to-day work of handling the affairs of the republic can go on a little more smoothly hereafter.

From Capitol Hill to the White House and the executive offices along Pennsylvania Avenue is a little more than a mile. Every President since Thomas Jefferson has gone along this mile to take the oath of office at the Capitol. The Avenue has changed, the nondescript buildings that once flanked it are gone, and sight-seeing buses roll along day after day, tireless guides reciting their patter about points of interest along the way. There are plenty of these—the great National Gallery, the massed buildings of the Federal Triangle, the National Archives, straight ahead the classic façade of the Treasury Building. The picture the Avenue presents is much changed from a generation or so ago. But the sense of living history still rests upon it.

Many soldiers have used this Avenue. In 1861, when the city lay defenseless and no one could be sure that Confederate troops would not move in at any moment, the crack New York Seventh Regiment hurried in and paraded gaily down the length of Pennsylvania Avenue. Other regiments came later, scores of them, tramping along this street, flags afloat and bands playing; and processions of laden ambulances jolted along here, too, carrying the human debris from dreadful battlefields to the Washington hospitals. At the Seventh Street corner one can recall another procession that eased tension in the early summer of 1864, when Jubal Early's Confederate army was out in Silver Spring, seemingly ready to capture the capital and win the war.

The 6th Corps, crack combat outfit from the Army of the Potomac, came up from the Virginia peninsula in the nick of time and tramped out the Seventh Street road to bar the way— lean, sun-browned soldiers in stained uniforms, who displayed a strong tendency to break ranks and run into saloons for refreshment as they marched to battle. Follow this road far enough, by the way, and you will come to the reconstructed fragment of Fort Stevens, where the shooting took place and where Lincoln himself, top hat and all, stood on the parapet to watch; stood there until Gen. Horatio G. Wright had to order him down to safety.

Long ago there was a railroad station at about the spot where the National Gallery now stands. No reminder of it remains, but it is worth a thought; for in it, on a summer day in 1881, Garfield was shot by a disappointed office seeker.

The White House, of course, is the magnet that pulls one along the Avenue. It is no longer the visitors' stamping ground; the President is no longer compelled to set aside certain hours every week to allow citizens to shake him by the hand. Lincoln shook so many hands just before he signed the Emancipation Proclamation that even his tireless muscles grew numb, and he feared that his almost disabled right hand would put a shaky signature on that famous paper. He recovered in time, and the signature is as firm as any. But even now a great many visitors can get a brief look at the White House, if not at the President himself. Every morning of the week (Sundays, Mondays and hoildays excepted) a group of thirty-five or forty is taken on a brief tour, the lucky ones being selected on recommendation of a Government official—a senator, for instance. They do not meet the President, but at least they see the house where he lives. Anyone who plans to do this had better apply weeks in advance, for the list is limited and is made up far ahead of time. Besides, on the same five mornings each week, the White House gates swing open at ten o'clock and stay open till noon, and anyone can walk through without a pass.

But no one needs to go into the White House to catch its historic flavor. This building—modest enough as palaces go —quietly but effectively dominates the whole city, and a bench in Lafayette Square, just across the street, offers an excellent place to meditate upon that strangest of all American institutions, the Presidency. If the Rotunda of the Capitol catches something of the American's inborn faith in the processes of democratic government, so too the White House speaks for a mighty intangible. From the beginning we have believed that a fellow citizen, chosen by ourselves, given enormous powers but always answerable to the electorate, would do everything for us that emperors, prime ministers and dictators could do for other peoples, and do it better—a tremendous affirmation of faith. And the cool white building in the classical style, set about with green lawn and great trees, protected by a wrought-iron fence, guarded efficiently but unobtrusively without any parade of glittering uniforms or bayonets, expresses this faith.

Lean back on that park bench and take a long, long look at the white mansion across the way. It is the most remarkable building in America.

Its history is by turns homely and dramatic. Abigail Adams, in the years before the fire (this building, like the Capitol, was put to the torch in 1814 by the invading British army), hung the family washing in the East Room, and Thomas Jefferson kept bear cubs on the lawn, brought back from the West by Meriwether Lewis. Lincoln's children played at soldiers here, condemned a doll to be shot as a spy, then went to the President's office and got him to write out a formal pardon. Robert E. Lee came here to talk to President Grant, seeking aid for a railroad-building project in the valley of Virginia, and showed no amusement when Grant remarked that he and Lee had had a good deal more to do with destroying railroads than with building them. Rutherford B. Hayes refused to serve wines at state dinners, and never did find out that some of his guests armed themselves for such occasions by bringing brandied oranges for their refreshment. Theodore Roosevelt sparred with professional boxers, put his Cabinet to tossing a medicine ball, and lived the strenuous life in the White House as well as out of it. And tough Andrew Jackson sat in a White House chair while a surgeon cut from his shoulder a pistol ball put there in a duel with Sen. Thomas Hart Benton twenty years earlier. At the time of the operation, Jackson and Benton had become close friends, and Jackson sent the bullet to Benton as a keepsake. Benton promptly returned it, remarking that after twenty years' possession the President had clear title to it.

The White House is the present day and the old times all at once. From this building, many years ago, came news of the Louisiana Purchase, and the Emancipation Proclamation, and the signature on the treaty that brought Alaska from Russian to American rule; Presidential papers calling for war—with Mexico, with Spain, with Germany, with Japan—were written here. The decision to proceed with the search for a way to harness atomic energy was made here, and so was the decision to use the bomb which was devised as a result of this search.

Presidents have lived in other places than the White House. A few short blocks to the west is the Octagon House, where James and Dolly Madison lived after the fire of 1814. Across Pennsylvania Avenue is Blair House, where Harry Truman lived while the White House was being restored. Blair House has its own stories from the past. It was once the home of Francis P. Blair, the ruthless politician who rose to power with Andrew Jackson and retained a good deal of his power all the way through the Civil War. In Blair House, in the early spring of 1861, Robert E. Lee was offered, and declined, command of the Union armies.

Washington, the city, was laid out according to the grandiose plan of Major L'Enfant. The plan was substantially modified—although the basic framework was retained—and even if L'Enfant's dream has not been completely followed, Washington has become the monumental city that he imagined. Central to it now is The Mall, the long open parkway that runs from the base of Capitol Hill due west to the curve of the Potomac. It forms the city's axis now, bisected at right angles by the secondary axis that runs from the White House to the Monument; and when it reaches the Potomac it sends a long, graceful diagonal across the river, the Memorial Bridge, to reach the heights of Arlington.

Look at this vast parkway, first at night, perhaps from the Lincoln Memorial at the western end of the Mall. Far to the east is the Capitol dome, gleaming white under its floodlights. In line with it, and nearer, is the lighted Washington Monument, another lofty white symbol.

Then, off to the south, on the dark heights of Arlington, is another floodlighted building, with classic white pillars shining in the night—Arlington House itself, once the home of Robert E. Lee, tied to the Mall by the Memorial Bridge which leads from Lee's house straight to the building that was built in tribute to Abraham Lincoln.

This is a symbolism that we take for granted, yet it speaks of one of the noblest turns in our whole American story. Lee, after all, was the great soldier who fought against the Government founded by Washington. With devotion, endurance and amazing skill he served for four tragic years as the most

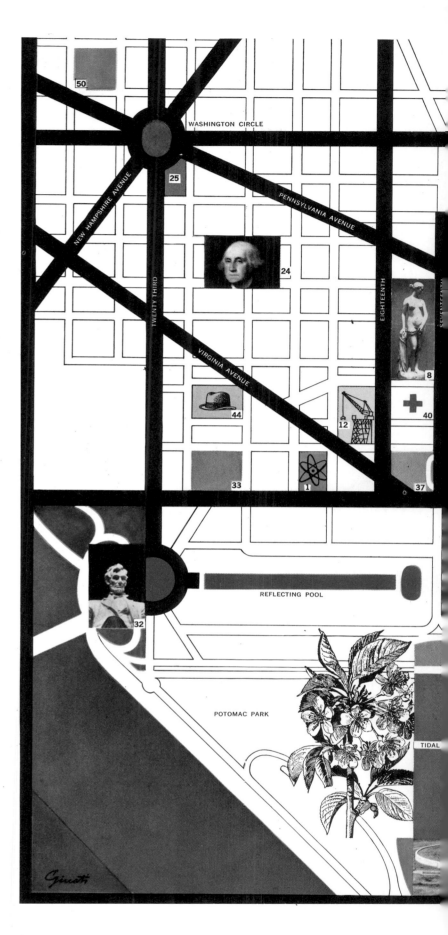

WASHINGTON

1 ATOMIC ENERGY COMMISSION
2 BLAIR HOUSE
3 BOTANIC GARDEN
4 BUREAU OF ENGRAVING AND PRINTING
5 BUREAU OF ENGRAVING ANNEX
6 CAPITOL
7 CHURCH OF THE PRESIDENTS
8 CORCORAN GALLERY
9 COSMOS CLUB
10 DEPARTMENT OF AGRICULTURE
11 DEPARTMENT OF COMMERCE AQUARIUM

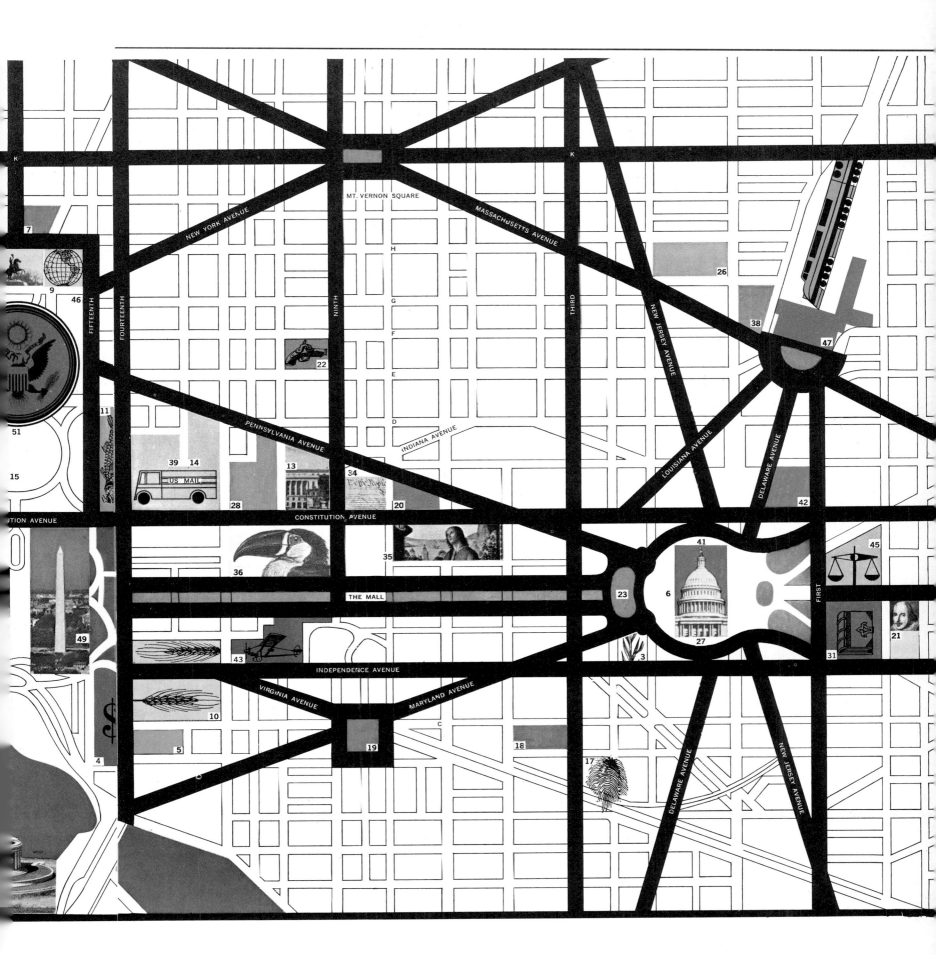

12 DEPARTMENT OF THE INTERIOR	**23** GENERAL GRANT MEMORIAL	**34** NATIONAL ARCHIVES	**45** SUPREME COURT
13 DEPARTMENT OF JUSTICE	**24** GEORGE WASHINGTON UNIVERSITY	**35** NATIONAL GALLERY OF ART	**46** TREASURY DEPARTMENT
14 DEPARTMENT OF LABOR	**25** GEORGE WASHINGTON UNIVERSITY HOSPITAL	**36** NATIONAL MUSEUM	**47** UNION STATION
15 ELLIPSE	**26** GOVERNMENT PRINTING OFFICE	**37** PAN AMERICAN UNION	**48** UNITED STATES CHAMBER OF COMMERCE
16 EXECUTIVE OFFICES	**27** HOUSE OF REPRESENTATIVES	**38** POST OFFICE	**49** WASHINGTON MONUMENT
17 F.B.I. IDENTIFICATION DIVISION	**28** INTERNAL REVENUE	**39** POST OFFICE DEPARTMENT	**50** WEATHER BUREAU
18 FEDERAL SECURITY AGENCY	**29** JACKSON STATUE, LAFAYETTE SQUARE	**40** RED CROSS	**51** WHITE HOUSE
19 FEDERAL SUPPLY	**30** JEFFERSON MEMORIAL	**41** SENATE	
20 FEDERAL TRADE COMMISSION	**31** LIBRARY OF CONGRESS	**42** SENATE OFFICE BUILDING	
21 FOLGER SHAKESPEARE LIBRARY	**32** LINCOLN MEMORIAL	**43** SMITHSONIAN INSTITUTION	
22 FORD'S THEATRE	**33** NATIONAL ACADEMY OF SCIENCES	**44** STATE DEPARTMENT	

effective warrior fighting to destroy American armies. Call the war of that day what you choose—Civil War, War Between the States, or what not—it did, under any name, represent a violent attempt to break the nation into halves. The attempt failed, at last, after North and South together had paid a heartbreaking price in lives, and Lee went off to join the shadows, a tremendous fighter who, in the eyes of the Government that had beaten him, was after all a rebel. Transpose that story into any other country and time you can think of, and you can do nothing but cast Lee in the role of the destroyer, the antagonist, the enemy who tried to bring the nation to ruin. He might be remembered with respect, as an able soldier, but he would inevitably rank as one of the villains in the annals of the nation that won.

But look at what has happened. His home is now a shrine, preserved because he lived in it; the lights strike it out of the summer darkness, just as they strike the Capitol dome and the great Monument itself and the memorial to Lincoln; the progression, from Virginia shore to Capitol Hill, is inescapable and unbroken—Lee, Lincoln, Washington and the lofty building that speaks for the final hopes of American democracy. In all history, unsuccessful rebellion never had an aftermath like this.

This is not to say that the American people are more magnanimous and forgiving than any other, but rather that they may have realized how little they have to be magnanimous or forgiving about. This was a fated chapter in our history, a terrible price paid by all of us in our progression from a small

Necks craned, visitors inspect the Capitol.

nation to a great one, another painful and tragic adjustment that this country had to make to the changing shape of the world. Perhaps it had to be; if not, we have at least discovered that gains, losses and wrongs were in the end a common responsibility. Neither Lee nor the Confederates he led ever asked or were granted anyone's forgiveness. What has come instead is understanding.

The Lincoln Memorial is simple enough. It is an oblong block of a building, surrounded by pillars and sited at the top of broad steps, looking east to the Monument and the Capitol, with a soft light, in the dusk, playing on the great statue of the seated Lincoln. It does not express triumph and it does not voice certainty: it is the memorial to a man who saw doubt and mist and the dim shapes of a great and sustaining possibility, and who left to his countrymen nothing much more than the right to hope that the possibility would some day become real.

On the walls there are no flags, no murals, no engravings; nothing except the words of two great speeches, the Gettysburg Address and the Second Inaugural. The words that come after these utterances, we have to find within ourselves.

First, there is Gettysburg: the brief paragraphs saying why it was necessary to remember that terrible battle, and the triumphant affirmation of faith. Government of the people, by the people and for the people: it shall not perish from the earth, because what the people are is the earth's final meaning, outlasting granite mountains and wide plains and all the other visible realities. Then, following that—sixteen months later, words spoken in the light of victory and the shadow of the waiting tomb—the Second Inaugural: the loftiest words, probably, that any American ever spoke to his fellows.

Here is the brooding quality that lies over every consideration of the meaning of the American experience. The strong affirmation of the words at Gettysburg is gone. Instead, we get honest puzzlement and the shadow of a sustained hope; there is an unanswerable riddle to human existence, no one can finally be certain about anything, the truth is something shared between men who contend bitterly with one another.

"Each looked for an easier triumph and a result less fundamental and astounding. Both read the same Bible and pray to the same God, and each invokes His aid against the other.... The prayers of both could not be answered. That of neither has been answered fully."

American history, it may be, leads to a question to which no mortal can give an answer. If the Gettysburg Address deals with the problem of America's destiny, the Second Inaugural deals with the fate and meaning of man himself.

The statue is here in the dim lights, looking out toward reflecting pool, gleaming Monument, and the shining dome of the Capitol, and off to the south the pillars of Lee's mansion take the light in the deep darkness; *the prayers of both could not be answered. That of neither has been answered fully.*

Leave it at that. The great story of history goes on, pulling contradictions together, touching the edges of everlasting riddles. We know nothing for certain. We can only see, by all that Washington says and is and means, that we are on our way in a quest for a magnificent final truth.

THE SOUTH

The South is a living complexity—a myth of Eden,
a memory of defeat in war,
a pattern of two races who share the soil as
economic neighbors but social strangers.
James Street wrote of the land of his birth,
of its past and of the crucial
changes which loom in the future.

A while back a Northern writer sent me a questionnaire and explained that he was doing an article about the South. (Of course, it was contrary to custom for him to come down and see for himself.) One question was: "What is a Southerner?"

I replied that a Southerner is a fellow who doesn't know the words of *Dixie* but who wants to holler when he hears the tune. That didn't satisfy, so I tried again.

A Southerner is a man who doesn't read many books but has sense enough to know that Steinbeck's *Cannery Row* is not all the Pacific Coast, that Sinclair's *Jungle* is in the Midwest and the Midwest not in *The Jungle*, that Weidman's *I Can Get it for You Wholesale* is not typical of the Northeast, and then is flabbergasted by folks who think all the South is in Faulkner's *Sanctuary.*

The inquisitor thought I was trying to be facetious and he was right.

Another request was: "Give me a brief summary on what the South is."

I replied that if he expected to put the South in an anagram then the word is "controversy."

Again he thought I was trying to be facetious. He was wrong because the South *is* a puzzle and the key is "controversy"; there's no agreement even on *where* the South is, much less on what it is or how it got that way.

The Westerner will say the South is back east, and that's fair enough if you want to think of Texas as the East.

The Northerner will say that the South is below the Mason and Dixon's line. That's all right, too, although that includes the District of Columbia and Maryland, Baltimore and Washington. And yet quiz programs have paid off that Houston, Texas, is the South's largest city. (Baltimore has been described as the city where Northern white folks think they are down South and Southern Negroes think they are up North. Now to me, Baltimore *feels* more of the South than does Atlanta, Georgia, and much more than Miami, Florida. The all-Southern deep South city to me is Memphis, Tennessee.)

If the Mason and Dixon's line is not an accurate geographic boundary, then what about using the former slave states? Go right ahead, but now you're including Delaware.

The Confederate States of America? Now you are leaving out Maryland and also Kentucky, West Virginia and Missouri.

The "solid South"? Oh, come now. Except for the Roosevelt years, the South has not gone solidly Democratic on the national level since 1916.

The error here is in describing the South as a geographic, political and economic unit rather than a land of vanishing agrarians whose sons now hear the factory whistles as far as papa ever heard the dinner horn; as more than 40,000,000 Nordics and Negroes looped together, but not welded, by our bi-racial mores, who share the soil as economic neighbors but social strangers.

And that brings us to the primary, thorny difference between the South and all other sections: roughly, every fourth Southerner is a Negro.

Some Negroes, Southerners as well as Northerners, live as high on the hog as white people do, and higher than many, but this is the exception; and yet in the South, Negroes contribute immeasurably to our folkways from manners to music, from language to languor, from food to frivolity, from mirth to violence.

Therefore, to understand the Southern song we must never forget that the Negro sings bass in the quartet.

Only two states—North Carolina and Georgia—have Negro populations of more than a million each, and Georgia has a total population of about three and a half million, North Carolina about four million. No state in the South is predominantly Negro although you will hear arguments that Mississippi, for example, has more Negroes than whites. Don't bet—you'll lose; the Negro-white ratio there is about five to six. Incidentally, there are three times as many Negroes in Illinois as in Kentucky and more in New York than in South Carolina.

Simply because we must have a base from which to operate, let's identify the South as the former Confederate States plus Maryland and Kentucky, and then shading into West Virginia, Missouri and Oklahoma. This sprawling region has three common wells which water Southern folkways: the Negro-white ratio, the lack of immigrants for almost a hundred years and our resultant homogeneity, and the fact that our grandfathers went down together in a war of ruin.

Nothing will solidify a people like standing together against an invader and being beaten, for there is brotherhood in defeat and misery; and, remember, we were clobbered. The patter chorus of those who see us from afar, know us not at all and analyze us intimately is that we still are fighting the Civil War. Could be. Nevertheless, the battleground for States' Rights, the basic issue of the Civil War, now is the Midwest and this has made a prophet of Jefferson Davis, who said, long after the struggle, "The principle [States' Rights] for which we contended is bound to reassert itself, though it may be at another time and in another form."

It's not that the South remembers the Civil War, but, rather, that we can't forget it. It frowns at us from a thousand courthouse monuments and haunts us from a hundred thousand tombstones. It speaks to us from hotels named for our generals, from highways named for our heroes. It smirks at us from a thousand war books that either call us dull, brutal schizophrenes or puff us up as heroic gallants, bowing and scraping and "honey-chiling" all over the place.

Be that as it may, what does that Chesapeake fisherman tonging oysters have in common with that Florida conch drying sponges? That Tennessee mountaineer at Oak Ridge?

That Louisiana Cajun growing sugar cane? That Texan punching cattle? Always this: their folks stood together in the Civil War and went down together, kicking and clawing.

It seldom fails—let two Southerners meet on the other side of the world and they won't talk about the Civil War at all. Each will assume that the other's grandpas got shot at and did some shooting. They'll talk about Southern food and Southern music. Southern football and Southern girls—and wind up in a hollering argument over the Negro question. But let a Northerner join them and up pops the Civil War.

Almost a century has passed, and yet our homes, gadgeted to the last push button, still have an invisible Civil War niche. Perhaps we are not always aware it is there, and when it is pointed out to us by strangers who see it more clearly, we are likely to get aggressively defensive.

We do not choose to scrub the niche and put there the bust of a living hero. Maybe someday, but not yet. For the Civil War is the epitaph to the Old South, and the Old South was a sort of never-never, ever-ever land.

Oh, sure, we know that the Old South mostly is a myth; but the Garden of Eden story has served man well for a long time and the Old South legend touches us the same way: once upon a time, long, long ago, all the land was beautiful and all men were brave and all women were ladies. We know it is mostly myth, and we also know that only a few had it mighty good in the Old South while most folks had it mighty rough.

but we ourselves are no slouches at the grab bag. When it comes to money, the Southern hand often is quicker than the Yankee eye, and our smile is wholly disarming. Beware the quaint character who takes off his wool hat and scratches his head and drawls, "Well, now, I tell you, mister. I'm just a po' boy from up at the forks of the creek." He might be right out of the Harvard School of Business, so nail down your skin because pelt and pelf are fixing to fly.

The South has changed more in the past fifteen years than it did in the previous fifty. The old mule-and-mud go-round is gone. The machine has us in its maw and some of us like it and some of us don't. There's no Southern accent to a tractor's exhaust, no dos-à-dos to a loom, no hush puppies on the assembly line and no buttermilk in an oil well.

We have busted out in an epidemic of industrialization. Miles and miles of brand-new factories, as modern as day after tomorrow, line our countryside. Our new plants have brought payrolls and unions and things, and, with schools and churches, have done much to crack the racial barriers. They are not splintered, mind you, but they are cracked.

But it's not the fact that influences us, it's the fancy. There's a nebulous connection between an Eden that never was and the aching muscles and sweat of today that you either feel or you don't, and if you don't then no explanation will suffice.

Southernism is a sort of malady, sometimes pain and sometimes pleasure, but a vaccine has been discovered. This vaccine is wealth and it's bound to cure some of the old pains and cause new ones. For the first time in our twisting history, money no longer is confined to the carriage customers.

The South still does not quite trust big money, and that's a hang-over from the old days, but we esteem Mammon without idolizing him. We disdain some folks who grub for money,

The last of the Texas-deck sternwheelers gives a nostalgic look to Old Man Mississippi.

THE MISSISSIPPI

All who would truly know America,
says Hodding Carter, should travel the Mississippi,
for on this 2500-mile journey from the
north country of Minnesota to the Delta and
New Orleans the multiple sources of America's
strength and America's heritage are all to be found.

The story of the Mississippi and the violent Eden that is its valley is a thousand tales, spun for four hundred recorded years and along 2500 twisting, treacherous miles. It is the anthology of a wilderness that was a European pawn and an American challenge; the heady record of man against man, and man against fever and flood; the chronicle of the woodsman, felling the pine and the cypress and the oak beside the swift brown waters and dreaming of the ships and cities that would follow after; and the soberer annals of men in the cities that grew, their dreams reversed, musing upon the laden dugout and the Choctaw war whoop, the crack of the Decherd rifle and the glad hooting of the stern-wheeler.

But these many tales are joined by one strong thread, the river that gives identity to the valley it created and to the people who were drawn to its banks. For the topic of the Mississippi antedates the red men and the white men who slaughtered and dispossessed them, and even the shadowy mound builders who came before either. It is an epic that begins in the vast whiteness of the glaciers which, receding, left a barrier mass through which dammed-up waters would hack presistently toward an ancient sea. But that part of the Mississippi's story is too remote and too unrelated to man for elaboration. It is needful to remember only this: that the Mississippi took a long time to get from where it started—and you can choose between Lake Itasca and Little Elk Lake, beneath the birch and pine and tamarack of Northern Minnesota —to its thick discharge into the blue and tropic Gulf; and that the nature of its progress has made it both an enemy and a friend of those who live beside it. From the northern woods, where the first tributaries join, to the Mississippi's five-tongued thrusting into the Gulf of Mexico, the river is strong, defiant and unpredictable, and the taming of which men boast is in truth only the curb of ceaseless vigil. For the river created a great alluvial plain, incredibly rich yet presenting man but

A ferryboat slants across the Mississippi at Baton Rouge.

few high places from which to escape its excesses; and it remains unpredictable even today, especially along its lower reaches, mocking men's effort to restrict or define its channel and reminding its puny adversaries from time to time that it offers them no certainty.

The Mississippi is also the Red and the Missouri and the White, the Ohio and the Tennessee, the Black and the Tallahatchie and the Yazoo, the Kaskaskia and the Arkansas and the Illinois, forty roaring allies, hell-bent beneath the towering divides, blessing a valley with their earth gleanings and scourging it on occasion with flood, while the levees rise higher and higher and the spillways and cutoffs and reservoirs are constructed in the unending strife.

Perhaps this is what the young Frenchman, De Tocqueville, sensed one hundred and fourteen years ago when he described the Mississippi's valley as "upon the whole the most magnificent dwelling place prepared by God for man's abode," but likened the river itself to "a god of antiquity, dispensing both good and evil in its course."

For the first century of its settlement there was no safety anywhere along the Mississippi; the usual uncertainties of the frontier were compounded here by the dreadfulness of endemic plagues that ravaged the lower valley with the slow death of malaria and the quicker death of yellow fever.

The man who managed to survive yellow fever and brown flood might find his life held as cheap by human scourges: the river pirates and the bandits of the Natchez Trace, the insult-hungry Creole and American duelists and the trigger-tempered buckos of the flatboats.

Death came swifty, too, among the river's snags and sawyers that could rip a keelboat to splintered wreckage; and even when the steamboats pre-empted the river traffic, in the golden years after Nicholas Roosevelt's maiden journey downriver in the winter of 1811-1812, there was no certainty to river travel. The crude, overtaxed boilers sometimes exploded, creating hazards in which only the hardiest found humor.

"This is the last time I ever mean to put my foot in one of these infernal contrivances," called back one riverman, deserting a wayward paddlewheeler.

"I have been five times run high and dry on a sandbank, four times snagged, three times sawyered, and twice blown up skyhigh. I calculate I have given these creatures a pretty fair trial, and darn my breeches if I will ever trust my carcass in one again."

Above the river stands the Louisiana State Capitol, 450 feet high.

The story of the Mississippi is an epic of the conflict between the river and man, and the river has a new trick around every bend. Here, looking deceptively placid, it winds past Illinois.

But it was the yellow fever that for nearly 150 years chiefly retarded the development of the lower Mississippi, destroying its people by the thousands and sending other thousands in terrorized flight.

Though the first epidemic recorded by the Spanish was in 1767, yellow jack was almost as old as the settlement of New Orleans. And from 1767 on, only a very few years passed without its curse.

The cautious and the cowardly turned from those whose faces became flushed and yellow, and the brave ones, remaining to nurse the delirious victims, brushed impatiently at the whirring little mosquitoes, not understanding that their bite meant death.

In 1858 the creaking yellow-fever carts hauled away 4845 bodies in New Orleans alone. As the 19th Century grew older, the toll became relatively as great in the smaller towns and on the plantations, and then came the epidemic of 1878.

Memphis was a city of the dead that year. Twenty-five thousand of its population took flight during the first few days of the fever, and of the twenty thousand who remained, fourteen thousand were smitten and five thousand died. Among the dead were four thousand of the six thousand whites who stayed behind, a majority of them Irish newcomers; but of fourteen thousand Negroes, seemingly possessed of a strange immunity, less than one thousand perished.

Memphis, already impoverished by war and Reconstruction, took a long time to recover. It was not until twenty-two years and many lives later that Agramonte and Reed and Carroll proved that the *Aëdes aegypti* species of mosquito was the murderer, and by their proof brought security to the Mississippi.

There were other affinities than those of slow or sudden death, of flood-borne disaster or the angry cohesion of war. Despite all these, the people of the Mississippi had known intermittently the fulfillment of the valley's fertile promise. The Scandinavian loggers of the north woods, the Iowa farmers whose green corn nodded by the riverbank, the merchants of the river ports and the cotton and sugar planters of the South alike could profit from the rich surging of nature. Life could be lush on the river, and graceful, too, as the traveler might discover from the colonnades of Natchez, the symmetrical, spacious homes that lined the river between Natchez and New Orleans, and the Latin joyousness of the Creole city. Or perhaps that gracious culture, however real, was only a façade behind which roared the frontier. This may be true even now, for the river people are still frontier in spirit. They have no truck with the moralist in the port towns, and the Memphis Negro knows what he means when he sings:

Mister Crump don't 'low no easy riders here,
Mister Crump don't 'low no easy riders here,
Ah' don' care whut Mister Crump don't 'low,
Ah'm gonna barrelhouse anyhow,
Mister Crump can go and fetch hisself some air.

The easy riders of both races, the fancy men and their pleasure ladies, have not yet surrendered to propriety. Here on the Mississippi the nation's "spo'tin'est towns" persist: St. Louis, Memphis, Vicksburg, Baton Rouge and New Orleans. Especially New Orleans. Reform has come slowly to them and rests lightly, and a man can find whatever he is looking for, be it fight or frolic, though this is not something of which their chambers of commerce boast.

There is also a less perceptible kinship that joins them to each other and to far places. Since its settlement the Mississippi has been almost as much a highway for the world as for a nation. The French voyageur, bringing his furs to New Orleans, could exchange not only his goods for the useful or ornamental products of a dozen lands, but also his ideas for those of the men who brought their cargoes to him. The trader, flatboating down the Ohio to the Mississippi, linked the interior with the more cosmopolitan folk of the East; and the red plush and mahogany saloons of the gaudy paddlewheelers were sophistication incarnate, their cabins crammed with curious Easterners and crop-rich planters, gambling men and great merchants, their decks laden on the downriver trips with the produce of the valley and upriver with the goods that the produce earned. The river towns were not provincial in the way that other inland settlements were, and by the same relative standards they are not provincial today.

They have been set apart, or have set themselves apart, from their back-country replicas, politically, culturally and —for lack of a more precise word—morally. It is no happenstance that the valley people go to the port towns for their good times; no simple coincidence, for instance, that in legally dry Mississippi the outnumbered and outvoted river towns and counties show their disrespect for prohibition by ignoring it. The outside world has put its mark upon the river people, and to their neighbors of the hills and distant prairies it is the mark of the ungodly. For where else would the shiftless spin out their days on idling shantyboats or in such sinful and lawless pleasures—the rich and the poor alike brazen in their esteem for wicked New Orleans and the virtues of the bottle and the dance?

This is but one way of looking at the Mississippi, one quick and sidelong glance at a timeless panorama. Others have seen and found other things. Among them are observant men who wrote of what they saw, and strong, dissimilar men about whom books have been written. Their ghosts outnumber the relics they have left behind. The Sangamon raftsman, Abraham Lincoln, watched helplessly the black slave consigned down the river, and his soul sickened because of the Mississippi's cargo. At Galena, a hard-drinking failure named Grant looked at the near-by Mississippi despondently, not knowing that one day, at Vicksburg, he would conquer it. Far below, from the bluffs of Natchez, Jefferson Davis likewise stared at the river, deeming it Southern and separate there, and the aloof, inward man did not find it difficult to choose between state and country. James B. Eads, a quiet engineer of St. Louis, was to design ironclads with which Porter would sweep the middle river; and later he would aid those he helped to defeat by constructing at the river's mouth those jetties which today guarantee safe entry and egress.

The procession begins before these and extends long after them, to this day when the stature of the river's men seems shrunken. On this river, seven years before Lexington and Concord, five obscure Frenchmen died at New Orleans before a Spanish firing squad, and became the New World's first martyrs to the vision of a free country. In the hidden bayous to the south, Jean Lafitte traded in pirated goods and slaves, and then joined Andrew Jackson, the English-hater from Tennessee, in the destruction of the British at Chalmette. Aaron Burr, his dark mind reeling with yet undeciphered purpose, journeyed down the Mississippi to final repudiation and disgrace. The American settlers around Baton Rouge in Spain's West Florida followed a ducal leader, Fulwar Skipwith, and the giant Kemper brothers in a rebellion from which a brief republic was born only to be annexed by the United States. At Memphis and on the Missouri side of the river, Thomas Hart Benton dueled and loved, and gave up his light-skinned mistress when he departed for the Senate in more staid Washington; and here David Crockett roamed before he found death at the Alamo. Along the river, in Arkansas and Tennessee, Nathan Bedford Forrest, slave dealer and Confederate cavalryman, directed his shadowy Klansmen in the grievous days of Reconstruction. Mississippi rivermen from Arkansas followed Albert Pike to Buena Vista, and from its banks Beauregard led his Creoles to Manassas. John Murrell, his Mystic Brotherhood a by-word for terror, murdered the wayfarer in the forests beyond the river, and plotted a slave insurrection for which many men, white and Negro, died. The upriver flatboatmen acknowledged the legendary mallet-fisted Mike Fink as their deity; their downstream brothers added to the bawdy lore of Annie Christmas, six foot eight inches of woman. And, later, there was Stackalee, a double-jointed legend, too, born with a veil over his face, and whose tracks could not be distinguished from a horse's or a mule's; and black John Henry, who weighed 44 pounds at birth and entered the world with a cotton hook for his right hand.

To the Mississippi also came men of a different stamp. One such was to become a symbol, Maine's Elijah Lovejoy, zealot for man's freedom, whose abolitionist sentiments were too vigorous in a state which later would fight to make men free, and who was slain by a mob in Alton, Illinois, while defending his newspaper plant from destruction. Far to the north, when the 19th Century was well along, came Cleng Peerson, pioneer among the Norse emigrants, and behind him a sturdy people to create a new Scandinavia among the tall pines.

There are others, quieter-spirited yet enduring. Thure Kumlien, the gentle-born Swedish naturalist, who brought his bride to Wisconsin and who lived with nature, seeking out and identifying the flora and fauna of the upper valley. Isaiah T.

Montgomery, the Negro house slave of Jefferson Davis' brother, who founded an all-Negro town, Mound Bayou, that survives in Mississippi today. Memphis' and Alabama's William C. Handy, the Negro composer, whose mournful blues are the projection of his people's spirit and the white man's unperceptive joy; Handy, and Beale Street on a Saturday night, redolent with the smell of frying catfish and the succulent little river shrimp, loud and happy and sometimes dangerous, and all around the ardent reminders of a St. Louis woman with her diamon' ring.

And so many others, heterogeneous and vital, good and bad. The demagogue Huey Long of Louisiana, who crowned and proved himself The Kingfish, cynically alert to the material demands of his followers, rearing behind the levee the sky-scraper capital that was his monument and his place of final reckoning. His contemporary and antithesis, William Alexander Percy, the Yazoo Delta's gentle poet and mystic, who proved in his too short lifetime there was at least one man in the river's history to whom the thing called *noblesse oblige* was no lifeless romanticism. But among them all, from De Soto to Ed Crump, two men stand forth as the archetypes of the Mississippi's spirit. One was truly a son of nature, John James Audubon, more at home in the forest's depths and the bayou's mud than in the galleries where the city-bred questioned the authenticity of his art. The other was Samuel L. Clemens, Missouri's Mark Twain, whose mocking despair of humanity was assuaged in the pilothouse and in the loving tales reconstructed from a river boyhood. What if they could have journeyed together, the one alert to the snowy heron's soaring, the other with the river's own current surging through his heart? Measured in danger or the clashing enterprise of men, theirs were no great adventures, though Mark Twain was briefly a soldier and Audubon knew privation beside the river. But they perceived the Mississippi as have no others, the one attuned to its wilderness and the wild things there, the other to its hardiness and humor and the epic quality of an inarticulate frontier.

But these dissimilar giants can be met in libraries, and it is not in libraries that the Mississippi is discovered. A man must live awhile beside the Mississippi and travel upon it, though this is difficult now because the barge has largely replaced the packet and the spirit of leisure has all but died in the age of speed.

And yet it would seem that all who would truly know America should travel it, slowly, and perhaps only a segment at a time. The north country first, in the pleasant summer, along the placid blue concourse in the bluff and prairie country between Minnesota and Wisconsin, Iowa and Northern Illinois. The middle river in the late spring, to sense the mounting strength as the Mississippi's great tributaries enter the river, from Mark Twain's Hannibal to Memphis, past the joining of the Illinois and the Missouri and the Ohio, where the current quickens and the river's face changes color and even the tenderfoot recognizes the danger of untamed force. And in the cool early autumn the lower river, down to the reedy passes, where the wet earth is almost indistinguishable from

Delicately wrought gates and classic columns— such reminders of ante-bellum South, like souvenirs lovingly kept, give busy southern cities a special charm and graciousness.

the spreading water; past the white-bolled, flat fields of the Yazoo-Mississippi Delta, past the proud, safe bluffs of Vicksburg and Natchez, past storied Baton Rouge and Latin-tempered New Orleans to the stilt-raised rendezvous of the bar pilots and the warm, embracing Gulf. For on this 2500-mile journey is to be discovered the multiple sources of America's strength and America's heritage.

It is the American cornucopia that one finds on this journey, the outpouring of earth's blessings upon a valley not yet awake to the earth's need of them. Such is the valley that the Mississippi made possible by its creativeness, by its navigability, by its promise; an Eden that is violent and abused, and yet is indestructible; a once buffeted land that may yet be the buffer for the nation whose true heart it is.

MY SOUTHWEST

Barren, bleak, red-raw and elemental,
the vast sweep of the Southwest—
New Mexico and Arizona—was created as much by
what it lacked as by what it had.
It is, says Jack Schaefer, a land of deficiencies,
ancient and immovable.
Time passes over it and the
pattern of the past remains.

Many people have come to my Southwest in search of many things, of gold and health and farmland and rangeland and business opportunity and simple vacation playground.

Some have found what they sought. More have not. Its deficiencies have defeated them. But all have found an incomparable place in which to search. And many of those who have failed have yet succeeded, have found riches other than those sought, and have stayed to become rich in living.

But first, a defining. What piece of land is covered by that name Southwest? There are definitions by the dozen. Some expand it eastward to take in Texas; others northward to include part of Colorado and Utah; still others westward to the coast. Nonsense like that robs it of all unity except a vague geographical kinship. My Southwest consists of New Mexico and Arizona.

Two states and yet one area. It has always been so. In the American territorial days these two, roughly what they are today, were a single piece, New Mexico Territory. Before that, a single province of Mexico. Before that, major part of a single province of the Spanish colonial empire. And before that, the range of the Amerindians whose descendants still hold much of it: the nomadic Navajos and Apaches, who roamed and raided through it, and the Pueblos and Hopis and Zunis and Papagos and Pimas and Yumas, who dotted almost every part of it through the prehistoric years with weathering remains of their stone-and-adobe dwellings.

That is my Southwest, west of the South and south of the West, Indian range and Spanish-Mexican province and American territory-become-states and still all three together and at once. Time passes over it and the pattern of the past remains. History makes markings upon it and these are small scattered lonely lost scratchings on the surface of the huge indifferent land. What it was it is and will be.

Three cultures exist here now, side by side: Indian, tracing back to man's beginnings in North America; Spanish-Mexican, tracing back to conquistadores and mission padres; American, called Anglo here, the latest, the still adjusting to the land. These three have played out the old familiar story of man's inhumanity to man, the Spanish conquering and exploiting the Indian, the Anglo in turn conquering and exploiting the Spanish-become-Mexican. Yet each culture despite minglings and overlappings, retains much of its individual character and in-

Mission San Xavier, just south of Tucson.

Sunset silhouettes cactus in Saguaro National Monument.

tegrity. And nowadays, to a surprising degree, the peoples of the three live together with a tolerance that is slowly conquering the animosities of past injustices and present rubbings.

Canyon de Chelly, deep in the Navajo reservation, holds many secrets of my Southwest. Its stark loveliness is a superlative backdrop for the lesson of the land. On hollowed ledges of the towering cliffs are ruins of the dwellings of many peoples who lived here in successive periods, more than 400 prehistoric sites and 138 major ruins in the one canyon area. Best known of these, because easily accessible, is the White House, once containing at least 175 rooms, three stories still standing, plastered with a whitish clay, giving the name. Seen from the opposite rim, distinct against a thousand feet of red cliff, it is truly "the house made of dawn...finished in beauty." Here lived those known to archaeologists as the Anazazi, who started this structure about the time William the Conqueror invaded England. Here, later, lived Hopis, who began remodeling about when Shakespeare wrote his plays. Here, still later, came the Navajos, to make this canyon their last stronghold against white domination.

Not far up the branch Canyon del Muerto, the canyon of death, are petrographs on the cliff wall, painted long ago, showing Spanish soldiers riding across the rock. High on a nearby ledge lie bones of Navajo women and children slaughtered in hiding when Spanish raiders discovered them. All through here, when this had become American territory, tramped Anglo soldiers under Kit Carson when he was forcing the final surrender. Nowadays Navajos with their flocks roam through the canyons. It is theirs again, because that same Kit Carson insisted that they be given the reservation promised them. The wise among these Navajos know what is really here. Beauty surrounds them, the living beauty of the land and the time-softened beauty of remembrance of recurrent tides of human history, and with it they wander.

Ancient ruins? There is hardly a square mile of the whole region, save the highest mountain slopes, that has not been a homesite for some prehistoric people. (Prehistoric here means pre-Spanish, before the keeping of written records, white-man style.) Local archaeological clubs turn up new traces everywhere. Highway construction is often interrupted by the uncovering of previously unknown ruins.

The whole long record is here. Ventana Cave alone runs through almost the entire gamut. It has yielded relics ranging from Folsom man about 8000 B.C. to modern Indian about the time of the Spanish conquest. Quite possibly it was more or less continuously inhabited for 10,000 years....Go to Aztec ruins (misnamed, no connection with the distant Aztecs of Mexico), a particularly well-preserved example of apartment dwellings and of what is known as the Classic Pueblo Period. ...To Casa Grande, massive watch tower built about the time of Europe's Crusades by the Salados, or Salt River People.... To Montezuma Castle, again misnamed, five stories high in its snug cliff recess, complete with penthouse, perhaps the best-preserved cliff dwelling of them all....To Wupatki, where occurred an early land rush. Here, nearly a millennium ago,

Sunset Crater erupted, covering a wide area with black moisture-conserving ash. At least four tribes converged upon it to take advantage of the new nurturing soil. But the blanket of soil faded under the sweeping winds. Within little more than a century the villages were abandoned to stand as another chapter in the long record held by the land.

Those are only a few items picked at random.

Real live Indians? The region has the 18 modern pueblos, various in size and population and appearance and flavor. It has 17 other reservations whose combined area is about the size of New England. It has thousands, too, of nonreservation Indians scattered through almost every section. It even has a small but increasing quota of eastern Indians, chiefly Cherokees, who have come here to live.

Make the reservation circuit. You will be welcomed everywhere or at least tolerated with that courteous reserve that in time may impress you with the distance between what we are pleased to call civilization and the ageless dignity of so many Amerindians.

Start, say, at Taos, superb in its mountain cradle, northernmost of the modern pueblos, and follow down the Rio Grande, then over to Zuñi, visiting them all, not forgetting fading Nambé and tiny Tesuque and remote Cochití, where the best drums are made, and quite modern San Ildefonso, where pottery is again an art, perhaps lingering awhile at Acoma, the sky city, with its neighboring Enchanted Mesa. That, too, is only a beginning. You have two Navajo reservations in addition to the tremendous main one yet to cover, three Apache, two Papago, two Pima, not to mention the Paiute, Hopi, Hualapai, Maricopa, Yavapai, Cocopah, and Mojave....

The Spanish influence? It is everywhere. Spanish-Americans still form a good third of the total, a majority in many areas. They, too, have the right to look upon us Anglos—even those whose families have been here for generations—as johnny-come-latelies. Old Spanish missions, antedating those touted in California, are spotted through the region. Some of the old churches are still in service at the modern pueblos. Some stand now with cities grown up around them.

Along the highways are old Spanish towns with an overlay of blaring signs and service stations. Off the main tracks, deep in the hills or in hidden lowlands, are equally old or older Spanish villages, clusters of "mud huts" that seem to grow out of the earth, as many abandoned as still occupied.

The Spanish *ricos*, the land-grant holders with their fine haciendas, are gone now with the wind of change. The little man of the village, with his small house and small fields and few head of stock, lives on, much as he lived several centuries ago. For him life still revolves around the cyclic swing of the seasons and around his small village churches, some of which in simple loveliness of outline and crudely ornate interior drive artists into ecstasies—and for some of his tight-lipped neighbors it still revolves around starkly sinister Penitente chapels on remote lonely hilltops. How quaint, you say. Aren't these people interested in stepping out and pushing ahead? Don't they know they live in the brave new world of the mid-20th Century with a braver new world budding at Los Alamos? Is their well-known shoulder shrug of strangely unsad resignation any answer to the riddles of existence? Why should it nudge you with a tiny seed of doubt of the transcendent value of the imperative push of progress?

The wild West of Indian-fighting days? This is the part of the United States where white men first fought Indians—and last fought Indians. Here, well into the 1880's, handfuls of Apaches, the hardiest warriors of the continent, were still keeping much of the entire U. S. Army busy.

The woolly West of the cattlemen and sheepmen heyday? My Southwest is the country of Zane Grey's two-gun men and stalwart cowpokes, of Stewart Edward White's and Owen Wister's finest stories. It is the country of Billy the Kid and Pat Garrett and Elfego Baca and Wyatt Earp and Doc Holliday.

It was sheep country from the first Spanish comings and is sheep country today. It was cattle country from the first Spanish comings and is cattle country today. Push out into the open spaces where sheep and cattle and horse ranches, and often all three at once, run from 20,000 acres on up, way, way up, and if you are lucky you will still bump into Charley Russell and Frederic Remington characters, as authentic as the rangeland itself. They use jeeps as much as horses, drive stock to market in trailer trucks instead of on the hoof, no longer carry Mr. Colt's hardware as standard equipment. They may even put on sober business suits when going to town to avoid being mistaken for the phonies who strut Western stuff for show. But sight a few of them out on the range, hunkered down on heels by a fire, taking a breather in branding time, and hear one start drawling about the little ol' hoss that tried tricks on him yesterday—the breed, out where the land sets the limits, hasn't changed much with the years.

Wilderness areas? Not just sparsely inhabited land but real wild wilderness? The national forests, more than 22,000,000 acres of them, offer plenty of that. The vast Pecos Wilderness at the headwaters of the river, much of it wildlife sanctuary, is still country to satisfy a Daniel Boone. The Gila Wilderness, larger than Delaware and Rhode Island combined, rugged beyond belief, is still largely inaccessible except to those hardy enough to pack in.

Shows, shirdigs, ceremonials? There are some such somewhere all the time: rodeos by the dozen; ski carnivals in the mountains; fiestas in the towns; festivals in the cities; Indian dances at the pueblos and the colorful four-day Intertribal Ceremonial at Gallup; stock shows, fairs, pioneers' days, old-timers' weeks—

My Southwest has more than enough of everything they come to see to keep visitors busy every moment!

And all that, of course, is arrant nonsense!

To come here and dash about, determined to *do* the region, is to defeat yourself at the start—to bring into it something foreign. My Southwest is not a collection of sights to be seen, a museum to study, a zoo to visit. It is an experience to be shared, a romance to be lived, a beauty with which to wander.

Slow down. Perhaps simply stop and stay awhile. There is no need to dash about trying to cover it all. There is always tomorrow, or the next visit, or the one after that. Mary Austin said it a half century ago. *This is the sense of the desert hills, that there is room enough and time enough.*

WEST COAST JOURNEY

*When Horace Greeley counseled young men to
go west, he couldn't have known that
his would be the most heeded admonition in
American history.
They went, young and old, and they stayed.
And what they have done to and for
the Coast from San Diego to Seattle surprises even
an old Angeleno like Robert Carson.*

"The Coast," as it is invariably called in Manhattan. Twelve hundred and ninety miles, give or take a few, separate Seattle from San Diego. These two cities represent the north-south boundaries of a slightly unbelievable region.

A woman in San Diego, grimly studying a crowded beach, said: "I can remember when we used to have wienie-bakes down here and get scared because it was so lonely. What'll we do in another year or two, go back in the desert and perish? Well, anyhow, it's only a hundred miles to the sagebrush and rabbits." I resisted an urge to tell her the deserts were filling up too.

Farther north they are also feeling the influx. A filling-station attendant in an Oregon coastal town said to me, "There were such mobs pulling salmon in, the conservation guys lowered the boom. Cut the season to two months. There are just as many salmon as before, but too many fishermen. I might haul for Alaska pretty soon, where bears walk down the streets in the middle of the day, and you have to slow on curves at night for fear of knocking your brains out on a moose."

In my book, however, the passage of time has wrought more good than harm. Gone are the days of Victorian hotels with spittoons in every room, indestructible hot-roast-beef sandwiches bathed in floury gravy, and towns where asking for a drink of strong waters was received with revulsion. The scenery is still viewable despite roadside advertising: tremendous stands of fir, clogged by bracken and ferns upon which the sun never shines, march mile after mile; great improbable mountains thrust up into the air, controlling the climate—and climate makes the Coast what it is; rivers come boiling down to the sea, clear, cold and attractively curved; and there are beaches, deserts, fleshpots, growing crops, fat women in tight jersey pants, and Disneyland.

Naturally, it isn't quite the way the chambers of commerce would have you believe. In the north, where the flashing green of the forests and the gold of the Scotch broom are nourished by frequent rains, wry stories prevail of the two main seasons, wet and dry; the dry one is August, unless it rains. Southward, long before you reach San Francisco, the country becomes open and less soft, dotted with scrub oak and covered by a vegetation which turns brown and arid in warm weather. Farther on it suggests the aspect of the desert, and a few miles inland it is frankly dusty and hot in season. The Pacific, notwithstanding the name, isn't the most peaceful of oceans; winds blow hard on exposed cliffs and beaches, the surf is high, and you can turn blue from immersion with remarkable speed, even in July. Coastal skippers will tell you this is one of the roughest stretches of water in the world, and the shore line is marked by old wrecks from Point Conception to Cape Flattery.

This is a fat and smiling land, though. What strikes one above all, in driving through, is the distinctive glitter of new roofs. Men are busy everywhere building homes, schools, factories, motels, retail establishments, superhighways, steam-generating plants—and dreary zoos for the display of fearsome wildlife. Apparently the itinerant public loves to stop, stretch its legs, air the kiddies, and goggle at hooded cobras and Gila monsters. If you wonder where the menagerie parts of the smaller circuses and carnival shows went, I can tell you. They've come to rest beside the highway. But I looked in vain for the cooch dancers and the men with snake oil and shell games; presumably they have transferred to TV.

Portland, the principal city of Oregon, appears to be a trifle flower-happy, which is all to the good. The abundance of blossoms and trees to shade them in the residential districts' is occasionally overwhelming. Every June, for fifty years, a Rose Festival has been celebrated, complete with the coronation of a queen, a floral parade, fireworks and a baton-twirling contest. What's more, in June of 1959 the state celebrated its centennial here with a 100-day Exposition and International Trade Fair that is said to have drawn eight million persons. In between times, Portlanders are not averse to golfing, boating, skiing on Mount Hood sixty miles away, and attending horse and dog racing.

When not engaged in sports, we were told, the citizens prefer to stay home and attend to mulching their plants, and the lack of night clubs and the nocturnal peace of the streets seem to bear this out.

In fairness, it must be said there is a darker side to Portland. The town is crawling with amateur and professional historians. Unless one takes care, one is very apt to be taken to see the Old Oregon Trail or the statue of Sacagawea, an Indian lady who was of immense assistance to Lewis and Clark in their expedition. And other Indian trouble abounds. A certain Multnomah tribe, which was benevolent toward white intruders in the early days, has its name perpetuated in everything from stadiums to hotels, inducing a degree of confusion. A resident I talked to said he'd even proposed that, since there were already too many Portlands in the United States, the city's name be changed to Multnomah. This, he added, became a serious campaign waged in the newspapers, generated a good deal of heat, and provoked factionalism. Having pored through a folder, I suggested that perhaps a better choice would have been Stump Town, Portland's old nickname (because the town was then full of uncleared stumps which had to be painted white so people wouldn't break themselves in two over them at night). The tone of our conversation became less cordial.

Mountaineer's eye view: *From a glacier
on Mount Rainier's flank, the rugged Cascades
seem to roll southward in mighty billows.*

One hundred and fifty miles north on U.S. 99, most of the distance by divided freeway running through parklike scenery, is Seattle. The tall buildings of the downtown district, mounted on hills, stand facing the imposing expanse of Puget Sound. From our room in the excellent Olympic Hotel, we could look in any direction and see forests and water. This is Venice in a larger, freer, unhallowed dimension, not hampered by stone and custom.

Although the shops are smart and the traffic on the ineffable one-way streets brisk, one never loses the conviction one is in some sort of national preserve. There are forty-five parks, including a primeval forest. Although the population is up around the six-hundred-thousand mark, having zoomed in the last ten years, natural resources are so close you can reach out and touch them.

We were taken in tow by a kindly couple and shown the sights. My wife said, "But it isn't like a city at all—no dust, no crowding, no real amount of paving. Trees wherever you look, and coveys of sailboats heeling over to the wind when you unexpectedly turn a corner. It's heavenly!"

"It rains a lot in the winter," our host said, "and the skies are gloomy. We like to spend two or three months every year in Palm Springs."

"Or go to Honolulu," his wife said. "That's more heavenly."

Our friends live in an area called Broadmoor, in a house beside a golf course, where lawns and flowers abound, and, of course, there are dense stands of trees. Distance to the center of town by car: ten minutes. I thought wonderingly of other people I knew coming in from Bucks County or driving the freeways from Glendale.

Another day, we were picked up by a pretty, generous lady who took us to her home on Lake Washington. The pretty lady lives in a spacious house with lawns running down to the edge of the water. One had the feeling of a mountain resort, except for the four-lane floating bridge crossing the lake in the distance. The lady's teen-age daughter, dubiously submerging a foot, said the temperature was too low for her taste most of the time; she preferred the heated swimming pool nearby. We were told the head of the family often parked his car on the Seattle side and covered the intervening distance, morning and evening, by boat, reducing his driving time to and from the office to ten minutes.

Our friend had a twin-engine cabin cruiser in a slip at the bottom of a path, in company with an outboard and a fast launch. When more people had gathered, we departed in the large craft for a sunset cruise, picking up additional passengers. Cocktails were served aboard, and then we moored at the lakeside country club for another drink. I thought everything very nearly perfect, if perhaps too close to lotus land.

"It does give you a feeling of guilt at times," the lady said, and smiled. "As if you were having too good a time. Seattle resembles one of those fabled marriages that are one long honeymoon."

A genial man, from the chamber of commerce, explained that boats in Seattle are a way of life. There are seventy thousand yachts here, in the pleasure-boating capital of the world.

Portland at dusk: *City lights twinkle and the snow cone of Mount Hood turns red in the sunset.*

"If you get bored with Lake Washington," he said, "which has a fifty-mile shore line, and Lake Union, you can always go out in the Sound and cruise indefinitely. Can you imagine just taking off, stopping anywhere you want on a deserted beach, catching some crabs, and barbecuing them in a Japanese *habachi* on the fantail? We issue the only travel folders that are for real."

I told him I believed him implicitly, in glorious Technicolor.

Since Lake Washington is higher in elevation than Puget Sound, trips between the two bodies of water are made via locks at the end of Salmon Bay. A visit to them during a summer week end provides a unique spectacle. Pumping water in and out, the locks raise and lower boats all day and into the night. The larger lock is over seven hundred feet long and eighty feet wide; the onlooker is stunned by the rush-hour sight of every variety of craft penned in like sardines, row on row, in this heaving expanse of fluid. Traffic men on the concrete borders of the basins resemble subway guards, ruthlessly wedging boats in spaces where the owners are bound to grieve for their paint and desperately throw out bumpers. As the conglomeration surges up or down, everybody aboard is mustered to fend off neighbors fore and aft and on either side. Romances have started here, deals have been made, highballs exchanged, and an occasional nose punched.

Notwithstanding the heavy traffic, sportsmen will be heartened to learn that salmon also use the locks, bound from fresh to tide water or vice versa; more than five thousand of them are counted in transit annually, and only 10 per cent are chumps enough to struggle up the fish ladders thoughtfully provided—the remainder, in company with their human opposite numbers, float happily and let the Government hoist or lower, without charge.

Overhead in Seattle, as in most other cities, is the sound of the future—the banshee wails of Boeing's turbo-jet 707's. And the smell of the future, which is evidently that of kerosene; when these expensive argosies take off they leave trails of greasy smoke behind them, like badly trimmed lamps. The engines are equipped with sound suppressors, but the high-pitched shrieks they emit at ear-muffed personnel on the ground, and the rolling thunder they pitch across the sky, make one doubt that airports or houses around them will be spots for a Sunday-afternoon nap after the next year or so.

Since we were city folk and ill-equipped psychologically or otherwise for that stunning snow-capped wilderness of mountains and valleys across the Sound called the Olympic Peninsula, or the fishing and exploring to be done in the Strait of Juan de Fuca, well-wishers advised us to retain our Sulka cravats and Irene suits and head south.

So we went back to Olympia, the uninspired capital of the state of Washington, and thence to Aberdeen, on Gray's Harbor, in the heart of the lumbering country. One passes through grim little towns set in lovely scenery, the latter as pretty as that of Bavaria, and occasionally comes to a jewel of a place

*The redwood trees of California, the world's
most ancient living things, tower like the columns
of a mammoth natural cathedral. Carpeted
with delicate ferns and grasses, softly lit by
sun rays filtered through the branches, the redwood
forests live in quietness and a sense of eternity.*

like Raymond, or the picturesquely neat South Bend, which is almost a replica of a fishing village in Maine. Everywhere, in barges or in piles along the shore, are whitening heaps of oyster shells waiting to become an element in chicken feed and fertilizer. Presently we came to the vast, dun-colored expanse where the Columbia River meets the sea, and a ferry took our car across to Oregon.

From here begins a resort area stretching intermittently for hundreds of miles. We had been told beforehand that the Oregon coast is the most beautiful in the world, and were prepared to resist; but after two or three days we were entirely conquered. Nothing in our experience compared to it, even the shores of the Mediterranean, Brittany, the Caribbean, the British Isles and Ireland, and the Pacific side of Central America. To a generation steeped in the wonders of Cinerama, and more inclined to look at Lawrence Welk, the region is a constant delight to the eyes. The unending and almost bewildering succession of sandy beaches, bold cliffs, towering forests, and clean little towns dressed for holidays is incredibly pleasant. If one grows tired of sparkling water and the swell of bold mountains, it is easy to turn to fields covered with azaleas, rhododendrons, Canterbury bells, tiny white daisies, and yellow and blue lupine. Around Tillamook, fat cows ruminate in landscapes Constable might have painted, and in the cheese factory they make tasty yellow slabs of the Tillamook Cheddar, which is favorably regarded by connoisseurs. All along the fisherman is paramount, either on the beach or in the rivers and streams, in search of salmon and steelhead. And clamming and crabbing rate high in popularity.

California's coast is nowhere near the equal of Oregon's, and the road decently turns inland shortly after the town of Eureka. But south of Garberville no traveler would want to miss the redwood belt; nor can he, for the highway threads straight through the groves of fantastically large and ancient trees. The silence of centuries which seems to invest them, the gloom their three-hundred-foot-and-over heights cast beneath, and the spectacle of their incredible trunks, devoid of branches in the lower parts, marching off in the distance like frozen giants, add up to an awing experience.

San Francisco, long the darling of the city collectors, is still doing business at the old stand. The Golden Gate is there, the hills, the bridges, the fog, the escape-proof pokey on Alcatraz Island, and the carefully preserved cable cars. And at night a traditional excitement motivates inhabitant and visitor alike— the colored signs begin to flame, the myriad saloons spread beckoning arms, and people begin to tuck away martinis on top of the Mark Hopkins Hotel and consider where to go next— not including Oakland or Berkeley, which continue to offer peace, quiet lodging, and meetings of the P.T.A. unlikely to attract the traveler.

The Bay City has room for all of them, with roller-coaster taxi rides and startling views of ocean, bay and miles of scroll-saw wooden flat buildings resembling small firehouses. Animation is not confined to the metropolitan area, but goes on down the Peninsula, to Burlingame and beyond, where drive-ins and large, deliberately quaint roadside restaurants beguile the drinker and eater. You may be tired and footsore from traversing the magnificence of Golden Gate Park or inspecting the Embarcadero and such ships as the militant water-front unions allow to use the port, yet the rush and promise of an evening here will catch you up, wash away your fatigue, and set you in motion toward Jack's or Trader Vic's or the Fleur de Lys. Pizza, charcoal-broiled hamburgers, sea food, smorgasbord or the Russian fish stew called *selyanka*, it's all waiting for you.

Idolatry aside, perhaps a few words in dispraise of San Francisco are not out of order. To begin with, it is a convention town. All the Coast cities are, but San Francisco's compactness makes the crowding very apparent. The vehicular traffic is paralyzing, and parking one's car is a major effort. Market Street, the principal avenue, is broad and should be dignified, and instead is shabby and unimpressive. An elevated freeway hurtles through the center of town, bound for the Bay Bridge, spoiling the looks of the area and complicating wheeled life under its ponderous buttresses. There is smog, despite boisterous winds, and the smell of internal-combustion engines.

The eating in San Francisco is not as good as they would have you believe. If you are a Chinese or Japanese food buff, you will, of course, have come home; otherwise the fare is satisfactory, and occasionally excellent, but something less than superlative. Even the famous Fisherman's Wharf, once uncluttered and unbedizened, is now highly commercial, doing business on an enormous scale and full of second-rate restaurants and night clubs. With a bedrock formed of Italian cooks, the city's restaurants tend to feed you fully, at decent prices. Evidently the San Franciscan is not in the mood to pay for the utmost in cuisine. He has no objection to checkered tablecloths, candles stuck in Chianti bottles, crowding, noise and indifferent service. His digestion is quite capable of overcoming gooey sauces and generous portions of spaghetti between soup and entree. Of late, he is inclined to cross the Golden Gate Bridge in his car and dine poorly in picturesque Sausalito. The red plush and paneling of the '90's is apt to please him more, I think, than a deft hand with the sour cream in the Beef Stroganoff or the proper shape and taste of the gnocchi Romano. Following a night on the town, he will infallibly smell of garlic —it covers a multitude of sins.

Down the Peninsula, they're eating steaks and baked potatoes full of chives, and topping it off with chocolate sundaes. And moving back into town and rebuilding old flat buildings at great expense because the traffic is growing so heavy. The co-operative apartment is rearing its menacing head, and Jackson Square, only recently a slum, is now an interior-design center, full of painted, exposed beams, stylish gentlemen in unpadded coats and unpleated pants, and nervous women in hats who are doing Japanese-modern apartments on Telegraph Hill. A tradition tenaciously clung to could go down for the count before long, as the population mounts and the automobiles multiply and scientists at Berkeley and Stanford and Sunnyvale devise fresh horrors and accelerate the populace along with the particles in their cyclotrons. The days of the gold rush and the land-and-railroad barons are long gone. The city is beginning to feel the cold hand of a hurried uniformity.

Southbound, the tourist is well advised when he forsakes U.S. 101 to take the Skyline Boulevard through pretty, wooded, hilly country to Santa Cruz, a resort town. The road then follows the inward sweep of Monterey Bay to Monterey itself, where Juan Cabrillo put in toward the middle of the 16th Century, and didn't land because of rough seas; Cabrillo has departed permanently, but the seas are still around, and frequently rough. General Sherman spent some time here, before he marched through Georgia, and Robert Louis Stevenson wrote a bit for local publications. Although the historical aspect is a talking point, the fact is that Monterey is now a thriving place, and there are more filling stations and motels and cut-rate appliance shops to look at than old adobe buildings and relics of the Bear Flag state.

Beyond is the Seventeen Mile Drive, quite as entrancing in its rocky, spume-filled seascapes as advertised, and thick with the rare Monterey cypresses. When you leave your car to breast the stiff onshore winds, you can readily understand how the trees became so gnarled, and why they infallibly lean to the landward side. The wonders in this region include Pebble Beach Golf Course (there's nothing like shooting in a spanking breeze, and losing your ball in an authentic ocean), the arts-and-craftsy village of Carmel, Naval and Army establishments set in scenes of great natural beauty, retired officers from every branch of service, at last integrated by the pension system, driving their station wagons in an eccentric fashion, Robinson Jeffers and his stone house, one of Bing Crosby's innumerable homes, and a variety of attractive lodges featuring television and Continental breakfasts.

Continuing southward—on State Highway 1 now—the traveler begins to sweat out a lot of curves on a mountainous, treeless, rather arid coast. Less than a hundred miles south of Monterey is the fantastic Hearst-San Simeon State Historical Monument, lately opened to the public. On 240,000 acres dwelt Mr. William Randolph Hearst at one time, in a great unfinished castle called La Casa Grande, flanked by imposing guest houses named La Casa del Mar, La Casa del Sol, and La Casa del Monte, and surrounded by gardens, wild animals, exotic trees and statuary.

Not much farther away, seemingly, begin the suburbs and signs of Los Angeles. They are prefaced by a sedate, uncommercial little city named Santa Barbara, full of shining white Spanish colonial period walls and red tile roofs. Here the richer, more leisurely citizens endeavor to escape the clangor and smoke of the southern reaches of the state, and to preserve a decorous peace and quiet. Nothing is supposed to happen, and it is rare when anything does. To be sure, a prominent member of the community was accused not long ago of taking photographs, through a one-way window, of the bared torsos of many Santa Barbara ladies (they were submitting to chest X-rays), but that hardly comes under the head of industrialization, which the inhabitants fear most.

In Oregon the Pacific forests come down to the edge of the sea along a coastline that is jagged, wild and spectacular. Remote promontories, like Cape Kawanda with its lonely beauty and shifting moods, jut far out into the cold Pacific.

A friend of mine, an early settler who came from the East when sound invaded the movies, sums up Los Angeles in this fashion: "It's a wonderful place to live, but I wouldn't want to visit it." His opinion is apparently shared by the majority of the other transients, who aren't transients at all but people who arrived with bag and baggage, children, pets, appliances and, unhappily, motorcars—the autos registered in the area are approaching three million in number. The newcomers are arriving at varying rates, but one figure commonly accepted is 2600 more inhabitants every week. The city is the third largest in the nation, there are more than five and a half million souls in the county, and qualified seers predict that within twenty years one semi-unified, sprawling collection of suburbs—still vainly searching for a metropolitan section—will stretch for two hundred miles along the coast, from the Mexican border to a no-longer-peaceful Santa Barbara. Just behind the visionaries the freeway builders work frantically, pouring eight-lane layers of concrete that are inadequate before they are completed.

Despite my friend, Los Angeles is a fine town to visit. There are more suburbs and complete, detached shopping centers than the mind can encompass, enough swimming pools to form a Gunite Lake Mead if they were combined, vast distances to drive, lined on either side by wholesale outlet stores and desperate dealers in secondhand Cadillacs, a Civic Center where a tax-happy administration is recklessly building soaring new edifices to house additional filing cabinets and bureaucrats, several new hotels, the majority of the sports cars in the Western Hemisphere, splendid ten-automobile wrecks on the freeways, and a so-called Oceanarium near San Pedro where a whale known as Bubbles entertains daily.

To conclude, the Pacific Coast has everybody's stamp of approval, not just mine and Duncan Hines'. It's certainly worth seeing, apparently just before it takes off from its launching pad into the wild blue yonder. Come early and avoid the rush, because I think the rush in the next few years is going to be awful.

Make the trip by car, if possible. You've never seen so many motels enticing you with swimming pools and free ice for your highballs, or so many clean service-station restrooms and courtly gas-pump attendants in white, pressing upon you maps and tip sheets on the sights to be seen.

The truck drivers are fully courteous as the trucking associations allege—they'll pull aside for you when they can, they'll help you when you're in trouble, and at night they'll blink their marker lights several times when it's unsafe to pass and once when it's clear.

And lovely and interesting as it is all guaranteed to be please go home and stay when you're finished. We've got enough satisfied customers here already.

THE WORLD OF LOS ANGELES

Los Angeles, a dynamic creation wrought
by sun, oil, and automobiles,
lures more thousands of people every year.
Life there may be as haywire as the Keystone
cops, as the city's numberless critics say.
But as Sean O'Faolain sees it, Los Angeles
may also be a world in the making, a dazzlingly
unconventional world busily creating its
own and, very possibly, the entire country's future.

Let us pretend that it is January and that you are flying here from the East. Your plane takes off from Idlewild in a cloud of snow dust flying back from the four propellers like the storm-blown hair of four screaming, withered Valkyries. You leave behind and below you sea-rimmed marshes edged with gray-green ice, inlets rimmed with tall sedge as stiff as spears with cold; and then, for hour after hour, the whole vast continent of America keeps passing beneath you as one fence-ruled and road-streaked plain of whiteness. Even in the heated plane you are so conscious of the intense cold outside that, for some time, you may well be unwilling to remove your overcoat.

You are relieved when, over Denver, the pilot's voice on the intercom blandly informs you that the temperature outside is now rising to zero. In the twilight you see the Las Vegas Strip all ruby and amber on the dark desert, for the snow has by now been left behind, although even down there the glass has only risen to 18°. Presently you become aware that you have lost the race with the sun; you see more and more lighted homes; the San Bernardino mountains come up darkly, closer and closer to your plane—almost too close, you feel—and you sense the loss of speed, the loss of height, the muted panting of your four Valkyries. And then....

Far beneath and ahead there opens up a great, wide valley falling slowly toward the Pacific, glowing with pools, lakes and oceans of lights upon lights, lights beyond lights, lights laid out in row after row, in line beyond line, pulsating across Hollywood, Beverly Hills, Westwood, Pasadena, south, south-west and southeast Los Angeles, light fading westward toward and among over the dusky hills of the Santa Monica range lights dimming eastward around Mount San Jacinto, lights in dots, blurs and angled streaks sloping gently southward toward the invisible beaches and the soundless sea. It is one of the greatest aerial night views in the world.

It takes you about fifteen minutes, now almost volplaning, from the San Bernardinos down to the tarmac of the International Airport, about two miles from the beach at El Segundo. From force of habit you wrap yourself in your greatcoat, clutch your gloves and your scarf, and emerge on the gangway. Do you remember T. E. Lawrence's phrase about the heat of Arabia coming out like a drawn sword? The people hanging about in the blazing lights to meet friends are in shirt sleeves or cotton frocks. The deep blue of the night sky is as pure and

clear as a morning-glory or the eyes of a virgin. But what you are feeling is far more than an alien summer's warmth. It is true that you take off your overcoat, stuff away your gloves and scarf, doff your hat. But you also expand, you smile, you may even laugh with pleasure. And then you feel the miracle beginning to happen to you: the flutter of wings within you trying to escape from the cage of your body, as if your very soul were taking flight in release from all mortal constrictions.

This has always been the response of the traveler to Southern California. The West has always expressed its instinct for leisurely living in terms of the pueblo sprawling over the wide and warm desert, from the days when the arid land was of such slight value that a man short of ready cash would as soon pay a creditor with a hundred acres of what is now Los Angeles as with a cord of wood: there is a recorded instance of this actually happening. But not every land where the sun is god, and where land was once called land, not real estate, has produced these low-flung homes set in spaciousness. It is not so in North Africa, Southern Italy, Cyprus: one thinks of the cramped lanes and alleys of Tangiers, or Naples, or Nicosia. Los Angeles has spread flatly, exploited the room at its disposal, because more than any other modern city it is the child of Nature and of Science. It has met, one does not say solved, all its problems in the American version of the Age of Reason. It is what it is chiefly because its natural advantages have been improved and its disadvantages minimized by two kinds of skill, agricultural skill and engineering skill; the first coping chiefly with water, and the second with water and oil.

It was on the basis of these two natural elements that Los Angeles began to grow, but it was the invention of the internal-combustion engine that broke down the last of its theoretical boundaries and let it grow as freely as it did, and does. Most cities give one the impression of having been built around Man. This one seems at first sight to have been built around the Automobile. It is the impression anybody might get from those six-lane urban freeways, endlessly flowing, never for a moment empty; from the swooping clover-leaf crossovers and crossunders; the helitrafficopters radioing down to the ground squads on motorcycles; the tickets handed out for dangerous slowing—in practice motorists run up to seventy miles per hour on the freeways. And nobody can fail to be irked by the parking problem downtown and the mounting death toll on the freeways. The stranger is constantly astonished by everybody's seven-league-boots attitude to distance, by the relation between distance and speed, and the profound and various effects of both on the life mode of the people.

I recall the young man who complained to me about one of the minor hardships of lovers in Los Angeles. His girl lives in the Valley, near a place sweetly called Tarzana after that famous film character Tarzan of the Apes. The young man lives about thirty-five miles to the south in Gardena. Every evening, after driving home from work, he has to spend about two hours in going to and coming from the home of his beloved, without

The Hollywood Freeway, one of the Los Angeles'
futuristic highways, cuts through the
Santa Monica Mountains to the San Fernando Valley.

reckoning any further driving in between, to get down to the sea or up into the hills. After a year of this nightly routine, I thought the poor young man was beginning to show signs of strain. But, then, a papa living in Tarzana who wants to take his youngsters to Disneyland will have to cover eighty-five miles going and coming, and spend between two and three hours behind the wheel, if he is not caught in a traffic jam. (I have on occasion seen cars backed up three deep for a mile and a half behind a breakdown.) They think nothing here of covering ninety miles for the sake of a dinner. No wonder the average driver will tick up 17,000 miles a year merely going between his home and his work.

There, then, it lies between the hills and the sea, a many-armed Shiva, spread-eagled in the browning sun, its outstretched fingers always creeping farther and farther up the valleys and gullies and gulches to clutch at more wild earth for its domain—which is already so big that nobody can see it in its entirety, not even from the highest plane. Bits of it are always hidden even from the eye of the sun. Its populace can only get to know it, over the years, by taking it piecemeal in sampling tours, savoring gobbets of their vast urban universe like connoisseurs. As when, one evening after dinner, a friend driving me back to my hotel in Beverly Hills chose to climb up behind Sunset Boulevard, along the high-flung ridge of the Santa Monica range on Mulholland Highway, for the sheer pleasure of seeing again, far below us on the one side, the spreading lights of Hollywood, and on the other, the level lights of the San Fernando Valley. And then, instead of cutting down through Laurel Canyon or Coldwater, we persisted on into the darkness of Topanga Canyon Boulevard just for the fun of approaching the soft hiss of the Pacific waves between Santa Monica and Malibu.

These remoter canyons winding back into the hills that encircle the city are to me the most affectingly beautiful parts of Los Angeles, and the remoter they are, the better. These canyons start as crumpled cliffs that open up roadways that go clambering back into the hills like galvanized snakes. Up here at night it can be so oddly lonely and silent and dark that the natural end of every party is the driver saying, "Know something? I dunno *where* we are." One feels miles away from the city proper. If the hills are touched by wisps of fog the effect is eerie. If we diverge a yard the road has an impish way of suddenly changing into a red-dirt track, for fresh development is always going on among the brushwood, the mesquite, the scrub oak and the manzanita; and an unexpected yellow blob of light from some new cliff dwelling will startle rather than guide us. If, as we probe downward, we should halt and turn off the engine, we might hear a coyote or a quail, or get the smell of sage and kelp and that salty air that speckles every western window by the sea and pockmarks every outdoor metal fitment unless it is painted at least twice a year.

One sometimes gets lovely night views from the western hills out over the coastal line of lights stringing down toward

Malaga Cove and the Point Vicente light. Visiting one evening out beyond Santa Monica and, I think, up Las Flores Canyon—but I cannot be certain for, as usual, we got lost several times—I met an old lady just arrived from Italy. She said happily and excitedly, as we stood in the balmy, aromatic darkness of the February night looking south and east at the line of lights: "I just cannot believe I am so far from home." And, indeed, it is very like that wonderful night view from the heights of Genoa along the Riviera di Levante.

But how little does such a tiny excursion as I have described show us of Los Angeles as a whole! If we took a similar sweep in the opposite direction, eastward this time for some thirty miles out to the Santa Anita racetrack and returning by South Pasadena, we should not have encircled in both trips a tenth part of the consecutive and continuous pattern of streets, boulevards, avenues, roads, freeways, highways, drives, cities, towns, villages and plains that are comprised under the name of Los Angeles.

The end of this unique blend of city life and country tempo is that every true Angeleno has bifocal eyes. He alternately suffers, or better say profits, from shortsightedness and farsightedness. At times he will see no farther than the fruit tree outside his door when he steps out to pluck a lime or an orange to concoct a drink; at most no farther than the barbecue or the blue-lined pool. This is his townsman's Sabine farm. And as Horace looked down at Rome from the Sabine Hills he looks down into his city from inside his wooden palisade. To this narrow camp he seems geared, for this and by this alone he seems to live.

But if he is a true Angeleno, and not a mere Johnny-come-quickly, a transient, his memories, loyalties and longings will soar to the farthest Sierras. His Los Angeles stretches from San Diego to Monterey. Carmel is his suburb, Robinson Jeffers is his poet; he knows the statue to Garces, the explorer of the San Joaquin Valley, as well as he knows the Cabrillo monument on Point Loma; he thinks of wine not only in terms of some cool Cucamonga cellar, comparatively near at hand, but also of the farthest vineyards of the San Joaquin, a hundred and more miles from City Hall. He will tell you, his eyes widening with poignant recollection, of the first time he got his Balboa view of Los Angeles, as a youth standing on one of the heights of Turnbull Canyon, a sweep of fifty miles from Mount San Jacinto around to where, far out on the purpling sea, Santa Catalina Island floated like the shell that supported Botticelli's naked Venus; he may tell you how he knew then that Los Angeles claims not only its farthest hills but its ocean spaces from the isle of San Miguel to San Clemente.

The ultimate source of this farsightedness, this roving view, is no doubt the traditional love of space and the open air, equally evident in the star-lit symphonies of the Hollywood Bowl, the outdoor libraries, called parasol stations, in the downtown plazas and parks, the drive-in restaurants, the proliferation of motels, unconventional but comfortable fashions in dress, health-and-strength cults, as at Muscle Beach, the widespread love of sport—all of which, as yeast in bread, aerate the common claustrophobic pattern of city life to which the world must submit elsewhere.

And yet, though this apparently triumphant humanism of the West may at first fill us with a delighted awe, it soon begins to fill us with apprehension. At first one throws up one's hand in unqualified delight at this man-made miracle, this return to the spirit of the Renaissance that made men feel that nothing on earth was impossible of achievement. In one's first flush of joy one feels like crying out: "How great is man! How infinite in faculty!" In each of those millions of homes, one fancifully thinks, there is an Adam and an Eve starting the world again as it was before the Fall. And then? One cools....

Adam and Eve are probably at that moment listening to the radio or watching the television screen. She may even, as in a recent and unexpectedly savage *New Yorker* cartoon, be saying to him where he lounges beside her, idly tinkling his Scotch-on-the-rocks, "Surely, honey, there must be more to life than this?" Los Angeles has coped with everything; with "this" she has yet to cope—that is, with the enlargement and fulfillment of her culture.

It is an extraordinary thing that this vast urban area, with a greater population than Chicago, cannot support a regular theater, has no major periodicals and no important book publishers, and has to rely on newspapers that—not to speak of the East—do not measure up to the best of the Southwest and Middle West. The regular routine here is to travel three thousand miles to New York for one day's business and a week of plays, the ballet and the opera. There is, however, a fine symphony in Los Angeles; and there are some fine rare-book dealers; and painting thrives.

Culture in Los Angeles is a secret society, a few tiny clumps of besieged colonies. You see it at its liveliest when a few painters get together to chat, or a group of musicians who have spent all day recording for the movies gather at night to play what they really want to play, whether it be free-wheeling jazz or a Vivaldi sonata. The city, indeed the whole state, has as yet produced few outstanding works of literature. Its native philosophy, if it has such intimations of immortality, has yet to find expression.

What we have here is a wonderful vessel, a genuinely new shape of urban life, waiting to be filled. That is possibly why Carey McWilliams, in the best book yet written about the whole region of which Los Angeles is the center and clearest expression—*Southern California Country*—was so much struck by a sense of loneliness among its newcomers twenty or thirty years ago—as of people who had been uprooted from their own folkways and come to live in a place that had not yet developed its own: whence that strange rash of fancy religions, or those groupings into societies named after the newcomers' original state.

But that *was* thirty and twenty years ago and those state societies and fancy religions have faded or are fading out. The Los Angeles of today strikes one as a city that is settling down and growing up. One would dearly like to be able to come back in, say, ten years or so and see whether the prophets of today are justified—whether Southern California is, indeed, rocking the cradle of the city of the future, and someday one of the most wonderful cities the world has ever known will cover the whole land between the Sierras and the sea.

SAN FRANCISCO

*Wise and worldly, San Francisco is one of
the world's truly great cities,
loved by nearly everyone who has known it.
Hamilton Basso admits that he carries a torch for
the city, and adds, with a shrug,
"Who doesn't?"*

In the unabashedly sentimental mythology of San Francisco there is a story that goes like this. Among the residents of the city, on the morning of the big earthquake, was a solid, sober-minded citizen of German extraction. Thrown from his cot by the earth's violent shuddering, he rushed to the bedroom where his wife and daughter slept. He found them clinging to each other, frantic with terror.

"Papa! Papa!" they cried. "It is the end of the world. We are going to die!"

He smiled at them gently. "Well, what of it?" he said. "Aren't we going to die in San Francisco?"

More than that privilege, as any good San Franciscan will tell you, no man could rightly ask. Although it will not be argued that San Francisco is heaven itself, there is a general agreement among its approximately 800,000 inhabitants that a happier steppingstone to heaven could not be found. Countless other Americans, moreover, lean to the same point of view. Of all the cities in the United States, San Francisco comes closest to being everybody's town. "San Francisco!" said Richard Henry Dana. "The emporium of a new world!" And another writer, George West, wrote: "Nowhere in America is there less in evidence the cold theological eye, the cautious hand withheld, the lifted eyebrow, the distrust of playfulness." More could be added. These are merely random selections from the long litany of admiration that has been chanted in San Francisco's praise. Not so very long ago I had the whole of it summed up by a Nevada ranch hand in whose company I was spending the evening. "Now there," he said, "is one hell of a swell town."

It was easy for me to agree. I would be inclined to regard with deepest suspicion anyone who didn't. Not to like San Francisco, to me, is as odious a heresy as not liking springtime in Paris, the lights of New York City as seen from Central Park at dusk, or the view of the Umbrian countryside that one gets at Orvieto. In other words, I carry a torch. And like most men in that predicament I find that language is far too limited to do the city justice. To say that San Francisco has character and personality, that it stands with New York and New Orleans as one of the three cities in the United States that rise in their own uniqueness above the national plain—this, I am afraid, is not enough. It wants a closer, harder, more intimate look. And for a first look it should be seen from one of its own eminences, a place like Twin Peaks or Telegraph Hill.

From such a height as this, looking down upon the whole conformation of the town, you come at once upon the largest secret of its sorcery. Geography is the key. Washed on three sides by the sea, built on the tip of a peninsula whose containing waters are spanned by two mighty bridges—one of which, flung across the piece of water known as the Golden Gate, is correctly esteemed as the most beautiful in the world—it is given a kind of high, soaring excitement by the drama of its fourteen hills. The place is assertive. It rises and dips and rises again. It lifts the eye up. It commands you not to look down.

In sunny California (which despite all the wisecracks *is* sunny), San Francisco is not always as shimmering as it might be. Although it can relax in sunshine for two thirds of all the daylight hours of the year, it is often shrouded in a cold, gray, penetrating fog.

But this, too, adds to the city's special flavor and tone. It keeps its all-year-round autumn from getting monotonous. It lends variety and makes for enchantment. The streets take on a new, mysterious dimension when the fog comes rolling in, just as they do in London, and if there is anything more beautiful in this world than the lights of the Golden Gate bridge shimmering in the still of the night when everything else is lost in the fog, I don't know what it is.

Fog experts like to point out that San Francisco has two kinds: the white, ordinary fog that forms in huge blankets, sometimes as much as 1700 feet thick, and which swallows up the entire city; and the tule fog, low-hanging clouds of condensed vapor which roam about the bay in long, restless, serpentine drifts, and sometimes completely cover one section of the city while another is bright with sunlight. Downtown San Francisco has an astonishing way of being fog-free. It is something of a standard joke in the city that stay-at-home housewives, mist-bound for days at a time, deeply resent their husbands' being able to work in such nice weather.

Then, too, between October and May, it is frequently likely to rain. The department stores advertise raincoats and umbrellas as accessories to what they call "liquid sunshine" but native San Franciscans tend to be less euphemistic. I have never known a people who entertain such strong feelings about rain. Fog they take in their stride—actually, since it is so uniquely theirs, they are tremendously proud of it. But let there be a somewhat heavier condensation, let so much as the slightest mist begin to fall, and every man, woman and child in the city begins to regard it as a personal affront. All in all, however, the true San Franciscan would just as soon let his weather stand as it is. "You can say what you like about the fog and the rain," I was told, "but at least it keeps all that sunlight they have farther south from baking out our brains. You'll notice that the yogi-swami-lunatic belt has never pushed up this far. If it wasn't for the fog and the rain, this place—God help us!—might turn into another Los Angeles."

The greatest appeal of San Francisco is the spectacle of San Francisco itself. "I love to go there," a service-station attendant in Sacramento told me when I was last driving cross-country. "I can have a wonderful time and it hardly costs me a dime." In no way was he exaggerating. Most of the best things that San Francisco has to offer are free. All that is demanded is a pair of legs strong enough to climb a few hills. To truly appreciate the city it is necessary to wander about its

From the dark-brown hills of Marin County, the Golden Gate Bridge soars across the harbor entrance to the peninsula.

streets. It wants to be savored slowly. Only then does its elusive quality gradually reveal itself. Take, for instance, its "picturesqueness." Picturesque it certainly is. Its port, its Chinatown, its Fisherman's Wharf, its Italian quarter, its cable cars —here, surely, is picturesqueness enough to be spread out over half a dozen cities.

But the picturesqueness of San Francisco, it gradually begins to appear, is of a rather particular kind. Its port is an economic artery of tremendous importance; its Chinatown is the largest Asiatic settlement this side of the Orient; its Fisherman's Wharf is the seat of an extremely sizable industry; and its quaint cable cars continue to be a vital part of its transportation system. In other words, the picturesqueness of San Francisco works.

But let's wander around for a bit. There is always Market Street to be explored, since it is the town's principal thoroughfare, but Market Street, which used to be to San Francisco what Fifth Avenue is to New York, has rather come down in the world. It seems to me that the hot-dog-and-hamburger stands have increased considerably over the past several years, that a few more miles of neon tubing have been added, and that it is mistakenly trying to turn itself into another Broadway. However, it is still the place where the cable cars that clang up and down Powell Street are reversed on their turntable, with passengers and pedestrians sometimes lending a hand, and it remains the address of what every San Franciscan knows in his heart to be the world's greatest hotel.

The Palace, naturally. There are other excellent hotels in San Francisco—the St. Francis; the Clift; the Fairmont; the Sir Francis Drake; the Mark Hopkins with its world-famous view—but The Palace is more than a hotel. It is a monument, a landmark and a legend. San Francisco could no more do without it than Paris could face the future without the Eiffel Tower. The original Palace, which opened its doors in 1875, was billed as such a supercolossal production that even a town with gold dust in its eyes began to take a cynical view. Wrote one local columnist: "The ground covered [is estimated] to be eleven hundred and fifty-four square miles, six yards, two inches. . . . A contract is already given out for the construction of a flume from the Yosemite to conduct the Bridal Veil Fall thither, and which it is designed to have pour over the east front. . . . The beds are made with Swiss watch springs and stuffed with camel's hair, each single hair costing eleven cents. . . . There are thirty-four elevators in all—four for passengers, ten for baggage and twenty for mixed drinks. Each elevator contains a piano and a bowling alley."

The reality almost outdid the exaggeration. The Palace cost $4,000,000 in the hardest of hard dollars and was so sumptuous that even the Emperor of Brazil, Dom Pedro II, had to break down. Said he: "Nothing makes me ashamed of Brazil so much as the Palace Hotel." By 1900 The Palace was already a legend —Grant, Sheridan and Sherman had been honored in its banquet rooms; Oscar Wilde had lent it his own elegance; James J. Jeffries had thrown a champagne party for an army of ad-

mirers; the "Nevada Four" had instituted their poker sessions, which called for an original take-out of $75,000; it has played constant host to "the great, the near-great and the merely flamboyant."

No ordinary climax could have capped the tale—there is a certain dramatic correctness in the old Palace's coming to an end and in the great earthquake. But even to the very end it kept its legend alive. Among the guests registered at the time was Enrico Caruso—the stories still tell how with a towel wrapped about his famous throat, he and some fellow members of the Metropolitan Opera Company came out into the street carrying a large portrait of Theodore Roosevelt.

The present Palace was built on the site of its predecessor in 1909. If, perhaps, its glory is less, it may be that the glories of the time are less. However, it still plays host to "the great, the near-great and the merely flamboyant," and it still possesses an extraordinary appeal. Like San Francisco itself, its character is unmistakable—go to sleep in The Palace and when you wake up you don't have to think twice to know that you are not in Kansas City.

No true San Franciscan would forgive a visitor who does not at least glance at a monument it knows as Lotta's Fountain. It stands on Market Street diagonally across from The Palace, and it is, I am afraid, a most commonplace adornment—a tall cast-iron shaft ornamented with lion heads and brass medallions depicting various California scenes, and with a fountain at its base. The fountain was presented to San Francisco in 1875 by Lotta Crabtree, the toast of the town in the age of gold.

Old-time San Franciscans can work up as much sentiment about Lotta as old-time New Yorkers can about Lillian Russell. One venerable great-grandfather, looking back to the time when he and the other blades were gay, told me that Lotta was one of the world's greatest actresses. "Tiptop that girl was, an absolute corker." Others of this generation appear to have agreed. So successful was Lotta—literally showered with riches by the affectionate miners who threw gold nuggets, gold coins and even gold watches on the stage—that she was able to retire at forty-four. Her professional career, which began when she was a child and which swept her on to a huge success in New York when she was only seventeen, ended in 1890. She died in 1924 in her late seventies, leaving an estate valued at $4,000,000.

But let us be on our way. Not far from Lotta's Fountain there are a number of buildings on Market Street that might be classified as landmarks—structures named after Hearst, Bancroft, De Young and others who helped to make San Francisco the city it is—but I do not think anyone will be quarreled with for passing them by.

The Nevada Bank Building, however, on the corner of Market and Montgomery streets, is one of the places that make San Francisco such a wonderful free show. No architectural gem, a prosaic twelve-story granite structure with the neo-Gothic ambitions of the early 1900's, it is the home of the Wells Fargo Bank & Union Trust Company, the oldest in the West and a direct descendant of the famous Wells Fargo Company. Busily engaged in cornering its share of San Francisco's multi-billion-dollar yearly banking business, the bank none-theless finds time to keep one eye peeled on its long, noisy, romantic past by maintaining a Wild West museum on its ground floor.

A wanderer in San Francisco is bound to be struck by the number of little alleys in town. Each is a repository of some nugget of local history. Not quite so picturesque as the older, quainter alleys of London, they nonetheless add incalculably to San Francisco's special Old World air. Far more interesting, however, is Grant Avenue, deceptively ordinary at first glance, but perhaps the most interesting street in the United States—four blocks of Mayfair with smart, expensive shops and smart, expensive women; nine blocks of China with all the sights, smells and signs of the Orient; and eleven blocks of Italy. During my several visits to San Francisco I must have strolled its length some fifty times—it is one of my ambitions to stroll it fifty more.

But the most fun had by most people who go to San Francisco is had in Chinatown. Grant Avenue is its principal commercial artery. Knowing San Franciscans say that the real Chineseness of the quarter is to be found along the side streets that run crosstown from Nob Hill, an opinion with which I have come to agree, but Grant Avenue, even to the residents of Chinatown, is still the big drag. Like anything else worth describing, it wants to be seen—the colorful bazaars; the grocery stores with their displays of bamboo shoots, bean sprouts, dried fish, and golden rows of roast ducks glazed with a kind of salty wax; the apothecary shops where all sorts of remedies are sold that to the untutored Western mind are completely mysterious; and all the rest of this teeming parcel of old Canton that lives its own life and goes its own way in the heart of a great American city.

Old Chinatown—the Chinatown that lasted from the bonanza days until 1906—was in many ways as sinister a place as San Francisco's notorious Barbary Coast of the same era. But along with the hatchet men and tong wars—one of which lasted seven years and cost sixty lives—there was always the sober, hard-working Chinatown of respectable merchants and industrious laborers who tenaciously held to their ancient customs, religion and traditional family life. It was this element that took over the control of the quarter after 1906 and raised the new Chinatown upon the ashes and embers of the old.

The new Chinatown, however, was rather a prosaic place—a collection of small, plaster-colored buildings that looked as Chinese as the Grand Rapids furniture that some inhabitants of the quarter were finding much more enchanting than the teakwood of their homeland. Today's Chinatown owes its appearance to an American corporation. Finding it necessary to put up a telephone exchange in the section, it decided, in one of those bursts of imagination that sometimes overtake the corporate mind, to design the building along the lines of a Chinese pagoda. Dazzled by its glory, the whole of Chinatown was soon going native, bursting out all over with golden turrets, fanciful cornices and pagoda tops—and this, paradoxically enough, at a time when its ties with China were beginning to grow more and more attenuated.

There are between 60,000 and 70,000 San Franciscans of Italian birth or ancestry who make up the city's largest and most powerful national minority. Some of them, who no more think of themselves as Italian than the Roosevelt clan thinks of itself as Dutch, have been putting down their roots in American soil since as early as 1830, but it was not until the late 19th Century that the Italians began to arrive by the thousands—laborers, mechanics, skilled craftsmen, farmers, shopkeepers. The majority settled in the Telegraph Hill section which, although now preponderantly Italian, was originally a polyglot community of Irish, German, French, Spanish, Mexican and Latin American immigrants. But in the Italian section, as in Chinatown, the yeast and fermentation that is part of the American experience has been at work—old ways, old customs and old habits have given way to the new.

The Latin Quarter's southern boundary is called Broadway, an annoyingly unfitting name by day, but one that lives up to its implications by night. For here is one of the centers of San Francisco night life—with bars, night clubs, cocktail lounges and some of the best restaurants in a city world-famous for its cuisine. Enough has been written of gastronomical San Francisco to make any further comment superfluous. Even so, I have to add my own tribute—after weeks of French, Italian, Chinese, Armenian, Indian, Mexican, Japanese and Polynesian cooking, I invariably find myself yearning for the exotic pleasures of cornmeal mush.

No excursion up Grant Avenue would be complete without a side trip to Nob Hill, perhaps the most famous of all San Francisco's ups and downs. Nob Hill got its name from the "nabobs" of finance and industry who built their mansions on its crest. Robert Louis Stevenson, whose stay in San Francisco is commemorated by a plaque in the city's Portsmouth Square, where he liked to loaf in the sun, knew Nob Hill when it was one of the highest pinnacles to which an up-and-coming tycoon could aspire. "The hill of palaces," he called it. "The best part of San Francisco." And Philip Guedalla, remembering its dizzying height, had this to say: "I estimate that a cent dropped on the crest of California Street would gather enough speed to kill a horse on Market Street, unless it hit a Chinaman on Grant Avenue."

Along with so much of the rest of old San Francisco, all but one of the great mansions of Nob Hill were destroyed by the fire of 1906. Today its golden age of compulsive ostentation is over, but it still remains a hill of palaces. One of its prize adornments is the Mark Hopkins Hotel, which occupies the site of the mansion which Mark Hopkins, one of the "Big Four," built in the 1870's. Nineteen stories high, the "Mark" looks down upon the most spectacular panorama of any hotel in the United States. The view from its penthouse cocktail lounge—"The Top of the Mark"—has become world famous.

Of the original Nob Hill mansions, the only one that remains is that of James C. Flood, one of the "Nevada Four." It was built of Connecticut brownstone at a cost of $1,500,000 after Flood made a trip to New York and had his imagination completely laid low by the mansions of the Fifth Avenue rich. The structure is now occupied by the Pacific Union Club. Its membership is restricted to an even 100—no more, no less —and wayfaring strangers who are invited to cross its threshold are apt to be regarded with the same awe as those who

Grant Avenue, San Francisco: *Gay, noisy Chinatown.*

have somehow managed to insinuate themselves into the inner mysteries of the Great Temple of Tibet.

But the club for which San Francisco is famous is a considerably less lamalike institution called the Bohemian. Not part of the Nob Hill scene, located in the downtown part of the city, it is as established a fixture of San Francisco as Fisherman's Wharf. "Weaving spiders come not here," says an inscription over the entrance of its five-story home, and but few weaving spiders are foolhardy enough to ignore the warning. The Bohemian Club now has a world-wide membership of about 2000 and a waiting list of hundreds. Once a year it has a kind of combination cook-out and house party in its Bohemian Grove, a rural hideaway some seventy-five miles from San Francisco, where an original play has been produced every year since 1880.

But there is really no end—one could go on and on indefinitely about the things to be seen in and about San Francisco. To sum it up—to bring it into a last, final focus—is almost impossible. All I can say is that I hope to see it soon again. Suddenly I am lonesome for it, and although its hills and towers lie on the other side of the continent I am somehow comforted to know it is there. As I said earlier, I carry a torch for San Francisco—but then, among those who have been privileged to know this lovely place, who doesn't?

San Francisco/Hamilton Basso **317**

ALWAYS SOMETHING TO DO IN SALINAS

When John Steinbeck was a boy, Salinas was
a town in the swamp. It wasn't much,
and it wasn't pretty, but it did have everything
a boy needed—rodeos and circuses and revivals; misers
and madmen; and over all a brooding sense
of violence just beneath the surface.

Early memories of Salinas are so confused in my mind that I don't know, actually, what I remember and what I was told I remembered. I am fairly clear on the earthquake of 1906. My father took me down Main Street and I remember brick buildings, spilled outward. Our own wooden house was not injured, but the chimney had completely turned around without falling. And my sharpest memory is that a phonograph we had obtained by subscribing to the *San Francisco Call* for two years—our first talking machine—leaped from a shelf and destroyed itself. There were two thousand five hundred people in Salinas then, but boosters confidently predicted that it would some day be a metropolis of five thousand.

Tradition was strong in Salinas and my town never forgot nor forgave an injury. For example, in the Fourth-of-July hosecart race in 1900, run against Watsonville, the Salinas team ran out its hose smartly and with a substantial lead, then found to its horror that the threads of the coupling had been filed smooth. They could not couple up and get water and so lost the race. Watsonville had obviously cheated. For a decade after, a man could get a fight in a bar at any time simply by bringing up the subject. I thought of Watsonvillians as foreigners and cheats. I wouldn't have thought of trusting them.

The old Camino Real, the royal road that threaded California together, moved up the valley and did not come near Salinas for a very good reason. The place that was to become Salinas was a series of tule-grown swamps, which toward the end of the summer dried and left a white deposit of alkali. It was this appearance of salt that gave the place its name. The stagecoaches on the royal road stopped at Natividad, a pleasant little town on the higher ground of the Gabilan foothills, free of fog and swamp and mosquitoes, protected from the fierce daily winds which funneled up the valley center. Natividad had a small college, perhaps the first in California.

There is no understanding the impulses of humans. Someone built a blacksmith shop in the swamp and houses clustered around it; Main Street went in, and little bridges were built over the dark and noisome swamps. On this least likely site, Salinas grew while Natividad died. The adobe college lost roof and windows. The royal road became a country lane. By the time I came along much of the swamp had been filled in, but there was plenty left so that the night roared with frogs. I was

A moisture-rich morning fog rolls in to freshen
the green, fertile fields of Salinas.

pretty big before I learned that silence was not made up of a wall of frog song.

Salinas was never a pretty town. It took a darkness from the swamps. The high gray fog hung over it and the ceaseless wind blew up the valley, cold and with a kind of desolate monotony. The mountains on both sides of the valley were beautiful, but Salinas was not and we knew it. Perhaps that is why a kind of violent assertiveness, an energy like the compensation for sin grew up in the town. The town motto, given it by a reporter ahead of his time, was: "Salinas is." I don't know what that means, but there is no doubt of its compelling tone.

As the swamps were drained and the black odorous mud exposed, it became known that this land was rich beyond belief. And Salinas became rich, the richest community per capita, we were told, in the entire world. I suppose this was true. Certainly we Salinians never questioned it even when we were broke. It was a town of wooden frame houses, the trading center of the valley, the social center of the whole world as we knew it.

The social structure was a strange and progressive one. First there were the Cattle People, the First Families of the Salinas Valley, gentry by right of being horsemen and dealing in gentry's goods, land and cattle. Theirs was an unassailable position, a little like that of English royalty. Then Claus Spreckles came from Holland and built a Sugar Factory (in capitals) and the flatlands of the valley around Salinas were planted to sugar beets and the Sugar People prospered. They were upstarts, of course, but they were solvent. The Cattle People sneered at them, but learned as every aristocracy does that not blood but money is the final authority. Sugar People might never have got any place socially if lettuce had not become the green gold of the Valley. Now we had a new set of upstarts: Lettuce People. Sugar People joined Cattle People in looking down

A farm laborer takes a break from his work.

their noses. These Lettuce People had Carrot People to look down on and these in turn felt odd about associating with Cauliflower People. And all the time the town stretched out— the streets extended into the country. Farm land became subdivisions. Salinas became five thousand and then ten thousand. Enthusiasts thought that twenty thousand was not too high a mark to shoot at. We had a brick high school and a National Guard armory for dances. And we had the rodeo in the summer to attract tourists.

We had many of what are now called characters in Salinas. Looking back it seems to me now it was solid characters, but at the time I thought everyone lived that way.

There was Hungry Anderson, who was known to be a tight man with a dollar. He and his wife lived about a mile out of town. He got his name on an occasion when he had some carpenters working on the roof of his house. At noon it took them about six or seven minutes to get down off the roof, and by the time they did, Hungry had eaten their lunches. He explained that when they were late, he had thought they didn't want to eat. He was called Hungry Anderson from that day on, and people began to say he was a miser. To prove that he wasn't he bought a shiny Chalmers automobile, but his instincts were too strong for him. He kept the car in a shed in town and came in with his horse and buggy, motored about town, put up the car and trotted back to his farm.

And we had misers, lots of misers. Heaven knows what they were, but we needed misers, perhaps with visions of counting gold pieces and hiding treasures. In those days many transactions were carried out in gold. Paper was highly suspected simply because it was unusual. One of our rich men used to sweat with nervousness when he had to pay a bill in gold. Paper saved him considerable painful emotion because it didn't really seem like money to him.

We had, however, one whooping dolager of a miser who gave us a great deal of pleasure. Of course now I know he was nuts, but then it was a different thing. He and his wife and his daughter lived in a dark little house in an apple orchard right in town. He was reputed to be a miser. My father had a feed store at that time and this man used to buy five pounds of middlings, which is somewhere between flour and bran. Every week he bought middlings and apparently that is all he bought. That is what the family ate, middlings and apples.

First the daughter died and a year later the wife died. The doctor who signed the certificates was said to have said, four times removed, that they had died of starvation. And now our miser was living all alone in his dark house in his dark orchard.

Naturally he was a pushover for us kids. We used to creep up close to his window at night and peek in at him sitting beside a kerosene lamp writing in a big ledger. Every once in a while he would stand up and make a speech to no one at all. We could hear his voice and see his gestures but could not make out his words. Then we discovered a delightful thing. If he sat still too long we could stir him up by knocking gently and in a ghostly manner on the wall. He would leap to his feet and deliver great speeches, waving his arms and shaking his fist while his face contorted with emotion and saliva dripped from his mouth. If we worked him over for quite a while, we could sometimes get him rolling on the floor. There was always something to do in Salinas.

Then one day he was gone and we were very sad because we thought he had gone away. But he hadn't. He was inside there and in about ten days somebody found him and the coroner had to take him away in a rubber blanket and spray the house with creosote.

Well, gold fever ran through us. We dug holes at the roots of every apple tree in his orchard. We got a window open and searched the house, holding handkerchiefs over our noses. The big ledger was there and we could make out sentences like: "Go good god goodily like liver line god do devil darn dawn." It didn't make any sense except to a psychiatrist and they hadn't been invented. Anyway we tried to find secret hiding places, rapped on the walls and even took up some floor boards. Finally we had to give it up. Then a distant relative looked in a place we had neglected, under the sink in the elbow of the u-trap. He found a flour bag containing eight thousand dollars in gold. I still get the shudders when I think we might have found it. It would have changed our whole lives and our parents' lives.

Salinas had a destiny beyond other towns. The rich black land was one thing, but the high gray fog and coolish to cold weather which gave it a lousy climate created the greatest lettuce in the world, several crops a year and at a time when no other lettuce in the United States matured. The town named itself The Salad Bowl of the World and the refrigerator cars moved in a steady stream out of the railroad yards toward Chicago and New York. Long packing sheds lined the tracks and the local iceman, who had used to bring a fifty-pound block on his shoulder for ice cream, made a vast fortune.

The need for labor became great. We brought in Filipinos to cut and chop the lettuce and there were interesting results. No Filipino women were allowed in and the dark, quick little men constantly got into trouble with what were called "white women." The Filipinos lived and worked in clots of five or six. If you had a fight with one, you had six on you. They bought automobiles co-operatively by clots and got women the same way. The wages of five or six mounted up and they could afford to buy themselves a pretty fair communal woman. For some reason this outraged the tender morals of certain of our citizens who didn't seem to be morally sensitive in other directions. There used to be some pretty fine gang fights in the pool rooms of Market Street of a Saturday night.

In addition to the Filipinos for chopping the lettuce, the cutting and packing sheds required labor. Women and men to prepare the lettuce for the crates, and icers and nailers.

Eventually, as was inevitable, these people decided that they wanted to have a union. It was happening all over and they didn't want to be left out. The owners yelled that communists were behind it all, and maybe they were. Nobody ever proved anything one way or another, but the union got formed. I guess wages were pretty low and profits pretty high. So, now they had a union, the shed people made demands for higher wages and when they were refused, went on strikes.

Now what happened would not be believable if it were not verified by the Salinas papers of the time. A man suddenly appeared, went to the owners and the sheriff and announced himself as an expert in handling strikes. He must have been a commanding figure. The sheriff turned the situation over to him.

The General took a suite in the Geoffrey House, installed direct telephone lines to various stations, even had one group of telephones that were not connected to anything. He set armed guards over his suite and he put Salinas in a state of siege. He organized Vigilantes. Service-station operators, owners of small stores, clerks, bank tellers got out sporting rifles, shotguns, all the hundreds of weapons owned by small-town Americans who in the West at least, I guess, are the most heavily armed people in the world. I remember counting up and found that I had twelve firearms of various calibers and I was not one of the best equipped. In addition to the riflemen, squads drilled in the streets with baseball bats. Everyone was having a good time.

Down at the lettuce sheds, the pickets began to get apprehensive.

The General sat in his guarded suite at the Geoffrey House issuing orders and devising tactics. He may have believed that Salinas was in danger of being annihilated. I have no way of knowing. Suddenly he issued the information that the Longshoremen of San Francisco, a hundred miles away, the most powerful and best disciplined union in the State, were marching on Salinas, singing *The Internationale*. A shudder of excited horror ran through Salinas. Orders were issued from Headquarters. The townsmen marched to the outskirts determined to sell their lives dearly. The sheriff seems to have become a kind of runner for the General.

Then a particularly vigilant citizen made a frightening discovery and became a hero. He found that on one road leading into Salinas, red flags had been set up at intervals. It was no more than the General had anticipated. This was undoubtedly the route along which the Longshoremen were going to march. The General wired the governor to stand by to issue orders to the National Guard, but being a foxy tactician himself, he had all of the red flags publicly burned in Main Street.

All might have gone well if at about this time the Highway Commission had not complained that someone was stealing the survey markers for widening a highway, if a San Francisco newspaper had not investigated and found that the Longshoremen were working the docks as usual and if the Salinas housewives had not got on their high horse about not being able to buy groceries. The citizens reluctantly put away their guns, the owners granted a small pay raise and the General left town. I have always wondered what happened to him. He had qualities of genius. It was a long time before Salinas cared to discuss the episode. And now it is comfortably forgotten. Salinas was a very interesting town.

It is a kind of metropolis now and there must be nearly fourteen thousand people living where once a blacksmith shop stood in the swamp. The whole face of the valley has changed. But the high, thin, gray fog still hangs overhead and every afternoon the harsh relentless wind blows up the valley from King City. And the town justifies the slogan given it when it was very young . . . Salinas is!

Salinas/John Steinbeck **321**

OREGON TRAIL: ADVENTURE WITH HISTORY

*Only a dream—the dream of California
and Oregon, of the unknown that lay out yonder
somewhere—could have led people to attempt to
cross half a continent by
the incredibly difficult Oregon Trail.
Yet they went, scores of thousands of them.
As he follows the trail across
deserts and mountains and rivers,
A. B. Guthrie, Jr., sees why so many perished
along the way. The wonder is that so
many lived to see the Pacific.*

We rolled through the town of Gardner, Kansas, and pulled up. It was a June day not long ago, a century and more since the ox teams of emigrants to the western shore had started tracing on the land one of the great stories of the world.

"It was near here," I told my son Bert, "that the sign said 'Road to Oregon.'"

The Road to Oregon. Now at last, two hard days out of Independence, Missouri, longer out of New England or New York or Pennsylvania or Ohio or Kentucky or Virginia, the wayfarers west might with a fragment of reason have considered themselves on their way; here the road forked from the older Santa Fe Trail and so became their very own—their own, that is, except as contested by Indians and brutes and, worst of all, the same fickle nature that had scoured a sort of highway for them.

In other summers and by other routes, Bert had come to love the grand reaches of the West. "It looks like the country's already opening up," he said now, in his voice an echo of that forward hope, that swelling expectation that earlier travelers must have felt or else turned back to the tired routines of cornfield and counter.

I answered yes. Let it grow on him, as we retraced the old way, that history offers no other markers like this one at the forks of the trail—none so bland, so understated, so wonderfully preposterous. Before the travelers lay an eternity of sod and sand and rock, of plain and peak, of pitch and drop, of desert and river, all to be paced by the sore feet of oxen, all to be ground under iron tires, all to be won, if won they were, by such sweat and fortitude and resource and faith as appall us today.

But onward! Onward with the stout new gear, with wagons wide-tired and falling-tongued, with sheet-iron stoves and churns and feather beds, with flour and bacon and saleratus, with medicines and schoolbooks for a bookless land. Onward to the Platte, the Sweetwater, the Southern Pass, the Green, the Bear, the Snake, the Columbia, the Willamette, home. Or to the Raft or Soda Springs and by tangent then to California and to gold. Or to Black Fork and westward to the Great Salt Sea and the New Jerusalem.

Indians had been this way long before white men. They had been up the Platte and over the pass and along the Bear and Snake and through the Blue Mountains and down the Columbia and everywhere the trail ran, following again the old rule of easy movement, though no single tribe knew or used the trail in its entirety. It was not peculiar that the white man kept encountering the red; this was a primary primitive highway even if here and there closed by primitive enmities.

So it is in a sense false to speak of the discovery of the trail. Discovery can mean only the white man's first coming on it, and even by this definition the honors are divided or uncertain or lost in the years. Who knows who found the way from Independence to Grand Island before the first had being or the latter its name? Going and coming, expeditions financed by that large promoter, John Jacob Astor, approximated the trail when they did not tread it. For twenty years or more, from the

Farm buildings near Moscow, Idaho, are the hub of a great wheel of wheat.

1820's on, the seekers of beaver went this way, learning in their travels all sections of the route by which men of different purposes were to go.

In those years, too, missionaries attached themselves to fur-company caravans and took the long road west, justified and elevated by tales of trusting Flathead Indians who had traveled clear to St. Louis to plead the need for interpreters of the white man's "Book of Heaven."

In 1842 the first emigrant train headed for Oregon. Upward of a thousand people, composing what remains known inappropriately as the "great migration," hit the trail in 1843. The ball was rolling then. The pattern was set. History could look ahead. Fourteen hundred men, women and children rolled across the continent in 1844, three thousand in 1845, thirteen hundred and fifty in 1846, four to five thousand in 1847. And the Oregon Trail was just coming into its great years. Thirty-five thousand forty-niners alone followed it to the points of departure for the gold fields of California. Western population doubled, trebled, quadrupled, increased by ten- and twenty-fold.

The travelers left land scars that railroads and macadam and time and weather haven't healed. The wheel cuts of their wagons still show in gullied soil and rutted stone. I have seen them on Windless Hill, near the present Lewellen, Nebraska, on the hills outside Scott's Bluff, along the river bottom close to Guernsey, Wyoming, along the reaches of the Sweetwater, at the Grande Ronde near La Grande, Oregon. More diligent and practiced eyes can see in an off-hued strip of wheat the track that wagons ran.

From Independence, Missouri, on you'll see the rivers—the Wakarusa, Kansas, the Little and Big (now Black) Vermilions, the Big and Little Blues and the fabled Platte—all points of old interest. You'll want to give an extra moment to appreciation of the valley of the Wakarusa.

. . . From Grand Island, Nebraska, you'll roll along the Platte, that sand-freighted, quicksandy, mile-wide-and-inch-

*Scott's Bluff is on the wide and windy tablelands
at Nebraska's western edge. Not many years
ago this highway was the Oregon Trail
and these fields a highland home of Indians.*

deep, thousand-mile-long wash of sluiced and island-spotted water, as the old travelers described it. Some river, they said. No good for navigation. (It wasn't.) Too thick to drink. So sandy it must flow bottom-side-up. Washington Irving called it "the most worthless of rivers." Worthless? A river that had worked a roadway from the mountains to the Missouri? Whose tributary, the Sweetwater, led to South Pass?

. . . Five or six miles east and south of Kearney, Nebraska, is the site of old Fort Kearney. No buildings remain there, only old and indicative disturbances of earth, but there is a stand of cottonwoods, planted by soldiers when the fort was built in 1848, the like of which you seldom see these days.

. . . The lower and upper fords of the South Platte were near Brule, Nebraska, and Julesburg, Colorado, respectively. You may want to see what the travelers had to contend with, though in these days of irrigation and lowered water table you may be misled. Ash Hollow and Windlass Hill are just across the North Platte from Lewellen. Physical evidences of the migration are abundant here. Outside Bridgeport are two musts: Courthouse Rock and Chimney Rock. As landmarks they were as famous as any on the trail. Early observers predicted a little dolefully that they couldn't stand against the weather long, being composed of nothing but a crumbly, indurated clay. They were wrong in their predictions if right in their analyses. From the floor of the valley these "rocks" stand prominent yet, mysteriously resistant to wind and wet. One bluff outside Scott's Bluff has become a national monument. There's an interesting museum here, and information and literature to be had for the asking. Both close to the river and farther south among the bluffs are the marks of trailers' wagons.

. . . Don't miss Fort Laramie, Wyoming. It's a national monument, too, and though what is preserved of it belongs to its later, military history, it is immensely interesting. Here the Laramie and North Platte join, and trees and green grass grow, and a man understands with what relief the dusty pilgrims looked down from the barren slope and saw shade and buildings, and Mom knew for a little while she'd have a chair to sit in. In early years this was the first place to reoutfit and to rest.

. . . Just south of Guernsey, Wyoming, is Register Cliff where, as elsewhere, trailers carved names still visible today. Look for wheel ruts too. They're not hard to find. Casper has reconstructed an old fort that our travelers antedated. They forded the North Platte and struck across for the Sweetwater.

. . . West of Casper, Wyoming, are the Red Buttes and the Fiery Narrows of the Platte that the Astorians named. Farther on, fifty-three miles from Casper, is Independence Rock, the Great Register of the Desert, a piece of granite bulging from the bank of the Sweetwater. Here the trailers of yesterday—aped by the dunces of today—inscribed names and dates with nails and chisels and paint. It is not impressive from a distance,

Oregon Trail/A.B. Guthrie, Jr. **325**

The Columbia River Gorge cuts through the Cascade Mountains. On the far bank lies Washington State; in the foreground the green fields of Oregon.

yielding to higher, farther hills and to the far-seen gash of Devil's Gate. Closer, it assumes size and dignity. It isn't hard to climb, and you will want to climb it if only to scan the old names, if only from its top to realize what space is. A few miles west is Devil's Gate, where a shard of mountain parts a crack to let the river through. Still farther on, up the looping Sweetwater, is Split Rock, which you can hardly miss. For a time the highway runs as did the old trail. Then it leads away, north of west toward Lander. Eight miles short of the town, it comes to South Pass Road, and you turn sharp left there and climb to Atlantic City and to South Pass City and are on the trail again. And you're also on top of the continent.

The way to Pacific Springs, leftward from the paving, isn't too well marked but it is worth a try. Then you can roll down to the Sandys and the Green.

. . . Fort Bridger, Wyoming, was the second scheduled stop for early overlanders. Like Laramie it is more reminiscent of the later, military time than the anterior civilian. It supports a museum and, like Laramie, is a kind of oasis, shady with big cottonwoods, aspens and pines. The highway takes you off course from Bridger but soon makes a correction and has you approximating the old trail along the fertile Bear. At Soda Springs still flows the naturally charged water that was the wonder and delight of wagon-train travelers, especially of young ones. Nothing remains of old Fort Hall, north of Pocatello on the Snake.

. . . This is Snake River country, where parties Oregon-bound had the devil's own time. Often the Snake was so canyoned they couldn't get water either for themselves or their stock. There wasn't any forage, or not enough of it. Sore-footed and overworked draft animals weakened, sickened, refused to answer to the whip, lay down, died. Loads had to be lightened. Out went grindstones, anvils, cherry chests. Food was short. And as if this weren't enough, there was the chancy first fording of the Snake. Retraveling the trail today, you'll want to see American Falls, which is still spectacular enough, though a dam sits just above it. The Raft River, where the California trains swung off, is a place of interest, complete with historical marker. The Thousand Springs still spring from the Snake's right bank, I guess from a thousand places. At Glenns Ferry, near which the trailers forded, maybe you will be able to figure how much it would be worth to you to try a crossing in a prairie schooner—or, once across, to head into a high, three-day-long desert beyond which, like the doubtful hope of Heaven, lay the lovely Boise valley.

. . . Nothing remains of old Fort Boise, Idaho, either, but, traveling to Nyssa, you won't be far from the old site, which was on the right bank of the Snake downstream from the mouth of the Boise. South of Huntington is Farewell Bend, where the trail said a final and not-too-reluctant good-by to the Snake. A sign tells you that some famous precursors of the trailers camped there—Wilson Price Hunt, leader of the west-

ward Astorians, in 1811; Captain Bonneville, colorful but unsuccessful fur trader, in 1834; John C. Frémont in 1843. Beyond La Grande the road climbs into the green and timbered Blues, where wild flowers shower the mountain parks. A tremendous hill falls down from the Blues to the Umatilla River and to Pendleton.

You're home free now, or almost. Here comes the Columbia. At Celilo Falls you may see Indians netting salmon in the fashion of their ancestors.

. . . You can travel down the terrific gorge of the Columbia or cut south and round Mount Hood as a great many overlanders did after the Barlow Road was made passable, barely, in the mid-forties. It's a good idea to go by one route and return by the other. The visual and historical rewards are great both ways. Bonneville Dam at the old Cascades, though an anachronism in our re-creation, is a place you'll want to see. Vancouver used to be Fort Vancouver, a Hudson's Bay post

presided over by Dr. John McLoughlin, who received the intruding Americans with generous courtesy and got small thanks for it. Here and at Portland, just across the river, and at Oregon City to the south are many things to see.

So now it is over. Now it is done. The far traveler is home, the traveler who marched ghostly beside you, visioning his home as he went. What home was like this, so new in the seeing, so old in the hope, so dear-won, so splendored with wages for hands and for hearts?

Stake out the rich land. Put up a cabin. Pick the wild fruits. Seed for the harvest. Rejoice in a family. Plant a nail here and it'll come up a spike.

There isn't any Oregon any more, no California, either, except as they exist in old imagination. As nearly as dreams do, our dream has come true, and here are Tyre and Alexandria and London, the swelling capitals of vision as our eyes look more and more across the western sea. Here is the thriving husband-

man. Here are the realizations of hopes hoped and dreams dreamed, but the dream is gone as the bird in the bush is gone when it comes to hand. Out yonder somewhere, in the beckoning nowhere, in men's remembering minds, lies Oregon, and we chase after it, setting pistons and horse power to the recapture of a dream. And it is a mark somehow of our success that though the dream is gone we exult in the signs of its having passed here and here and here. It is with a sense of discovery, though everything has been discovered, that we push along the Platte, the Sweetwater, the Southern Pass, down to the Spanish River and up into the Blues, seeing Hood and St. Helen's rising grim and lovely as of yore, and in time come to Portland, that rich proliferation of a squatter's cabin, and to Oregon City, where a man listening hears beyond the noises of today voices ardent for the virgin soil. Oregon. California. The dream. The fact. The poignant vestige. The proud development. And where do we go from here?

Oregon Trail/A.B. Guthrie, Jr. **327**

In the wastelands of the Kenai Peninsula,
only fifty miles from Anchorage,
the weirdly sculptured barren ice glitters
blue-green in the chill of Portage Glacier.

Alaska

*The forty-ninth state is a land where
superlatives are commonplace. It is the northernmost,
biggest, highest, and ruggedest state in the union,
a country so vast that even the wide-striding Alaskans
haven't got around to seeing all of it in the hundred years
that it has been part of the United States.
Alaska, says James Warner Bellah,
has no common denominator in our past experience.*

Alaska should be entered slowly, by boat or by road; its vast spread makes it impossible to assimilate in the four easy flying hours from Seattle to Anchorage. Its magnitude is untrammeled; its grandeur grows upon the consciousness, like hunger. It cannot be explained by comparison. It offers no common denominator to past experience. There is no instant Alaska.

By ship from Vancouver to Juneau, the capital, you steam three days between the islanded shores of the Inside Passage, through thick-growing timber, and along that entire eight hundred miles there is no scar of forest-fire damage, no smoke wisp of a campfire. You hear no honk of a car horn, no whistle of a train. No one is there to drop a cigarette, to be careless with fire smolder. No one is there at all. In places, no one has *ever* been there.

The Tongass National Forest, in the southeastern part of the state, says the Forestry Service, alone could provide much of the newsprint for the newspapers of the world. United States Army Engineers estimate that a Yukon River dam at Rampart would form a lake as large as Ontario, that would take nine years to fill; and the resulting water power would produce

half as many kilowatt-hours as are produced at present in all the other forty-nine states.

Yet in Nome, on the Bering Sea, a guide, after spotting a polar bear from the air, can telephone a Wall Street broker that if he will hop a plane he can enjoy some fine shooting and be back at his desk a few days later.

Arrived at Juneau, you have barely entered Alaska. You must continue westerly about *thirty-four degrees* of longitude before you reach Little Diomede Island in Bering Strait—a scant two and a half miles from the U.S.S.R. You must travel north more than a thousand miles across the entire northwest shoulder of North America before you reach Point Barrow on the Arctic Ocean. You must go almost to Asia before you reach Adak in the Aleutians. Alaska is a *damn* big land.

Despite Edna Ferber's implication to the contrary, there are many respectably-come-by mink coats in Fairbanks and considerably more in larger Anchorage (although the parka is more suitable winter garb). Lilly Daché hats and Irene gowns are sold in both towns—and to prove that this fringe of luxurious insanity is no latter-day innovation, Klondike Kate wore a Worth gown brought from Paris at Dawson's St. Andrew's Day Ball back in 1900—and every gentleman with her in the extant photograph wore tails, except one who came black tie deliberately or was a waiter. And Dawson, fifty miles or so across the line in Canada's Yukon Territory, is a bare 128 miles south of the Arctic Circle.

Alaska is a solidly, stubbornly, prideful American land. You can live and work there in reasonable comfort the year around —despite the mere two hours of summer darkness and the scant two hours of winter daylight.

There is no Skid Row in any Alaskan town. With seasonal employment a condition of life, some Alaskans plan their liv-

ing better than others, thus live more comfortably in the slack winter season. Some have more, some less—but there are few bums; it is not an environment in which a bum can survive.

Newcomers have difficulty adjusting to the high costs of food, clothing and rent; but wages are high, too, and it isn't long before a balance is struck. Then life settles into a routine much like that in any small town Stateside. There are Scout troops, Cub packs, the Y.M.C.A., bridge clubs, cocktail parties, lodges, luncheon clubs and country clubs of sorts.

The first winter can be a morale hazard if you make it one. Children go to school in darkness and return in darkness. But again, in compensation, the sun is still shining in summer when you come out of the night picture show.

Alaskans work hard, on a seasonal schedule; they are imbued consciously or unconsciously with the challenge of their vast land. They marry young, raise large families and their children for the most part remain in Alaska.

There is a cheerful get-rich-quick flavor to life that seldom pays off; it probably persists from the gold-rush days which never paid off either. This may be due to the absence of huge corporations to dominate commerce and mold organization men. A young Alaskan will get a local job—but he usually keeps one hand free for himself. He fishes and hunts as a routine of life and, as a further routine, he eternally casts about for an opportunity to go into business for himself—however modestly. He has an extremely self-confident and independent character. You cannot be otherwise in the eternal grandeur of this vast land.

There have long been two schools of thought in Alaska about statehood—for and against. The "Fors" wanted their destiny in their own hands, regardless of the taxes needed to support a state. They wanted to be rid of territorial status, to pass their own laws to govern their living—for there is a Great Dream in Alaska, and it can come true only if the individual is untrammeled by Federal paternalism.

The "Againsts" were acutely conscious that the permanent population of Alaska is small and they believed that the economic health was due in great part to the vast military and naval installations. They wanted no curtailment in the largess of Uncle Sam. They saw financial ruin in statehood.

The "Fors" wanted statehood now. The "Againsts" wanted it too—but after a while. Now that the die has been cast, however, most Alaskans seem gratified. They have attained voting representation at last—as a balance to their taxation. Statehood is American—no matter what it costs.

Now that Alaska is a state, it is expecting—and preparing for—an influx of visitors. There is no Hilton Hotel yet in Alaska and no Forum of the Twelve Caesars to dine in, but if you write for summer-travel information, you'll get enough material on off-trail sights—natural wonders, totem poles, fish, moose, bear and Mount McKinley—to top seven pounds on the bathroom scales. For to Alaska tourism is an essential industry highly organized by the Alaska Visitors Association.

From June to September you can travel Alaska's tenuous net of paint-shy, neon-lighted towns by your own car, hitchhiker's thumb, bus, boat, train or any of a dozen airlines in a reasonable expectancy of comfort. In winter, hitchhiking will freeze

The fertile Matanuska Valley, bounded by the jumbled Chugach Mountains, grows 60 per cent of Alaska's farm products. The summer sun shines here for eighteen hours a day.

your thumb stiff, and the waterways are iced in, but with foresight and respect for weather, travel is not entirely restricted.

There will be a virile echo of the raw frontier in this Alaskan junket, a sense perhaps of the latent sacrifice that has always attended the March of Empire, a feeling that the Donner Passes and the Death Valleys that have been long forgotten Stateside are still nebulously just around the corner in Alaska, in a grandsire's living memory.

Before you reach Ketchikan on the Inside Passage, there is the rusted wreck of the steamer *North Sea* on the easterly shore a few miles north of the Indian Village of Bella Bella. She went down in 1947—with no loss of life. In Juneau, at the Museum, there are two water-stained life rings of the *Princess Sophia*. She sank above Juneau in 1918—and there were no survivors. The North Country can be a hard country.

Ketchikan is the first port of call on the Inside Passage, and there the frontier forthrightness strikes you abruptly in a hand-lettered sign: "No dogs. No drunks allowed." This is not tourist stuff. The proprietor means it. It bears the indelible mark of anger—of long-suffering patience exhausted at last. You *feel* for the man who lettered that sign.

The average age of the Alaskan today is twenty-seven, which in all sports—including the challenging one of making a new country—is about the peak championship age. Bred in Alaska, in many instances for three generations, his grandfather knew the '98 Gold Rush. His father knew the lean years after 1918—and his children find the houses too big when they visit the older states, and the waters too warm for good swimming. "Outside" for a few weeks, they want to go home—to the snow-capped mountains, the salmon, the fast, trout-thick creeks, the bear and moose in the broad and empty reaches of the Big Land—a land that has already grown its own vital people.

There is the natural friendliness of youth in the Alaskan. It is innate to his character that he offers himself and accepts you without guile. He passes you from town to town to his friends and neighbors. Alaska is the biggest small town in the world. Trump your partner's ace on Monday in Petersburg and it's known—by mukluk telegraph—in Kotzebue on Tuesday.

Its Main Street is only four blocks long—Southeast Alaska, the Interior, the Arctic and "Westward"—which ends at the tip of the Aleutian Islands, close against Asia. This Main Street, though, has a cultural texture that could give a scholar a lifetime of research.

Aboriginally, there are the ancient Indian tribes of Southeast Alaska and the offshore islands that shelter the Inside Passage. There are the Eskimos of the northern Arctic rim. There are the Aleuts (give that three syllables, please), an Eskimo stock differing from the Arctic Eskimo in head shape and in development of basic language, with their culture

Evoking ancient conquests of the warlike
Chilkat Indians, one of their descendants wears a
wolf costume. The nose and lips are
of copper, and real wolfskin forms the cape.

In the judge's files, there is a photostat of a document that had long been mislaid in Washington, and which the judge finally located when he was a delegate: "To the Treasurer of the United States, greeting. Pay to Edward de Stoekle, Envoy Extraordinary and Minister Plenipotentiary of His Majesty the Emperor of Russia, or order, out of the appropriation named in the margin—Seven million, two hundred thousand dollars, being in consideration of certain territory ceded by the Emperor of Russia to the United States as described in treaty of 30th March 1867." That Warrant, Number 9759, made Alaska a part of the United States at a price of about two cents an acre. A right smart real-estate deal.

Arctic Alaska is the comparatively small strip along the Bering Sea and the Arctic Ocean that gave the forty-ninth state its "outside" trade-mark of the igloo. The word means house but the Eskimo's permanent home is not of ice. It is a fairly large skin-and-driftwood shelter tunneled into from beneath. Or it can be a cottage, or a Nissen hut, or an apartment in Fairbanks, depending on his job. He builds small igloos of ice blocks only when hunting far from home. He is a pleasant, round-faced person with the ready, incandescent smile of the Himalayan Gurkha—and a capacity for technical education that, in the opinion of Air Force officers, could eventually qualify him to handle any specialized job on the installations of the D.E.W. Line. He has inherited a flair for tools and engines from his Oriental ancestors who, thousands of years ago, probably helped invent the wheel.

He has been reviled in the past for his "barbarity" in leaving his old folks in provisional ice igloos when hunting was bad. But to him it was not barbarism. It was for the good of the greater number; the handicapped being left so the others could go on and survive. He has been reviled, too, for polygamy; but this again was self-preservation. In mid-June and July he goes after whale. Last year some Point Barrow hunters were caught on rotten shore ice with an offshore wind; they were saved, but in years gone all the men of a village have been lost. So polygamy was a matter of survival too.

Of all the original people of Alaska, the Eskimos cling most tenaciously to their tribal customs and their language—probably because their race memory is deeper. They have held precariously to life along the Arctic and Bering Sea littorals for centuries, sustaining themselves on game, fish, berries and roots, and the transition to modern dietary habits at first caused a high incidence of previously unknown diseases—especially tuberculosis. But medical science came with the change of diet and soon brought things into balance.

There is an unfathomable plasticity to the Eskimo mind that is probably the fundamental ingredient of his survival. He adapts. A product of primitive tribal government since the beginning of known history, he was amenable to the overlay

adapted to a raw, wet climate rather than to subzero cold. The islands of the Aleuts curve under Siberia—almost to Kamchatka.

In hill-sprawled, jumbled Juneau—named for Joe Juneau who discovered gold there in 1880—it is easy to go back the first ninety-two years of American Alaska's culture. You can do it in conversation with Edward Keithahn, curator of the Museum—or academically with the records and exhibits kept under his helpful and scholarly hand. Or you can climb up to Ruth Allman's house and cover the subject informally over sourdough waffles and Russian tea. Ruth's house hangs on the hillside with most of Juneau below, framed by the bow windows in which Judge James Wickersham's old desk and chair still sit. Her stepfather, James Wickersham, was a United States District judge in Alaska from 1900 to 1908—often as not riding circuit by dog team—and thereafter delegate to Congress from Alaska for fourteen years. He introduced the first statehood bill in 1916—forty-two years before final passage. He was the moving spirit in the founding of the University of Alaska. His old house is a pleasant home still and a repository crammed with mementos of his service to Alaska—including a five-foot shelf of his personal diaries.

A pure-blooded Eskimo, of Kotzebue, Albert McClellan,
models his seal-hunting outfit. His kayak is
made of sealskin and he wears a white
parka for camouflage on the ice fields. Behind
him is a sea-going umiak of walrus hide.

of democratic concepts. Early in territorial history he began to sit in the Legislature, so that his place already was firmly established as Alaska became the forty-ninth state. He *is* the Alaska National Guard—organized in Scout Battalions with modern light weapons—and he knows how to handle modern heavy equipment. Eskimo teenage girls look more at home in sweaters, nylons and high heels than Indian girls do.

At Point Barrow, a two-day or a three-day packaged air tour from Fairbanks in July will give you a chance to witness the Nulikatuk, that celebration of a successful whale hunt which is supposed to appease the whale spirits so that there may be a successful hunt next year. It's a time of laughter and roughhousing. Take a sweater.

The Eskimo from time immemorial has made tools and weapons of walrus-tusk ivory and the whalebone of long-gone corset days—his only durable materials. Then the traders got after him to turn out tourist catchalls, and today the shops are full of all sorts of ivory gewgaws that the Eskimo himself never uses.

Come back from the Arctic to Fairbanks and look in on the University of Alaska. Judge James Wickersham, after years of selling the project to Congress, laid the cornerstone in 1915. It was originally an Agricultural School and a School of Mines, but has expanded its courses into Arts and Letters, Biological Science, Business Administration, Chemical, Civil and Electrical Engineering, Education and Geophysics—with graduate work in most of them. The summer-school students may make an air trip over the North Pole which is almost as painless as going out to Montauk, Long Island, from Columbia University in New York.

In interior Alaska, around Fairbanks and Anchorage—eight hours south of Fairbanks by train—you pick up the huge installations of the Armed Services, Eielson and Ladd Air Force Bases near Fairbanks, Fort Richardson and Elmendorf Air Force Bases near Anchorage. These are huge, self-contained military cities, the nuclei of the outer line of defense for the entire continent. Here the line is held along the entire westerly and northerly front of the Cold War. Daylight or dark, winter

*Alaskan Indians gather for a
tribal festival, with sealskin drums,
pretty faces in furry hoods, and
inevitably fish—muktuk, a treat of
raw whale meat for the children; racks
of dried fish for everyone all winter.*

new California subdivision, except that the ranch houses are smaller for the $30,000 or $50,000 they bring. Smaller, therefore easier to heat against the deep-freeze of winter.

You can drive from anywhere in the United States to Anchorage, by way of Fairbanks. The road roughly parallels the railroad, through the beautiful Mount McKinley country. The Department of the Interior runs the railroad. Coffee in the dining car is twenty-five cents a cup, and no free refill. All over Alaska the price is fifteen cents a cup, with copious refills. A moral lesson here, and a solid pocketbook reason for statehood.

In Anchorage you are two hours by air from Kodiak Island, the United States Navy and those Big Bear. They weigh considerably over half a ton and the pelt cures to more than eleven by ten feet. A hundred and twenty-seven pounds of rug, without the head. Call Alf Madsen—and if he's not home he's at Karluk Lake after bear. Alf is in his thirty-eighth year of guiding with no client hurt beyond a mosquito bite—and fourteen-year-old boys have killed their bears under his competent hand.

Donnelley and Acheson in the town of Kodiak is the oldest store in Alaska. Only the Spanish missions outdate it in point of outlander establishment along the American Pacific littoral. It has been at its present location since 1796. You can buy anything there from a Cadillac to a package of chewing gum.

Up the street is the B and B Bar, the seventeenth-oldest licensed bar in Alaska, which is like holding a low-numbered *Fédération Aeronautique Internationale* flying license, for there are as many bars in Alaska as there are lakes on the Kenai Peninsula—or mosquitoes in summer.

Off Kodiak Island the halibut weigh hundreds of pounds, delectable king crab measure six feet across, salmon are thick in season and the Dolly Varden trout follow them upstream to feed on their eggs. The green of Kodiak is as brightly iridescent as in Ireland and Scotland. It shines wet green even at night.

The Navy's Alaskan Sea Frontier—the utterly last frontier in America—stretches down the Aleutians to hang under Asia. This is the last block on Alaska's Main Street. Here are the tiny fishing towns of the beckoning names—Dutch Harbor and Scotch Cap, Ouzinkie, Halibut Bay, Kanatak, False Pass, Squaw Harbor and Unga—down to Adak, which again is Navy and the only installation west of Kodiak that approaches the dimension of civilization, with good docking, good housing, good food, four-engined strips and the finest harbor in the Aleutians. There is no bear or moose or reindeer at Adak, but the Marines have put a caribou herd out to breed. Lonely and isolated under a not unusual seventy-knot wind, and the williwaw that blows 125 knots on occasion, Adak is the farthest western reach of the tangible sovereign dignity of the United States, but children are born here, men work here and this *is* the United States—under the new 49th star.

A Big Land, my masters, which is what Alaska has been called in the language of its older people since long before Christ. The *Main Land* as opposed to the islands that fringe its coast, hence the *Big Land* as opposed to the smaller land of the islands—for that is what the word Alaska means.

and summer, defensive air patrols are maintained. Our pilots see the red-starred planes patrolling their side. A thin line of dynamic alertness lies between the two—vast sinews of retaliation tense and readied.

Anchorage is much larger than Fairbanks—say a hundred thousand people and miss it by twenty thousand or so—but it started as a camp for the construction of the Alaska Railroad, so the aristocratic gold-grubbing tradition does not cling to it. The frontier feeling does, however. There are forty-four bars on Fourth Street, the main drag.

Anchorage has log cabins that are still lived in and two of them stand in the shadow of the fourteen-story Mount McKinley Building. If you want Jack London texture surge into the Cheechako Bar on Fourth Street, just a short step from the svelte Chart Room of the Westward Hotel.

There are smart dress shops and it costs $2.50 to have slacks and a sport coat cleaned and pressed. It is a growing town of new apartment houses and housing developments. Drive through Turnagain-by-the-Sea and you might well be in a

As the sea rushes across the rocks at Lumahai Beach, on the Island of Kauai, a native fisherman tries for a catch in the ancient Hawaiian fashion: with a weighted circular net skillfully flung out and into the oncoming surf.

Hawaii

For many Americans, Hawaii has been a technicolor dream of Paradise. Today, as the fiftieth state, it has an exploding population and a booming economy, tangled traffic and juvenile delinquency. But however it has changed, says Robert Carson, it is still Hawaii—a country of extraordinary beauty with a simple friendliness and courtesy that the mainland has never known.

One night not long ago my wife and I took a cab to Los Angeles International Airport and, after the usual delay, boarded a huge jet aircraft in company with a hundred-odd other travelers. We were bound for Paradise. At least that is how our Fiftieth State, Hawaii, looks in photographs and reads in the travel folders. And though we hadn't been there in almost twenty years, that's how we remembered a rather sleepy and pleasant former Territory.

To whet my anticipation, I had done a bit of preliminary reading. I knew we were going to eight islands of varying sizes stretching for three hundred miles, 6435 square miles which outrange Connecticut and wouldn't be noticed in Alaska, and that with a little diligence we could see snowy mountain peaks and deserts and jungles, sugarcane and pineapple plantations, an active volcano or two, tremendous military installations, and enough palm trees to make a camel homesick. I was intrigued by the thought of living for a few weeks among 585,000 people who were operating their own do-it-yourself melting pot, in which Caucasians are outnumbered three to one by

fellow citizens of Oriental, Filipino and Polynesian extraction. And I knew from experience that we would encounter the kind of climate California and Florida have advertised for years.

What I didn't know was that Hawaii is enjoying, more or less, a boom that has blasted off like one of the more successful Cape Canaveral projects. This seems to me, upon reflection, the essence of the new Hawaii, a modern, streamlined, supersonic, somewhat numbing manifestation, both fascinating and enjoyable.

Presented from left to right, traveling a southeasterly course, the islands are Niihau, privately owned, devoted to agriculture and barred to the tripper; Kauai, undoubtedly the prettiest, with scads of blossoms and a miniature Grand Canyon and barking sands; Oahu, which has the city of Honolulu, Waikiki Beach, 70 per cent of the state's population, gaggles of pink and candy-striped jeeps bearing fringed-canvas tops, the sworn allegiance of Tin Pan Alley, and the nearly undivided attention of tourists. Then a cluster follows, beginning with Molokai, site of a leper colony that lives walled off by cliffs from the rest of the land, and of the village of Kaunakakai, whose name inspired a song about a cockeyed mayor; Lanai, wholly owned by the Hawaiian Pineapple Company, and covered by its product; Maui, containing a ten-thousand-foot mountain, magnificent beaches and waterfalls, and a towering natural formation known as the Iao Needle; Kahoolawe, small, barren, deserted, used by our armed forces as a target for bombs and shells, not recommended by anybody. Finally there is Hawaii, the "Big Island" (it has nearly two thirds of the state territory), an unsettling scene of volcanic eruptions, informal skiing in season, extensive cattle ranches, cacti, dismal craters, black-sand beaches, coffee farms, expanses of twisted lava grown cold, the faraway, sleepy, South-Sea-Island Kona Coast, and the bay

In a bamboo jungle a young couple picnics next to one of the Seven Sacred Pools on the island of Maui.

where Capt. James Cook, presumably the first white caller, got killed and parboiled and perhaps devoured on his second visit to Paradise.

Vacationists should not allow Captain Cook's unfortunate experience to deter them from coming to the islands. Oahu, the first port of call for everyone, has charms to suit the most attenuated tastes. Its climate is flatly perfect, with sea currents and trade winds providing the air conditioning. In summer the days are a little hot, but the nights are cool.

Honolulu has been on a mad building spree since 1955, and there is plenty of accommodation. Unlike many other resort areas, here the whole tourist concentration is on a narrow, man-made finger of land bounded at one side by the Pacific and at the other by the Ala Wai Canal, and dominated by a strip of beach slightly more than a mile long—famous Waikiki. At the far end looms Diamond Head's squat, extinct crater, probably as well known to humanity as the Sphinx or Gibraltar, and from here almost to the Yacht Club's harbor are crowded sixty-two hotels and an overpowering array of shops, restaurants, auto-rental agencies, drugstores, camera establishments and cocktail lounges. Lack of space (Waikiki ground often sells at fifty dollars a *square foot)* has forced a vertical development, and the new caravansaries tower fifteen or twenty stories in the air. They are constructed in the modern cellular style, violently painted, and each room features an open porch known as a *lanai.* Interspersed among them stand co-operative apartment houses of late design, and in the shadow of Diamond Head bulk two more, giving the romanticist in search of the land of Dorothy Lamour and Jon Hall a bit of a turn.

.Kalakaua Avenue, the main artery running through these scenes of pleasure, is undistinguished except for the attire of tourists. The opening move of a nonresident is to get into shorts and bra or a blindingly patterned Aloha shirt and trunks and hit the beach or the bricks. A common additional touch is a straw hat with a fringe of loose ends around the brim. Some ladies slip into an ample, shapeless, highly colored garment called a *muumuu,* a latter-day adaptation of the Mother Hubbard introduced by missionaries. An elderly broker on leave, in gray-flannel shorts and wickerwork shoes, is unlikely to attract the least attention in this crowd, nor is a woman in a black tubular Chinese gown slit up the sides to the thighs.

Amid these figures of fun—and I use the term advisedly, for if anybody doubts that the American public is overfed, he has only to go to Waikiki—I had no difficulty spotting occasional descendants of the early settlers. They are the people wearing suits and dresses and bemused expressions, and they come by the expressions legitimately. Oahu, and Hawaii as a whole, has a double heritage deriving from theoretically joyous and amoral natives and from duty-ridden missionaries. The result is a conflict between a romantic ideal shaded by waving palm fronds and a Bostonian devotion to orderliness and discipline; it engenders a curious schizoid attitude toward Waikiki among *kamaainas* (Hawaiian for old-timers), who both approve and disapprove of its new manifestations.

A couple of miles or so from this enclave of costumes and games is the central part of Honolulu. Climbing above an ordinary United States business district through three main valleys to a spiny central ridge of mountain are residential areas, which also follow the curve of the shoreline toward Pearl Harbor along the flanks of the Punchbowl, an extinct volcanic crater transformed into a superb National Cemetery for the war dead. Beyond is an industrial section, and then the tremendous concentration of military might that constitutes our principal bastion in the Pacific. Fifty thousand members of the armed forces are stationed on Oahu, and more than 20,000 civilians work with them.

Today Hawaii has all the doubtful attributes of a state on the mainland: an exploding population and economy, the dizzying potentials of boom-or-bust, tangled traffic, juvenile delinquency, the necessity for long-range planning. Statehood, long debated, is a mixed blessing; at last the islands are fixed in the American mind and glum Honoluluans are spared the task of informing United States correspondents that dollars are standard currency and nobody need bring his passport or get a visa, but departure of the Federal administration means a new state government and more taxes.

In Hawaiian, haole means "white person." Not so long ago, the word also carried the implication of higher social status. Now it's beginning, in the minds of some unreconstructed haoles, to represent a minority group. At Honolulu's oldest club, the Pacific (once called the British Club), America's nearest approach to pukka sahibs sit brooding over their domino games and awaiting the end. The good-looking, aging, colonial-style clubhouse is to be torn down, and elsewhere on the grounds modern buildings are under construction.

"Now we're going to have a swimming pool," a testy, gray-haired gentleman said. "No doubt so our new people can bring their children on weekends and make existence hideous for the rest of us. It is a trend, of course—another in a succession of disasters." He shook his head mournfully, recalling the monuments of ruination. "First there was that Japanese task force, then Harry Bridges and his International Longshoremen's and Warehousemen's Union, then one-way streets, then Henry J. Kaiser with his confounded bulldozers and optimism. If I weren't old, I'd emigrate to Tahiti."

One successful youngish man I met has a home in the highlands beyond the Pali, with acreage sufficient to take care of his horses, and is surrounded by the same kind of neighbors. The tack room with its riding gear is more important to his family than display or formal living. As an individual who has imported the Bucks County way of life into paradise, his adjustment matches his ingenuity.

"None of us denies that the history of the Big Five control of Hawaii was spotted by forceful paternalism, racial distinctions and opposition to the unions," he said, over a very dry Martini. "The point is, that's finished. We don't control any more. The unions have won their battle, and we're only too anxious to work with them—we have to in order to stay alive. Color bars are coming down so fast in Honolulu that it's a question whether they continue to have any real validity; certainly they won't in the next decade because any man who tries to enforce them will be shutting himself off from the labor market. My company's problem, like that of the others, is the handling of our growth. As with any United States corporation, we have to diversify our efforts, get into other industries and countries. We're doing that." He smiled at my mention of despondent *kamaainas*. "It's the same as at Waterloo. The Old Guard didn't surrender, it died. Most of the dominant families have simply run out of gas and suitable representatives. The sole vestiges of them are lawyers adminis-

A narrow Hawaiian war canoe slices through the water off Molokai Island.

tering their trusts. Don't you Southern Californians use a phrase, 'going Hollywood'? Well, Hawaii is 'going mainland' —in short order."

What do you do on Oahu? Sand awaits, and a tepid ocean conveniently screened from breakers by coral reefs. There are terraces to dine and dance on, hula girls to watch, beach boys to teach you board-and-body surfing or how to paddle an outrigger canoe through the waves or sail a twin-hulled catamaran, and swimming pools with handy bars in case salt water palls. You can learn native dances and how to strum a ukulele, and add enough Hawaiian words to your vocabulary to arouse the resentment of *kamaainas* who overhear your hep conversation. For strenuous athletics, you can go out toward Diamond Head to Castle Surf and use your board to find how a rocket feels when it is taking off from a launching pad. Yacht trips are available, sport fishing, water skiing, skin diving, and foreign cars, pink jeeps and the plain old for-rent variety. If you bring the children, they are sure to have a wonderful time.

We found the Big Island, Hawaii, to have the largest area —more than 4000 square miles—and the widest variations in climate and topography. Attractions include our remotest national park and Volcano House, a hostelry perched upon the edge of an immense crater and presided over by Uncle George Lycurgus, aged 100; a periodically erupting mountain, Mauna Loa; fields of orchids around Hilo, the principal town; tree-fern forests and a falls in the Wailuku River that makes constant rainbows; and plenty of roads difficult enough for the stanchest drivers. And the highway department has a sense of humor—on one rough, mountainous stretch between Hilo and Kona, a sign carries the warning, "Improved Road Ends."

While we were on the Big Island, Mount Kilauea, Mauna Loa's disastrous pal, chose to blast off in a spectacular fashion. Coincidentally we fell in with Slim Holt, another agent of the omnipresent Hawaiian Visitors Bureau, who took us with him in a light plane to inspect his paradisiacal development of Warm Springs, scene of a number of tropical movies.

The eruption was operating on full throttle as we circled it, pushing a column of fire and molten lava and spewn rocks six hundred feet high in the air. Beneath, more burning lava pushed in a broad river to the sea, ruining in its course Warm Springs and the village of Kapoho.

Such a close-up of hell in action left us speechless, and Slim, a tall, bronzed man of part-Hawaiian descent with an awing fund of energy, was also pensive. We understood and sympathized. Although Slim's main business, seconded by an amiable lieutenant named Ducky Goo, lies in the supplying of tour and U-drive cars and arranging fishing expeditions, hunting for wild sheep and boar, and jeep journeys in the upcountry with camping equipment, his special pet enterprise had been the Warm Springs resort. Nevertheless, by the time we were back at the Hilo airport, he had recovered his habitual forcefulness.

"Now you can see what I mean about the future of tourism in the Big Island," he said, with a certain glum pride. "There's something for everybody, no matter who he is. We even furnish smog for homesick Californians from real live volcanoes."

Having come to Hawaii, you must go to the Kona Coast. There are regular flights from Hilo, but the trip by automobile is too scenic to miss. You leave damp lowlands, with tin-roofed shacks peeping from the jungle, and climb to high country both forested and bare, encountering herds of cattle and green crops and desertlike expanses studded by cacti. Then, dropping gradually through coffee plantations along an excellent highway, you arrive at the coast and the town of Kailua.

Kona is warm, dry and languid. Kailua runs for perhaps a dozen blocks along the shore, cross streets vanishing into hill-

The 32-foot canoe with outrigging was carved from the trunk of a koa tree.

The oldest and most northerly of the Islands, Kauai confronts the Pacific with these great cliff bastions, the Na Pali Cliffs. Here a group of hunters makes its way 1000 feet above the ocean.

sides, and offers few conventional tourist seductions except the Ocean View Restaurant, a Chinese-family affair that can be rewarding if the cook is in a good mood. They tell the story of the visiting nabobs who went especially to the Ocean View to get a Cantonese shrimp dish enjoyed on a previous visit; a daughter waited upon them, took the order expressionlessly, retired to the kitchen to confer with her father, and as expressionlessly came back. "He don't feel like it tonight," she reported.

The Polynesian and Hawaiian influence is strong here, and the Oriental spirit of compliance relatively weak. Running a hotel on the Kona Coast is a delicate matter; help is brought directly from the backwoods, and Hawaiians do not take kindly to scoldings or rigorous time schedules. During moments of stress, they are given to smiling and agreeing—and disappearing.

Assuming there are delicate souls who will be oppressed by the brassy expressionism of Waikiki, I can heartily recommend the outer islands to them. Anyone with a taste for incredibly green verdure rising abruptly from the sea, for tangles of mountains and tropical undergrowth, for picture-book surf breaking on a coral reef and Miss Sadie Thompson's rain, shouldn't miss these refreshing alternatives.

Hawaii, Kauai and Maui are the best. Virtually no interisland surface transport exists, but all are served by two excellent airlines, Aloha and Hawaiian. The longest trip isn't much over an hour, and we had the chummy feeling of belonging to the mob when traveling in a plane containing enormous brown ladies in *muumuus*, pretty Filipinas, grizzled men talking local politics, and attractive children of mingled bloods good-humoredly called "chop suey" in Hawaii. It is not unknown for a Hawaiian family to board an aircraft accompanied by a pig, and the freight versions of the lines carry laundry, dry cleaning, produce, fresh bread daily, hindquarters of beef and live calves.

On Kauai, you land amid cane fields near the county seat town of Lihue, and can take in fish ponds, wet and dry caverns where tribal chiefs are supposed to have gathered, geyserlike coastal rocks, old Russian forts (this isn't the first time they've bothered us), and a huge depression in volcanic stone called Waimea Canyon. Still better, you can enjoy the handiwork of Miss Grace Buscher. She is a demure, handsome Pennsylvania lady, an expert on island lore, and manager of Coco Palms. With her partner Lyle Guslander, a frenetic Madison Avenue sort, she has created a hotel set in a thirty-two-acre palm grove formerly *kapu*—taboo—to any but Hawaiian royalty.

Coco Palms fronts on a broad beach beside the mouth of the Wailua River. On either side and over a lagoon stretch buildings and thatched-roof cottages, with lanais and crimson carpets. Drums serve as nightstands, large white clamshells as wash basins, and planters hold small coconuts which have

Hawaii's familiar face: *Waikiki Beach, most famous strip of sand in the Pacific, continues to symbolize the pleasures of Hawaii. The great extinct volcano, Diamond Head, looms above the beach.*

sprouted. Attached to some suites are private walled-in-gardens and outdoor lava-rock bathtubs. Nobody is about to encounter *this* every day in the week, and it's fun.

Indomitable strangers on the island of Maui will probably have a look at the attractive port town of Kahului and the neighboring county seat of Wailuku, gaze in surprise at a brief divided highway and a modern housing development numbering nearly a thousand homes, and make the twenty-two-mile drive to Lahaina. This coastal village, regarded as romantic by compilers of travel folders, was the capital of Hawaii until 1845. Here, in the mid-19th Century, Antarctic whaling crews spent winters drinking, gambling and committing various deadly sins. Missionaries in concert with the monarchy put an end to the high living, and when the whaling trade played out, Lahaina went back to sleep.

Nature lovers are obliged to see the Iao Valley, handy to Wailuku, and then head upward to the ten-thousand-foot-high Haleakala Crater, where they can join a guided tour on horseback and explore the pit.

Except for the trade winds, which tend to lift you off your feet when you get on the weather side of islands, and the overbook-and-explain-later policy of a few hotel operators, and a certain provincialism induced by self-enraptured advertising. I thought Hawaii precisely as advertised—a dandy paradise with all the comforts of home. The new quickstep era and booming expansion were, I felt, an improvement on twenty-odd years ago. With the outer islands as an alternative to the discordances at Waikiki, all can find some fulfillment here. Of course, this is no spiritual refuge for pale city sophisticates who bridle at the pleasures of sea, sun and sand. Prices aren't cheap, but even for residents living is 20 per cent higher than on the mainland.

In spite of crowding, increased competition and an accelerating tempo, Hawaii continues to express a simple friendliness and courtesy that dates from its brown-skinned past. The old Hawaiian life, perhaps doomed, is still romantic and inviting. So these beautiful islands, no longer remote, slightly fevered by the Hawaii Visitors Bureau, beckon to you. Come in the fall for Aloha Week, a grass-skirted version of Mardi Gras, or Prince Kuhio Day in March, or any other time. The tourist industry will thank you to come from as far away as possible, and in as large numbers as convenient—conventions and expense accounts are always welcome. Fiftieth Staters, happy with the privilege their children have of attending classes barefooted until of high-school age, would like to buy them shoes anyway.

Qualifications for the visitor are simple, as witness the story of Garry, a Japanese man who literally runs the whole show at the Halekulani Hotel. Queried on a form by a New York travel agent as to the kind of guest desired (a polite mode for finding if racial or religious restrictions were in force), Garry wrote: "Nice people."

Lake Moraine, not far from Banff, is backed away
in the Valley of Ten Peaks. The visitor feels like
a small intruder in a landscape made for titans.

Canada

*The half continent between the Great Lakes
and the North Pole has begun to wake.
It is a massive, exhilarating land, proud of
the progress that has swept across it in
the last twenty years, bursting with
resources that have not yet been measured.
What their future may be, Hugh MacLennan
says, the Canadians do not know.
They only know that they have at last grown
up sufficiently to face it.*

"Methinks I see in my mind a noble and puissant nation rousing herself like a strong man after sleep and shaking her invincible locks."

So Milton wrote of England 300 years ago; so, without exaggeration, could one write of Canada today. The change that has crept over my country in the last dozen years is taken for granted by the children of Canada who grew up during the war, but those of us with somewhat longer memories still find it hard to accept.

When we were born Canada was a quiet country of farmers, lumbermen, fishermen, small manufacturers and merchants, of no real account politically but always stiff with the pride of the economically sound. Now she is ranked sixth among the industrial producers of the world, she is the fourth trading nation, and another forty years may find her a land of 50,000,-000 people. After the long, silent growing, Canada is beginning to respond as though a morning alarm had rung.

The first people to realize something of what has been happening up here are, naturally enough, our nearest neighbors. After a century of scarcely thinking about us except as a vast game preserve, they are now examining us more closely, and the scrutiny is as revealing to us as it is to the Americans. But the best thing this examination of Canada has produced is the

illusion that the country can at last be seen and understood as a whole.

Look at Canada on the map. From east to west the country extends from the lichen-coated granite of Cape Race—oldest European landfall in America north of the Caribbean—to the Alaska boundary where the glacier-capped bastion of Mount Logan rises 19,850 feet into frigid air. South to north the country extends from the busy traffic intersection where Windsor looks across the river at Detroit to the northernmost cape of Ellesmere Island, less than 500 miles below the North Pole —where there will never be land traffic of any kind.

The map, in other words, tells us that weather and living habits prevalent in Canada are not only more varied than those that are to be found within the borders of the United States but also that the major part of Canada is devoid of any human habitation.

Notice where the dots of towns and cities are clustered and then think for a moment about space again. From Montreal to Fort Chimo, at the northeastern tip of Quebec, the air distance is 1215 miles; pilots who fly back and forth pass over an expanse of spruce forests dotted with shallow lakes and threaded with streams that appear on few maps. Our most northerly city of any size is Edmonton, in Alberta, but it is only 350 air miles from the border of the United States, while it is nearly twice that far from Edmonton to Yellowknife, on Great Slave Lake, up in the Northwest Territories, and from Great Slave Lake issues the Mackenzie River which runs its 2500-mile course through the gray-green barrens to the Arctic. That's another way of pointing out how empty of human beings Canada really is. The great majority of us live within 150 miles of the American border.

Yet it is out of this apparent wasteland of the North that Canada's destiny is now being forged. From Great Bear Lake came the uranium that went into the first atomic bomb, and there's still plenty there. Incalculable power will result from the damming of Rocky Mountain lakes; gold, silver and 90 per cent of the free world's nickel are mined from the rock of the Canadian Shield; and now a lode of iron ore larger than the state of Connecticut is being made available in the waste ex-

panses of Ungava and Labrador. Oil and natural gas in Alberta are making millionaires of farmers and promoters; copper is being mined on the shores of the Arctic Ocean; more than half the world's newsprint is supplied by our forests.

So far, Canadians have not been sold from childhood the notion that they must maintain a "Canadian Way of Life," to paraphrase a slogan familiar to us all. We have been Nova Scotians, Quebeçois or British Columbians when we thought of ourselves, because only in this way could we grasp the meaning of who we were and where we lived. Thus the country has retained natural divisions not only geographically but also psychologically. First there are the maritime provinces of Nova Scotia, New Brunswick and Prince Edward Island, to which

lately has been added our youngest province, Newfoundland. Quebec, long known as Lower Canada, and Ontario as Upper Canada, are places and ideas distinct in themselves. The prairie provinces of Manitoba, Saskatchewan and Alberta allow themselves to be linked together, but British Columbia stands alone.

Those who know the great, weighty bulk of Canada to the north are doubtless adept at distinguishing its parts, but to the rest of us it is a single incredible unit composed of barrens, tundra, rock and ice. From here on let's consider these six sections in turn.

Beauty, says the philosopher, lies in the eyes of the beholder. To me it seems absurd to apply the word beauty, with all its subjective overtones of truth and understanding, to landscapes

Nova Scotia: *seascapes, landscapes, and a friendly remoteness from the rest of the world.*

so vast the mind is unable to comprehend them. Most painters, given a choice of the Canadian Rockies or a fishing village on the Atlantic coast as a place to work, would choose the latter simply because it is small enough to allow a man to make some of it his own.

So it is with me when I come to talk about this part of the world which I consider mine. I have known much of it intimately and it is always to me beautiful, yet I still have difficulty in condensing my knowledge of it into a few words.

New Brunswick is crisscrossed by cold salmon streams like the Tobique, the Restigouche and the Miramichi, and its forests shelter moose and deer. At its southern juncture with Maine, the lovely expanse of Passamaquoddy Bay (with Campobello and Deer Islands in its mouth) is flecked with white sails on fine summer days.

Everyone knows that Prince Edward Island is the scene of *Anne of Green Gables,* but those who pay it a visit discover that it is also superb dairy and potato country, a producer of the finest oysters that come from the sea (let us not argue unless you have met a Malpeque oyster and know it by name), and that its obsession with the breeding and racing of trotting horses extends from small boys to old men.

No part of Nova Scotia is more than fifty miles from salt water and nearly all its people live within ten miles of the sea. On its Fundy side the Annapolis Valley, scene of Longfellow's *Evangeline,* foams for eighty miles with apple blossoms in late May. The Atlantic coast is wild and ragged with countless coves and granite promontories. It is also prodigal with expansive harbors and sheltered bays. Americans have journeyed to Nova Scotia for many years, long before we built fine roads and improved our table. So it must always have given them something they couldn't find at home. Perhaps it is as simple as time to think, to talk, to observe at an unforced pace.

Once when we were in Halifax an American naval squadron put into port, first the carriers *Midway* and *Leyte* and later the heavy cruiser *Columbus* accompanied by five destroyers. While they were there, each day saw more than 10,000 American seamen thronging the streets, walking through the public gardens and sitting with girls in the parks as sailors have done in Halifax since the days of Nelson. When I was young they were always British sailors. I remember particularly those from the *Hood* that was blown up by the *Bismarck,* and the *Repulse,* sunk off Malaya by Japanese torpedo bombers. Did these Americans with accents of the Carolinas, Kansas, Oklahoma and Illinois realize the magnitude of the compliment they received when hundreds of citizens of this old Royal Navy port told each other they had never seen a finer or more likable body of men?

The future of Newfoundland lies probably in the hands of the engineers who are tapping its almost untouched resources of coal, lead, zinc, copper and iron. Its past has belonged to lumbermen and to the heroic characters who fish for cod in the icy, bleak waters of the Grand Banks. Their ancestors came to Newfoundland in the reign of Queen Elizabeth; in the outport fishing villages one still hears the idiom of Shakespeare's England and folk songs equally old. Something of Elizabethan poetry has survived in the haunting place names of the island,

tremendous names with the roll of the ocean in them: Conception Bay, Bonavista Bay, Placentia Bay! And the names of the tiny villages where fishermen's houses nest like gulls on the granite cliffs: Heart's Content, Seldom-Come-By, Topsail, Conche, Trepassey, Bonne Bay, Twillingate and Joe Batts Arm!

The province of Canada most familiar to Americans, the one which rings up nearly half the border crossings and seems most like home to them, is Ontario. Six American states—New York, Pennsylvania, Ohio, Michigan, Wisconsin and Minnesota—border it and it can be entered in a variety of ways.

The rich peninsula bordered by Lakes Huron and Erie is the most thickly populated region in all Canada. Ontario to the north and west of this peninsula is mostly rocky, lake-dotted bush. Near Niagara the climate is mild enough to grow peaches and wine-producing grapes. Along the shores of Hudson Bay and James Bay it is very, very cold.

Toronto, which seems more American than Cleveland when one first encounters it, is in fact the essence of Canada as it thought of itself before the war—Yankee in accent but in spirit more British than the Queen. Its two chief hotels, the Royal York and the King Edward, dutifully sound the loyal note in their very names.

For years Toronto has been the butt of jokes in Canada, particularly jokes made in Montreal, where the Ontario capital is characterized as part dead-end kid, part Fauntleroy. Actually it is a rich, competent city of nearly a million inhabitants with a fine university and excellent hospitals, the center of Canadian book publishing and the home of our national magazines.

East of Toronto along the shores of Lake Ontario to the St. Lawrence, and north in forested lake country are the vacation spots which attract hundreds of thousands of Americans every year. Nights in the Thousand Islands pulse with the beat of marine engines; speedboats throb over the blue waters of the Muskoka Lakes, Lake Simcoe and Lake Nipissing; the island dwellers in Georgian Bay would be unable to bring in provisions were it not for motorboats; fishers for muskellunge in the innumerable northern lakes use outboards and canoes. As for sails, the largest yacht club in Canada is located in Toronto.

But the aspect of Ontario which appeals to me most is its particular contribution to Canadian culture, to Canada's awareness of her own meaning and of her own kind of beauty.

About the time of the First World War some native artists who later became famous as the Group of Seven began to exhibit pictures they had painted on trips into this land north of Toronto: wind-torn pines writhing on the shores of Georgian Bay, the somber mass of the Algoma Hills, lonely forest lakes scarlet and gold with the reflections of the trees that ringed them; islands in Lake Superior as austere as icebergs. Here, caught in paint, was the wilderness that has kept our population penned into narrow strips of fertile ground beside the American border, but the painters showed us this wilderness as a well-loved enemy, as a wildly passionate creature who tore her hair and threw it to the gale so that in autumn along Georgian Bay the air itself grows red with streaming leaves. They also showed us that we could say something new in a universal language and say it about ourselves.

The finest of these paintings are in the National Gallery in

Ottawa, where they belong. For Ottawa, the nation's capital, is probably the only single Canadian city which comes close to symbolizing our enormously diversified land, a city shared now by both French and English, austerely splendid where the Peace Tower rises over Parliament Hill, its business quarter that of a provincial town, its embassies growing in importance year by year.

On the American plains only North Dakota gives me the kind of emotion I discover in our prairie provinces. In most of your western states the legends are different from ours. Sweet Betsy from Pike was on her way to California and the followers of the mountain men used the plains as a broad highway to Oregon. But in Canada for more than a century the prairie has been the goal of homesteaders who were willing to work cruelly hard in the hope—sometimes fulfilled—that the alluvial earth would yield them a fortune. Then and only then could they go on to settle in Vancouver or California.

Stand on the prairie and listen to the larks sing. Stand in that ocean of grass and listen to the wind. *Listen to the Prairies* is the title of one of the most beautiful movie shorts I have ever seen; made by the National Film Board of Canada, it is based on the annual Winnipeg Music Festival and links that open-to-the-wind city with the prairie about it, the towering sky bowl, the combine reaper swaying like a ship through the wind-swayed wheat while through it all surges a Bach chorale. If ever Canada breeds a great musician he will probably come from the prairie, for only music can translate fully the quality of emotion given out by that boundless sky of visible wind and that sea of singing grass.

The sky and the grass—the one a bowl, the other a sea—between them they formed the prairie landscape until aircraft began flying through the sky bowl and perspectives changed. How sudden those prairie cities of Canada look when seen from the air! They lie on the flat green or bronze plate with rivers curving through their hearts and some with no rivers at all—Winnipeg facing the French-speaking town of St. Boniface across the Red River, Saskatoon on the south branch of the wandering Saskatchewan, Regina stark and lone, Edmonton on the northern Saskatchewan and Calgary on the aquamarine waters of the Bow.

All the transcontinental trains stop in Winnipeg, chief city of the prairies and once the capital of the Hudson's Bay Company's empire. Today this open-eyed city has become so enterprising and independent that it has fostered our first ballet company, now touring as the Royal Winnipeg Ballet. One reason for this prairie upsurge is the mixture of races that live in Manitoba—Ukrainians, Scandinavians, Estonians, Hungarians, Icelanders, German Mennonites and Hutterites along with the English, Scots, Irish and Welsh whose parents moved west from Ontario and the Maritimes. Canada has never been a melting pot, so most of these people have retained at least some of their own folkways and many of their traditional skills.

We once traveled to the West Coast by rail and after the train left Winnipeg we pounded west through Saskatchewan.

Here the earth was brownish, aspens grew where they had been planted to serve as wind-breaks and soil binders and the land rolled in slow surges like mile-apart combers of the Pacific.

For hours we never struck a real town. Our few stops were at tiny platforms dwarfed by gigantic grain elevators.

At Calgary the train took on an observation car and we headed into the mountains with two locomotives pulling us. We were bound for Banff and over the Divide by way of the Kicking Horse Pass. No matter which route you take, the journey across the 400-odd miles of mountain ranges to Vancouver taxes anyone's power of description. The C.N.R. passes north by Edmonton and threads its way through the valley of the Athabaska to Jasper and then across the Divide through Yellowhead.

It is in the two lofty national parks, Banff and Jasper, that most travelers see the Canadian Rockies. Banff includes Lake Louise and Lake Moraine, Mount Eisenhower and many, many stalagmitic forms that pierce the clouds. In Jasper are Lake Maligne, Mount Robson and the Columbia Icefield.

There is a highway between the two parks and as you drive along or ride over the trails on horseback you see big-horned Rocky Mountain sheep, straight-horned goats and antelope, and on the whole you are lucky if you do not see a grizzly bear.

From Banff (or Jasper) the journey through the mountains to the coast passes through a montage of scenery that can only be called overpowering. Let nobody tell you the Canadian Rockies are beautiful. That homely, human word is far too intimate for this spectacle. No one has yet been able to paint the Rockies without making them look like exaggerated posters. Men will have to live here for centuries, they will have to suffer in these mountains, die in them and for them, hate and cajole and outwit them, and seek desperately to understand a few fragments of them before it will make any sense to call them beautiful. Now they appear as though gods had built cathedrals for themselves and departed after losing their religion, leaving their old places of worship vacant for the grizzlies, the sheep and goats and antelope and marmots, the clouds and the colors of dawn and sunset on glaciers and lakes, leaving them finally to the human beings who blundered into them a few years ago and built castlelike hotels to remind themselves of pictures they saw as children in novels of Walter Scott.

Next morning the train rumbled down the Fraser Valley into Vancouver, a city I am always willing to call handsome until I stop to consider what I mean. Is Vancouver so lovely? Certainly the prospects from its streets and water front and the roof of its fine central hotel are more than eye-filling.

Here the mountains are held at arm's length as a backdrop rather than forming a megalithic cage. But there is a pleasing untidiness about the city itself that makes it too young to be handsome. When the Lion's Gate Bridge was built to cross the harbor, men faced nature and caught a fragment of it in a net, thus reducing some of its tremendous formlessness to order.

Everyone who knows Vancouver loves it. It grows fast and it sprawls because there is plenty of space. Nearly all the houses have gardens, magnolias scent the nights and roses grow on trees as they do in England. Its lawns are lush green as a reward for its many drizzly days. The city faces south and west, south toward California and west beyond Vancouver Island to the Orient. Behind it are the forests of Douglas fir, the truck farms of the Fraser Valley, the orchards of the Okanagan, and farther

Peggy's Cove, west of Halifax on the southern shore of the Atlantic.

still above it are the hinterland and upperland of the third largest of Canada's provinces, overloaded with untapped wealth and power.

Across Georgia Strait on Vancouver Island is Victoria, the provincial capital, with its neighboring naval base at Esquimalt. Victoria is regarded as the most "English" city in Canada. It is kind to roses, complexions and bad hearts and is one of those blessed places more beloved by children and old men than by youths and the middle-aged. Its Empress Hotel is one of the most famous inns on the continent and wealthy Easterners return year after year to pass the winters in its brown-paneled rooms: mustard on the breakfast table, a boar's head for the Yuletide dinner, tea in the lounge every afternoon and holly growing on the lawn. In Victoria there are boys in blue blazers with school crests and little girls who curtsy at formal parties and show black-stockinged legs under dark jumpers when they play in their school grounds. Victoria may be 6000 miles away from England, but it is still closer than any other place in Canada.

Methinks I see in my mind a noble and puissant nation.... What makes a nation noble and what keeps it puissant is not the wealth it breeds out of its rivers or the metals and grains it wrings from the soil, but the love the people bear for it and the vision they create of it.

Nearly three centuries had to pass from the time when De-Monts and Champlain built their first stockade on Annapolis Basin in Nova Scotia until the day came when the scattered peoples in what is now called Canada were willing to declare themselves a nation. Three quarters of a century had to pass after confederation before Canadians dared to love their country, for to love rightly means to accept responsibility for what love entails, even responsibility for the unknown. Before Canada awoke it was easier for the people to fix their affections on the areas where they were born. Nova Scotia seemed far from Ontario and Ontario farther still from British Columbia.

Then came the Second World War. From 1940 until June in 1944 the bulk of the Canadian fighting army was either in camps in England or in the line in Italy. As armed representatives of a small Allied power, the Canadian troops abroad were neither British nor American. They felt themselves singularly alone. In the months and years while the men waited for the signal to cross the Channel they dreamed of home and at last met Canadians from all parts of their enormous country. They talked late at night, they formed plans and exchanged ideas, and gradually was built up in their minds the vision of a united Canada which seemed to them both a goal to strive for and a reason for their existence. This feeling for the country they had never before thought about coherently grew into a fire of passionate love.

When the men came home in 1945 they brought the fire with them and it swept Canada from Halifax to Prince Rupert. We do not know, any more than our American neighbors, what the future may hold for this continent. We do know that at last we have grown up sufficiently to be able to face it.

Fortress-like Château Frontenac rises from the upper town of Quebec, heart of metropolitan French Canada. British troops of General Wolfe forced Montcalm from these heights in 1759.

French Canada

As poor as they were proud, the French-Canadians were for generations a withdrawn minority in the country which they founded. But today, Hugh MacLennan points out, they are abandoning their isolation, and the creative French heritage is at last being woven firmly into the colorful new bicultural pattern of Canada.

The French-Canadians are the senior North Americans (the Indians, of course, excepted) above the Rio Grande and the Caribbean, and their awareness of this fact lies close to their awareness of themselves as an extraordinary people. They know their own story, every aspect of it, as members of a proud family know theirs.

Though French-Canadians live in all the ten provinces of Canada, their heartland is the old Province of Quebec, once known as New France. Quebec now has a population exceeding four million; it is the largest Canadian province, and after British Columbia, the most varied in scenery, climate and terrain. But though Quebec is so vast that its total area is more than double that of Texas, most of the province consists of the rock and scrub of the Laurentian Shield, so useless for habitation that even from the ramparts of old Quebec City you can look north into the wilderness.

This scarcity of good land has been the second conditioning factor in the French-Canadian story. Without enough soil to provide sustenance for their teeming offspring, the French-Canadians were poor for years, and for years thousands of their sons had to emigrate from Quebec or leave a settled community in order to break new land in terrains terribly harsh. Until recently, luxury on any substantial scale was unknown in French Canada.

Yet the province is as beautiful as it is stern, and at last technology has unlocked some of its riches. Quebec contains forests which supply the United States with an enormous percentage of its newsprint. There are thousands of lakes large and small, the mineral wealth is incalculable, there is hydroelectric power for a population far greater than Quebec has now.

It was the rivers which gave French Canada her life: first the St. Lawrence and then those majestic tributaries, each a major stream in its own right: the Ottawa, the Richelieu, the St. Maurice and the Saguenay. To this day most of the people live in the river valleys, and the St. Lawrence is so entwined in the French-Canadian story that it is impossible to imagine French Canada without it. As early as 1608, Champlain recognized this as the most strategic waterway on the continent. So did Queen Elizabeth and President Eisenhower, when they opened the International Seaway in Montreal in 1959.

No one making a home beside such a river could have escaped the consequences. From the first settlements, the St. Lawrence—and to a lesser extent the Ottawa and Richelieu—guaranteed the French-Canadians that dubious blessing, an interesting history.

No statements about a country as huge as Canada can be made without qualification. Montreal may be Canada's heart in the sense that it is here that the largest number of French and English-speaking Canadians encounter one another. But it is not the provincial capital—old Quebec is that—nor is it quite accurate to call Quebec merely a province. The French-

*The Gaspé, rugged eastern peninsula of French Canada.
Visitors like particularly the fishing-farming
village, Percé, on the Gulf of St. Lawrence.*

Canadians are a racial island in North America; Quebec is therefore a nation in spirit, enclosed within the federal state of Canada.

There is no minority in America remotely as self-conscious as the French-Canadians. So many things have conspired to keep them a people apart. They have married hardly at all with their English-speaking neighbors because most of the English are Protestants and practically all the *Canadiens* are Roman Catholic. Even language has been something of a barrier to their association with their English-speaking coreligionists. But often I think that the greatest barrier has been an almost mystic feeling that their overriding duty is to exist as a separate community.

I suppose most French-Canadians would be startled if anyone called them exclusive. As individuals they are friendly, gregarious, democratic and exquisitely courteous. But as a group they seem to their English-speaking compatriots as exclusive as the Jews must often have seemed to the ancient Romans. Often I think the French-Canadians desire to believe that the nation's English-speaking majority is opposed to them. Often they seem to require outward and visible signs of political and social opposition, as though only in this way they could keep vividly alive their sense of mission and their image of themselves as a people. I do not mean that there has ever been a conscious policy in French Canada to make trouble. Far from it; these are the most peaceful people I have ever known. Yet they seem to have an emotional need to emphasize every aspect of a tradition that sets them apart.

The motto of Quebec is *Je Me Souviens*—I Remember—and the French-Canadians forget neither a slight nor a favor, nor any important event connected with their past. No people in America are so conscious of their ancient roots. As recently as the last war, two candidates for Parliament wrangled on a platform about the status of each other's ancestors in the Norman hamlet their families had left three centuries earlier. When Jean Drapeau was elected mayor of Montreal a few years ago, one of his first acts was to display to the press a picture of his family tree, which demonstrated that the roots of the Drapeau family were sunk deep in some of the most historic soil of Old France.

The emblem of French Canada is the fleur-de-lis of the French Catholic kings, and when Louis XVI was guillotined by the atheists of the Revolution in 1793, Quebec was permanently estranged—not from the French people but from the French secular nation. The French-Canadians have hated British imperialism so much that the Boer War seemed to them a monstrous crime. Yet they have always preferred the British Crown to the French Republic, and in 1776, when Benjamin Franklin came to Montreal to win them to the Continental Congress, they turned him down flat.

This preference for monarchy is deep in their character and history, for they are, ironically, the only people in the Western

world who have never offered allegiance to anyone save a legitimate sovereign. The English had their Cromwell, but not the ancestors of the French-Canadians. They sing *Vive le Roi* or *Vive la Reine* and mean it, with the understanding, of course, that *La Reine* is at present Queen Elizabeth I of Canada, and not Queen Elizabeth II of Great Britain. French-Canadian troops serving the Queen, who is the honorary colonel of their most famous regiment, have finally won the right to receive their commands not in English but in the language of Frontenac and Montcalm.

It is in terms of his historical past that the French-Canadian understands his loyalty. In the past century, when Canada was technically a British colony, the first loyalty of English-speaking Canadians was to Great Britain. But ever since the cession of New France to England in 1763, the first loyalty of *Canadiens* has been to their Canadian home, which was all they had left. Loyal to the federal nation they certainly are—they will die for it if they must—but their emotional loyalties are reserved almost exclusively for their own province. Cardinal Léger, speaking at the funeral of Premier Paul Sauvé early in 1960, described him as a great leader of *"notre petite patrie."* Again and again speakers on patriotic occasions will use the phrase, *"Ici, nous sommes chez nous."* And in this idea of French-Canadians being at home only in Quebec is contained the further idea of being at home in an intense form of the Roman Catholic faith.

For years Protestants have called Quebec more Catholic than Italy, and when you travel the countryside you can see why. Crosses stand on many of the larger hills, Catholic institutions in grim gray stone are attached to community after community, the black soutane of the curé flaps as he strides down the village street, and his parish is dominated by a church with its roof shining in aluminum paint, its size ample enough to serve as a cathedral. At hundreds of crossroads there are wayside shrines. Life-sized crucifixes, some of them outlined in red neon after dark, stand in front of many farmhouses. Almost every Quebec village bears the name of a saint. In some regions originally English—there are several near the American border —the French have moved in recently and appended a sacred name to the original English one. There is a Sacré-Coeur de Crabtree Mills in Quebec; there is a Saint-Claude de Dudsville; there is—or at least there was for a time—a hamlet on the American border called Sainte-Suzanne de Boundary Line. Frank Scott, a Montreal wit, poet and constitutional lawyer, once saw a notice in a downtown office: THIS ELEVATOR WILL NOT RUN ON ASCENSION DAY.

Yet so sure of itself is Quebec Catholicism that in recent years it can tolerate an open, and at times ribald, anti-clericalism that would horrify a Boston Irishman. Not even the clergy themselves are immune to it. A priest of great charm and erudition once said to me with a smile: "I would like to consider myself the leading anti-clerical in Quebec, but I have many rivals in that line."

French Canada/Hugh MacLennan **357**

Possibly because I have lived in Montreal for twenty-five years, possibly because I am a Highland Scot whose minority language and folkways long ago disappeared into the Anglo-Saxon maw, the drama of French Canada's fight for survival has fascinated me ever since I first became conscious of it. Visitors from Europe always find Quebec the most interesting part of Canada. Since World War II English-speaking Canadians have been forced to revise their notion of the senior province. And with good reason. For what has happened in Quebec is one of the most encouraging stories in postwar North America.

Under British rule the French-Canadians enjoyed freedoms they had never known under their own kings, but the Conquest was a traumatic shock from which the community has only now recovered. In 1763 some 68,000 *habitants*, their captains departed to France, found themselves isolated on an English-speaking, Protestant continent. From that moment their policy became starkly simple: to survive as a people. So the long struggle of *le fait Français en Amerique* began, and the Catholic Church of Quebec assumed the intense nationalism it has never lost.

In this curious struggle, probably without precedent in history, the French-Canadians were never persecuted. Their aristocratic British governors infinitely preferred them to their own English colonists, the dissenters of New England. The Quebec Act of 1775 granted the French-Canadians everything they needed for their security: the official use of their language and their own civil law, and it also confirmed their church in the privileges it had enjoyed under the *ancien régime*. Indeed, the Quebec Act was suicidally damaging to England, for it enraged the New Englanders and was one of the prime causes of the American Revolution.

The American revolutionists, at first sympathetic to Quebec, sent Benjamin Franklin to Montreal to win the French-Canadians over. But their leaders clearly recognized that, if the Americans won the Revolutionary War and Quebec became a state in the new republic, *le fait Français* would be swallowed in the federal nation Jefferson was planning. So Franklin was sent home empty-handed. But when the war ended, the irony which has dogged Canadian history ever since made its first appearance. In nearly every region of America where English was spoken, the Union Jack had been hauled down. In French-speaking Quebec it still flew.

The long, slow struggle continued into the next century. Canoe men of unbelievable endurance mapped Canada to the Beaufort Sea and the Pacific Ocean, while along the St. Lawrence and the Richelieu French-Canadians settled into the quiet pattern of the stereotype. Slowly their politicians learned to work with the English-speaking leaders of the Maritime Provinces and Upper Canada. In the 19th Century the scattered provinces of British North America formed a new kind of nation called a Dominion, the inspirational prototype of the British Commonwealth. Again, the French-Canadians' instinct for self-preservation decided the issue. Though they had no particular love at that time for their English-speaking compatriots, they feared annexation by the United States.

The struggle continued. The French-Canadians, outnum-

Nova Scotia holds a proud claim as gateway to a continent, but its special charm is an amalgam of English, Scots, and French historic background.

bered by two to one, were inferior economically to *les Anglais*, who had the edge over them in commerce and finance. The French élite preferred the humanist training of their classical colleges to business. Then came the 20th Century wars. In the First World War the French-Canadians were so embittered by the Conscription Act that the fragile Canadian unity was almost shattered. But in the Hitler war the nation at last came together. In Italy and in France, French-Canadian troops mingled with their English-speaking fellow soldiers. Les Fusiliers Mont-Royal went onto the beach at Dieppe side by side with men from Ontario and the western plains. And as the war dragged on, French-Canadians at home rubbed their eyes in wonder. For years they had assumed—or had been taught to assume—that the prime loyalty of *les Anglais* in Canada was not to Canada but to Great Britain. Now they knew that this was no longer true. An ardent spirit of nationalism swept Canada from coast to coast. English-speaking writers and journalists began to take the side of Quebec. Suddenly the French-Canadians realized that *les Anglais*, even emotionally, were their countrymen after all.

The wars did more than broaden the French-Canadian outlook; they forced upon Quebec an industrial revolution which turned her life inside out, and within a generation and a half changed her from an agricultural to an industrial society. For hundreds of thousands of French-Canadians this was a bewildering, even an agonizing, experience. They became uprooted; they left the familiar rural parish for the unfamiliar factory town; they suffered hunger, misery and fear in the depression. They learned the dreary routine of strikes and lockouts, labor disputes, wage fights and picket lines. French Canada underwent the painful process of creating a new middle class in a continent where the middle classes had ruled for years.

The war ended, and Canada entered the most dynamic phase of expansion in her history. Significantly, it was a French-Canadian, Louis Saint-Laurent, Prime Minister of Canada from 1948 to 1957, who guided the country through most of this period. French-Canadians fought in Korea, and as the Canadian boom continued at home, signs of it appeared everywhere in Quebec. So much new building has been going on in Montreal that in places the city looks as though it were recovering from a bombing attack. And in the midst of the boom, French-Canadian energy exploded into commerce, industry, art, literature, drama, television, athletics and crime.

Montreal at the moment is so stimulating that it is almost exhausting to live in. Throbbing with reckless traffic, it has become a Balzacian city in swing time. Stores which used to cater solely to *les Anglais* are now crowded with French-Canadians buying with American abandon. On hockey nights the Forum thunders as the most rabid fans north of the Mexican bull rings cheer their new national heroes: Rocket Richard, Jean Beliveau, Henri Richard, Boum-Boum Geoffrion and the

other violent men of Le Club Hockey Canadien. You can seldom pick up a Montreal newspaper without reading of a new holdup—a bank, a store or a filling station; the price of liquor, sharp clothes, girls and night clubs has gone up.

Native art, most of it *Canadien,* has become so profitable that at the moment there are eighteen commercial galleries in Montreal alone, most of them selling contemporary pictures. French-Canadians have also taken to the ballet; the troupe called Les Grands Ballets Canadiens is now eight years old.

Before 1937, almost the only French-Canadian novel anyone had ever heard of was *Maria Chapdelaine.* Now Ringuet, Gabrielle Roy, Robert Choquette, Roger Lemelin, André Langevin, Germaine Guevremont, Robert Elie and the poetess Anne Hebert are not only widely known in Quebec but are also published in France. Gabrielle Roy, without making the slightest effort to write for European taste, became the first foreign writer to win France's coveted Prix Femina. It is no nest of simple folk that this literature depicts: these are the descendants of the Chapdelaine family who are now living in cities with the uncritical, greedy, passionate eagerness of Balzac's people in *La Comédie Humaine.*

Because the Canadian market is too small to support a native novelist, most French-Canadian writers turn out radio and television scripts to supplement their incomes. The result has been astonishing. The language barrier protects Radio Canada from American competition and to a great extent from American influence. Television in the French channels has done even more than the Industrial Revolution to transform the habits, values and ideas of the French-Canadian people.

The energy of some of these new *Canadien* writers is also reminiscent of Balzac. Lemelin—he turned novelist after a pair of broken legs ended his career as a ski-jumper—for years turned out two episodes a week, one in French and one in English, of his serial called *The Plouffe Family,* a fictionalized portrayal of Quebec in transition. Marcel Dubé is not yet thirty, but already he has written fifteen dramas which have appeared on the stage and on television. Recently an eighteen-year-old girl was discovered in Quebec City with more than a dozen manuscripts of publishable plays and novels and an outlook like Francoise Sagan's. Jean Gascon's Le Theâtre du Nouveau Monde has become a kind of *Canadien* Comédie Française performing original modern works and on one occasion playing Molière to acclaim in Paris. Gratien Gelinas, who might be called the father of the French-Canadian theater, for years did four men's work on a shoestring: he was writer, actor, producer and business manager at the same time. Now, with the financial help of the Quebec government and the Montreal Conseil des Arts, Gelinas operates in one of the most modern playhouses in America.

There is nothing anywhere like these *Canadien* theater groups. After each play has had its run in French, a translated version is offered in English, and the same players, all of them bilingual, enter a second run in a second language.

Nobody knows the future of *le fait Français en Amerique.* The French-Canadians, after two hundred years of struggle, have won their victory. They have seen their vision of Canada as a bilingual nation accepted at last, at least in principle, by their English-speaking compatriots. Energies kept frozen for two centuries have thawed out, and French-Canadians have learned and are learning science, industry, engineering and business administration. A son of one of their most honored families, Major-General Georges Vanier, war hero and diplomat, is the nation's second native-born governor-general.

But now that the French-Canadian has gone to town in every sense of the phrase, he cannot help realizing that his very success has destroyed all possibility of maintaining his old isolation. Nor should this worry him. It is not by weakness and withdrawal that a people survives, it is by strength. And French Canada is quite strong enough to meet the full competition of North American life without anxiety.

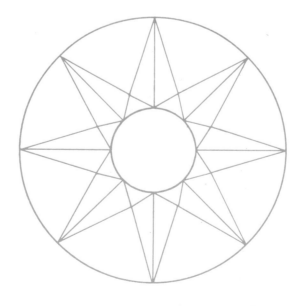